MARTIN SHERMAN

Martin Sherman
Skipping Over Quicksand

Tish Dace

McFarland & Company, Inc., Publishers
Jefferson, North Carolina, and London

LIBRARY OF CONGRESS CATALOGUING-IN-PUBLICATION DATA

Dace, Letitia.
    Martin Sherman : skipping over quicksand / Tish Dace.
        p.   cm.
    Includes bibliographical references and index.

    ISBN 978-0-7864-6662-7
    softcover : 50# alkaline paper ∞

    1. Sherman, Martin — Criticism and interpretation.
I. Title.
PS3569.H433Z63 2012
812'.54 — dc23   2011041135

BRITISH LIBRARY CATALOGUING DATA ARE AVAILABLE

© 2012 Tish Dace. All rights reserved

No part of this book may be reproduced or transmitted in any form or by any means, electronic or mechanical, including photocopying or recording, or by any information storage and retrieval system, without permission in writing from the publisher.

On the cover: *Martin Sherman*. Portrait by Nick Cuthell, 2010. Oil on canvas. 65 × 45 cm. Courtesy of Nick Cuthell.

Manufactured in the United States of America

McFarland & Company, Inc., Publishers
  Box 611, Jefferson, North Carolina 28640
    www.mcfarlandpub.com

In memory of Ross Wetzsteon,
who in 1975, as theatre editor of the *Village Voice*,
gave me my start as a theatre critic

and Christine Lavren,
who gave dozens of hours late in life
to sharing memories of Sherman

Table of Contents

Acknowledgments — ix
Preface — 1
Prologue: First Performance of Bent — 2

1. Crucibles and Satires (1938–1960) — 3
2. Songs (1960–1962) — 11
3. Fat Tuesday (1963–1966) — 16
4. Crises (1966–1972) — 22
5. California Dreamin' (1973–1977) — 33
6. Pink Triangles (1977–1979) — 45
7. *Bent* on Broadway (1979–1980) — 67
8. Rachel (1978–1984) — 83
9. Isadora (1983–1988) — 95
10. Vanessa Times Two (1986–1991) — 104
11. Ian Again (1989–1991) — 126
12. A Future in Film (1990–1993) — 137
13. Magic (1994–1997) — 146
14. Celluloid (1994–1997) — 160
15. Dreams Fulfilled (1994–1997) — 173
16. Judaica (1998–2000) — 187
17. Italy (1999–2003) — 199
18. India (2000–2002) — 212
19. Oz (2001–2003) — 221
20. Laura (2003–2005) — 234
21. More Controversy (2005–2011) — 247

Appendices
    A: Bent *on Stage* — 267
    B: Messiah *on Stage* — 270
    C: When She Danced *on Stage* — 273
    D: A Madhouse in Goa *on Stage* — 275
    E: Rose *on Stage* — 277
    F: Films on Screen — 281
    G: Mrs. Henderson Presents *on Screen* — 287

Selected Bibliography — 295

Index — 323

Acknowledgments

I thank Martin Sherman's friends and colleagues who generously shared their memories with me. During periods varying from short snatches to dozens of hours, they provided primary-source material that would otherwise have been lost to the future study of the dramatist's life and work: Robert Allan Ackerman, David Aukin, Verna Bloom, Simon Callow, Robert Chetwyn, Alan Cumming, Judi Dench, Mary Dolan, Olympia Dukakis, Tom Erhardt, Judy Flynn, Robert Fox, Stephen Frears, Gale Zoe Garnett, David Marshall Grant, Rupert Graves, James Hammerstein, Norma Heyman, Judith Ivey, Daniel Kramer, Christine Lavren, Maureen Lipman, Leila Livingston, Tim Luscombe, Sean Mathias, Judy Mauer, Ian McKellen, Philip Wm. McKinley, Nancy Meckler, Roger Michell, Tim Miller, Helen Mirren, Eileen Mitchell, Joan Plowright, Alan Pope, Corin Redgrave, Vanessa Redgrave, Jacqueline Russom, Antony Sher, Howard Schuman, Stanley Silverman, Jenny Topper, and Wendy Wasserstein.

I likewise thank Sherman's childhood friends Myrna Caplan Fineman, Michael B. Grossman, Angela Ciccotelli Mulloy, Nancy Lemerman Hermann, Ellis Katz, Don Lundy, Anita Ciccotelli Miller, Irvin Molotsky, Helene Goldman Singer, and Barbara Sarli Thomas.

I thank my theatre critic and scholar colleagues for helping me to learn about productions and supplying me with other elusive information: Sherry Eaker, Jane Edwardes, Derek Elley, Arlene Epstein, Robert Faires, Antonia Forster, George Hatza, Jay Handelman, Ian Herbert, Damien Jaques, Yun-Cheol Kim, Michele LaRue, Elizabeth Maupin, Tomasz Milkowski, Sanja Nikcevic, James Cary-Parker, Joe Pollack, Peter Roberts, Alvina Ruprecht, David Sheward, Catherine Stadem, Caldwell Titcomb, Irving Wardle, Steve Warren, Travis Weekes, and William Proctor Williams.

The following theatre practitioners assisted me in various ways: Turgut Akter, Margaret Chuang, Rebecca Fuller, James Leverett, Ernie Lijoi, Christopher Martin, Robert Moss, Ali Poyrazoglu, Nava Semel, Karen Sunde, Arnold Wesker, Jonathan West, and Doric Wilson.

I likewise feel grateful to the following libraries, librarians, other reference personnel, journalists and agents who have assisted my research: Amherst College Library, Michael Kasper; British Library, Stewart Gillies; Camden High

School Media Center, Kathy McBride; Contra Costa County Library; Kansas State University Library; Library of Congress, Arlene Balkansky, John Buydos, Malea Young; Theatre Collection of the late London Theatre Museum, now at the Victoria and Albert Museum, Barry Norman; Minnesota Historical Society Library, Alison Porgy; Jackie Willoughby, Warren Platt, Stephen Shepard, New York Public Library; its Billy Rose Theatre Collection, Rod Bladel; San Francisco Public Library; SUNY Stony Brook Library; Toronto Public Library; University of Arizona; UMass Dartmouth Library; University of Wisconsin Library, Rebecca Payne; Ruth Arnaud, Adrian Bryan-Brown, Chris Boneau, Michael Borowski, Barbara Carroll, Michael Constantinides, Vivien Goodwin, Jackie Green, James Harvey, Kellee at *Poz*, Heidi McKenzie, Arabella Neville-Rolfe, Joe Perrotta, QX's staff, Steve Sanderson, Jodi Shields, and Abbie Van Nostrand.

I acknowledge the generous help of family and friends: Roger Burnham, Hal, Ted, and Zak Dace, Elaine Fisher, Fernando Garcia, June Golden, Sally Hall, Julia Herd, Dabney Lassiter, Marcia Leatham, Rita Marinho, Susan McClaren, Kenneth Milford, Smoky Moak, Adam Szymkowicz, Dolores Walker, and Tanya Wesker. Thanks to Yusuf Parkar for replacing my defective computer so I could complete this book!

Finally I thank Martin Sherman for putting up with dozens of interviews, tolerating hundreds of additional questions, and writing so many challenging scripts.

Preface

Martin Sherman dramatizes the "other," outsiders—gay, female, foreign, disabled, different in religion, class or color—skipping over quicksand.

I've based this book about him and his work largely on primary sources. These include interviews I've conducted with Sherman, his friends and colleagues; letters, cards and e-mails from him; and his plays and screenplays, including unproduced and unpublished work.

I analyze and evaluate reviews of Sherman's plays and films, identifying those critics who appear to doze, garble facts, or grind axes. For each play and film, I endeavor to establish the nature and flavor of the critical debate.

This book doesn't constitute an "authorized" critical biography. Sherman didn't welcome a biography and doubtless will disagree with some critical interpretations and evaluations.

I would appreciate receiving notice of any errors.

Although not uncritical of Sherman's work, I would not have taken 15 years to research and write this book had I not admired his craft. Few others of his generation have produced such varied scripts; he never writes the same play or film twice. He likewise imitates no other writer. He takes risks; his daring prompts some outraged responses as well as huge applause.

I offer this book to those often clapping.

Prologue:
First Performance of *Bent*

Tonight Sloane Square's Royal Court Theatre presents the first performance of a new play by Martin Sherman.

Producers have imposed a vow of secrecy on everyone connected with the production. Theatre listings describe the drama as "gay," so some curious gay men turn up. Others like to see anything on offer at the Court.

Spectators watch the first scene, evidently set in 1979 London. A hungover man tries to elicit from his boyfriend information about the night before. A naked blond hunk enters, and Ian McKellen, as the amnesiac suffering a headache, double takes. Laughter continues as gay domestic comedy unfolds. At scene's end, however, two SS officers burst in and slit the hunk's throat. A sign descends: "Berlin 1934."

By Act 1's end, viewers know they witness an historic event.

During the interval, some slip away to buy flowers. Others read a leaflet explaining Sherman has based his characters' victimization on the historical record. Such events happened under the Third Reich. Tonight spectators will learn about concentration camp prisoners wearing pink triangles.

Act 2 depicts two Dachau inmates moving rocks back and forth. Sounds dull, but, as they perform the monotonous task, the drama occurring between them and inside them rivets attention.

As the play ends, everyone leaps up to give it that tribute unheard of in London, a standing ovation. Those who prepared themselves rain blossoms upon the startled actors. Thunderous applause continues even after the house lights come up. Surprised performers take final curtain calls while watching an audience as brightly lit as themselves.

Two hours earlier viewers knew nothing about the evening ahead. The play has astonished them, shaken them, transformed them. Only rarely, a play changes those who see it. That happened tonight. Dazed, some still weeping, spectators stream onto the street. Some seek the author, stammering, "Thank you. Thank you so much." The play, called *Bent*, has rocked their world, as it has continued to do, for new viewers, for over thirty years.

This book tells the story of the man whose *Bent* so profoundly affects us, and it elucidates the scripts with which he has enriched theatre and film.

1. Crucibles and Satires (1938–1960)

Martin Gerald Sherman's parents, Joseph T. Sherman and Julia Shapiro Sherman, lived in Camden, New Jersey. Julia's mother gave birth to her shortly after emigrating from Russia; Joseph was born in Yultishka, but immigrated at six.

Joseph, a lawyer, took on too many criminal and divorce cases for people who paid poorly. Julia didn't work outside the home. She gave birth to Martin on December 22, 1938, in Philadelphia, but he grew up at 1417 Wildwood Avenue in Camden and attended Parkside.

Sherman's mother died when he was 30, but his father practiced law until nearly 90 and tried a murder case at 86. By 1999, at 92, Sherman's father had survived his second wife, Laura Daisy, but suffered from declining health. He died in December.

Lawyer Sherman remains a Camden legend. Martin's childhood friend Michael B. Grossman heard the tales from attorneys: "Hundreds of less affluent clients saw him as their savior. He would come into court empty-handed. When the case was called, he would pull a piece of paper from his pocket and work from that. Next case, next piece of paper."

The playwright adds, "The best part of the story is all the papers were blank."

Sherman appreciated his mother taking him to the theatre in nearby Philadelphia, beginning when he was six, and encouraging his theatrical interests. But later she failed to nurture him and embarrassed him. She sat silent, her gaze fixed, her condition increasingly vegetative. Only much later, when, at 18, Martin left for college, did his father explain that his mother suffered from a degenerative neurological disease, Huntington's Chorea (now Huntington's Disease), which caused the heretofore unacknowledged peculiarities as her brain atrophied.

Sherman explains the constraints that kept him ignorant: "It was a Russian Jewish family from the shtetl, where things weren't talked about, and people were superstitious and afraid." He describes his confusion as "an absolute nightmare."

Fear he would develop this hereditary disease haunted Sherman for years, and he has peopled several plays—*Next Year in Jerusalem*, *Messiah*, and *A Madhouse in Goa*—with characters afflicted with the disease's characteristic aphasia. As eccentric as such characters seem, the nearly universal sense we all grew up in dysfunctional families makes this aspect of Sherman's work recognizable. It likewise provides one of several bases for his sympathy for those regarded as different or "other."

Sherman endured neglect as a child. His mother grew less able to give him attention, and his father worked long hours. An only child, Martin lived with a mother not "present." He read, he wrote, he reflected, and, beginning at 12, he went alone to Philadelphia theatres.

Sherman didn't learn basic skills or receive a nutritional diet. He lacked parental role models, and his paternal grandparents spoke only Yiddish. His salvation lay in summers in Atlantic City, where his maternal grandmother worked in the Pierrepont Hotel.

Sherman survived his childhood, but friends would later tease him about what he had failed to observe. He never learned chicken must be removed from plastic wrap before roasting, vacuum bags must be emptied or replaced, or how to use a screwdriver—things inquisitive youngsters with more usual childhoods absorb.

Sherman felt an outsider. As he grew in sophistication and as he came, at six feet, to tower over his father from the shtetl, he might have assumed he had been dropped from Mars into this household.

Nevertheless, during his early childhood, his mother gave him love of theatre. With her and later on his own, Sherman attended Philadelphia Broadway tryouts and post–Broadway road companies. James Hammerstein produced, directed, or stage-managed Broadway shows during Sherman's childhood, and he reports young Martin, between 12 and 18, saw every Broadway play running in Philadelphia.

His mother took him to *I Remember Mama* and *Where's Charley?* Alone, he saw *Guys and Dolls* (1950) at 12, *The Constant Wife* (1951), and *The Chase* (1952). He preferred Kim Stanley in the latter and in other roles to the more famous actors—Katharine Cornell, Tallulah Bankhead, Helen Hayes, the Lunts. He found those performers too "actory," especially Cornell. He concedes, however, Lynn Fontanne and Alfred Lunt gave good performances in *The Great Sebastians* (1955) and later in *The Visit*. Besides Stanley, he especially admired Jo Van Fleet in *Camino Real* and *The Trip to Bountiful* (both 1953), Viveca Lindfors and Eugenie Leontovich in *Anastasia* (1954), and Paul Muni in *Inherit the Wind* (1955). Also in 1955, he enjoyed *Cat on a Hot Tin Roof*; Williams has remained a favorite.

Sherman began acting because his poor diction prompted his parents to pay for "elocution" lessons from Mae Desmond, who had taught speech to Clifford Odets. "She was exactly the way her name sounds—a very dramatic actress. Theophilus Thistle thrust three thousand thistles through the thick of his thumb—that's what I studied. We did Shakespearean monologues; at ten, I was doing Lear."

From those exercises, Desmond promoted Sherman to her touring production of *Snow White and the Seven Dwarfs*, which played in Pennsylvania and New Jersey schools. Sherman can't recall which dwarf—incongruously tall—he played, but Desmond followed up with *Snow White and Rose Red*, in which Sherman also toured "until a blizzard or hurricane or something closed the roads." His parents resented Desmond's insistence they get him to the performance anyway because the show must go on, so they made him quit. Later he appeared in a Philadelphia community-theatre production of Ibsen's *An Enemy of the People*.

Like many stage-struck children, Martin wrote plays. Helene Goldman Singer went from first grade through 12th with Sherman. She suspects they co-authored *The Return of Ulysses*, their fifth-grade play at Parkside. Sherman remembers at 12 writing *Black and Midnight*, a comedy concerning "the witches from Macbeth coming to a small town in New Jersey." Shortly thereafter, he wrote *The World and Maylon Horn* "about a teenager whose parents have died in an automobile crash and who is desperate to escape from his town. He is helped by a nice lady in a bus station who is passing through." The same year, he wrote a screenplay, *Aspirins and Chickenfat,* about "a hotel in Atlantic City like my aunt's. I fear it was influenced by Jerry Lewis."

Sherman's writing didn't confine itself to school and neighborhood "stages," but expanded to a regular radio series called *The Adventures of Don and Henry*. He wrote and directed it, and he and his friends from Hatch Junior High performed it on WCAM twice a month on Saturdays as part of *Your YMCA on the Air*. Martin played Don and best friend Nate Ginsburg played Henry, while four or five other children did smaller roles. Grossman remembers playing a police officer in one of these dozen or so 15-minute episodes and still finds amusement in "this bunch of nervous Jewish kids doing a show to benefit the Young Men's Christian Association." Since the children always started laughing, Sherman fears his program consisted mostly of giggling.

Despite such away-from-school diversions, Martin hated Hatch, where he felt miserable and friendless—apart from his thespian pals. He acknowledges few young people at his "horrible" school were happy, as gangs kept students fighting and scared, and the education appalled him. He stayed sane by writing but also by reading assiduously, not assignments or anything his contemporaries might have read, but what interested him, such as novels by Fitzgerald, Faulkner, Ferber, and Hemingway. These and Philadelphia plays provided Sherman his own private education. "Because I wrote well," he recalls, "I could fake my way through classes, except for mathematics, in which I required tutoring." Otherwise, he easily earned high grades.

Life improved at Camden High, during a period he remembers as the only happy part of his childhood. He made more friends and gave parties his buddies vividly recall because he served chocolate-covered ants and fried grasshoppers and hung their history teacher in effigy. "We were so cool," enthuses Ellis Katz, while Nancy Lemerman Hermann says, "He was clever, with a savvy eye for the ridiculous."

Sherman remained after school to work on shows or the yearbook or the magazine, but, Grossman recalls, didn't play ball in the park. The other Jewish students "made nothing of it except to recognize he wasn't the picture of eye-hand coordination." He also rarely showed up at the soda shop to hang out on the sidewalk and watch girls. Katz didn't recognize his friend was gay, but noticed "only that he was different. It was that difference that made him so interesting and appealing." Grossman says the guys who understood the nature of that difference never taunted him. "It was a non-issue in our crowd."

Gangs from outside Sherman's immediate neighborhood, however, could rough him up. Shrewdly, he befriended a tough classmate, who protected him. Irvin Molotsky, also Camden High class of 1956, explains this protector later murdered his girlfriend and was executed (NJ4).

In tenth grade, Sherman wrote, directed, and, with an eight-millimeter camera, filmed a Shakespearean parody called *Homlio and Roulette*. Angela Ciccotelli Mulloy played the Juliet role, and Sherman still calls her "Roulette." Don Lundy appeared as Homlio, while Angela's sister Anita, Katz, and Ginsburg took on assorted others—in Katz's case called Corpulent (Capulet)—and passed themselves off as "the multitudes." They changed headdresses or props and Martin shot them repeatedly, hoping to suggest a cast of thousands, or more than five. He filmed in the Cicotelli's yard and Farnham Park.

He wrote in Angela's yearbook, "Dear Roulette, the finest little actress since Marilyn Monroe, who laughs when she should cry (last scene)." Perhaps that explains why he didn't cast her the following year in *Omelet*, his send-up of *Hamlet*. A play rather than film, this Sherman satire featured an evil king— enacted by Katz—who drank from a bottle labeled "kindness." When the poison in that bottle dispatched him, he died with the rebuke, "Thou hast killed me with kindness."

Something in the bottle upset the actor's stomach, so Ellis missed the next performance. Martin drafted Ernie Tsonis to play the part, while, as Ellis later learned, "Martin crouched behind the throne and whispered the lines to Ernie. After he drank the poison, he spent a full three minutes expiring. He brought down the house, but, even so, I don't think Martin ever forgave me for not showing up."

Sherman became associate editor and, as a senior, editor of the literary magazine, the *Record*. During sophomore year he published a satiric short story called "Socrates Jones," which he topped junior year with "Socrates Jones in 'Tickets, Please.'" As a senior, he followed his earlier amusing pieces with an editorial defending young Americans from unjustified accusations of juvenile delinquency.

Despite this earnest message, Martin's friends remember him as amusing. Among the school shows he wrote, his friend Barbara Sarli Thomas describes a quiz-show script for her, Nate, and himself. He took the largest role, the emcee, while she and Nate played contestants. She laughs now at her effrontery in trying to improve some of his jokes and praises his restraint in not complaining.

Grossman describes the big annual Speech Contest senior year. Auditions determined which three boys and three girls would appear at night in a packed auditorium. "Martin did 'The Treasurer's Report' by Robert Benchley. Nate did FDR's 'Nothing to Fear' speech. I did Stephen Vincent Benet's 'John Brown's Body.' Martin was hilarious; the audience loved it. Nate was boring, and I tried for drama. The audience preferred Martin's performance, but the judges gave me the prize."

Myrna Caplan Fineman attended Bethel religious school with Goldman and Sherman. After their confirmation in 1954, they enjoyed their reward of a weekend in New York, where she remembers roaming the theatre district with Martin. She loved the "Come as You Were" party Sherman gave on June 11, 1956, to celebrate their graduation. She enjoyed Martin's jokes and clever banter between him and Ginsberg.

Sherman's new happiness made leaving for college in Boston difficult. His father, however, encouraged him to get away. Sherman notes the financial sac-

Confirmation Exercises of Beth-El Synagogue, Camden, New Jersey, June 7, 1954, Sherman back row, third from left (courtesy Myrna Caplan Fineman).

rifices his dad made and the extra legal work he took on to make possible his son's private education.

By the time he left to study acting at Boston University, Sherman had attained considerable mental sophistication. Nevertheless, he describes himself as "thrown into a new city where I was with only strangers and at such an odd period, 1956, in a theatre school cut off from the rest of BU. What is now the Huntington Theatre was our building, where all our theatre courses met. It was incestuous. A kid from New Jersey, I was thrown into a sexual and emotional caldron."

Sherman's appearance hampered his acting aspirations and psychological health. He had buckteeth, a poor complexion, and an abnormally skinny frame—the latter a testament to his lack of proper nutrition. Department secretary Judy Flynn remembers him as gangly, uncoordinated, and unskilled in first-year Theatre Practice—the crews who built and ran productions. The technical director agreed to pass Martin if he stayed out of the way.

By the end of freshman year, Sherman began to find his footing although he didn't succeed as an actor. He understood that craft cerebrally, but his disquiet about Huntington's and his insecurities undermined his confidence and the focus acting requires.

He appeared as a mechanic in *A Memory of Two Mondays* and in the chorus of *Agamemnon*, starring graduate student Olympia Dukakis as Clytemnestra. Composer Stanley Silverman recalls his performing effectively as the Arab in *The Time of Your Life*. Other cast members included Verna Bloom, Walter McGinn, and John Cazale, who became professional actors.

Perhaps appearing with such performers helped him relinquish his acting aspirations and instead begin writing satiric sketches, usually based on plays BU staged. These parodies earned him a reputation as "the writer," as Silverman thought of him while they collaborated on revues.

Summer 1957 Sherman worked as assistant to Michael Gardner, producer of American Mime Theatre. He also wrote a play. He lived in a tiny Greenwich Village apartment, where his high-school friend Ellis visited him for a weekend. They went to bars and bookstores, a club featuring female impersonators and another where Odetta sang, and they attended *Most Happy Fella* on Broadway. "It was the highlight of my young life," says Katz. It also kept Martin away from Camden and his mother's continuing deterioration. At summer's end, he visited home briefly and attended *West Side Story*, which wowed him by successfully combining every theatrical element into musical tragedy.

When Sherman returned to BU for sophomore year, he had grown brave enough to demand from the department head the main stage for a revue he would write. The administrator acquiesced, and Sherman wrote *The Obscure Revue*, well received in fall 1957. He penned another success, *Eight to Hate*, for the small theatre/dance studio in spring 1958. Sherman had earned a position of importance.

Then something happened which stopped him. Michael Weiner had directed the spring 1958 revue. Sherman describes him as

> very neurotic and very talented. I had a huge crush on him. He directed it brilliantly, but was disappointed some of the actors—you know, young, temperamental—hadn't listened to him, so he said he was never going to direct anything like that again. And I didn't have enough faith in myself to direct my own work. Also, I thought I'd come to the end of the line. You can't go on writing parodies. So I coasted for the next two years. I wasn't as creative and productive as I had been. I still had a reputation, but I coasted.

Classmate Stanley Silverman met the playwright as soon as they arrived in September 1956. He majored in music but, because he liked theatre and hoped to write musicals, he volunteered to write incidental music for the Theatre Division's plays. By their sophomore year, Sherman and Silverman lived in an apartment of a Back-Bay brownstone, sharing it with two others.

Sherman grew close to Silverman, the late Speedy (Walter) McGinn, and Bloom, who remarks, "I never had another friend with whom I could confide the way I could in him." She became the first of several especially close lifelong friendships Sherman has developed with women.

Sherman couldn't cook, except for tea and vanilla pudding. But Silverman recalls him as "great fun" even though clearly worried he would develop his mother's genetic illness. While worrying, Sherman created comic works, spoofing BU productions and the Oscars.

The surviving sketches from *Eight to Hate* represent the earliest extant scripts of plays he wrote. They parody productions their audience had seen recently, and they were performed and directed by people who knew how to lampoon their targets. Their ridicule therefore must have prompted hysterical laughter. Reading these juvenilia 50+ years later, we can only try to imagine ourselves into their context. Therefore, Sherman's sophomore sketches sometimes seem sophomoric, even as they suggest the cleverness that informs his mature work.

"Louella" Sherman receives credit for *What Makes Oscar Wild: A Loving Tribute to Hollywood Tradition*, in which he ridicules the Academy Awards. *The Golden Sicks* parodies Maxwell Anderson's last play, *The Golden Six*, concerning Caligula and Claudius. Sherman's third surviving sketch from *Eight to Hate*, *A Song for a Penny: A New Intermission*, satirizes spectators as well as BU's director, Pressman, who turned the intermission for John Whiting's *A Penny for a Song* into a performance.

Eileen Mitchell remembers the sardonic attitudes which must have prompted Sherman to write his revue sketches just before she arrived there as a graduate student. She, Sherman, and Weiner used to deride their peers, tearing productions apart. They enjoyed criticizing others. The playwright later grew out of such negativity. Although he retained his wit, he acquired empathy.

Sherman remembers other theatre majors as mostly misfits, a tragic group. Even the talented often didn't have the required survival skills. They stood out as freaks, different, the "other" in a world of squares. He explains, "In the '50s, we were the only ones. The '60s, for all the destructiveness, were healthier." He feels James Baldwin captures the alienation in *Another Country*. "That was so familiar—the torment of those days." He cites "the obvious tragic famous cases like Speedy (Walter) McGinn, one of the best actors of his generation, but an alcoholic who died in a car crash. Another actor drank himself to death. One of the best actresses in the school gained about 300 pounds and hasn't acted in years. The mortality rate was high." These friends of Sherman's—"wonderful, exciting, creative"—born out of their proper time, so strange in the '50s, provided the playwright another basis for empathizing with the "other."

His survival in this era partly depended on his friendship with Peggy Nicholson, a splendid actress who lived outside Boston with siblings, mother, and mother's companion, Kip Tiernan. That nurturing household provided a refuge of sanity. Tiernan had written a musical called *I'll Tell the World*, so Sherman helped with the book. Later she achieved fame as a social activist who, among other accomplishments, founded the first U.S. women's shelter, Rosie's Place. This household encouraged Sherman's developing respect for strong women.

Silverman speculates he and Sherman remained stable when other BU students didn't because of their fathers' work ethics. It never occurred to the playwright to stop focusing on his goal of writing. "I think he saw his father working, responsible and dealing with adversity. He continued his work despite the strain of the situation with the mother. Martin had this model of somebody sticking to a path."

Sherman's world-class sense of humor also helped him deal with challenges and adversity. He could see the humor in anything.

Sherman had developed survival skills during his bizarre childhood. Because nobody around him acknowledged a problem with his mother, he "lived through hell. It produced all kinds of conflicts. Years later, my therapist said of all her patients my childhood was the worst. I should have turned out crazy and been institutionalized. Yet I had both feet planted firmly on the ground."

When he received his BFA in theatre, graduation took place in an arena where the circus had closed the night before. The incongruity didn't escape him. Dumfounded, he discovered he had graduated cum laude. His work ethic about his writing had not extended much to his courses, yet he had succeeded.

When he arrived in Boston in 1956, Sherman felt insecure, confused, even tormented. In 1959, he left BU an aspiring writer, clear about his goal and confident in his ability to achieve it.

2. Songs (1960–1962)

After graduation, Sherman moved to New York, where he received money from his father. Initially he shared a flat with BU friend Mitchell.

She recalls he wrote easily, without blocks, and never found excuses for not writing. She admired his sense of self and purpose and believes he felt comfortable later in London because he didn't fantasize about theatre, but did it daily. She also admired Sherman's wide reading, not just in theatre, but in history and politics and how to change society He asked her to join CORE, which soon would take him south to register voters.

Since his budget wouldn't allow him to pay for tickets, Sherman adopted a practice common to impoverished theatre people: He would mingle outside at intermission, find an empty seat, and watch the rest of the play, a practice known as "second acting."

In April 1961 Sherman moved into a cheap apartment at 445 West 49th St. He had already started writing musicals, yet no longer could ridicule college productions, but instead had to create plots. He regards his work then as mostly terrible. *Attitudes*, for example, had "a couple of backers' auditions," Sherman says, "but wasn't done. It didn't deserve to be." Next he wrote a children's musical (with composer Ed Kresley) based on *The Emperor's New Clothes*, which received production as *We Love Adventure* at Judson Hall in 1961 and as *The Emperor's New Clothes* in L.A. in December 1962.

Shortly after graduation, Sherman had written lyrics to Silverman's music for *Ten Nights in a Barroom*, an old chestnut about temperance. John Savoca, Marcia Taradash, and Robert Alvin had adapted W.W. Pratt's play. The show opened—"to our chagrin," says Sherman—on October 28, 1962, when Alvin directed it at the Greenwich Mews Theatre on West 13th. "We were embarrassed by this awful production." Echoing Sherman's distaste, Silverman recalls, "The first run-through was so atrocious we got hysterical giggles."

Their score lampoons the original's serious intentions. For instance, Sherman's dactylic meter mocks corny sentiments in "Mary's Hymn." A young woman on her deathbed reassures her father, "Now that I'm certain your path will be straight, /I happily head for the heavenly gate." In "Switchel-Mehitable Duet," a woman rebukes her suitor's drinking, he swears he's stopped, she fears he'll begin again, but he silences her protests by proposing unromantically,

"Mehitable, Mehitable, I won't be askin' twice. Let's have a joint stock partnership. I mean let us be spliced." Sherman follows this with lyrics for a "gay waltz," "Charity, Grace and Romance," in which the groom insists he won't backslide: "No man is more rum proof than I, more warranted to wear." These lyrics speak of love in terms suited to commerce.

While Sherman wrote in New York, Silverman had studied composing with Darius Milhaud at Mills College in Oakland. After he finished his masters, Mills invited him to present an original musical, so he asked Sherman to write book and lyrics. He created an urban-angst, largely plotless affair. He regards his book for *A Solitary Thing* as "another adolescent embarrassment" but judges "some songs quite nice and weird." Performances occurred on November 9 and 10, 1962.

Jacqueline Russom, who, as Jacque Haring, played Sylvia, remembers Sherman as "skinny, gawky and earnest—a nerd." Russom described her role as an exotic bohemian. As the plot's catalyst, Sylvia breaks up central character Connie's relationship with her boyfriend. Connie—the title's "solitary thing"—then can find a better man.

A Solitary Thing's songs reflect the characters' angst. Sherman feels his "lyrics were ahead of their time. They didn't follow the usual rhyming patterns. They were, if not mature in execution, mature in attempt. Stanley's music was wonderful. The show was a mess because my book wasn't good. But there were things in the score I'm proud of."

As that begins, Connie mournfully contemplates "ashes to the sea, free flowing." Sherman's odd image suggests lava running down a mountain, or perhaps a cortege casting the deceased's ashes upon the waves. Literally, the refrain refers to her cigarette ashes, yet evokes Connie's soul as ashen.

Silverman shifts tempo, moving into the sprightly "Why Do I Feel So Free," in which Sherman establishes Connie has left the city for the seashore. The sea lifts her spirits, but she returns to a slower, contemplative "cool and clear, to the sea" as this number ends.

Another song musically resembles Erik Satie's "Gymnopédie." Connie considers "The face /The face on my pillow /Is handsome /Oh so handsome /And it smiles a secret smile /A hint of something deep /Deep within the smile. /Morning is the gentlest season of love." Yet she perceives it as "childlike," reflecting "foolish dreams." This number, deceptively simple, hints at a common dilemma, physical attraction luring us into relationships with people we later find unsuitable.

Connie complains, "Why Can't I Like the Guy I Love." This up-tempo jazz features ad-lib solos for piano and drums and wit such as "I like Lenya when she sings, /Adlai when he speaks, /Burton when he—. /I like Mailer when he writes, /Pablo when he plays, /Lenny when he sweats, /Liston in the first, /Nixon out of work." The playwright would eventually win respect as a man who uncannily appreciates how women feel. We notice that capacity even here, in the work of 23-year-old Sherman, as this song concludes, "Why must my mind be so damn clever? /Why on the subway do I want to shove? /Why can't sunsets last forever, /and why can't I like the guy I love?"

"The Pace Is Fast" establishes Connie's job as a photographer, which suggests he identifies with this woman so unhappy with the man in her life. A quarter-century later he used that profession again for *A Madhouse in Goa*'s David, a photographer who also resembles him.

The title song, a duet for Connie and her mother, alternates voices. The widow recounts situations parallel to her loneliness, and Connie pleads for tolerance of her need for solitude. In music patter close to recitative, Mrs. Peterson sings, "Mister Finley has a son who's been gone five years, /trav'ling over Europe they say." Her tempo then diminishes for "Mister Finley's all alone, /while his son just wanders off. /Mister Finley's very sick, /always has a nasty cough. /But there's no one ever there since his son went away. /No there's no one ever there." To each tale of children neglecting their parents, Connie responds with something similar: "Please try, try to realize /there's more to life than what you see. /Please try, try to understand /a solitary thing like me." The sense here requires emphasis on "you"; Silverman instead emphasizes "see," rendering the line hard to comprehend.

Sherman repeats the contrast, substituting for Mrs. Finley's son Mrs. Weinstein's negligent son and daughter, who never visit or phone but put their mother in a home. Then Connie's mother sings of summer nights reminding her of long ago. She speaks part of one line, "The world changes before you even know it," and the two sing together Silverman's haunting melody, as Connie begs her mother to understand and Mrs. Peterson insists "I try to understand. I try."

Connie gets more solitude than she bargained for after the break with her boyfriend. She sings "Leave Me Alone," then follows with the bitter "All a Joke," which beats Sondheim to imagery of clowns mocking her misery. Sherman and Silverman conclude with another party, where Ruth introduces Connie to a wonderful new man.

Christine Lavren, who, as Chris Donelly, played Ruth, remembers the audition director Ronald E. Barnes held. She saw this "strange-looking man in a puffy lavender mohair sweater wrong for his body. He was so skinny he was bizarre looking. I kept watching him."

Barnes set up a group improvisation requiring the aspiring thespians to pretend they attended a New York cocktail party. "The others began creating these phony little conversations. I lit a cigarette and just watched, and when somebody tried to do one of those conversations with me I snapped, 'Fuck off!' Every time I could hear Martin laughing. So I kept doing it. I was very aware I was getting a response. Finally he came loping up to the stage laughing and asked, '*Who are* you?'"

Lavren and Sherman became instant friends. She recognized he wanted her to play the lead, but Mills wouldn't permit a freshman to do that, so she settled for a supporting role as a bitch. Her part kept growing as her relationships with the authors developed. When Silverman arrived, she sang "I Enjoy Being a Girl" for him, and they began an affair. But Lavren grew especially close to Sherman as the three hung out together, Jules-and-Jim style.

Lavren contrived to get out of the dorm each night to go to their off-campus apartment. "I remember," she recounts, "all these sexual high jinks. Martin loved that and participated in the French farce aspects. He and Stanley weren't thrilled with the girl playing the lead, but they were with me. So I gradually got more lines, and they wrote a new scene and added a dance where I attacked the lead." The Peppermint Lounge, a hot new spot on West 45th St., had introduced what quickly became a dance craze in New York called the Twist. Sherman and Silverman taught it to Lavren, and she performed it. "Outside rehearsals, we became this threesome, but it was really Martin and me. I was Stanley's first shiksa, and for me he was just entertainment. But Martin and I bonded."

Lavren describes Sherman at nearly 24 as terminally shy, yet "in your face, full of life, just spit-and-vinegar humor." He alternated between silence or mumbling or discomfort and wit his listener mightn't get until two sentences later. He still suffered from acne and horrible hair as well as awkwardness in moving his long body, which resembled Ichabod Crane's, but he proved emotionally generous to his friends, who trusted him instinctively.

A Solitary Thing drew good houses both nights, but critics mangled Sherman. While they appreciated Silverman's music, they missed Sherman's contribution as lyricist. Russom found it "a very good play." She remembers laughing at lines and liking songs. She recalls the man playing the romantic male lead as so poorly cast—because the woman's college had few options—that he damaged credibility.

While in California, Sherman and Silverman wanted to meet Ira Gershwin, whom they both admired. They wrote asking if they could visit him. The lyricist agreed and sent Sherman an autographed copy of his *Lyrics on Several Occasions*. After *A Solitary Thing*, Silverman was performing with the Los Angeles Philharmonic, so they went to L.A. They spent a day with Gershwin at his home, asking him questions, chatting, discussing their work.

Sherman hung out with Silverman in L.A. They attended a post-concert party at Dorothy Chandler's, chauffeured there by Leonard Stein, Arnold Schoenberg's assistant, accompanied by Schoenberg's widow, and they later attended with her a Bernstein concert. Silverman had entree to a heady world; his friends included Glenn Gould, Pierre Boulez, Paula Prentiss, and Dick Benjamin. Sherman remained in L.A. until *The Emperor's New Clothes* opened at the Music Box in December.

He might have enjoyed a career as a lyricist, but nobody could stimulate him to do that after Silverman. Whenever he started a project with anyone else, he found it boring, because he missed the adventuresome music of his former collaborator. Silverman had commissions for symphonies and other work to occupy him, so they worked together little after 1962.

Sherman needed "someone with Stanley's brilliance by my side. And lyric writing isn't something you can drop in and visit occasionally. It's a demanding discipline you must continually work at and grow with." If circumstances had differed, Sherman might have made his whole career as a librettist/lyricist. However, he didn't achieve a place in musical theatre until 40 years later.

Instead, he earned his laurels as a playwright. In 1963, while attempting to market the Sherman/Silverman opus and flailing around with unproductive attempts at other musicals, he began for the first time as an adult writing a non-musical script.

3. Fat Tuesday (1963–1966)

When Sherman returned from L.A., he rented an IBM electric typewriter to revise *A Solitary Thing*. He wrote Lavren on February 9, 1963, hoping she wasn't in "the Stockade, or wherever they jail their Wayward Girls." Instead she slit her wrists and landed in Alameida County Hospital. Her father, a psychiatric social worker, wouldn't help get her released, and she had no money to return home. Sherman borrowed Christine's fare from his friend Weiner.

A pariah back in Philadelphia (and miserable living with her family), she married the leading actor, Pat Cronin, from the theatre where she worked that summer. They moved in September to New Orleans. There, Pat began Richard Schechner's MFA program at Tulane, while Christine worked in the Dean of Students' office and read plays for *Tulane Drama Review*. The same month, on September 15, Ku Klux Klansmen bombed the black 16th Street Baptist Church in Birmingham, killing four girls.

Throughout 1963 the south had seethed with racial tensions. Efforts to desegregate Southern schools met with fierce resistance, and some state governors sided with white mobs. Many pro-civil rights demonstrations and marches occurred from late–March through mid–June. Medgar Evers was murdered on June 12, and the Ku Klux Klan held a gigantic rally in Georgia on June 23. In July, protestors staged sit-ins to desegregate diners. Finally, on August 28, 250,000 marched on Washington, D.C., where Martin Luther King delivered his "I Have a Dream." Racism, violence, and efforts to achieve social justice went into the mix of influences on the play Sherman soon began.

Meanwhile, in November, Sherman wrote Lavren that he and Silverman "have a semi-nonofficial agent helping us get the script to producers." Frieda Fishbein had served as agent to Moss Hart, George S. Kaufman, Elmer Rice, Jean Anouilh, and Jean-Paul Sartre. "She's about one hundred and two," he continued, "and I doubt if she can do much good with the show—everyone she knows is dead—but we're so damned flattered she likes it." He likewise considered offers to write lyrics; he accepted some.

Sherman escaped to New Orleans to visit Lavren shortly before Mardi Gras on February 11. Also known as Fat Tuesday, it precedes Ash Wednesday. The first of two occasions during 1964 in which he visited the Cronins on Freret St. beside the Tulane campus, the February trip made Sherman feel as though he must have lived there in a former life because he seemed already to know the city, its streets, its culture. He instinctively found Marie Leveaux's grave. His fascination with her and with voodoo colored his New Orleans play and, years later, cropped up again in *Some Sunny Day*. He so loved the Big Easy and it so fired his muse that, although he had planned to stay for ten days, he remained two months.

Daily Sherman alternated writing, discovering New Orleans, and registering voters. The Congress of Racial Equality had moved its headquarters to New York in the late '50s, and in early 1961, Sherman had joined. CORE's motto, "Making Equality a Reality," represented a lifelong Sherman goal.

CORE had started organizing voter registration drives in '61. These involved teaching Southern African Americans how to pass registration tests and accompanying them to register, when aspiring voters faced refusals by racist registrars. Just before Sherman's arrival in New Orleans, the 24th Amendment—on January 23, 1964—had abolished the poll tax designed to prevent poor Blacks from voting, but that didn't guarantee African Americans could vote.

Those trying to register and those helping them faced danger, especially during summer 1964. CORE recounts in nearby Mississippi "37 black churches and 30 black homes and businesses were firebombed or burned that summer, and the cases often went unsolved. More than 1000 black and white volunteers were arrested, and at least 80 were beaten by white mobs or racist police officers" (www.core-online.org).

At night, Sherman and Christine, sometimes accompanied by her husband and/or her lover, would go out to eat, drink, talk. The other three fed him. He couldn't have picked up the checks. Lavren and Sherman palled around late at night. *Jules and Jim*, the 1961 French film, inspired them to dress her like a boy, wearing dungarees, with her hair under a cap.

Mardi Gras and the New Orleans experience of February–March 1964 sent Sherman into sustained work on a new play, which he first called *Dark Comedy* before settling on *Fat Tuesday*. He based the central female character on Christine, then 20, but worldly-wise beyond her years. He made her 22, later adjusting the age to late 20s.

Sherman returned to New York in early April and continued writing *Fat Tuesday*. Dan Rodden, Artistic Director of Music Theatre in Philadelphia, returned *A Solitary Thing*, saying he found it in "the Noel Coward tradition"— a tribute to its playfulness and epigrams.

On June 21, 1964, "Surfside Sherman" writes Lavren he's on Collins Avenue in Miami Beach, visiting his stepmother, Laura, on whom he doted. He intends to stay two months and revise *Fat Tuesday*, although he caught his "typing finger" in his front door the week before and so can't type for a week or two. He failed to mail this letter immediately because he couldn't afford a stamp.

On July 1 he typed a letter, enclosed the earlier letter, and explained the cause of his precarious finances: "I arrived at the airport, cool, calm, unhurried—but minus my ticket. I had to buy another, and thus screwed up my finances completely—and so there was a week minus buses, stamps, food." He explains he doesn't feel like writing a letter "because I'm so sick of this damn typewriter. The only thing worse than writing is reading what I've written. I am now rewriting."

The day he wrote his "Surfside" letter, June 21, three men disappeared outside tiny Philadelphia, Mississippi, about 200 miles north of New Orleans. As Sherman arrived in Miami, CORE's "Freedom Summer" got under way. The 20-year-old Queens College student Andrew Goodman, among the first to arrive in Neshoba County, had volunteered to coordinate the local African-American voter registration project. New Yorker Michael (Mickey) Schwerner (at 25, a year younger than Sherman and new director of CORE's Meridien office) had been working with a local black volunteer, 21-year-old James Earl Chaney. The three vanished. Because Ku Klux Klansmen held government offices and served on local law-enforcement agencies, the search lasted six long weeks. On August 4, FBI agents finally located the murdered civil-rights workers' bodies.

Sherman returned to New Orleans, where he stayed with the Cronins, poised to move to Memphis. He again registered black voters. Christine recalls, "That August was very hot and very dangerous"—not least because these civil-rights activities occurred at a time of heightened racial hatreds. But violence continued to galvanize Sherman. During this visit, he "was asked to hide civil rights workers in the French Quarter. They had escaped from Mississippi after the triple murders. Because I knew the city well, I seemed the natural person to find them refuge, which I did."

Back in New York in September, Sherman completed revising *Fat Tuesday*. Yet he still remained glued to his typewriter, preparing (in the days before copy machines) additional scripts. After expressing to Christine his frustration about this typing treadmill with "Ahhhhhhhhhhhhhhhhhhhhhhhhhhhhh," he continues, "My script is being wonderfully unproducable." He will return to New Orleans, not to see his friend, who no longer lives there, but "to complete a cycle" by attending Mardi Gras again.

Sherman vowed to avoid agonizing about *Fat Tuesday*. Although excellent for so young a writer, it remains unproduced. Yet it was this script he submitted the following year with his application to the playwriting program of Actors Studio.

Sherman provides two author's notes. The first quotes Lawrence Durrell in a passage illuminating the mixed genres of nearly all Sherman's work: "We know that the history of literature is the history of laughter and pain. The imperatives from which there is no escape are: Laugh till it hurts, and hurt till you laugh." The second author's note explains the title refers to Mardi

Gras, or Shrove Tuesday, which Catholic countries celebrate as culminating Carnival.

Sherman takes, not the plot, but the situation, ambience, and kinds of characters from his surroundings in New Orleans and his life. He draws upon Christine to create Rosalyn, aspects of both himself and his New York friend Mylo Quam for Christopher (a poet), some also from Quam for Bobby, and some of both himself and Weiner for Lucas (a songwriter). He also loosely bases Christopher's parents on his mother and father and Weiner's father. Placing the characters in Mardi Gras loosens their inhibitions, thus prompting them to depart from their usual guarded behavior.

The opening creates mysteries that sustain suspense throughout. Christopher Gold, 23, lives in "Poor Bobby's" apartment. We know Bobby painted, for he has left unfinished canvases. But who was he, and what happened to him? Christopher lives downstairs from Lucas, late 30s, whose face we usually observe "masked in sardonic lethargy." We hear carnival noise and music sporadically.

Sherman draws upon not only people in New Orleans but also his understanding of bohemian misfits derived from BU and Manhattan. He contrives an intricate plot, marred only occasionally by padding and inflated rhetoric imitating Durrell's *Alexandria Quartet*, his favorite fiction, and *Camino Real*, a favorite Williams play.

Sherman could, if he chose, turn the play into an interesting period piece, authentic to its era and bearing the Sherman hallmarks: mixed moods and dual themes—outsiders and threats to survival. A gay songwriter, a Jewish Yankee poet and his messed-up parents, a charming female drug smuggler, and an African-American friend, Isaac, variously incarnate "the other." Although Wendy sometimes seems extraneous, she also serves to demonstrate that a white Southern woman can rise above the racist indoctrination of her '40s and '50s upbringing to rescue Isaac from lynching.

Fat Tuesday reflects its era, including racism, more accurately than most other American mid–'60s plays. Perhaps that, rather than its flaws, caused every agent in New York to turn it down. Its characters' cultural diversity would have guaranteed most readers and viewers would find something unwelcome. The two interracial plays produced on Broadway in 1964, both by black writers—Baldwin's *Blues for Mr. Charlie* and Hansberry's *The Sign in Sidney Brustein's Window*—didn't run long, and Baldwin's *The Amen Corner*, in spring 1965, closed even faster. Agents didn't beat the bushes that year looking for *Fat Tuesday*. The dramatist acknowledges the play's pretentiousness and overblown passages, but his timing also stank. That he juxtaposed melodrama and comedy increased its "unproducable" nature.

New Orleans lured Sherman again. After the Cronins moved to Memphis in autumn 1964, Sherman returned for Mardi Gras. Because Easter fell late— on April 18—Fat Tuesday came on March 2, 1965, five days before Bloody

Sunday in Selma, Alabama. While Sheriff Jim Clark, his deputies, and state troopers attacked civil rights marchers on the Edmund Pettus Bridge, Sherman helped black voters register in New Orleans.

Shortly after Sherman returned to New York, Christine left her husband. Sherman urged her all summer to move in with him, so she packed her bags and arrived at Manhattan's Port Authority on her 21st birthday, September 7, 1965. Although out of town, he had sent her the key to his Hell's Kitchen apartment.

After he returned, Christine kept nagging him to introduce her to Michael. "There was always a way Martin spoke about Michael," she remembers. "He never indicated they were lovers. But it was Michael was this genius, and Michael knew everything, and Michael taught him everything. It was clear he loved Michael. And I just assumed they were lovers. So I begged to meet him, and finally, in November, we went to his place. I'm thinking I'm going to meet Martin's lover, but when Michael opens the door, he's incredibly handsome, incredibly sexy, and a genius. I was completely thrown. I wasn't looking to feel interested in him. I couldn't have been more shocked."

Christine kept feeling drawn to Michael and was upset by it. But she began to appreciate that he and Martin weren't a couple. After that evening, the three began going out together. Late in 1965, they went to a party and then "walked to Central Park and all around the zoo until dawn, playing games. Animals came out. We were dancing and leaping, just this incredible magical thing. By the end of the night, I was convinced this man is in love with me, and I'm in love with him, and this is the great love of all time. Martin made clear to me he recognized what was happening, and that it was good. I was not worried he would be hurt. I was stupid. So Martin watches me, this girl he loves, hook up with this guy he loves."

Just as Sherman became part of his second real-life *Jules and Jim* triangle involving Christine, Silverman asked him to write lyrics. Silverman had known Jules Irving and Herbert Blau in San Francisco. When they took over the theatre at Lincoln Center, he became their musical director, and, in fall 1965, he asked Sherman to collaborate on *The Country Wife*.

He feels Sherman's lyrics succeeded admirably. They occurred juxtaposed to Wycherley's own rhymed couplets ending scenes; these also served as lyrics. The men modeled a street scene on a 17th-century piece called "The Crys of London"; they created a market where vendors hawk their wares. Silverman knows his music for this section resembles the Modern Jazz Quartet and acknowledges the scene he and Sherman wrote belonged at New York City Opera.

Sherman cringes recalling Robert Symonds's failure to mount the street scene. "There was chaos—a crowd scene with all these street songs, but no direction. And then Stanley and I were on stage *directing* this scene. And I remember thinking, this is *nuts*! I'm not even listed as lyricist in the program, and I'm co-directing at Lincoln Center, yet I'm *nobody*. Staging it wasn't our job."

"New Exchange Cries" played simultaneously with "New Exchange Fugue." Performers spoke some of the cries but sang most of this section. Sherman invented Town Crier, Flower Girl, Drunken Sailor, Prostitute, Pimp, Meat Seller, Book Seller, and Rug Seller, whose segments frequently overlap contrapuntally.

Sherman begins with pimp and prostitute, and their dialogue continues as a gag running under the street sequence music. Pimp keeps lowering her price, until finally she protests. Meanwhile other vendors hawk their wares—roses, hot sausage, oysters and eels, almanacs, ballads and rugs—while from the din emerge snatches of a drunken sailor's ditty, which near the end reappears as "Drinking Song." Silverman alone receives credit for the songs, but Sherman wrote the lyrics save bits of recitative from Wycherley.

Although this production—opening December 9, 1965—received mixed reviews, some critics liked Sherman and Silverman's contributions, singling those out for special praise even while complaining about production flaws. Cooke praises "the director" [!], who has

> contrived on the large revolving stage colorful and descriptive scenes of late 17th-century London peopled with the gallants, bawds, sailors and ladies in extravagant silks with low-cut bodices. Stanley Silverman's background music adds further to the atmosphere, and in fact this production is suggestive of modern musical comedy production standards [16].

Hipps also praises the crowd scene: "The business made good sense" (62). Gottfried, however, begins, "The Repertory Theatre of Lincoln Center produced 'The Country Wife' last night as if it really didn't like the play at all" and rebukes the market-place scene (25).

Shortly after the opening, Christine moved in with Michael. Disillusioned with New York theatre after his Lincoln-Center experience and failure to secure a production of *Fat Tuesday*, Sherman also found himself odd man out when Christine and Michael married on April 24, 1966. Other aspects of his life also troubled him.

That spring he began therapy, and he received good news: based on *Fat Tuesday*, the Actors Studio had accepted him into their playwrights unit. People who understood theatre appreciated his talent.

Both depressed and looking forward to his fall studies, Sherman went to Europe.

4. Crises (1966–1972)

In mid–May 1966, Sherman flew to London, where he stayed with his friends the Gardners. He further economized by using Arthur Frommer's *Europe on $5 a Day*.

He hadn't felt at home in the U.S., but he recognized immediately he belonged in London. "I knew it would take me a long time to move there," Sherman recalls, "that it wasn't something you could just do. But I knew my destiny lay there." He would spend the next 14 years working to make relocating possible.

On May 30, he wrote the Weiners he had seen three productions at the National Theatre. He describes conditions in his friends' flat as chaotic because pneumonia has hospitalized Patty Gardner. Yet he has feasted upon plays. "The bad theatre is on a level so much higher than ours," he writes. "It is simply unsatisfying, not embarrassing or unbearable. And there even is good theatre. Think of that!"

Concerning his ventures to the National, he writes succinct reviews:

> A brilliant production of Congreve's *Love for Love* was not played for the usual Restoration leers and caricature, but rather with realism, and the result was warm and charming, as well as funny. (It was everything *The Country Wife* should have been, though it's a much better play.) Olivier played a fop with great comic skill, and the entire company (Joyce Redman, John Stride, Lynn Redgrave) played like the well-knit unit repertory companies are supposed to be. Pinero's *Trelawney of the Wells* is a dreadful old chestnut, but I found myself crying and laughing at the silly old thing. Maggie Smith was in it, which means a lot, and another joy was Robert Stephens, who suggests an enormous range, indeed the possibilities of a great actor.

He signs off by reporting "the Gardner children are throwing jello at the walls, so I suppose one must do something."

In subsequent letters he elaborates about productions he relishes and those he doesn't. On June 12 he exults, "I have been to the theatre nineteen times in a row, and I am staggered. I must say the London theatre is worth going to nineteen times in a row (more than I saw all season in New York). It exists in an atmosphere and under conditions that lend themselves to honor and perception instead of boredom and inanity."

Of another production, he writes, "The most exciting modern play I've seen—a play that carved its way into the soul of today's youth—probed deeper into 1966 than anything I have encountered. The play is *Hamlet*, Peter Hall's production at the RSC with David Warner. The production angered me at first because I was detached; I wanted to cry, but I couldn't; all I could do was think. When on earth does *that* happen in the theatre? Even *Sound of Music* can make you weep, but you have to be dragged screaming into thought."

After appraising other plays and productions, he considers costuming: "The city is dressed by Salvador Dali; the common everyday form of clothing is the epitome of Op Art, and it is all outrageous and wonderful. It makes London truly the most modern city I have seen, because it adapts modern art forms into living reality, and I think it is absolutely deserving of its reputation as 'the city of the sixties.' I leave in two days for 'the city of the twenties.'"

When, on June 14, Sherman arrived in Paris, he learned his friend Elisabeth hadn't joined him, instead opting to travel with a boyfriend. He continued alone to Nice, then Florence and Rome, where he arrived on a scorching July 4. He writes the Weiners on July 6 "OLD ROME is magnificent—all those ruins and churches—but NEW ROME is a dud—Dolce Vita has moved to London. The Riviera was marvelous."

Of depression and financial troubles, he hints not a jot to the Weiners. His two cards from Greece sound ecstatic. On July 12 he writes from Corfu, which he reached by boat from Brandisi. He addresses it to "MRS. Michael Weiner" and begins "*THIS IS NOT FOR YOUR HUSBAND!* He is a non–Durrell-loving infidel and thus cannot receive a card from Corfu, the home of the master. Did one ever doubt Durrell's wisdom, even in choice of home? It is an enchanted island. My first touch of Greece, and now the trip becomes so much more vivid. At last it is all unreal, and at last it is all real. I'd end with an Hellenic proverb, like Durrell always does, but I don't know any." He signs it by referring to two writers in *Alexandria Quartet*: "Would-Be Pursewarden and/or Darlay."

Had he packed Durrell's *Prospero's Cell*, however, he might appropriately have quoted "Other countries may offer you discoveries in manners or lore or landscape; Greece offers you something harder—the discovery of yourself" (11). Indeed, Sherman speaks of the trip as "one of those rites of passage," especially a coming-of-age in Greece. It became a home-away-from-home after he moved to London; later he built a house there. Greece also figures in his work.

In 1986 he used Corfu as setting for Act 1 of *A Madhouse in Goa*. He stayed in Benitzes in an inn overlooking the Albanian coast. Two brothers ran it, as in his play.

When he left Corfu on a ferry, he relished "the beauty and the little islands we passed popping out of the water. There was fog, very romantic. That is when I fell in love with Greece."

Sherman mailed from Mykonos his last postcard to the Weiners. He rhapsodizes: "IT IS SO BEAUTIFUL HERE—When the Gods smile, surely they are thinking of Greece."

Since his first visit there, Sherman has returned often, to soak up sun, think about his work-in-progress, tussle with any problem it presents, recover from his latest production or deadline, or write to meet deadlines looming. He feels a special affinity to "the light. I love the color of the light. I've never seen light like it anyplace else. It has great clarity. Clears my mind. Makes me think."

Sherman acknowledges he feels connected to the ancient Greek past. "It's inescapable, timeless. If it were just beaches and sun, I wouldn't have that connection. When I first went to Athens, the Parthenon thrilled me. Most of the places I'm attracted to have a huge sense of connection to a past."

Sherman notes he doesn't necessarily go to a place to see ruins. He reveres the land. He can take "a boat to a beach and pass rocky terrain and I'm incredibly aware it's been there forever."

In Greece, Sherman discovered male beauty—"nothing to do with my attraction to men. Men on Mykonos didn't feel constrained by conventional fashions. They felt free to draw upon their feminine—but not effeminate—sides." He admired the otherness of Greek men who permitted themselves to look beautiful before this grew more common among jetsetters, models, and stars.

Sherman's own appearance altered in Carnaby Street clothing. Previously ill at ease in his skinny frame, he now had clothes that fit and even seemed designed for his body. Suddenly his shape became an asset. He let his hair grow long and grew sideburns. Buses stopped so tourists could photograph him. He developed his own style, before it became known back home as "hippie." He embodies this in a speech for Gideon in *Cracks*.

After Sherman stayed in Athens and Mykonos, he planned to visit Santorini, but a boat problem caused him to head instead to Samos, which he disliked, and then to Crete. There he had so little money he slept on a hotel roof. He went from Crete to Rhodes, which he hated, and then to Israel, another place where he felt that link to long ago: "I connect with places having ancient histories because I'm aware how fragile our civilization is and our hubris in thinking it's going to last, where so many amazing civilizations that preceded us disappeared." He set *Next Year in Jerusalem* in a Holy Land temple.

Sherman describes himself by the time he reached Israel as "a complete neurotic, screaming mess." He wired his father for money because he couldn't face another boat or train. He flew from Israel, stopping over in Amsterdam, en route to London, where he stayed another couple of weeks, gorging himself on more plays, during "the great glory days of the British theatre."

Sherman reflects, "I rediscovered my love for theatre. It was the heyday of Olivier's National, of the RSC. That summer in London opened up whole new areas for me in terms of classical technique and repertoire and the whole range of theatre."

4. Crises (1966–1972)

On August 31, 1966, Sherman sent Bloom a postcard bearing the message "RETURN ENGAGEMENT by popular demand back from European Tour 'Who's Afraid of Martin Sherman' reopens Wednesday, Sept. 7, New York, 1:40 pm."

Once home, Sherman began courses at Actors Studio. He terms his acceptance "the first thing that ever happened to me of any consequence." For that year only, Harold Clurman was running the playwrights unit. Instead of attending only those classes, however, Sherman went to the acting and directing sessions, too. In acting classes, Lee Strasberg taught his interpretation of Constantin Stanislavsky's techniques. What he inculcated in Marlon Brando and James Dean, for example, had become known as "the Method."

Sherman says, "Strasberg could teach acting for film, but he ruined actors for theatre. When he got away from sense memory, etc. and went on to specifics about theatre, he had resources of practical knowledge I ate up. Strasberg taught me, if you have a play in previews and something is wrong, they're going to give you specifics about what it is, and almost always the specifics will be wrong, but the area they're encircling is right; look at that. His side issues were the best education I've had in theatre."

Although Sherman had one therapy session right before leaving for Europe, he undertook therapy in earnest in September 1966. He says, "I'm fairly sensible, and my depression was not uncalled for. I had a depressing life." Although he loved Europe, his trip had intensified his depression. Years later, in *A Madhouse in Goa*, David, the young American in Corfu whom he based on himself, anguishes because Michael doesn't love him. We can assume similar feelings in Sherman that summer, but he accounts for his misery by noting his friend Elisabeth never joined him in Paris. "I was on my own—little money and alone." While traveling in Italy, Greece, and Holland, "I was miserable and suicidal."

Nevertheless, Sherman found the experience strengthened him. He managed to stretch his money to meet expenses and found he loved the places he saw. "As sometimes happens," he explains, "it was an endless nightmare that was the best thing in the world. I fell in love with Europe. And I knew I had come home." He recognized "my emotional resources were strong."

He also recognized if he could fall in love with Europe while depressed and anxious, that meant he wasn't falling for some phony fictitious Europe. He had confronted the realities. He notes, "There was nothing sentimental or romantic or pretty about my attraction to it because I had a miserable time. I think that's why I have such a healthy relationship with Europe and why I feel so comfortable here. There were no illusions to shatter."

Sherman had a lot to talk about in therapy and found it helpful, but "the '60s got me out of my depression as much as therapy did. I couldn't have done it without therapy, but I also couldn't have done it without the late '60s."

Sherman's spirits began to lift. Friends who knew him then speak of his joy of life, his talent for fun. Silverman says, "I admired his ability to laugh despite the 50 percent probability he would develop Huntington's Chorea. He had learned to live with that anxiety. He laughed a lot."

With Silverman, Sherman went to New York Philharmonic concerts, listened to contemporary music, and had meals in the north Bronx with Silverman's family. His mother, Eva, loved Sherman, whose skinny frame challenged her; she made it her mission to fill him out. When he got the flu, she went down to West 49th St. with chicken soup and her finest delicacies. "She just loved him," Silverman says, "and he loved her." She supplied him mothering he hadn't known.

Another older woman entered his life in the late '60s, dancer Leila Livingston's mother, Jorie. Sherman met her through Mylo Quam, who studied voice with her. Jorie Livingston adored Sherman as a son. Leila says of her mother's closeness to him, "She felt he wasn't yet at home with himself. She stood by him and encouraged him to go for what he wanted."

In the late '60s Sherman wrote several scripts. Although these prolific years produced nothing of lasting worth, they helped the dramatist prepare for his mature work. These plays also won him agents in both the U.S. (Mary Dolan) and the U.K. (Peggy Ramsay).

Next Year in Jerusalem grew out of Sherman's trip abroad and his examination with his therapist of the crisis his mother's illness precipitated. He completed it by early 1967, shortly after he enjoyed seeing Bloom play Charlotte Corday in *Marat/Sade* on Broadway. Sherman's play received a spring staged-reading at Actors Studio, where Walt Whitcover directed Kevin O'Connor, Boris Tumarin, and Russian Anna Sten. The next year, beginning June 8, 1968, HB (the Herbert Berghof Playwrights Foundation) presented it; Terry Kiser replaced O'Connor.

Sten had made noteworthy films in Russia and Germany but didn't transfer well to Hollywood. Her films there proved such legendary flops she achieved fame as a Cole Porter song lyric: "If Samuel Goldwyn can teach Anna Sten English then heaven knows—anything goes!"

In this explicitly Jewish play, painter David and his parents, Aaron and Deborah—the latter barely able to walk because she suffers from a degenerative disease, here dubbed "Hovington's Cortea"—visit in Israel's Negev Desert the country's oldest ruined temple, erected to a Phoenician sun-god. Aaron insists on bringing his wife from the car. David hopes "there might be one magic moment in which she would care enough to speak—really speak.... I thought a land of miracles would produce one."

Both men express impatience at Deborah's infirmity. David wants to discuss institutionalizing her. Aaron refuses to acknowledge the gravity of his wife's condition, and David urges her to fight her illness, as though she could somehow resist a degenerative disease. He also petulantly destroys her cigarettes—the one thing she still values enough to prompt her to talk. David clearly suffers his own denial, plus narcissism that turns Deborah's horrifying condition into his own personal drama and converts his fear of ending up just like her into rage directed at her.

David's nascent narcissism precedes, without equaling, the full-blown megalomania of such later characters as nearly everyone in *Cracks*, Sergei in *When She Danced*, Barnaby in *A Madhouse in Goa*, Horatio in *Some Sunny Day*, Allen in *The Boy from Oz*, and Onassis. Sherman's radar easily detects this trait, and, as his dramaturgical skills develop, so does his deft portrayal. Other Sherman characters evince it without this quality controlling their every act.

Next Year in Jerusalem depends too much on exposition; the characters speak about what they've said before or already know. The dialogue occasionally resorts to clichés, as when Aaron tells his son, "I need you. You're the only one I really care about. You don't know what you mean to me. You were the answer to my prayers." Nevertheless, it dramatizes a dramatic confrontation among members of a frightened family, and it includes original theatrical elements, such as picnicking on the altar and David and Deborah scuffling as he destroys her cigarettes, which in turn metaphorically embody her illness, the real source of David's rage. It also prefigures the studies of disability later given mature form in *Messiah*'s Rebecca, *A Madhouse in Goa*'s Daniel, and *Rose*'s Sunny.

The play's strength lies in characters dreading the future: Aaron doesn't really want to reach Jerusalem because he worries it will change nothing. Deborah fears she is losing her mind and will be institutionalized. And David dreads turning into his mother. Sherman reflects the night thoughts everyone harbors about what lies ahead.

Sherman incorporates autobiographical elements, characterizing himself as young David, out of college two years but still supported by his father, casting Joseph as Aaron, and drawing upon his mother's degenerative disease, which David, like Sherman, fears he might have inherited. He gives David a speech that describes Sherman's boyhood perceptions: "When I lived at home I never knew you were ill. No one told me. It started quietly when I was just a child. You would be clumsy, you would fall. You began to have trouble preparing our meals. And it grew slowly.... By the time I reached high school you were dropping everything and wearing disheveled clothes and withdrawing from the household and from me. You used to sit in a chair in the living room and stare—just stare—into space." Like Sherman, David didn't learn what was wrong with his mother until "when I went to college, [and] Father decided it was time—oh yes, time—at last—to let me know."

Although he created a deeply personal script, Sherman here imagines a confrontation that never took place and a family visit to Israel that didn't occur. Instead he went there alone, in 1966, encumbered by thoughts of the sort David articulates. The family also resembles one in *Fat Tuesday*, in which the mother drinks and Christopher feels she could and should stop; he likewise rebukes his father's denial of her alcoholism. Like Christopher, David insists his mother control the uncontrollable.

Sherman describes the play as "very young and indulgent. But it was a big step for me," he adds. "For all its excesses, for the first time I was completely honest."

When Whitcover directed the Actors Studio reading, Clurman fell ill, so Strasberg led the discussion. He admired spots in the script, calling them "pure playwriting." Sherman recognized he had written those because of what he had learned in acting classes at BU. This involved dialogue discussing something different from the scene's real subject.

Whitcover loved the play. When he persuaded HB to do it, he suggested Sherman write a short companion piece to its 70 minutes. Because Sten's husband was designing a comeback for her, Sherman made clear he wouldn't write a short play for her. "She's too unusual," he argued. He had something else in mind, a little romance. Sten's husband agreed.

So Sherman wrote the 20-minute *The Night Before Paris*, suggested by his own experience, about a New Yorker scheduled to fly to Paris the following day. She leaves her therapy group and picks up an ice-skater. Sherman concedes it's "a disguised gay play, heterosexual and funny, cute, charming." He filled it with group-therapy jokes. He wrote it for Bloom, but then Sten wanted to do it. Sherman refused to let 60-year-old Sten play the role, so HB only presented *Next Year in Jerusalem*.

Sherman had managed to protect the role for Verna once, but when Actors Studio decided to do it in January 1969, Sylvia Miles, a Studio member, wanted the part. What Bloom describes as "that lovely little play" went to Miles. She played Eileen and Fox Harris played Troy, a precursor role to the diver in *Passing By*, a gay romance.

By the late '60s that decade had become what people mean by "The Sixties," the hippie era of psychedelic clothing, LSD, flower children, love-ins and Woodstock. An era of social upheaval, this decade spawned racial hatreds and the beginning of racial healing, homophobia and the beginning of gay pride. What seemed like an isolated event when Lee Harvey Oswald gunned down John Fitzgerald Kennedy on November 22, 1963, recurred: On February 21, 1965, Malcolm X died. On April 4, 1968, Martin Luther King, Jr., died. On June 5, 1968, Robert F. Kennedy died. Such events influenced the three scripts—all musicals—Sherman wrote during and just after 1968.

First his *Candide* play, *Things Went Badly in Westphalia*, secured him Mary Dolan at Gloria Safier as his American agent. She loved the title and represented it effectively, getting it published in Stanley Richards's *The Best Short Plays: 1970* and presented at least once in 1971 (Storrs, Connecticut) and thrice in 1973 (Wisconsin, May; Oakland, June; Long Island, July). She remembers him as sweet, gentle, and skinny. Like others recalling youthful Sherman, she cites Ichabod Crane.

Political satire *Westphalia* features an American gay hippie stand-in for Voltaire's Candide. Sherman mocks homophobia, racism, prejudice against anybody different. Joshua roams the country, singing and playing guitar, while avoiding bombings, brandings, lynchings, mutilations, slaughter via bows and arrows and machine guns, autodafés—violence threatening "the other."

Joshua experiences conflicts about whether to live or die, but reaches conclusions such as "something good is going to happen" (396)—Sherman's equivalent of Candide's insistence we live "in the best of all possible worlds." Joshua longs to reach "Flower City," but, when he does, finds everybody he cares about has been crucified. Yet even then he chooses survival rather than suicide or capitulating to murderous bigots.

Although *Westphalia* critiques the era, Sherman also satirizes literature, drama and films that misrepresent gay men as sporting limp wrists, slit wrists, or both. These caricatures he derides in *Westphalia* before providing accurate portraits in *Passing By*.

Following *Westphalia* Sherman wrote *Change*, with Ed Kresley and Drey Shepperd providing the score. Producers optioned it but never presented it. Each time they altered it at producers' insistence, it grew worse. On May 20, 1969, Lehman Engel's BMI Musical Theatre Workshop presented scenes from it, with a cast including Bernadette Peters, David Cryer, Patrick Fox, and Jonelle Allen.

Shortly afterwards, on a hot June night, Sherman and Miles walked up Seventh Avenue and crossed Christopher Street. He saw a crowd outside a gay bar, the Stonewall, where police were tossing drag queens into a van. He remembers the queens as funny, feisty and angry. But the Stonewall didn't appeal to hippie Sherman, who preferred Janis Joplin to Judy Garland—who had just died. Jonelle approached him, and they watched briefly before they plotted a ruse to get her a cab. Since drivers wouldn't stop for Blacks, he hid her, hailed a taxi, then hurried her into it. He pondered racism as he and Miles continued walking.

Sherman didn't understand the evening's significance. Much later he realized, "I had witnessed the birth of another movement, one that would color my life and that of every lesbian and gay man from that moment on. There had been a raid, and queens had fought back. Fought back! I was there, but I wasn't. Actually only the drag queens were really there that evening. I had seen it, but I hadn't. I had stumbled across history. And I didn't know it" (*Stonewall 2*).

Finally, Sherman and Shepperd wrote *Delta Lady* for Miles, who would have played "a Martha Raye-like USO entertainer who gets lost in the Mekong Delta with her troupe. It wasn't me," reports Sherman. "It wasn't terrible. It was clever but manufactured." Producers optioned it, but no production followed. "If it had been produced when we wrote it, probably it would have succeeded," he speculates. But it would certainly have misled audiences as to what sort of play Sherman writes. Following this play with songs and musicals *Change* and *Westphalia*, he created no more librettos for over 30 years. In 2002, however, he revisited that night outside Stonewall in his book for Broadway's *The Boy from Oz*.

While Sherman spent late 1969 and early 1970 in London, he sent his plays to England's premier agent, Peggy Ramsay. She agreed to represent him and submitted *Westphalia* to Oscar Lowenstein—who wanted to produce it but didn't—and *The Night Before Paris* to the Traverse Theatre's Michael Rudman, who presented it at Edinburgh's adventurous playhouse in June 1970. Job Stewart directed Claris Erikson and Robert Hamilton in Sherman's first production outside the U.S. That year, the Traverse presented Wesker's *The Four Seasons* and Pinter's *The Caretaker*, along with less memorable new plays. Sherman had begun establishing a presence in his adopted country.

Back home, he took part in an early Martin Scorsese documentary. The director filmed *Street Scenes* during two rallies against the Vietnam War. Both took place in May 1970, one on Wall Street, the other in Washington, D.C. Oliver Stone participated as a cameraman. Sherman and his friends Bloom and husband, Jay Cocks, led the students holding cameras "into the 'hot' spots, meaning we were always getting tear-gassed." The film also contains a postmortem. Scorsese, Harvey Keitel, Cocks, Bloom, and Sherman sit down to discuss the protests. All except Sherman participate. He explains, "I'm just sitting there like an idiot, saying nothing, because I was sooooooo tear-gassed."

Also in 1970, Sherman joined the board of Curt Dempster's Ensemble Studio Theatre, which held a reading—just cast, Dempster, and Sherman— of a new play. Only 15 pages, all from Act 1, have survived. At 5 A.M., painter Toby sleeps beside attorney boyfriend Daniel. The phone wakes Toby, who learns his sister Rachel will soon arrive. Panicked, he rouses groggy Daniel and tells him to leave immediately. We assume Toby doesn't want his sister to find him in bed with a man. Wrong! He wants to prevent Daniel from learning Rachel's dead boyfriend Simon has possessed her. When "they" arrive, Daniel refuses to believe in Rachel's dybbuk. This leads to laughter when Act 1 ends as Daniel rebukes Simon—as though he exists.

This fragment resembles later plays. Toby and Daniel's interaction suggests *Passing By*'s banter. Rachel possessed by Simon predates *Cracks*, with its woman possessed by her dead therapist. Sherman named *Messiah*'s protagonist Rachel and gave the name Daniel to Hosani in *Madhouse*, and he used "Perlow" again in *Rose*. Years later Sherman modernized Ansky's *The Dybbuk* as a film. When, in 1972, Sherman abandoned his draft of this early dybbuk play, he turned to *Passing By* and again employed the names Simon and Toby. Both Tobys paint. Perhaps Dempster found a dybbuk intriguing because he gave *Cracks* a reading at EST before its staged reading at the O'Neill Center in 1975.

While Sherman worked on the dybbuk draft in 1970–71, he and his lyricist/composer collaborators tried to get their musicals mounted, but projected productions of both *Change* and *Delta Lady* fell through. Sherman's disappointment about the aborted *Delta Lady* with Miles in spring 1972 occurred as he came down with hepatitis.

Severe hepatitis sent him to bed for three months, thus breaking a debilitating routine of seeing people whose self-destructiveness had been damaging him.

Sherman feels "hepatitis saved my life. If my bottoming out hadn't taken that form, it would have been another more dangerous. I needed to stop everything I was doing and reassess and change my life. My enlightened doctor agreed, though I had bad hepatitis, to send me home instead of to the hospital." Sherman couldn't move, but friends brought him food. After six weeks, he went to Florida and stayed with his stepmother.

While recuperating, from August 26 through September 11 Sherman watched the summer Olympics. He especially relished the diving. Small wonder, later that autumn, as the playwright shaped a gay romantic comedy about two men suffering from hepatitis, he decided to make the hunky one a diver. *Passing By*'s Simon has even won a bronze medal in the '68 Olympics.

Sherman felt he had found in hepatitis a great, theatrical subject. Nobody had done that before; playwrights then didn't write about illness. Although he doesn't show his earlier plays to others, in *Passing By* he created a work in which he still takes pride. He likes its warmth, and he calls it a "watershed," his breakthrough both in dramaturgical skill and in gay subject. It threw the dramatist completely out of the closet—an unusual self-outing for 1972.

After his mockery of gay angst in *Westphalia*, Sherman presents homosexuality as normal. He dramatizes a budding gay relationship, for the first time, in a completely positive light, without any agonizing about sexual orientation, or coming out, or persecution, just as natural and a given of these men's lives. Although a politically important act, this romance doesn't make an explicit political statement.

Passing By contains some of Sherman's most economical writing. He deftly sketches the men's first wordless encounter at a movie theatre—probably watching *Jules and Jim*—and their developing relationship under unusual circumstances, as first New Yorker Toby contracts hepatitis and then out-of-towner Simon finds himself stricken. A charming, light, gentle comedy about men initially strangers, it dramatizes them caring for each other during their mutual illness. Written before the advent of HIV, *Passing By* has no connection with AIDS plays and movies that came later, first from others and eventually from Sherman in *Alive and Kicking*.

Toby and Simon's relationship changes their lives. For example, Toby finds he can paint again. But their love doesn't cement them. New York artist Toby will soon depart for Paris. Simon has arrived in the Big Apple from Miami for an interview, but fails to land the job. Their meeting as they are "passing by" sends Simon pretending to just "pass by" the wine store where Toby works, yet the diver admits he has tried six stores. After surviving a serious illness together, their affection has grown. They want to stay together, but Toby must embark on his postponed painting in Europe.

This upbeat play dramatizes the value of loving and being loved, of tenderness together, of laughing together, even of fussing and feuding together when love buttresses the aftermath. Yet Sherman retains a realistically practical perspective about Toby and Simon's need to stick to their career plans.

He employs a plot construction similar to one he chooses five years later in *Bent*. Toby and Simon in Act 1 occupy varied locales—a movie theatre, an apartment, a wine store, a park bench—but in Act 2, neither man can leave the apartment. In *Bent*, Max and Horst can't leave because the second half takes place in Dachau, whereas only illness prevents departure from Toby's flat.

Act 1 ends as Simon discovers he has caught Toby's hepatitis. Sherman conveys this in Toby's query to Simon, "What colour are your eyes?" (111). Act 2 ends, after they test free of hepatitis, as Toby leaves for Paris.

The clear structure, dialogue that wastes no words, and clever situation exemplify the craft of spare yet effective playwriting at which Sherman since has proven a master.

After recovering from hepatitis and considering his options, Sherman, like Toby, prepared for a change of scene.

5. California Dreamin' (1973–1977)

When Sherman sent out *Passing By* in late 1972, nobody in New York would do it. He had treated his usual themes of "the other" and survival affirmatively. Producers had never seen a gay-romance like it. Soon Doric Wilson, Lanford Wilson, and Harvey Fierstein would dramatize gay relationships in this matter-of-fact fashion. But then, Sherman took a bolder approach than New York producers could stomach.

He wanted to relocate to London; therefore he moved to Los Angeles. Antony Sher explains this circuitous route to achieving his dream by insisting, "Martin did this to make himself dislike America so much he'd have to leave the country." Actually he needed to make money and establish a reputation that would enable him to meet British Immigration's requirements concerning income.

Sherman arrived in L.A. just in time for the February 21, 1973, 5.3 Point Mugu earthquake and subsequent mudslide. He stayed with friends and later lived in Venice and right off Santa Monica Boulevard near Barney's Beanery.

Sherman met producer Allan Carr, who, between 1973 and 1976, gave him work contributing to television and film projects. He began writing story outlines to sell to TV series, and he bought a '64 Ford Thunderbird because the City of Angels didn't offer useful public transportation.

He wrote the Weiners on March 2, 1973, about L.A.'s weirdness. One paragraph easily could have turned up in *Cracks*. He quotes a guy saying, "I go to group therapy at Synanon, even though I'm not a drug addict, because it's close to my house, and besides, junkies really know how to criticize. I discovered the spirit is *permanent*. I mean, if you're going down on somebody in a subway john, that's temporary, you know, but once you enter the spirit world, you have continuity."

On August 8, Sherman wrote Lavren saying he has sold a Movie-of-the-Week story outline, the "most sophomoric, inane, embarrassing thing ever to come out of my typewriter—and naturally Hollywood loved it." His outlines paid his rent.

By late summer Carr hired Sherman to contribute to Cass Elliott's last TV special, *Don't Call Me Mama Anymore*, which she did with Joel Grey on CBS. By the time it aired on September 28, Sherman had gone to Taos on a

Wurlitzer-Foundation Residency Grant. On the Rio Grande, between September 20 and December 17, preceding his 35th birthday, he wrote *Cracks*.

On September 25 Sherman wrote Lavren, "I have this huge house, even a music room, two studies. And I'm going crazy. There ain't no one else around. I'd like two words of conversation a day. There are no newspapers, and you can only get one radio station, which is fine if you like Indian war dances. Christ, am I lonely! Listen, I gotta' go pace."

Introducing *Cracks*, Sherman explains the place to write his grant provided.

> Outside my house lay an astonishing ... landscape that featured breathtaking canyons and gorges and the Rio Grande—God's country, surely ... and a fiercely alcoholic and unhappy Mexican community and an occasional sound of gunfire and wandering tribes of shell-shocked hippies mourning the sixties and a secret Catholic cult named Penitentes who each Easter crucified one of their members.... In this soothing calm, I wrote *Cracks* [vi].

Sherman sets it in 1973 in California. His '60s iconic characters include a rock megastar, a cross-dressing bodyguard, a woman who plays Monopoly with her dybbuk, an actress based on Miles, and a Jewish former Buddhist becoming a monk who worries the monastery won't offer him any cocaine "until they're sure I'm cool." The playwright understands these misfits and ridicules their hedonism and narcissism good-naturedly, relying on irony, not venom.

Sherman had trekked up to Bethel, New York, for the August 15–17, 1969, rock-and-rain Woodstock and had told Dolan about "groupies making plaster casts of rock stars' private parts," which he gleefully incorporates into *Cracks*.

His title suggests several meanings: wisecracks, cracked nuts who slavishly follow fads, cracking a multiple murder case, cracks of gunfire, cracks caused by earthquakes, but also fissures in human character of self-absorption, which rendered impotent the counterculture's high ideals.

Sherman generates a more suspenseful and coherent whodunit than Agatha Christie's 1943 *Ten Little Indians* (a.k.a. *And Then There Were None*). In her version, we can't tell whether anybody survives, whereas his leaves no doubt. In the guise of a comic thriller, this farce appreciates and yet mocks and kills off the hippie counterculture, both free-spirited and intensely egomaniacal—hence the term the "Me generation"—which abandoned its flower-power ideals and wallowed in self-indulgence. He farcically sets up the one "normal" character to take the rap for murdering the "others"—an interesting perspective on what happened to flower children who failed to protect themselves. He needs only nine actors to play ten people because one enacts a woman possessed by the dybbuk of her dead shrink. *Cracks* sends viewers into giggle fits. The ending shows the joke's on us because our mortality will fell us.

Sherman observes in this comedy the neo-classic unities for tragedy. It takes place in "real" time, its four Act 1 scenes separated by moments, and the intermission covers a few minutes. Act 2 unfolds in one continuous scene. He sets everything in one set, the rock star's living room, study and garden. And once begun, the action's inevitability takes charge. Ever the ironist, the playwright embraces the "rules" for tragedy but won't let us stop laughing.

He begins and ends with one-person segments, opening with nearly naked Rick adorning himself for a ritual but, after a shot rings out, falling dead. Another shot cracks periodically and somebody else dies, until, finally, only Irene remains. She convinces herself she must have shot the others and rejoices "It was me!" as a shot kills her, too.

Irene's combination of logic and panicked dementia resembles that same amalgam in Heather's speech in *Madhouse* as she recounts trying to choose healthy food. In *Cracks*, Sherman also anticipates the annihilation he lets loose toward the end of *Madhouse*, which emphasizes death will claim everyone. Certainly on one level *Cracks* dramatizes and satirizes the death of the '60s, but this black comedy also demonstrates the inexorable *process* of death. We can't make sense of it, it has no motive, but, no matter how hard we might struggle to survive, we cannot.

After killing off Rick, Sherman builds suspense about when the others will find the body. We meet Jade, a 17-year-old groupie; Clay, Rick's lawyer who makes pornographic films; Gideon, a guitarist in Rick's band who perpetually smokes joints; Maggie, who stopped acting when she became a celebrity; Roberta, a transsexual tough guy who wears a dress; Nadine, a young woman possessed by the dybbuk of her shrink; Irene, Rick's uptight cousin; and Sammy, who in some ways resembles Sherman: gay, Jewish, longhaired, and he used to register black voters in the South. Several are gay or bisexual.

After completing this comedy, Sherman continued living in L.A. and doing projects for Carr. He also wrote narration for KNBC–TV news and documentaries. His plays as well as personal matters, however, continued periodically to take him back east.

He learned Robert Moss had scheduled the first production of *Passing By* at the new Playwrights Horizons, so he spent several weeks in New York for casting, rehearsals, and March 5, 1974, opening. Director Joseph Cali encountered predictable problems casting the show, even though it only required two men. "It was hard to get good actors to play openly gay roles that didn't end with their suicides or weren't excessively camp and therefore character parts," Sherman explains. Established actors wouldn't risk their careers playing happy, well-adjusted gay men. Sherman summarizes, "We couldn't cast it properly."

That year, Dempster gave *Cracks* a reading at Ensemble Studio Theatre. The cast included Stockard Channing, James Woods, Jerry Zaks, and Bloom.

Sherman spent 1974 working on TV projects, but he returned to New York in early October because Jorie Livingston had fallen ill. Worry about Jorie began to help shape his next play, *Rio Grande*, a script which caused a brief rift between him and her daughter Leila. A deeply private person, she objected to his basing the play's central character on her mother.

One year after the unsuccessful Playwrights Horizons' attempt to do justice to *Passing By*, on March 14, 1975, TOSOS (the Other Side of Silence), a gay theatre run by Doric Wilson and Peter del Valle, began presenting it for four weekends. Del Valle directed Joseph Hardin as Simon and Jerry Tobin as Toby. TOSOS served an historically important function by staging work other theatres wouldn't touch, but the remounting encountered the same casting obstacles as the premiere.

Sherman's next Big Apple production, *Soaps*, a ten-minute comedy, on April 26, 1974, opened at Playwrights Horizons with nine other short shows as part of *New York, New York*. In three tiny but hilarious revue sketches, it satirizes soap operas. Subsequently Robert Allan Ackerman directed *Soaps* for a benefit performance at the Shubert Theatre with a cast including Susan Sarandon, Madeline Kahn, Gilda Radner, Jill Eikenberry, Chris Sarandon, and Steven Collins.

Sherman read in *Variety* Drew Griffiths and Gerald Chapman had formed a company in London called Gay Sweatshop, so he asked Ramsay to send them *Passing By*. She submitted it, and, by coincidence, Michael Rudman, by then Artistic Director of Hampstead Theatre, also sent it to them.

Gay Sweatshop had been invited to mount a season of gay plays (jointly termed *Homosexual Acts*) at Ed Berman's Almost Free Theatre. They accepted the script. Drew Griffiths (important to *Bent*'s genesis) directed, while Simon Callow played artist Toby and Michael Dickinson appeared as diver Simon. Sherman went to London for rehearsals and the June 11, 1975 opening.

McFerran lauds acting and production, but pronounces the play "polished and enjoyable pap" (15). Church recognizes as significant "that absolutely no tension is felt between this enclosed world and the 'straight' heterosexual world outside" (13). He praises the "exemplary" production and says the script "sets itself strictly limited objectives which it then proceeds brilliantly to achieve." He concludes, "Much of it is funny, some of it moving." For his first London production, Sherman had won a rave from the *Times*. That professional accomplishment generated a personal milestone as well: he used the review to come out to his father.

Passing By also generated a notice unconnected with its merits, but instead reflecting a political rift. British gay men had created Gay Sweatshop, yet its founders had chosen American plays—three by Robert Patrick, plus *Passing By*—for the first season. Some members resigned over this, and one critic panned Sherman's play because the company was "dredging the history of Off-Off-Broadway" (36). Gilbert, who soon became a Sherman supporter, termed the script "fearfully misty and sentimental," but his real objection concerned the absence of "home-grown" work. Gilbert raised this issue as Sherman was becoming part of Gay Sweatshop and the London gay community.

"It was the first really good production I had," Sherman recalls. "It was the first time I saw anything of mine that worked, that captured what my kind of theatre was about."

On July 23, 1975, Inter-Action administrator Martin Turner wrote Ramsay, reinforcing Sherman's self-respect. Gay Sweatshop presented the play under Inter-Action's auspices. Its head, Ed Berman, decided to increase Sherman's previously agreed upon royalty. Sherman had received £10, but Berman decided to increase the fee to £30, so that "Martin Sherman should receive at least as much as the cast."

Passing By has received productions in Sydney in 1976, in Stockholm by 1977, in Hartford in 1979, in Richmond and Rome in 1994, and in Philadelphia in 2009.

Second Stage in New York scheduled it for summer 1983, but Sherman had to withdraw permission. Because of AIDS' advent, he feared "it would be seen as a play in which the characters have a major problem, which is illness. It would be hard for audiences to respond to the lightness and charm and humor." Sherman feared critics would scapegoat the men, equating their sexual orientation with disease. Withdrawing the play broke his heart, because it would have appeared at a major New York theatre.

Sherman's fears about the play's flippancy misfiring proved well founded when Proctor complained, "Any play that attempts to draw laughs out of a situation in which a man sexually transmits hepatitis to another man is a poor production choice in the era of AIDS." This critic's anger permeates his review and demonstrates how history made *Passing By*, for a time, dangerous.

The 1975 Gay Sweatshop production proved the playwright's turning point professionally and personally. Sherman joined Gay Sweatshop. He returned to London the following year and continued to give advice and participate in this company, and that led him, in 1977, to write *Bent*.

Those weeks in London during June 1975 introduced Sherman to Callow, Antony Sher, Alan Pope, and Pope's boyfriend Peter Whitman. Beginning that summer, on each London visit Sherman stayed with Pope until relocating in 1980.

During the three years subsequent to Gay Sweatshop's production of his romantic comedy, while Sherman continued to live in L.A. and then New York, he visited London frequently. He slept in Alan and Peter's living room, and they fed him. Pope remembers when he appeared in "a biblical rock musical called *King David*, Martin turned his scathing wit upon this awful project. That's how I got to know him well. He settled into our household quickly then."

But back in June 1975, Sherman's "real life in London" began.

Callow had imagined the author as short and plump, but, when Sherman arrived, found him "wonderfully thin and willowy. He picked a delicate way across the rehearsal hall. He's a delicate goat of a man who picks his way carefully across the stones of life.

"When I read the play," Callow continues, "I instantly adored it. It's extraordinary because it's about two men who fall in love—just a rather ordinary little romantic affair. The hepatitis adds a hilarious dimension. I recognized it as in the vein of Neil Simon, with this radical difference; it's about two guys, and it has a tenderness you don't feel in Simon."

Callow praises Sherman's support of the actors in rehearsals. "He was utterly affirmative, and also witty, subtle, interesting, and original. We became good friends immediately. He's a very gifted friend, good at the processes, loyal and shrewd."

While appearing in a long-running West-End play, Sher also performed in another Gay Sweatshop lunchtime show. "I remember being very taken with *Passing By*," says Sher. "I liked it enormously and wanted to be in it, and I liked him enormously. He's very arresting—the wit and gentleness and sensitivity. He also was physically very striking, so I wanted to whip out my sketchpad." He believes the season of gay plays and the discussion groups proved immensely valuable. "We had a lot to learn about being gay. Martin was prominent immediately because he's so articulate and wise—one of the truly wise people I know. I started to turn to him for advice on gay issues." He saw so much of Sherman for the rest of the decade he assumed his friend lived in London.

Pope, a member of Gay Sweatshop's advisory committee, notes, "Drew did a fabulous production, with show tunes sung in harmony, very wittily done and specially recorded and used like a movie sound track. When they're first diagnosed with hepatitis, the line says, 'Your eyes have gone all yellow,' so during the scene-change Drew used 'Jeepers, creepers, where'd you get those peepers?' He used music with a gay sensibility Martin responded to."

After London, Sherman headed for the Eugene O'Neill Theatre Center/National Playwrights Conference in Waterford Connecticut, where *Cracks* received two staged readings. He met excellent actors he respected and Dena and Jamie (Geraldine and James) Hammerstein (son of Oscar), who became close friends.

Previously he had tended to spend time with people not good for him "because their negativities dragged them down. Until the O'Neill, a lot of my friends were good people, but subsequently self-destructed. When I reached the O'Neill, for the first time in the U.S., people who had the answers surrounded me. I made some wonderful friendships there. I found the social side of the O'Neill phenomenal and loved every minute."

The O'Neill had rejected *Cracks*. The month before the National Playwrights Conference, a weekend occurs when the writers go to Waterford and read their plays aloud and people comment. A few days before that preliminary weekend, a playwright dropped out, so *Cracks* got that slot. Hammerstein first remembers seeing Sherman at the preliminary reading in the mansion's living room. "Martin read his play dryly, and I loved it. It was a scream, incredibly funny. I tried to get assigned to direct it, but failed. Lloyd Richards gave it to Tony Giordano. I found it bloody brilliant."

Sherman calls 1975 his "golden summer"—*Passing By* in London and then his black-comic satire in Waterford. After obscurity, he achieved some stature in the U.K., and the O'Neill thrust him into a U.S. spotlight. Despite criticisms about the O'Neill "process," he calls this reading "very important" and feels grateful. He also loves actors and enjoys their company. "I think I'm a playwright," Sherman muses, "because I love the combination of solitary and communal." He adored the communal experience there. And *Cracks* "caused a sensation. It was a huge hit."

For the staged reading presented on July 31 and August 1, Giordano drew a remarkable cast: Ben Masters as rock star Rick; Joe Grifasi as Sammy; Rosemary De Angelis as Nadine and her dybbuk; Meryl Streep as Jade; Ed Zang as Clay; Christopher Lloyd as Gideon; Jill Andre as Maggie; Louis Giambalvo as Roberta; and Jill Eikenberry as Irene. The theatrical gods had blessed Sherman, and those fortunate enough to see it showered *Cracks* with praise and laughter.

Hammerstein loved how this farce first shocked and then reduced viewers to helpless hilarity. "I sat behind two of the local blue-haired ladies. When the plaster cast held the man's phallus in an erection and a transvestite with an ax chased him, they stopped whispering 'We must go' and almost fell into the aisle laughing. *Cracks* transformed uptight people into idiots laughing out of control. It really cleans up psyches."

In the famed "O'Neill process," everybody criticizes the scripts, but Sherman observes he has "seen this criticism harm plays" as writers tinker while attempting to please everyone.

Nobody criticized *Cracks*, even though they should have. "There's a five-minute section [presumably while they try to remember who else attended the party] that treads water. It has no dramatic momentum. At both performances spectators responded hysterically, but that section doesn't work. Nobody at the O'Neill mentioned it, and I've never been able to fix it because it's part of the internal structure. But I saw the problem because of a staged reading by wonderful actors, not because of any comments. I'm grateful to have had the opportunity to see that, but the 'O'Neill process' of extensive criticism isn't constructive."

Following *Cracks*' success in Waterford, the Changing Scene in Denver rushed it into rehearsal for a mid–November opening, and Theatre Communications Group gave the playwright a grant to attend rehearsals. There he met Judy Mauer, who stage-managed and remembers she and Sherman "were the only Jews in cow town." Nellhaus raved its "incisive wit chronicled today and demolished it," so performances sold out (26).

While spectators cracked up during *Cracks* in Denver, Dolan negotiated with Adela Holzer to produce it at the Theatre De Lys, beating out Hammerstein for the privilege.

Giordano again directed, and he managed to retain Lloyd as Gideon and Giambalvo as Roberta, the transsexual in transition, while securing fine performers for the other roles. Gale Garnett (now Gale Zoe Garnett and called Zoe) played Nadine/Cynthia, the woman possessed by a dybbuk. She reminisces,

"The first morning of rehearsal, I greeted Martin, 'Good morning, playwright,' and he replied, 'Good morning, star.' And we have called each other that ever since."

She remembers Holzer's misunderstanding of *Cracks*. After Sammy and Nadine dance, she tries to thank him, but Cynthia disagrees. Garnett had a piece of business she loved. "Cynthia slapped Nadine, who subsided. The audience understood immediately there were two people in one body. It got a laugh of recognition. Martin loved it, but Tony cut it after the first preview. Adela and Martin had rows about the funny parts."

Later convicted of actual crimes, but at that time only guilty of the moronic misconception Sherman had written, not a romp worthy of Aristophanes, but a solemn drama, Holzer coerced Giordano to eradicate any timing, inflections or stage business prompting laughter. She forced horrible rewrites. While she vacationed, rehearsals and early previews proved hilarious, but when she returned she insisted she hadn't put her money into a comedy. "In making her happy," Hammerstein reflects, "they ruined the production."

Robert Allan Ackerman conveys just how miserable Sherman felt. "Once while sailing in Greece, we were overcome by seasickness. We stood on the deck throwing up into plastic bags. Our clothes were soaked as waves washed over us. My partner Franco's cotton sweater was stretched down to his ankles by the water. I said this was the worst experience I could ever remember. Green around the gills, Martin replied, 'That's because you weren't at the De Lys for *Cracks*.'"

Sherman wanted Mauer there so badly she agreed to serve as wardrobe mistress even though she couldn't sew, and she agreed to understudy Jade even though she couldn't act. She kept Sherman laughing during the Holzer ordeal.

Because the producer ground into dullsville psychedelic farce, satire and black comedy that had delighted Waterford fans, she had to trap spectators by eliminating the intermission. But she couldn't control critics; most panned it. Richard Watts' review bore the headline "The Season's Worst Disaster" (13). When the play closed the next day, presumably Holzer took pleasure in Douglas Watt's description "unfunny" (78) and Glover's AP judgment "boring." Others who gave it thumbs-down include Barnes, Gottfried, Sharp, and Madden.

Da Silva appreciates the play as "very funny" (9). Oliver blames production, not script, because she has seen it in Waterford. Feingold defends it as a "trashy pleasure" (106).

After opening on February 10, 1976, *Cracks* closed the next morning.

Although Holzer destroyed this *Cracks*, she made a bigger mess of her life. Arrested for fraud in 1990, she served four years in prison. Afterwards she undertook a scam using the name Adela Rosian, and, on May 25, 2001, she was arrested on new fraud charges. In August 2002, she received a sentence of nine to 18 years. As she was hauled off in handcuffs, she threatened to kill the prosecutor.

Sherman returned to L.A., where Carr asked him to write the English dubbing script for a dreadful Mexican flick called *Supervivientes de los Andes*.

Sherman calls it "the single worst film ever made." It depicts the same plane crash in the Andes as *Alive*.

According to Hollywood legend, Carr and John Schlesinger attended a dinner party, where the director said he was going to do *Alive* and also mentioned a terrible Mexican film about the same crash doing boffo box office there. Carr supposedly left the dinner party, took a plane to Mexico City, bought the rights, and thus killed *Alive* until 1993, when Frank Marshall directed it. Carr and Robert Stigwood produced the U.S. version as *Survive!* It provided a profitable return on a small investment.

When Sherman began writing new words, he discovered "the Mexican film didn't make any sense. I couldn't write a dubbing version until I created a coherent plot. I revised the structure while an editor followed my instructions. It's still the worst film ever made, but it's vaguely coherent now." Sherman then wrote an English version, and Clay Blair, Jr., revised it to make every syllable match the actors' lips.

After spending four months on *Survive!* Sherman used his fee to escape to Europe. He planned to move back to New York, so he asked Garnett's help finding an apartment there and then flew to Paris, where he arrived on June 22, 1976, and stayed through July. While living at a little hotel in Montmartre, near Leila Livingston's flat, he began writing a play partially set in Paris. Like *Cracks*, it concerns death.

"I loved very deeply Leila's extraordinary mother Jorie," Sherman explains. "She had died about two years earlier." That summer he wrote *Rio Grande* about them both. Leila had lived and danced in France, Italy, and Sweden, and she became, with little disguise, the play's daughter, while her late mother served as model for Cassie Ferber, taking her last name from novelist Edna. He named the daughter Clea, lifted from Durrell.

Both women function as Sherman "outsiders." The mother feels alienated from those around her and from her ill body. The daughter has gone into exile from her country and feels alien when she visits home and can barely remember how to construct an English sentence.

We meet Cassie in 1929 Paris, where she prepares to audition for the Paris Opera. Sherman segues to Cassie in 1976. She lives on Central Park West, where she coaches a young actor for an audition and advises him—much like Mrs. Honey speaks to David in *Madhouse*—to unbutton the top buttons on his shirt. Her shocked student quits.

Cassie never leaves the stage. Sometimes her rambling fails to make literal sense, but her refusal to answer the frequently ringing phone builds suspense. We learn she loves the Rio Grande because nothing can stop it. The river survives, whereas Cassie will soon die of cancer. Sherman relies heavily on exposition, spelling out themes in dialogue instead of trusting us to perceive them in action. "You're a survivor," another character tells her dying friend, as though we could fail to notice the playwright dramatizes exiles and survival.

Notable for its originality and focus on women—a favorite form of "the other"—and as a precursor to *Some Sunny Day*'s alien, *Rio Grande* doesn't succeed but provides a bridge to more mature work.

Cassie's lover Marco, frightened by her illness, abandons her; Cassie's daughter Clea has declined to live in New York; and her student has quit. Having emphasized Cassie's isolation, Sherman pulls the rug from under us when Cassie begins talking to a green man from outer space, a true alien and, thus, a kindred spirit. She can read his mind, so the character doesn't speak. She suggests he visit Taos, where people stare up at the sky waiting for UFOs. She sings "The Bell Song" from *Lakme* for him and then begs him to take her with him. He agrees and tells her to go out the window at six o'clock. She accepts his invitation to suicide.

Clea surprises Cassie by expressing concern. "I don't have to go back to Paris. I'd take care of you, if you needed me," Clea offers. Reassured her daughter cares, Cassie lies, which permits Clea to continue to enjoy the Paris career denied her mother. This resolution to the parent-child relationship proves more credible than the angst-ridden conflicts in *Fat Tuesday* and *Next Year in Jerusalem*. Working this out in *Rio Grande* made possible the advancement on the topic he achieves in *Messiah*.

Clea's love and selflessness help Cassie choose to cancel her appointment with the alien. Her father had killed himself when life turned tough, but she resolves, "I got things to do." She's energized and relishes her career again, even plans to write a book and accept new students. She will make the most of her remaining time and survive the illness right up to her natural death.

Sherman feels that "*Rio Grande* has a nice opening and beautiful last scene, but in between it doesn't work. I thought Peggy Ramsay'd like the Jorie character, but she hated the play and said, 'Oh, darling, you wear your heart on your sleeve. You have to toughen up.' She was right, so taking her advice very much to heart, I wrote *Bent*."

He spent August in London, returned to L.A. to pick up his possessions, then headed for New York, where he moved into an apartment on West 12th St., soon known as "the hovel." Playwrights Horizons had offered him a position as Playwright-in-Residence.

L.A. had served its purpose. It helped him achieve an income-earning professional track record required to show British Immigration he could support himself.

At Playwrights Horizons Leland Moss directed *Rio Grande*, which previewed November 11, 1976, opened November 12, ran through the 20th, then played four performances in Queens.

Sherman acknowledges his script threw audiences a curve: "It's disorienting because, for the first hour and twenty minutes, it's a realistic afternoon in a woman's life. And then a man from outer space appears." Later, when Hammerstein wanted to produce it, he thought of it as "the strangest play

Martin ever wrote" and, sure enough, he couldn't raise the money. The script, likewise, proved too challenging for Playwrights Horizons and critics.

Sherman describes this as "another of my dreadful New York productions. Irene Daily as Cassie gave an impressive performance, but the director wasn't really a director, and the young woman who played opposite Irene wasn't really an actress."

Worst of all, the director and designer chose a ludicrous and unintentionally hilarious way to represent the alien. Since the character never speaks, they could have used a green follow spot or more generalized green lighting. Or they could have put green grease paint on an actor. Instead, they created what Bloom describes as "a laughable, giant, serpent thing," wrecking any chance we might care about Cassie's conflict concerning whether to kill herself or see her disease through its terminal course. It also undermines appreciating her courageous choice. A different design decision would have permitted spectators to decide whether Cassie hallucinated the alien or pretended he existed so she could talk to somebody, like an imaginary friend, to work out whether, when, and how to end her life. This would have produced better reviews.

Although most critics praise Dailey's performance, most deride the play. Feingold pens a mixed review. He judges this "an extremely risky sidestep into fantasy expressionism," but feels Sherman "has three fully realized characters onstage"—Cassie, her friend, and her boyfriend. "Even the untenable fantasy scene in which Cassie confronts death directly has genuine power and humor mixed into its awful Woody Allen cuteness" (97).

As the holidays approached, Garnett asked her boyfriend, Tom, to take to Sherman "a scarlet silk scarf, lightly fringed, very pretty. Ten minutes later Martin called and said, 'It's so beautiful. I want to thank you from the bottom of my heart for my present. I love it. And the scarf is nice, too.' And I said, 'You send him back!' And he asked, 'Do I have to?'"

Although he didn't lose his sense of humor, a circumstance during his season as resident playwright prevented Sherman from benefiting from that as expected, i.e., by writing new plays.

Robert Moss, Artistic Director of Playwrights Horizons, had invited four dramatists to serve as playwrights-in-residence. The theatre hadn't done this before, yet they didn't anticipate snags. Philip Magdalany, Kenneth Pressman, Marsha Sheiness, and Sherman would spend the season writing. Actors' Equity, however, blocked the deal. A playwrights' theatre couldn't give preference to playwrights. The actors' union insisted playwrights couldn't earn stipends until actors received Equity-scale salaries. This forced the dramatists to work full-time as office staff to justify their earnings. Instead of writing, they answered phones and stuffed envelopes.

Fortunately, Sherman had written *Rio Grande* during the summer, but he couldn't conceive and create another play quickly while drudging in an office. Therefore, the theatre revived *Cracks*, which opened on June 16, 1977.

Finally it received a production that worked.

Director Larry Carpenter's wife, Julia MacKenzie, played Irene, so Sherman "couldn't complain about the actress to the director." But the play's excellence came across this time, and nobody forbade audience laughter. Judy Mauer, who stage managed Sherman's plays that season and had worked on both previous *Cracks* productions, pronounces it the best. "We had really good actors and real support from the theatre."

This *Cracks* had to live down the previous year's horrendous notices, yet critics greeted it more positively. The least laudatory reviews came from Baker, who, nevertheless, calls the lack of a solution "Sherman's best joke" (43), and from Eder, who faults the missing solution (C22). Harris calls *Cracks* "immensely entertaining" and the dialogue "very clever" (48–49). Gold judges it "an amusing trifle" which "deserves more than a one-night stand" (42). And Syna raves about "a brilliant and hilariously funny spoof," the "freshest stage satire I've seen this season," and "perfection" (12).

Few London reviewers made the trek to see *Cracks* at the Coliseum Theatre, Oldham, on October 10, 1981, but Shorter, while eager to learn whodunit, praises the "snappy writing" in the "unusually entertaining spoof" and the "priapic" gag worthy of Aristophanes (17). Coveney terms the comedy of death "a trash classic" and "Agatha Christie on an acid trip" (11).

Vindicating *Cracks* for the ages, Tim Luscombe directed it at the King's Head, London, from April 23, opening April 29, 1993, 20 years after Sherman wrote it. His friend Whitman played Roberta. Critics piled on the praise: "fab, fab, fab" (Venning 55), "fun" (Wardle 21), "loopy" (Wolf 106). Peter praises "a bouncy, entertaining and utterly and completely mad little play" (sec. 9, 23), while Kingston lauds "the funniest and cleverest portrayal of that doped and dopey generation you could hope for" (34).

Since that historic mounting, U.K. productions have included those in Leeds in May 1998, Chorlton in March 2001, Brighton in May 2003, and Edinburgh in August 2010. *Cracks* has received a Tel Aviv production and probably at least one in German-speaking Europe since a producer on June 17, 1993, bought the rights for 36 months.

Meanwhile, after *Cracks*'s opening at Playwrights Horizons and the dramatist's release from clerical hell, Sherman visited London again. There he attended a Gay Sweatshop rehearsal that inspired him to write the play that made him famous.

6. Pink Triangles (1977–1979)

On July 1, 1977, Sherman left New York for Europe. When he reached London, he stayed with Pope and Whitman. Once more he steeped himself in performances and delighted in his hosts' company.

Gay Sweatshop premiered *As Time Goes By* on August 26, in Nottingham, for the Campaign for Homosexual Equality, then presented it at the Edinburgh Festival's Fringe on August 30, where Sherman attended. While still rehearsing in London, the company had asked him to advise them about American accents for the final section, set in Greenwich Village.

Noel Greig and Drew Griffiths depicted gay men living in Victorian England (1896), Weimar and Nazi Germany (1929–1934), and New York City during the Stonewall riots (1969) (*Two Gay Sweatshop Plays*). Concluding the German segment, a lyric referring to pink triangles worn by gay concentration-camp victims caught Sherman's attention.

He immediately began work on *Bent*, which he conceived and wrote for Gay Sweatshop. Having written in *Passing By* a romance in which being gay poses no problem, he now wrote about the death sentence a gay identity guaranteed.

Sherman conducted research at London's Wiener Library, specializing in the Holocaust and Nazis. A librarian assisting him suffered from the misconception, then widespread, gay men during the Third Reich served in the SS, not as prisoners behind barbed-wire fences. The library's materials concerning homosexuality, however, proved the reverse. They established Hitler and Himmler's systematic efforts to identify, arrest, incarcerate, and exterminate gay men. At the Wiener, Sherman found information in "a sentence here, a footnote there."

While visiting Paris, the dramatist created Uncle Freddie. Still pondering his play-in-progress in London, he discovered Plant's "The Men with the Pink Triangles." Like Sherman both Jewish and gay, Plant survived the Third Reich by escaping to Switzerland.

In *Christopher Street*, Plant notes evidence the Third Reich "exterminated countless gays," who in concentration camps "were often beaten, tortured, or killed" (4). Plant explains the Night of the Long Knives, then describes the subsequent terrorizing and incarcerating of gay men. He describes the hat trick

SS officers employed to murder their prisoners, who "worked in a quarry surrounded by a high voltage fence. If they stepped within five feet of the fence, they were shot. The SS would throw a prisoner's cap against the fence and order him to retrieve it. He would be electrocuted if he touched the cap, or he was shot for disobedience if he refused to go after the cap" (8). Sherman employs this scenario to powerful effect in *Bent*'s penultimate scene.

Back home, Sherman used two books as sources for information about the Holocaust in general (but not regarding gay prisoners). He didn't read, know, or draw upon Heger's *The Men with the Pink Triangle*, despite widely circulated assertions to the contrary. In *Bent*, he created an original play; he didn't adapt anything. Heger's book concerns a different sort of man in quite different situations, which makes this mistake preposterous.

Sherman derived some details about Nazi concentration camps from Kogon's *The Theory and Practice of Hell*. A political prisoner at Buchenwald, he based it on a report he compiled for U.S. forces after that camp's liberation, drawing on personal experiences, interviews, and documents.

Kogon discusses Dachau as the original concentration camp, the model for others, and the place where commandants for all camps trained. He explains the claim of protective custody which Max takes seriously, but which actually signaled the end to the right of habeas corpus (12). Kogon makes his own distaste for homosexuals evident (e.g., 39), but he nevertheless calls the position of these prisoners "very precarious" and their fate "ghastly" and "consigned ... to the lowest caste in the camp during the most difficult years. In shipments to extermination camps ... they furnished the highest proportionate share.... Theirs was an insoluble predicament and virtually all of them perished" (35).

Sherman found in Kogon the hostility the SS directed towards intellectuals, especially those who wore glasses [81], and he used this detail to doom Rudy. He learned some camp work proved useful, but some "was utterly senseless, intended ... [as] torture" (83), and he used this to devise a senseless assignment for Max and Horst. Kogon cites building a wall one day, tearing it down the next, then repeating this sequence. Sherman also learned "about one in every three inmates was actually in a position to receive money from his family" (121), so he has Max receive from Uncle Freddie funds to bribe the guard to move Horst to work with him. Sherman read "to become sick in a concentration camp meant to be doomed" (137), so he thus motivates Max to get Horst medicine.

Sherman read German Jews "were not arrested as a matter of general policy in the early years of the Nazi regime. Merely a portion of them were picked up and sent to the concentration camps..." [169]. Hitler didn't implement his Final Solution with gas chambers until August 1942, when Jewish "mass liquidations began" (176). Max and Horst die in 1936, six years earlier.

He also read about "muslims," the men broken by the camps (233), but he learned more about them from a different book, Bettelheim's *The Informed*

Heart, which calls them "moslems" (151–58). A Jewish inmate for a year during 1938–39 at Dachau and Buchenwald, Austrian Bettelheim deals with inmate psychology (not extensively examined by Kogon), so Sherman drew upon this book to understand how Max and Horst react to their treatment by the SS. This survivor likewise illuminates SS psychology and methods they used to break and control prisoners. He demonstrates how "the total mass state ... sets out to destroy individual autonomy" (288) but the informed heart preserves autonomy.

"I based the psychology of the play on that book," Sherman says, "so I always make director and cast read it if I'm involved in a production."

A psychoanalyst, Bettelheim hoped those skills would help him survive. He found psychoanalysis "by no means the most effective way to *change* personality. Being placed in a particular type of environment can produce much more radical changes, and in a much shorter time" (26). He also notes psychoanalytic theory held "the test of the well functioning, well-integrated personality, the goal of psychoanalysis, was the ability to form freely intimate relations, 'to love'..." (27). Sherman dramatizes a personality who rapidly improves under environmental pressures. Max vows to survive, but he does better: He grows. He and Horst evince healthy personalities by loving each other.

Bettelheim's remarks about autonomy and self-respect also illuminate Max's growth, under extreme conditions, from helplessness to taking control of those decisions open to him. These include bribing a guard to bring Horst to work with him, changing the rock-moving pattern, or using leisure time to do pushups.

Max's survival instincts prompt him to seek Horst's companionship. *The Informed Heart* instructs, "To survive, not as a shadow of the SS but as a man, one had to find some life experience that mattered, over which one was still in command" (147). The pair's relationship keeps them alive and increasingly autonomous, autonomy illustrated in their lovemaking.

Bettelheim discusses loss of freedom that prevented determining "the time and conditions of death"; self-destruction would constitute "the only true act of self-assertion" (104). Sherman dramatizes first Horst and then Max reclaiming that right. Horst refuses to obey the order to electrocute himself, but instead dies attacking the SS captain. Max chooses his "time and conditions of death." Both defy the Nazis, refuse submission, and retain autonomy. Moreover, their lovemaking goes farther than Bettelheim could imagine as an action defying their tormentors, refusing to play by their rules, and asserting autonomy.

Bettelheim explains a Nazi goal "to break the prisoners as individuals, and to change them into a docile mass, from which no individual or group act of resistance could arise" (110). Although Sherman dramatizes Max and Horst's resistance, his play would lack drama—as well as credibility—unless we at first see the Nazis' goal realized.

During transport, Max undergoes extreme trauma of the sort Bettelheim describes: "Their 'initiation' to the concentration camp, which took place while on transport, was often the first torture prisoners had ever experienced and was, for most of them, the worst torture they would be exposed to either physically or psychologically" (120). If the distance to the camp seemed insufficient, the train would slow to allow time for guards to break prisoners (124).

Horst cautions Max against trying to help Rudy, and the guards force Max to beat his lover. Bettelheim writes sometimes "a prisoner got killed, but no prisoner was allowed to care for his or another's wounds. The guards also forced prisoners to hit one another ... any failure to obey an order ... or any help given a tortured prisoner was viewed as mutiny and swiftly punished by death" (124–125).

Occasionally some naysayer mocks Sherman's second act, insisting Nazis never wasted laborers by setting them meaningless tasks like moving rocks. Such carpers might feel surprised to read, "New prisoners in particular were given nonsensical tasks, such as carrying heavy rocks from one place to another, and after a while back to the place where they had picked them up" (134).

Other details Sherman gleaned here include swapping rumors (112, 229), relief provided by conversation when guards didn't interfere (117), bribing a foreman concerning a work assignment (117), even inequitably ladled soup (178). He read, "To enter the camp with hornrimmed glasses was tantamount to a death warrant" because they signified the intelligentsia, whom the SS despised (203). He learned inmates worried about growing impotent, so masturbated to check their virility (195–196). Yet critics have doubted inmates could experience desire. Bettelheim also discusses denial such as Max lapses into on the train, as he insists the nightmare isn't happening (128–129), and an inmate's inability to remember "names of their closest relatives," as Max blocks Rudy's name at the end (166, 193).

Lest anyone doubt a prisoner might grow in Dachau, Bettelheim attests, "I did not leave the camps the same person I was when I entered. But the notion that spending time in a concentration camp could be a growth experience did not occur to me until many months after I was gone" (127).

Bettelheim explains regarding his fate and that of fellow Jewish prisoners, "As late as 1940 many of them were being released if they could immediately emigrate" (199, 253). He had the resources to do that. This preceded the Final Solution and contrasts the fate of gay men, marked earlier for extermination.

The playwright selected as his title the British slang term "bent," a derogatory synonym for "gay" possibly derived from the fact a gay man bent over exposes his bum. Max and Horst bend to pick up and put down rocks. But the title conveys the play's essence, not only its gayness but also that the men endure SS persecution bent but unbroken. Max bends circumstances to his advantage, and Max and Horst bend Dachau's rules, promoting their spirits' survival.

By late November 1977, the dramatist had completed his breakthrough play. Throughout the 12 weeks he took to write it, he remembered something he had scribbled in his notebook: "Think Ian McKellen"—his ideal actor to play Max. He wrote the play for McKellen without knowing such casting might occur. Then he applied to the Eugene O'Neill Center's National Playwrights Conference for its 1978 season. He also sent *Bent* to agent Ramsay and to Gay Sweatshop's Griffiths.

They reacted identically. They told him his script deserved a bigger production and wider audience than a gay theatre could provide. Sherman recalls Griffiths saying, "You're crazy. We can't do this. Give this to the Royal Shakespeare Company." When Ramsay likewise baulked, the loyal playwright insisted he wrote *Bent* for Gay Sweatshop. Other company members as well as Griffiths, however, felt the play belonged in a major theatre. "It was extraordinarily generous of them," Sherman acknowledges.

Sherman dedicated the published play to two of them, Pope and Whitman. He had stayed with them when he first conceived it, and he stayed with them while awaiting a London production and during rehearsals, the premiere, and the West End transfer. Moreover, says Sherman, "they had helped create a climate for gay theatre that made *Bent* possible."

Callow still recalls how he lost his chance to play Max. Before thinking better of mounting it, Griffiths offered him Max. "I was utterly bewitched by the character," says Callow. "I understood him so well."

When the search for a more prominent theatre began, Callow was working as a reader at the Royal Court for then–Artistic Director Max Stafford Clark. Callow told Clark about *Bent* and got Whitman to supply a copy. When Ramsay discovered Callow had given it to Clark, she sent Sherman

> a ferocious telegram, saying, "Some actor has been meddling in the affairs of the agency. If he continues, consider yourself unrepresented." So I got a frantic letter from Martin imploring me to stop. It was too late to prevent Clark reading it, but he didn't like it. When Ian put his weight behind it, and Eddie Kulukundis put money into it, the play landed again at the Royal Court, and I was considered for Horst, although I'm singularly ill suited to playing somebody thin. Later, Martin asked me to go to Peggy's office to pick up something, and we became close friends. I once said to Peggy, "I take Martin's advice." So she asked, "Is he very wise?" And I replied, "Almost terminally so," which made her laugh. From then on, she called him "the wise one" or sometimes W.O. I don't think she ever called him Martin from that point on. He *is* very wise.

Ramsay sent the Wise One's script to Michael Rudman and David Aukin at Hampstead because Rudman had done Sherman's *The Night Before Paris* in 1970 while running Edinburgh's Traverse Theatre. Both men loved the play, so they sought a director. They miscalculated, however, by assuming they should hire a gay director; each one they tried shunned it.

While awaiting production, Sherman wrote a short comedy called *Blackout*, which Ensemble Studio Theatre presented April 21 to 23, 1978, in their

Marathon 78. Hammerstein directed it; he felt it didn't work: "Two people mistake each other's gender in a blackout. The gay man thinks he's with a boy, and the woman thinks she's with a girl, until they light candles. The audience laughed, but it wasn't a brilliant cast."

During rehearsals they cut it from 14 minutes to 10 by deleting sections the actors performed least effectively. Although hampered by his cast, Sherman seems more interested in building bridges between the gay man and the lesbian than in humor. This comedy would elicit more laughs if the two people engaged in courtship longer and only later discovered their mistake.

Lloyd Richards, head of the National Playwrights Conference, initially rejected *Bent* for the 1978 staged readings. Hammerstein, then second in command to him at the Society of Stage Directors and Choreographers, recalls Richards "saying 'Michael McClure has withdrawn his play.' I insisted 'Then you've got to put *Bent* in!' He asked, 'You think so?' and I replied 'Absolutely. It's a great play.' I went berserk. He said, 'I'll think about it.' But of course it went in."

Dennis Scott, assigned to direct McClure's play, thus inherited *Bent*, which Sherman thinks Scott didn't especially want to do. But Sherman met Robert Allan Ackerman that summer and "felt a kinship with him artistically. I told him then I would like him to direct it in America."

Sherman again enjoyed getting to know actors at the O'Neill. "In fact," he recalls, "Lloyd admonished me for spending my time with actors. 'Why aren't you sitting with the playwrights at dinner?' And I replied, 'Because the playwrights are talking to themselves, complaining. They should be with the actors doing their plays. The playwrights also happen to be rather boring, but that's why they're boring, because they're not part of the theatre community.'"

Sherman felt he got a wonderful cast: Ben Masters ("one of the best Maxes ever"), Jeffrey De Munn ("one of the best Horsts, who turned down Horst on Broadway to do *Modigliani* instead, a great career mistake"), Chris Sarandon as Greta, and David Marshall Grant as Rudy.

Grant remembers meeting Sherman on the porch of the big house that forms the heart of the Playwrights Conference.

> Martin told Bob Ackerman I should play Rudy. I hadn't been cast as Rudy originally. Dennis Scott had Alan Rosenberg, and Bob had me, so Dennis and Bob traded. Martin had the greatest sense of humor. He was continually good natured and a source of calm and reassurance. People said unhelpful things at the critique, like that when Greta turns in Max and Rudy, they should die immediately and the play should become about Greta. And for one or two Jews—because Martin said the Holocaust didn't just happen to Jews—*Bent* pressed a threatening button.

Grant explains he has a Jewish mother but doesn't covet the Holocaust as exclusively Jewish.

A Jewish critic took offense. Sherman, however, maintained his vision. He likewise refused to rewrite Act 2 to interrupt the rock moving, something Richards demanded.

Remembering a handful urged him to revise extensively, Sherman identifies the paternalism of the O'Neill process, which assumes anybody there knows more about what the play needs than the playwright. Both the Playwrights Conference and Ensemble Studio Theatre, where he served on the board of directors during the '70s, fostered paternalism that turned dramatists into "children who have to be told what to do, rather than encouraged. I was a founding member of EST, and I admire many people there, but I had to leave because I had no right to pass destructive judgment on other playwrights."

Sherman has given writers workshops, where he stresses "Never revise anything simply because someone has told you to, and never tell writers they should have written a different script, the script you'd have written."

Grant remembers spectators at the O'Neill readings, despite a few cavils, gave the play "a heartfelt response." He recalls, "I felt when I read *Bent* I was in the presence of a great play. It has a genius opening, but I remember being amazed by the play's courage in every respect, thematically and linguistically, especially in the second act."

Garnett saw *Bent* there and praises "Ben Masters' remarkable performance. He was straight but had no problem playing all that part. During the performance," she continues, "I watched Katharine Hepburn's brother, the doctor, with the family face. And during the 'My mouth. My cock. My mouth' section, he was vibrating with indignation at having to listen to this sort of talk. But by the end I heard him saying, in that Hepburn voice, 'Well, it is, actually, very moving.'"

Shortly after the O'Neill, Sherman still had no production, so some of the Waterford cast read it again in a private performance at the Public Theater for Joe Papp. (Grant missed it because he had to film *French Postcards*.) Hammerstein and his wife saw it for the first time there because a scheduling conflict had kept them away from Waterford. Ackerman also attended, and Sherman, and a few of Papp's people. Everybody except Papp loved it.

Hammerstein deplores Papp rejecting it: "I think he was afraid it might offend Jews. If that's the case, Joe was less than the courageous person he was made out to be." After the opening, Papp relented and told Ackerman he "felt it was much better than he first thought."

The O'Neill reading and subsequent admiration for *Bent* prompted Jack Schlissel that autumn to offer Sherman a Broadway production. Ramsay kept pushing him to sign the contract, but Sherman held out for a British premiere starring McKellen. That possibility had developed—thanks to serendipity.

In late August 1978, W. Stephen Gilbert, then producing drama for BBC Birmingham, ran into writer Howard Schuman on an Edinburgh-bound train; both would attend the Television Festival. Gilbert had a copy of *Bent*, told Schuman about it, and let him read it. Schuman

> read it with increasing excitement. The first act was gripping, but it was the second act that really startled me, with its overwhelmingly moving depiction of the love,

erotic and mental, between Max and Horst. I asked Stephen if he could get a message to Sherman in New York asking if he would be okay with my long-time companion Robert Chetwyn directing. Bob was hungry to find a challenging modern play. I also thought the part of Max might attract McKellen, with whom Bob had worked. A message came back from Martin, via Whitman and Pope, that Martin would be pleased for Bob to read the play and that he had written Max with Ian in mind.

Chetwyn previously had directed McKellen for the 1963 Ipswich season. There he played his first leading Shakespearean role, Henry V, and in the spring essayed Luther. In 1971, McKellen selected Chetwyn to direct him in *Hamlet* for Prospect.

Chetwyn recalls, "Reading *Bent* was a powerful experience. Shamefully—as a gay man—I knew nothing of the Nazi persecution of homosexuals. I was gripped by the Act 1 narrative, although I thought some of the language a bit flat. However, I found the second act absolutely remarkable in its conception and incredibly brave—combining the growing intellectual/erotic connection between Max and Horst with images as hauntingly bleak as a Beckett play."

Chetwyn sent it to McKellen, who was producing and performing in two plays for the RSC. The tour began in August in Edinburgh, so that's where he received the script. Just that week he had met young Sean Mathias, who would soon become his lover and afterward his partner for nine years.

Mathias remembers:

> Ian asked me to read it. We stayed up all night talking about the historical context and the persecution of gay men in Nazi Germany. We talked about the way it starts as a boulevard comedy and then becomes a tragedy, but also a black comedy. I loved this mixture of styles and different theatrical form. It spanned from Neil Simon to Samuel Beckett. I found that exciting. It seemed unlike any play I had seen or read before. I thought for those reasons, the eloquence of its compassion, and its stylistic bravery, it would make very exciting theatre. And happily my young voice was heard by Ian and proven right.

McKellen tilted in favor of accepting Max, but, distracted by his responsibilities on the RSC tour to 12 other cities, he didn't immediately tell Chetwyn.

About two months passed while McKellen toured. After he returned to London, Schuman explains, "Bob organized a reading at our flat so Ian could hear the text. Tim Curry and a fine actor called Philip Sayer read Max and Horst, and I took all the others."

Chetwyn picks up the story. "Even this kind of reading confirmed *Bent* was gripping, moving and tremendously powerful. At the end, Ian said, 'I have to do this play, don't I?'"

McKellen later regretted his delay in accepting Max. Because no firm offer for a London production seemed near, Ramsay insisted Sherman sign the Broadway contract the New York agency Fifi-Oscard had negotiated. Reluctantly, Sherman did so on December 15, 1978. This caused problems.

Only with difficulty did he bargain for Ian to appear in the world premiere and delay the New York mounting. The deal included a "by arrangement with Jack Schlissel" statement on the London program, but the Broadway postponement also cost Sherman money.

Possibly McKellen's new agent, Jimmy Sharkey, cautioned the star against doing the play. If so, he proved mistaken, because, while beginning to perform *Bent* in the West End, McKellen in June received the CBE. Subsequently he also won the SWET (Society of West End Theatres) Best Actor Award for Max. (In 1984, this award became the Laurence Olivier.)

McKellen performed *Bent* in 1979 while remaining in the closet, something he later termed "a bit stupid." He didn't come out until 1988.

He agreed to play Max because he recognized a wonderful role and valued the play's potential impact: "It is socially and politically an important play that changes attitudes, reduces prejudices. It focuses on being a gay man in a repressive society. Yet, as a metaphor, it can reduce injustice towards other minorities. Martin does that without relinquishing its theatricality. It is moving, empowering."

Once Sherman had a director and his chosen star, they needed a theatre. Producer Eddie Kulukundis liked *Bent* so much he determined to help the Royal Court fund a production; he would move it if box-office warranted.

Stuart Burge, the Royal Court's Artistic Director, didn't care for *Bent*. Chetwyn recalls Burge took three months to decide, but he reluctantly agreed to house it because his theatre would only need to cough up running costs. Kulukundis funded the mounting, and the theatre got to enjoy its sell-out business without risk. By early January 1979, Sherman hoped he had his production, so he went home mid–month to await spring rehearsals. Kulukundis arranged on March 16, 1979, to lease the play from Schlissel. Finally all concerned had a firm deal.

Before rehearsals began, but after the Royal Court had announced the production, a friend of John Dexter's tried to talk Sherman into replacing Chetwyn with Dexter, who presumably smelled a hit. Since Chetwyn had obtained McKellen as leading man and Kulukundis as backer, betraying Chetwyn struck the dramatist as preposterous and unethical.

In late March, Sherman wrote to Garnett, "Rehearsals begin today. Tom Bell is playing Horst, which is considered a coup as he is a major star and an electric actor. Ian has been a total marvel. He will be a thrilling Max."

Chetwyn says, "The important casting decision was Tom Bell. I felt Ian's innate theatricality, so right for Max, needed balance by a more unadorned naturalistic performance from the actor playing Horst. Tom provided superb balance to Ian, and their chemistry on stage was tremendously exciting."

Sherman reports Burge hated the play so much he occasionally phoned the playwright during rehearsals to try to persuade him to tone down the sex. Sherman didn't.

The Royal Court didn't embrace *Bent* as theirs until 2006, when the theatre finally began selling copies along with their other successes.

During rehearsals Sherman switched Americanisms to British equivalents, substituting "flat" for "apartment," "bloke" for "guy." He added one line, referring to the Olympics, to alert spectators that the play ends in 1936. Also a stage direction regarding Max unpinning the pink triangle from Horst's jacket changed to Max donning Horst's jacket. Chetwyn says, "I was glad the text was so clear we didn't need to do the extensive rewrites often required on new plays."

Sherman occasionally pared dialogue, notably the end. By eliminating clutter, he threw remaining lines into starker relief. McKellen's script illustrates some of this process. Readers can compare the multiple endings contained in the scripts published by Amber Lane, U.S. Samuel French, and Methuen.

The latter contains the ending at its most economical—and powerful. Grant terms this economy "percussive. Martin writes rhythmically, especially in *Bent*. It's poetic. You could almost not understand the language, yet it would have resonance, especially the second act, particularly the sex scene. It's drums."

Chetwyn feels "Martin's text played wonderfully. Before previews, however, Burge watched a run through and said the camp's menace wasn't felt sufficiently. I asked our sound designer to produce a nearly subliminal hum, to remind the audience the fence was electrified. This created constant tension during Act 2 and prepared for the powerful climax."

Chambers in *Peggy* illuminates the vital role the dramatist's agent played, and not just in contracting for productions. He recounts how worried Sherman felt because "a difficult scene change ... had been a terrible mess at the technical rehearsal." Distressed, he had gone to see Peggy the next morning. "'You mean it's roaring like a lion when it should be purring like a kitten?' she asked." An hour later Sherman found "extra technicians on hand and seemingly the whole staff trying to sort out the problem, which they did. Afterwards one of the stage crew went up to Sherman and said, 'It purred like a kitten'" (217).

A subconscious influence as Sherman wrote *Bent* came from Mary Renault's *The Mask of Apollo*, a gay romance. A gay actor appears in Aeschylus's lost play *The Myrmidons*, about Achilles and Patroclus. Only a few lines have survived in quotations by other writers. This "great tragic gay love story," which figures centrally in Renault's novel, got Sherman interested in "writing a modern version."

He read the novel for the second time while recovering from hepatitis in 1972 and started trying to write about the love of this ancient Greek pair. Fueled both by the novel and by John Barton's RSC production of *Troilus and Cressida* in 1966, Sherman "tried to find a way into their story, but I couldn't. Then I realized I had sublimated all that into *Bent*"—which became the great tragic gay love story.

Max won't allow himself to love, indeed insists, "Queers aren't meant to love" (Methuen, 121). Because he suffers his family's rejection, develops self-contempt, and then experiences the Third Reich's oppression, he won't risk loving men to whom he feels attracted. When we meet him, even having sex requires booze and drugs. But the man who can't love learns to. In a love story free of sentimentality, he summons courage to care.

In *Bent*, Sherman wrote the world's most famous coming-out play, yet Hammerstein stresses, "You could say it's about standing up for who you are, but it's not that; it's about standing up for who you love." Sherman ridicules homophobia by observing "the object of one's sexual desire is so unimportant, which makes homophobia ridiculous and inexplicable." That attitude underlies *Bent*. He dramatizes the slow development of Max and Horst's love to create sympathy, understanding for them, and contempt for their tormentors.

Sherman constructs his plot episodically in six Act 1 scenes (each set in a different location) and five for Act 2 (all set in the same place). Each contains significant dramatic action revealing character and driving plot, as Max's humanity evolves.

Scene 1, the apparently contemporary sitcom, misdirects us. Sybarite Max deals cocaine, gets drunk and high, has rough sex with strangers. He makes deals and hustles to get by. His dissolute life has no purpose beyond immediate pleasure. He lacks self-esteem.

The biggest error some commentators make about *Bent* identifies the ending as a despairing suicide. Max instead kills himself after traveling a long journey towards self esteem. He has come out to his tormentors and accepted his identity. He thereby reclaims his self-respect and drops his desperate efforts to survive.

Practically speaking, this means the SS captain will kill him. Max has told Horst, "He'd kill me if he knew I was queer" (133), because Max obtained Horst's medicine by giving the captain sexual pleasure. Max triumphs and achieves redemption by determining the moment and means of his death.

Nobody who has read *The Informed Heart* would think Max acts from despair. The notion he loses the will to live imposes upon this time, place and character a simplistic psychology irrelevant to Dachau and foreign to *Bent*. Earlier, Sherman has carefully contrasted the "moslem" who cannot go on and the act of free will whereby an inmate takes his destiny into his own hands. (Concern about unintentional religious slurs has prompted Sherman to cut this term.)

Psychoanalyst Bettelheim, based upon his comprehension of the human psyche in general and in particular his observations, at Dachau and Buchenwald, understood the action a prisoner like Max takes. He defies the Nazis. He wins the one victory over them possible in that circumstance, one the SS want to prevent.

Most people watching *Bent* instinctively understand this. Although they grieve Horst's and Max's deaths, as well as Max's loss of his lover, they feel elated at the spirit in which both men die, fiercely resisting SS ideology and methodology.

Many of us never face an ethical challenge of catastrophic proportions. Max faces two—participating in killing Rudy and killing himself. In the former instance, he must choose between only Rudy dying or both dying. In the latter, he could again choose survival. Instead, he makes the brave and heroic choice. A few months and an inspirational role model have altered his character.

The playwright employs a repetitive structural device to underline several crises Max undergoes. Four times his protagonist counts to ten. The first contributes to the opening's comedy, as Max suffers a hangover. The second occurs after he has repeatedly struck Rudy in order to preserve his own life. On the third occasion, after Max confesses how he obtained his yellow star and expresses self-contempt, counting to ten ends Act 1. Finally, counting constitutes the play's last words but precedes Max picking up seven more rocks and his courageous final acts. Placed there, instead of helping him block out actions prompting shame, he uses the counting to steady himself, stop crying, and then, while moving rocks, make his last choice, his most important dramatic action.

Sherman employs additional structural parallels. Max embraces two corpses, the dead 13-year-old girl whom he chillingly mentions late in Act 1 and Horst, whom he holds late in Act 2. Sherman likewise creates three closeted men. Greta relies on marriage and children to keep him safe; Freddie hides his real orientation; and Max does so during and after transport to Dachau. The playwright also employs a structural contrast. On the train, Horst advises Max. In early Act 2, Max advises Horst.

The dramatist frames the post-transport action by Max entering the closet (a pragmatic choice) and Max emerging from it (an idealistic choice stemming from his achieving self-respect and autonomy).

Sherman uses the interval—as he often does—to transform his play. He strips away the populated universe and relatively realistic surroundings and substitutes a minimalist world à la Beckett. He imposes a spare, repetitive movement on his two central characters. The Nazis, in a sense, do the imposing because they order the rock carrying, but Sherman chooses this example from Bettelheim to illustrate an SS methodology that destroys inmates. *Bent* shows victims can turn the tables and achieve autonomy despite this torment.

Sherman acknowledges, "On some subconscious level, if Beckett had never existed I might have written that act differently." Yet his second act's vitality and truth to life and history don't duplicate the moment-to-moment Beckettian life in the void. We know with *Bent* what moment in history and what geographical spot these men occupy; indeed those factors cause their suffering. We also know their goals, more exact than waiting for Godot to come, even though no more attainable. They want to survive, they want a relationship, and they identify shortly before the end a desire to live together in Berlin.

Those who complain nothing happens in the camp except moving rocks miss all that does happen: the confession, guilt and remorse, deal-making, gradual falling in love and lovemaking, the men trapped when Max's deceit with the Captain comes to light, the Captain's ploy to kill Horst, Horst's declarations of love and Max's resistance, Max's declaration of love and coming out and defiance. What a lot of action in an act sometimes damned as lacking any. Only the physical activity repeats; the dramatic action varies enormously. Those who object consider only the static situation and miss the drama.

Sherman devises recognizable characters in Greta and Freddie, but our sympathies go to Max, Horst, and Rudy.

In Max, Sherman creates a narcissist and hedonist who, initially, compromises anything resembling a principle. However he grows beyond narcissism. This opportunist becomes responsible, willing to sacrifice for Horst and lay down his life for principles. He displays enough complexity that, before he participates in killing Rudy, he loyally refuses to leave the country without him. He knows he passes up immediate passage to safety when he pushes away the envelope Freddie proffers, but the threat during transport poses immediate, fatal consequences. He exhibits courage and loyalty when facing the possibility of dying, but not when facing certain death.

Sherman also imparts to Horst believably human, because contradictory, behavior. A foil to Max, he teaches the older man how to survive by stifling his desire to help Rudy. He instructs Max to deceive to save his life. Yet he rebukes Max for his choices. When Max experiences self-contempt, Horst tries to diminish that. Yet he never allows Max to forget he should wear a pink triangle.

Leila Livingston reports Sherman put what she said into dancer Rudy's mouth, which gives his lines about dance authenticity. "I was always raving about dance floors, about needing a wooden floor, not cement, and worrying about injury," she recalls. "And Rudy has my discipline. Even when they're fleeing, he wants to go to dance class." Discipline and dedication to craft make Rudy oblivious to political realities as well as self-absorbed. He also spouts most of the anti-Semitism, worrying more for his plants' feelings than for his landlord. His casual prejudice parallels but also contrasts Nazis' deadly hatreds.

Sherman typically mixes moods, and *Bent*, despite its grim subject, proves no exception.

The sense of inevitability Sherman generates suggests tragedy. He depicts probable events, linked necessarily. Max and Rudy and, later, Max and Horst experience Nazi persecution. Once initiated at the end of scene one, Max's flight works its way inexorably to Dachau and the likelihood he will die there. Yet Max makes deals to survive that create dramatic tension to sustain suspense.

As we observe Max grow from narcissism towards altruism, we suspect he could take action that will cause his death. Ironically, when he tries to help Horst survive a bronchial infection, he dooms them both.

Sherman foreshadows, planting information to ensure we feel no surprise at later events and understand their significance. Sherman puts into Horst's mouth what we must know in advance about suicide in a concentration camp: "It doesn't mean anything if a moslem kills himself, but if a person who's still a person commits suicide, well ... it's a kind of defiance, isn't it? They hate that—it's an act of free will" (Amber Lane 59; Methuen condenses this). The dramatist makes this do double duty: It both serves to explain why Horst's "barracks had to stand outside all night" (Methuen 118)—which causes Horst's illness, which leads to the men's deaths—and it foreshadows Max's similar choice to end his life to defy his Nazi tormentors. When he chooses death, spectators experience catharsis.

Sherman supplies the finality tragedy requires. The action begun in scene one decisively ends with Max's last decision. Yet *Bent* doesn't altogether feel like one, unless we remember Aristotle explains ancient Greek tragedy could end happily. Max avoids dying passively. We approve his defiance. We cheer the SS's failure to break his spirit. We applaud his growth in stature to the point he can equal Horst's heroic gesture of defiance—his attacking the captain instead of passively obeying the order to electrocute himself.

We want to congratulate Max at the end—after we stop crying. He has learned to love, to commit, to stop putting survival first. He has achieved sophrosyne; he knows himself, as the Delphic Oracle instructs. And he claims his identity publicly.

If *Bent* involved merely the good dying and evil prevailing, we would have melodrama. But so much more happens. A selfish coward has evolved into a man capable of loving and heroic action. The Nazis didn't kill his spirit, and we feel thrilled.

Although not a comedy, *Bent* makes us laugh. Its first scene contains comedy of wit and manners similar to Wycherley's or Wilde's. It also employs farce. Sherman designs Wolf for his sight-gag value as well as to illustrate Max lying. When the SS sweep into the flat, shoot Wolf, then slit his throat, the horror hits us harder because we just laughed.

When Max staggers on reeling from a hangover, Sherman draws on overindulgence, a source of humor employed since Thespis and buffoonery honoring Dionysus. Max's lament "Oh God" ([55]) underscores suffering that soon will seem paltry. As Max requests information about last night, Rudy stalls, teasing. That and Max's responses amuse.

First he puts his hand over Rudy's mouth to silence him. When Max threatens to kill Rudy's plants, the dancer apologizes to them. Challenged to supply an explanation for Max's bruises, Rudy will only say, "You fell" (59). Rudy corrects Max's suspicion regarding a "threesome" to "not a threesome. A twelvesome"(60). Sherman builds a sequence about Max drinking to combat depression to conclude with Max saying he doesn't remember what caused his depression and Rudy retorting, "Then drinking worked, didn't it?" (60).

Here Wolf enters naked, and the hilarity grows. Max learns he identified himself to Wolf as a Polish baron, and meanwhile Wolf dons a bathrobe too short for him—funnier than nudity. As Wolf's incredulity grows, Max confesses he lied about his country house and car and hits up Wolf for a loan to pay the rent to landlord Abraham Rosen, even now knocking. After Rudy's pseudo trumpet fanfare, Max throws open the door. The mood shifts from laughter to horror. Surprise, often a comic device, gives way to murderous mayhem.

Sherman wrests humor from Rudy's naïveté and Greta's biting sarcasm in the next scene and, in 3, from Max and his uncle passing the envelope back and forth and Freddie's swish-ness and Max offering a deal to marry: "Our button factories can sleep with her button factories" (77). Freddie's inquiry "Can I phone you?" and Max's response "In the *forest*?" amuse even while they convey the uncle doesn't grasp Max's situation.

That scene's comic spy-flick quality contrasts to 4, which builds the requisite tension over the couple's impending arrest. While contriving to render us increasingly apprehensive, Sherman lightens 4. Max complains of the nearby tents, "There's no one to talk to in any of them" (79), a funny remark yet one that also foreshadows Max moving Horst to his work site so he can converse. Max and Rudy quarrel, as Rudy insists on calling the forest a jungle and declares, "I'm a dancer, not Mowgli" (82; in the U.S. Samuel French text Sherman switches to "not Robin Hood," 39). This echoes McCoy's *Star Trek* refrains, "I'm a doctor, not.... " Romantic comedy ends with their capture; the contrast between warmth and terror constitutes one of several coups de theatre.

Only scene 5, on the train, lacks humor. Six provides hustler Max telling Horst he worked a deal to get his yellow star and the latter's incredulous query, "With the Gestapo?" (94). This light moment contrasts with the next dialogue, as Max explains how he earned his yellow star.

Act 2 humanizes the pair's interaction with levity—as a survival tool. Form reflects content: The dramatist writes one-liners; the prisoners joke to cope with their nightmare.

Concerning the guard, "We had a kid like that in school," Horst quips in scene one, "Used to lead us in 'Simon Says'" (102). When Max regrets they'll miss the Olympics, Horst responds, "I knew there was a reason I didn't want to be here" (109). After their lovemaking, Max expresses amused disbelief that they did it in three minutes (118). When Max later suggests sex, Horst replies, "I have a headache" (125). Max's menu rumors become a running gag. Preceding the final burst of violence, Sherman intersperses humor in a romantic scene. Max quotes Rosen as saying "I owed him rent" (133). Horst enjoys a last wisecrack with "I saw you by the river. You were making a fool of yourself. And I said 'Someday ... I'll be at Dachau with that man, moving rocks'" (134).

The black-comic sight of Max holding Horst's corpse at attention and talking to him creates a more complex set of emotions than laughter, but it does change the mood slightly, between Horst's courageous actions and, subsequently, Max's declaration of love.

Bent dramatizes Sherman's twin themes: outsider status and survival.

The Nazis and the other prisoners regard homosexuals as scum because they differ from the straight majority. The law classifies these "other" as outlaws. Sherman dramatizes bigotry so virulent the Third Reich attempts systematically to exterminate gay men.

Since their "alien" nature dooms them, Max, Rudy, and Horst must struggle to survive, yet Sherman considers survival of Max's body but also of his self-respect, his capacity to love, and his humanity. At first, Max will do anything to live, but he evolves to where he finds some prices for survival too high and some principles worth dying for.

Max's desire to survive conflicts with his need to accept his sexual orientation and deem himself worthy to love and receive love. Sherman dramatizes Max overcoming his internalized homophobia and attaining psychological health.

Nobody had ever written a play like this before. The production team asked everybody to keep the secret. Although announcements described *Bent* as gay, nobody told the press about the play's setting and subject. Spectators entered the theatre, began watching the first scene, and thought it a contemporary comedy. Then they gasped as Wolf dies and Max and Rudy run for their lives. Of course, that surprise could only occur until reviews appeared.

At the interval, viewers received a one-page leaflet providing background information. It lists events beginning in 1871, when King Wilhelm adopted the Bavarian Code; its Paragraph 175 outlawed "lewd and unnatural behaviour," and the country's subsequent gay-rights movement attempted to persuade the Reichstag to repeal it. It covers founding the SA and SS and then, on May 14, 1928, promulgating the National Socialist Party (i.e., the Nazis) position on homosexuality, which concludes, "Anyone who even thinks of homosexual love is our enemy."

The next year the Nazis "were swept into power," and on January 30, 1933, Hitler became Reich chancellor. Two months later he established Dachau and the following month the Gestapo, and the Nazis ransacked and destroyed Hirschfeld's Institute of Sexual Science. The leaflet then lists The Night of the Long Knives; shipment to a concentration camp of a gay activist in summer 1934; in 1935 the criminalization of a kiss, an embrace, or even gay fantasies; and in 1936 Himmler's speech calling for exterminating homosexuals. The leaflet ends by explaining the gay death toll in concentration camps. This information establishes the factual nature of the material Sherman dramatizes.

Bent began previews at the Royal Court on April 26, 1979. During that night's standing ovation, flowers rained down upon the stage. McKellen told Sherman, "Don't ever forget this. It will never be like this again." Well-wishers,

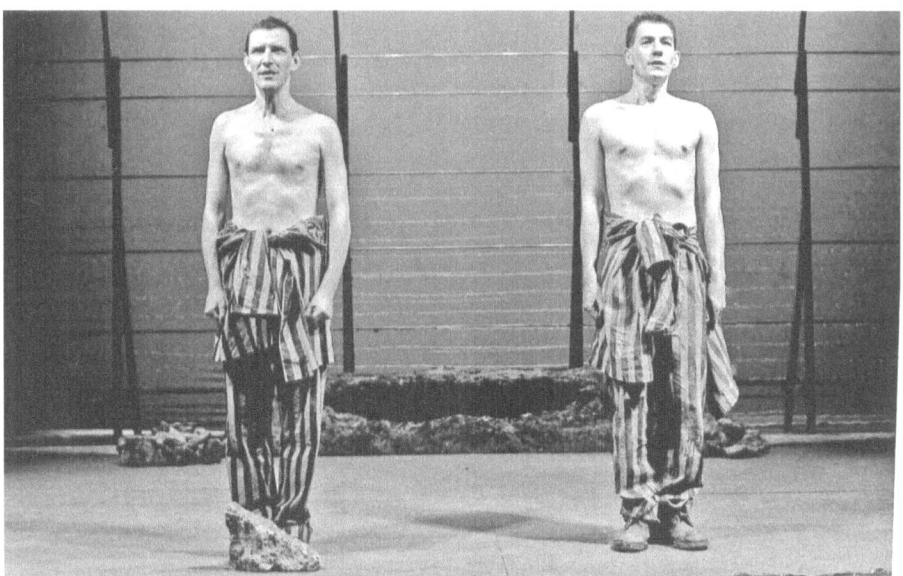

Tom Bell (left) and Ian McKellen in the world premiere of *Bent* at the Royal Court Theatre, May 3, 1979. (Photograph: John Haynes/Lebrecht Music & Arts.)

instead of chattering, stammered out thanks because the play had moved them so deeply.

Chetwyn describes that first preview as "the most exciting performance of *Bent* (or any play I was involved in). The effect on the audience was tremendous." Schuman remembers his partner coming home that night and saying he'd "never experienced an audience reaction like it."

"By contrast," Chetwyn continues, "although the press night went well, it came nowhere near the first preview. After curtain down, I celebrated in Tom's dressing room, where we drank copiously, and the rest of the evening is a blur of warm feelings. The reviews the next day were unsurprisingly mixed—given how daring the play was at the time, but reactions continued overwhelmingly positive."

Schuman saw *Bent* at the opening. He felt elated at this experience he had helped to midwife. He found it "stunning, and the chemistry between Ian's theatricality and Bell's pure naturalism was electrifying, the now famous verbal love scene tremendously moving, and the end shattering."

After *Bent*'s May 3 opening, the party celebrated both the play's impact and Eddie Kulukundis's birthday. Judy Mauer describes "this big affair with the crème de la crème of British theatre. Martin, Alan, Peter and I went home at 4 A.M."

The General Election on opening day, May 3, brought the Conservatives to power. The next day Maggie Thatcher became Prime Minister.

The Royal Court had scheduled just over one month—sold out—from April 26 through June 2. Not until shortly after the last performance did Kulukundis, urged on by Chetwyn, reach agreement for transfer to the Criterion. It would have to close in November to make way for Simon's *Last of the Red Hot Lovers*. The transfer ran four months, but could have run much longer had a theatre become available.

Critics greeted *Bent* variously, some cheers, some jeers. A strike prevented the *Times* and *Sunday Times* from publishing reviews; both papers' critics disliked it. *Bent* received seven negative reviews, nine mixed, and 11 favorable.

Shulman pens the most hostile notice, arguing Sherman "has given us something akin to a Homo Holocaust ... a theatrical shocker relying on violence and sensation to achieve its effects." He condemns the ending as "too melodramatic and too incredible to be moving." He finds the sex scene unimpressive and the pair's "romantic exchanges ... dramatically banal" (15).

Young rebukes *Bent* as "really two plays" (21). He believes Horst dies from electrocution, calls the theme "a cliché," and labels events and characters stereotypes "gathered from existing writing and films about Nazi Germany." King acknowledges the importance of dramatizing homosexuals suffered under the Nazis, but calls Sherman's attempt to do so "sadly ineffectual" (14). After cataloguing the four deaths, the critic announces "each such event leaves one unmoved and even vaguely embarrassed by its sadism or sentimentality."

Simo mistakes *Bent*'s period as World War II. He calls it "sensationalist" because it concerns "the problem of being gay" (98). The play proves Sherman has "no visible ability ... to develop dramatic situations through character-interplay." He doesn't understand why Max kills himself. Stewart opines Sherman "may know the facts but has not the skill to dramatise them convincingly" (1634). He finds Act 2 "sadly undramatic" and complains because thus "it is the first half that, undeservedly, sticks in the memory." Trewin feels Sherman "is so sincere that I am sorry to dislike a piece that hammers its points too hard" (931).

Bennett's *Gay News* notice trashes *Bent*: "Even an actor as gifted as McKellen, onstage throughout, cannot breathe life into dialogue as dead as Mr. Sherman's," he declares (33–34). "*Bent* is distressing. But so is blood in a fight outside a pub."

His condemnation and other negative press prompted the newspaper's editors to urge readers to see *Bent* (16). They argue they perform one of the greatest services they have ever done for readers. "Only when you have emerged from the theatre ... will you appreciate just why and how we can make such an apparently extravagant claim." They continue, "The number of people who seem to have emerged untouched ... by the evening appears to be infinitesimally small." If *Bent* fails to transfer, then "a handful of journalists will have robbed us and a wider public of the most provocative gay play yet seen in the commercial—perhaps any—theatre."

Among the mixed reviews, Cushman knows the year (1934) and initial event (Night of the Long Knives). He understands "this is the 'coming out' play to end them all," a "celebration of homosexual love," and the play's value "as a cautionary tale" (14). But he fears the setting "overwhelms the play" and can't believe two people in a concentration camp could "form a relationship." He admires the playwright's skill in keeping the second act's scenes going but also finds them "mawkish."

Elsom praises "some powerful scenes," especially in Act 2, and notes, "Even in Britain, there must be many Horsts and Maxes." To them he feels *Bent* "is a heroic myth. It has the laughter which Yeats asserted lay at the heart of tragedy, a determination to proclaim one's nature in the face of death. My criticism of *Bent* is that the surrounding horror story distracts you away from its powerful theme" (689–690).

Chaillet charges Sherman "is an extremist in theatricality, regularly advancing the action with a violent reversal of the dominant mood" (23–24). He enjoys the opening as "distinctly Noel Coward" and finds some later scenes "chilling" but terms the ending "cliché-ridden and unconvincing" and finds Max insane. Thus he misses Max's development and mistakes an affirmative conclusion for the pair's "stupidity."

Brown echoes Chaillet: Initially "you'd be forgiven for thinking 'Bent' ... Noel Coward's 'coming out' play" (31). He argues "Sherman's attempt to move gay laughter in the throat of death is salutary, and certainly witty." Then he reverses himself: "for all its powerful passages," it fails to shake "loose from its sensational historical trappings, which render Sherman's clarion cry for the oppressed muffled, muddled and a trifle meretricious. This reviewer ... is not bent, just lopsided."

Hepple calls the script forceful and moving, but then complains of the "largely artificial first act" which detracts from the "strongly dramatic second half" (13). Hirschhorn calls it "harrowing" and "undeniably powerful but to be avoided by those with tender constitutions" (22). What begins positively shifts to barbs.

Tinker writes, "I admire the courage of this piece enormously. It would be blind and churlish not to" (3). He observes the "sell-out run" at the Royal Court and move to the Criterion indicate "London is still brave enough to take on a serious and compelling theme." Yet he finds the work "depressingly arid despite— or possibly because of—the author's high-flown aspirations." He faults comic moments amidst the drama—a mixture that becomes a Sherman trademark.

Coveney finds "it impossible to be either cool or enthusiastic" about an "unsettling play, part horrific comedy, part concentration camp love story" (23). He terms it "less memorable for its writing than for its sensationalism." He applauds its education of Britons about the gay Holocaust, noting even many Jews had no idea gay men died in the camps. Coveney concludes, "It is performed with dignity, conviction and grace."

Barnes raises an issue no British critic mentions, speculating, "the play could offend particularly susceptible Jewish sensibilities" (40). He praises McKellen (misspelled "McKellan") and Bell for "giving two of the greatest performances in London's theatrical decade," but objects, "the play struck me as needlessly melodramatic, overwritten and poorly constructed. It is said that at every performance homosexuals weep openly in the audience—for the situation perhaps, and for the performances certainly, but not, I imagine, for the play." He makes a distinction without a difference: the situations and characters played by the actors inhere in the script he disdains.

Other critics publish glowing notices.

Billington's *Guardian* review terms *Bent* a play of "dignity and passion" illuminating a little-known subject "without indulging in special pleading or gratuitous sensationalism"(10). He finds *Bent* "a fascinating historical document" but also "a parable about the way selfish survival gives way, under pressure, to a hunger for interdependence." He prefers some scenes to others, but won't "carp at a play that deals in historical persecution without an ounce of facile self-pity." He concludes, "I admire the way it puts the case for the declaration of one's sexual feelings in such a sane, measured and eloquent way." Billington's second review ends, "Mr. Sherman has handled the theme with an impassioned restraint. I hope ... the play now gets a showing in New York" (24).

Barber approves the informative pamphlet supplied. Writers of negative notices seem not to have read it. He prefers the second half, which he calls "a grim study of a friendship" to the "thriller" preceding it (9). He uses "friend" to refer to Rudy and Horst. This suggests he finds homosexuality distasteful, but he doesn't bash the play and even tells his readers it received "a particularly warm reception."

Nightingale might have penned his notice as a response to naysayers (692). He notes, "There are times when Mr. Sherman's attempts to particularize his horrors seem lurid and extravagant.... Yet the magnitude of the atrocity tends ... to reduce such complaints to the niggling niceties of a sheltered mind. How can a critic presume to accuse hell of being melodramatic? Or anything that occurred in or around Dachau of being improbable?" He applauds *Bent* as "a V-sign defiantly flourished at all forms of oppression."

De Jongh judges the train scene "ranks with the most brutal in modern theatre. It is horrifying and appropriate to its theme," and he compares it to Webster's *Duchess of Malfi* (11). He explains the transport and Act 2 dramatize "the peculiar genius of the Nazis ... to inspire the very worst in people." When the men reach Dachau, "The play enters an infernal world ... of endless punishment, entire humiliation." He justifies this because "the loathing of sexual minorities still exists today. *Bent* gives an idea of where and how that loathing can culminate. It is a play of importance, power and pathos which should concern us all."

Grant approves Sherman's "powerful and defiant study" (30). "Rather than merely exploiting its Nazi setting the piece explores a historical situation which doubles as a compelling dramatic metaphor for the most hideous kind of human oppression: the inability to love in the face of sheer terror and the power to overcome that terror by love itself, even in the hell of Dachau." He commends the "strong linear narrative," terms it "a triumph" and reports feeling "much moved."

Leech calls *Bent* "not to be missed" and "a harrowing play that makes you think and reflect" (50). He explains, "Even now it is possible that people are being tortured in Argentina and Chile, and fascistic ideas are far from being eradicated." He concludes *Bent* "serves to remind us that the theatre is not just for 'entertainment.'"

Three other critics publish raves. Morley doubts "there has ever been a better play about homosexuality; it is *The Boys in the Band* rewritten in blood" (908) He terms it "chilling" but also explains the early scenes remain "a comedy, albeit a very black one." He calls the section with Uncle Freddie "a little comic masterpiece" and the "throwaway references to Berlin ... closer to the truth of that time than many of Isherwood's." Like all the positive reviewers, he praises the actors.

Gilbert writes "When I first read the play more than a year ago, I thought it simply the best gay play ever written.... There was so much to bite on—plot, tension, wit, characterization" (33). He feels the second half will "be seen as one of the supreme achievements of modern theatre. It is a love duet ... pure theatre in which one man draws another man into full humanity."

American Reed raves "a shattering new play ... has electrified London. It is far and away the best play I have seen in my three-day splurge" (12). "Its subject is grim and often painful. But it is so skillfully written and magnificently acted that it builds hypnotically from first scene to last, gripping the audience in its suspense and humanity until you are thoroughly wrung out by the final curtain."

Shortly after *Bent* transferred, Barber, who had reviewed it favorably, reversed himself (8). He argues people shouldn't want to see *Bent*. In remarks misleading and sometimes homophobic, he describes Max beating Rudy (dramatized), Max having sex with the dead girl (not dramatized, but Barber implies Sherman does), and the "suicide." He announces, "I resist such material" and "Hitler's torture chambers ... should not appear on stage." He objects: "It seems to argue that being a homo is all right because it blossomed even in Hitler's torture chambers" and it "seeks to glamorize homosexual love by presenting it as coming to valiant birth amid the most succulent horrors in recent history."

McKellen responds to this diatribe, unusual in its attack on a play the writer already reviewed favorably. He doesn't directly address words like "homo," or the notion showing incarceration of gay men in Dachau glamorizes their sexual orientation, or the implication homosexuality is unacceptable.

Instead McKellen challenges the call to banish historical horrors from stage as well as how Barber distorts the experience of *Bent* by mentioning some actions but ignoring others. He terms "the semi documentary revelations ... a metaphor for much modern violence against minorities" (14). He identifies the subject as not homosexuality but "oppression, whenever it occurs, using horror, as Shakespeare constantly used it, to celebrate love, fortitude, and dignity." He cites the scene in which Max and Horst make love, "a scene of quite startling tenderness and joy," and concludes his challenge "Worryingly, Mr. Barber's piece doesn't mention it. What makes a play is all its scenes. Some in *Bent* ... are even funny."

Plays and Players presented its 1979 award to Peter Shaffer's *Amadeus*. *Bent* came in second, supported by *Time Out*'s Grant, *Punch*'s Morley, and *New Statesman*'s Nightingale. Tom Stoppard's *Night and Day* received two votes, and Harold Pinter's *Betrayal* received one ([12]–13). What a season!

McKellen recalls, "It was thrilling to see lines outside the theatre." He enjoyed the full houses and concluded "It's one of those few plays critics might not like but audiences do."

He received a letter from a Jewish writer "reviling the play as a disgrace, designed to lessen the experience of his race under the Third Reich. He couldn't see the connection between the treatments of Jews and gays. Other Jews wrote favorably, and survivors on the street showed me the numbers on their arms."

McKellen's fan letters ranged from an actor in Chiswick who writes, "I have never before been so deeply emotionally affected by a play" to a chemist in Portugal who praises *Bent* "for the courage of its emotions and the purity of its beliefs. Appalling and beautiful at the same time, it evokes in this spectator a tremendous charge of compassion. I hope I'm a better person after having seen it."

McKellen's Criterion box-office records show *Bent* had its poorest week initially but thereafter did well, earning its highest gross the last two weeks. Only in the first three did the gross fall below £10,000, and in the last two, the weeks of October 27 and November 3, it took £14,447.06 and £18,860.86.

Bent closed because Ian Albery had previously booked the Simon comedy. However, efforts occurred to move to Wyndham's. Shortly before the last performance, Christopher Miles saw it and offered McKellen the lead in *Priest of Love*. Miles was moving into production; he needed McKellen immediately. The actor stalled while negotiations continued for Wyndham's. Although moving looked likely, nothing firm existed, so McKellen signed and began filming. He later blamed Albery for keeping his commitment to the Simon play; Chetwyn blamed McKellen for taking the film.

After *Bent* opened at the Royal Court, Sherman visited Berlin with Pope, flew to New York, returned to London for the West End July 4 opening. Then he prepared for Broadway.

7. *Bent* on Broadway (1979–1980)

After the O'Neill reading, Jack Schlissel found *Bent* "a work of great meaning, substance and importance" ("'Bent'" C–20), but later he objected to the rocks.

Hartford Stage Company had planned to present *Bent* as an out-of-town tryout, but freeing up its star for six weeks in Connecticut proved impossible, so the production began on Broadway.

Schlissel's co-producer, Steven Steinlauf, invested nearly a quarter of the $400,000. Also investing: Lee A. Minskoff; Alvin Nederlander Associates; and Philip Langner, president of the Theatre Guild ("Why Are There So Many Off-Broadway Shows" 1, 3; also "Co-Producer Steinlauf Has 88G Piece of 'Bent'" 83). Liz Smith reported dress designer Bob Mackie as a "major backer"; if so, he must have invested as "Nedra Corporation of Beverly Hills," $36,000 (8).

Ackerman would direct *Bent* on Broadway. Designers Santo Loquasto (settings), Arden Fingerhut (lighting), and Robert Wojewodski (costumes) joined the team.

When Richard Gere accepted, he had appeared in *Looking for Mr. Goodbar*, *Days of Heaven*, *Bloodbrothers*, and *Yanks* and had filmed *American Gigolo*. His stage experience included regional theatres and on and off–Broadway. He had appeared in *Taming of the Shrew* in London and New York and played the lead in *Grease* on Broadway and the West End. The producers, Ackerman, and Sherman didn't just grab a movie star for Max. They selected a skilled stage actor who could build box office.

Ackerman and Sherman met Gere in L.A. on his 30th birthday. He lived in a Doheney Drive apartment once home to Marilyn Monroe. After discussing the script, they wanted him. He asked for the weekend to think about it. Ackerman explains, "We were both nervous about his answer. You had to be secure and brave to play a gay role for fear of committing career suicide. That Sunday we had breakfast with him and his agent, Ed Limato, who supported Richard doing it, and they gave us a 'yes.' We were thrilled."

David Dukes accepted Horst after Jeffrey De Munn turned it down (though De Munn replaced Dukes in June 1980). Michael Gross took Greta, and David Marshall Grant repeated Rudy.

Grant emphasizes the working relationship Ackerman had with Sherman. The direction "trusted the play. It was about finding the play's rhythm. The hardest thing for Bob on Broadway was the scene changes, six in the first act. You go from the apartment to the club to Uncle Freddie to the forest to the train to the soup line. Six realistic sets in an hour."

Gere differed from the older McKellen, and Ackerman had his own interpretation. Gere developed a more externalized build to climax than the Brit had used. His thrusting pelvis surprised those who had seen McKellen's immobilized torso during this scene. Ackerman reports every night at the end of that sex scene, "The audience went wild. It was like the end of a great aria in the opera." Gere also decided to scream as he hit the electrified fence at the end. Ackerman liked this and had it taped and amplified, a more chilling effect than sparks flying off the wire in London.

Dukes, Gere, Ackerman, and Sherman lived on the same West Village street. Ackerman reports, "It wasn't unusual for the doorbell to ring at any hour, and I'd find one of them there. Nor was it unusual to open the door and see Richard sitting on the stoop looking in despair. 'What's the matter?' you'd ask him. 'I have to kill myself tonight,' he'd answer."

Ackerman explains late in previews the producers said they had something to discuss.

> This was our first Broadway play. We were blindsided. They wanted us to rewrite and restage the second act to cut the rocks. "Can't they be doing something else? Moving rocks is really depressing." Two guys in a concentration camp for no reason other than their sexual orientation, being degraded by hostile guards, tortured, starved, and dying, and they only now, right before opening, realize they're not producing *Oklahoma*? Martin asked if they had read the play and if they had been there earlier in the evening when the audience was applauding wildly and throwing bouquets of flowers onstage. But they chalked that up to being a preview audience. They were concerned about the reaction of people from New Jersey.

It doesn't seem to have occurred to them the playwright came from New Jersey. To stiffen his resolve, Sherman must have envisioned Adela Holzer wrecking *Cracks*.

Ackerman concludes, "After much wrangling and Martin threatening to go to the Dramatists Guild, they agreed to retain the rocks, which were a brilliant and brave idea signifying so much existentially. The monotony is the point, and the image is primal, like the end of the world."

Producers had already encouraged director and writer to emphasize humor. Ackerman introduced a new sight gag in scene 1. Rudy turns the radio on, hungover Max turns it off, and Rudy turns it back on. Sherman added a new line for Max who, after coming, notes, "It's awfully sticky" (Samuel French, 77).

To compose "Streets of Berlin" Sherman selected Silverman, who insists the music "wrote itself" because "it's right in the words." He scored it for violin, tuba, accordion, cymbals, drums, and guitar (which he played). (The score shows piano, viola and cello as well.) His "brilliant chamber musicians" recorded the music on November 12, the day before the scenery load-in. Focusing lights occurred on November 14 and 15, and the tech rehearsal on the 16th. Ackerman scheduled two dress rehearsals for Saturday November 17. On November 19, previews began.

On December 1, *Bent* played a benefit performance for Playwrights Horizons, which said *Bent* demonstrates "Playwrights Horizons' commitment to developing writers.... Since 1974, all his other plays ... have been produced at Playwrights Horizons." A party afterwards followed at La Rousse, on Theatre Row (42nd St.). Many who think they remember the opening describe that party.

The opening occurred on December 2. Sherman sent Grant a card reading, "If Bo Derek is a ten, you're a ten and a half. You know there has been no other Rudy since you first walked on that O'Neill stage. You not only make Rudy everything I ever dreamed he could be, but very much more. I'm very happy and very grateful. All my love, Martin."

Pope flew in and stayed with Mauer, and they drank champagne in the limo. They took charge of Sherman's father and stepmother. Lavren, who by that time had separated from second husband Weiner, also attended the opening and sat with Sherman and his parents at Sardi's.

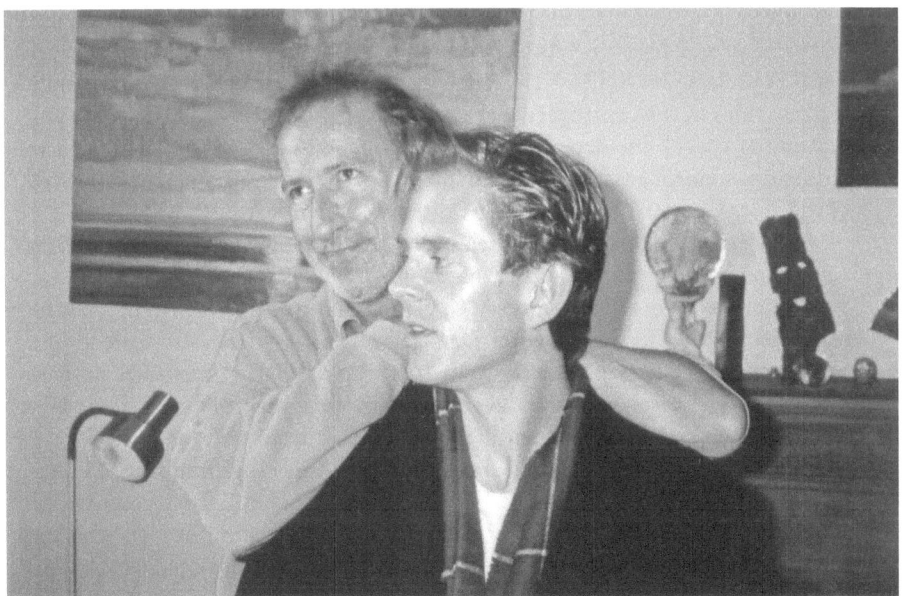

Sherman (left) and David Marshall Grant at Sherman's home, mid-'90s (courtesy Martin Sherman).

As reviews appeared, McKellen won the SWET Award as Best Actor for Max. Sherman sent him, on December 4, a telegram reading, "Your award has given me even more pleasure than a Broadway opening. I'm so proud. All my love, Martin."

Sometimes *Bent*'s detractors have engendered controversies. Some have termed it "sensational" only because it depicts homosexuals, as though playwrights should ignore gay people. In 1979, some reviewers felt no shame objecting to a gay play—one sympathetic and affirmative—as unsavory. The problem lay with those critics' prejudices, but, instead of seeing their bigotry reflected by on-stage Nazis, they blame *Bent*.

Other complaints occasionally surface.

In 1991, a drama teacher at Rhydfelen secondary school in Glamorgan, Wales, John Owen, resigned after a disciplinary committee began to investigate him. In 1990, he had taken 30 sixth formers (16 to 18) to the National Theatre to see *Bent* and allowed them to perform scenes from it. Their parents knew its subject when they permitted their offspring to attend. Nevertheless, one mother filed a complaint against the teacher ("School Drama over Bent"). Presumably the school pursued her "very serious allegations" because of Clause 28, anti-gay legislation passed by Thatcher's government. (See chapter 11.)

Bent's scheduling at St. Louis's HotHouse upset a Missouri legislator, who complained to the state Arts Council. Pollack reports its head told the theatre they couldn't use their $2,250 grant to mount the play in April 2001 (2). The company added to its flyer the statement "Due to the controversial subject matter of *Bent*, Missouri Arts Council funding is not available for this production." Pollack quotes Judith Newmark as inquiring, "Controversial? What would the two sides of the controversy be? Pro-Nazi and anti–Nazi? Killing gays and not killing gays?" She declares, "The state of Missouri is going to make sure it does not sponsor art that might offend Nazis." Missourians who disapproved of the Arts Council's action couldn't discover which legislator to oust.

More often bigots disguise their prejudices by citing aesthetic flaws. They complain about anything except what troubles them.

Another kind of "controversy" occasionally greets *Bent*. Some viewers object to Max preferring to enter Dachau wearing a yellow star instead of a pink triangle. Those who voice outrage at this plot device insist Jews suffered more than gay prisoners could have. Such viewers ignore the play's period.

Sherman sets *Bent* between 1934 and 1936. It begins on the Night of the Long Knives, the purge of homosexuals in the SA, lasting from June 28 until July 1, when his captors executed SA chief Ernst Roehm, Hitler's second-in-command. His murder put virulent homophobe Heinrich Himmler, who ran the SS, into that spot directly under Hitler. This "night" launched a campaign of violence aimed at gay men that preceded genocide against Jews.

Plant records 300 men not members of the SA died the night of June 28, 1934 (211). He notes on July 3 the Ministry of Justice approved these murders as legal. He further records "the first large wave of arrests of homosexuals" occurred throughout Germany in October and November. On October 24, the Gestapo ordered police departments throughout the country to supply "lists of all men known to be, or to have been, homosexually active." In December, "The Ministry of Justice issued new guidelines stating the homosexual offenses did not have actually to be committed to be punishable; intent was what mattered" (112–113).

On May 22, 1935, SS magazine *Das Schwarze Korps* demanded the death penalty for all gay men (212). On June 28, Paragraph 175 was strengthened to criminalize "any conceivable contact, however tenuous, between males." However, that more draconian law proved unnecessary because the next month the courts decided, "any action can now be punished without a judge's referring to a specific criminal statute." Himmler thereafter reaffirmed his intention to exterminate homosexuals (213–214).

For contrast, Plant (himself both Jewish and gay) supplies the following dates: deportation of German Jews began in 1940; forced transport of Jews to the Warsaw Ghetto in 1941; first tests of gassing late that year; and in 1942, "the first systematic gassings" at Auschwitz began on June 23 and transport of Warsaw Ghetto inmates to concentration camps began on July 12 (218–220).

Those who accused Sherman of setting up competition in suffering between gay men and Jews missed the consecutive nature of two murderous Nazi assaults. Jewish and gay, Sherman grieves both slaughters. Others had memorialized the Jewish Holocaust; in 1977, he chose the virtually unknown gay version. In 1998, he would write the Jewish, partially–Holocaust *Rose*.

Sherman could have avoided rage from a few quarters had Max requested some badge other than a yellow star. Had he done so, however, Max couldn't have met his landlord Rosen in his barracks, gained respect for him and other Jewish companions there, and reduced his anti–Semitism—all integral to the arc of Max's character development. Sherman chooses the irony of minorities despising "the other" without actually knowing its members. He also slyly allows terrified Max to make a stupid choice. Directors sometimes emphasize this.

Sherman explains, "*Bent* is a very Jewish play. My Jewishness affects everything else." He learned from his culture an imperative to protest inhumanity towards anyone. Would a non–Jewish writer have put an anti–Semite into a Jewish barracks and made his life there a growth experience? Yet an occasional Jewish viewer equates gentile Max with Jewish Sherman, missing the playwright's criticism of his protagonist.

Before *Bent*, people bought wartime Allied propaganda depicting Nazis as gay. This "calumny" took advantage of prevalent homophobia and further contributed to it. Sherman corrected this misconception publicly and internationally. Out of ignorance, some assumed Sherman lied about the elimination of gay men's human rights initiated shortly after Hitler took power in 1933.

The concentration camps began early in the Third Reich as detention

/labor camps; their first, and the model for the others, Dachau (established March 1933), Sherman selected as his second act's setting.

By the time the Nazis introduced gas chambers in mid–1942, the government systematically had exterminated or driven into hiding, escape, or the army most potential gay victims. Hitler and Himmler then concentrated on eradicating Jews. During different periods, the Nazis focused on different primary goals and employed different methods of mass murder.

Historians' poor coverage of gay genocide caused ignorance. William Shirer, for instance, doesn't discuss it. He ignores anti-gay incidents and laws. Moreover, surviving homosexual inmates hid the reason for their incarceration to avoid imprisonment after liberation. Germany didn't decriminalize homosexuality until 1969, so those victims didn't give interviews. The Allies jailed inmates whom they identified as gay. The German government didn't pay gay survivors reparations every other former inmate population received. The gay Holocaust remained invisible until *Bent*, followed by studies by such historians as Rector, Plant, and Grau.

As a result of such efforts, the German Bundestag (lower house) voted unanimously on December 7, 2000, to apologize. Austria, however, has refused recognition of gay Holocaust victims (rainbownetwork.com).

Both the 1979 and 1990 London productions supplied spectators with facts. The more extensive inserts for 1990 contain the 1871 Paragraph 175 criminalizing homosexuality: "A male who indulges in criminally indecent activities with another male or who allows himself to participate in such activities will be punished with jail." It likewise quotes Himmler's February 1937 "It is vital we rid ourselves of them; like weeds we must pull them up, throw them on the fire and burn them. This is not out of a spirit of vengeance, but of necessity: these creatures must be exterminated" (Trans. David Benedict. For contrast of 1871's 175 and 1935 revision, Grau 64–67. For fire passage, Grau 97).

Gay prisoners faced more than Nazi determination to eradicate them. Other prisoners formed alliances, and those allegiances doomed gay inmates. Political prisoners and convicted criminals vied for dominance and used their positions in the camp hierarchy to protect others wearing the red or green triangle. (Kogon, a political prisoner, details how this system worked.) These powerful prisoners' homophobia also contributed. Like the guards, they regarded pink triangles with contempt.

Head prisoners' prejudices ensured gay inmates received the least food and the worst work assignments, those most likely to kill them. Thus, the green-triangle Kapo ladling soup gives Max some solid food but skims only the liquid on top for Horst. This incident faithfully represents camp life.

Thus Nazi policy *and* internal camp politics elevated gay death rates.

Bent polarized New York critics, moving them to raves or rage. Although British critics hadn't felt Sherman insults Jews, some New York reviewers, many Jewish, grew apoplectic.

Sherman had thoroughly researched early Third-Reich gay persecution, so he knew more about this than reviewers could. Angry critics misapplied facts concerning Jewish slaughter in gas ovens (1942–45) to 1934–36. They knew about the Nazis' subsequent Final Solution but didn't know about earlier systematic extermination of homosexuals. Therefore, otherwise decent men and women lobbed false accusations again Sherman regarding his supposed distortion of history. Soon Woods would fantasize *Bent* caused "rioting" in Israel (255).

Sherman notes most Jewish spectators haven't shared the views of a few outraged critics. He cites the play's reception in Israel, where it opened on May 7, 1983, at the Haifa Municipal Theatre and ran in repertory for about two years, including touring. "There were no problems. Audiences throughout Israel responded to and appreciated it. Most spectators had either been in a concentration camp or their close relatives had." *Bent* assaults viewers' feelings; some people resist emotional involvement. Israelis, on the other hand, automatically felt emotionally vulnerable to this Holocaust play. They couldn't refuse access.

Bent produced a change in Israeli law. The new country had adopted British legal codes, including one prohibiting homosexuality. After *Bent*, people from the theatre approached the left-oriented party RATZ, says Nava Semel, who has translated Sherman's other plays. The party's head, Knesset member Mrs. Shulamit Aloni, led the successful effort to legalize homosexuality. Thus, Sherman's play enabled Israeli gay men and lesbians to emerge from their closets.

A misconception exists concerning U.S. Jewish responses to *Bent*. Years later Clum said, "Jewish groups angry at its gay appropriation of the holocaust" picketed (124). Ackerman can't imagine what Clum refers to and, initially, Sherman couldn't either. Later, he remembered a handful of people standing outside the theatre before a tiny number of performances—"the most minor picketing possible."

Yet polarized New York critics gave *Bent* 15 negative reviews, 12 mixed, and 17 positive. (Subsequent criticism grounded in historical fact—e.g., Sterling's, Clum's, Seifert's, and Hammermeister's—proves appreciative.)

The list *Variety* published on December 5 shows critics who hated *Bent* included Cunningham on WCBS-TV, Klein on WNEW-TV, Lyons on WPIX-TV, and Siegel on WABC-TV. Currie's pan evinces incomprehension: "Max is an unattractive, unexplained character whose final suicide is strangely unmoving, and the play is an unhappy amalgam of naturalist drama and homosexual self-indulgence." Of the sex scene, he observes, "The play goes down the tube right there."

Watt labels *Bent* a melodrama and therefore "arresting, but unmoving" (29). "Strong stuff," he continues, "but we aren't deeply involved, because 'Bent' is more Grand Guignol than serious drama." He dismisses it as "largely a waste of time." The next day Liz Smith counters with praise in Watt's newspaper, calling *Bent* "thoughtful" and "a strong plea for tolerance and humanity" (8).

Christian Science Monitor's critic alleges *Bent* "reduces the Holocaust to sensationally twisted melodrama" and "includes scenes of sordidness, decadence, and offensive sexual explicitness" ("Bent" 19). He calls it "grim and exploitive drama" and "a luridly sensational piece of special pleading" which "trivializes his subject."

Unlike British producers, those presenting the play on Broadway failed to provide historical data. This oversight prompted some critics to charge Sherman invented the gay Holocaust. Munk accuses him of "mythmaking" or "fictionalizing history" and complains he says "gays suffered 'more than' Jews" (104). Munk, therefore, concludes he has "corrupted his purposes." Gerard writes from a similarly infuriated sensibility, insisting, "*Bent* comes across as mere cheap commercial manipulation of both history and of its audience" (18).

Simon alleges *Bent* "ahistorical and preposterous" and "a kind of combination homosexual wet dream and Steigian dream of glory" (110–111). He adds, "Credibility goes out through the fourth wall from the outset" and the three major gay characters rank in perfection "only a little lower than the angels." Max an angel? Simon can't have paid attention. He ends his jeremiad by terming *Bent* "hack writing."

Sharbutt begins, "Really bad dramas don't come along all that often on Broadway. But *Bent* ... may easily qualify as the worst of 1979 (23). He reviles it as "a badly done, unbelievable tale of homosexual love marked by dialogue that is mundane, grotesque or just awful."

Kauffmann tries to come to grips with the play, but fails to understand it, especially the ending, which he condemns because "it's sentimental to see uplift as the inevitable result of suffering" (30, 32). He misses that Sherman dramatizes redemption by means of love. He terms Sherman's leavening of pain with a comic sensibility "a macabre vaudeville." Because he doesn't understand the source of Max's redemption, he also refers to Act 2, in which Max and Horst fall in love, as "filler-material."

Hobe Morrison covered *Bent* for *Variety*. A family man in his mid-70s at the time, he nevertheless pens a far less venomous pan than some colleagues. He doubts "there is sufficient public for an essentially harrowing drama" (88). Concerning what he terms a tragedy, he reports, "Although some of the scenes grip the audience in utterly silent attention, the production doesn't figure to have popular appeal. Explicitly descriptive passages about homosexual acts may represent calculated sensationalism to many playgoers."

Stasio trots out charges of sentimentality and character growth through suffering and the one against "the shabby theory that homosexuals somehow suffered more than Jews or political prisoners in the Nazi death camps" (30). She mislabels these early labor camps and even insists the play has no relevance for contemporary homosexuals. If so, why does she think *Bent* still occupies a Broadway house more than six months after opening? Where Simon sees an angel, Stasio dismisses Max as "a man whose main interest in life seems to be muscle tone."

Goldfarb despises everything except Dukes; his attack includes critics who admire *Bent*. Currie lets off another broadside about the second act not working.

Among numerous mixed reviews *Bent* received, Mackay judges only designs. The others fall into two groups, those that, like some negatives, object to what they perceive as a competition between Jews and gay men and those that don't. Richardson, Kroll, Feingold, Brustein, Eaker, and Rich raise the issue. Wallach, Bowne, Barnes, Wilson, and Watt don't.

Watt? But didn't he pan the play? Yes, but he reviewed it again when the replacement cast went in; then he understands and appreciates *Bent* more than before (79). He also spells out more clearly what he doesn't care for, plus he explains what he likes about the play. He finds Max's decision to refuse the ticket to Amsterdam not credible, but he refers to *Bent* as "this smartly-written thriller."

Barnes still mostly dislikes *Bent*. On the other hand he prefers Ackerman's direction to Chetwyn's and the U.S. sets and costumes to those in London. Barnes argues, "The first part of the play has a certain atmosphere and, in its loosely written way, is interesting. The second part is repetitious, boring and worst of all melodramatic" (19).

Wallach posits Sherman "has generated considerable impact in individual scenes without quite managing to make the marriage work" (32). He rebukes the playwright for striving for a "Big Statement," a "tedious" second act, and "reaching for profundity," but "before the weakness becomes manifest, he has written enough absorbing scenes to give abundant evidence of his playwriting talent."

Where Wallach objects to Sherman combining gay love and "Nazi horror," Wilson feels "survival," "the Holocaust," and "homosexuals" belong in three different plays (22). He argues a playwright cannot combine these subjects so a gay man tries to survive the Holocaust. But he avers, "The story is forcefully told. Mr. Sherman has written a number of striking scenes, some frightening, others quiet and intimate."

Bowne applauds *Bent*'s "great courage" (7). Yet he finds Ackerman's direction execrable, the sets "slow-moving," and the writing "pedestrian, repetitious and meandering" except for its peaks, which he terms "strong." He would cut all scenes depicting Max and Rudy's flight, which other critics call thrilling. He deplores the length of rock carrying.

This brings us to mixed reviews that damn Max masquerading as a Jew. In addition to that complaint, Eaker regrets Sherman fails "to elicit empathy," praises "a series of short, fast-paced scenes which build tension and impact," and derides the "entire repetitious and lengthy second act with the exception of the final scene" (51).

Kroll judges, "It is a jolting, troubling, worrisome play that at times rises to real power and at times sideslips into special pleading.... But it's ... a strong, serious play on Broadway ... and anybody who claims to bring a thinking head to a Broadway theater should confront this play" (115).

Brustein argues inmates couldn't have orgasms (23–24). He confuses the gaunt specters released in 1945 with healthy young men in early labor camps. Concerning Sherman's dramaturgical skill, Brustein alleges *Bent* lacks depth: "It might have been a major play; here, at best, it is merely an interesting one." He prefers the first scene to the rest and the remainder of the first act to the second, complaining Sherman "goes on to ruin it in the second act by turning his play into a love story with a melodramatic conclusion." He believes Max fell in love with Horst first, and bribed the guard to move him afterwards—a factual error. Brustein concludes, "Still, the subject is a potentially interesting one, and it has not been wholly trivialized. The failure, at least, is not of nerve or daring, which alone makes the play an oddity in a theater for clever journalists."

Muddled Richardson asserts Max "tries to convince himself that he is not a homosexual" but really Jewish, a misunderstanding of Max's deal-making (71–75). He also believes Max meets Horst at Dachau. He finds the play "simplistic" and "given to fits of sentimentality." Yet he feels "for most of the evening one remains sympathetic to *Bent*, for the play does, with some humor and a great deal of earnest conviction, come down on the side of life and human courage."

Rich notes two "superlative" roles, but faults "too much clunky plotting and overwriting in Act 1, too much repetition in Act 2, too much anachronistic language " (C16). He argues "debates about Max's capacity to express love are the digressionary stuff of soap opera." Because *Bent* dramatizes a narcissist who cannot love and puts his own survival first, but who learns to love, the section Rich condemns proves pivotal to plot, character development and theme. Remove that, and you have no play. Rich concludes, "Mr. Sherman's feel for theater is keen, and he can grab an audience whenever he really puts his mind to it.... *Bent* cuts a distinctive swath across the Broadway stage."

Feingold believes sexual preference easy to conceal, so most homosexuals surely didn't endure arrest, incarceration and death (105). When he writes Max's "presence in the camp is based on a fluke," he fails to understand the Gestapo's effectiveness at spying. He concludes, "The play still packs power, raises knotty, troubling questions, and is emphatically worth seeing."

Among positive reviews, one appears in the *Village Voice*, providing *Bent* from that weekly one pan, one mixed notice, and one rave, from Bell, a roving commentator rather than theatre critic, who attended a late rehearsal. He conveys a gay spectator's gut reactions. Bell judges this "brilliant theatre" which "will be the most controversial and powerful play since Albee stunned us with *Virginia Woolf* 17 years ago. The climax is staggering—it ends with a scream that chills—and though the main characters are homosexual, *Bent* is about injustice, courage, and love" (39). His tears left him speechless.

Book reviewer Molyneaux writes the script communicates "viscerally the homosexual experience of living in an antagonistic society. This technique allows the author to craft his play with illuminating economy and to create a taut, highly charged (though not sensational) theater piece.... We might very well have acted as Max Berber does—if we finally had his courage" (1536). Sherman has created a "homosexual hero as everyman."

Clurman pens a somewhat grudgingly favorable notice. He begins, "Though at moments embarrassing, *Bent* ... is not boring" (701–702). He discerns "divergent minorities who in so-called normal circumstances might be inimical to one another may, under common duress, come to realize the folly of such division. We are all equal in suffering and thus in need of universal compassion." He predicts a fine future for Sherman. Instead of just expressing his distaste for the verbal lovemaking, he shares that most spectators disagree with him.

Patterson offers psychological analysis of dictatorships. He perceives "this remarkable perception has been brilliantly conceived and executed" (14). He notes the rock moving, but then elucidates, "In the course of this murderously dull task they build a detailed, cunning and intricate relationship which possesses as full a range of emotions as one can imagine."

Gill begins, "To be overly ambitious is a good failing in a young and gifted playwright, and I am quick to forgive Martin Sherman for most of the flaws in *Bent* ... a play that is well worth our serious attention.... What passionate, blood-drenched theatre he offers us" (100). Gill explains, "The message of the play isn't a despairing one." When Gill reviewed the replacements, he grew still more enthusiastic, applauding the play as "even more tragic" than it had seemed before and proclaiming, "What a gifted playwright Martin Sherman is!" (55).

Kerr published two reviews, one long, another longer. He judges Sherman has "got a powerful sense of theater going for two-thirds of his bizarre, bloody journey. Along the way he may be willing to use the tricky surprises of suspense melodrama to make sure we're startled to attention, but he never uses them cheaply" (C15). He urges, "Any serious theatergoer on the lookout for energy and originality in writing, staging ... and performing would find it necessary to see 'Bent.'"

Subsequently, Kerr argues at greater length *Bent* deserves attention. "It plays as crackling, sobering authentically dramatic event, as something to be believed in, something all too possible, something to be pursued—avidly—from one plausible step to the next" (sec. 2: 3, 34). He explains Sherman's "instinct for the tangled psychological realities underlying the brutality of his narrative ... does most to command our sustained interest, our acquiescence" and praises "intelligence," "judicious use of language to get where the psychic secrets are," and "drama, the original, and forever harrowing, plunge of the knife."

Rabkin feels *Bent* "moves beyond the past to contemporary resonance, and ... is exceeding well crafted ... a powerful and moving theatrical experience" (65–66). Concerning Max's disguise as a Jew, he argues, "Sherman's point has to do with identity, not with competing degrees of anguish." He explains *Bent* "succeeds in grabbing us viscerally" and its humor underlines its theme as "human determination to resist dehumanization by defiantly asserting the capacity to give oneself to another. Despite its grim conclusion, *Bent* is essentially optimistic in this affirmation."

Kalem raves about "this gritty, powerful and compassionate drama" (84). He describes it as "pro-gay" but "not proselytizing. He wants to show us the brute cost of survival, the deep need and sustaining force of human affection in dire adversity and the taxing journey to the root core of one's identity." Kalem concludes, "*Bent* is not 'entertainment' ... but in its tensile strength and nervy risk taking, it is audacious theater."

Kissel understands "to survive in such conditions throws into question the value of survival" (12). Concerning Max electrocuting himself, he explains, "In the context of Sherman's harrowingly conceived play, it seems the only alternative to madness." He praises "a series of theatrically brilliant dialogs," "an electric current rarely seen on Broadway" and "an explosive, overpowering experience."

Johnson calls *Bent* "gripping and passionate" and notes it treats its subjects "with clarity and great depth of feeling." He predicts Sherman "will be long remembered for the subject he has dared to write about with such remarkable directness." He admires how the playwright "develops a relentless forward drive that pulls us ever deeper into the pain of his characters," which ends "in wrenching tragedy." He feels the safe-sex scene brims "with both sensuality and, surprisingly, humor." He concludes, "It is a strong, even revelatory theatrical experience" (F1, F9).

Cizmar proclaims, "*Bent* is a powerful, chilling, upsetting, and important play. But the impact of *Bent* far surpasses the historical, political, or social importance of its subject matter" (23). It explores "human instincts of survival and the love of one human being for another. The plot is well-structured." Act 2 provides "all the drama that is needed." She suggests *Bent* could have concerned other pairs because it demonstrates "relationships can triumph over even the worst of human ugliness and power-induced persecution."

Reed counters by calling *Bent* the most "profoundly important play about homosexuality ever presented on the New York stage ... that must be seen and experienced" (56). He reports some spectators wept and others grew enraged. "Rarely have I heard so many heated debates in the lobby and in the street....

When was the last time you saw that in a New York theater?" He praises the play as "a life-affirming work about courage and valor and standing up for human rights in the face of destruction." He calls *Bent* "brilliant."

Raidy greets *Bent* as a "riveting portrait of the Nazi persecution of homosexuals" and a "strong, intensely moving play" (24). He judges Sherman "has written an extraordinary drama, as gripping as it is provocative." He notes, "Camp comedy ... turns into grim tragedy" and concludes, "*Bent* takes fire. It is a fire, intense in its impact as well as its message, you will never forget."

Christopher Street had to go to press before the opening, so Ortleb evaluated the script and published a scene. He offers accolades to *Bent* "as one of the most important political and cultural events of the last few years. It is not to be missed" (10–11).

Bent became *the* play to see that season. Callow remembers going backstage with Sherman to Gere's dressing room, where they found Francis Ford Coppola, Steven Spielberg, and the like. Grant recalls "celebrities in my dressing room—Diana Ross, Bianca Jagger, Andy Warhol. *Bent* was a big deal. I met Laurence Olivier!"

Had reviews provided more support for sales, *Bent* could have run longer. Nevertheless, it enjoyed an over seven-month Broadway tenure, impressive for a "straight" drama. When Gere left the cast after June 7, 1980, ticket sales dropped. Michael York lacked his box-office power, so *Bent* closed on June 28. Its Tony nomination hadn't produced a Tony win.

Bent won the Dramatists Guild's Hull Warriner award and received inclusion in *The Best Plays of 1979–80*. An error has circulated on websites, in theatre programs, and even in print that the play received either a Pulitzer Prize or, more commonly, a nomination. (See, for instance, Harris, who states, "*Bent* won a Pulitzer Prize.") It didn't win, and back then the Pulitzer Committee didn't release nominations, so Sherman doesn't know whether *Bent* made the short list. For their performances, Gere garnered a Theatre World Award, and Dukes received a Tony nomination as featured actor.

After *Bent* opened, Sherman finally met Richard Plant. As they lunched at Joe Allen's, a misunderstanding occurred. Plant asked whether Sherman had read Heinz Heger's *Die Manner mit dem Rosa Winkel*, i.e., *The Men with the Pink Triangle*, and Sherman replied no, but he had read Plant's article and had used some details from it in writing *Bent*.

The playwright perhaps failed to convey audibly his negative regarding Heger's book. Plant likewise missed the change of subject, from that book to his own article "The Men with the Pink Triangles" in *Christopher Street*. Compounding the confusion, the English translation of Heger's title differs from the title of Plant's article by only one letter, the "s" which Plant uses to provide plural triangles.

Thus, Plant must have thought he heard Sherman acknowledge a debt to Heger's book rather than to Plant's article; he records that misinformation in his book: "Martin Sherman's play *Bent* (1979), which based some of its plot on material in Heger's book, was widely discussed" (14).

The error seems especially preposterous given huge differences between play and book. Heger writes of a 22-year-old Austrian, arrested in 1939, and incarcerated at concentration camps other than Dachau. This man, so different from Max in age and circumstances and imprisoned during a different period, doesn't have an experience resembling Max's.

Plant's error has perpetuated itself ad nauseum in countless press releases, theatre programs, publications, and websites, including Wikipedia, all dead wrong when they claim Sherman based *Bent* on Heger's book (e.g., "Love Against the Odds"). These widely disseminated mistakes eventually prompted Sherman's agent to insert in contracts for *Bent* productions a clause stating producers mustn't say Sherman used this book as a source. Nevertheless, the error continues to circulate.

Plant didn't appreciate the dramatist couldn't read a book published only in German, a language he didn't know. The English translation appeared in 1980; Sherman wrote *Bent* in 1977.

Ironically, Plant confided to Sherman doubts concerning the authenticity of Heger's book, which struck him as possibly fabricated. That Heger's reputed source could have survived so successfully in contrast to the suffering and deaths of his fellow gay inmates struck Plant as implausible. Nevertheless, he appears to have based his own remarks concerning "dolly boys" upon Heger.

As Sherman packed to move to London he couldn't know the profound and international influence his play would have. Decades later it would continue, 'round the world, to shatter those, gay and straight, who see it. Productions would occur in 54 countries by the early 21st century. Theatres in world capitals would revive it again and again. On film it would reach millions more.

Bent's impact on individuals, especially gay men, cannot be overstated. All sorts, from teenagers to elderly closet queens, after exposure to *Bent*, came out, or if already out, found support for their evolution. The play educated but also produced gales of laughter and gallons of tears, and it *changed* people, profoundly and irrevocably changed them. Great theatre should do that; *Bent* did and does.

Among those who have worked with the play's author, let a few examples stand for thousands. Tim Luscombe reports,

> *Bent* changed my life because it moved me more than anything ever. It was colossally great, took gayness out of stereotypes, told a chapter of gay history I knew nothing about. It blew apart drawing room comedy by setting it in a drawing room and then destroying it. It filled me with joy, hope, love and sadness. It's one of those rare plays that change the nature of theatre and a movement. *Bent* was seminal, part of everybody's coming out. I was already out, but it changed me.

Sher hadn't yet come out when he saw *Bent*. Like McKellen, he didn't emerge from his closet for several more years, but the play stayed with them both and helped them reach their decisions. Sher remembers Ian phoning and thanking him when he followed McKellen's example. Sher says, "*Bent* had a huge impact on me. I left the theatre shaking and weeping. It was one of those remarkable evenings in the theatre that leaves you assaulted. It's still one of the absolute best things. It's so original, such a brilliant concept, done with such passion. He takes on a big, grisly theme and fills it with life and light and love. It's a life-enhancing work."

Grant explains both he and Ackerman inhabited closets then. They created illusions when they gave interviews. Grant would mention his girlfriend; Ackerman would mention his wife and son. Regarding Max's internalized homophobia, Grant explains:

> That notion in the gay community is more recent than the play. So much of our behavior has been dictated by our self-loathing, based on what we're taught as children. We refuse to allow ourselves to be loved because we're not worthy of love because we're "bad." Nobody but Martin was telling that story then. Everybody in *Angels in America* except Belize acts horribly. They're terrible people. Martin was ahead of his time. He tells us, before Kushner wrote his play, why they're terrible people. That's prescient. No play addresses that issue as clearly as *Bent*.

Performance artist Tim Miller, one of the "NEA Four" who lost their grants because of the sexual nature of their work—or rather because of the conservative nature of the government—believes

> Martin's influence on a whole generation of playwrights and performance artists is massive. *Bent* was a highly significant moment in the development of queer culture. It politicized a generation of English actors. It was a huge influence on my work, so inspiring and validating. *Bent* claimed hidden history and popularized the pink triangle as a signifier of gay identity. That's one of the most important things an artist can do, to create a space for a community around the world. *Bent* is hugely transformative for young actors. *Bent* gave me permission to do the work that got me into trouble with Jesse Helms and the NEA.

Bent became the most produced play worldwide written by an American during the 20th century's last quarter. It entered global consciousness to such an extent that familiarity with it provides common ground across dozens of different cultures that otherwise have little in common beyond YouTube, cell phones, and McDonald's. Only Muslim areas, most of black Africa, and dictatorships so far haven't made room for *Bent*. (See Appendix A.) Those countries that most virulently discriminate against gay men—and therefore most need the play—don't stage it. (Witness homophobia in Nigeria in 2009; Uganda, Malawi, Kenya, and Zimbabwe in 2010; ongoing in Iran.)

Israeli director Eytan Fox and his writer/producer and partner, Gal Uchovsky, include a scene from it in their love story, *The Bubble*. This 2007 film dramatizes love between a young Israeli and a young Palestinian. They attend *Bent* in Tel Aviv. Young-adult novelist Barthe Declements uses *Bent* when two characters in her popular *Seventeen and in Between* see it. Not many works enter pieces by other artists. *Bent* likewise proves the answer in a crossword puzzle in *Henry Hook Trivia Crostics* (21). Sumner's volume providing solutions to theatrical design problems presented in frequently produced plays also includes *Bent* (199–200).

Bent informed millions about slaughter of gay men under the Third Reich and brought the pink triangle to public consciousness. In the 1980s, gay men and women fighting for their civil rights while their friends died of AIDS adopted the pink triangle to symbolize their pride and resolve. Later, the badge worn by Nazi victims gave way to the more affirmative rainbow of inclusivity and diversity.

Bent's indictment of bigotry and genocide offers increased resonance over three decades since its premiere. Subsequent to Rwanda, Kosovo and Darfur, not to mention terrorist attacks, we need its powerful warning not to demonize those deemed "different" and its elegy to those already slaughtered.

Sherman had decided before *Bent*'s production that he would write no more plays because his career hadn't panned out. The play's success, however, changed his mind. And now he could fulfill his dream of moving to London because it proved to British immigration he could support himself.

After *Bent* opened on Broadway, Sherman bought a flat in Bayswater in early 1980. Away from tourist throngs, yet convenient to Central London, this peaceful oasis has nurtured his craft and spirit.

8. Rachel (1978–1984)

Before *Bent*'s premiere, the BBC commissioned Sherman to write a teleplay called *Movement*, a 50-minute dramatization of Cuba's oppression of gays, due March 31, 1979. Producer W. Stephen Gilbert—who helped bring *Bent* to the stage—invited Sherman to write this teleplay, which would have begun the second season of a series. Sherman wrote and delivered the script, but, before filming could begin, the BBC canceled the series (Howes 15–16). Sherman had to wait until 1993 for one of his teleplays to air.

Another producer in 1979 asked Sherman to write a film for Barbra Streisand, but the dramatist didn't like the property, *Third Time Lucky*. He therefore declined.

The year 1980 brought Sherman a National Endowment for the Arts Fellowship and his own London flat.

After launching *Bent* in New York and between his trips round the world to attend other productions, Sherman made his first adult attempt at directing. His pal Pope and Alex Harding had conceived a cabaret called *Point Blank*. Pope wrote book and lyrics, and Harding composed music. Pope would perform, while Harding accompanied him. Somebody needed to serve as their eyes in the stalls. So *Point Blank*, directed by Sherman, received its first London performance at Oval House on June 18, 1980.

During winter 1981, Sherman completed a film begun the previous summer for director/producer Fred Zinnemann. Based on Vladimir Volkoff's 1979 French novel *Le retournement* (*The Turnaround*), this espionage tale concerns the KGB and the Russian Orthodox Church. Zinnemann never filmed it.

While Sherman considered what to dramatize next, renegade Rabbi Josef Scharf-Wilner gave him a note containing the words "Sabbatai Sevi." The rabbi said, "Read about this man. You'll want to write about him." The playwright wrote Garnett on September 21, 1981, "I may be writing a new play. Leave for Paris tomorrow for previews of *Bent*."

Sherman had begun reading about Sabbatai, the 17th-century Sephardic rabbi widely greeted as the Messiah. Scharf-Wilner had expected Sherman would find him fascinating, but, as the playwright read, he grew more interested in Sabbatai's impact. A lesser writer would have dramatized this "Messiah" as his protagonist, flanked by followers. Not Sherman. He writes about a Sherman trademark: a strong female central role. He (or God) tests the faith of his female Job. Sabbatai doesn't appear.

Sherman chooses an outsider protagonist in Rachel—a woman, a Jew, a rebel, and ugly to boot.

Within three months of writing to Garnett that he might be starting a new play, Sherman had completed *Messiah*.

The dramatist imagines a Jewish community in 17th-century Poland, on the Ukrainian border. A holocaust has occurred in which marauding Cossacks have killed one third of the region's Jews. Fear of further genocide has left survivors eager for a savior. Sherman chooses the village where, in the early 20th century, his father was born. Sherman grew up steeped in this shtetl's lore; he then thought it was called Yultishk, and he uses or refers to it in three other works.

Readers will recall the Shermans regarded themselves as Russian, yet will know contemporary Russia lies far from the Ukrainian/Polish border. People born there 100 years ago, however, thought of their country as Russia. Sherman explains, "As far as I'm concerned, I'm a Russian Jew. That's how I was brought up."

Sherman constructs *Messiah* in 35 scenes; nearly half these—16—employ only Rachel, who speaks her monologues to God. This skeptic carries on perceptive, wisecracking, argumentative dialogues—albeit one-sided—with that unseen character. Generally Sherman alternates prayers and more populated scenes.

Rachel reacts differently from her companions to news the Messiah has arrived. After extended internal and external conflicts, she leaves home seeking Sabbatai. Eventually she and her companion, Asher, differ about Sevi's apostasy.

What should someone raised in a faith do when it appears unsustainable? Asher kills himself. After losing her mother and her lover while she sleeps, Rachel goes on living and doubting and addressing those doubts to a God who might or might not hear her. Her last words address this: "Oh God. After all of this, I still don't know" (200).

Sherman terms this often-amusing work "my most painful and personal play. I've absolutely stripped myself naked in it." Rachel has the buckteeth and pimples that had plagued young Sherman, but the character also reflects him on a deeper level. In addition to his perception of his youthful self as homely, she embodies Sherman's intelligence, analytical nature, and wit. He identifies with Rachel, whose conversations with God constitute fresh, funny and insightful monologues. Her independence yet her yearning for love, her doubts yet her yearning for faith, her propriety yet her yearning for a handsome young lover, might exemplify Sherman's conflicts—but they speak to us all.

So do two other women, Sabbatai's wife, Sarah, and Rachel's mother,

Rebecca, the latter woman disabled by her inability to speak, who thus embodies another form of "other." In their scene we glimpse what sort of sensual life Sabbatai must lead. Though largely subliminal in its sexuality, this sequence culminates in a long kiss. The scene dramatizes the characters' sexual repression just outside their conscious thoughts.

Sherman acknowledges the gay undertones of this erotically charged scene. He recalls, "When I wrote it, I was caught in currents I couldn't control. My hand was pushed. I think good playwriting, anyhow, is having the craft to channel your subconscious. And my subconscious flowed during that sequence."

This scene also provides us insight into the silent Rebecca, who can't develop in the usual way through dialogue and monologues. A victim of Cossacks pillaging her shtetl in 1648, she suffers from post-traumatic stress syndrome, though nobody in the 17 century calls it that. Sarah gives Rebecca kindness, understanding, and affection. The Messiah's wife heals Rebecca, who therefore can take care of Rachel.

In *Fat Tuesday*, *Next Year in Jerusalem*, and *Rio Grande*, Sherman turned his maternal-nurturance deficit into drama. In *Messiah*, however, he does this more successfully. During Act 1, instead of receiving a mother's love, Rachel must mother her mother. In Act 2, Rebecca gives Rachel affection and protection. Without arguments or confrontation, the mother offers what the daughter needs. Sherman here utilizes actions, not words, to touch us.

Both Sarah and Rebecca, the Cossacks' victims, recognize a literal Satan who pushed marauders to such barbarity they killed Rebecca's father by sewing up a live cat inside his belly. And both women long for Sabbatai to save their people from a recurrence. Because Rebecca recognizes evil as so palpable and powerful, she twice surrounds her daughter with a circle of wool to protect her.

Rachel's husband, Reb Ellis, likewise suffers from an easily identifiable modern disorder, religious psychosis, like those California cultists who believed Hale Bop a gate to Heaven and therefore killed themselves, or members of Jim Jones's People's Temple who drank cyanide. But Sherman doesn't focus on *Messiah*'s male characters. The self-destructive men, fanatics both, die. They exist to illuminate his protagonist, one of four women, all of whom live. Rachel suffers, and she experiences a metaphysical conflict usually reserved for a Hamlet, an Oedipus, a Willy Loman. Fully conscious of the horror she is enduring, she exhibits a powerful will to survive.

Rachel refuses to accept mindlessly dogma others embrace. She rejects religious fanaticism and obsessive orthodoxy. Rather than endangering her survival, her independence keeps her alive. In contrast, her husband jumps off a roof, and her lover stabs himself. Men of blind faith, blind obedience, and blind fanaticism, each believes he is following God's will. Rachel instead learns to rely on herself. She exhibits not mere independence but also heroic courage.

A Sherman outsider, she behaves in ways we don't expect from most people, certainly not a 17th-century Jewish woman.

Sherman, as usual, mixes genres. This audacious, provocative, witty play convulses us one moment and chills us the next. Ultimately it devastates. Especially in Act 1, however, Sherman employs satire and farce as Rachel deals with a garrulous husband and a mute mother and God. He supplies enough one-liners for an episode of *Saturday Night Live*.

Messiah's resemblance to Chekhov or to Beckett's metaphysical work might elicit the label "dark comedy." Yet its violent deaths might prompt terming it "black comedy" in the first act, or "melodrama" in the second. Certainly Sherman writes the section leading up to and including Reb Ellis's death in a style as black comic as Orton. *Messiah*'s catharsis seems appropriate to tragedy, yet the action shows us Rachel will endure. Therefore, the plot doesn't arc into tragic finality. The action ends only in that Rachel receives, by the final curtain, everything she asks for in her opening prayer, although God's answers take ironic forms. This device unifies the play, but doesn't make it tragedy.

Sherman achieves something richer and more diverse. It's as though *Carousel*'s Julie Jordan had a keen mind and a sense of the absurd. The shifting moods embrace the multiplicity of human experience and a mixture of pain and humor somehow very Jewish—and wise.

As Callow observes, "Sometimes Martin's plays are deceptively light, but they have at their center a very subtle, precise analysis of some part of the human heart."

The playwright's craft generates suspense throughout: We want to know what will happen. During the opening 60 seconds, Rachel's prayer asks that Mama get well, the Cossacks not return, someone love Rachel, and the Messiah come. Will these occur? As events unfold, we want to learn whether Rachel will marry Reb Ellis, whether he will believe in Sabbatai, and whether he will make a literal leap of faith. Later we wonder if Rachel will receive a sign to leave and travel to Turkey, if Rebecca will ever speak, if the nature of Rachel's relationship with Asher will change. Will we finally see Sabbatai? Is he the Messiah they await? Will he go to Constantinople and be crowned? What impact will Sabbatai's fate have on Rachel, Asher, and Rebecca, and will Rachel lose her faith in God? Sherman piques our curiosity repeatedly.

As in *Bent*, Sherman employs the interval to shift the script's locale and to change its style from largely representational to predominantly presentational. After the first act's brimming-with-life-but-claustrophobic folk tale set in a shtetl, Sherman offers us, in the Turkish second half, open spaces and more minimalist accouterments. Think of *Waiting for Godot*'s selective action and setting. The startling shift in locale also conveys theme: The exoticism of the Islamic marketplace scene visually establishes the characters' "otherness," as they find themselves exiles from their country, their language, their religion, and their customs.

8. Rachel (1978–1984)

Sherman and Maureen Lipman at her birthday dinner, London, probably May 1996, (courtesy Martin Sherman).

Sherman contrasts the Ashkenazi Judaism of the shtetl in cold, landlocked Eastern Europe, where Rachel has never seen a boat, to the dancing and music and freer Sephardic-overlaid-with-Turkish atmosphere in Act 2's early scenes. Although Sherman hadn't yet visited modern Turkey, Gallipoli lies closer to modern Greece than to Istanbul. He knew the Aegean, where Sabbatai was born in the same town as Homer, and brought its white light, wines, and mandolin music to creating his contrast.

Sarah has transmogrified from the daughter of a strict family like Rachel's into a Mediterranean siren. Poised as it is among European, North African, and Turkish ambiences, Greece steeped Sherman in an appropriate cultural cauldron from which to concoct Act 2, especially the bazaar and Sarah's scene. That cultural reversal occurs during intermission.

Sherman also shifts the mood after the interval. Had he done so without that pause, we might feel uneasy. But he allows us during intermission to forget how much we have laughed in Act 1, and thereafter he successfully shifts into something more hallucinatory and nightmarish.

When Aukin, Hampstead Theatre's Artistic Director, accepted *Messiah* for December 1982 production, he suggested his wife, American Nancy Meckler, as director. Sherman, however, feared working with another husband-wife team after his experience on Playwrights Horizons' *Cracks*, so he wouldn't agree. He subsequently regretted this decision, both because she would have directed the play better than Ronald Eyre and because he later loved working with her on *Alive and Kicking, Rose, A Passage to India,* and *Onassis*. Sherman calls his decision to reject Meckler "the biggest mistake I've ever made professionally."

Hampstead sent the script to stage-and-television star Maureen Lipman, who had never met Sherman and hadn't seen *Bent*. She recognized an excellent role and found she adored the writer: "He's the dearest person, genuinely sweet, without demeaning his strength. He has a natural good, a sort of spirituality. At rehearsals he was as delicate as a gazelle. He doesn't have the ego problems a lot of writers have."

Lipman agrees Eyre proved the wrong director. She describes him as "a cerebral man, so we didn't explore enough possibilities." She finds the script

> impressionistic, such a rich tapestry and so different from his contemporaries, so traditional yet modern, blending humor and tragedy. He chronicles the present using great swatches of the past, like a Bronxville Jane Austin, the opposite of the biopic. By making us understand the heartaches and poetry of individuals, he illuminates civilizations and why they behave badly. It's very Jewish even when he's not writing about Jews because it's full of pain, but out of that comes laughter.

Eyre turned *Messiah* into a piece of comic local color, deemphasizing the darker, fearful emotions. Although he diminished the impact on spectators, his leading lady understood the play so well it devastated her. Lipman endured buckteeth for years until she got her dentist to correct the problem. When, ironically, she asked him to create false buckteeth caps for her, she fiercely identified with her role. "The only person she could talk to in the world was God, and suddenly God gives her a tiny glimpse of passion and then takes it away. She suffers so."

This identification went beyond the character and extended to her creator. Lipman recognized "a brother, a twin" in the playwright, and they grew close. "There's only so many of those people you meet in a lifetime."

Lipman feels she let down the play because she couldn't take off her top to show Asher her breasts. "It's a fantastic coup de theatre, but I couldn't do it. I worried they would decide to get another actress."

Messiah began performances at Hampstead on December 3, 1982, and opened on December 9. In addition to Lipman as Rachel, Eyre cast Matyelok Gibbs as Rebecca, Clive Swift as Reb Ellis, and Jack Klaff as Asher. A quarter of a century later, Aukin reflects, "Eyre made a complete mess of the casting, other than Maureen Lipman in the lead. Although the production was a success, it was soft and romantic, whereas it should have been tough and hard." Meckler observes, "It was so different from the way I would have done it."

Critics who saw it at Hampstead rebuked Sherman for what Eyre did and credited Eyre for what Sherman did. Some couldn't keep track of the characters' names, others profoundly misunderstood the writer's attitudes, and most lambasted the play. For reasons as various as the reviewers who made the pronouncements, critics regarded the script as inept.

Barber begins, "A good play lurks beneath the coziness and sentimentality." He complains about "the author's flat writing and labored efforts to be lovable at all costs" but lauds Lipman, the direction and design (11). Billington praises the production while dismissing the script as "a flawed fable" (10).

Some critics fault *Messiah* because they'd have written it differently. King, who disliked *Bent*, writes, "Mr. Sherman once again shows both his aptitude for finding an arresting subject and his inability to do it adequate justice. One fatal error is that Sabbatai never himself appears"(12). Grant, likewise, complains, "Sherman's piece is extremely thin and long-winded and quite unforgivably ditches the most interesting male character ... after the first act" (105). Edwards rejects *Messiah* because he wants it serious: "Why does there have to be humour here at all?" (52). Elsom wants a sweeping historical drama and. hence. objects to the love story, which fails to achieve "its epic potential" (35).

Amory makes *Messiah* sound ridiculous, then candidly concludes, "Martin Sherman wrote *Bent*, which was much admired, and I did not like that either" (48–49). Young belittles *Messiah* as "a tolerable first draft for an interesting melodrama, but no more" (12). Cushman laments, "His audacity and his stagecraft run considerably ahead of his actual writing" (29). Fenton begins his harangue, "Martin Sherman, in this as in his previous play 'Bent,' is unable to present his contemporary theme in a way which arises naturally from their historical settings" [sic] (40). He condemns each detail.

Some reviews refrain from play bashing. Wardle seems to mean as a muted compliment "The conceit of the play is to present a modern heroine in historical context," which he compares to "Edward Bond with jokes" (11). He likes Rachel, saying, "You swiftly warm to Rachel as a Yiddish comedian in a rabbinical society." He understands Sherman's twin themes of survival and a beleaguered "other" suffering hardship.

Other critics loved *Messiah* at Hampstead. Barkley has only good things to say about what he describes as an "ironic comedy" (22). Shulman also enjoys the humor: "What might have been a ponderous religious statement is saved by Mr. Sherman's witty and cynical pen. With the help of Maureen Lipman, as Rachel, he gives us a play that examines the Jewish dilemma with humanity and humour" (30).

Pascal praises how Sherman has "given his central intellectual debates to a woman. It's unusual to hear a woman speaking frankly to God about her sexual longings and her doubts" (55). She enjoys the intelligent, witty character" and "truthful writing."

Morley understands *Messiah* concerns fanaticism, the "narrowness of any orthodox religious belief," and the "contrast between an unashamedly modern heroine, gossiping to us in the audience while also trying to deal with age-old historical and doctrinal mistakes" (6). He lauds a playwright "prepared to take on in a two-hour, two-act evening, themes of life and death, religion and humanity, of the broadest possible scale. That and his talent for good, acid, black jokes continue to make Sherman an admirable if underrated writer."

Herbert predicts "it will be a big success on Broadway. It has all the ingredients for a New York smash, and there would be no shortage of actresses to try and match Maureen Lipman's brilliance" (4).

Because audiences loved it and critics supplied usable quotations for advertisements, Eddie Kulukundis, on December 30, 1982, arranged with Michael Codron to move *Messiah* to a West End theatre the latter controlled, the Aldwych. Between 1979 and 1982, both producers had separately commissioned Sherman to write untitled plays, which became the same play, produced by one and housed by the other. *Messiah* began performances there on January 26, 1983.

This unfortunate venue, the mammoth home of Aldwych farces, lacked Hampstead's intimacy. Lipman believes,

> It couldn't survive in there. But Martin would pop in and see us. Even when we were complaining, he would comfort us with this wonderful wry acceptance. There is no malice in him at all, as a writer or as a person. Often when we have gotten together since that time it has been for a sad occasion, a funeral, but I've also seen him glowing. I think he's gorgeous. He doesn't think so, but he is.

Although *Messiah* landed in the wrong theatre, notices improved.

Critics continue to contradict each other. Roper puts down the play (13), complaining of its "stark seriousness," but Petty praises its comedy until her last paragraph, when she concludes, "The comedy of this play is haunted by tragedy, but unfortunately the cast seem haunted by the difficult task of allying the two moods" (25).

Hirschhorn damns *Messiah* as "a pointless, rather embarrassing curiosity" (23). Carne censures both script ("strangely pedestrian") and direction ("suffused with ... reverential dullness"). She repeatedly inquires, "Who cares?" (15). Masters loves the play and its star, but faults the direction in the final scene. Yet his review approaches a rave, and he notes, "The present-day parallel is too close to be unintentional.... It will stand for any idealists anywhere whose dream suddenly shatters" (11).

Stewart likes script and Lipman better than direction (447). Asquith offers the same contrast between "intriguing" play with "profound" message but unsatisfactory mounting (50). De Jongh faults production, including its star, but elucidates play and its connection to *Bent* (12). Gordon praises everything except for wishing the second half "might have attempted more" (25). Yet he stresses the play's importance ("It is of fundamental concern to us") and concludes, "It's a moving, intelligent evening."

Nightingale chides critics who panned it before, including his colleague Edwards, "But, judging by the empty seats ... he and others may well be carrying the public with their animadversions on its supposed clumsiness, flipness and anachronism" (32–33). He compares its structure to *Bent*'s and notes Sherman's understanding of the "blessing and curse of being Jewish." He praises *Messiah* as "a pithy, direct, even blunt play."

Readers will note none of these notices comes from those who judged *Messiah* at Hampstead. Only two critics reviewed a second time; one further castigates and one further praises. Or, rather, Barber quotes the play he hates in order to praise Lipman's acting, as though she had written her own lines (13).

Morley raves about the play—"superb"—and playwright—"an extremely exciting writer" (44). He further extols Sherman in another notice, beginning, "Martin Sherman is one of those dramatists whom nobody much likes except the public" (10). Morley believes "Sherman is the most exciting dramatist to have come out of America in the last decade."

Messiah didn't last long in the West End.

After it closed, Sherman went to Israel to see *Bent*, which began performances on May 7, 1983. He knew he would be returning soon for *Messiah*, so instead of lingering in Haifa, he embraced the opportunity to see Egypt— finally. He took a bus to Cairo and explored the country for a week. Insufficient time, but he revisited during filming *The Clothes in the Wardrobe*, when he again found the country breathtaking. He wrote Lavren, describing that first trip as his "*most* overwhelming and intense and thrilling experience" ever.

The same Israeli theatre that had presented *Bent* arranged to mount *Messiah*. It began performances at the Haifa Municipal Theatre on New Year's Eve 1983 and continued in repertory through February 1984. Ackerman directed this production, which Sherman calls "brilliant" and "inspired."

During rehearsals, he escaped to London for two weeks and completed *Unseen Angels*, later re-titled *When She Danced*.

Although *Bent* caused no controversy in Israel, *Messiah* nearly shut down Haifa's government, pitting Jews against Jews. The Orthodox ultra-right-wing objected, while others—both secular and religious—found the protests without merit, even silly. Most Israelis had no problem with *Messiah*. But tiny political parties can topple the Israeli government because they must participate in coalitions in order for a large party to take or maintain power.

"So," explains Sherman,

> the Orthodox wielded disproportionate power. One saw the play and ostensibly objected to the moment in the last scene when Rachel curses God. He called this blasphemy. This party really objected to the whole sweep of the play. Sholem, the great writer about Jewish mysticism, one of the great Jewish thinkers, and Sabbatai Sevi's biographer, wrote an article in *New York Review of Books* comparing Sabbatai's followers with West-Bank settlers. He provided parallels between the two false messiahs. The protestors really objected to those parallels, but they had to claim they objected to blasphemy.

Because the censors had approved *Messiah*, extremists couldn't close it for blasphemy, so they pressured Haifa to stop the play. Then they tried to shut down the theatre. Then Orthodox rabbis threatened to remove all Orthodox Jews from Haifa. "Orthodox terrorists planted bombs in the theatre," Sherman relates.

> Furious debates erupted in the Knesset. For two months, it was the only subject besides Lebanon on the front pages. Three members of this party, by pure fluke, were sitting on the committee that controlled the national purse strings. They withdrew the following month's subsidy from the municipality of Haifa, so 20,000 workers weren't going to receive paychecks because of *Messiah*.

> The chief Orthodox rabbi issued a proclamation saying anyone who saw *Messiah* had to observe 24 hours of mourning, had to tear their clothes, had to say prayers for the dead. But because Israeli television had broadcast the last scene, every Israeli had seen it. Finally the Israeli president had to step in. A year previously, peace protestors had marched against the war in Lebanon. It was nearly the anniversary of that "peace now" march. Members of the Orthodox right had thrown a grenade into that march. It had killed one marcher and injured several others. On that anniversary, the first march since then would occur in Jerusalem. The president needed some sort of trade-off with the Right to prevent violence during this march. So he pleaded with the theatre to remove the line where she curses God. And the theatre removed it.

Sherman didn't want bloodshed. He also wanted those 20,000 people to receive paychecks. So he didn't protest the deletion.

Some published accounts of the protests and the deletion include more than the curse, covering as well Rachel saying she hates God and/or that God doesn't exist, but only one sentence fell victim to objections: "God damn you, God!"

Franco Zavani (left) and Sherman while *Messiah* previewed at Manhattan Theatre Club, Thanksgiving, 1984, at the NYC home of Verna Bloom and Jay Cocks (courtesy Verna Bloom).

Nava Semel, who translated *Messiah*, explains, "The audience knew exactly the missing words because of the scandal. We could hear the audience mumbling them in Hebrew, 'Arur Tiyhey Adonay, Arur Tihye.' I used the exact biblical phrase used by God, cursing the snake in Genesis." (For additional facts, see Handelzalts.)

To whatever extent protestors in Israel really objected to Rachel's cursing God, they ignored that this lasts only a millisecond. Her faith persists despite her fear God doesn't deserve it. We should equate Rachel with Job, not Nietzsche. Events test her faith and leave her skeptical—a state of mind we observe elsewhere in *Messiah*.

Sherman feels "it's my most painful play." More painful than a play set in Dachau? Rachel and her family experience the pogrom that killed her father by sewing up a live cat in his belly and killed her brother by ripping him apart and roasting the pieces. Rachel's husband leaps off a roof in the grip of religious mania that convinces him he can fly. Rachel's lover turns against her, blames her for his own decisions, and kills himself. This and more devastate us. Max dies heroically, while Rachel survives. Perhaps we must judge perishing defiantly an easier fate.

Manhattan Theatre Club's Artistic Director Lynne Meadow had wanted to present *Messiah*, but Sherman found the original space on East 73rd St. too tiny and intimate. The larger of the new theatres at City Center, however, provided room "to breathe. It's not a piece of domestic naturalism. You need that little bit of room to capture its theatricality." So when MTC moved, he agreed to a December 1984 mounting. (See Appendix B.)

While in New York for the MTC production, Sherman received, at an awards luncheon on December 6, a $1,000 1984 Drama League Special Playwriting Assistance Award, and subsequently he won a 1985 Rockefeller Fellowship. These both contributed to his support as he wrote and awaited production of his next two plays.

The BeerSheba Municipal Theatre revived *Messiah* in Christmas week 2008. Instead of inspiring right-wing protests aimed at canceling the production, this mounting the following week succumbed to Hamas bombardment of Beersheba; rockets temporarily closed the theatre. Juxtaposition of Jewish and Islamic in the play and in real life underlines the work's continuing pertinence to adversarial relations of near-cousins. Indeed, in spring 2008, a Turkish theatre inquired about staging it there. That marks the first interest in that Muslim country in Sherman's plays.

9. Isadora (1983–1988)

In New York, Sherman came to love Martha Graham's company and New York City Ballet. Later he grew close to dancer Livingston (to whom he dedicated *When She Danced*). *Rio Grande*, *Bent* and *Alive and Kicking* also feature dancers. He knew others, and, like Degas, he depicts them with respect and understanding.

After completing *Messiah* in autumn 1981, Sherman read sporadically about Isadora Duncan, who gave birth to Modern Dance. In 1983, he started shaping a play. He began before leaving for the Haifa Municipal Theatre's fall 1983 *Messiah* rehearsals. When he returned to London for two weeks, he finished *Unseen Angels*, within a few weeks retitled *When She Danced*.

Sherman chose Duncan because of "the ephemeral quality of her art, the impossibility of describing it or knowing what it was. And yet it had and has still such profound influence. She's one of the biggest influences in the 20th century. But no one knows what she did. That became compelling."

Concerning her influence, Sherman details her invention of modern dance, her reinvention of ballet via her influence on Diaghilev and Nijinsky, her influence on sculpture, her influence on Stanislavsky by using herself in her work, and her influence on how women dress and behave. "She was a feminist far before her time. Some others, particularly artists, lived as freely as she did, but they didn't talk about it to the press. That was astonishing then and incredibly brave. She also had a radical sense of the world as a small place."

Sherman selects as his subject an artist whose work, though much revered, hasn't survived. Thus, he can celebrate her gifts through contrasting types of admirers and take as one theme the impossibility of describing or paraphrasing art. Duncan's life abroad, surrounded by a polyglot coterie of friends and hangers-on speaking nine languages, permits him to dramatize another difficulty—communicating, because of language's limits, whether in art or life. He also dramatizes his overriding themes—survival and outsiders, in this case expats and a larger-than-life female bohemian superstar.

Sherman selects a locale he has loved since 1966. Confused by a city where he knew nobody and couldn't speak French, he nevertheless found the spots the play mentions fascinating: rue de Rivoli, rue de la Pompe (Isadora lived at 103), rue Jacob, rue de la Paix, rue Bonaparte, rue des Beaux Arts. He found his soul's true home in Paris and Greece, something he shares with Duncan. *When She Danced* occurs in 1923, when Isadora lived in Paris, and Greece inspired her.

He populates Isadora's milieu with "the other," outsiders, not only aliens or L'Etranger (except for Jeanne), but, in three cases, artists. Furthermore, he selects a Jewish character, a gay character, and several women, and he understands Isadora so well he seems to channel her. He identifies with Isadora, Esenin, and Alexandros; he feels living as an exile "fuels my work." Yet he identifies with another outsider, the mousy Belzer, a non-artist uneasy among glitterati.

The play's events take place four years before Isadora's death, between when she wakes up and the time she falls asleep—less than 24 imagined hours in a legend's life. This fictional day occurs sometime between Isadora's return home to Paris in February 1923 and her arrival in Moscow with Sergei on August 5. Though Sherman creates the action and most dialogue, he researched Duncan's life and quotes a tad from her autobiography, *My Life*.

Among Isadora's actual remarks, she tells her students, "Listen to the music with your soul" (76) which he converts to her explanation, "I listen to the music within my soul—and I dance" (43). Isadora enjoins children "come forth with great strides, leaps and bounds" (343), which Sherman incorporates in Isadora's plea to Christine, "Touch your *own* spirit, feel it, nourish it, release it—and then come forth with your own great strides, no one else's. With your own leaps and bounds, no one else's" (49). More important than her words, he captures the essence of her distress when "disciples" merely imitate movements they believe she has performed rather than discovering their own talent.

Duncan writes "genius has always had a fatal attraction for me" (251), which Sherman improves as "I am fatally attracted to genius" (26). The dramatist also distills into her speech to Luciano (44) her remarks on observing Botticelli's Primavera and determining afterward "to translate all this to my dance" (113–114). Elsewhere, he found "When in doubt, always go to the best hotel" (*Isadora Speaks*, 123), which he renders as "When in doubt, head for the best hotel" (18).

Those characters he invents represent types who figured in her life. Although Sherman creates translator Belzer, Isadora hired in Wiesbaden Lola Kinel, who describes an argument somewhat similar to one Isadora and Sergei have late in Act 1.

Sherman also invents Luciano, to whom he gives the last name of director Ackerman's late partner, Franco Zavani. Duncan approached people for money, and, in Paris, went to the Italian embassy and asked for money for a school. There she mistook somebody unimportant for a vice consul.

He uses three characters named Duncan: Isadora; her true artistic progeny, piano prodigy Alexandros, whose mother saw Isadora dance and gave him the middle name "Duncan"; and Christine, a phony imitator of Isadora's dance, which she has never seen. She merely mimics what one of Isadora's students mistaught her. Sherman invents both these Duncans, but they represent young artists who clustered around Isadora and pseudo-disciples who plagued her.

Isadora's husband, poet Sergei Esenin, and her friend Mary Desti existed, as did her maid Jeanne. Sherman accurately portrays Esenin's alcoholism and violence as well as his jealousy regarding how she cherished her children's memory. His insensitivity did entail reciting to her "The Song of the Dog" ("Pesn'o sobake").

Duncan did consider the least painful way to kill herself and did try to commit suicide in Nice by walking into the sea. She also evinced compulsive generosity.

Desti, mother of Preston Sturges, met Duncan during his infancy. Under her influence, Desti dressed him in a toga. They traveled with Duncan, so Sturges grew up as a member of her household. Sherman concluded Sturges's screwball films must reflect that atmosphere.

The first Hollywood writer-director, Sturges released seven fine films between 1940 and 1944. Sherman discovered in Sturges an original genius who moves instantly from farce to drama or back, who writes witty dialogue, and who devoted the war years to mocking many American verities. Sherman absorbed the Sturges manner.

Toto in *The Palm Beach Story* speaks no English, the Claudette Colbert character in this film tries to score a big bankroll, as does the gold-digger Barbara Stanwyck character in *The Lady Eve*. The issues in *Sullivan's Travels* concern wealth versus poverty, as well as the relative merits of comedy versus drama. The Veronica Lake character disguises herself as a boy wearing a cap, just as Sherman had encouraged Lavren to do. Eddie Bracken in *Hail the Conquering Hero* plays a Sherman-style outsider, and the film depicts the ersatz versus the authentic. *The Miracle of Morgan's Creek* provides a splendidly anarchic model for *When She Danced*'s wildest farce. So does *The Beautiful Blonde from Bashful Bend* (1949), in which Betty Grable's dancehall cutie hurls crockery, pots, pans, and kettle in a comic fusillade resembling Isadora's. Yet Sherman hasn't seen this film.

Among Sherman's international characters, Isadora speaks primarily English and French; Jeanne only French; Sergei Russian; Mary English and Italian; Belzer English and Russian; Alexandros English, Greek, Italian, and a bit of Yiddish; Luciano Italian; and Christine Swedish. Isadora also exclaims in German, Spanish and Russian. Of the play's nine languages, in her short opening speech Isadora speaks five.

Sherman speaks and reads only English. He's built a house in Greece, and that led him to acquire a smattering of Greek, but he continues in awe of the multi-lingual. Growing up near paternal grandparents who spoke only Yiddish, he has understood the humor and pathos of not understanding or making himself understood with people he loves.

Sherman believes spectators feel comfortable hearing all those languages because they "identify with Isadora, who doesn't understand." He muses, "If there weren't a character at the center who also didn't understand, it would be a problem for the audience. But the central character is in the same position they are. Plus the actor playing Sergei, who says the most in a foreign language, must give an expressive performance, so we know what he's thinking."

Like much Sherman comedy, the subtlety of having Isadora awaken spouting Russian, English, French, German, and Spanish might amuse us unconsciously. Sergei also communicates to Isadora in pantomime, plus we laugh at the misunderstandings. Ironist Sherman, however, shows the inability to communicate might preserve a relationship.

He also dramatizes the arts and artists. Belzer and Mary have seen Isadora dance, as did Alexandros's mother. In the only departures from realism, each delivers a presentational soliloquy outside the action to speak of her artistry. They convey little, however, about dancing. Mostly they dwell upon themselves, for Isadora's performance turns them inward. This revelatory experience of art illuminates them for themselves but also highlights their narcissism.

Mary and Belzer explain her dance only in terms of self. When Alexandros recalls what his mother told him, he quotes her sage remarks upon art's ineffable nature. In the play's last line, through him, she mourns, "'Then mboro na to exiyi so.'—'I can not explain'" (63). We cannot paraphrase art.

Alexandros longs to see her dance, but never does. He appreciates his loss, unlike the philistine Luciano, who expects a verbalizeable description and thinks he has seen a replica of it in the travesty Christine performs.

Sergei has seen her dance. He holds her evanescent artistry in contempt compared to his permanent poetry and yet—hilariously—tries to hang himself to protest the world's failure to appreciate her genius.

Desti's experience of Isadora dancing leads her into the delusion of seeing herself in Isadora and fancying herself another Isadora.

Isadora's dancing has deeply touched Belzer. If her reaction, likewise, smacks of narcissism, perhaps we are permitted that in response to artistic genius, refracting its dazzling light through the lens of self. As Gerard Manley Hopkins observes, "It is the blight man was born for. / It is Margaret you mourn for" ("Spring and Fall: To a Young Child"). When we see ephemeral beauty (in Hopkins' case dying autumn leaves, in Isadora's case her dance, which didn't survive her), we grieve our own mortality. And that, too, Sherman incorporates into this play, which concludes as Alexandros speaks, at a later date, about Isadora dying before he could see her dance and his mother dying without sharing with him what happened when she danced.

Although Sherman demonstrates we cannot adequately describe or paraphrase art, he permits us to observe a genius's inner creative process, when, for two minutes and 35 seconds we watch Isadora, motionless, listen "with power, force and passion" (35) to Alexandros play Chopin's Etude, Opus 10, in F Minor. Sherman instructs us "She is on fire—but inside."

The Amber Lane edition's cover encapsulates the play's essence—thereby doing what the play tells us we shouldn't attempt—in four Russian words, which loosely translate as "There is beauty" or "Here is beauty" or "This is beauty." After watching the characters' hilarious but misguided attempts to put into words what Isadora did "when she danced," we must appreciate that beauty simply *is*. When critics try to talk about it, we make fools of ourselves. When we try to copy it, we desecrate what we imitate. When art has perished with the artist, we can only revere the memory of one whose equal might never move among us again.

Sherman mocks Mary, Luciano, and Christine. This amuses us, but also indicts narcissism. That characteristic occurs more spectacularly in Isadora and Sergei. Isadora's self-preoccupation victimizes Belzer, who can't reply to the primadonna's rare questions. Belzer exhibits sensitivity to others' feelings when she declines to translate Sergei's insults as well as his horrific poem. She thus attempts to shield Isadora from pain.

Sherman characterizes his dramatis personae through dramatic actions such as these, a series of telling choices veering from pathos to hilarity and back.

Selfish Sergei insults dance because of its impermanence compared to poetry. Ironically, he doesn't appreciate his own triviality outside Russia, since elsewhere few people can read the language in which he writes, and poetry translates poorly. "Isadora," he proclaims, "shall disappear" (30).

Despite Sergei's contempt for her dance, when he recites a poem, she shushes everyone to listen, and, afterward, she rapturously "throws herself in front of Sergei and kisses his foot."

Sergei insists Belzer translate his poem. She narrates briefly its story about a dog who gives birth and then watches her master drown the puppies. This scene has turned from farce to gloomy, almost Russian, pathos. It ends as Isadora, suffering, speaks of a woman, not a dog, losing her children, and Sergei rants in Russian "I do not care about your children," rips up their photo and leaves. As she collects the photo's pieces, Isadora laments, "My babies" and the act ends (34).

The poet's psychological violence demonstrates his cruelty and egomania. Because the couple speak no common tongue, Isadora hasn't previously understood these aspects of his character. She has experienced the ardent lover and drunken bravura fellow artist. Belzer's translations make this day different: Isadora learns the truth and recognizes Sergei has exploited and degraded her pain over her children's death in a poem about dead dogs. When she objects, he destroys the cherished photo, a decision worse even than his choices to write the poem, to recite the poem to her, and to insist Belzer translate the poem. These actions make him monstrous—perhaps another side of "the artist."

In addition to pathos, Sherman provides verbal wit and visual farce. He gives Isadora such delicious lines as "it's highly overrated—language. We never had it in America" (12). Some farcical high points include Christine's dance travesty, Sergei's long attempt to hang himself, and, interspersed with that, men removing the dinner table before the guests have finished.

Belzer tries to persuade Isadora to stop Sergei, Alexandros wants to "rescue table," and Christine indulges in Swedish laments. As Sergei ties his noose to a light fixture, Luciano acknowledges his identity and praises Christine's dancing, which causes Isadora to hurl her champagne glass at him (55).

In her fury at learning she has sold her furniture to wine and dine a clerk—whom she mistook for a diplomat—she flings the plates and remaining glasses at him, smashing everything. Alexandros and Sergei join in. Admiring his wife's spirit, the latter abandons suicide.

The play's final minutes, however, shift moods again.

As usual, we can't pin down this play's elusive genre with one word. Shall we settle for "poignant comedy" or "witty drama," a marriage of Feydeau and Chekhov (including the veiled references to *The Three Sisters* and returning to Moscow)? *When She Danced* achieves the mood shifts of a Sturges film—appropriate since Sturges grew up in Duncan's household.

Sherman satirizes, as when Sergei ridicules Desti in pantomime and when Desti protests Isadora hiring Belzer even though Desti brought the translator to her. Sherman sends up pretensions with words and actions but also in music when he has Alexandros play the Marseillaise, to mock melodically the French maid Jeanne after she protests in French that nobody in the house speaks French. He follows that with wordplay based upon the confusion attendant upon "nay" in Greek meaning "yes" (20–21).

Jeanne repeatedly pops in and out, giving her reiterated requests for money the comic effect of a jack-in-the-box. The dancer's colloquial American speech also provides humor, as when she incongruously calls out "Good girl, Belzer!" (24), inquires "Honest injun?" (29), or exclaims "Yikes!" when Alexandros explains Luciano is asking for a date (42).

We chuckle at Alexandros's incredulity after he watches Isadora remain motionless during her dance rehearsal. We laugh at her explaining "I do not move my feet" and his puzzlement when she mentions angels (27). He plays straight man to her jokes and later to Sergei's comic jealousy (28).

During the dinner party Sherman contrasts the authentic and the inauthentic, the real and the ersatz, using the philistine clerk Isadora mistook for the vice consul and Christine, who thinks she performs like Isadora but instead travesties the artist. Sherman ridicules the frauds before moving into the slapstick assault upon Luciano.

The play mixes madcap comedy and eccentric characters with moments of compassion, humanity, and serious insights into human nature and the nature of art.

Of the eight characters, only Jeanne fails to qualify as an oddball. Her gravity and ordinariness, the normal way she reacts to her impecunious and drunken employers, by contrast to them, proves hilarious.

Despite its humor, *When She Danced* dramatizes the difficulties outsider Isadora faces surviving, sorrows she experiences, and pain she feels.

When She Danced joins the Sherman oeuvre as another highly original mixture of pain and often-ironic mirth, focusing on a larger-than-life iconoclastic, iconic woman whose image he refracts through the lens of a wise gay fellow artist, Alexandros. Over time, spectators have embraced it, and theatres have loved to produce it, despite the formidable challenges all those languages present.

Yet after Sherman completed it in late 1983 it didn't move quickly into production. He and Ackerman, who was directing *Messiah* in Israel, shared a flat in Haifa, so Sherman showed it first to him. The director recalls going into his bedroom to read it "and when I came out I felt like I had several glasses of champagne. The play sparkled with wit and life. I thought Martin had done it again, tackled a complex and difficult subject with humor and pathos." Ackerman admired Sherman's courage writing scenes in which the characters can't understand each other.

Ackerman shared Sherman's bravery by agreeing to direct it. Knightsbridge Theatrical Productions (Kulukundis) undertook to produce it within one year in a contract signed on February 7, 1984. Efforts began to find an Isadora.

In December 1984, Sherman speculated Dorothy Tutin would star, but that hope gave way by April 1985 to the reality, as described in a letter to Lavren, Tutin "loves it, but will not commit herself." Knightsbridge extended its option through December 31, 1985. Sherman and Ackerman considered Judi Dench, but she "doesn't read plays," and Joan Plowright, but "she only wants to do plays John Dexter directs. Unless we find an Isadora soon, She May Not Dance," he bewails, and concludes, "I've got to go now, walk the streets, looking for an Isadora."

Finally producer Kulukundis, who hoped to move the play to the West End after its run at the Yvonne Arnaud in Guildford, southwest of London, offered the part to Pauline Collins. Sherman calls her "seriously miscast."

Ackerman provides more detail about this demi-debacle. "Pauline wasn't right for Isadora. There's nothing about her physicality that would suggest she was a great dancer. Perhaps the most memorable thing about Isadora is that she danced in bare feet. Well, Pauline thought she was too short, so she refused to take off her shoes. Where do you go from there?"

Ackerman also blames himself.

> The play is about eccentric geniuses, and I had no idea how to create the proper behavior for the actors to make an audience believe they were seeing the spontaneous madcap actions of artistic bohemians. The play swings between wild farce and poignant, almost terrifying and painful drama. Sometimes it has to turn on a dime. I tried, but it wasn't at all convincing. So, despite a beautiful set by Carl Toms and some wonderful performances, especially Belzer, played with an insane Cheshire cat grin by Angela Pleasence, the production didn't work. I never faulted the play. I always blamed the production's inadequacy.

Not only did Pauline Collins fail to embody a dancer and free spirit, but Alexander Arbatt's sole qualification as Sergei, his Russian origin, only permitted him to speak the lines, not to perform the poet's wild passions. Yet the two best actors, Angela Pleasence as Belzer and Kevin Elyot as Luciano, appeared in the next British mounting three years later, and Elyot, whom Sherman describes as "an absolutely delicious comic actor," appeared also in the 1991 West-End staging.

When the production opened on November 27, 1985, it received eight reviews, some mixed, some positive. The *Herald*'s headline concurs with judgments by playwright and director: "Play about Isadora Duncan a Little Too Sedate" (6). P.B. judges Collins "is not an Isadora" and finds Ackerman's direction "imaginative, but for some reason it did not entirely convince." The critic concludes, "It is a play worth seeing nevertheless."

The *Surrey Advertiser* understands "in the central role, Pauline Collins is only intermittently engaging" (23). This critic praises the dinner party for its "moments of wonderful comedy and glorious incongruity" and enjoys the play's "startling ironies." Tatlow commends Sherman's "remarkable new play" (24). Tims applauds "an absorbing play, tense with emotional trauma and laced with comedy" (9).

Sherman recalls, "The audience identified strongly when it touched on suburban concerns—the fact Isadora worried about money for daily essentials, for instance." Because he wouldn't move the play with the wrong star, absence of ovations didn't matter.

Sherman and Ackerman tried again in Israel the following year, at the Haifa Municipal Theatre. This production, which opened September 6, 1986, starred Gila Almagor, the mother in *Munich*. The actors spoke Hebrew in place of English. Neither playwright nor director understood that language, so interpreters augmented the din.

Ackerman reports, "I suffered the same problems. It still lacked authenticity. You couldn't believe the people onstage were the uninhibited geniuses Martin wrote. I couldn't unleash that behavior, and when I tried to invent it, it wasn't clever or brilliant enough to make the play real."

Sherman met Sheila Gish at Suzanne Bertish's New Year's Eve party and thought instantly, "My God, that's Isadora." He sent her the play, and she wanted to do it. Her determination made the next production occur in 1988 at the King's Head.

Gish telephoned Tim Luscombe and asked him to go to Sherman's flat to talk about directing her in it. He felt thrilled to meet Sherman because "*Bent* changed my life. I wanted desperately to work with and know Martin."

Luscombe loved directing Gish: "You give her a little tiny thing, and she runs with it, and she's never afraid to make a fool of herself in the rehearsal room. With Isadora Duncan, that's what you need. You need someone who has the freedom to find her spirit. Not only was she physically like Isadora, but she worked to get the San Francisco accent right."

Sherman reports, "Sheila was a wonderful Isadora—blowsy and feminine and maternal and seductive and funny." He raves about the supporting cast as well. Owen Teale "showed brilliantly you didn't have to be Russian to play Sergei." And they retained Elyot and Pleasence.

Luscombe found Sherman in rehearsals to be "kind, supportive, a fantastic politician, humble, generous, selfless, and funny." By "politician," the director means Sherman's diplomacy, never saying, "Just do that, trust me," but always offering encouragement, support, and tactful, indirect advice.

At the King's Head, *When She Danced* began performances on September 15, 1988, and ran through October 22. When it opened on September 19, spectators loved it. It received no negative reviews, six mixed (Hurren, Gardner, Edwards, King, Peter, Wardle), and 13 positive (Shulman, Hirschhorn, Tinker, Edwardes, Hiley, Kemp, Coveney, Billington, Chamberlain, MacDonald, Morley, Nathan, Spencer). Among the latter, many of them raves, Kemp uses an especially expressive simile to describe Daryl Back's dance as Christine: "The sequence suggests someone attempting semaphore while simultaneously trying to deal with a wasp in her dress" (12). Several reviews call for a transfer to the West End.

Most critics admire play and production, but they fail to agree concerning themes, genre, and attitude towards Duncan. Their preconceptions about her color what they see. Those who respect Duncan generally assume Sherman does. Some who scoff at her assume he satirizes her. Sherman has written such a complex role in such a complex script that no one review could entirely explicate it. Interpretations attest to the play's rich texture and emphasize paraphrase cannot convey a work of art.

Sherman loved this production and hoped it would move to the West End. Many producers wanted to transfer it, but they refused to accept Gish. Sherman explains, "She simply wasn't a big enough name. I said this play will make her that kind of name. I refused to move it without her." Thus, it closed on October 22, 1988, and moved nowhere.

When Sherman finally okayed another London mounting in 1991, he knew "every avenue to do it with Sheila had been exhausted. But Sheila never forgave me. I could never bring myself to tell her every manager had turned her down; I knew it would be too hurtful. So this estrangement continued until her horrible and untimely death. She was a wonderful woman and actress and single-handedly rescued *When She Danced* from the rubbish. If it hadn't been for her, it would still be that play that closed at Guildford."

Meanwhile, Luscombe had another shot at *When She Danced*, when Sherman asked him to stage it in New York, where it opened on February 19, 1990. (See Appendix C.)

This touching yet hilarious valentine to genius finally made it to London's West End in 1991, but that subject requires introducing into Sherman's life and career Vanessa Redgrave.

10. Vanessa Times Two (1986–1991)

Sherman spent four weeks in Jerusalem in early 1985. The city had invited him to stay at the Mishkenot Sha'ananim, apartments facing the old city walls, so he could "absorb" Jerusalem.

While there, Sherman completed his HTV pilot for a series set in Israel, based on James Michener's *The Source*. This concerns excavations in the Holy Land and flashbacks to ancient times about each artifact archaeologists find. Sherman created a modern framestory about Israelis and Palestinians. The producers loved his pilot, but no network would touch this topic.

There, Sherman also wrote lines for a woman who evolved into Mrs. Honey in his next play. Intervening between the single speech for an unknown character and a finished script came casting, rehearsals and performances of *When She Danced* at Guildford.

In October 1986 Sherman completed *A Madhouse in Goa*, a metaphor for an insane world.

The script's initial reception by theatre managements matched its author's bleak view of humanity's future: The Royal Court, National, and Hampstead rejected it. Then Ramsay sent it to Robert Fox: "I loved it, because it's extraordinarily funny but also has huge heart. So we had lunch at the San Lorenzo to talk about how to do it. Having loved the play, I was happy to find I liked the author."

Plans jelled in November 1986 for a production the next year at the Lyric Hammersmith. Ackerman would direct, and Fox would move the play to the West End if box-office prospects warranted. And they would, because Vanessa Redgrave had agreed to star, playing different roles, 15 years apart.

When a movie star and a film director agree to do a play, other commitments intervene. Redgrave's and Ackerman's changing schedules caused three postponements during 1987. A 1988 production proved impossible as well.

That year gave Sherman and Redgrave opportunities to get to know each other. Fox took her to see *When She Danced* at the King's Head. She loved it and treated the cast to champagne afterwards. Her admiration for the author turned to friendship as she began to involve Sherman in her projects. Despite his shyness, she coaxed him into public appearances, giving speeches and readings.

He participated with her in a benefit for the Arab Women's Association in November 1988. With Frances Barber, he read the simultaneous translation for the Moscow Jewish Theatre Shalom's *The Train to Happiness*, which she and the Russian Theatre Workers' Union produced at the Lyric Hammersmith in February 1989.

By June, Sherman had gathered the confidence to play Shakespeare in Tom Stoppard's *Ten-Minute Hamlet* at the rally to save the Rose Theatre. Redgrave appeared as Gertrude at the event, designed to prevent builders from obliterating the recently uncovered remains of this Elizabethan theatre. Sherman's role that afternoon—alongside Redgrave, Steve Martin, and a Bolshoi Ballet star—attests how much he had become part of London theatre.

Madhouse had already opened, first at the Lyric Hammersmith on April 28, 1989 (performances there from April 21 through June 10), and then at the Apollo on June 15 (beginning June 14 in a limited run of 12 weeks).

Program covers feature a northern white rhinoceros, a species humans have nearly eradicated. This suggests the human race also heads for extinction. The only animal featuring a horn in its face rather than on top of its head, a rhinoceros likewise represents "the other."

In addition to Redgrave as Mrs. Honey and Heather, the splendid cast includes Rupert Graves as David, a Jewish, gay nerd, and Barnaby Grace, a nincompoop Hollywood producer; Ian Sears as Greek seducer Costos and Heather's son Dylan; Larry Lamb as inn co-owner Nikos and gay nurse Oliver; Francesca Folan as mysterious Aliki; and Arthur Dignam as nearly speechless Daniel Hosani.

Sherman draws upon his early trips to Greece. References to Durrell and Albania might suggest he sets the first act in or near Kalami on Corfu's northeast coast, a mile from Albania. This village where Durrell, living in his White House, wrote *Prospero's Cell*, lies near a taverna in Agnistini called Nikos's.

Sherman creates a hotel identical to one in Benitzes (owned by two brothers) where he stayed briefly in 1966. Benitzes lies south of Kirkira town, whereas Kalami lies north. Nevertheless, Durrell did dine at his hotel right before Sherman arrived, and the king did plan to go to dinner there right after he left.

He sets Act 2 on Santorini, an island he visited shortly before conceiving *Madhouse*. He stayed in a tiny hotel on the cliff below and slightly to the left of Franco's bar, but he sets this act in a home.

Neither act takes place in Goa, yet the title came first. Sherman saw a documentary referring to the incident in Goa described in 2. A former Portuguese colony, Goa lies on India's west coast. "The documentary included an interview with a woman in a madhouse because she had lost her passport. She spoke three languages, and I was very impressed with her lucidity and haunted by her."

He had never visited India, but he knew Greece well, so he set the play there. He returned there in *Alive and Kicking* and *Onassis*.

He pondered the play in London, on Mykonos, and in Tokyo. But he wrote *Madhouse* in London, except for that speech that came to him in Jerusalem.

Durrell's *Alexandria Quartet* influenced Sherman, not only in this play, but earlier, in *Fat Tuesday*, and later, in *The Summer House* and *Some Sunny Day*. Clea's name in *Rio Grande* he lifted from the fourth novel. His play derives from Durrell its structural daring, which he uses to strip away layers of illusions, but he invents the novel-within-a-play device.

The Alexandria Quartet explores love in all forms. As *Justine* opens, the narrator, Darley, tells us about Justine and Nessim Hosnani, from which Sherman derives Daniel's last name, Hosani. Durrell's "Note" to *Balthazar*, the second novel, tells us he bases his quartet on "the relativity proposition." He recounts events from roughly the same period thrice ([9]). In *Balthazar*, we must discard as false truths we thought we knew in *Justine*. There, deceptions, misleading "facts," misinterpreted appearances have prompted erroneous conclusions. *Balthazar* appears to set the record straight. Durrell writes the third novel, *Mountolive*, as a third-person account. Our reliable narrator turns upside-down everything we thought we knew from the first two. Justine hasn't betrayed anyone, but all other key players have. Durrell employs multiple betrayals to keep shifting our perceptions. In *Clea*, the Nazis have occupied Paris, and Egypt resembles the Cairo Sherman later dramatizes in *Some Sunny Day*.

The *Alexandria Quartet* presents illusions we mistake for truths and then offers other possible truths to replace them. *Madhouse* does the same, and not just when Sherman takes us after the interval to the different universe of Act 2. Although it corrects our original misperceptions, it provides more: that Daniel lacks lucidity, nurse Oliver enjoys good health, Santorini offers a safe retreat for Dylan and Heather, Barnaby reveres Daniel and co-producer Jesus. It also misleads about Aliki's nationality and interest in Barnaby and Dylan.

Sherman has hoodwinked us *twice*. Although reviewers don't quite understand why so many grow angry at the final minutes, that second set of deceptions underlies critics' rage. Furious reviewers blame authorial incompetence. The more perceptive appreciate early in 2 that the world has gone mad and heads for the abyss, and also that we cannot trust wise governments, a benevolent deity, or our own judgment to protect us. Thus, when apocalypse arrives, those critics feel not bamboozled, but satisfied.

They can take pleasure because Sherman has chosen a form for *Madhouse* reflecting its content: A pleasing order, easy to comprehend, but unreal in 1, and a (to the naysayers) displeasing disorder and multiple disasters in 2. Ironically, some find off-putting the very expression of theme by form others regard as genius. Sherman does what Daniel didn't do when he wrote the novel we see staged in Act 1: He tells the truth about the world he observes. *Madhouse* enrages or enraptures viewers.

Sherman populates the play with Americans. He dedicates it to two Americans: Philip Magdalany, a Playwrights Horizons playwright who died of AIDS, just as we learn Oliver will do, and Sue Fleming, a New Yorker who died of cancer after Sherman completed the play.

In Act 1, the American woman (Mrs. Honey) and a young American man (David) visit a Corfu hotel, where two Greeks—Nikos and young employee Costos—manipulate and control them. Act 2 features an entirely foreign (i.e., non-Greek) group: a British male nurse (Oliver), a Mediterranean woman (Aliki), and four Americans—Daniel Hosani, his friend Heather, her son Dylan, and film producer Barnaby Grace.

Sherman's dramatis personae exemplify aliens abroad, of course, as well as three gay men and two women, all outsiders. Yet the play focuses as much or more on his survival theme, and for once he devises the action to call into question humanity's survival.

We understand that by the apocalyptic ending, but the evening begins quietly. Act 1, titled *A Table for a King*, initially appears a comedy of wit by an American Noel Coward. It finds David, early 20s, writing in his journal. Gay, Jewish, shy, insecure, self-deprecatory, and self-pitying, he speaks in the dark before we see him, inappropriately dressed in Corfu's blazing heat in slacks and long-sleeved shirt.

David mocks his own diary entry's purple prose. "What's an illuminated teardrop? What a dreadful sentence!" ([5]). Sherman used his own youthful journal, personality, and experience in creating David, and Rupert Graves, who originated the role, tried to imitate Sherman's accent and intonations. The playwright even gave him kvetching lessons. On the other hand, David doesn't physically resemble the young Sherman—in 1966 a hippie with long hair.

The comedy continues with what Sherman wrote in Israel, as an imperious Mississippi matron rings a bell and deplores the Kistos Inn's poor service. She likewise complains she lost her table to Durrell on Friday night. Two older American women stayed at Sherman's little Corfu inn. One resembled Mrs. Honey's garrulous manner, and the other, an American, traveled incessantly. "I based Mrs. Honey on those two," plus a New Yorker, he explains.

Think also a lady three-quarters Williams, one-quarter Wilde. As Sherman's friend Pope observes, "Mrs. Honey resembles a Tennessee Williams character, but Williams couldn't have written *Madhouse*." He couldn't have written the second act, and he wouldn't have written the first act's seduction scene.

Although he writes light comedy in Act 1, Sherman also provides David and Mrs. Honey with choices. Nikos asks her to give up her table again. She figures this time he must want it for the author of a quintet, but, no, he wants to seat the king there. She refuses, so a power struggle ensues.

While singing snatches of American pop hits, Costos seduces David, but then asks for his watch or his ring or his camera. When David realizes Costos didn't act out of attraction, he refuses, until Costos threatens to scream for the police and accuse David of molesting him. To avoid prison, David relinquishes his watch.

Next morning David's watch and the bride's ring appear in Mrs. Honey's jewel box. David admits the watch belongs to him. When Mrs. Honey asks how it got into her jewel box, he says he doesn't know (39). Mrs. Honey emphasizes the importance of his moral choice, but he lies.

Mrs. Honey capitulates, leaving both her table and her room. In his final voiceover, David explains the king canceled his reservation because rain fell. Ironically, Nikos wasted his blackmail, David sold his soul for nothing, and Mrs. Honey departed unnecessarily.

The American visitors in 1 know nothing about the king, to whom Nikos wants to assign Mrs. Honey's table. In 2, however, several characters know King Konstantinos II, in 1966 around 24, roughly David's contemporary. A right-wing monarch, he damaged Greece, though not to the extent the subsequent colonels did. Corfu had escaped the Turkish rule that had plagued most of Greece for nearly four centuries (1458–1834) and even had prospered as a British protectorate for half the 19th century. Thus, on Corfu especially, inhabitants took for granted certain liberties the king and colonels infringed upon.

In Act 2, Heather knows Daniel neglected to mention in his novel the political realities, and Aliki resents this. Daniel, the guilty party, knows but can do nothing to atone because, ironically, this aphasiac writer has lost control of words.

Act 2, *Keeps Rainin' All the Time* (a lyric from "Stormy Weather"), takes us to Santorini "some time in the near future," to quote the program, or the summer of 1990, to cite the text (42). Theatres presenting it more recently have had to set it in the late '80s because, otherwise, Heather and Daniel would have grown old since 1966. Yet the play dramatizes, not a fantasy of what did happen, but what could happen in our own future unless we change.

Drenched by fallout-laden rain after nuclear accidents and because global warming has altered world weather patterns, Santorini proves home to David, actually named Daniel, older now and suffering from aphasia, cared for by Oliver, and hosting visits by Heather, her son Dylan, philistine producer Barnaby Grace and his girlfriend of the week, Aliki. Sherman satirizes the film mogul, who peppers his speech with such monstrosities as "grow-tired experience" and "look-strange place" and plans to sanitize *A Table for a King* by cutting everything controversial.

The charming and amusing first half moves, by way of its touching conclusion, to an act darker, more sinister, more alarming. Nothing in the first part prepares us—nor should it—for the shift from urbanity to apocalypse. Not that the second lacks its share of amusing badinage. On the contrary, the producer who speaks in hyphens keeps us in stitches, and this act features a seduction paralleling David's erotic entrapment by the waiter. Yet the humor in 2 functions as a survival kit to keep us, and the characters, from succumbing to the despair beneath the grins.

Sher's *Beside Myself* sheds light on the genesis of the second act's shower scene. He recounts the night in 1984 on which Harvey Fierstein didn't win the Olivier Award for *Torch Song Trilogy*, starring Sher. After the awards dinner, Fierstein invited the cast plus director Ackerman, his partner Franco Zavani, and Sherman back to his room at the Savoy for "one of Harvey's famous shower parties" (184).

Sher explains only "two young (straight) actors" took up "the shower party idea and went into the bathroom, leaving the door ajar. The rest of us sat working our way through Harvey's mini-bar, taking turns to stroll to the door and glance in.... Then, on one of her visits, Miriam Karlin suddenly said, 'Oh my God!' She spun round, intending to return to her seat, but was trampled in the rush to the door. This closed in our faces." Sherman places Dylan in the shower while Heather and Oliver observe him with Aliki.

Aliki "proves" she will see Dylan in Athens by giving him her jewel box—as in the first half, a device to betray.

That betrayal's extent Oliver includes in his bravura final speech, an almost comical catalogue of mishaps. Heather's cancer has returned; she has only a few weeks to live. Dylan's plane exploded, killing everyone. Investigators discovered from the wreckage a jewel box had held a bomb. Aliki, real name Maria, real nationality Lebanese, had tried to kill a Palestinian courier who escaped when he canceled at the last minute. Maria had slit Barnaby's throat on Crete, thereby destroying the film deal and Heather's dream of a fortune going to good causes. Oliver has AIDS and remarks, "I suppose it can be classified as ironic. The last time I was with someone was five years ago. And only for a minute" (79–80).

Oliver will leave, not to wait to die, but to try to heal somebody he could really help. He tells Daniel, "If you have gifts, you should use them, shouldn't you? It's a way of facing the madness and shouting 'stop'" (80). No line in *Madhouse* better conveys what Daniel (and Mrs. Foster/Honey) did wrong. They shirked responsibility to try to stop the madness.

In writing *Madhouse*, Sherman confronted his own responsibility to try.

The dramatist concludes his play quickly. A distant noise suddenly increases. Oliver doesn't recognize it, but Daniel knows. He tells his nurse, "The apricot is erupting," and he starts to laugh, while the "noise grows very loud" as annihilation approaches.

Madhouse dramatizes Sherman's primary themes, exile and survival. Sherman wipes out the characters, but he uses a lighter touch, too. He provides Heather a frenzied monologue about foods, all dangerous. Redgrave found in this the humor, but also the nightmare.

Madhouse likewise dramatizes multiple deceptions. Mrs. Honey proclaims, "I see deceit everywhere." Costos misleads David about his motives for seducing him. Nikos lies about suspecting Mrs. Honey of stealing the watch and the ring. David lies to avoid jail. Daniel has lied about Greece in 1966. Barnaby has raised lying to the only art he practices in filmmaking. Aliki lies about her identity. Truth tellers Mrs. Honey, Oliver and Heather can't save the world, although political activist Heather tries.

David's narcissistic loneliness in Act 1 previews self-absorbed isolation in 2's characters. Sherman dramatizes their narcissism not only by their words and actions but by their Walkmans—so they needn't listen—and by Daniel's aphasia, which cripples his ability to say what he means when he still wants to.

"If I could lamb chop," he laments (44). And when he senses the danger Aliki poses, all he can muster as warning comes out as "Don't sneeze" (68). Don't trust her? Don't let her take control? Like Heather a Cassandra, Daniel warns, but nobody heeds him. The others suffer less extreme isolation, yet each exists in a private world.

Sherman devises distinctive lines for each. He provides the miserable, mumbling geek with self-consciously flamboyant expression of his self-pitying melancholy, while to more practical Mrs. Honey he gives stream-of-consciousness rambles and the ability to deflate David's hyperbole with teasing and such candor as, "Watching the dentist disappear before your eyes. Cancer. That's an abyss.... Not being loved is nothing. Easy. Fact of life" (20–21).

Nikos, who studied political science at Oxford, Sherman characterizes as suave in attempting to persuade Mrs. Honey to relinquish her table but too impatient to sustain that tone in order to obtain what he wants. "Now my dear Mrs. Honey—I must ask you for another favor," he begins, but he interrupts himself during solitaire, "Bloody hell" (10). The lady's uncooperative response soon reduces him to "I could choke you, Mrs. Honey" (12). He resorts to guile because he lacks the charm to sustain persuasion.

Into the cunning young waiter's mouth Sherman puts lies such as "Greece happy with King" and snatches of American pop songs (24). Costos sings a phrase or two from several. Then he explains, "How I learn my English, Sonny. Cher. Mamas. Papas. Simon. Garfunkel. Good teachers. My English good?" (25). Eventually Sherman makes a private joke when Costos warbles, "We'll sing in the sunshine. We'll laugh everyday," and then explains, "Gale Garnett" (26). Costos grows more blatant as he seduces David, of course, but his speech still comes out in choppy phrases. "Put hand here," he commands (27). "Sputnik. You go up like Sputnik," he observes as he arouses David (28). And when David climaxes quickly, he complains "So soon? Sputnik land so soon?"

For the assemblage on Santorini, Sherman also concocts distinctive speech. To match Daniel's aphasiac garblings, Oliver speaks in short, soothing phrases. Thus Daniel begs, "Don't discover me," and Oliver replies, "I don't think I can." "Please," Daniel continues. "Don't worry," Oliver reassures him. "Tangerine," Daniel says. "Don't know tangerine," Oliver responds. "Tangerine!" Daniel again implores, and Oliver urges, "Let's calm down" (43). When Heather begs for reassurance to combat her paralyzing anxieties, Daniel doesn't try to soothe her. He tells it like it is, replying, "Applesauce" (66).

Heather's impassioned ideals impel her to make longer speeches, sentences tumbling out regarding what causes money from the film will support. For Dylan, who mocks his mother's wisdom and activism as psycho, Sherman devises a lingo at once laid-back and callous. He explains his father "was this poet from Chile ... and they arrested him because of his poetry and put him in a stadium and they threw kerosene on him and set him on fire. Mom thinks I should get into politics because of that, but that isn't, like, a positive example" (76–77).

Aliki speaks broken English: "Here we are. Little island. Funny little island. Looks like no place else. Like moon" (66). This speech does more than describe Santorini. It provides a clue. A Greek wouldn't describe this popular Greek tourist destination like this. That should alert us to her disguise.

These varied patterns economically characterize the speakers. Sherman gives Barnaby, however, extra verbiage to hang himself. He hyphenates words, describing *A Table for a King* as "a life-affirmer rather than a down-in-the-dumpser" (70). He has invented a "think-positive aspect" (71). When Daniel yells, "Oysters!" and starts to choke Barnaby (72), the latter complains about the unexpected "tension-factor" (73). When Heather tells him he can make his film, Barnaby rejoices with an incongruous juxtaposition, "The Lord's been with me, he's my shepherd, he's clinched my deal," then pats Aliki's head and orders, "Come on, Sunshine, we're leaving" (73). Sunshine, huh? Barnaby proves as poor a judge of her character as he does of artistic merit. Sherman reveals that as much from Barnaby's language as he does from his choices.

Both a gay play and a woman's play, *Madhouse*'s unsympathetic (or largely so) characters include two Greek men (Nikos and Costos), Barnaby Grace, and Heather's son Dylan. On the other hand, those who constitute "the other," the sympathetic (or somewhat so) characters, include an older, wise widow, a gay Jew, more or less the same gay Jew, but now also disabled (another frequent category of Sherman outcasts), a gay male nurse, a female political activist, and a female terrorist.

We can appreciate the sources of Aliki's anger, even while recognizing terrorism as part of the problem, not an appropriate solution. The play dramatizes victims and exploiters, which explains why Dylan and Barnaby belong in the same group, although not in the same circle of hell. Materialism drives them both. Despite her destructiveness, Aliki has turned from victim to victimizer, a not uncommon path. Sherman's later creation, Rose, would understand her while deploring her. Both Heather and Aliki strive to change the world; Aliki goes about it wrong.

Greed drove Daniel. Had he told the truth perhaps that would have made a difference for those who came after. But how many people would have read his book had he done so? The high price he pays earns our sympathy, just as Max's suffering does. And, like Max, he comprehends his sins and shows signs of growth and remorse.

David allows Costos and Nikos to blackmail his friend. Yet he does so because he believes he will go to prison if he doesn't.

Sherman employs a representational style except for the presentational segments in which we hear David's thoughts as he writes.

He constructs *Madhouse* using a series of parallels and contrasts, and he employs a radical shift during the interval to emphasize the contrasting acts. His structure forces us to reexamine 1 in light of 2. This illuminates three levels of reality an artist can create: the authentic, the commercially fictionalized, and the bastardized. Sherman recounts the real facts, Daniel creates the second version as *A Table for a King*, and Barnaby Grace relishes the third. This witless producer plans to eliminate any value in Daniel's fiction. Daniel's sin surpasses clueless Barnaby's, because Daniel knew better when he sold out.

Among his parallels, Sherman cites radiation poisoning: Living in a downwind town caused Mr. Honey's death, and fallout from a nuclear meltdown will kill many more. Seductions carried out for unprincipled purposes (Costos of David and presumably the bride; Aliki of Barnaby and Dylan) provide the vehicles for betrayals in both acts. These also employ a jewelry box, the first to blackmail Mrs. Honey and the second, given to Dylan as a pledge of trust, holds a bomb. Each act involves selling out artistic integrity: The first exemplifies it, since Daniel falsified personal and political realities to create it. The second contains Heather's retaliation by taking Daniel's selling out to its logical extreme, both for revenge and to obtain funds to do good.

Another parallel dramatizes sex's dangers: It destroys dignity and causes anguish to David and Mrs. Honey, and it kills Dylan, Barnaby, and Oliver. In each act, somebody cancels a reservation—for a table, for a plane ticket—when, ironically, the king and the Palestinian courier don't show up. The change in plans fails to save others from harm.

In both parts, Americans abroad, aliens on treacherous foreign isles, lack power to protect themselves. David and Mrs. Honey lose self-respect or dignity. Years later, the Americans, no longer innocent, perish because the world has gone mad. Paradoxically, Sherman has put his insights about this into the mouths of seemingly batty women, but actually wise sages, Cassandras others ignore at their peril. Ironically, critics who regard Sherman in this play as barking mad miss his sagacity and prescience.

Perhaps the most important link between acts dramatizes David shirking the ethical choice of telling the truth when Costos blackmails him and Daniel creating David as an autobiographical character, yet making the unethical choice to falsify the truth of his experience by popularizing it for profit. Daniel made that decision after the events that only partly resembled Act 1 but two decades before Act 2.

Daniel has no more chances to make ethical choices. He has become helpless even though he clearly wishes to refuse the film producer's money. The way he has misused his life, his gifts, his funds has prevented his finally choosing correctly. We infer the world can no longer mend its ways and avoid annihilation. Indeed, this cataclysmic comedy about the end of ethics and everything resembles Bernard Shaw's *Heartbreak House* and David Mercer's *Duck Song*.

In Act 1, Sherman contrasts Corfu's blazing sun and blue skies with his alter-ego's depression. Sherman makes David's determined misery hilarious. He pokes fun at himself as a young man, but he likewise appeals to whatever readiness we possess to fess up to our own lapses into self-pity, angst, despair.

Mrs. Honey perceives similarities between herself and David. They share the fact they travel alone. They also have no function; nobody needs them. They drift. Yet she has a keen sense of self and asserts herself, whereas David reacts instead of acting.

David's ludicrous inhibitions contrast to his relaxed Greek surroundings and Mrs. Honey's chatty informality. Sherman also contrasts David and seducer Costos, so sure of himself, breezy, in control. Not that we should regard David as out of control. He clamps down hard on himself as though he would otherwise disintegrate.

Sherman contrasts the one-upsmanship game of Nikos and Costos to the deadly game in which Aliki engages. And he contrasts the dishonorable characters to the three more selfless souls, Mrs. Honey in the first part and Heather and Oliver in the second. These three provide the play's moral compass.

Sherman likewise contrasts Mrs. Honey and Heather. Mrs. Honey stands up for something trivial and self-serving: She takes a stand so she can continue enjoying the veranda's best view. She doesn't consider how Nikos feels about providing it for his country's king. Empathy for him would have spared her humiliation.

Heather cares about humanity. Although lacking sustained empathy for Daniel, she compensates by determining to do good by selling the film rights. Observing her helps us appreciate what Mrs. Honey's stubbornness might have accomplished had she used it to oppose atomic testing and later nuclear plants. Retreating into a madhouse pleases her, but it won't save the world. Only Heather's engagement on major issues could accomplish that. This contrast stems as much from their different eras as from character differences.

The second half's setting builds suspense because the volcano could erupt; the location foreshadows this will occur. David thinks he teeters on the edge of an abyss. But Santorini's Fira really does, and this set metaphor suggests the doom in store for a world out of control, due for annihilation by several forces it has let loose: cancer-causing tobacco, pollutants, greed and lust, terrorism,

AIDS, nuclear weapons, nuclear energy, our prodigal dependence on fossil fuels, and altered world weather patterns.

Sherman needs a decisive event to conclude. Fallout doesn't slaughter quickly enough. Having already killed some characters, he needs to eradicate the rest. As Oliver speaks of helping somebody who needs him, Sherman signals he won't live to do that. Everyone will have died shortly after play's end.

Does that make this a tragedy? It might for those who pick up on the way the characters inevitably hurtle towards oblivion. Sherman generally mixes moods and baffles or angers those intent on pinning down a play to one genre, but he outdoes himself in *Madhouse*. Here, in both acts, he uses the stuff of melodrama, drama or tragedy but puts it to largely comic use, and he shifts moods instantaneously.

Take Heather's aria to Daniel about her fears, including "Dylan going to Paris. Dylan upstairs with that girl. Dylan getting nuked. Dylan getting AIDS. Dylan getting religion" (65). Further on, she hilariously laments, "I can't even have a meal without panic" because eggs cause heart attacks, chickens contain antibiotics, etc. After rejecting every possible food, she says she relaxed and ate a banana split. Finally she considers "I'm here courtesy of chemotherapy. I have only seconds left. But the kids, the kids.... What can they eat? What can they breathe? Who can they sleep with?"

After a bittersweet first act—what Barnaby describes as "a real smile-on-face tang with a slight seem-sad taste" (53)—Sherman darkens the second act to make this his bleakest play, at least prior to *Onassis*. And rarely has a play engendered such a sense of impending doom. Yet the moods continue to shift, and we keep laughing. In both acts he employs sex farce, Chekhovian dark comedy of futility, comedy of wit, and satire. Could we have here a black-comic, farcical, satiric tragedy? Or should we view it as a funny, touching wake-up call to humanity to rescue itself from oblivion and thus, in a sense, a positive force, conveying a tad of optimism that perhaps we can forestall Armageddon?

Madhouse also uses a mystery's conventions. We must figure out in Act 2 we've been watching a novel rather than real life. We must work out that Daniel created David as a partially autobiographical character and recognize Heather accompanied him on his European adventures. As we put together those pieces, we must pick up subtle clues that Aliki, beneath the sex-comedy trappings of her ménage-à-trois, poses a threat to both men.

We eventually recognize Heather's fears don't represent paranoia because she displays appropriate concern with survival. She correctly inquires, "How can anybody not be frightened?" (64). Nevertheless, since the world has passed the point of no return towards doom, her efforts seem, not misguided, but futile. In this dramatic universe, the characters cannot take any action that will avoid everyone dying. It's *Cracks*, except now we know the killer's identity: The human race kills itself.

Among the devastating contemporary events to which Sherman responds, AIDS—in a decade offering no effective treatment—perhaps tops the list. Sherman's friends sickened and died as he planned and wrote this play. They died from AIDS but also from cancer and self-destruction bred of despair. The play expresses anguish at loss of friends but also of the larger planet, succumbing to nuclear disasters, climate change, deadly foods and medicines, and technologies run amuck. The prophetic inclusion of environmental havoc and terrorism makes the play especially resonant in the 21st century.

Irony—sometimes comic, sometimes dramatic—permeates the play. Only the mad offer sane and sage perceptions. Writer Daniel, as dormant as the volcano, cannot communicate his simplest thought or need. A born-again Christian will film his Jewish novel, cleansing it of controversies. Dylan prefers to ignore politics, but politics will kill him. Heather believes Dylan will remain safe if he stays on Santorini, but the erupting volcano will kill everyone there. Oliver believes he "will not end my days" with Daniel, but moments later he will.

Performing in such a complex play pushed the cast hard to comprehend it and give it their best, but Graves recalls rehearsals fondly because Sherman proved so supportive and helpful: "He was careful not to tread on Robert's toes. But you don't feel a fool asking him how to do something. When he taught me to kvetch, he wafted over and agreed I didn't sound like a Jewish boy. So he sat there, very feline, like a cat with his tail going under his nose, with that little smile, and then his kvetching took off as an improvised skit, so funny."

Graves loved the challenges rehearsals presented—playing two such different roles, mastering the gay and Jewish aspects of the nerd and singing and carrying on extravagantly as the born-again producer. He especially loved playing David, who faces such a quandary, and also because throughout he must function "while his heart is shrieking inside, shrieking to be loved, but being tangled, clumsy, feeling so bad. It's a beautifully written role, yet tough."

Redgrave faced a challenge with Mrs. Honey. Ackerman correctly sees this matron as "a refined, rather elegant Southern belle wandering the world aimlessly." But she latched onto a description in the second act of the real woman who inspired Daniel to write his novel as "a crusty old dame." Despite the fact playwright and director saw the role as, in Ackerman's words, a "sort of faded Scarlett O'Hara," Redgrave ran with the second act description of a different person.

Ackerman continues,

> She started talking in this gravely voice, took on a masculine persona. She wore a baseball cap and pedal pushers. She is supposed to ring a little dinner bell, but Vanessa opted for a cowbell. At first we were rather put off. I argued she was heading in a totally wrong direction. But Vanessa can be very convincing, and because she is one of the greatest actresses alive, she can make you believe anything she does is

beyond brilliant. I remember coming home every night thinking, "She's a genius. I would never have thought of doing it that way. But that's why she's who she is." I was in awe of her inventiveness and her imagination and marveled at her ability to see something even Martin could never have imagined.

Then came the tech rehearsal. One day for the first act, one day for the second act, and on the third, a full dress, and that night, we open. We started teching the first act, and there was Vanessa up there with a cigarette dangling from her lip and growling away in that awful voice, tromping around in her baseball cap and pedal pushers, and I thought, "Holy shit. She's dreadful." The whole thing was wrong. It had worked in the rehearsal hall, but on stage it was a caricature. It destroyed the play.

My stomach was doing somersaults when suddenly Vanessa broke character, looked out and said, "Bob darling, I feel totally fake."

"Thank God," I thought. "Go on," I told her. "Let's get through this tech and then we'll talk."

After the rehearsal, Martin and I took her out to an Indian restaurant and talked about southern women. She said very little, mostly just listened. Martin got her the tape of *Gone with the Wind*, and we all went home. I kept wondering, how do we fix this? We have to tech act two tomorrow, and then the next day, we open. The tech of act two went fine.

When I showed up at the theatre on the third day, the opening day, Vanessa wanted to show me something in her dressing room. She had a soft white wig, put a flower in her hair, and showed me a lovely matronly dress she had bought that morning at Marks and Spenser's. She held a small white fan. She had transformed herself into the Mrs. Honey Martin and I had originally envisioned. I told her I would do whatever was needed to help her get through that day's rehearsal, and I also told her I thought she was very brave. "You have to be," she said, "when you're that stupid." She went on with a reinvented characterization and was brilliant.

Only three critics hate *Madhouse*; many reviews praise the production but pan the play.

Hiley regards the halves as one-acts that find the playwright "on shaky form" and insists they "should either be more vividly contrasted, or unnervingly similar. Instead Sherman opts for a miscellany of one-liners" (31). Herbert finds "no great dramatic substance" (527). He mocks "the play's apocalyptic coda ... has all the sound of a frustrated dramatist at the end of a hard day's useless work consigning his output to the shredder." Paton calls the transfer "deeply eccentric drivel by the self-indulgent Martin Sherman" (32). Troubled by his usual mixture of moods and genres, she likewise complains it "degenerates into farcical melodrama."

Barnes pulverizes the play, employing invective rather than details. It would "make my short list of 100 worst" and "should never have seen the light of night" (32). He quips, "Take *A Madhouse*, please" and "There is not one single event in the whole preposterous evening of fantasy purporting to be profound that bears any relationship to any truth, either inner, outer or in-betweener." Having dismissed Sherman, he mocks Redgrave. This review could have caused the long delay between the London mounting and its U.S. premiere.

One more negative response came, not from a critic, but from the president of the U.K. branch of the Goan Association, who lodged a protest over "denigration of what Goa and Goans stand for" ("Londoner's Diary" 6).

Among mixed reviews, Wardle's tone contrasts to Barnes's because he likes the play at first and enjoys the performances. He correctly appraises Mrs. Honey and David as "two outcasts" and finds *A Table for a King* "quite neat and touching, with an amusing homosexual interlude, but fruitily overwritten." He calls the double casting "a delicious shock," and he praises the "marvelous solo turn" when the Hollywood producer pitches his film concept. He objects to the ending, however. "Not content with logically contained plotting," the playwright expands "his fable to apocalyptic dimensions" (14).

Wardle's views epitomize other mixed reviews, some less kind. Roberts calls the script "a total mess," but recommends seeing it for the performances (26). Pitman finds *Madhouse* "funny, depressing, unnerving, confusing and eventually way over the top" (65). He judges the first part "far the better one" and, concerning it, elaborates, "The material is spare, comical and suspenseful, offering fine character studies and pressure cooker atmosphere, including a gay seduction scene." Yet "Sherman's taut, artful touch goes off the rails in the closer"; he calls it "a disappointing hash compared to the moving and subtle opener."

Watt pronounces the play "something of a madhouse in itself" (45). He prefers the first act, and seems to have grown inattentive for the second, which he believes transpires "at the same hotel." Kissel also prefers the first half to the second but admires a country which can present such an evening successfully. He feels the U.S. has "very few producers canny enough to market a play like this. The British still have a *professional* theater with producers who know their business and *theater stars*, who sell tickets regardless of the critics" (35).

Edwards likes the first part, but not the second. (43). Hepple advises Redgrave "to stick to the classics if she cannot find anything better than" this (11). He terms the first half "the more amusing." Spencer parts company with some colleagues by preferring Act 2 to Act 1. He calls the first "dismayingly thin" but the second "a little livelier" (17).

Billington can't resist beginning, "Beware of plays set on Greek islands" (21). Like some other mixed reviews, his relishes the performances but reviles the script, although he enjoys David's seduction. Ratcliffe begins, "Martin Sherman, whose talents are considerable, is a brave man" (41). Yet he calls the play "with one seductive exception, an unresolved mess." He compares the script to a Kaufman and Hart comedy, evidently not intending this as a compliment.

Hurren adores Redgrave but notes she appears in a "self-chosen disaster" (36). He praises the performers but judges "all is beyond salvage in this realm of the Higher Bosh—no, forget the 'higher.'"

Arditi notes "considerable incidental pleasures" but then dismisses it, complaining, "the plays [*sic*] appear utterly different in both intention and effect" (46). Hirschhorn terms the play "imperfect, albeit stimulating" (19). Hornby feels "there is a good play here somewhere," but urges revision (631).

Coveney's first review proves positive, but the second, upon the West End transfer, seems mixed. He first describes the evening as "this strangely personal and intriguing double-bill" (19), but when he pens his short notice he refers to it as "the unsatisfactory but vitally intriguing play" which "has its high comic moments" (19).

Edwardes largely favors the enterprise. She lauds Redgrave for "lending her support to a new play," and she judges the seduction scene the funniest. She concludes, "Sherman should surely have limited his targets, but it seems a long time since a play as ambitious and thought-provoking as this landed in the West End" (49).

Hutera greets *Madhouse* still more enthusiastically, praising the hilarious seduction. He extols, "With grimly merry, messy daring Sherman fashions his Pirandellian conceits into a restive meditation on the artist's responsibility to the truth, and a blackly comic cry at our diseased age. Perhaps his only way out is to end the play not with a whimper but a literal bang and a manic cackle. Give the man a cigar for setting his sights on—and actually hitting—so many targets" (40). Smith proclaims it "a bravura display of the playwright's craft, deftly structured around a clever narrative device that creates an accumulation of passion and tension" (132).

Robinson prefers *Madhouse* to *Bent*. He calls it "structurally fascinating ... a play with subtleties to send you chattering into the night" (71). Wearing raves, "Martin Sherman's brave new play presents a wry vision of apocalypse. First the past and then the future, first a fiction and then another kind of reality, make a lucid sense of the 'madhouse' that is now, right now" (36). Wearing concludes "Human, passionate, serious theatre."

Morley rebukes those who dislike *Madhouse* and says, "Sherman is among the most ambitious of contemporary dramatists, and his tricky, treacherous, intermittently manic play is wonderfully and coherently dire" (7). Nathan observes Sherman "goes over the top in a number of interesting directions" and praises "this engaging extravaganza" (15). Tinker begins, "Martin Sherman is a writer never afraid to bare his soul, take the outside chance and trust his viewers to share his vision" (30). He avows, "One comes away giving it the benefit of not a few doubts in thanksgiving that there are artists around who will still strive to challenge our conscience as well as our imagination."

McAfee refers initially to Sherman's "complex new play" and thereafter largely explicates rather than judges (41). Yet she makes sense of the ending so troubling to some critics: "Nature itself takes revenge on the arrogant treachery of man, Sherman suggests."

Renton argues, "Grace and his concepts are delicious parodies and all the characters of the 'true' story are larger than life. Only in fiction, Sherman seems to be saying, are people credible" (13). Renton prefers *Madhouse* to *Bent* because "the essence of Sherman's new play is a moment of similar brilliance; but in structural, rather than dramatic effect." Shorter concurs about structure, calling this "the most ingeniously linked double bill in modern theatre" (xx).

Tyler and Gale praise *Madhouse*, then conclude, "It's an impossible play to review without revealing the plot. It has nothing new to say about being gay, gay writing, or facing disaster, but it says it with panache" (76). They find a way to explain where the play heads: "Cleverly constructed, it delivers a series of wrist slaps to us for daring to assume that we knew what direction it would take."

Henry III raves about "the best new play of a fecund London year that has already brought new efforts from half-a-dozen top dramatists" (59). He further extols the two parts of this "sprawling, ambitious piece" as "linked by one of the cleverest devices in memory."

Rich recommends *Madhouse* "for the unexpected." He continues, "It has its obvious flaws, but it also has Vanessa Redgrave and guts" (C15, C20). He continues, "Mr. Sherman has pertinent points to make about American writers who are 'famous too soon, thrown aside too quickly' and about those who smooth out life into commercial fiction that favors so-called universal truths over unpleasant political imperatives." Dace praises *Madhouse* for "its startling combinations of wit and anxiety, topicality and universality, originality yet relevance.... Sherman's play reminds us why we ever acquired a taste for theatre in the first place" (38).

Producer Fox observed young spectators relating to it: "Martin touched a chord with them. That's why some critics don't get it. You either plug into Martin or you don't. If you don't, I'm sure it's like Swahili," but such a person lacks soul because "Martin is so wise." Fox adds he especially "connects emotionally with the second act of *Madhouse*," amongst all Sherman's plays.

Jenny Topper, who would present *Some Sunny Day* at Hampstead, ponders some critics' failure to understand why *Madhouse* ends in apocalypse: "Anybody who's got a head on their shoulders and a big heart and keen eyes would know those things he says are those any sane playwright would be trying to find a vehicle to say at that time."

Subsequently, Clum anthologized the play and perceptively analyzed it.

Madhouse speaks even more powerfully today than when Sherman wrote it. World climate change challenges us, terrorism terrifies us, and disaster at Fukushima Daiichi augments our dread. As we continue to destroy our planet and its populace, we need this *Madhouse*, reflecting our own, to shock us out of complacency before time runs out.

Redgrave would have toured the U.S. during summer 1991 in Peter Shaffer's *Lettice and Lovage* had she not announced her opposition to the Gulf War, which caused producers to cancel the tour. Therefore she had time to take on something else. In April her son-in-law Fox offered a West-End engagement in *When She Danced*. As a child she had hoped to become a dancer, and she had already played Duncan in the 1968 Karel Reisz film *Isadora*, for which she received an Oscar nomination.

He wanted to produce it because he loved the play and also felt an "emotional connection" to its subject: "My father was Vanessa's agent when she did *Isadora*, and my brother appeared in it, but I thought the movie didn't quite do justice to either Isadora or Vanessa, and I thought Vanessa would be extraordinary in the play." Fox and Redgrave even discussed a possible film version of *When She Danced*, a play she had adored when Fox took her to it at the King's Head.

She explains, "I adore Martin Sherman and love being with him and working with him." She accepted *Madhouse* because "his unique thinking about our times was extraordinary." By the time the opportunity to appear in *When She Danced* came along, she had concluded he "is *the* foremost playwright today." Of course she accepted.

Providentially, Ackerman had time available to direct.

To find a Sergei, in May, Fox sent Ackerman, Sherman and Redgrave to Moscow and soon joined them there. They auditioned actors, they saw plays, but at first to no avail. Ackerman recalls:

> Martin and I had dreamed of seeing Russia, the home of our ancestors and Chekhov. We auditioned all the most talented young actors in Moscow. The food was awful and the vodka too, and the hotel was a nightmare. Martin and I shared a room and peanut butter and jelly sandwiches. One night we saw a rat in our room. We both freaked out, but the people at the front desk thought we were a pair of hysterical queens. They shrugged. Robert finally arrived and took us to sumptuous meals at Pizza Hut and the like.

The translator's parents invited them to dinner at their apartment. Ackerman assumes from "the incredible spread they laid out they had used up all their rations for a month on this lovely meal." During it, Sherman went to the bathroom but failed to return. Finally he replied to questions and knocking "in a quiet and embarrassed voice, 'I'm locked in.'" The others worked to release him. "Robert Fox and I were laughing so hard we couldn't breathe, as people walked by with knives, screwdrivers, pieces of rope. While we laughed, Vanessa pressed her face against the door and tried to calm him while telling him how terrible his two friends were for laughing."

The director had just gotten a camcorder, so he videotaped the whole farcical episode. "One has to know Martin and his inability to negotiate anything mechanical to appreciate this. When a light bulb burned out, he would call Franco and me to change it for him. He also has a natural propensity for creating chaos. Once in Israel, when he turned on the faucet, the whole sink fell off the wall."

Finally they attended a small production of Camus's *Caligula* and found the star breathtaking. Ackerman remembers, "Playing the lead was a young, gorgeous, sexy, Russian genius named Oleg Menshikov, who has gone on to become Russia's biggest male star." Ackerman notes he has since appeared in films, including *Prisoner of the Mountains*, *Burnt by the Sun*, and *East-West*. "We knew on the spot we had found our Sergei. We were thrilled to find he was dying to do it because Esenin is still a major icon in Russia. Oleg couldn't speak a word of English, but it didn't matter." Neither does Sergei.

Frances de la Tour joined the cast as Belzer, and Michael Sheen, straight out of RADA in his professional debut, took on Alexandros. He went on to stardom, playing Tony Blair in *The Queen* and David Frost in *Frost/Nixon*. At the time, Sherman felt, "I have never ever had such a wonderful cast."

Rehearsals began on June 16. Ackerman rejoiced at getting a third chance at a play he had failed before. "This time we finally got it right," he exclaims. Obviously that began with casting. "If you are doing a play about a genius, it helps to have a genius in the role."

He reflects,

> For the first time, the actors embodied and understood their characters' eccentricities. I could allow them to invent the lunatic behavior. One day Oleg got on the piano and grabbed the chandelier and flew across the stage attacking the women. Then he suddenly dropped to the floor and in an instant became a remorseful, inconsolable little boy needing the love of mother or wife. Isadora's failed efforts to comfort Sergei became numbingly sad. That transformation from slapstick comedy to painful poignancy came from improvisation. When Sergei regards Alexandros as a presumed rival for Isadora, Menshikov threw Sheen down to the floor and rolled him up in the rug like a sausage and sat on him. We howled. No one had ever seen anyone do something so absolutely outrageous. But it was in keeping with the play and the character and a joy to watch.

> Vanessa played the scene when she first meets Alexandros as if she had just emerged from the shower, wearing nothing but a sheet. It suggested the Duncan toga.

She performed the scene in which Isadora rehearses her new dance in that sheet, and Ackerman found it "unforgettably moving."

He also remembers "at the beginning of Act 2 when Sergei is trying to cheer up a despairing Isadora and win back her favor, Oleg took a sheet that covered furniture and did a fantastic parody of Isadora dancing. At the end of it, he ran from the room holding the sheet over his head so that it was a flying cape, and as he exited he let the sheet go, and it drifted to the floor. That moment and the symbolism evoked as the sheet floated to the floor were beautiful."

After the dinner party they lifted the tablecloth containing the remaining dishes and swung it "like a sack backward and forwards" and threw it across the room. "It was wild and thrilling. All I had to do was edit the actors' behavior and knit it together. Yes, leave that in. No, that doesn't work. They created brilliant moments bristling with energy, humor, and life. I'm sure no other production could ever equal what those actors were doing."

Performances began in Brighton in mid-July, and the play opened at London's Globe August 6, 1991, and did a limited run (all Redgrave could manage) through December 20.

Redgrave recounts when her ex-husband, Tony Richardson, lay near death in Los Angeles, Sherman for two weeks went home with her each night and sat at the kitchen table and held her hand (343). She flew to L.A. on November 13, and he died on the 14th (344). Small wonder Redgrave terms Sherman "my dearest and most treasured friend" (333).

The day before she left for L.A., Redgrave received the *Evening Standard* Best Actress Award for her Isadora. Later, Oleg Menshikov won the Laurence Olivier Award for Best Actor in a Supporting Role for Sergei, and Frances de la Tour received the Best Actress in a Supporting Role Award for Belzer.

Few critics dislike the West-End *When She Danced*, but those who do wallop it. Paton hates Duncan herself, the play, direction, and performances, except for Menshikov, who, she notes, makes "his British acting debut in jersey boxer shorts, another good reason for having raised the Iron Curtain" (29). She calls this "a truly ghastly partisan play" offering "no interesting critical perspective."

(Left to right) Vanessa Redgrave, Simon Callow, Sherman and unidentified woman at the *Evening Standard* awards, November 12, 1991, the night Redgrave won for Isadora in *When She Danced* (courtesy Martin Sherman).

Four others concur in panning it. Hurren calls it "an irksome piece" with tedious dialogue (33). Macaulay attacks Redgrave as "all wrong" for Isadora (9). He calls the script "neatly tacky" and insists Sherman's Isadora and Sergei "aren't real." In contrast to those who object to Sherman adoring Isadora, he believes Sherman doesn't like her and "does not want to portray Isadora's intelligence." Gore-Langton dismisses the play as minor, a "rather camp celebration of creative folk" (15). He also terms it "a not over-funny boulevard comedy." Shuttleworth dislikes it because it "never gets to grips with its chosen issues, and is seldom more than facilely dramatic while circumventing them, culminating in a ludicrously polyglot dinner party" (57).

Six critics pen mixed notices. Morley still likes the play, but judges Redgrave less effective than Gish (7). Bayley disagrees, proclaiming, "Vanessa Redgrave is utterly right as the dancer" (34). She describes the poignant Act 1 ending and argues, "Sherman powerfully captures an essence of the relationship," and she calls the fact we never see Isadora dance "a clever conceit." Yet she concludes the play should have dramatized Belzer's "tragedy" and therefore dismisses this comedy as "rather thin."

Koenig also suggests Sherman focus on another character: "Couldn't an entertaining play be written about Mary Desti?" (42). She identifies Christine as Isadora's "pupil" and believes her dance ends the play. Christine dances, however, on 49, but the play concludes on 63. Perhaps Koenig dashed away to catch a train? No, she says the first act ends during Act 2, when Isadora "dances," instead of much earlier when the dancer weeps over her drowned children's photograph . Edwards faults the play for Isadora's life, a "touristic vision of la vie bohemienne" (40–41). Dance critic Newman terms it "insubstantial" but admires Redgrave (1116). Gross's review proves less mixed than contradictory (XII).

A total of 17 critics published glowing notices. Shulman approves "this delightful account" and the "sharply-written dialogue of Martin Sherman's sparkling play" (36). Wardle prefers this production to that at the King's Head (15). Nightingale praises the play's fun and "delicious" moments (16). Edwardes believes the "Tower of Babel" Sherman creates "effectively" dramatizes "the incomprehension that confronted Duncan during her lifetime" (102). Hirschhorn terms this "Sherman's splendid comedy," a "fascinating eavesdrop on Isadora," and "not to be missed" (60). Nathan declares, "It works, works triumphantly, eloquent performances and skilful direction uniting with Sherman's subtle exploration of the ephemeral nature of dance as art" (20).

Peter errs in believing it "subtly but substantially rewritten, with greater depth and resonance, haunting and melancholy, but also ribald and savage and poignantly funny" (sec. 5, 9). Sherman changed the placement of Isadora and Sergei at the end. Instead of pinned under him, she faced him, as they drank champagne, took sleeping pills, and talked—with a few tiny changes in the lines there. The text otherwise unfolded exactly as it had at the King's Head.

Any other perceived differences came from the different director and actors, which helped Peter and others see the play afresh.

Coveney loves the production so unreservedly we must assume he likes the play. He had praised it at the King's Head (49). Lipman reports, "This is a wonderfully paced, brilliantly performed exploration of the communication not just of art but of frail human beings" (15). Raymond terms it "an entertaining, sometimes moving portrait of Duncan ... highlighting the ability of art to communicate without language" (30).

Isadora authority McVay calls *When She Danced* "fascinating" and elaborates, "Subtly and tantalizingly, Martin Sherman never shows Isadora dancing" (33). He regards as the evening's highlights Belzer's description of seeing Isadora dance 18 years earlier, Esenin reciting his "Song about a Dog," and Christine trying to imitate Duncan. He feels Sherman "achieves a technical tour de force ... hilariously funny." Although McVay pens a positive notice, he expresses discomfort at Sherman's comic use of Esenin's pretense at a suicide attempt. McVay regards this as bad taste because he still assumes Esenin killed himself, although scholars have evolved a new theory that murder caused the poet's death.

O'Connor's positive review likewise raises a quibble based on his expertise, in this case in music (17). He objects to using a 1938 song to set the scene in 1923 Paris and to including a blues recording despite Duncan's hatred of jazz. He otherwise approves and singles out the "daring stroke" that Sergei speaks only Russian.

Taylor writes, "It's one of the achievements of the play and of this fine performance that they convince you that there was genuine goodness and an indomitable idealism in Isadora despite all the artiness and strenuous Bohemianism" (15). Concerning Duncan hearing the dog poem, he comments, "Expertly played, the sequence flickers through conflicting moods and ends with gulping sobs from Miss Redgrave so harrowingly real that this reviewer had to turn away."

Four other critics published raves. Tinker acclaims, "Sherman's brilliantly conceived tragic-comedy ... conveys a haunting, insistently triumphant note throughout" (3). He identifies "a magnificently comic coup de theatre" in the dinner party and concludes, "It is one of the bravest, finest, funniest and most poignant pieces to illuminate the West End in many a long, dark month."

Billington tells us in its King's Head production it "seemed a witty and moving play about Isadora Duncan in decline. But in the hands of Vanessa Redgrave at the Globe, it becomes an infinitely more mysterious work" (29). He observes, "It is an unusual play to find in the West End: one that deals with the mystery of performance, the limitations of language, the elusiveness of art." Linford likewise rhapsodizes about it as "an oasis of poignant beauty and charm" boasting Redgrave's stunning portrayal (11). He concludes, "This is a mesmerizing play, written with consummate skill and finesse."

Pitman also relishes every aspect. "The production, staged with matching wit and satisfying vitality ... pays off in every department" (92). He pronounces the play "a work of intelligence and satisfying dramatic flair" and "easily one of his more confident and witty efforts." He concludes, "The show meets the first and most basic requirement: it's very good entertainment. It's not only thoughtful, but effortless fun that at times explodes into delightful farce."

Garnett says of Menshikov and Redgrave, "He would risk just as much as she would. She doesn't have that experience a lot. She could just go. And anywhere she went, he could go, and he was going to take her places that she was going to have to run to catch. I got little bumpies. Nobody was left on a shoreline waving."

Kurth writes in the preface to his *Isadora*, "Only when I saw Redgrave playing Isadora onstage in London, in Martin Sherman's enchanting play *When She Danced*, did I decide to go ahead with the book.... I remember thinking it was lucky that Martin's play was closing, because if too many more people saw Vanessa as Isadora—live, in the flesh—I wouldn't need to write a word" (xii).

While *When She Danced* ran at the Globe, efforts continued to film Redgrave in it and to mount *Madhouse* on Broadway with her. Neither effort succeeded. Fox couldn't fund the film, and producing *Madhouse* on Broadway "didn't want to happen." Andre Bishop briefly considered doing it at Lincoln Center. Actors Equity wouldn't permit the original cast to come to Broadway with it. Vanessa's brother Corin subsequently appeared in a Sherman play, however, and her friendship with Sherman continues.

Ackerman says of his West End *When She Danced* not moving to Broadway, "Vanessa was looked on as a liability to any American production because of her politics and her supposed anti–Semitism. About that, she was a great friend to two American Jewish guys, and at no time did I ever hear her say anything remotely anti–Semitic. That charge was nonsense. Or as the script says, it was all 'chipuka.'" The fact Playwrights Horizons had produced the play the previous year didn't help convince New York investors to underwrite it again.

Ackerman staged it a fourth time—in Japan. Because he had seen the inspired West-End cast, he could tell his Japanese actors what he had learned. "The extraordinary and beautiful Rei Asami of Takaratsuka fame played Isadora. She was fantastic. As Sergei, we cast Russian ballet dancer Andris Liepa. This production was a joy."

Ackerman illustrates Isadora's allure by noting, "The Kabuki star Tomasabaru Bando, an onagata (a man who plays women) and a Japanese 'national treasure,' saw the play in London and wanted to play Isadora." Perhaps that will produce another Ackerman mounting.

11. Ian Again (1989–1991)

By the late '80s, partly influenced by Redgrave, shy Sherman, who as a younger man had felt uncomfortable with his looks, grew distinguished looking and confident. Gay politics also brought him out of his shell and into the limelight. A Belzer had developed the flair of an Isadora.

McKellen changed, too. He had a secret in 1979, and he kept it while playing Max, who keeps the same secret. *Bent*'s influence took years to prompt action. In 1988 he risked coming out. In January, he mentioned his sexual orientation on three programs—BBC World Service, Radio 3, and TV's "Wogan." He emerged from the closet while battling Clause 28. As the U.K.'s most respected actor, his willingness to stand up and be counted made a difference. Others followed his lead.

Galvanized by Clause 28, Sherman (always open about his sexual orientation) and McKellen emerged among leaders in the nascent British gay rights movement. This clause, Section 28 of the Local Government Finance Act 1988, took effect on May 24, 1989. It stated, "A local authority shall not a) Intentionally promote homosexuality or publish material with the intention of promoting homosexuality; b) Promote the teaching in any maintained school of the acceptability of homosexuality as a pretended family relationship." This constituted restriction of freedom of speech and action, directed against one segment of the British population.

It appeared to ban a teacher reprimanding homophobic remarks or actions by students, a theatre which received government support presenting a gay play, or a library having books on its shelves that presented homosexuality in anything but a negative light. Perish the thought anyone should read *Heather Has Two Mommies*. During an AIDS epidemic, disseminating information concerning safe sex could violate this law. It muzzled government employees, particularly teachers and librarians and medical staff. It likewise censored theatres and writers, but only those not homophobic.

Meanwhile, homophobes in the press launched a witch hunt, denouncing ministers and judges suspected of homosexuality. Multi-millionaire John Hall declared, "What I really think about gays is this: you should put the whole pack of them on an island; encircle them with a fence; and surround the whole place with sharks" (Cotton 49).

Britain needed *Bent* again.

As *Madhouse* moved towards and enjoyed its production, events transpired that produced a major revival of *Bent*.

First, on June 5, 1988, Sherman co-produced (with McKellen, Mathias, and Michael Cashman) a benefit to fight Clause 28 called *Before the Act*, i.e., before the Local Government Act of 1988, containing Clause 28. Richard Eyre directed this variety show at the Piccadilly, comprised of material written by gay men and women. It lasted over four hours. Performers included the Pet Shop Boys, Peggy Ashcroft, Joan Plowright, Alan Bates, Alan Bennett, Derek Jacobi, Juliet Stevenson, Vanessa Redgrave, Judi Dench, Harold Pinter, Eileen Atkins, Kenneth Branagh, Maureen Lipman, Edna O'Brien, Antony Sher, and Simon Callow. Appearing in *Bent*'s park scene, McKellen played Uncle Freddie, while Hugh Quarshie took Max.

A year later, on June 25, 1989, as a one-night benefit for the newly formed Stonewall Group and the Iris Trust, Sherman, McKellen, and Cashman arranged to present *Bent* at the Adelphi.

Mathias, who had persuaded McKellen to appear in the play's 1979 premiere, agreed to direct, even though this dredged up old emotions because they lived together for nine years and had broken up only a couple of years before.

McKellen repeated Max. Television star Cashman (gay Colin on *EastEnders*) took Horst, Alex Jennings appeared as Rudy and Ian Charleson as Greta. Ralph Fiennes and Richard E. Grant played Nazis, with over 100 other actors appearing in the Dachau scenes. McKellen describes the audience as "absolutely overwhelmed" at the end and applause so thunderous and long "there was time for Martin and Sean to come from their position in a stage box and join us on stage."

The charity performance might have played no more. Yet, Mathias explains, "this night had created such an epic stir people thought this production must be seen. West-End managements wanted us." The National Theatre's head, Richard Eyre, suddenly had to postpone a scheduled production of *Celestina*. He saw in *Bent* a substitute, something to run in repertory with *Salome*. Thus, the National would do it, and it would move to the West End.

This unprecedented revival by the country's leading theatre of a play only 11 years old, written by an American, solidified Sherman's reputation in Europe as a major dramatist. It also brought him new fans.

A major theatre had taken the chance of doing a gay play, risking prosecution under Clause 28 or reduction or elimination of its Arts Council subsidy. This production, written and directed by openly gay men, also starred two openly gay actors. By producing *Bent*, the National's management, led by Eyre and Aukin, took a highly visible stand against this discriminatory law and its accompanying homophobia. Sherman felt deeply moved and regards the National's decision as "very brave."

McKellen and Cashman would star, but with a new supporting cast. They

Sherman (left) and Sean Mathias at Ian McKellen's home, London, late 1989, as the revival of *Bent* directed by Mathias, starring McKellen, prepared for its National Theatre run (courtesy Martin Sherman).

couldn't expect actors of Fiennes's stature to accept a small role in something playing more than one night. Stevan Rimkus took over as Greta, Paul Rhys as Rudy, Robert Eddison as Uncle Freddie and Dominic Rickhards as Horst. Michael Vale designed the set, Tracy Klyne the costumes, and Ben Ormerod the lighting.

Seven months after the benefit, on January 19, 1990, *Bent* had its press opening. Sherman's opening-night note reads, "Dearest Ian, No matter what city, what country, what theatre, what language, what revolution, for me, there has only ever been one Max. And now I am twice blessed. Please, can we do this every ten years? All my love, Martin."

Why did McKellen agree to perform a role he had already appeared in to acclaim and for which he already had won a SWET award? Appearing in the same role a second time does not usually enhance an actor's reputation. McKellen explains, "I could return to the play after coming out. I also thought it desirable *Bent* should have the imprimatur of the National as a classic which should constantly be revived. That it should star two openly gay men and be directed by a third was making history at the National."

Bent played 30 sold-out performances and then transferred to the West End for a run limited by McKellen's previous commitments. It opened at the Garrick on March 6, 1990, but most critics attended press night at the Lyttleton.

Shulman again panned *Bent*. His second paragraph stunned London: "A rather unfortunate spin-off from this effort to combat anti-gay prejudice is that it could arouse anti–German prejudice just when Europe is in no mood to be reminded of the Nazi past" (33). *Bent* has proven perennially popular on German stages, matched by its popularity in Japan. We can infer Germans and Japanese regard this reminder of their past as salutary. Sherman says, "Shulman's comment is the subject of more laughter in London than any review I can remember."

Shulman's distaste for Sherman's gay men colors his language. He terms Max and Rudy "anti–Semitic creeps" and says of Max, "This reptilian character is played by Ian McKellen with clammy detachment and cold-blooded passion." Then Shulman rebukes any enthusiastic viewer thus: "The dramatic impact of these moments, as well as the melodramatic denouement ... will no doubt hold audiences whose emotions have been crassly lacerated and shrewdly manipulated." Finally, Shulman quotes his 1979 summary condemnation and adds he sees no reason to change it.

Hurren refers to McKellen as "the fervent street campaigner" rather than, say, the acclaimed actor, and calls the play "grindingly boring" (32). He sums up, "Forget it, Ian. It's a cringe-maker." Koenig objects, "The characters are stereotypes, the arguments are bogus, and the premises phony" (42). She insists homophobia doesn't exist. Edwards confuses the SA with the SS and asserts Wolf dies only because he resists arrest. He attacks the dramaturgy, opining, "The exchanges between Max and Horst give off no dramatic charge whatever" (45–46). Smith objects, "Sherman tries to hit too many targets" and complains *Bent* fails to move him (37). Hirschhorn scolds *Bent* as a drama of "suspect quality" (38). He further castigates Sherman for "acutely embarrassing" verbal lovemaking and adds, "Nor was I moved by their horrific deaths."

Gross blames Sherman, because "at no point in the Dachau scenes did I escape the feeling that I was watching actors going through a charade. The true edge of despair isn't there" (49). Hewison argues *Bent* concerns anything except its actual subject, Nazi persecution of gay men. He associates the play with AIDS, even though it predates that disease, and with the '70s and subsequent decades' gay pride movements, turning it into an anachronism and an allegory (E7). He claims it lacks impact.

Time Out lists *Bent* as a "Critics' Choice" (37). This unsigned mini notice sends readers to the play because of its importance, provided by political context, as accusations against possibly gay judges force them to resign.

The mixed reviews vary. Kemp approves *Bent* until he reaches the second act, which he says "some factors enfeeble" (11). He enumerates the actors' failure to appear emaciated, some "clichéd attributes of gay couples," and some use of principal characters as "icons." Yet Kemp concludes, "The only time he embraces Horst is when he too is a corpse. Images like these, not psychological or social insights, are what linger at the end of this ferocious theatrical cry for sanity about sexuality."

Hiley's ambivalent review notes he avoided seeing the premiere because he feared the play would reinforce "the homosexual's role as victim" (43). Yet *Bent* "deserves a permanent place in the repertoire of every national theatre." He protests Sherman's connecting "private, consensual sado-masochism with Nazi brutality." Yet he adds, "*Bent* is as subtle as it is shocking." Then Hiley offers a wise take on the issue that has prompted some hostile U.S. reactions: "Sherman shows that, sooner or later, the struggles of all oppressed people intersect—as when the landlord turns up in the camp, sharing the fate of the erstwhile tenants and abusers."

Williams praises the first half but dislikes the second, which he deems a "gay manifesto" (38). He notes as especially "tremendous" the scene with Uncle Freddie. He acknowledges, "The audience applauded as if it were Beethoven's Fifth."

Osborne, who panned it in 1979, writes, "The play now seems, in Sean Mathias's staging, to strike resonances beyond its immediate subject. Sherman's principal characters are male homosexuals, but their plight could be that of men or women of any race, religion or sexual preference, subjected to violence, degradation and torture" (13). Strangely, given that view, Osborne likes the first scene and the park bench scene but finds the second act "less convincing" and "merely depressing." Mars-Jones also finds Act 1 "works best, and particularly the first scene" (91). He judges the opening "funny and touching" but the second half "mildly dated."

Miller admires *Bent*, saying it bears "witness to the Nazi torture and massacre of homosexuals with passion and intelligence" (76). Yet he judges this revival "the worst directed production to have been allowed on stage at the National since Peter Hall left." Therefore he prefers Act 2, when McKellen and Cashman, "left alone," succeed.

Hoyle also prefers 2. By the interval, he describes feeling "the mixture has, dramatically speaking, curdled rather than jelled" (13). Yet in Dachau the play "comes into its own as a study of the salvation of a soul." The sex scene Hoyle judges "more harrowing, erotic and moving than I remember ... perhaps, paradoxically, because it is more lightened with humour." Then he considers the second lovemaking scene, in "which they imagine only holding, touching and protecting one another," as "infinitely more powerful than I remember it" from the premiere.

Van Werson admires McKellen's performance even more than the play and prefers Act 2. He argues, "Sherman has an eye for a flashy theme, a striking talent for duologues, and a very imperfect command of dramatic rhythm and structure," but notes the latter half "presents no dramatic problems for Sherman" because it consists of "a static conversation piece ... a gripping episode, with suggestions of the vaudeville of En attendant Godot" (14). Despite the play's "stark and terrifying theme," it "rarely falls into polemic" as it depicts "the desolation of our terrible century and its terrible emblem, the electrified fence and guard tower."

Cook's rave concurs Sherman's script "is no soap box" and continues, "Instead he has created a tragedy for us all" (33). Cook reasons, "Despite such bleak subject matter, this show is consistently entertaining. Sherman lends a light and tender touch to each set piece, rendering *Bent* fascinating viewing throughout. In the face of unending cruelty, his characters retain fun, affection and above all love. This is what lends this tragedy its indelible hue of optimism, and its triumphant conclusion."

Nathan matter-of-factly notes Max and Rudy's casual anti–Semitism and Max's belief wangling himself a yellow star will help him stay alive. He understands the play as "a fierce and passionate plea for acceptance which does not pretend that homosexuals are especially virtuous" (18). He sums up, "Mathias's direction even manages to wring dark laughter from Sherman's bitter account of the barbarous extremes of homophobia."

Nightingale expresses pleasure the National has revived *Bent* because "contemporary plays rarely get revived these days, especially at posh addresses" (Review, 41). He continues, "It was always an intelligent, feeling play, and time has actually sharpened its edge." Nightingale notes horrific incidents on the train, then asks "Are such touches excessive? Maybe; but to say so would be a bit like calling Hell melodramatic." He terms it "an eloquent play."

Tinker reverses his previous condemnation to praise *Bent*. "Of its moral courage," he continues, "I never had the slightest doubt" (3). The passage of time has increased homophobia, and thus, in "the backlash of intolerance which is now raising its head in the distinctly ugly guise of moral rectitude, the play takes on a fresh and vivid clamour. It stands, as I am sure it was always intended to, as a metaphor for all witch-hunts, whether they involve the human horrors of the concentration camp or simply the mindless trampling of careers and social standing."

Herbert, likewise, changes his view. He praises the National's "bravery" in reviving it and continues, "Ian McKellen's personal triumph in *Bent* is also a reward for his own bravery in promoting the gay cause: the play's plea for a persecuted minority has acquired alarming resonances.... I found myself much more responsive now to a play I had dismissed at first as melodramatic exploitation" (59).

Also reversing himself, Coveney feels homophobia causes *Bent* to appear "a necessary play" (60). He compares the vilifications practiced by the Nazis and the British government (in Section 28), and refers to George Gale, who, in "the *Daily Mail* last August, suggested that all homosexuals were likely to spread the disease of Aids and were therefore incipient murderers." He continues, "The leap still to be made is the full acknowledgement by a predominantly straight society of such a thing as homosexual love. On the merely visceral level, this is now the challenge of *Bent*, and the audience's response at the performance I attended was of a shattering intensity."

Billington likewise specifies right-wing intolerance has increased since

1979. "'Pulpit Poofs' screams *The Sun* while *The Times*" decrees, "'It is not advisable for senior judicial appointments to be offered to practicing homosexuals'" (38). He contrasts his reaction to his response in 1979. He liked it then, but now, "more than I first realized, the play is also about the moral education of its hero, Max." He recognizes Sherman disagrees with Max's goal of surviving. Billington has learned, "It is a subtler play than I first realized." He concludes, "A demanding, fascinating play ... it reaches beyond the specialist appeal of gay drama to offer a sane and timely warning about the brutality of sexual intolerance."

Morley calls *Bent* "chilling" and reflects upon its "extraordinary mixture of black comedy ... and naked human tragedy" (7). He praises "the timeless strength of the play as an anthem to gay endurance, even at the worst of political or social or medical times." Rees rejoices that the National has chosen it and explains, "*Bent* doesn't bash you over the head with its politics, thank goodness, but they're as clear as a bright spring morning" (9). Paton begins, "The great strength of Martin Sherman's famous play about fear and loathing in the Third Reich is that it never romanticizes its characters" (37). She notes his "ironic sense of humour never allows the piece to become maudlin." She understands Sherman "writes from the double perspective of being both Jewish and gay and can thus appreciate better than most the paradox of one despised minority attacking another."

Shortly afterwards, Sherman gave an amused summary of conflicting reactions: "Audiences have responded tremendously, and the reviews are better than the original production received. But you just can't believe all these critics attended on the same night." He explains critics love the humor or hate it, fault the production as low key or praise it as understated, note audiences feel nothing or say, "I've never been in an audience so deeply moved."

Others reacted to this revival. Summers praises *Bent* as "shattering" (382) and "a celebration of gayness in the face of oppression. Its tenth-anniversary revival in London, again with McKellen, was akin to a religious experience for gay men, bristling under laws forbidding positive portrayals of lesbians and gay men in government supported theatres" (194).

More personal responses reached McKellen. Maggie Smith writes, "I hadn't seen the play before and was really knocked out by it.... I'd heard about the wire at the end but my hair stood on END when it happened."

A man from Stoke on Trent who had spontaneously bought a ticket and missed his train home writes, "It was funny, warm, witty, sad and very dramatic and totally theatrical." He hopes this production will counteract the bigotry encoded in Clause 28. A woman from London praises the "shattering play." Another writes, "I cried so much during the last scene, the tears ran down my neck."

A woman from Newcastle upon Tyne says, "We traveled down particularly to see 'Bent' and it was worth the journey and more. My friend's mother was in the Warsaw Ghetto, and she lost family in the camps, but we had been less aware than we should have been of the sufferings of other groups."

A woman from Middlesex feels, "'Bent' should be seen by everyone, not only because of the superb acting, but because everyone must know the truth about homosexuality, must realize the dangers of prejudice and persecution — from Clause 28 to the media's hostile portrayal of homosexuals and the general public's acceptance of such opinions and stereotypes.... 'Bent' is the best, and most moving, play I have ever seen."

A woman from Manchester explains, "The love shown between Max and Horst in the play was so strong and so real that it touched my heart and my awareness to homosexual relationships has changed drastically. I was drawn in so much I was scared, really scared, and I was so touched, but disturbed, and I was in tears by the end, and realized what terror and victimization homosexuals must go through. *Bent* is the best play I have ever seen, and I would gladly see it again and again." A woman from Leeds says, succinctly, "'Bent' is such an important play."

Andrew Rowe, MP, writes "it was good to be reminded of the perils of trying to interfere in the private lives of individuals." A man from Sussex comments, "I was moved beyond tears and the play will continue to haunt me. Unfortunately 'what it says' has not dated!" A woman from the country, who describes herself as a "non-gay, nearly middle-aged, mother of two young children" suggests "it should be compulsory viewing for supporters of Clause 28. However, I guess they would only respond by wanting to ban it."

A London woman inquires, "Is there a chance of 'Bent' being filmed? If so, every school and college in the country should have a copy." Theatre entrepreneur Michael Codron terms it "a shattering and memorable experience." A woman who has seen the play four times rhapsodizes, "It still has to be the most wonderful theatrical experience I've ever had."

A heterosexual Londoner who has seen the play twice and plans to go again writes:

> I wanted to tell you how deeply moved I have been by this brilliant play.... Such an unbelievably intense, dramatic, stirring and emotional piece, full of dignity and passion, and of man's inhumanity to man, but also of the human spirit's ability to triumph over oppression. And so superbly portrayed. Watching "Bent" is a shattering experience. I have sat with tears in my eyes, and have left the theatre numbed and emotionally exhausted, even too moved to speak. But it has also stimulated countless discussions amongst my friends and me, and it has thus made us more aware not only of the little-known persecution of homosexuals by the Nazis, but also of the continued oppression in the form of such things as Clause 28. We should all be working towards a time when all men and women are equal, regardless of their sexuality.

A 19-year-old lesbian of color says she left "with tears streaming down my face and a very damp handkerchief in my hand; I was so incredibly moved and saddened. No play has ever had this effect on me before." Another London woman confides, "I sat with tears rolling down my face. The play remains with me still. Clearly it's a play with a vital political message for us now." Teachers write, generally to complain of Clause 28 prohibiting their reproving their pupils' homophobia. One closeted man notes, "I was struck by the way the scene on the train reminded me of 'The Crucible' and the McCarthy trials—the whole business of persecution and trading person for person is similar and horrible. I can also not forget the line 'We are not meant to be loved,' which is both haunting and probably all too true. The persecution seems to be going on all the time."

A woman from Essex says, "I found when Max was telling Horst how the Nazis made him prove he wasn't gay my hands were clutched so tightly my nails made marks in my palms and my eyes were wet and hot. A horrible, tragic love story. When Horst rubbed his left eyebrow I thought my heart would break—more wet eyes. *Bent* will be with me for a long, long time." A female "A-level History student studying Hitler and Nazi Germany" credits the play for so vividly portraying that world that she "was sick in the interval.... I felt I was living it too."

The word "shattering" appears in several letters. A lesbian couple writes, "Neither of us has stood in tears at the end of a play before." Another writer explains, "Having seen it in June at the Adelphi, I was knocked out by its sheer force and brilliance. In June, it was the unexpectedness of the wit and comedy in the face of so much evil and intolerance which affected me. On Friday, it was the power that came across. *Bent* must surely rank as one of the greatest plays of the 20th century."

A young man told McKellen, "I was overwhelmed and left the auditorium trembling and with tears trickling down my cheeks." Another London man says, "It's appallingly harrowing but at the same time extraordinarily uplifting, really I can't imagine theatre being any better." A young woman from Henley on Thames writes she "felt the power of this play greater than anything else I have ever experienced in the theatre."

An American teacher says,

> *Bent* is a remarkably successful work of art. I saw this production twice and each time the audience (and they were otherwise quite different) confirmed my own sense of the play at first reading: that it is impossible to see it honestly, to empathize with Max, to experience that world and later to leave the theatre and make faggot jokes or hear them. Your audiences are devastated, yes, but there is a sense of something more: the audience understand what some critics have chosen not to—that this play is as much a warning for the present as a record of the past.

A woman in Croydon echoes these sentiments:

> Forty eight hours after seeing the play, I'm still shaking, angry, and screaming out at—what? The way things were, and still are.... What we saw was the happy ending—Horst retaining his dignity by standing up to the Nazis at his death, and Max

regaining his, by accepting his pink triangle and electrocuting himself. Happy?! Yes, let's say happy—and the whole audience shattered, harrowed, wracked ... the most important play I've ever seen.

This writer also supplies a five-stanza poem about the play, using "fence" as metaphor.

One letter encloses another, which the writer has sent to the editor of the *Sunday Times*, dated January 29, 1990:

Dear Sir,

I write to object strongly to a comment by Robert Hewison in his review of the National Theatre's production of "Bent." It is generally impossible to criticize a critic as so much of what is said is subjective judgment. However, in this case where he says the play has almost no impact, he can only fairly relate that to the impact on an audience. My wife and I go to the theatre every two weeks or so, generally but not exclusively to the RSC and the National. Neither of us can think of any play in the last five years or so that has had so dramatic an impact on ourselves and the audience around us. I have never experienced such rapt stillness or such a long, shocked silence at a final curtain; followed by lengthy applause and cheers. Mr. Hewison's comment seems to indicate a less than splendid isolationism. His considered view that "Bent" has almost no impact is not just a palpable nonsense but from our experience it is also an untruth and should not be left unchallenged.

Sincerely,

Laurence James [Roydon, Essex]

The *Sunday Times* failed to publish Mr. James's remarks.

Another testament to the production's impact came from the Laurence Olivier Award judges, who nominated McKellen for the Best Actor award for his Iago and his Max.

Nearly a year later, when the Queen's New Year's Honours bestowed a knighthood on McKellen, Derek Jarman denounced him in the *Guardian* for accepting this honor from the government which had enacted Clause 28's discriminatory strictures. Sher and Sherman wrote a letter supporting McKellen and solicited additional signatures.

The *Guardian* published the following statement:

As Gay and Lesbian artists, we would like to respectfully distance ourselves from Derek Jarman's article (*Guardian*, 4 January) in which he argues that Ian McKellen should have refused his knighthood. We regard his knighthood as a significant landmark in the history of the British Gay Movement. Never again will public figures be able to claim that they have to keep secret their homosexuality in fear of it damaging their careers. Ian McKellen provides an inspiration to us all, not only as an artist of extraordinary gifts, but as a public figure of remarkable honesty and dignity. Simon Callow, Michael Cashman, Nancy Diuguid, Simon Fanshawe, Stephen Fry, Philip Hedley, David Lan, Bryony Lavery, Michael Leonard, Tim Luscombe, Alec McCowan, Cameron Mackintosh, Pam St. Clement, John Schlesinger, Antony Sher, Martin Sherman, Ned Sherrin, and Nicholas Wright [18].

These reasonable words from Sher and Sherman, plus support by other important figures (some of them never before open about their sexual orientations) derailed Jarman's effort to bring McKellen into disrepute in gay politics.

As the Millennium neared, the National Theatre management listed the 20th century's most significant plays. They included *Bent* among 100 NT2000 Plays of the Century, along with Shaw's *Pygmalion*, Coward's *Private Lives*, Eliot's *Murder in the Cathedral*, Wilder's *Our Town*, Williams' *A Streetcar Named Desire*, Miller's *Death of a Salesman*, Beckett's *Waiting for Godot*, O'Neill's *Long Day's Journey into Night*, Delaney's *A Taste of Honey*, Pinter's *The Caretaker*, Albee's *Who's Afraid of Virginia Woolf?*, Stoppard's *Rosencrantz and Guildenstern Are Dead*, Shepard's *True West*, Mamet's *Glengarry Glen Ross*, and Wilson's *Fences*.

Bent has become one of the most frequently produced plays 'round the world, staged in 54 countries. (See Appendix A.) It receives major revivals, with actors eager to test their skills against Max and Horst as they also hope to tackle Hamlet or Lear.

12. A Future in Film (1990-1993)

Prior to 1990, Sherman had written little for celluloid. In 1976, he created a dubbing script for Carr and re-edited that film, *Survive*. In 1978, the BBC commissioned the Cuban *Movement*, never filmed. In 1980, he worked with Zinnemann on a project, never filmed. In 1985, he wrote the pilot for a series set in Israel, never filmed.

His agent kept suggesting Sherman, but an American living in England seemed too American to British producers and too British to U.S. producers. The Carr project predated Sherman moving abroad. The others had foreign settings, which eliminated concern about whether he could write American or British characters.

In February 1990, while attending rehearsals for the New York production of *When She Danced*, Sherman tussled with how to turn a trilogy written from three viewpoints into one movie. Producer Norma Heyman had offered him this Durrellesque television film commission. She sought a foreign writer because the third novel provides such a perspective. She wanted someone sympathetic to central female roles, as well as a writer of intellect and wit, and one who understood religion's power. His plays demonstrated all that. *A Madhouse in Goa* also showed his skill at dramatizing freedom, disillusionment, and disdain for convention, central to the property she offered. "He knew how to write about unconventional people in unconventional surroundings," Heyman observes.

When she met Sherman, she found his understanding of postwar England "quite astonishing," and she likewise relished his appreciation for how "older people can change things. Martin's very sympathetic to the old." She also responded to him personally: "Martin can create joy around him."

Sherman felt eager to write another film. He explained in 1990, "It's a great thing to do between plays. You make money and if you're adapting, you exercise your muscles. And I want to prove I can write British, which, after ten years in London, I ought to be able to do."

He would adapt Alice Thomas Ellis's trilogy *The Clothes in the Wardrobe*, published in the U.S. as *The Summer House*. He embraced the opportunity to focus on survival issues confronted by outsiders: a young woman bereft of defenses, an old woman bereft of joy, and a foreigner who flouts strictures the bourgeois '50s impose upon her gender.

During 1990 and 1991 he conceived, wrote and revised his film.

In Ellis's trilogy, trauma on an Egyptian holiday impels a young Englishwoman, after her return, to make a ludicrous mistake. So dysfunctional has Margaret become, when Syl proposes, she doesn't reply. When he takes that as assent, she can't protest. Without accepting, she finds herself engaged.

Margaret considers recent events and her impending doom in *The Clothes in the Wardrobe* (1987). Syl's mother reflects about the engagement in *The Skeleton in the Cupboard* (1988). The sexy, exotic Lili considers interfering in *The Fly in the Ointment* (1989).

The trilogy appears in the U.K. under the title of the first novel. This led U.S. critics to assume Sherman draws only upon it. To avoid confusion, we refer to trilogy and film as *The Summer House*.

Ellis writes about three generations. Each first-person account describes only those events she participated in and only from the perspective of her own years—teenage, senior, and middle-aged. The narratives never approach straightforward chronology. Instead, they record introspective reflections.

Margaret, 19, narrates the first novel. She had an affair in Egypt with Nour, a young man she adored until he forced her to help him dispose of a gypsy girl he murdered. Tormented by guilt at her complicity, she punishes herself by permitting her arrogant neighbor to announce they're engaged. She longs to become a nun in an Egyptian convent. Immobilized by shame at her sin and convinced God cannot forgive her, she drifts passively toward her wedding until rescued by a woman self-absorbed but intent upon performing this good deed.

Syl's mother, Mrs. Monro, who narrates the second novel, at nearly 80 assumes she soon will die. Like Margaret, she drifts. Also like Margaret, she tolerated marrying a man she didn't love. She, too, had an earlier passionate affair, which, in her case, produced a child. Although she confides such intimate details, she never reveals her first name, and she calls her pet by the impersonal appellation "dog." He dies as her narrative ends.

Mrs. Monro knows Margaret and Syl shouldn't marry. Despite having once caught Lili having sex with her husband, Mrs. Monro befriends her and prods her into preventing the marriage. In her narrative, she doesn't witness the denouement.

Both Margaret and Mrs. Monro like Lili, the third novel's narrator. The half-Egyptian, half-English Lili—like Syl and the young woman's mother Monica in her 40s—went to the English school in Alexandria with Monica and has always lived in Egypt. A free spirit—partly from courage, partly from hedonism—she shocks Monica, but fascinates Margaret, who admires her, and Mrs. Monro, who befriends her. Saucy Lili induces joy and renewed zest for life in the old lady.

Lili reveals dark secrets and meanness. Sherman wisely took some quips and incidents from this third novel but retained for his script the more idealized version of Lili as seen through the two earlier narrators' eyes.

Understanding the novels and film requires historical perspective. Repressive '50s' mores bred hypocrisy as well as alcoholism (presumably to lubricate hypocritical behavior and, later, deaden shame). The women all regard men as "the other." Male sexual predators drive women into imprudence. These women deserve better men or fewer constraints. Instead they suffer from a double standard, requiring virginity before marriage and monogamy afterward. Ellis and Sherman subvert this patriarchal system.

Monica's pedophile ex-husband Derek molested Margaret when she was four and later left Monica for another woman. Nour sexually exploits Margaret, and Syl cheats on and patronizes her. His father cheated on Mrs. Monro. Small wonder Monica, Margaret, and the old lady feel sour about their lives until liberated Lili waltzes in. She has also married a libertine, but husband and wife behave alike. Lili's sexual allure gives her power to take control and save Margaret.

Sherman feels all the women "have delicious voices," but he also recognized immediately "they're three people who would never say what they feel." This made the novels hard to dramatize.

He had an ally among the characters, the distasteful Syl, whom no narrator likes. Therefore, all three women dread the approaching marriage, which provides them a common goal.

Sherman begins and ends in Egypt. Just after the credits, Nour stabs an Egyptian woman. We hear about Monica's life there and Margaret's birth there, and we keep observing moments in the young woman's recent months. In a scene Sherman invents, Syl and Margaret discuss their plan to honeymoon there, and, in another scene Sherman largely invents, the middle-aged characters agree this destination must change. The paintings Robert exhibits depict Egypt, specifically the immediate neighborhood where Margaret visited.

Initially we infer Margaret still loves Nour, but then understand she repudiates her passion.

The filmmakers use the Temple of Karnak to advantage. Obelisks and columns tower as tall as eight stories, dwarfing humans. This intimidating scale suggests Margaret lacks control of her life.

Sherman uses snippets from Ellis effectively and juxtaposes material to make it revelatory. For instance, he expands upon Lili's account of passing in Alexandria a bloody bride's nightdress hung out to prove virginity. Then he shows Margaret's face as she guzzles a martini, worrying about Syl discovering her secret when he draws no blood. Immediately afterwards, Sherman's Lili tells Mrs. Monro Derek had sex with his daughter when she was four. Margaret doesn't remember this, but we appreciate, from the juxtaposition, Nour didn't take her virginity.

To devise dialogue, Sherman uses most conversations from the novels, turns thoughts into speech, and invents some. Inventions include some of Lili's witticisms, such as her addressing Cynthia by a series of incorrect names beginning with "c." Ellis merely has Lili call Cynthia "Eve" once. And only Sherman's Lili bedevils her hostess by greeting Monica with the phrase "So much water under your bridge," as though Monica alone has aged.

Only in the film does Lili ruminate "Happiness? Good God! One must never expect that from marriage. A few quiet moments, if you're lucky, and an occasional day that doesn't incite you to murder." Only the cinematic Lili responds to Margaret's mundanely about Egypt—"It was very nice"—by remarking, "It's always best not to gush." Right before Margaret's insipid judgment he tells Lili to put "down her fork in anticipation."

Sherman gives Lili a new line when she greets the others on her first morning in Croydon: "Can you believe our luck? Another day!" He continues improvising additions: Lili responds to news that Monica has run out of coffee beans by asking for "hemlock" and greets instant coffee by exclaiming, "Pure joy!" When Monica laments, "I'm short of a chop" for dinner, Sherman's Lili pretends to misunderstand by replying, "Nonsense, you look fine" before offering to buy it. Lili asks Margaret to accompany her by saying, "We're going to practice walking."

Sherman embroiders the conversation on the walk. When Margaret explains how Syl proposed, his Lili employs irony: "I had forgotten how romantic the English are." He gives her a playful fantasy: Lili suggests Syl might be a masochist because "on nights when you don't fancy anything else, it's relatively easy to crack a whip," and then she muses, "I wonder if he wears lace panties. Egyptian men don't as a rule, but the British are a breed apart."

Sherman's Lili references Ellis's title by telling Monica and Margaret, "You should never underestimate the power of clothes." He frequently finds unexpected ways to illuminate the ordinary, as when Monica inquires about what has occurred when Margaret's thumb bleeds. Sherman's Lili replies, "Greek tragedy." When Monica turns her planned wedding canapés into a source of eternal rejoicing, Sherman gives Lili the sarcasm "I feel much better now." When Mrs. Monro wonders "if Margaret's anemic," Sherman's Lili rejoins "I think she's a little low-key for anemia."

Sherman provides Lili with new lines to needle her husband about his affair with Nour's mother. When the characters say Margaret isn't well enough to return to Egypt on her honeymoon, Lili speculates Marie-Claire has exposed others to germs, mischievously hoping Robert will fear he might have contracted something. When Monica complains they couldn't find her the night before, she explains, "I was in bed," implying she shared it with another man.

Although Sherman especially writes new dialogue for Lili, he also gives others new remarks.

He provides Monica with an afterthought when she gives Margaret breakfast in bed. "Were you dreaming about Syl?" she inquires, and her daughter replies, "Who?" So we know from the top Margaret doesn't dote on her fiancé.

To show Lili as outrageous even in childhood, Sherman's Monica describes their first meeting: "You know, she was in the sixth form when I first went to school. She walked over to me—(proudly) picked me out actually— and punched me in the face. I knew I had made a friend." Much later, when Lili speaks unkindly of Derek's second wife, Sherman's Monica says, "You are wicked. I do adore having you here, Lili."

Sherman devises revelatory new lines for Syl, Nour, Mother Joseph, and others, most importantly Mrs. Monro. For instance, she tells Dog, "That girl is too quiet"—a shrewd suspicion. Sherman follows Mrs. Monro's comment from Ellis about the aged of other cultures flinging themselves off ice-floes with his own supplementary line, "But there are no ice-floes in Croydon." During Sunday lunch, when Mrs. Monro observes Margaret's loathing of her son, Sherman rejects Ellis's "just look at those cows" (217) in favor of a line Plowright renders both elegant and sardonic, "Shall we risk the trifle?"

The night before the wedding, Sherman's Mrs. Monro deliberately spills her drink on Derek's lap, then tells Lili, "I'm not behaving well. I'm bordering on hysteria. I can't bear to look at Derek. He's evil incarnate. His wife is a goose. Monica's a fool. And Margaret's drunk. The old are powerless." This enables Sherman's Lili to reassure her, "I've given you my word. It will not happen." Sherman invents much of this party and the wedding breakfast.

In addition to augmenting the novels' material, Sherman reshapes what he uses from Ellis. Take the passage reviewers most often quote. Ellis wrote, "I thought—it isn't just me. Nobody likes Syl. I'm marrying a man whom nobody likes" (36). Sherman reduces this to "I'm marrying a man nobody likes. I thought it was just me." In so doing, he makes an ordinary remark succinct and quotable. Likewise, where Ellis's Margaret has a nightmare that Syl brings her breakfast in bed, Sherman improves upon this by making Syl essentially naked as he enters carrying the tray.

Whether or not drawing directly from Ellis, Sherman writes short scenes to create a feeling of forward movement even when little occurs. As he draws scenes from the novels, he must arrange them in an order that makes sense, and he must invent action bridges between the bits from Ellis.

He also invents longer sections, even whole scenes. He interpolates the early scene in which we meet Mrs. Monro when Syl brings her a breakfast cup of coffee in bed. This parallels Monica bringing Margaret breakfast in bed (from Ellis) and provides exposition. Towards the end, Sherman inserts Monica's excitement at how Margaret looks in her wedding dress, her invitation to come to the summerhouse to see the flowering cactus, and the rest of the scene. This includes Mrs. Raffald and Father O'Flynn liking miracles and everyone, champagne in hand, parading across the lawn to peek inside the summerhouse.

Sherman creates a date in which Syl takes Margaret to a club, he appears silly, and she finds him foolish. When he takes her home, she turns her face so his kiss lands on her cheek, and she slips out of the car quickly to escape him. Each line reinforces their unsuitability. When Syl lets slip he remembers her as a baby, and she mocks this admission, he doesn't appreciate it emphasizes he's twice her age.

Ellis conveys the developing relationship between Mrs. Monro and Lili with their private thoughts. Sherman instead must dramatize their growing friendship. He expands their scenes and dialogue, making them drinking buddies cavorting.

The pub scene's opening doesn't derive from Ellis. Lili says she's sorry, and when Mrs. Monro asks, "Sorry?" Lili mentions her husband's death. We expect Lili instead to say she's sorry she had sex with Jack. To Mrs. Monro's relief, Lili doesn't, thus avoiding disrupting their new friendship. This suspenseful moment leads to a more interesting confession by both women concerning their pleasure in widowhood, achieved or anticipated.

Mrs. Monro sings and Lili laughs as they walk arm in arm after leaving the pub in a scene 100 percent Sherman's. They both laugh, and Mrs. Monro expresses her satisfaction in Lili: "It's been years since I've been able to say things as they come into my head—to a non-canine, that is—knowing that I would be understood."

At Mrs. Monro's house, they dance and fall in a heap, laughing at Syl's disapproval. He exacerbates this by rebuking his mother for behaving like that "at your age." This section Sherman likewise invents, as he does in most of the scene in which Lili tells Mrs. Monro that Derek sexually abused Margaret and both women disparage men.

Sherman expands the Egyptian material from the first novel. Margaret cannot confide in anyone, so he writes flashbacks for her as nightmares and memories, both montages and dialogue. He makes good use of paintings of Egypt Lili's husband exhibits.

This gallery opening provides us the most glimpses of Margaret's experience in Luxor, and finally Sherman shows us the rest as she broods in front of the painting Syl insensitively presents her as a wedding gift. This depicts the crocodile pool where she and Nour threw the corpse.

Among other alterations, Sherman inserts Monica inviting Nour to the wedding; Ellis includes his mother but not Nour. In the first novel, Margaret confesses her sin to a priest, but Sherman instead has her leave after telling the priest, "This is between me and God." Sherman recognizes if the priest absolves Margaret she might find the will to end her engagement, thus depriving us of Lili's solution.

In constructing his scenario, Sherman provides several sources of suspense. He prompts us to wonder what happened in Egypt. Will Margaret marry Syl, and why has she passively endured this intolerable engagement? Will Mrs. Monro forgive Lili for having sex with her husband? Will they manage to stop the wedding? If so, how? Will Margaret fulfill her dream of becoming a nun?

Sherman avoids dialogue when visual action will do. However, his first draft didn't always perceive each opportunity. And he tended to write multiple scenes involving the same action. For instance, Monica originally fitted the wedding dress on Margaret more than twice. Bits of padding fell away during his work with Heyman. She admired the way he provided the actors with meaningful pauses they could fill. She commends this talent he shares with a few other great screenwriters of "letting the pauses speak as much as the words."

Sherman didn't collaborate with the film's original director, Malcolm Mowbray, whom Heyman replaced with Waris Hussein after shooting had already begun. Instead, the notes he received came directly from Heyman; they agreed on the final shooting script. As for Alice Thomas Ellis, she had no say in what Sherman did with her novels, but Heyman reports the script impressed her.

Sherman wanted Jeanne Moreau for Lili, but worried she mightn't accept. Heyman elaborates, "There were few actresses who could have played Lili. We discussed only Jeanne. She faxed me the day after she received the script, saying, 'Whoever thought of me for this impudent role I thank from the bottom of my heart.'"

Given his fascination with *Jules and Jim* and his admiration for Moreau, Sherman must have felt he had died and gone to cinema heaven.

Sherman also got his first opportunity to work with Joan Plowright, who accepted Mrs. Monro. "I love the Ellis books, I thought the adaptation excellent, and I wanted to act with Jeanne Moreau." The two relish their scenes together.

Heyman recalls, "Martin and I got our dream cast!" She describes Sherman's participation as

> examining each actor in relation to the rest and sensitively and astutely asking delicate questions which enabled the actor to answer what he could do. Martin would be sparing with those questions, but he would give the actor freedom to say whatever he wanted. He knows which actor will get to the heart of a character.

Production began on February 1, 1992, and ended in late March, with shooting in Egypt and Cockfosters (standing in for Croydon). The film would have wrapped sooner, but the second director, Hussein, had to reshoot some after BBC executives sacked Mowbray.

Heyman feels Hussein understood the screenplay's spirit. In Egypt he supplied the purity of the lilies, changed the nuns' garb from black to white, and shifted the convent's focus outward. Mowbray had enclosed the nuns in a walled fortress. Hussein changed this to an open structure, high, airy and filled with light. This conveys the convent's spirituality as liberating and its joyous appeal for Margaret.

The cast enjoyed each other, and David Threlfall had the chance of a lifetime. Heyman recalls, "A friend of his who was opening at the National said, 'This is a great moment in my career.' And he responded, 'It might be a great moment in your career to have the lead in a Williams play, but next Tuesday I'm going to fuck Jeanne Moreau. That's a great moment.'"

Sherman received his own bonus. He had been percolating an Egyptian play. Creating *The Summer House* in 1990 and 1991 and returning there in 1992 helped prompt his writing *Some Sunny Day*.

Heyman had intended *Summer House* for BBC 1, but they rejected it for prime time, so BBC 2, the arts-oriented network, took it and aired it at 10 P.M. on January 17, 1993. Its popularity won it a rebroadcast in July 1994. It also was shown at the 36th London Film Festival.

Heyman resisted selling it to Goldwyn for U.S. theatrical release, but that company's Tom Rothman, who had seen it on television, held a U.S. screening and telephoned her while sitting with the audience. She recalls, "I heard this incredible noise, and I asked what it was, and he said, 'Norma Heyman, it's called laughter.'" Her doubts as to how U.S. viewers would respond evaporated, and she agreed Goldwyn could have it. It proved popular with arts cinema viewers and received generally excellent notices, although not the uniform raves it commanded in the U.K.

There Peachment notes, "Acting honors of the weekend go to Jeanne Moreau" (13). Wilson calls it "very funny" (xii). Listing it as "Pick of the Day," Day-Lewis lauds "a lovely debut television drama script" (xxvi). The *Times* praises it as "lively" and "packed full of delicious lines" ("10.00 Screen Two." 17), while Catchpole pronounces it "a class act" (34). The *Observer* terms it "sheer delight from beginning to end" ("10.00 Screen Two" 54). E.P. proclaims, "Martin Sherman has skillfully woven the strands of Alice Thomas Ellis's 'The Summerhouse Trilogy' to comment acidly, but hilariously, on the tyranny of marriage.... As an anthem for the common woman this is unbeaten. Don't miss" (153).

Payne writes, "A new season of feature-length films makes an excellent beginning with Martin Sherman's adaptation" (sec. 8, 27). Amery rates it "the best thing I watched the entire week" and "memorable" (17). Venning pronounces it "a cracker" (23). Paton refers to it as a "winsome fable about freedom," "ethereal fantasy," "earthy satire," and an "exotic cocktail." She notes Sherman's "filleting" the novel "almost to the bone" and adds, "The result vividly captured a Bohemian invasion of frigid Fifties Croydon" (31).

Paterson raves, "Martin Sherman's screenplay achieved the transition from page to screen with its spirit triumphantly intact.... Quite the most enjoyable piece of television in ages, not least for its unfashionable theme that the old can still influence events" (34). Anwar judges, "Martin Sherman's extremely deft adaptation," complete with "acidic aphorisms," provides "a more cinematic" experience "than any reader of the novels could have hoped to see" (55).

Several U.S. critics predicted Oscars, and Goldwyn officials hoped Moreau would receive a nomination. Academy-Award rules, however, prohibit consideration of films that have aired on television prior to showing in theatres in L.A. Nevertheless, they must have felt pleased at the critical reception and brisk box office for a British period piece, an urbane comedy not written for 13-year-olds. (See Appendix F.)

The film received a Writers Guild of Great Britain nomination and a BAFTA nomination for "Best Single Drama (for television)."

At the ceremony to announce the BAFTA nominations, Sherman found himself with three people with whom he would work again. Olympia Dukakis, who would originate Rose, read the nominations in his category. Heyman accompanied him. And Stephen Frears had directed *The Snapper*, another television nominee. In 2003, Heyman would commission and Frears would agree to direct another Sherman film.

The Summer House gave him entrée into that cinema world. Eventually his agency would move him from their list of playwrights to the more remunerative category of screenwriting.

13. Magic (1994–1997)

In the mid–90s, Sherman wrote three scripts employing the supernatural. The play features an outsider possessing superhuman powers. The first screenplay adapts a magic-realist novel in which a central character turns into a fish. The second features a protagonist possessed by a dybbuk. Each script dramatizes threats to outsiders' survival.

Although the first film's producers commissioned Sherman in summer 1994, he didn't immediately begin. Before *Alive and Kicking* went into preproduction, he scheduled a vacation on Mykonos. There, in early September, while considering how to adapt the novel, he licked a decade-long difficulty. He had pondered this during previous Mykonos vacations. This time, he suddenly knew how to make his protagonist work.

Elated, he returned to London to tackle that play, which he completed by January 1995. He also drafted the film *See Under: Love*. Likewise in early 1995, Sherman tutored screenwriters for Equinoxe in Bordeaux and learned that his alma mater, Boston University, would present him with an award on April 24.

Even before Sherman titled the play, Robert Fox agreed to produce it. It would begin in a non-profit venue, but Fox's option included the West End and Broadway. Sherman and Fox joked about alternatives, but they stuck with *Some Sunny Day* from Vera Lynn's "We'll Meet Again."

Ramsay sent the play to Hampstead, where Topper had replaced Aukin as artistic director. She loved it and scheduled it from April 5, 1996, through June 1.

She especially responded to Emily and Horatio's marriage, which she calls

> the most insightful and searing account of what love's folly can do to a person's perception of their world and place in it. It's so beautifully written, so profound and funny and tragic and frightful that anybody who has been wronged in love must cheer. For anybody who has come up against that moment in their relationship where the other person says black is white and, oh, by the way, given that black is white, you simply don't figure in this landscape of inverted colors, he's telling it how we've heard it and witnessed it.

Yet Topper saw more to *Some Sunny Day*: "This imagines beyond the beyond. It is as funny and wise as anything I've ever read."

It boasts Sherman's most varied characters, set in his most exotic location. He dramatizes in conventional form his most unconventional material, because the difficulty he mastered involved employing an alien protagonist, from outer space.

Sherman had used an alien briefly in *Rio Grande*, but now he chose an extraterrestrial as the largest role, the person we most respect. He knew this throughout the ten-year gestation.

In September 1994 he discovered he must tell us from the outset. He drops hints early, even has the man say he's from outer space. Therefore, when he turns into an orange blob at the end, we shouldn't feel surprised. He also embeds this alien in a place, time, and situation where nobody knows for sure who anybody is; the characters distrust each other. With the potential for characters in disguise, characters spying, characters endangered and behaving oddly, Robin assuming a false identity shouldn't startle us.

Sherman sets *Some Sunny Day* near the British Embassy in Cairo, early July 1942, hours before the battle of El Alamein. Everyone not Egyptian wants to flee because they expect the city to fall. The British have pulled their ships out of Alexandria, which German forces bombed heavily on June 29.

Sherman employs linear plot construction and episodic development. The action unfolds on a single set; the playwright employs unity of place, time and action. As catalyst he uses a stranger, Robin.

Sherman drops his first hint immediately. Ostensibly a Maori journalist from New Zealand, Robin stares out the window at 3 A.M. while singing "Twinkle, twinkle, little star. How I wonder who you are" (7). Sherman has changed "what you are" to "who."

Officer Alec, Robin's landlord and lover, joins him and learns that the embassy is burning papers. If Robin filed a story, the censors would kill it. The play dramatizes such killing of the truth by lying about it, disguising it, omitting it, or otherwise interfering with learning it. Robin inquires whether Alec ever wonders "what's out there" in the sky, but his companion evinces no interest.

In scene 2 Horatio, Embassy propaganda officer, pays Hamid, a fortune-teller, to lie and say the British will win. Horatio admits spreading lies, and Robin admits he lied about being a reporter for the *Aukland Herald*. "I'm not really. I'm from outer space" (13).

Horatio tells Robin, "I could never have imagined that one day Cairo's most important belly dancer would love me so" (14). Robin finds Horatio's self-importance and inflated rhetoric so side-splittingly funny he makes the Brit promise you'll "never make me read your novels" (15). Horatio resents Robin failing to take him seriously. This great love of his life "composes a song for me as she dances," to which Robin responds, "You read her hips?" (15). When Robin objects Horatio is married, he responds, "You live in the past."

Having established Horatio's egomania, Sherman introduces a Russian duchess Horatio pronounces an impostor (16). She begs Horatio for an embassy pass to Palestine.

Alec suspects Horatio's belly dancer of spying, and possibly Robin as well. Horatio assures Alec Robin is "from another planet," to which Alec responds, "Too true" (21). Alec shoots and destroys a cup and then places the pistol in a drawer, so it remains onstage.

Alec's leave has ended and, as he prepares to depart for his desk job, Robin begs him not to volunteer to fight. This prompts the closeted officer to protest, "Don't call me Darling in daylight" (23). Robin reminds Alec he has paranormal powers. Robin knows Alec will die if he fights, but Alec chooses to request a transfer to the front. Robin mocks himself by singing the Carmen Miranda refrain "I, yi, yi, yi, yi, I like you very much," Alec joins in, they hold fruit on their heads à la Miranda and samba. Just then Horatio enters and announces, "Suddenly—for the first time—I know we will win the war" (24–25). Alec leaves with only a "bye, old chap." Having failed to save his lover's life, Robin tells Horatio and the Duchess, "He's going to die" (25).

In scene 3 a Dixieland band plays a dirge as Horatio's wife, Emily, manipulates a voodoo doll and chants the voodoo verse Sherman used in *Fat Tuesday*. She puts Tahia's hair in the doll's wig and a thread from Tahia's costume in its dress. Emily describes the humiliation Horatio has inflicted on her, which has led her to stick a pin in the doll's belly. She apologizes to Robin for giving "a mad scene" (32). When she exits, Robin tells the Duchess everybody suspects Emily of spying.

Robin knows things he can't have learned by ordinary means, such as German forces have killed Nigel in Greece and the Duchess isn't Russian, but Polish and Jewish. She admits this and tells him she is lesbian and that Nazis killed her lover. Robin uses his powers to see the future and assures her she and her beloved will be reunited in another life. This gives Robin a headache and causes clocks to spin and cutlery to bend.

Robin confesses his identity, but she has left so doesn't hear this or that her lover has returned as a cockroach. Hamid brings another "secret" document, half-burnt lyrics to Vera Lynn's song. "We'll meet again ... some sunny day" (44) suggests the reunion in reincarnated lives that Robin predicts.

In 4 Horatio dismisses the war as mere "background" to "my heart," and Emily responds, "Do you know what upsets me—what really upsets me—is that I typed phrases like that in your manuscripts time and time again and I never laughed" (46).

After smelling Tahia's oils and perfumes on her husband's hands, Emily laments, "All the perfumes of Arabia" (48). She regrets giving "another mad scene," especially "someone else's mad scene." We perceive this as simultaneously funny and painful.

He orders her to fetch a knife to open a package containing a pearl necklace he steals for Tahia. He rebukes her, "If you loved me, you'd be happy for me" (52), and he accuses her of making him suffer and treating him badly. Emily observes she became colorless "because you drained the reds and greens and yellows from me, which I allowed, because you absorbed them and took sustenance from them, and became, in your way—using my colours—a rainbow" (53). He plans to bring Tahia to the house so Emily can meet her and be happy for them. Emily begs for a pass to escape, but he refuses and, as she grows hysterical, he plunges the knife into her, then exclaims, "Look what you've made me do" (56). Robin enters in time to catch Horatio murdering Emily.

Sherman gives us the intermission to recover from the most compelling character's death. As authentic as Horatio's narcissism seems, especially to women, we haven't anticipated until he commits murder that he will.

If we believed Sherman would restore her to life, we appreciate, as Act 2 begins, this won't happen. Instead Sherman restores, seemingly from the dead, Alec, who has returned and plays Mozart while waiting for Hamid to locate Robin. We assumed he went to the front before; now he must go.

Alec begs Horatio to tell Robin British officers suspect Robin of spying. When Alec tries to send his regards to Emily, Horatio freaks. He gives the boy his word that he will warn Robin about the authorities' suspicions, yet he fails to do so when Robin appears from hiding the moment Alec departs. Robin couldn't bear saying goodbye to his doomed lover a second time.

Robin assures Horatio Hamid has hidden the body. Horatio insists Emily is better off dead, but Robin demands he fulfill his part of the bargain, a pass to Palestine for the Duchess. Horatio refuses, and Robin blackmails him.

Scene 2 finds the Duchess with her pass departing for the mosque to pray. Horatio directs his paranoia at Robin. The embassy has determined Robin invented his cover story. Horatio pulls the revolver out of its drawer and announces he will be a hero when he shoots a spy who killed Emily.

Desperate, Robin says he's from another planet. When Horatio mocks him, Robin asks,

> Why is it so difficult to believe? If you have no trouble at all accepting that a virgin can give birth, and that the father was an unseen spirit, and that the child of this bizarre union is able eventually to walk on water, cure lepers and the lame, restore a blind man's sight, turn water into wine, and most impressively feed thousands of people with only a few loaves of bread, not to mention resurrecting himself after he has been killed, why can't you believe that I'm a two foot orange blob? [83–84]

Robin tries again. Horatio accepts electricity, the telephone, radio, and photographs without being able to explain them. Why not life on other planets? Horatio remains determined to murder Robin, who must therefore give himself another headache. As Horatio pulls the trigger, Robin's telekinesis bends and melts the pistol and freezes his assassin.

In scene 3, Robin instructs Hamid to return Emily's body and put the knife in Horatio's hand. He should wake up about the time the police arrive.

If they execute him, he will mature in his next incarnation "in an age when selfishness is truly appreciated" (91).

In 4, Robin relishes life à la Emily's ghost in *Our Town*. She loves clocks ticking and her butternut tree. He delights in lemons, Alec's arms, Carmen Miranda, jasmine, the sea, traffic, Mozart, and the moon over Cairo (92). In 5 Robin in his natural form flies out the window.

The Duchess returns for her luggage and mashes a cockroach, her reincarnated lover. She leaves to save her life again. Of six characters, two have died, and four have, what else, survived? For Sherman, that constitutes a happy ending.

Sherman constructs the play to engender suspense we might associate with a thriller or spy caper. He employs foreshadowing, including Robin and Hamid's predictions. The characters suspect each other of spying. He drops clues about Robin's origins. He provides partial information by writing dialogue in short interrupted spurts, thus divulging only parts of answers to questions.

The characters sometimes lie, and often we can't tell the difference between truth and falsehood. We wonder about the real identities of Robin and the Duchess, wonder if the Brits will betray their country, wonder when Rommel will attack, whether he will take Cairo, and whether he will kill or capture our characters. (Sherman can count here on most people not knowing this bit of history.) Will Alec go to the desert? What will happen to Emily? Will Horatio be caught? Will Horatio kill Robin and frame him for Emily's murder? Will the Duchess get her pass? Sherman keeps us guessing.

Although a few reviews mention *Casablanca* (probably because the Duchess and Emily want a pass to escape), only Herbert mentions the *Alexandria Quartet*. Durrell's Alexandria becomes Cairo, and, as in *Madhouse*, Sherman gives us a superficial level of truth and then invites us to penetrate it. Sometimes we think we know, but later learn we erred.

Beyond the war play, the spy saga, the thriller, the sci-fi or fantasy and the deceit, lurk truths about humanity. Mischievous Sherman encases his wisdom in magic, but beneath the voodoo, fortune telling, disruption of time and space, spoon-and-pistol bending, clocks spinning, and freezing a living body, he dramatizes how people treat others. We laugh, but we also emerge from the experience shaken.

Their emotions control these characters. Fear of death rules the Duchess. Romantic illusions about military gallantry propel Alec. Jealousy drives Emily in and out of madness. Greed grips Hamid. Horatio suffers from hubris and narcissism, loses his way because of lust, and becomes a sociopath who destroys the good life he had. His encounter with human emotions also motivates Robin, who has never had such feelings before, but it leads him to a selfless action. Can only aliens act humanely?

Only Robin grows. Like Max and Rachel, Robin has found love and compassion. He will forget his holiday when he returns to his planet, but surely his soul has benefited from saving the Duchess and singing at the Pyramids.

Sherman dramatizes his usual twin themes: aliens try to survive.

Threats to survival emanate from several sources. The characters expect the Nazis to kill or imprison them. In Greece they have killed Nigel. They killed Anna before; in her new incarnation she dies again. The Duchess, a Jew, must flee or perish. Alec will die at the front. Horatio kills Emily and might face execution. He tries to kill Robin, who fails to keep Alec alive but saves the Duchess and attempts to give Horatio a chance. Hamid, an Egyptian, not an outsider, faces no dangers.

Sherman dramatizes his outsider theme clearly. At least three of the six characters we can identify as gay. Sherman hasn't written a gay problem play. Yet he foregrounds gay characters, even two gay couples if we count Anna, a cockroach—but in a larger-than-usual role for the species.

Emily and Horatio represent heterosexuality. Their fate suggests we shouldn't fear "the other"; we should fear our partners or "normal" straight folks. The one straight, white, Christian male proves a loathsome, lying lecher.

The Christian woman suffers psychological abuse. Women experience a shock of recognition at Horatio's behavior.

Five characters are foreigners, "exiles" in Cairo. An extraterrestrial qualifies as Sherman's most "other" protagonist. Because we see events through his eyes, we have an alien's perspective. We become alien voyeurs.

Irony abounds. The British burn secret documents so ineffectively anybody can read them, and they pay Hamid to tell a lie that's the truth. Robin admits his identity, but nobody believes him. The Duchess suffers survivor guilt about her lover and yet kills her again. Horatio denies wanting to kill Emily yet does so. Horatio calls Robin's blackmail immoral. The only non-human acts humanely.

Like *Cracks*, *Some Sunny Day* explores narcissism in a life-threatening setting and ends so as to irritate spectators if they weren't laughing so hard. Yet this play contains less farce and more dark comedy and black comedy than *Cracks*. It matches *When She Danced* for wit and *Madhouse* for satire. Shaw, late in his career, might have written it. It has that quality of imagination and bite.

Callow identifies this as his favorite Sherman play: "I think Martin threw caution to the winds. The goat leapt onto the top of the mountain and stood on its hind legs."

Director Roger Michell selected the play because it contains an orange blob. "The ending is an audacious, theatrical coup. It also contains brilliantly observed writing. The scene between Horatio and his wife is savage, real and human."

Sherman asked for Rupert Everett as Robin. Corin Redgrave took the more difficult role of Horatio. The two female roles attracted talented women who mightn't have accepted such small parts: Sara Kestelman consented to play the Duchess and played her wonderfully, and Cheryl Campbell took Emily and gave a tour-de-force performance so superb nobody who saw it will forget. David Bark-Jones and Eddy Lamar played, respectively, Alec and Hamid.

Rehearsals included a visit by psychic Uri Geller, who spoke about what bending spoons and so on feels like. Sherman had read Geller's autobiography, in which he details the relationship between his paranormal abilities and his contact with aliens. He believes he channels powers of extraterrestrials trying to prevent humanity from destroying itself. This book might have suggested Robin could possess the kinds of abilities Geller says he taps into.

Corin Redgrave describes Sherman's presence at rehearsals as very helpful, offering pertinent advice, and notes he watches with a "director's eye." Redgrave adored his role, an "extraordinarily well-written character I hope will last on stage or in dramatic literature for generations. Horatio is one of those towering figures." He exclaims only a writer of "protean talent" can create such a range of characters. "It's a testimony to his genius. *Some Sunny Day* is brilliant. It made me sing with happiness."

Sherman knew he'd written another challenging play: "It starts out on the surface as my most conventional, but becomes my least conventional. I assumed some people would want to cart me off to the loony bin."

Nevertheless, in a brilliant production with superlative cast and director, the play proved a tremendous success, receiving some of Sherman's best reviews, and any remaining tickets sold out.

Five critics trashed *Some Sunny Day*. Obviously angered at the orange blob at the end, they seem not to have noticed the orange blob in the opening. Had they observed it where we then notice Robin, perhaps they mightn't have felt embarrassed or angry.

Peter gets his facts wrong. He believes Alec must go to the front, thinks the action occurs in Horatio's home, and misquotes. He doesn't know who the Duchess is. He finds Robin "coldly cruel" toward Alec. He asks, "If it's meant to be a comedy, where's the humour?" (10*14).

Nobody bludgeons it as much. Nathan writes, "Sherman is determined to be seriously weird and tries a little too hard" (38). Hirschhorn rejects it as an "absurd mishmash" and judges Sherman "fails. Period" (42; 59). Morley praises the acting but doesn't detail what he dislikes.

Herbert astutely mentions the *Alexandria Quartet*, praises Dudley's set, then objects Sherman does "nothing" with characters "worthy of Durrell" (449–450). He objects to the cast's abandonment "by an author who can't be bothered to make a play out of their efforts, copping out instead with idiot fantasy."

Eleven critics praise *Some Sunny Day*, except for its ending. Rarely do mixed reviews convey such agreement about what they value and what they deride. Nightingale applauds it as "diverting" and the cast as "fine" (17). He asks, "Is it wise to give a play so eloquent about human unpredictability a twist that lifts it out of the realm of the human?" Hanks terms it "acutely and tenderly perceptive about people's emotions, theatrically astute, and at times very funny" (Critics, 15). He finds "the strategy is bold, the transfiguration of what has gone before literally jaw-dropping." Yet he feels, "In trying to turn the audience's preconceptions on their head, he's ended up capsizing the drama."

Trevelyan calls the play "masterly" yet concludes the "dazzling, but downright bizarre ending" makes it a "memorable disappointment" (17). Smurthwaite opines, "Sherman is funny enough and perceptive enough and original enough to manage very nicely without a lot of mumbo-jumbo" (24). Poole objects to the end, even while praising "the bleak anatomization of Horatio and Emily's childless marriage" as the "truest thing in this play" and admiring the production (19).

Others who laud the mounting and some of the play while rejecting the Geller elements include Christopher, de Jongh, Sierz, Cash, Hughes, and M[urray].

Redgrave asks those troubled by fantasy why they take *A Midsummer Night's Dream* seriously, but not *Some Sunny Day*, because "it also looks at human beings from the viewpoint of one not human. It's a brilliant premise."

Fifteen critics praise the play; many pile on superlatives. The most subdued, Kellaway, expresses some reservations but also lavishes much praise and concludes, "It is fun and, in its demented way, original" (11). Tinker also extols its originality. Of the ending, he explains, "We roar with delight at the cheek of it all, and—this, I swear—we actually do want Mr. Everett to survive his horrible experience as a visiting alien" (52). Billington discerns a comedy concerning "the possibility of tapping into one's real feelings while being an outsider in a foreign land." He compares this play and *Bent*, explaining, "Here, too, Sherman suggests that it is only in moments of extremity that people shed their protective exteriors and embrace their true identity." Paton calls it "provocative" and recommends it as entertaining (7).

The others write raves.

Spencer calls it "one of the most entertaining and unexpected plays of the year" (14). "It is one of those rare dramas when you genuinely long to know what is going to happen next." He praises its combination of "anguished, touching emotion, with a sense of the ridiculous." The ending Spencer admires as not only "delightful in its utter unexpectedness, but curiously haunting too, revealing a real generosity of spirit and a touching affirmation of what it means to be fully human." Spencer commends "a play that deserves that overworked adjective astonishing."

Woddis appreciates Sherman as master of "the art of the eccentric" and "possessor of one of the quirkiest views of the English to have surfaced in some time" (52–53). She notes, "The whole play rebuffs the idea of English stoicism on the one hand, and gay love as outside the norm on the other."

Benedict praises Sherman's "simultaneously affecting, funny and illuminating" play (sec. 2, 26). He appreciates the remarkable roles: "Actors will tell you that meaty characterization is woefully rare, but it's one of Sherman's trademarks that signal the genuinely theatrical nature of his plays." He concludes, "The characters all dream of leaving but by the unexpected end of this impressive play, it is the audience who have traveled furthest."

Among others who approve, count Gross; Selavie; Barnsley, who calls it a "brilliantly witty new play" (16); and Thaxter, who says it "seems certain to transfer" (12). Harley terms it "hilarious satire" and "superb parody," notes "hysterical laughter," and calls the comedy "almost genius" (17). Rieden finds "part of the charm comes from Sherman's sharp balance between comedy and pathos" and "this is a compelling and atmospheric piece which stays with you long after the curtain falls" ([6]). Wilson praises the play as "full of fun and intrigue" and, like many others, judges this Everett's best performance ever (28).

Wolf enthuses, "The principal purveyor of the evening's magic is the playwright himself" (100–101). He calls the play "a lovely piece of writing that manages to be the most moving when also at its weirdest." He believes "Sherman closes the play with a potentially preposterous surprise that, in retrospect, seems both sensible and inevitable." He thanks Sherman for restoring "to the theater a sense of wonder."

Some Sunny Day broke Hampstead advance sales records and set attendance records, while hundreds of unsuccessful ticket-seekers begged for a seat. The excitement made reaching the box office by telephone nearly impossible. No playwright could have asked for more.

Except Fox decided not to transfer it.

This will go down as one of the great mysteries of London theatre history. A mega-hit closed at the end of its Hampstead run. Nobody has presented the play since.

The West End season had done poor business, so Fox got cold feet. Plus Everett, who had all along said he couldn't move to the West End because of a film commitment, meant that.

Fox and Everett were close enough that Everett had joined him in a prank that landed Fox in prison for a night. Readers of Everett's autobiography can learn about that and read his claim—which others dispute—that he didn't land the role in *My Best Friend's Wedding* until after he had rehearsed the play. Possibly Fox counted on the cinema role going to somebody else or Everett finding the part and the pay insufficient. Fear of losing a fortune prevented Fox from making one. This constituted a bad judgment call for him, a catastrophe for the play.

Asked why he didn't move *Some Sunny Day*, Fox concedes, "I was sort of involved in helping to put it together. Then I decided it didn't have huge commercial potential. Certainly without Rupert it didn't. And I wasn't very popular with anyone involved. Nor was Rupert. It looked as if we had ganged up to make it not happen. My instinct was to protect the play rather than expose it." As ensuing years have proven, this protected the play into oblivion. But Fox continues, "I thought it was kind of great, but I didn't think it would work commercially."

What about the reviews and sold-out performances? "It was very popular and got great reviews, but it wouldn't have appealed to a broad public without Rupert. He had a lot to do with selling the tickets at Hampstead. He was a big name, even then. Without him there was no other big name."

Not Corin Redgrave? "No other producer came running into the breach saying, 'I'll take it. I'll move it.' I know everyone was pissed off at me, but you can't produce to be popular."

London producers hadn't come to see the show because they knew Fox would move it, and tickets had sold out. Then Fox abandoning the play put a stigma on it for other producers. In order to keep the stellar cast—minus Everett—somebody had to move the show quickly.

Michell explains, "After the first preview, Fox said how much he enjoyed it. After another preview, he thought it even better. At the opening, he said, 'Well, let's start talking about theatres if the reviews are decent.' The reviews were great, so we traipsed off to Robert's office and talked about theatres. Three days later, he said he wasn't going to transfer it. If he had concluded that a few days before, another producer might have stepped in. The timing was the kiss of death."

Michell and Fox knew all along that Everett couldn't transfer. Michell believes that wasn't an issue. They had talked about his replacement and didn't find that a problem. Fox lost his nerve; Michell doesn't understand why.

Topper agrees somebody could have taken over Robin: "We were exploring who when Robert pulled the plug. I don't think of Rupert as an actor. It would have been interesting to see a trained actor play the role."

Topper disagrees with Fox's belief Everett's presence accounted for the huge advance sale.

> Hampstead consistently has been patronized by the Jewish community of north London, and when they realized Martin had another play here, they reclaimed him. That was one of the reasons tickets sold so rapidly. The combination of Corin, Cheryl, and Rupert was also heady for anyone who wanted to get the best value theatre outside the West End. The poster was attractively playful, and the setting was romantic and intriguing. For those in the know, having Roger Michell direct and Bill Dudley design was seductive. And the title is quite wonderful. It delighted people. It was a play everybody wanted to see. It was a huge hit in a tremendous production. There wasn't a play in town that had as high production values. But London has no off–West End. If we had one, it would have had a further life. I'm perplexed at the way Robert went about disentangling himself. But my theory is that Robert always had an arms-length approach to it.

Fear of orange blobs?

"Yes. He couldn't, because of his deep respect and love for Martin, bring himself to say from the outset, 'I'm not sure I want to produce this. I'm not sure I want to take this into the West End.'" Topper believes some of Fox's friends didn't care for it and their views

> weighed heavily on him. My instinct is, he felt more ambivalent about it than he let on, and he tried to protect his friendship with Martin. I'm sure he thought he was being kind, but he was cruel. It would have risked everybody's relationships less if he had been more straightforward earlier. If a producer as respected as Robert says yes and then no, everyone else is jolly wary, so it became damaged goods. In 1996, from mid–February onwards, the bottom fell out of theatre. Suddenly, from ticket sales in the West End having been erratic but always seeming to recover, it seemed there was a downward plunge occurring we'd never recover from. 1996 was the year London moved closer to New York in its perception of entertainment in West End theatre.

Redgrave explains he felt flabbergasted when *Some Sunny Day* didn't move because he didn't see how it could not succeed: "So I worked to get it on. Thelma Holt was happy to come in with another manager."

Oh? Fox said no other manager would touch it.

"She didn't have the means to do it alone, but she would have come in on a 50/50 basis. She suggested that to Fox. But he didn't want to do that either."

Another motive for Fox's decision has surfaced. Everett has published a memoir in which he trashes pretty much everybody he has ever known, burning behind him his career bridges. Indeed Denby, in his review of *Shrek III*, says of him, "Rupert Everett, so snide that he has become uncastable as anything but a voice" (86).

Red Carpets and Other Banana Skins gives an error-filled, mean-spirited description of Sherman's play. Does he really think his character was green, not orange? His mockery might mean he was making wisecracks to Fox while in the play. This private badmouthing might have, indeed should have, alarmed Fox and set him worrying that Everett would publicly ridicule it. That would explain Fox's change of mind.

Sherman and Fox remain friends, and Fox has produced another Sherman work.

On May 18, Sherman flew to Greece. He had opened a play and prepared for a transfer that never occurred. He had shot *Alive and Kicking*, prepared for rehearsals of his *Bent* film to begin in ten days, and prepared to write, after the second movie finished shooting, a second version of his dybbuk film for Nick Hytner. He had worked himself into a state he describes as "dimensions beyond exhausted; sort of subtextually tired." He should have rested longer, but he spent the week he could manage in Mykonos.

In June, Uri Geller announced he had "used the power of positive thinking" to prompt the critics to write favorable reviews (Reynolds). To whatever extent any critics had disliked the play, they based their complaints on its magical and extraterrestrial aspects. Ironically, to think Geller influenced a critic one would have to believe in exactly such possibilities.

Geller's revelation, like the play's failure to transfer, saddened Sherman, because he loved the production: "It was extraordinary. The cast was uniformly brilliant and impeccably directed, in a way that honored every moment and never called attention to itself. The set was magnificent. I couldn't possibly have been happier. It got wonderful reviews. If it hadn't been successful, if it had been badly done or badly reviewed, if nobody had come, I wouldn't feel this way. It would have succeeded in the West End, because there was nothing else to see that summer."

This period marked the height of the alien bonanza as the 50th anniversary approached of 1947's purported UFO crash near Roswell, New Mexico. Filmmakers rushed to make outer-space epics. In 1996, as the media reported evidence of life on Mars, *Star Trek: First Contact*, *The Alien Agenda: Out of Darkness*, and *Alien Chaser* joined *Independence Day*. The following year studios released *Men in Black*; *Contact*; *The Alien Agenda: Endangered Species*; *The Alien Agenda: Under the Skin*; *Alien: Resurrection*; *Starlight*; *Starship Troopers*. The frenzy extended to fashion. As *Some Sunny Day* wasn't transferring, UFO-inspired clothing and accessories sold briskly. Had Fox not suffered last-minute jitters, he could have capitalized on this alien craze.

Sherman had no leisure to mope. On top of the two films he had in production, he simultaneously wrote two films.

Ann Scott and George Weiss in summer 1994 had asked Sherman to turn Israeli David Grossman's Holocaust novel, *See Under: Love*, into a film Mike Newell would direct.

"It's a brave book," the dramatist enthuses. "The style and invention take your breath away. I could see it would be impossible to make into a film, so of course I wanted to do it."

It presented Sherman with "irresistible" challenges. Boasting multiple narrative personas, periods, and settings, it disregards chronology and sometimes logic and science. Briefly the ocean serves as narrator. The novel contains a story within a story within a story. The narrator of one plot sometimes chats with the narrator of another or stands aside and watches another story unfold. It mixes levels of reality in one novel rather than a quartet. Given his success at representing several viewpoints in *The Summer House*, Sherman must have seemed the perfect choice. Besides, *See Under: Love* concerns "the other" and survivors.

Sherman restructured it and focused on fewer characters. Originally he tried to include an unworkable amount, including all the magic-realist material. Eventually he decided, "I either must use all the magic or none of it." He chose none, instead throwing the concentration camp scenes into greater prominence.

A character furiously protests, "We can't have another planet in this story"—perhaps an inside joke mocking reviewers furious because Robin hails from outer space. He also sneaks in a reference to his father's shtetl, Yultishka.

While simultaneously writing and going through the production process of two plays and three other films, Sherman wrote four drafts for Newell and one more for Christopher Hampton, slated to direct beginning in 1997, after Newell left. These drafts overlapped completing *Some Sunny Day*, *Alive and Kicking*, the *Bent* film, *The Dybbuk* film, and *Rose*. As late as 2000, Sherman still anticipated funding to film *See Under: Love*. The subject, however, lacked commercial appeal to attract investors.

During summer 1996, wedged between filming *Bent* and vacationing on Mykonos, Sherman had dinner with Wendy Wasserstein at Veronica's and they tied the knot—metaphorically. She had seen her niece's Orthodox ceremony in which the bride walked around her husband seven times. Wasserstein walked around Sherman seven times. He took her hand and said, "It's official."

During winter 1996 Sherman had begun writing *The Dybbuk*, a film suggested by Shloyme (Solomon) An-ski's Yiddish play. Hytner would direct for the Samuel Goldwyn Company. Sherman wrote his second draft in autumn 1996, after *Bent* wrapped. He wrote three subsequent drafts and finished his fifth only 18 months after his first. During summer 1997, he learned Samuel Goldwyn, Jr., hadn't liked his last version. "I never heard from him, but he

Sherman and Wendy Wasserstein at a London gallery, probably summer 1996 (courtesy Martin Sherman).

fired me, I'm told. Several weeks later, his own company fired him." Although Goldwyn himself owned the script, he instead produced the lighter-weight *Welcome to Woop Woop* and *Tinseltown*.

Sherman takes from An-ski a dybbuk possessing a bride. The old Yiddish play and Sherman's script differ in nearly all respects, but share possession by a young man who loves her but dies when her father betroths her to another; the dybbuk's conviction he and the bride are destined soul mates; and an exorcism.

Hytner and Goldwyn asked Sherman to reset the action to turn-of-the-century America, but instead he chose Atlantic City during summer 1953. He had spent summers there during the '50s because his grandmother's sister owned the Pierrepont Hotel and his grandmother worked there. He selected this time and place to change Channon to a Holocaust survivor and to threaten the wealthier characters with McCarthy-era inquisitions, often directed at Jews.

Leah's father, Sender, owns a hotel Sherman names the Majestic. The film occurs there, along and under the boardwalk, in the ocean, and on the Ferris wheel. Sherman faithfully reproduces the marginalizing of women during this era, never letting us forget Leah's status as "other."

Sherman supplies two additional "others": a black maid and Channon. Both these foreign-born characters serve as a second layer of "other" among the Jewish characters who have money, U.S. citizenship, and respect. Channon describes his father stuffing him up a chimney in Yultishka when the Nazis came. Everyone else in his village perished, burned alive while locked in the schoolhouse. Sherman had learned about this fate of his father's shtetl (as well as its correct name) from an actor in the Moscow Jewish Theatre. He uses the story again in *Rose*.

Channon survived the Holocaust only to die of love for Leah. In this Jewish *Romeo and Juliet*, his spirit lives on in her.

Sherman revised this and then, in mid-October, went to East Hampton for the film festival, where *Alive and Kicking* won Audience Favorite. Still busy redrafting two films and on *Bent* post-production, Sherman spoke for International Artists Against Racism at Westminster Central Hall on December 5, 1996. He remained in London through this hectic year's end.

14. Celluloid (1994–1997)

Following *The Summer House*'s success, Martin Pope asked Sherman to write for the BBC a 60-minute teleplay for a series of AIDS films. John Schlesinger would direct.

Sherman had tried to write an AIDS play for years. "I even went away to Paris for a month to try to write about it," he explains.

Then Sherman recognized he shouldn't take protagonist Tonio to the end of his life. He could write a life-affirming script about a man who refuses to waste his remaining days. "I wrote the first draft in Switzerland, in Jeanne Moreau's house. I couldn't have done that without her. All the drafts afterwards were extensions of it."

The BBC asked Sherman to deliver this teleplay by October 16, 1993. The contract called it *Movement*, the title Sherman had used for his 1979 Cuban script. Its series had been canceled, and the second *Movement* met the same fate because higher-ups at the BBC found it distasteful and rejected it, even though Sherman had just been nominated for a BAFTA. Pope then took it to Aukin at Channel 4. He commissioned a full-length version called *Indian Summer*.

Schlesinger asked for changes. Sherman made these, and the director loved it. "He couldn't have been sweeter," says Sherman. "But he was offered a huge Hollywood film for lots of money. Rather than do this one which he loved, he did that one which he liked."

Aukin's decision to commission it as a feature for Channel 4 Films and release it to theatres gave Sherman his first original film—by that time retitled *Alive and Kicking*—to make it into cinemas. Another benefit derived from signing Nancy Meckler to direct. Having erred by refusing to use her to mount *Messiah*, Sherman eagerly accepted her for this project.

The script Sherman completed by August 1994 takes a radical approach to writing about AIDS. At that time, the disease carried an automatic death sentence, yet Sherman writes about living with AIDS, not dying from it. Before the film's release, however, history caught up with this perspective in the life-prolonging combination therapies. To clarify the action occurs before the advent of these protease inhibitor cocktails, filmmakers added a caption reading "London 1995."

Meckler didn't know Sherman when she received the offer. She had seen him in the Hampstead Theatre foyer, they had said hello, but they had never conversed.

> A few things I wasn't entirely happy with. So we agreed Martin and I would work together for three afternoons to see whether we could get on. I wasn't sure how amenable he would be to revisions, but he was very open to what I was talking about. A lot of the things I wanted to lose were the first director's ideas, not his vision, so he was happy to cut them. Sometimes we would discover the things I wanted to add were in a former draft. He would get it out and say, "Look, I did write a scene like that. We could put it back." After three days, we said yes, we can proceed.

Meckler felt "it was well written, beautifully constructed and told. I loved the humor. Also, the world of dance I have always adored. And I liked directing something very relevant."

Sherman, Meckler, and Pope knew casting would pose problems because the film contains so much dance. Every dancer had to act as well, and in most roles actors must dance. The film's success, above all, would depend on finding the perfect Tonio.

Meckler describes the casting process as

> difficult. At first we saw dancers or actors who were ex-dancers, but none of them were funny enough for Tonio. I had always thought an actor could play the role because modern dancers try not to look like dancers and often strive to make their movement look natural. I thought an actor could do that as long as he moved well. Jason Flemyng came in quite late. Martin Pope thought of him because Jason had done a small part for him several years before, and he turned out to be *the one*.

They knew they must cast as the therapist somebody who could avoid looking obviously handsome. Aukin urged them to see Sher because Aukin had seen something Sher had done recently in which he had been quite natural. Meckler feared Sher's tendency to give a big performance. "But we sent him the script," Meckler reports, "and he just adored it."

Sher recalls "reading the script in one go and being terribly moved by it. I told Martin, 'Whatever happens'—because I wasn't offered it, only asked whether I was interested—'I think it's your best work since *Bent* and the most heartfelt since then.' He wrote this directly from his heart."

Sher believes in both *Bent* and *Alive and Kicking* Sherman "takes on a very big, grisly topic and fills it with life and love and light. They're both life-enhancing works." He also admires the film's language. "Martin is an elegant writer. His dialogue is musical, short sentences beautifully phrased. And yet the spirit of his writing is very real, doesn't suggest artifice." In short, Sher yearned to play Jack. "They said, 'Nobody else is up for it, but we have to know the chemistry works.' So they asked me to read with Jason. Luckily I vaguely knew Jason from the RSC. We were there at the same time." As they read together, they immediately had what Luna calls "rapport."

Meckler, Pope, Sherman, and the casting director selected Dorothy Tutin as Luna (her last feature-film role), Anthony Higgins as Ramon, Bill Nighy as Tristan, Philip Voss as Duncan, Diane Parish as Millie, Aiden Waters as Vincent, and Linda Bassett as Tonio's doctor.

To choreograph, Meckler chose Liz Ranken, who was "brilliant at creating movement from the performers' own choices. She got them moving and chose from what they were doing. She would say, 'Oh, I love that. Can you do that bigger?' If she could see somebody was good at something, she used that."

Pope approved Rankin and also Peter Salem as composer, even though he hadn't done a feature film. Like Ranken, he had worked with the RSC and had done theatre with Meckler.

Somewhere between agreement on a shooting script and completion of pre-production, Pope confessed he couldn't raise the money. Channel 4 only backs a film 50 percent, and no other backers had signed on.

Sherman explains,

> I would have been crushed if it hadn't been filmed because it's an original, and I can't turn it into a play. The money wasn't going to materialize, so I went to Aukin and said, "We can't let it die." He asked, "Can you and Nancy and Pope cut the budget in half? If you film it in 16 millimeter, that will reduce the cost, and you can blow it up. And Channel 4 will break all our rules and finance the whole thing."

Asked about breaking rules, Aukin expresses admiration for Sherman's screenwriting skill: "He shows he is a subtle and adroit storyteller, with a wonderful economy, never using a word where a picture will do." Although they keep their careers quite separate, we shouldn't forget Aukin's marriage to Meckler. Yet Aukin commissioned this project long before Meckler became involved, so we can assume he would have continued to back it no matter who helmed it.

Once assured of financing, Meckler and company had the green light to rehearse—essential because of how Ranken worked with her performers to create the dance. Two weeks' rehearsals also developed bonding. They behave on-screen like a cohesive company because they knew each other better than they would have from showing up and immediately going on-camera.

Sher explains, "Rehearsals allowed us to work on our scenes in a way I haven't on other films. That was very productive, particularly charting Tonio and Jack's relationship, which would be filming out of sequence, yet must have a subtle development." Sher also believes rehearsals enabled them to develop a sense of spontaneity. "We could live through the dialogue rather than just presenting it. Without rehearsals, one might have learnt it on one's own the night before. Instead we grew, so the scenes came alive. And Martin was constantly helpful."

They had never before worked together, but Sher found Sherman supportive and as funny as usual: "In shooting, cameras film you and then move around to film me. Martin carries his bag with his thermos of herbal tea and camps where he faces the action, and then they have to change over. During one of those shifts, he said, 'Oh, filming is so Jewish; you have to keep packing and moving.' It's the gay—Jewish combination of viewing the world from an outsider's perspective."

They had hoped to start shooting in September, but found themselves still in pre-production, so they began on October 23 in Greece, shot for two days, then filmed in London for six weeks.

Sher "treasured that Martin was getting up at five and was there every moment while we filmed. I wouldn't have wanted most writers present all the time, but one does with him, and that's not just because he's a friend. His spirit contributes." When pressed for details, Sher adds, "Well, wisdom. There aren't many wise people about. Martin has warmth and humor, but others offer that. Wisdom is rare, and I prize his, and huge grace. His presence really helped."

Meckler agrees: "Close involvement by a writer during filming is unusual. But he was such an ally! He never insisted I focus on him but was there if I wanted somebody to bounce things off. He was there when needed, not to protect his material. He has no ego problems, and, like me, he loves to collaborate." She valued his advice, but also the ways he enhanced her confidence. "He makes people feel he trusts them completely. When I would say, 'What do you think? Should we play it like this or that?' instead of saying what he thought he would ask, 'What's your instinct?' which was a perfect answer."

Post-production occurred during winter and spring 1996. Meckler devoted special attention to the final dance, "Indian Summer." She had found it exciting in the rehearsal studio, but when she and the editor put it together, she felt it didn't work as well as she had hoped. "So we re-edited, chopped it up, made it more impressionistic. Then we slowed down some of it. It's not slow-motion because we didn't shoot with a slow-motion camera. We step-printed some of it, printing each frame twice, so it looks like slow motion. You don't get the distortion you do with a slow-motion camera." Most people who film dance try to record the choreography, so they stay at a distance. "But we needed to capture the characters' emotional experiences, so we filmed this dance as close up as possible." By extensive editing, Meckler and the editor captured the excitement she sought.

After seeing the completed edit, Sherman felt "as proud of that film as any work I've done."

In selecting his characters and setting, Sherman followed the Creative Writing 101 maxim "Write about what you know." Selecting a dancer as his protagonist and a dance company as his milieu made sense. AIDS was decimating the dance world, plus Sherman has known many dancers. He understands them thanks to strong bonds with several, among them ballerina Livingston and Broadway dancer Alan Peterson, who died of AIDS.

He could render visually the disease's impact on a dancer's body, craft, and life. Dancers' necessarily brief careers parallel the brief life expectancies the AIDS-afflicted then could expect. He had written about dancers in *Rio Grande*, *Bent*, and *When She Danced*. Indeed Luna's query, "Why must he dance with his feet?" might remind us of Isadora's rehearsal. Sherman received inspiration from a U.S. dance troupe which carried an ill dancer during a performance.

Sherman chose a therapist as the dancer's partner and drew upon his friendship with therapist Alan Pope. When Sherman began writing, Pope worked for "a voluntary agency rather like Jack does. He used to hear me complain. You work with the dying at a cost. It was hard for the doctors too. No matter how much you did, all your clients and patients died. Martin was aware of that from conversations and research. He spoke with doctors at Chelsea Westminster, which was seeing 25 percent of all Britain's AIDS cases. He gives an accurate picture."

The inspiration for Luna, the dance company's forgetful, sometimes demented founder, came from Sherman's observations of agent Ramsay, who had slowly succumbed to Alzheimer's as many of Sherman's friends sickened and died of AIDS. Seeing the two illnesses simultaneously ravaging those he loved gave him insights into contrasting personal tragedies, and this led to his portrait of Luna and also her epiphany, shared with Tonio: "You mustn't be afraid, dear ... of not growing old." Sherman reports Peggy continued to offer such sage counsel even as she deteriorated. "Luna isn't exactly Peggy, but she's more than suggested by her. I've used things she said."

The film reflects Sherman's experience of visiting dying friends and grieving their deaths, from AIDS but also cancer. He could see the positive ways his friends used their last months and weeks and days. He feels all his work combines optimism and pessimism, but to this one he brought more sense of affirmation, despite knowing one day Tonio will die. Sherman gives him an indomitable spirit.

During 1995, he juggled several other projects. He prepared for the *Some Sunny Day* run, wrote *See Under: Love*, planned to film *Bent*, and planned *The Dybbuk*. Yet he continued to visit dying friends, among them Alan Pope's partner, Peter. Pope reports Sherman visited their flat every day, taking buses across London. "Lots of people with less to do would have made excuses for fewer visits," Pope believes. "Our friends who owned cars came less often." Multiply that times all ill friends Sherman visited during the '80s and first half of the '90s, and we must wonder how he wrote. He felt, strongly, the sense of community his film dramatizes. He also observed how an occasional partner abandoned a dying lover when it got "tough," as Jack notes he might.

Shortly before, Sherman had survived a passionate relationship, which provided extra authenticity.

We mustn't forget among Sherman's sources Greece—its inspirational light, its antiquities, even its disappearance as a civilization, leaving behind its temples, sculpture, and mosaics, as well as the rocks that have endured beyond mere mortals. Sherman sets the pair's most important conversation outside the Temple of Aphaia, where "the two characters tell each other extraordinary truths." He selected the perfect setting to inspire such candor as Jack's "Actually, *you* don't love me. More than I don't love *you*. If you were healthy, would you look twice at me? Don't answer. I know the answer."

Sherman constructs his screenplay in short cinematic scenes, moving among Tonio's personal and professional lives and Jack's workplace and recreation. The disease and tempestuous relationship build suspense. Will Tonio's good health last? Will Jack and Tonio sustain their affair? Will Tonio perform in "Indian Summer"? Will Tonio survive his hospitalization? Sherman gives us a shot of friends near his hospital bed and in the next footage shows us the bed empty and attendants stripping off his sheets. Did he die? Sherman keeps us wondering until we see Tonio.

The action dramatizes Sherman's dual themes, "the other" and survival. Nearly all the characters qualify as outsiders. Even the pas de deux concerns a gay couple who parallel Tonio and Jack.

Sherman offers his most clearly gay perspective subsequent to *Bent* in this romance circumscribed by illness and arrogance. He doesn't offer viewers any straight perspective. Instead he provides us an entrée to AIDS's impact on the gay community straight viewers might previously have lacked. As the film entertains and amuses, it also engenders compassion.

The original title, *Indian Summer*, suggests sudden but transient warmth and vitality, which winter will replace, but *Alive and Kicking* implies sustained survival and the life force which animates Tonio. The film addresses other survival issues: Jack's precarious emotional survival or mental health, given the anguish which surrounds him; the similar situation of other therapists and doctors who attempt to sustain AIDS clients or patients; Ramon's death; the Luna Ballet's demise; the survival of the odd-couple relationship; and Luna's deteriorating mind. Her disease will eradicate all her memories and abilities. Lurking in this optimistic film's shadows, our mortality awaits us. We must seize the day and live each moment fully.

The screenplay offers vivid characterizations of the lovers—complex, imperfect, yet admirable and charming. Critics tend to stress Tonio's narcissism, yet he doesn't rival Horatio, Onassis or even Max. Self-absorbed, yes, but he also proves supportive to Ramon, Millie, and Jack. Like Max, he grows.

Tonio has his choice of partners. The fact he can respond to Jack's wooing, appreciate his good qualities and put up with the bad, however, shows his growth beyond egocentricity and impatience. He frequently laughs at himself.

Initially, we see Tonio injure himself. He complains to nobody. When Millie notices, Tonio understates his pain. He performs through it, joy on his face. Off-stage for a moment, he mutters the mantra "Get through it. Get through it." Sherman has quickly established his guts and dedication to his craft. He lives to dance. He won't let pain stop him.

Meckler says Sherman "has that remarkable gift of writing something serious underneath but using humor to tell the story." Sherman writes witty exchanges, finds humor in somber situations, and even combines sadness and laughter simultaneously. He loves Sturges films in which the mood shifts on a dime, but concerning *Alive and Kicking* he also cites his admiration for Howard Hawks, especially *Bringing up Baby*, in which characters played by Cary Grant and Katharine Hepburn—both notably self-absorbed and arrogant—fight while dealing with her baby leopard.

Before production wrapped, Taylor attacked Sherman for reviving the cliché of gay dancers. Since Hollywood films portray dancers as straight, no such thriving film cliché exists. The journalist hasn't read the film and, hence, gets his facts wrong. He says it "tells of a young dancer dying of AIDS who falls in love with his male therapist" (sec. 2, 8). Tonio has no therapist. Taylor spends much of his article parading male dancers married to women. He attacks a film not yet completed, viewed by nobody. Yet he dismisses it as sure only to "shore up a moribund old cliché that little bit longer."

Sherman responds. He explains Taylor doesn't know his film, notes nothing in the film identifies all male dancers as gay, names many famous dance films about heterosexuals (sec. 2, 7). He inquires, "Why then does one film that looks at the dance world through homosexual eyes cause Taylor to react so strongly?" He names three famous contemporary gay male dancers whom Taylor's article renders invisible. In his final paragraph he reasons, "If there are relatively few gay men in the dance world, as Taylor suggested, there must be very few incidents of AIDS. A simple examination of the *Independent*'s obituary pages, even in just the past few weeks, would prove that false. The truth, quite simply, is that there are gay dancers and straight dancers and one should not cancel out the other."

Producers successfully screened *Alive and Kicking* at festivals, first under its original title and later (after they discovered the Alan Arkin *Indian Summer*) under the new one. (See Appendix F.)

U.S. distributors, perhaps worrying people might have tired of AIDS films, felt reluctant to release it. A short synopsis made it sound depressing, and they couldn't see how to sell it. But festival screenings generated terrific word of mouth, and it won a couple of prizes. Shortly before it opened in the U.S., Holden called it one of the most eagerly anticipated summer openings. "The advance word-of-mouth about the film ... is extremely enthusiastic," he wrote. Allowing interest to build had worked.

Alive and Kicking opened first—on June 6, 1997—in the U.K., where it received at least fourteen favorable reviews, four mixed, and four negative. The major newspapers proved divided, with the more right-wing publications and tabloids less enthusiastic. No surprises there, since the film features nudity, simulated sex, and "offensive" language.

Gilbey judges the screenplay "finds a nice balance between optimism and realism" (Eye, 8). Thompson finds Sherman "deals in a courageous and unflinching manner" with his subject and "the show-stopping finale is extremely moving" (Review, 11). Brown enjoys its "winning and breezy spirit" and "well-rounded humorous treatment" (37). The *Times* includes *Alive and Kicking* in its "Do Not Miss Films" (21).

Malcolm considers the theatrical tone appropriate and the characters suitable to the dance world. He feels Sherman handles the lovers' relationship "with considerable tact and understanding" and calls the movie "both watchable and moving" (Review, 9). Previously, Malcolm published one after a festival, writing it "avoids a lot of the traps ... and ultimately builds up a forceful head of steam" (Reviews, 11).

Bradshaw observes, "Cogent and witty, it thankfully steers clear of the downbeat worthiness of the AIDS-drama ghetto (even while capturing a real sense of ravaged community) towards the more invigorating realms of contemporary gay courtship" (79). He identifies two comic scenes he especially likes, "Tonio and Jack co-opting those Häagen-Dazs ads; Tonio and a lesbian friend drunkenly failing to have straight sex."

Childs calls it a "sensitive, positive and humorous" film that "makes you laugh and see the positive side to a terrible situation" and shows "we are all the same. We are all human" (15). Hamilton judges "Martin Sherman's bold script soon has the audience rooting for this dysfunctional troupe" and "a fluid and humorous character study as good as any of Mike Leigh's slices of life" (46).

Tyler lauds "a compassionate and heart-rending film about love and living with AIDS" and finds the relationship "dynamically" portrayed in a "cracking" screenplay ([25]). Clinch terms it a "poignant romance," praising Sherman for "nuances with a gratifying degree of subtlety and humour ... albeit gallows humour" (86). Robinson describes it as a "joyous, life-affirming depiction of love in the time of AIDS" (23). He exults it's not "just a gay film.... *Alive and Kicking* is nothing less than a celebration of the will to live ... about facing up to life-threatening illnesses and not letting them take control of your life.... Directly after leaving the theatre I went out and partied the night away. It's that good. It's not only uplifting; it's empowering."

Cameron-Wilson likes its "startlingly frank look at the dilemma of living with Aids" with "sparkling dialogue" (16). Wilson raves about "this tender, passionate, remarkably uplifting film" he terms "a life-affirming experience you will never forget" ([8]). He elaborates, "This is a low budget film ... populated with interesting, believable and sympathetic gay characters and also features the most authentic and least-embarrassing disco dance scenes ever filmed."

Allan's mixed notice praises what some negative reviews fault: the long dance sequence and the attempt Tonio and Millie make to have sex. She also likes the ice-cream fight. But she complains the dance "only serves to remind us how unadventurous and stagy the film has been up until this climactic point" (35). She maintains "theatricality ... is the fundamental weakness of *Alive and Kicking*." She likes its humor, though, and its "admirably unsentimental script." Leith writes, "It's slightly more than you'd expect; there are funerals, discos, couplings in the dark, and lots of dance rehearsals. There is sodomy, but not as much as in *Crash*" (12).

Two gay newspapers likewise published mixed reviews. Stimpson judges, "Humorous dialogue and a sequence in Greece ensure that the story is not merely downbeat en route to its final proclamation in praise of love" (93). He finds Tutin's performance "amusing and touching, like the film itself." Although he declares it "has its heart in the right place," he also insists, "Where the film fails it is largely on account of Sherman." Richards, having two months earlier clobbered it, now praises Flemyng and Sher, then describes the film thus: "Like most movies of the genre, this one's got the lot: funerals, tears, deathbed scenes and moments of sacrifice and bravery. If you like weepies, you'll love it" (18).

In a feature, gay writer Feinstein reviles *Alive and Kicking* and many other AIDS films (12). He gets facts wrong, fails to substantiate generalizations, and implies it ends with Tonio's death. Landesman excoriates "lame one-liners that pass for homosexual wit these days" and complains, "This is another one of those let's-be-positive-about–Aids films that are so darn life-affirming you want to die" (5). Walter refers to AIDS as "this avoidable scourge," blaming the victim. He pans the film as "sentimentalized, under-written" and alleges Sherman "gives a once-over lightly feel" to Tonio and Jack's relationship. An anonymous critic terms *Alive and Kicking* "the biggest dog of the year so far" and claims, "No cliché is too hackneyed, no character too obvious and familiar" ("Dancing Queens" 26).

Before he saw it and penned his mixed notice, Richards had denounced it. In the "Express" section of a *Pink Paper* cover, he claims the film at the closing night of the London Lesbian and Gay Film Festival "has been panned as 'crude and embarrassing' by the kinder critics." In fact, film critics didn't review this festival showing, so these pans came from two spectators: "'That was terrible,' a young man said. 'Lamentable,' a film buff commented, rolling his eyes" (2). Yet Richards presumes it damned "by consensus, a truly awful film and a dull ending to a record breaking festival."

No U.S. critic published a negative notice. The least laudatory, by Lim, finds the film better than most AIDS movies, likes "laudably real and messy situations," but calls the writing "spotty" (78). Stamets objects to Sherman mixing "screwball dialogue" and "the sociology of grief" (NC 37). He admires "a deftly-scripted encounter at a throbbing disco," clever banter, "a nuanced love story." Byrne likes the romance and "well-etched, multi-layered characters ... but the issue of AIDS ... and the milieu of the English dance world ... are not as fully realized as the lead roles." Worth loves the stars, but credits Meckler for plot elements he likes so he can call the script "flawed" (51). He feels Tutin plays Luna solely "for laughs," ignoring dignity and pathos.

Elliott finds some aspects not credible. He notes, "The contrast and overlap of the lovers, candidly juiced with sex, is the movie's life (often wittily)" and adds, "There is heartfelt humanity and some grit of truth in *Alive and Kicking*, which is direct about AIDS" (Night & Day, 8). Schwarzbaum assigns it a B-, after calling it "heartfelt" and "so well performed, made with such fervor." She finds it dated "by the advent of protease inhibitors" despite appreciating its "arch banter, flirtation, moments of solitary despair, and passionate arguments." Donadoni judges, "Sherman's screenplay has its preachy and unintentionally funny moments, but the beautifully nuanced performances ... make the relationship feel mighty real." Williamson notes "a gay theme" and "the ballet world," errs in saying Sher plays a doctor, and calls both leading actors "highly accomplished and persuasive" (22).

Alive and Kicking's 35 other U.S. reviews range from good to spectacular.

Holden begins, "Screen acting that transports you into the skin of a character is so unusual that when encountered, it can actually be unsettling" and then praises Flemyng's "fiery visceral intensity" (C14). He feels the screenplay "goes further than most films in portraying the texture of an adult relationship." Satuloff writes, "A celebration of gay spirit and strength, the film approaches its subject with narrative sophistication, wit, energy, and clear-eyed humanism" (67). Skir enthuses, "Dear Jason, you don't need to be bisexual to make homosexuals happy. Just be beautiful, act up a storm in a great script/story and we're happy. Very." Huisman greets it as "spirited and insightful ... with a great script" and "verve and wit" (59). He adds, "Extra thanks should go to the filmmakers for allowing a character with AIDS to actually have sex."

Brophy rhapsodizes concerning complex characters and a "breathtakingly beautiful gay love story," in which, after the lovers find each other, then "comes the work of staying together, which is delineated more acutely here than we have come to expect from the cinema" (20, 30). He enjoys a "sharply funny look at the perils of romance" and "rumination on the power of art." He loves the "magnificent dance sequence called 'Indian Summer'" and terms it "one of the finest depictions of male same-sex desire ever seen in a movie." He raves also about direction, principal performers, Parish, and Tutin, who "conveys the heartbreaking sadness of her decline."

Graham says Sherman "avoids lapsing into clichés and creates a funny and refreshingly honest love story" (D4). After praising the actors and calling Parish "stunning," she concludes, "*Alive and Kicking* proves worthy of its vibrant title. It takes us to familiar places, and reveals something warm and new." Keough feels, "*Alive and Kicking* accomplishes everything *Love! Valour! Compassion!* tried for" and "invests new life in the prematurely moribund AIDS melodrama genre." He enjoys the "tumultuous, convincing, brilliantly choreographed love affair" and rejoices "*Alive and Kicking* makes a strong case that love and laughter can be, almost, a match for death." Shulgasser approves the script as "direct and unsentimental" (C5). She observes, "Part of what makes this film so real and moving is the way it portrays the devastation of AIDS as ... part of the routine of life."

Roca affirms "a small picture with a big heart, and one of the summer's sweetest surprises. With equal parts dark comedy and romantic melodrama and with nice touches of the old Hollywood show-must-go-on biopic thrown in ... the action is fast, the images vivid" (D3). "The romance," he says, "has the feel of a real relationship." A dance critic, he acclaims "the most accurate movie about dance since *The Turning Point*."

McBride speaks of the "richly textured original screenplay" concerning "a character who defiantly refuses to allow the disease to rob him of everything. Never falling back on melodramatic clichés or allowing his protagonist to succumb to self-pity," Sherman shows Tonio "fending off death with his artistry and a welcome dose of life-affirming humor." Summer refers to it as an "adult romantic comedy" (5C). The screenplay, she judges, may be "theatrical, but it's uncommonly human."

Heading it "Recommended," Smith commends "brave, straightforward emotional honesty," which "sneaks up on you and delivers a wallop." He predicts among films of the "AIDS-haunted gay romance genre," a few "will continue to have power and relevance due to strengths that transcend their overt, epidemiological themes. *Alive and Kicking* is one." Millar begins, "*Alive and Kicking* is powerful stuff that features a first-rate script." He adds, "Sherman writes terrific dialogue, funny in a high-culture, show-biz-wicked way, plain and intense when those qualities are demanded."

Ringel reflects Meckler and Sherman "have captured dance's insular, bravura, exceedingly body-conscious world, with all its backstage bitchery, banter and camaraderie" (18). She describes it as "a tart, smartly observed romantic comedy with somber undertones." Hartl greets it as "exceptionally well-written" and boasting dialogue "sharp and theatrical, like the bitchy exchanges in the best backstage comedies.... It's entirely convincing" (G7). He judges "this British comedy-drama may be the most aggressively vital" AIDS film.

S. Hunter begins, "Too many AIDS movies are really just World War II platoon movies with germs in the place of Germans but all other stereotypes firmly in place. That mold is happily broken in ... *Alive and Kicking*, which gets all the messy squalor and magnificent toughness of men trying to not merely live but to carry on in the face of death" (Weekend, 42–43). He adds, heroism against the "enemy is always impressive, whatever the enemy."

Thomas finds it "full of surprises. Its people are sharply, even rigorously, delineated. And it develops into an unexpected love story of uncommon honesty with a great deal of insight about life, art and values" (B9; F12). Bernard applauds, "Such intimacy is one of the treasures of this lovely love story," which she finds "refreshingly straight forward about human attachment" (68). Reed calls Sherman "brilliant" and the film "spiritually healing and morally uplifting" (29). He proclaims, "It is not a downer. In fact, the filmmakers have found just the right balance between art, humor and human dilemma to keep you laughing and enthralled while your eyes moisten." He terms the "Indian Summer" dance "one of the most moving finales ever devised for a film."

Kauffmann writes, "Mostly the film is about the hazards for two intelligent men of being alive and caring. Sherman quite clearly knows his people—the principals and others—and supplies some springy dialogue" (26–7). D. Hunter describes it "in turns disarming, downright funny and devastatingly poignant" and "a scenario that's awash in 'minority humor'—a tactic that softens the tragic milieu and offers some hope for the likable protagonists" (5, 33).

Sigesmund writes it "manages to be both thoroughly modern and charmingly old-fashioned," and "anybody who has ever been in a serious relationship will relate to the priceless dialogue between the 'married' couple. Shot in a spare style appropriate to its subject, the film elegantly examines the hardships of gay men living with AIDS." Another NBC affiliate, WNBC-TV, broadcast Jeffrey Lyons' favorable review.

Farber calls it "by far the best" AIDS film. "It also presents the most believable love story in the recent batch of gay movies. The film is gracefully directed by Nancy Meckler and brilliantly scripted by Martin Sherman.... Sherman writes laceratingly funny dialogue, and he's sketched all the members of the ballet company with revealing strokes (38).

Jessica Film Junkie posts, "The story is both heartbreaking and uplifting. A great modern tale about finding what you most need in the place you would least expect it." Ramos praises Sher and script, which "tempers the film's comic romance within an AIDS context." The Brussats call it a "touching love story."

Bookey feels it offers "a lot of humor and a lot of heart. At one point the audience laughed so hard that two whole minutes of dialogue were drowned out." Feeney concludes his rave, "*Alive and Kicking* is one of the best written, best acted films of the year. Its honest humor in relation to love drives its defiant confrontation with mortality."

Drobnic terms the script "astounding," and "at times bitingly funny," but addressing "some very heavy issues, not only about AIDS but also about the inherent power differentials in any relationship." Maltin calls it "this touching drama." Bleiler writes, "This moving tale of endurance, survival and the redemptive power of love is deeply affecting." Martin and Porter call this an "engaging tale" in which Sherman "explores a gay relationship without resorting to the usual clichés."

Sher earned a Best Supporting Actor nomination for both *Alive and Kicking* and *Mrs. Brown* from the Chlotrudis Awards, which recognize excellence in Independent films.

After release in the U.K. and North America, *Alive and Kicking* screened in Switzerland, Japan (as *Curtain Call*), Germany, France, and South Korea, and was televised in Brazil.

Despite laudatory reviews, it flopped financially. Sherman's second film released in 1997, his adaptation of *Bent*, would prove less popular with critics and cause controversy. It would, however, do better business.

15. Dreams Fulfilled (1994–1997)

In 1994, Sarah Radclyffe asked to film *Bent*. She would executive produce and Michael Solinger would produce. Sherman agreed, provided Sean Mathias directed. Mathias accepted, and producers began fundraising.

Two previous directors, both internationally renowned, had shown interest.

During *Bent*'s Broadway run, Sherman and Gere pitched the project to Rainer Werner Fassbinder. They arranged to meet at JFK, while Sherman waited to board a plane to London, Fassbinder waited for a connection from Germany to L.A., and Gere waited for his own flight west. Both director and star headed for the Oscars.

Sherman recalls, "Fassbinder was unpleasant, but he said, yes, he wanted to make the movie. He had strange ideas about an extension of the concentration camp that would be a factory." Sherman slyly pauses so the fact this occurred a decade before *Schindler's List* can sink in. "I didn't know what he was talking about, but I thought he was a genius, so it would be all right. He wanted to talk again," Sherman continues.

> About two weeks later I was going to Mannheim for the play, and he suggested I go from Mannheim to Munich, where he would be editing a film. So I schlepped from Mannheim to Munich, and I phoned his editing room, and he refused to speak to me. His editor finally said, "Herr Fassbinder will have nothing to do with *Bent*" and hung up. I phoned Richard and he said Fassbinder had asked Richard to do his next film as well. Richard didn't like the script, so he refused. If Richard didn't do that film Fassbinder wouldn't do *Bent*. So it was blackmail. Richard suggested, "Well, maybe I should tell him I will do the other film," and I said, "No, if it begins this way, think how horrible it will become."

Then Sherman and Gere approached Costa-Gavras. They arranged a meeting in Paris in October 1980, and he said he would do it. He hoped to cast Jon Voight opposite Gere and planned to shoot in summer 1981. Sherman wrote a screenplay, and United Artists came on board, but Costa-Gavras postponed shooting to late 1981, and again to 1982. Soon he abandoned it.

Because he loves the film Mathias made, Sherman says, "I'm utterly thrilled neither Fassbinder nor Costa-Gavras made it." And now, finally, he could fulfill his dream of working with a director he totally trusted and had already worked with during the National Theatre production.

Sherman and Mathias lacked the budget for a realistic film, and they didn't want to compete with *Cabaret* and archival footage of concentration camps. They understood Sherman wrote a love story about two men, not about a camp teeming with multitudes. Sherman chose Mathias because he would recreate *Bent* for a late-century audience. "I didn't want a play filmed," Sherman explains. "I wanted a riveting reinterpretation."

His choice made sense on another level. Mathias had adored *Bent* from the moment he read it in 1978, when he persuaded his then-lover McKellen to play Max.

Mathias brought to his first film the same process he used in theatre, a workshop approach to rehearsals. Author and director agreed this work-shopping would assist the playwright in deciding how much dialogue he could pare away to replace with visuals.

Producers would need to raise money and permit casting to occur and work by actors to begin before they received a script.

Despite this, they found backing. Channel 4 contributed because Aukin admires Sherman's work. Japanese investors signed on because repeated productions of the play have occurred there; its popularity would guarantee audiences. Producers also obtained subsidy from Britain's Arts Council. Eventually they put together their modest budget of a little over two million British pounds, small even by indie standards.

Mathias asked designer Stephen Brimson Lewis to come aboard, and Philip Glass agreed to compose the score and one song. Isabelle Lorente signed to edit, and cinematographer Yorgos Arvanitis joined them.

Casting didn't occur in the traditional manner. They needed actors who would work more for love than money, so they approached their friends and people whose work they adored and who, therefore, wouldn't need to audition. How could they hold auditions without a script? Because they couldn't pin down a shooting schedule until they had a completed screenplay and funds, they lost a few actors to commitments that later conflicted.

As Max, Mathias cast Clive Owen—whom he had directed in *Design for Living*. Brian Webber from South Africa, where the director lives, would play Rudy. French-Canadian Lothaire Bluteau loved the play, so when Mathias called him, he accepted Horst. McKellen says he would have felt hurt had he not received an invitation to play Uncle Freddie in Mathias's film-directing debut, and Sherman would have felt hurt had he refused. He had already done the role in a scene for *Before the Act*.

Sherman thought of Mick Jagger for drag queen Greta. He brings the perfect decadent allure to the Glass/Sherman song "Streets of Berlin" and an appropriately sinister quality to alter-ego George. Rupert Penry-Jones took the tiny role of the Nazi who, on the march to Dachau, strikes Max with his rifle, and Paul Bettany that of the captain towards the end.

The team collected extras from amongst their friends: Jude Law, Suzanne

Bertish, Sadie Frost, Rachel Weisz, Jamie Hammerstein's wife and son, Dena and Simon. They also recruited Jan de Villeneuve and relatives, as well as choreographer Wayne McGregor and his company. Other U.K. artists, actors, models and designers expanded the crowd at Greta's.

On the required day, the actor cast as the officer on the train couldn't appear, so they contacted Rupert Graves. Mathias barely had time to tell him the previous actor had decided to wear glasses, even though the officer persecutes those who wear glasses. Graves loved the idea. He delivered a splendid impromptu performance.

A Welsh director filmed a screenplay by an American, designed by a Brit, edited by a French woman, with cinematography by a Greek, using Welsh, French-Canadian, and South African leading actors, produced with Japanese and British money.

They also by then had a script, completed just before filming began. Sherman developed that in stages, some involving the actors.

Perhaps the adaptation would have stuck closer to the original had it occurred sooner, i.e., closer to its premiere as a play. Instead, Sherman creates a radically different opening and a dissimilar texture throughout.

Sherman drafted the first half before workshops began. Those started on May 27, 1996, with the play's text—reading it and discussing it—ensuring everybody understood the full script. Then they shifted to his half-written screenplay. He recalls, "I cut the play to shreds when I wrote the screenplay's first half. After we read that, I took away more, but I also put back lines actors thought their characters needed."

Initially, he creates much new material, some by turning dialogue into cinematic action. He intercuts Max and Rudy's flat with the club. If Sherman can devise a way for us to see a behavior or choice, he shows it rather than telling it. Drug dealing, drug using, and orgies establish Max's sybaritic milieu before he and Rudy flee the Nazis. This world resembles that of some gay men in New York City when Sherman wrote the play, in 1977, before AIDS. Later he takes all the play's scenes, in order, but reduces the text and adds visuals. For the total film he stripped away about 50 percent of the play's dialogue, but a larger proportion disappeared from the first half than from the second.

The four-week workshop followed by two weeks rehearsing prepared the actors to deliver extraordinary performances by July 8, when they began filming. Thanks to the workshop, Sherman developed his screenplay into a form he, Mathias and the actors love.

The production couldn't afford and didn't seek realism. Sherman explains, "It was Sean's brilliant idea to use only disused power stations and factories throughout." Designer Lewis selected the evocative locations Mathias desired. They turn what might seem a disadvantage—little money—into an advantage, a daring and unified vision. He creates Max and Rudy's apartment in one abandoned Scottish power station (in Dalmellington) and Greta's club in another (the Braehead station, also near Glasgow). In lieu of Dachau he uses an abandoned cement factory in Tring, Hertfordshire. This facility includes buildings that serve as the prison barracks as well as train tracks to deliver new inmates. Glasgow streets stand in for Berlin, and nearby woods serve as Rudy's "jungle." A London studio contained the boxcar set for the transport scene. Mathias filmed in these locations for 35 days.

The visuals and Sherman's screenplay produce a post-modern feeling that underlines parallels between discrimination and dehumanization in 1934–36 and now. This helps to account for the film's popularity with younger audiences, who see the underlying real event but also what people do to others in the name of whatever demented dogma makes them regard themselves as chosen and everybody else as alien. Younger audiences readily perceive the application to whatever "today" they inhabit.

Like the play, the film dramatizes "the other" and survival issues, but Sherman devises new strategies for treating these themes. Above all, he replaces dialogue with visual images. The first ten minutes contain almost no words.

The play opens with a sitcom scene that could take place in 1977, when Sherman wrote it. The film begins with a searchlight highlighting the title. At Greta's club, a spotlight hits Greta on her trapeze. The next frame shows a flat, the next Greta's face (revealing Jagger in drag), and the next Max's face on his pillow. This establishes the locales will alternate between the night before and the morning after, as the Night-of-the-Long-Knives' murders continue into the next day.

Seeing Max at play makes his growth seem even bigger than it did on stage. It creates a more negative picture of him at first: He more clearly cannot respect himself and cannot love another. Thus we admire more where his journey takes him.

In the park scene, Sherman adds a character, a demented woman who blurts out, "I think geraniums are best" and later begins rummaging in her bag, as Luna does in *Alive and Kicking*. While the men discuss Max marrying, this woman mutters, culminating with "get out, get out," as though warning Max to accept the single ticket. After this, we observe Rudy working on a road gang. In the forest, alternating shots of the lovers and the SS with dogs closing in to arrest them build suspense. On the train, reaction shots of Max's face enhance his pain at what "isn't happening," and a montage of partial and blurred images subtly suggests what Max does to obtain his yellow star.

Sherman alters dialogue between Horst and Max when Max calls a pink triangle "the lowest" and Horst corrects him by adding, "So's the yellow star." Despite the evidence demonstrating that during this early part of the Third Reich (in this scene, 1935) both guards and other prisoners treated gay prisoners worse than other groups, Sherman permits us to conclude Max has misunderstood and has thought a hierarchy exists when, in fact, none does. Yet the captain's action dramatizes his greater contempt for Horst, who wears the pink triangle and receives the order to fry himself on the fence even though Max, not Horst, has deceived him. The captain punishes the gay prisoner, not the "Jew," for the lie Max told.

Unlike the play, the camera can show Max cradling the dead girl's corpse and a guard brutalizing him.

After the prisoners enter Dachau, crowd scenes vanish and most color drains away. Thus Mathias and his designer reflect Sherman's choice to dramatize a two-person love story in the camp and the Nazis' choice to deprive their victims of the simplest satisfactions available beyond the walls.

New also, a fellow prisoner sheers Max's head and shaves his chest, and then Max, naked, turns to where another prisoner has thrown anti-lousing powder on a newcomer. Max is hosed down, and then handfuls of powder fall onto his body. Now wearing a concentration camp uniform, Max stands in profile for a photo.

The film achieves effects the play couldn't. Against mammoth ashen walls and floor, a tiny figure holding a tiny rock moves from one tiny rock pile across the frame towards another. After the progressive and silent dehumanization of Max, the rock thuds loudly as it hits the pile, and Philip Glass underlines the endless task with a repeating bass viol bar.

In *Bent*'s most famous scene, a new character enters. We hear a fly buzzing as they speak of missing sex. Then we see the fly. Max blows at it before replying, "Yes," he does miss it. He blows at it again and waves it away. When Horst says they don't have to miss it, he waves at it, too. In this accidental intrusion they break slightly the prohibition against moving just as they contemplate a greater rebellion.

The film shows the couple in the snow, and then Horst coughing in his barracks while others sleep. The snow deepens; the cough worsens. Visuals replace dialogue. We also see Max pretending he has a cough and the captain approaching him. We observe two pairs of legs away from the others—no dialogue required.

When Horst dies, the scene uses all the play's lines but with vivid visuals. The final minutes likewise resemble the play, but visuals enhance impact. After Max dons Horst's jacket and buttons it, he calmly returns to his rock, touches his pink triangle, and walks to the fence. He grabs it, screams as sparks fly, and sags, his left hand stopping next to Horst's cap. As the camera pulls back and up, we hear the wind. The screen slowly goes white.

The film moves from sensory indulgences to bleak, washed-out isolation and desolation, prefiguring the men's movement from life to death. Even had they enjoyed a lavish budget, a documentary style would detract. During the second half, in contrast to their surroundings, they find ways to inject love and joy into whatever days remain. Max undergoes a transformation; extras would diminish that and dilute the ironic contrast between Max risking love and suggesting they return to Berlin together and then, suddenly, Horst's death.

Like the play, the film dramatizes Nazis persecuting "the other," but it makes visually more vivid the play's second dominant theme, survival. Both play and film show Max's willingness to lose his soul in order to save his life, but design and direction here further emphasize the work dramatizes suffering, repeated dangers, and three gay men's deaths. We see more graphically how ill Horst grows and that Max saves his life by obtaining the medicine. Watching Max close up we also cannot possibly make the mistake of regarding his death as suicide. He takes control, makes an existential choice, and cheats the Nazis out of further opportunities to terrorize and kill him.

Mathias completed post-production during winter 1997 and then held a London screening for the cast and crew plus a party on March 25.

Bent contains something to annoy almost everyone, both the play's admirers and its detractors. Some dislike the subject and others blame the film for not reproducing the play.

The tender, touching, and funny love story *Alive and Kicking* appeals to most viewers, including most film critics, but the love story *Bent*—also tender, touching and funny, but, above all, powerful—doesn't. It drives homophobes up the wall and leaves some other straight critics wondering why anybody bothered making it. Nevertheless, many reviewers love it.

Mathias notes spectators feel horror because they have to look at how they'd deal with such crises. "How would one behave on a train to Dachau? How would one survive in a concentration camp?" Critics don't express such discomforts, but some do share his view "it's a hopeful piece because it speaks eloquently about fighting oppression."

When *Bent* screened on May 13, 1997, at Cannes, it won the Prix de la Jeunesse (Prize of the Youth). Nevertheless, Levy trounces Mathias, both leads, and Glass's score. He accuses Mathias of lacking "technical skills," putting the camera "in the wrong place," and "heavy reliance on cross-cutting and montage" (66). Based on this review, Sam Goldwyn insisted on additional editing, which reduced the film's length by nine minutes. Levy praises Sherman, saying, "It's an indication of Sherman's vigorous writing that, despite helming and thesping deficiencies, his anti-dictatorial statement and tribute to the indefatigable human spirit remain powerful."

Four days later Hunter published a favorable review. "The sheer theatrical intensity of the piece is slightly diluted in the translation," Hunter writes, "but director Sean Mathias makes a stylishly impressive feature debut and the emotional charge of the piece remains undeniably potent" (15). He concludes, "Mathias' study of love and Nazi repression is an eye-catching production that makes its modest budget its aesthetic."

Corliss approves *Bent* as the "strongest of the sad-gay films," likes "Mathias's chic, stunning visualization," and concludes it "has an artfully designed palette" (2, 4).

Sherman spent June 8 through 11 in New York to cast *Madhouse*. Mathias, meanwhile, cut *Bent*.

At Cannes, *Bent* ran 118 minutes. Still that length, it showed at the Moscow International Film Festival on July 26 and 28. During summer and fall, most countries received the longer version, but a few got a 109-minute edit. On October 30, Seattle's Lesbian and Gay Film Festival saw the shorter version.

Only then did the Motion Picture Association of America rate it NC-17, citing shots of simulated sexual activity at Greta's. The filmmakers had expected an R rating. MGM, which had inherited the film when parent Metromedia bought Goldwyn, declined to cut the film further for its cinema showings but likewise declined to challenge the rating because they felt the film's violence made it unsuitable for young viewers. The MPAA finally awarded the video an R rating when Mathias deleted five additional minutes. Otherwise the video would have landed on porn shelves. Only that final edit eliminated graphic sex shots at Greta's.

Bent had its release on October 4 in Japan because of its Japanese co-funding. At roughly the same time it showed in Germany at a festival. In early November, Chicago's Lesbian and Gay International Film Festival screened it, and it played at a Greek festival on November 23. Also in 1997, it won Lothaire Bluteau the Gijon International Film Festival's Best Actor award and there too gave Mathias a nomination for the Grand Prix Asturias for Best Feature.

In March 1998, it appeared at the Melbourne Queer Film and Video Festival. In October, it screened on the opening night of Bremen's Queer Film Festival. Also in 1998, at the Emden International Film Festival, Mathias received Second Place for the Emden Film Award, and at the Torino International Gay and Lesbian Film Festival he won for Best Feature Film. The movie also snagged a 1998 nomination for the GLAAD Media Award for Outstanding Film, and it screened at festivals in Barcelona, São Paulo, and Lisbon.

On its path from Goldwyn to MGM distribution, *Bent*'s coveted Prix de la Jeunesse at Cannes vanished from publicists' radar. Goldwyn's people knew about it; MGM's didn't. The poster failed to include the Cannes symbol, and the press kit failed to mention the award. Whatever advantage this honor would have conferred on *Bent* it lost.

Sherman arrived in New York on September 21. The long-awaited U.S premiere of *Madhouse* at Second Stage would rehearse six days a week, would begin previews on October 25, and would open on November 17. Shortly thereafter, the day before Thanksgiving, *Bent* would open in major U.S. cities. *Bent* went into limited release to big cities on November 26 and thereafter into general release.

More U.S. critics liked *Bent* than disliked it. Among the negatives, Ebert wielded the most influence because he broadcast his views plus published this pan, or a summary, in at least five newspapers. He says he hasn't seen the play.

He believes gay prisoners wore a "pink star." He rejects the film as "eroticism" designed to entertain. "The more deeply it descends into horror, the more alarming its agenda becomes, until finally I'd had enough." Hmmmmn. Would that be the "homosexual agenda" right-wing pundits reference? He enjoys one "thrilling" scene, when the Nazis chase Max and Rudy through the woods.

Another hostile response comes from the critic for a gay porn website. Adnum terms it "stage-adaptation hell," a "very stock picture of martyrs at the mercy of a cruel world" and "very unimaginative." He doesn't like the play either.

Taylor calls it "a film of bad ideas, notably the palatable but dumb and facile notion that suffering ennobles the victim." She finds the dialogue "stuffed with declamatory sentences ... designed to explain what the plot doesn't." She accuses Owen of mugging and labels *Bent* "confused vulgarity."

Elliott brags he walked out and hated the play as well. He erroneously claims the Broadway *Bent* boasted "full-frontal male nudity" by Gere, and he attacks the film for historical inaccuracy because it mentions Ernst Roehm "as being still around" even though Hitler had him killed on the Night of the Long Knives. He doesn't know the film begins that night.

Noh also dislikes the play, calling it "a shallow mix of camp, provocation, and emotional milking" and judging "Sherman has done nothing to improve matters for the film adaptation" (27). He slams performances, terming Owen "monotonously gloomy" and Bluteau "affected" and "a wormy, whining little drip." Noh says "no" to everything: Mathias "misses the mark," the stylization gives a "shallow" treatment to Dachau, and this creates a "repellent" absence of "dehumanizing filth and claustrophobia." Somebody at this newspaper, however, disagrees. The arts listings report, "*Bent* is a moving film about two gay men," etc. (32).

Several critics who dislike it call one of the two Dachau inmates Jewish as well as gay. White refers to Horst as "gay–Jewish" (58). He judges the Nazis' murder of Wolf "a misjudged fantasy raid," rejects the "orgiastic overkill of the film's opening sequence," and damns Mathias's direction as "big visuals, little sense."

Eight negative reviews call Max Jewish and gay. These confused critics include Patterson, Null, Rabin, Karten, Shulgasser, Saravia, Bookey, and Kehr. Kehr thinks the club belongs to Max, not Greta.

Fine writes two reviews, one negative, one mixed. The two intervening years explain the contrast. His first terms it "stilted and pretentious" and "lumbering," and he belittles Mathias's "pitiable efforts at cinematic expressionism" (F8). The second calls it "an impressive, important statement ... worth seeing."

Weitzman, Rozen, Bennett, and Gerhard supply other negative notices.

Three critics published reviews either negative or mixed. Holden offers a mixed response, framed as negative, but supplied with a neutral headline.

He concedes merit, saying it "still has some power to unsettle" and has "earned its place in cultural history. And it's still impossible to watch the scene set on a train transporting prisoners to Dachau ... without feeling a sickening shudder of dread" (B3). But he finds it too realistic; he wants it more minimalist, like the play. Holden also believes the Nazis would never have wasted the prisoners "on a meaningless task" and rejects sex occurring in Dachau (See Chapter 6 for evidence he errs.)

Strauss puts down the film, then supplies rather sympathetic plot summary, acknowledges homophobia still exists, says Mathias directed the original London production (nope), then explains he would have written the latter half differently by including several more characters and their own "personal tragedies" (Weekend, 22). Rule for critics: Don't revise the work.

Scheck's review carries two and a half out of four stars but contains multiple complaints: less powerful than the play, a "wildly overdone" first half, the "jarring" sight of Jagger in drag, the absence of Hollywood stars; big names "would help us identify more with their characters."

Among mixed notices, T. Adams begins, "I'm on the barbed-wire fence" about it (47). Unlike Holden's preference for the Beckettian latter half over what he regards as a realistic first half, Adams longs for a realistic film and rejects the symbolic "Robert Wilson piece." She praises it, however, as "a well-acted, impassioned drama" and calls the pre–Dachau scenes "as shattering as they are economical."

Savlov calls the verbal sex "one of the most erotically charged scenes—gay or straight—within recent memory ... *Bent* is a viscerally affecting film, ripe with sadness and pungent with the scent of misery and suffering." He rejects "leftover dialogue from the stage that could just as easily have been excised," but "the film is a punch in the gut and a kiss on the lips, and it works despite these flaws" (60–61).

Byerley praises the lovemaking scene as "incredibly affecting" and the two leads as "without fault." He concludes, however, Mathias "has not found a fluid way of translating *Bent* into something of visual interest on screen." Howe feels, in contrast, "It's Sean Mathias's visual direction that keeps you going, rather than the overindulgent, self-consciously theatrical dialogue they exchange."

A. Potter concurs, saying Mathias "conjures images of jolting intensity.... Yet the film's painfully stagy script usurps its visual power." Susman and Garner reject Mathias's stylization, demanding realism instead. Millar damns *Bent* as "far too stylized and overtly theatrical," but then praises Mathias because he "efficiently executes the conception of the film as a series of metaphors" as well as Stephen Brimson Lewis's "arresting production design"—a prime source of the movie's stylization and theatricality.

Several mixed reviews—by Tatum, K. Williamson, Dermody, and the critic on *Screen It!*—term this a World War II movie.

Some reviewers prefer the pre–Dachau scenes; some want to lose those but like the Dachau portion. Kauffmann complains Sherman "has written a long prelude to the camp section." Rickey describes the latter part as "hugely effective."

S. Adams likewise judges those scenes between Max and Horst "work best on screen" and feels "Sherman's writing is powerful stuff." Adams sometimes sounds homophobic. "Debauched" implies disapproval of homosexuality; so does "lifestyle" instead of "life" or "sexual orientation."

Among those mixed reviews preferring the pre–Dachau scenes, Robin Clifford calls the Nazis' targets "perverts," assumes anti-gay prejudice no longer exists against this "lifestyle," complains the film should "follow Greta/George and tell her/his story," and concludes, "There is a passion between Max and Horst, but it is a passion I, personally, do not identify with, so I felt no real empathy for the characters."

Like Robin, Laura Clifford likes the earlier scenes best. She finds the train segment especially "compelling," and, even though she feels the "pacing becomes ponderous" towards the end, she recognizes the later scenes dramatize "Max's redemption."

Morgan prefers the earlier scenes where Mathias "opens the movie up" to more stylized scenes (D2). Kitty Bowe Hearty praises the "strong" start but laments the later action "feels like a play." Alspector judges it "starts off provocatively" but condemns the latter half as "like a bad one-act. The subtext is so forcefully delivered that the text disappears" (sec. 2, 12). Tatara agrees, complaining, "The play's least cinematic qualities make it to the screen intact. This is a big mistake, but not completely unforgivable given the first-rate quality of the performances and the undeniably moving material." He identifies the Dachau portion as "the most stage-bound." Fox also finds "the first half still stands as a valuable dramatization" but the "austere" latter half fares "less well."

Johnson-Ott regards *Bent* as a World War II movie and its filming as unnecessary because "the nightmares of the Holocaust are well documented" (8). Berardinelli doesn't confuse the period and knows previous Holocaust movies don't deal with gay men. Like these other critics, however, he prefers the "more successful" first half and finds "once the movie reaches Dachau, it grinds to a screeching halt."

Other authors of mixed responses include Henrickson, Schwarzbaum, Litton, Martin and Porter, and Maltin.

At least half the film's North American reviews praise it. These critics ostensibly have little in common; they write for the gay press and straight press, major metropolitan dailies and alternative press, weeklies and monthlies, a Jewish paper and a film journal, websites and film guides, WNBC–TV (Jeffrey Lyons) and *Playboy* (B. Williamson, who warns his readers the film "may shake you" [19].)

Sokolowski judges *Bent* "most powerful as a tender love story" and "its message inspiring" (21). She also calls it "timely, considering the current wave of anti-gay sentiment sweeping through the legislative halls in Juneau." Bleiler, likewise, greets it as "a moving love story" and "a striking adaptation of the stage play."

Steinberg establishes he's straight, describes the sex scene as "breathtaking," then defines the scene's importance as a "stunning portrayal of sex as a fundamental expression of human connection and essential life spirit triumphing over even the most systematic and brutal attempts at its annihilation. And ... it is also ... as hot as any more conventional, hands-on interaction you're likely to see.... I was trembling at the end, both from the intensity of the sex itself, and from the giddy victory of possibility over impossibility, life triumphing over death." He urges his readers not to miss *Bent*.

Four gay critics agree. Period writes "murky, sad and yes, wrenching, it is a testament to the power of love." Pickett, after terming it "wrenchingly heartbreaking and shiveringly beautiful," urges "Support this film, see this film." Warren praises it, especially direction, acting, and score. And Stuart terms it "high-voltage, visually haunting" (77–78).

Graham pronounces it "arguably one of the most wrenching films in recent years" and the ending "devastating." She writes, "Max commits horrid acts to survive, but Sherman's extraordinary screenplay allows the heart to ache for his desperation." Verniere calls it "powerful" and celebrates "the slow, painful, but beautiful evolution of Max's soul." Obejas relishes *Bent* as "a powerful adaptation" and "a dark, dynamic film, excellently paced and acted" (C), while Vitello lauds it as a "masterful production" and "a taut examination of identity, strength, and love's power to sustain."

A. Williams labels it a "must-see" (48). He finds it "taut ... driven by Clive Owen's harrowingly believable lead performance" and says, "Intense but understated, austere but accessible, graphic but not sensational in its depiction of physical and psychological brutality, *Bent* is rooted in a specific nightmarish era, yet its spare dialogue, superb young leads, and slightly surreal visual scheme make it immediate and contemporary. More clearly than any stage production of *Bent* I've seen, the film conveys the primal struggle between Eros and Thanatos."

Nechak extols it as "brilliantly moved from the stage to the screen." Hartl loves the film even more than the play, saying Sherman "knows how to use theatrical conventions within a cinematic context" (E3). C. Potter proclaims *Bent* "takes a quantum leap into tragic wisdom" with this "marvelous film." He notes Max's betrayal of Rudy to save himself resembles the denial of Christ by "fearful Simon Peter."

Polunsky adjures readers, "It takes guts to watch *Bent*. But it's worth it." Baltake speaks of "the wrenching film version" and "a hauntingly austere work." Guthmann refers to *Bent* as "a sober, beautifully modulated film" and to its "spare, understated power" (E8). Dickson finds it "as powerful and deeply affecting as the play" and "a brilliantly executed film translation, from the striking cinematography to Philip Glass's haunting score to the riveting performances and the raw power of the words themselves." About the "amazing" sex scene, it proves "the most intense sex occurs not below the waist but between the ears."

Whitty relishes its "strong performances and haunting, evocative score" and its "passionate espousal of rights and respect for all." He values Sherman's refusal "to make plaster saints of its gay martyrs," include "the trappings of the typical Holocaust" movie, or indulge in "sentimentality and melodrama." He supposes others don't write about Hitler's pogroms against gays "because it sadly remains, to many people, the least shocking" and notes those who most need to see it will stay away.

A. Johnston judges *Bent* "powerful and haunting," delivering "its message with style and an impressive lack of didacticism" (77). He lists it under "Critics' Picks." Hammond calls it "provocative, yet macabre and heart-wrenching" and "masterfully effective." She approves the choice to "concentrate on how the human psyche reacts to the devastation" rather than to make a commercial movie and urges "Catch this film." Taubin judges *Bent* "baroque, violent, and terribly disturbing—which is as it should be" (84). Thomas terms it "powerful, galvanizing" and "a remarkably deft transposition by Martin Sherman of his successful play to the screen" (B10; F8). Thomas concludes, "*Bent* may be hard to take, but it's easy to admire."

Reed begins, "Get ready to be electrified!" (45). He judges it "one of the best films I've seen this year" as well as "one of the best films ever made about one of life's most important lessons: You can break the body but you cannot destroy the indomitable human spirit." He insists, "*Bent* is *not* depressing. It's uplifting and life-affirming—a film of rare power, passion and cinematic brilliance."

Kirkland terms it "bold" and "a harrowing descent into hell" (119). Burliuk concludes, "Were it not for the subject matter, I'm convinced *Bent* would be touted as an Oscar nominee for best film" and begs for at least an acting nomination. De Wolfe calls it "a drama that verges on Shakespearean tragedy." She feels Sherman has improved upon his play and refers to its "tragic conclusion." Monk also praises it.

Travers reassures us the play reaches the screen "with its outrage intact" and lauds its "fervent cry of defiance" (85). *E! Online* rejoices the play "makes a triumphant transition to the big screen." Maynard raves a "film of staggering power" and "brilliant, moving ... one of the year's best." Canaan predicts, "Sure to be on award lists this year," while Hofler pronounces it "that rare instance where the movie version of a play improves on the original." Natale especially loves the Dachau portion, in which "the power of Sherman's writing begins to burn fiercely." Charles praises the lovers' achieving "a triumph of lust, longing, memory and imagination." She notes it "leaves audiences breathless and believing" and urges, "See this film."

Chase commends it as "intense, moving, and completely unforgettable." Satuloff regards it as a "gut-wrenching experience" and judges "its dramatic story, powerful theme and historical importance are undeniable." Judell calls it "a love story that takes on the tragic proportions of a *Romeo and Juliet*" ([138]). Later, he terms it "a brave, brilliantly effective movie." Provenzano predicts *Bent* "is likely to be one of the hardest-hitting, most depressing and ultimately most moving films of the year." Bernstein refers to "Sherman's gorgeous, dark script" and praises it as an "incandescent stage play" which has "lost none of its power to disturb and move its audience" (9).

North American positive reviewers also include Meek, Pinsker, Chuck the Movie Guy, Hershenson, the Brussats, Valez, Hitchens, Thompson, hppub.com, Keogh, Maynez, Craig, and Jessica Film Junkie.

Most British critics posted notices either hostile or indifferent. Brown, for instance, dislikes the direction and complains (as do some other U.K. reviews) Sherman seems to suggest "Jews got off lightly in the Second World War" (37).

Walker suggests the death of homophobia has left *Bent* "an idea whose time has gone" (26). Hemblade faults writing, direction, acting, and mood. He calls the latter "broody, dark and depressingly downbeat," as though Mathias and Sherman should have made a light-hearted gay Holocaust movie (44). Billson labels it "no fun at all" (Review, 12).

Others either intend to pen mixed reviews or reveal indifference by taking no position. Gilbey prefers the first hour to the shorter second half (19 & Eye sec., 6). Sweet prefers the latter part to the former (sec. 2, 6). Simpson concurs, arguing, "The second half of this screen version is far more successful" (94), but T. Johnston praises the earlier portion (73).

Andrews prefers the play (22). Likewise, the *Mirror* calls the play "brilliantly harrowing" but the film "dully directed," though acknowledging its "moments of great poignancy" (Screen, 5). Van Kruyssen prefers the first part to the second because the latter resembles the play. She concludes, "Although this claustrophobic approach intensifies the sense of angst, you become baffled by just why the director was given the go-ahead to bring the play to the big screen."

Fisher writes, "It is a well-made but grim and dour drama with all the feel-good factor of a 14 lb. frozen turkey" and complains it "isn't entertaining" (30). French remarks it "seems both more theatrical and more abstract" than on stage, calls Greta "delightfully decadent," and criticizes the sets. Finally, R. Williams writes, "Theatrical artifice is part of its technique: stark, stripped, it demands attention" (sec. 2, 7). However, he means the play, not the film, and he complains, "The experience is not exactly cinematic."

Three U.K. critics like it. Porter commends, "It makes laudable use of the opportunity to add new scenes expanding on the hero's life before incarceration" (sec. 2, 11). Cameron-Wilson terms it "an ineffably touching and haunting love story" (44). Kimberly notes Sherman's screenplay repeatedly breaks "free to enter a realm of painfully hallucinatory spaces" (39–40). He continues, "The movie's arresting imagery is nowhere more apparent than when protagonist Max is carrying rocks." Kimberly concludes *Bent* renders the love story "as movingly as it reminds us of the depths of Nazi hatred."

16. Judaica (1998–2000)

Sherman imbued with Judaism *Next Year in Jerusalem, Messiah, See Under: Love*, and *The Dybbuk*. After the An-ski inspired film fell through, he began three new scripts in 1998. All reflect his Ashkenazi heritage.

During 1997 his father began experiencing declining health, forcing him into a retirement home early in 1998. This drained Sherman's finances and left him open to a new commission. Producer Amy Robinson asked him to write a 30-minute script for HBO, part of a series on seniors. The subject combined his concerns with "the other" and survival. Sherman drew upon his father's recent life as inspiration for *Tracking Jack*. He completed a first draft by spring 1998 and his second in July. HBO liked it but didn't make the series.

The same disregard for facts that has won him cases makes attorney Jack self-destructive. He imprudently avoids wearing a seat belt, saving money or paying bills. Nobody will hire him at his age. Bereft of his late wife, without work to provide structure and satisfaction, he bets at the racetrack. Sherman "tracks" Jack's gambling.

The second 1998 commission came from producer/director Simon Curtis. Would Sherman turn a book by a playwright into a film for BBC? Wesker's *The Birth of Shylock and the Death of Zero Mostel* recounts a theatrical disaster. Everything went wrong with the attempt to bring *The Merchant* (later renamed *Shylock*) to Broadway, especially the death of star Mostel during its Philadelphia tryout. Wesker conveys what a playwright suffers at the hands of a misguided, megalomaniac director (John Dexter), inappropriate actors, and critics unkind to his script.

Wesker's book concerns a British, Jewish playwright in New York and Philadelphia. Why not hire a Jewish playwright with dual citizenship, living in London but born in Philadelphia and a long-term resident of New York, familiar with putting on plays there?

All concerned reckoned without Sherman's wicked wit. Wesker wrote a serious book about a play likely to succeed on Broadway turning into a fiasco. Sherman sees the humor.

He creates a "documentary" in which Wesker, Dexter, and others address the camera. The film interpolates stock footage of Shakespeare's Shylock, an airplane flying, a train chugging. Sherman includes a lot of Wesker's play and captures that fine script's flavor. He permits Wesker insights into the grief piercing a playwright's heart. He also invents material. After Wesker and Dexter agree to work together again, they do a music hall act, in top hats and tails, singing "Friendship" and dancing soft-shoe and tap breaks. After a money meeting, Arnold sings "If I Were a Rich Man."

Towards the end a winged, dead Zero, recumbent upon a cloud, plays his harp. When Sherman's Arnold avers, "The play clearly needs a good actor as Shylock ... but not a star personality," we assume the off-camera Zero drops his harp to zap his author, for thunder booms, and a deluge falls "only above Arnold." The film's sardonic title, *Dead Zero*, says it all: Sherman has turned a sad, although sometimes amusing, book into a show-biz satire.

As Sherman wrote, he speculated, Wesker will "want to kill me." Yet he had warned he would write it "like Dennis Potter on acid." Curtis responded enthusiastically. By late 2000, Sherman suspected the BBC wouldn't film it, but reported, to his surprise and pleasure, "Arnold loves it." Although the BBC couldn't obtain co-financing, which killed the project, Sherman felt "pleased and touched by Arnold's enthusiasm."

As the Millennium approached, Sherman considered writing a pair of one-person plays, for a Jewish woman and a gay man. Octogenarians, they would look back over their respective lives. The woman would reflect upon fading Yiddish culture and the man would consider the birth of gay consciousness as a movement. Sherman never wrote the second play. He created *Rose*, during the summer of 1998, in Paris, Mykonos, and London.

He constructively critiques contemporary Judaism in this piece about a resilient survivor wracked by grief. She mourns two little girls' deaths, Yiddish language and culture's decline, and erosion of the ethical imperatives she's respected throughout 80 years. The playwright elicits laughter and tears and, from some spectators, anger. Never afraid of controversy, he explores a century of persecution first of Jews and now sometimes by Jews.

This play requires us to watch one person sitting, never rising, nor taking a step. Beckett's *Happy Days*, although it mires Winnie in earth, also provides her mobile husband for contrast. *Rose* fascinates so entirely, however, we soon forget its sole character, previously a wandering Jew, sits shivah on a bench and peoples the stage only with Sherman's evocative words.

Sherman considers 20th century Judaism by focusing on one 80-year-old's passage from childhood in the shtetl Yultishka, to motherhood in the Warsaw Ghetto, to retirement in Miami Beach—only Sherman doesn't skip all the years in between. His Rose remembers everything; we live it with her.

Sherman bases Rose partly on his witty maternal grandmother, Elizabeth Shapiro, to whom he dedicates the play. Born in 19th-century Ukraine, this immigrant didn't run an Atlantic City hotel, but her sister owned it, and Shapiro managed its kitchen. Sherman spent childhood summers there, so he used it as one of his settings. He invented his plot, however; Shapiro didn't have the adventures that befell Rosala, Americanized to Rose.

She represents a composite of those Sherman knew and a kind of strong woman he admires. His protagonist also reflects Sherman's own survival skills and outsider status. When Rose speaks of her childhood saying, "Each day I grew a little and each day I died a little, both at the same time. I did not belong" (*Plays* 1, 211), she speaks for herself and her creator.

Sherman took the personality of Rosala's mother from his paternal grandmother. She and her husband lived two doors down from Sherman but spoke only Yiddish, and Sherman's parents, intent upon assimilation, didn't encourage him to learn it. Forever alien, they represented the Old World to the young man, who immortalized what little he could understand of their outsider spirits in *Rose*.

The play's periods and locales fall into 26 segments, 12 in the first half and 14 in the second. The first part covers childhood in Yutishka with mother, father, sister, and brother; joy in Warsaw, where she meets and marries Yussel and they have a child, Esther, but she feels "still outside" (214); the Warsaw Ghetto and work in a factory, which she couldn't leave while the Nazis took her husband; her three-year-old shot on a whim by a passing Ukrainian soldier; her life hiding in the sewers for two years; her incarceration in a displaced-person camp; her voyage to Palestine on the *Exodus 1947*; the British attacking them; her five hours in the Promised Land; forced removal onto another ship, which returned her to Germany; the Allies tossing her onto a train to transport her to another camp; and American sailor Sonny Rose telling her to jump off and marry him. The second half dramatizes the New World immigrant experience.

Shortly before she speaks to us, she sees on TV her youngest grandchild, Israeli Doron, who has shot a nine-year-old Palestinian girl in the forehead. Therefore, she sits shivah for Nora el-Kareem and recalls son Abbie's fury at her on the phone, as he shouts, "Your world is dead" (245). She belongs nowhere. She struggles for breath and closes her eyes. Readers assume she dies, finally, from emphysema, having already mourned her own passing. Viewers of the play's premiere saw a woman still very much alive and about to resume talking, an outsider continuing to skip over quicksand. Sherman's nature balances optimism and pessimism. He wrote an ambiguous ending, but decided she survives.

Although Rose never moves and narrates rather than interacts with another performer, a great deal happens. Each segment involves dramatic action, i.e., moral choice, both Rose's decisions and those of people she embraces or opposes. Sherman laces drama with humor and ironies.

He constructs his plot so we learn at the outset Rose mourns a child killed in Israel, but we don't know that child's identity and who killed her until the closing minutes, when the information surprises, shocks, and devastates us. He likewise guides us through his plot's structure by initially employing humorously the words "on the other hand." This gives them special resonance when we hear them to different effect at the end. Rose says, "I'm inching towards dust, and sometimes I wish it would hurry, preferably in the middle of a thought, or a sentence, just like that ..." ([205]). Sure enough, Sherman gives her as her last words, "On the other hand ..." (247).

Sherman begins the second half in ways that echo how the play started, and he plants information throughout which enhances dramatic irony. By the end we appreciate Rose has sat shivah for two little girls, for her dying culture and values, and for herself. Such devices unify his plot and provide finality to the journey we've taken with her.

Rose delivers contradictions, contrasts, paradoxes—irony of every sort. The narrator describes her mother the Jewish saint, but also a pagan in the woods singing wild melodies. Rose likewise describes her father, dying of a "mysterious illness, which was very much like God, there was no visible sign of it, but some fanatical Jew kept saying it existed" (207). He survives for years until his medicine wardrobe topples and crushes him.

When the Allies arrive and Rose can leave the sewers, she must seek sanctuary in the safest place, Germany—in an irony supplied by both Sherman and history. As she passes through Dresden, she sees, crawling on the street, a child without arms, and she appreciates another irony, the "goodies had conquered the baddies, and saved what remained of our lives, but the child had no arms" (218). More ironies follow: "I found the Americans. They welcomed us. They gave us cigarettes. I had never smoked before. I smoked for the next fifty years. Now I can't catch my breath" (218). After living involuntarily 12-in-a-room in the Warsaw Ghetto, she turns hippie and voluntarily lives 12-in-a-room in a commune. After surviving Nazi massacres, she must endure Abbie's convert wife telling her, "'You don't deserve to call yourself a Jew.' I thought, well, just about the time my entire family was wiped out because they were Jewish you, my dear, were being baptized in Kansas" (244).

Ironically, because she strove to assimilate, Rose doesn't permit her son to hear Yiddish as a child, so he rejects the language. When she calls its death "Hitler's Final Victory," and he retorts "That's just Meshugge," she responds, "Meshugge is a Yiddish word" (240).

Rose mourns loss of life, but also a way of life, a people, Yiddish-speaking Jews, their culture and belief in serving to perpetuate a moral force. Rose and Sherman lament the erosion in the most fanatically conservative Israeli faction of the old obligation "to be better" (244), replaced by a convert praising the Jew who exterminated Arabs in the Hebron mosque massacre. Rose appreciates that a century has passed since the pogroms in her parents' youth, yet people still do the same awful things to others, and now some Jews also do some mass murdering.

But Rose doesn't preach. Sherman instead gives her jokes and, "On the other hand," images evoking sights and sounds, the numbing experiences she undergoes. As usual providing mirth amidst lacerating drama, he flips us, even in mid-sentence, between laughter and tears. When British warships ram the *Exodus 1947* just as Rose has sighted the Promised Land and Brits board the boat, initially she couches her description of the Jews' attempts to defend themselves with bottles of soda pop in comic terms: "Refugees were hurling cans of kosher corned beef at the steel helmets. I saw one of the sailors being clubbed. I saw a boy, only sixteen, his family wiped out in the camps, shot in the face" (221).

In mid-laugh, Sherman wrenches our hearts. Refugees hurling their food supplies at armed troops parallel crockery smashing in *When She Danced*'s dinner party, but it ends in pathos.

Repeatedly she perceives pain as fodder for humor and employs humor to survive pain. Recalling Cossacks pillaging her shtetl, she quips "I suppose if you have your first period and your first pogrom in the same month, you can safely assume childhood is over" (209). Remembering her in-laws' displeasure when Sonny returns with her as his bride, she jokes, "Their boy runs away to be a pirate and returns with a catatonic shtetl girl, when what they always wanted was a nice Jewish-American daughter-in-law named Sheila or Arlene" (226).

Sherman dramatizes his dual themes. Although the first half might appear to stress survival more and the second half might seem more focused on exile, in fact both permeate the play.

Rose's wise mother has hoarded kopeks. "I saved, Mama said, for when it's life or death" (211). When Rose objects that her going to Warsaw doesn't involve life or death, Mama disagrees. She feels Rose's survival depends on escaping the shtetl. This prescience saves Rose's life.

A quintessential survivor, Rose during the Holocaust loses everything except her life. She clings to it in the Ghetto, the sewers, and avoiding displaced-person status. Her survival skills include her humor, her fierce determination, and her ability to reinvent herself. Although composed of sterner moral fiber, her will to live resembles Max's.

Her father dies because he has given up living. Her mother and sister die when Nazis round up everyone in Yultishka, lock them in the schoolhouse, and burn it down—a true story. Rose's three-year-old daughter also fails to survive. "Esther ran for the soup. The soldier aimed his gun, the small gun. Esther reached the soup. The soldier pulled the trigger" (217). A fellow Ukrainian murders Esther. "He might have been from Yultishka. He was just passing by" (217). His random violence eclipses Nazis rounding up her brother, sister-in-law, and husband.

Rose survives physically, but her faith perishes. "I sat shivah in the sewers," she says. "There were no wooden benches, but God makes allowances. Except I stopped believing in God. God died in the Ghetto" (217). Shades of *Messiah*'s Rachel, but even she couldn't conceive of evil on the scale of the Holocaust.

Characters continue dying in Act 2, and echoes of mortality recur, as when a survivor hoards dinners in Styrofoam as insurance against famine or when Rose describes Morton's band, called Mort, which sings about death. Sonny dies, her third husband Mr. Feldstein dies, and self-righteous Doron shoots a nine-year-old in the face.

Rose describes young Israelis' "belief in the future" with awe: "Future wasn't even a concept in Yultishka or Warsaw or even in Atlantic City or Miami; on some subconscious level we knew we were skipping over quicksand" (234). That image evokes desperate efforts to survive. Rose, her relatives, and her people must struggle to survive because they differ from those who wield power and guns. Their outsider status prompts skipping over quicksand.

Rose's sense of alienation, instilled in her even in the shtetl, persists. Even in her beloved Yussel's arms, long before her exile to the New World, Rose feels "still outside, like that tumbleweed rolling through an empty town" (214). Here the dramatist uses a western image to express this eastern European's nomadic alienation and her status everywhere, with everyone, as "other."

Sherman includes characters different because they suffer disabilities. Yussel paints even though, like Sherman's great uncle, he has lost an eye. Sonny suffers the sort of degenerative disease that killed Sherman's mother.

Rose knows about Jewish bigotry towards others, those not of her race. Concerning Atlantic City, she remarks, "There were now black ghettos surrounding the hotel strip, and since victims of prejudice seem susceptible to the disease themselves, Atlantic City just packed up and moved to Florida" (234).

When she first visits Israel, she doesn't experience herself as an outsider because "everyone in the country looked like my relative," including the Palestinians (238). But her grandchildren laugh at Yiddish, and then she perceives Israelis killing for reasons other than self defense, and she sees "photographs of women and children picking their way through the rubble and the rubble wasn't ours, it was next door" (238–239).

In Israel, Rose appreciates her values have gone the way of her native tongue. She observes two Semitic peoples, each convinced they have God on their side, slaughtering each other, killing women and children, killing their humanity.

Rose responds by doing what an octogenarian can. She argues, she opposes her family, she insists on preserving the imperative against murder, insists on adhering to a better code. An outsider to her family, an outsider to the family of Nora el-Kareem, she grieves senseless slaughter of "others," slaughter based on perceived differences which prompt fear and hatred. Outsider Rose believes in banishing bigotry and allowing other outsiders to live and thrive. Still an alien herself, she strives to persuade her family to honor the commandment "Thou shalt not kill" and insists on sitting shivah for the "stranger" her grandson has murdered. Loving her neighbor as herself, she comforts the dead child in Yiddish.

As soon as Sherman completed *Rose* in late summer 1998, he sent it to the National's Artistic Director, Trevor Nunn, who rearranged the schedule so as to present it before the next century dawned and, moreover, decided to direct *Merchant of Venice* as a companion piece.

Meckler agreed to mount *Rose*. They needed a major star to play the role and to attract ticket-buyers to a one-woman play. One of Meckler's friends suggested Olympia Dukakis. Daunted by the length, Dukakis nevertheless accepted. She agreed to play Rose despite the money she would lose from turning down film roles. She loved the play that much.

To meet with Sherman and Meckler at Heathrow, she rerouted herself to London on her way home from filming a mini-series in Czechoslovakia. "We talked and talked," she recalls. "Then, on my way back to resume filming, we worked for three days in March at the National. We read through the play and talked to see if we could understand each other. How could I *not* do it? It's so extraordinary."

Dukakis accepted one of the most taxing roles ever. Although Sherman had written one long act, she eventually requested an intermission so she and spectators could stretch their legs. She worried about learning the lines and confesses, "A couple of times I got up to call my agent and say, 'Look, I can't, I'll never get this.'" The length worried her, and the complexity, depth, and variety challenged her. They also motivated her to persevere.

(Left to right) Sherman, Nancy Meckler and Olympia Dukakis rehearsing *Rose* in London, spring 1999 (courtesy Martin Sherman).

Meckler says of rehearsals, "We had an easy collaboration. Olympia was trusting. Martin's presence was supportive."

Dukakis concurs: "He was wise. Usually you don't want a writer there. They make you nervous. They don't understand your process and think what you're doing in rehearsal is what you'll do in performance. They don't get it. That's not true of Martin. His belief in me meant a great deal."

She describes the rehearsal process as "threading it together. If that's going to happen here, what can happen there? How does it affect action down the line? Nancy's work was absorbed, so it doesn't show." But both Dukakis and Sherman praise Meckler's contribution.

Sherman describes this as "bliss. I enjoyed it more than any rehearsal experience I've ever had. We investigated Rose's character and life. Nancy is so wonderful. Olympia had total trust in her, and Nancy and I had total trust in Olympia. It was very productive."

They didn't know running time until late in rehearsals, when, without an interval, it lasted two hours 30 minutes. Sherman cut it to two hours 15 minutes and added an interval to rest Dukakis and spectators.

Effectively paced by Meckler, Dukakis admirably embodied this outsider who "did not belong" even as an intellectual youngster who felt out of place in her shtetl (211). The actor comes from an immigrant family, understands the role of exile, and possesses all skills required. She has the presence to command a stage for over two hours. She inhabits Rose 100 percent.

After a brief try-out outside London, *Rose* began previews at the Cottesloe on May 19 and opened on June 24, 1999.

Most London critics liked or loved *Rose*. They also understood it. Three major daily reviewers used the word "unforgettable," and the play received an Olivier Award nomination.

At least 15 publications ran positive reviews. Ten other notices range somewhere along a spectrum of mixed to negative, more the former than the latter.

Barnes pans script, while appreciating star. He says Dukakis "finds the role of her life" and "is adorable, touching, dryly amusing, ironic, even at times tragic," as though she had shaped the action and written the words herself (32). Yet this review excoriates the play as "a long-winded, simplistic monologue" which omits "no contemporary Jewish cliché" and "seems as predictable as a calendar."

Macaulay faults *Rose*, calling it "ingratiating junk" and the character "a fake" (20). He makes factual errors, for instance, that she survived a "concentration camp" and witnessed Esther's death. He pronounces Dukakis "not quite theatrical," the text "manipulation" and the character "a type: almost a stereotype; almost camp; and slightly synthetic."

De Jongh terms the performance a "triumph" but says, "For all its witty astuteness and vivid eloquence, the reminiscing chatter too often takes on the quality of a leisurely charabanc tour down the arterial roads of a life" (10). Then he denounces the "offensive ... way Sherman makes" the Arab girl's death "seem analogous" to Esther's. "There may be Jews in Israel who murder Arabs. Such men do not, however, deserve comparison with Nazi assassinators."

Spence compares watching *Rose* to "being trapped by a bore on a park bench" but concedes, "For those who like this kind of thing, this is the kind of thing they like" ([20]). Billington prefers enacted scenes to narration. He grants, "At times, his writing is flecked with illuminating detail" and admires Meckler's "quietly austere production" and Dukakis's "performance of effortless dignity" (21). Clapp's mixed review can't forgive a one-hander. She describes Rose as "queen of the kvetch, the wry shrug, the pertinacious argument, the double edge.... It is often pungently expressed, and Dukakis ... holds it together as a tour de force. But in the end it's an argument against solo shows—not so much a monologue or portrait as a star turn" (8).

Gore-Langton extols "the play's blend of sentiment and muscle" (35). Yet he qualifies this, "Where it stalls as drama is the author's resort to implausible coincidence," before praising "a play that at its best laments not just a life but a vanishing culture." Wolf recommends the production, which "has London audiences on their feet nightly ... in a show that can only be Broadway bound." He lists this as one of "Four Musts" running in London, but he also terms it "overstretched" (July 27).

He predicts, "Dukakis has an annuity for as long as she wants it," but announces the play "not by a long shot" wins his comparable approval. He accuses Sherman of "belatedly catering to the carriage trade" by aiming at the commercial theatre. He notes previously the playwright has "seemed at great pains to avoid" this and terms *Some Sunny Day* his "finest work to date." Wolf objects to "a script overloaded with seemingly ready-made ethnic jokes." He prefers the latter half to the earlier and praises the end, in which "performer and play come together beautifully" (July 19).

Morley's mixed feelings apply to both star and vehicle. He terms her "seldom less than mesmerizing" yet objects, "The experience seems all too often just outside even her considerable grasp." He asserts the script contains "few jokes" as well as "no stereotypes, just an infinitely painstaking (and sometimes, it has to be said, ponderous) attempt to link up the dots across the Jewish map of the millennium," and he regards the result as "touching, chilling, overlong and sometimes random."

Wardle's mixed review tips more toward positive. He praises Dukakis's "stunning" U.K. debut and terms Sherman's text "a powerful contribution to the urgent and theatrically neglected topic of Yiddish-Israeli relationships" (Review, 8). "Rose's beloved Israeli grandson shoots an Arab girl and her son denounces her as an outsider.... Unforgettable."

Among positive reviews, Eaker predicts, "Rose is surely Broadway bound" (7) and judges, "Sherman has written a play that avoids all clichés and gets straight to the heart of the matter." Dace likewise praises it (22). Nightingale terms it "bold," "filled with unostentatious sympathy for outsiders" (Arts, 6). "Rose could easily be a case study rather than a character," he continues. "That this danger is averted says much, both for Mr. Sherman's writing, which compensates for its occasional longueurs with always lively, often distressing, sometimes hauntingly strange observation, and for Ms. Dukakis's acting."

Wright explains, "Rose is a Jewish everywoman.... Rose's monologue achieves an almost symphonic quality, interwoven with recurring leitmotivs" (sec. 11, 22). Foss speaks of "Sherman's brilliant new one-woman play" containing "wonderful Jewish humour" (62). Both Hepple and Edwardes praise play and performance (12 & 144), as does Taylor, who begins, "The only thing I didn't care for at the opening night of Martin Sherman's *Rose* was the standing ovation at the end of it" (10).

Butler observes, "The play draws its strength from her longevity. This perspective allows the questions of Jewish identity to return again and again in a new light" (6). He feels, "*Rose* is a sharply imagined, perfectly detailed story." Jennett greets it as "a poignant examination" of the Holocaust's "aftermath" and "an extraordinary play." Coveney calls the solo turn "riveting" and says of the play "Rose's story becomes, in fact, a story of our century, and a mighty moving one at that" (23). Brown pronounces Rose "good company—feisty, funny and wise, with an indomitable spirit. Just as vital, however, is Sherman's careful crafting, which gently imposes a satisfying dramatic tension" (Review, 73). She pronounces the ending "sad and haunting."

Spencer notes Sherman "is refreshingly difficult to categorize" (19). He continues, "Thanks to the wise compassion of his writing, and a performance from Dukakis that walks a skilful path between engaging Jewish humour and sudden glimpses of unimaginable pain, the piece emerges a real triumph." He adds, "There is no mistaking the play's great heart."

Herbert calls *Rose* "the highlight" of that issue of his magazine and "just riveting" (797). The play demonstrates "it's possible to have good and bad Jews; but it does much more." Sherman "gives us a profound glimpse of the twin motors of the Yiddish and Hebrew traditions powering Jewish achievement and Zionist ambition. It's a long evening ... but a most rewarding one."

Finally, Kingston proclaims Sherman "a master of the telling phrase and the unforgettable image" (19). Rose speaks from the present, with "elements from the past reappearing in very different contexts; one, almost as if in a fairy tale; another, finally, with the resounding horror of a tragedy."

Sherman met his late–July deadline for revisions of *Tracking Jack* and *See Under: Love* and then finished revising *Dead Zero* by his late September deadline.

As efforts continued to arrange for a Broadway *Rose*, in late December 1999 Sherman's father died. The year had begun with Jamie Hammerstein's January 7 death, followed by L.A. producer Allan Carr's June death. Thus that year took three men who had assisted him secure a living as a writer.

Sherman flew backwards and forwards, because of his father's illness, to attend his funeral, and to participate in arrangements for *Rose*. By the end of January, he had a commitment it would open on Broadway on April 12, 2000.

Every night at the Cottesloe Dukakis had received a standing ovation, unusual in London. *Rose* played to 97 percent capacity at the National (Wolf, Sept. 13, 1999). Fox described *Rose* as "an important play" and "Martin's best writing." Encouraged by the National's attendance, he thought he would move it to the West End and then to New York. Ultimately he didn't produce it, but he did help to involve Andre Bishop, former Artistic Director of Playwrights Horizons, now running Lincoln Center's theatres, who produced *Rose* on its behalf. *Rose* represented Sherman's first Broadway show in 20 years, but the next would follow three years later. Fox would produce it.

Sherman went to Tel Aviv in February 2000 for the Cameri production, popped over to Paris in early March to write, and on March 15 flew from London to New York, where *Rose* would rehearse for one week starting March 20 and then begin previews on March 28 for a run through May 20.

National Theatre officials expected *Rose* (reduced to two hours) to prove more popular than their *Copenhagen*, which opened on Broadway the night before. More popular with audiences and at the box-office, yes, that occurred, but not with critics. The thunderous standing ovations continued each night. Press agent Barbara Carroll reports the shows had the same advance sales, and *Rose* always played to at least 80 percent capacity, not true of the other play, which sent tickets to the half-price booth. She explains a typo in *Variety*'s figures for the week of May 8–14 created a temporary misimpression. That week *Rose* did 81.5 percent capacity, compared to *Copenhagen*'s 78.6 percent, but a misprint changed *Rose*'s figure to 31.5 percent (61). *Variety* deems *Rose* a hit because it was a financial success, just like *Copenhagen*.

New York reviews varied. Some critics loved *Rose*, and several predicted a Tony nomination for Dukakis (who didn't receive one). Yet others muddled plot details, peppered their pans with errors, and didn't understand it.

A few Jewish critics bridled at the playwright's criticism of Israel, and occasional spectators heckled Dukakis. (Contrast the Israeli production's excellent reception that didn't rebuke Sherman for taking to task some of their countrymen.) Sherman calls it "thrilling" on rare occasions when a spectator became so involved as to yell: "The audience was, by and large, incredibly supportive. But I'm sure it did upset some people, and I would rather they voiced their political objections honestly than do what some critics did and clothe political fears in allegations of bad writing."

Contrast the limited objections to Sherman's view with the furor that erupted over Carter's best-seller *Palestine Peace Not Apartheid*. The former president's charges of Israeli human rights abuses against Palestinians occupy a larger proportion of his text than does the complaint Rose registers. Nevertheless, both Carter and Sherman hit a nerve. (See Appendix E.)

When Sherman returned to London, comedian Ruby Wax asked him to direct her next one-person show. He had twice appeared on her TV program, and they had become friends. While he finished adapting William's *The Roman Spring of Mrs. Stone*, during May–June 2000, Sherman prepared Wax for a fall tour of *Ruby Wax Stressed*, then a run at the Tricycle. She also toured Australia and New Zealand.

Rose had done brisk box-office on Broadway and sparked enormous enthusiasm. It went on to become one of Sherman's most popular and most frequently produced plays.

Dukakis performed brilliantly, but Sherman builds the rhythms into the lines so well that any excellent actress of appropriate maturity can embody Rose effectively. In some spots, she speaks huge stream-of-consciousness gulps. A sentence that begins by defining shivah finishes 116 words later concerning the street where Einstein was raised (205). When she visits her grandson Rafi, a film editor, she tells him of Jews from the Old Country creating the Hollywood film industry, but by the time she reaches her sentence's end 139 words later she has shifted to Chernobyl's dust (241–42). Short or long, each sentence compels the actor to supply appropriate pacing and emphasis. But for towering talents such as Dukakis, this role of a lifetime will make or enhance careers. Rose has joined the short list of coveted great roles for women.

Wasserstein says of Sherman's Jewish plays "The voice is uniquely Martin. There's fancifulness *and* depth, and it's moving. His treatment of Jewishness touches on truths that aren't what's current in theatre. It's highly intelligent, but not pretentious. There's a Yiddish word; he's got a lot of saykchell. Saykchell is 'smarts.' He knows what's going on. And this is not a guy who's saying, 'This is how it should go.' He says, 'This is how it is.' Martin is virtually Talmudic in his depth, his wisdom."

Those who love *Rose* see in it that saykchell. The play's specificity gives it universal appeal and enables us to see through Rose's eyes, discover through her sense-memories, register shock through her heart. We join her as she strives to survive, and, belatedly, strives to ensure her culture will survive. She wins the first battle, but she loses the second—despite a certain triumph in personally upholding in the New World her Old World values.

17. Italy (1999–2003)

In September 1999, George Lane asked to become Sherman's New York agent, and director Franco Zeffirelli asked him to write the film *Florentines*, which Christopher Hampton had begun, then relinquished. Hampton recommended him. Sherman agreed to both requests.

In mid-October, he left for Rome, where he spent five weeks with Zeffirelli. The director's superb chef didn't diminish the pleasure.

In February 2000, he returned to Rome. Zeffirelli liked his script and offered him another commission to collaborate on a film about Maria Callas late in life. Her friend as well as director, Zeffirelli had an idea for a project titled *Callas Forever*.

Franco Zeffirelli (left) and Sherman in Positano, probably spring 2005 (courtesy Martin Sherman).

February produced another commission, also Roman. Sherman would write for Showtime a new adaptation of Williams' novella *The Roman Spring of Mrs. Stone*. The same month, he flew to Israel for *Rose* at Tel Aviv's Cameri.

Sherman continued to work with Zeffirelli. In October 2002, the director asked him to write a third script, a new version of Pirandello's *Right You Are (If You Think You Are)*, a.k.a. *It Is So (If You Think So)* for Joan Plowright. Sherman wrote rapidly. The play rehearsed in April 2003 and opened in May.

Florentines doesn't resemble Sherman's other work. A sprawling opus set in late 15th–early 16th century Florence and Pisa, it depicts Medici intrigue, young Clarice and Marco, and geniuses Leonardo De Vinci and Michelangelo. Others include Marco's cousin Lisa, Savonarola, Machiavelli, and a huge cast. Think mega expensive.

Although Sherman wrote *Florentines*, he built upon Hampton's efforts and followed Zeffirelli's directions. Leonardo paints Lisa and reroutes the Arno, Marco rides in Leonardo's winged flying-machine, Michelangelo sculpts David, artist and model interact, painter and sculptor meet.

Every time Zeffirelli raised the money for another revision the script expanded. The March 2000 version, 119 pages, ballooned to 236 pages in March 2003, still longer in autumn 2003 and spring 2005. Dino De Laurentis briefly grew interested. Yet Zeffirelli never filmed this interminable epic.

Sherman says, "I really, really love Franco. He's a genius." Nevertheless, the honor of Zeffirelli asking him to write *Florentines* couldn't have compensated him for spending months rewriting a film nobody would see and which has little to do with him as a writer.

The *Callas Forever* script does represent Sherman. The filmed version doesn't.

Sherman's September 2000 script finds concert promoter Larry arriving with the Rolling Stones in Paris in 1977. He picks up a young painter, then visits his friend and client Callas to propose a film series, *Callas Forever*.

The camera follows Callas about her Paris neighborhood. A car nearly hits her. She shops in a store blasting her "Casta Diva," but nobody recognizes her. When a woman on a bench does, she denies her identity. The completed film instead shows a woman who never leaves her flat.

The script continues as journalist Sarah decides Larry's plan might rescue Callas. She can renew her career by lip-syncing roles to her old recordings. Larry takes Callas to a screening room where she views her last concert, with her recent voice replaced by a dubbed earlier recording. Larry's new boyfriend, Michael, shows her his paintings and tells her she inspired him. This prompts her to consider Larry's idea.

They take her to a Rolling Stones concert. She joins in singing along to "I Can't Get No Satisfaction." Then Larry tells her Mick did some lip-syncing.

We trust Larry because his assistant, Annie, tells Maria he paid all the hospital and doctors' bills when her husband died. Then Annie asks, "There's nothing worse than *wasting* life is there?" The film doesn't contain Annie.

They will begin with *Carmen*, because she recorded it but never played the role on stage. Larry puts up 50 percent of the money, and others invest the remainder. She delights in rushes of her lip-syncing the "Habanera" and gains confidence.

They ask their waiter at Chez Maxim's to audition for them on the spot. He sings and dances Flamenco among the chic diners. Sarah quips, "I think I've died and gone to M-G-M." Sturges could have taken pride in claiming this scene as his own—had this remained in the film. But it didn't.

The early script continues with rehearsals and filming. Larry catches Michael cheating with the waiter, whom they have cast as the matador. Maria pursues the young man, Marco, cast as Don Jose, but then retreats. She enjoys the completed film and agrees to *La Traviata* next. Michael breaks up with Larry, who has been so absorbed he has neglected his painter. Maria, Sarah, and Annie discuss Onassis, but when Annie vanishes from the movie, so does that.

Maria refuses to film other operas but agrees to *Tosca*, on condition she will sing it in her 1977 voice. She asks to rehearse the second act with a live audience where she discusses Tosca's feelings towards Scarpia. She draws upon Onassis's mistreatment to motivate Tosca stabbing Scarpia. On film, nearly all this disappears.

The project's backers refuse to permit her to sing Tosca, and Callas asks Larry to destroy *Carmen* because it isn't honest. He agrees, as he does in each version.

By March 2001, Sherman completed a revision that attracted Jeremy Irons, Joan Plowright, and Fanny Ardant. Still a lot like the first draft, it substitutes a fictitious punk-rock band called Bad Dreams (or, as Sarah dubs them, Wet Dreams). Much of the original remains: Maria strolling in her neighborhood, Annie, Callas talking to the lead singer and dancing. The scene at Chez Maxim's remains, as does the Tosca workshop.

Sherman remained excited about his script as production neared. He had taken Zeffirelli's ideas and brought to life another strong and complex woman, another artistic genius. As filming approached, Sherman made a few tiny cuts, just minor tightening. He and his director went into production with a fine script, laced with sly humor, which revives interest in the diva and gives her stature late in life.

Zeffirelli hoped to cast Teresa Stratas. When she couldn't do it, Sherman suggested Fanny Ardant, whom he had seen play Callas in Terence McNally's *Master Class* in Paris. Plowright agreed to play Callas's confidante, Sarah. Jay Rodan took Michael, and Gabriel Garko Marco. Jeremy Irons accepted music entrepreneur Larry Kelly, and Manual de Blas stood in for another side of Zeffirelli as Esteban Gomez, *Carmen*'s director.

While on location, Sherman wrote a three-minute scene for the *N25*

Chain Play, celebrating the National's 25th Anniversary. Twenty-five writers created an episode, then sent the text to the next writer. The performance took place on October 26, 2001, the night after the anniversary lit up the National as a giant birthday cake with candles. Sondheim contributed a song, and he and others who wrote their scenes after 9/11 (not Sherman) worked that into the play. Although Sherman couldn't attend, perhaps writing his sketch distracted him from his Bucharest experience.

Production began in late July 2001, first a week shooting Paris exteriors. Most filming occurred in August and September in Bucharest. Although visually a reasonable Paris substitute, Bucharest unnerved Sherman. He found it "a strange place because thousands of wild dogs attack people. There are muggings, but I was more worried about the dogs. They bite pedestrians and bikers." Then terrorists struck on 9/11, and suddenly guards armed with machine guns patrolled his hotel corridor.

More than wild dogs and machine guns, departures from his text concerned Sherman. A team-player praised by directors for his collaborative and cooperative nature, he had always written every word of his films. He hadn't before worked with an auteur director.

Zeffirelli cut half the script. No, scenes didn't land on the cutting room floor. The director simply skipped them during shooting. He began with an 82-page script but omitted filming 43 of those pages. The scenes he deleted nearly all show Callas away from her flat and the studio, and often they depict her zest for life. She relishes the rock concert, an art gallery, meals, dancing the night away, and the hilarious waiter's audition.

Zeffirelli expanded the proportions devoted to Maria in her apartment late at night and especially *Carmen*. Instead of filming snatches of the opera, he shows us what Larry promises to destroy, Callas—or rather, her stand-in, Ardant—performing Carmen. We see all the famous numbers.

By cutting, the director shifts our attention. He makes a film less about the diva and more about her friend Larry, a.k.a. Zeffirelli. Under the guise of a tribute to Callas, ironically he makes a film that emphasizes her narcissism, temper, self-pity, and bad behavior towards Larry. She proves untrustworthy; he behaves nobly. He respects her wishes even though destroying *Carmen* will cost him a fortune. He breaks down, weeping; she mocks his grief. We're supposed to admire and empathize with Larry. Had not Ardant managed to impart warmth and humanity to her scenes, Callas would seem a monster.

Zeffirelli stresses he depicts fiction, but also acknowledges Callas's maid Bruna worried about her during summer 1977, when she claimed she went on holiday in Greece and Egypt but really remained in Paris. And he also concedes he tried, shortly before her death, to persuade her to perform Monteverdi's *Coronation of Poppea*. She would think about it, she told him, while on vacation. Then she died.

Zeffirelli's revelations about parallels between himself and Larry, as well as his friendship with Callas, whom he directed in five operas, encouraged critics to ignore Sherman's participation.

Nevertheless, some of Sherman's vision remains—witty lines, an interesting diva, and the Durrellesque multiple layers of reality: Ardant lip-syncs or sings along while playing the older Callas lip-syncing or singing to a younger Callas's recordings, as movie makers create a film within a film.

When asked about working with Sherman a second time, Plowright tactfully doesn't mention the film, but praises the writer whose script attracted her to the project: "I particularly like its eloquence and wit and admire his quirky sense of humor. He is a lovely fellow, has high standards, and is sensitive to other people's problems. He is not afraid to criticize when necessary, but does it gently."

Callas Forever received two award nominations, the Goya in Spain and Silver Ribbon in Italy—both for its costumes designed by Anna Anni, Alberto Spiazzi, and Alessandro Lai.

The producers received distribution slowly.

If they feared critics, they had good reason. But they also correctly assumed the film would find its natural audience, gay opera buffs, especially those who had seen Callas and relished the chance, essentially, to see her again, even preserve her *Carmen*—the one she never performed—on DVD. Durrell would have loved this: Larry didn't show *Carmen*, but Zeffirelli did.

Ardant enhanced her reputation with Callas. When the French Institute/Alliance Francaise sponsored a Fanny Ardant series in May 2007, they kicked it off with *Callas Forever*. Zeffirelli's tribute to Callas has succeeded as a tribute to Ardant.

Japan received *Callas Forever* especially enthusiastically. But wherever pockets of Callas queens thrived, so did the film. At NYC's Angelika for an afternoon showing right after the *New York Times* panned it, viewers filled every seat. Everyone remained through the final credits and then applauded wildly, as though at a live performance.

Because the film doesn't represent Sherman's screenplay, for reviews see Appendix F.

Zeffirelli and Sherman's third collaboration succeeded. Although Sherman wrote rapidly, *Absolutely! (perhaps)* garnered good reviews and several award nominations.

Pirandello's play appealed to Sherman. Its focus on truth's relativity, the impossibility of ever ascertaining *the* truth, coincides with similar themes in Durrell's work and, often, Sherman's. He subtly shifts the Nobel Prize winner's genre from melodrama of meddling to drama and comedy melded.

Sherman pillories prying gossips who damage those whose privacy they invade. As commentator Laudisi remarks, "But don't people have the right to behave how they choose in their own home?" (4). Think *gay*: Arrogant busybodies can harm homosexuals if private behavior becomes public.

Sherman retains the plot structure—each segment destroying our belief in a "truth" just established in the preceding dialogue—and Pirandello's theme, but he exploits a funny situation by emphasizing inappropriate interference and adding jokes. Working from a literal translation, Sherman produces an entertaining new play and substitutes a witty new paradoxical title.

Pirandello constructs his play in three acts and gives the first and last lines to his spokesperson, the skeptic Laudisi. Sherman does likewise. Snoops insist upon ascertaining the truth about Signor Ponza, his mother-in-law, Signora Frola, and his wife. As the townspeople interrogate each in turn, they fail to obtain a definitive answer because Ponza and Frola each say the other suffers from insanity. That occurs in Act 1.

The remaining acts flip the nosy neighbors—and spectators—back and forth. An earthquake has destroyed all records in the village they come from, so no evidence exists to support either claim. The compulsive inquisitors summon the daughter, but she refuses to satisfy them. Yet the town has damaged three lives.

In its usual stodgy translations, it seems a museum piece. Sherman livens it by employing contemporary idioms and finding the humor in prying. He adds satire and farce, and he enhances the dramatic impact by making Pirandello's play more accessible. We more clearly perceive the harm the townspeople cause. He improves Pirandello.

Sherman exploits the play's comic potential from the start, when Laudisi declares, "Let me get this straight—he's gone to the *mayor*??" (3). Sherman injects the irony that the skeptic who derides the possibility of reaching certainty insists on precisely that. Although spectators won't laugh out loud at this, we begin giggling as Amalia and her daughter Dina object to standing outside a door like "hitching posts" (3) and as Dina enjoins Laudisi "imagine that you are standing here," he retorts, "I *am* standing here," and she replies, "Imagine it anyway" (4).

As the meddlers' obsession escalates, tiny jokes encourage us to maintain our objectivity so we criticize them rather than join them. Thus when another snoop appears, claiming to wish to meet Laudisi's sister, but actually longing to hear gossip, the skeptic declares sarcastically, "My sister is suddenly very popular" (37). He then toys with and teases the newcomers concerning the surprise confrontation about to occur, which he describes as "Ponza and Frola! Together again!" (37). Not the vernacular of 1917, but funnier because it suggests a circus act.

Sherman opts for informality, and the cast performed naturally, as though spontaneously. Oliver Ford Davies, playing Laudisi, delighted in saying "Don't interrupt me; I'm on a roll," so much easier to snap than a polite request to permit him to continue (54). He relished how Sherman renders Laudisi's refusal to reply to the Mayor's question, "How about you, Laudisi?" by making "terrible noises as if his mouth has been taped" (56).

Zeffirelli already had Joan Plowright as Signora Frola when he commissioned this version. She explains this project "had been close to Franco's heart, and he had spoken to me about it for several years before we did it." She also loved the script and declares Frola her favorite of the roles Sherman wrote for her "because it required a bigger range and Frola was allowed a sense of humor. Martin adapted the play with great skill so that, though couched in contemporary language, it still sounds like a classic."

Sherman admires both Zeffirelli's understanding of Pirandello and his skill as a stage director. "He has a fantastic sense of theatre. He asked me to reverse a couple of lines, so a different line ended the scene. That was a strong line to end and sometimes got applause." He explains the director's style differs from the usual. "He gives line readings. A lot of actors find that difficult. But it was a cast of veterans, so they allowed it. It seemingly robs an actor of freedom, but when they got on stage and started performing in front of an audience, they had more freedom than I've ever seen. He directed them brilliantly."

Zeffirelli designed the scenery as a set metaphor. We cannot know the truth? We therefore see mirrors and patchwork mosaics which refract life into a crazy quilt, a maze, a distorted jigsaw puzzle, or funhouse mirrors which cannot reflect a true image, but instead suggest a person occupies more than one location simultaneously.

The production began in the West End on May 7 and opened on May 20, 2003.

With one exception, critics either loved it or liked it. The naysayer, Evans, despises Pirandello's play—"a creaky bauble by a dud genius"—and mocks the players as "marvelously adequate." He mentions neither Sherman nor changes in the 1917 script (42, 44).

Eight reviews range from positive to raves. Brown lauds, "Sherman's sparkling new version ... as well as teasing the brain ... tugs at the heartstrings" (69). Peter rhapsodizes about "dark intellectual magic," then concludes, "You must see this" (Culture, 18). De Jongh dislikes Davies but praises everything else, including "Sherman's fresh, witty version" (42). Foss rejoices "thanks to a bright new translation by Martin Sherman and his own immaculate good taste, Zeffirelli ... makes fantasy and reality dance together in ever-increasing circles until you are almost absurdly dizzy with deception."

Gross calls it "witty" and extols Sherman's version as "fresh, fluent and easy on the ear" (Review, 7). Nightingale notes "the questions and counter-questions start by dizzying the mind and end by justifying the title of Martin Sherman's colloquial translation" (5L). He praises the evening as "gripping and entertaining" as well as "tantalizing."

Macaulay likes "the balance of comedy and tragedy" and judges, "Although Martin Sherman's new English version is at times very free, it is admirably fresh, while elegantly keeping the audience's attention with a rich supply of polished sentences." Spencer raves that Zeffirelli "deftly balances the play's playfulness and its profundity, its fleet wit and deep pain," while he also praises the "crisp, colloquial new version" (20). He admits he found himself "surprised by tears in its astonishing final scene."

Among the nine critics who posted mixed notices, some disagree with this assessment about successfully mixing genres. Maxwell can distinguish only one genre. He likes the wit but finds no drama underpinning the comedy. Clapp agrees. She praises "Sherman's fresh and idiomatic new version," yet concludes, "It's a stylish, adroit occasion, but becalmed, pretty and playful rather than urgent, intriguing." Koenig complains about jokes and playable text (10). She prefers "formal diction." Gore-Langton reviews it in two sentences, cramming in praise but also scorn for the title. Shenton likes the mounting, not the play.

Bassett finds "Sherman's translation and the acting can be stiff, here and there" but praises "wittily observed comic behaviour" and finds the production entertaining plus more intellectually stimulating "than most of the West End's current pulp" (12).

Both Nathan and Billington seem not to understand Pirandello's play. The former says Plowright's mother-in-law, rather than her daughter (or whoever she is), is "mysteriously kept in doors." Billington concludes his review, "It is a good evening that would be even better if Zeffirelli focused more on Pirandello's domestic tragedy and rather less on games with illusion and reality" (24). This seems an odd comment about a writer—married to an insane wife—who dramatized the difficulty of distinguishing between exactly those poles. Neither review mentions Sherman.

Michael Coveney, however, approves the new version ("translated with subtle aplomb by Martin Sherman"), as well as the set and Plowright's performance. He doesn't care for much else (9).

Several months after its limited run had ended, *Absolutely! (perhaps)* received four Olivier Award nominations: In the Best Performance in a Supporting Role category, Oliver Ford Davies for Laudisi; for Best Set Design, Franco Zeffirelli; for Best Costume Design, Raimonda Gaetani; and for Best Revival, "*Absolutely! (perhaps)* by Luigi Pirandello in a new version by Martin Sherman." This nomination creates a paradox, a "revival" of a play in a new version never before produced.

During winter 2000, Showtime commissioned Sherman to write a new adaptation of Tennessee Williams' novella *The Roman Spring of Mrs. Stone*. Sherman simultaneously wrote this and *Callas Forever*. He created his initial draft before Showtime had selected a director. He completed it quickly, during summer 2000.

Time passed, he wrote *A Passage to India*, Zeffirelli filmed *Callas*, and finally, in January 2002, Sherman saw the final cut of that film and participated in preproduction on *Roman Spring*.

Ackerman would direct, and the cast would include Helen Mirren, Anne

Bancroft, French heartthrob Olivier Martinez, Brian Dennehy, and Roger Allam. Brazilian Rodrigo Santoro would play the silent Young Man, who begins and ends the film and follows Karen Stone.

Ackerman loved the screenplay: "I was blown away. He got every nuance into the script, but also opened it up in a way that made it more modern and improved the original. He knows the rhythm of film and how long or short a scene has to be."

Their 23-year working relationship made mutually agreed upon adjustments easy. In addition, Ackerman decided to film a few sequences Showtime had asked Sherman to cut—such as the Young Man peeing in front of Mrs. Stone. "I just shot them anyway," Ackerman explains, "and in the end everything they had made Martin cut wound up in it."

Filming began in mid April, but *The Boy from Oz* workshop caused Sherman to miss the interior sessions in Ireland. He flew to Rome.

Ackerman managed to shoot on the Spanish Steps, instead of having to satisfy himself with shots from above or below. He obtained this permission because, says Ackerman, "the Romans love Tennessee Williams and because Rome appears in the title." Although the script isn't kind to the city, they filmed along the steps, which hadn't been permitted in 20 years. "We were so lucky," continues Ackerman. "Memories of Audrey Hepburn and Gregory Peck were present in everyone's mind. We were also allowed to shoot in the Coliseum when no one else was there, and in the piazza in front of the Pantheon. It was marvelous."

Williams tells an unpleasant tale of a widow drifting and duped and dumped. A bawd and a gigolo exploit and mistreat Karen. They succeed because sexual obsession impairs her judgment and self-control. Never did Williams write anything more autobiographical and seldom did he write anything more distasteful than this degraded, humiliated, lonely middle-aged woman. Imagine what *Streetcar Named Desire* might have depicted had he given us Blanche at Belle Reeve rather than afterward in New Orleans. The subject matter challenged Sherman. The weak 1961 film starring Vivien Leigh, Warren Beatty, and Lotte Lenya made the challenge more enticing.

Sherman again created a central female figure, an actress and, thus, an artist. Her own actions imperil her survival. We cannot know when the film ends whether she will live through the night. An "exile" from her country, this American also behaves beyond the pale for her mid–20-century gender, which makes possible her enemy the Contessa terming her scandalous. She shares some characteristics with Isadora, but without that bohemian's devil-may-care attitude and entourage of supportive admirers. The usual Sherman elements— an outsider struggling to survive—seem familiar, but could he create a character we care about rather than a figure born of Williams' self-contempt?

Karen needs someone to talk to. Williams gave her Meg Bishop, a nasty writer. Sherman deletes her because she plus the horrid Contessa create misogyny overkill. Instead he devises as confidante Christopher, a Southern playwright, a theatre professional because in the novella, "You never believe she's an actress. She behaves like a socialite." He tries to lure her back to the theatre—thus providing a possible escape route. He understands the allure of beautiful boys. He also cares what happens to her; this encourages us to care. As played by Allam, Christopher becomes Williams on a good day.

Sherman increases our sympathy for Karen's lover Paolo di Lio by emphasizing the postwar setting. Williams ignores the war's effects, so his Italians behave with motiveless malice. Sherman, however, emphasizes the poverty shared by Anne Bancroft's Contessa, a fascist, and the young men she introduces to wealthy American women. These titled aristocrats need somebody to buy them dinner, and they loathe the Americans who pulverized their country and impoverished them.

Williams relies more on narrative than dialogue because he wrote notes to pitch this film idea to Greta Garbo. He described the action in the third person. When Garbo refused, he expanded what he had and published it as a short novel—minor work by a great dramatist. He also laces his prose with interior monologue, often her vague thoughts as she "drifts" through her months in Rome. Only towards the end does he insert as much conversation as Sherman could employ.

He goes way beyond inventing dialogue. He creates new scenes and Christopher, who appears four times. He and his lover Guido enter Karen's dressing room after her disastrous opening as Juliet. He doesn't lie. Instead he drawls, "I haven't seen such bravery since Dunkirk." Karen asks, "Didn't we lose Dunkirk?" and he replies "Valiantly," demonstrating why she values his friendship. He finds something to praise—her courage at getting through the performance. Sherman communicates this in 12 words.

Christopher encounters Karen at a party. He points out Paolo to her, remarking, "He's with Mrs. Jameson Walker, whose husband owns Texas." Christopher accompanies Karen to the Coliseum, where, after she scatters her husband's ashes, she says she has decided to stay in Rome. The playwright inquires, "Can nothing tempt you back onto a stage?" She replies, "Only amnesia. I have no talent."

Christopher returns to urge Karen to appear in his new play in a role he wrote for her. He argues, "You can retire from a profession, you know, but not from an art." When he cannot budge her, he asks if Paolo is a handful, and she, looking to him for understanding, says, "I thought you would approve." He has similarly indulged, so he responds with the movie's most often-quoted lines, "Beautiful boys are medicinal. Like penicillin, they should be taken twice a day until the course is finished, after which you should have—in theory—recovered."

Following further conversation, as Christopher prepares to leave, Karen finally acknowledges she cannot "recover." She now understands "the meaning of addiction." Christopher responds, "Then, Baby, you're lost." This sounds like Williams yet doesn't appear in the novella.

Sherman invents the Contessa introducing Karen to other men and her dates with them, Karen meeting Paolo, their first date and evolving romance, and all the lovemaking scenes. The latter include explicit sex, some nude, to communicate the powerful erotic attraction between Karen and Paolo. Williams mentions the Contessa has asked Karen for a large loan but she has offered a small one. Sherman gives us the full scene. As we watch Mrs. Stone outsmart the Contessa, we know the American has thereby unwittingly lost Paolo, whose bawd will insist he leave her for a more lucrative client.

Sherman dramatizes courtship and affair more visually than verbally. This includes Karen and Paolo in public and private. Happy home-movie images as they cavort together provide a final stark contrast between joy they took in each other and animosity as their affair ends. Similarly, Paolo sings "A tisket, a tasket, a little yellow basket" and then teases Karen into singing. Ackerman films part of this sequence through gauze curtains, giving us a voyeuristic feeling as we observe the laughing couple. Scenes like this emphasize Karen loses more than a stud.

Sherman follows this with the pair after lovemaking, when Karen wants to cover her body in a bathrobe, but Paolo sincerely tells her, "You are beautiful." Afterward, while Karen sleeps Paolo moistens his finger and touches her eye, then studies the makeup that comes off. The non-verbal here doesn't so much contradict Paolo's reassurance as supplement it, providing richer texture, contrasting truths.

The novella focuses on fear of aging and loss of allure. Williams also imbues it with his shame, his guilt, his pain. The screenplay communicates those, but as the affair's aftermath, not its essence. Previously we observe a full range of emotions, including Karen reveling in love and sexual fulfillment.

After an extended courtship and an exciting affair, Karen loses Paolo not because of wrinkles but because her pride won't permit her to pay a gigolo the required sums, and his pride—plus his financial necessity—won't permit him to continue without them. A culture-gap contributes—her American assumptions versus his Italian traditions. Sherman's heritage provides him a richer grasp of New World versus Old World than Williams intuited.

Sherman's complex Paolo loves Karen in his fashion, enjoys their good times together, but also suffers from pride and the belief his position as a count entitles him to wealth and prestige. He blames the U.S. for depriving him of these. Thus, he harbors conflicting feelings toward Karen. The Contessa successfully manipulates him by exploiting these conflicts about his self worth. She also offers him the promise he can become a movie star. Therefore Karen cannot win, and our hearts break for her. Sherman's script creates sympathy Williams' novella doesn't.

Mirren appreciates the screenplay and regrets the film aired primarily in the U.S. She praises Sherman as a "remarkable" writer, "the only one who could truly do justice to the delicacy and poetry of Williams' writing. He wrote a beautiful script that was psychologically complex, but understandable. He also has a marvelous economy. With a Sherman script there is no editing. It arrives in perfect form."

Roman Spring began broadcasts on May 4, 2003—three days before *Absolutely! (perhaps)* started its West End previews and four months before *The Boy from Oz*—which Sherman, meanwhile, had revised—began its Broadway run.

Roman Spring received two pans but otherwise good, sometimes great reviews. The negatives could stem from the Williams material, offensive to some no matter how adroitly handled.

Still, these critics blame Sherman. Garvin writes, "This purported tragedy of lost youth is strictly farce" (3E). Lazere finds Sherman's version worse than its Hollywood predecessor. "The screenplay ... lacks both tension and any tone of genuine decadence fitting the circumstances. His Karen Stone is missing the hard edge of a pampered star; she's too nice to make the turnaround satisfying."

In contrast, Fries finds this version "rings truer to the original text than" the 1961 film. She judges "Sherman distills the essence of the story—a repressed woman's sexual awakening—into a provocative piece." Gardella loves "this outstanding adaptation" and concludes, "This is one trip to Rome you won't want to miss" (63). Smith concedes she dislikes the situation in which Williams embedded Karen, but praises this version as "better than the original in many ways" (W11C). Stewart rates it an 8 (49). Either Mason or Connors praises the film's revelations "about the human condition at the mercy of false expectations" (18).

Storm feels it "can be disturbing, which is what good dramas should be" and is "beautifully acted and powerfully written." Gilbert praises the screenplay for providing the postwar bitterness towards Americans as a "context" which "adds weight to the story" (D1). Rosenberg calls it "classy" and raves about "an achingly on-point adaptation of Tennessee Williams' novella with a striking performance by Helen Mirren that ranks with her best." Richmond judges the screenplay "adapted for TV with sensitivity—if an occasional overabundance of melodrama," then terms the conclusion "wrenching."

Two critics ambivalent in their responses, Gates and Meyer, judge Mirren poor casting for Karen. Gates says, "Ms. Mirren gives a strong, touching performance, but she may be miscast" because she looks intelligent (E27). She notes, "Everyone seems a little more desperate and hungry in the new film," and she quotes a line approvingly. Yet she calls it "admirably faithful but heavy-handed."

Meyer judges Mirren lacks "the kind of fragility that Williams intended" (D1, D6), but she praises "some very hot sex scenes ... that weren't in the original.... She might be paying for it, but she's getting her money's worth." And she approves Sherman's choice of period, bringing "context to the desperation displayed by its postwar Italian characters."

The American Society of Cinematographers, USA, nominated Ashley Rowe. The Golden Satellite Awards nominated Mirren for "Best Performance by an Actress in a Miniseries or a Motion Picture Made for Television" and Bancroft for the corresponding "Supporting Role" award. The Screen Actors Guild nominated both women for "Outstanding Performance by a Female Actor in a Television Movie or Miniseries."

Roman Spring received five Emmy Award nominations: Dona Granata and assistant Gill Howard for costumes, John Altman for music, Mirren for "Outstanding Lead Actress in a Miniseries or a Movie," Bancroft for the corresponding "Supporting Actress" award, and Robert Allan Ackerman for "Outstanding Directing for a Miniseries, Movie or a Dramatic Special." Finally, the Golden Globes, USA, nominated Mirren for "Best Performance by an Actress in a Mini-Series or a Motion Picture Made for Television" and nominated the movie for "Best Mini-Series or Motion Picture Made for Television." *Angels in America* won this award.

Ackerman remembers when Williams saw *Bent* he loved the play and its mounting. Had he lived longer, he would have taken pleasure in the same writer and director's rendering of his *Roman Spring*.

Fast forward to spring 2008. Ackerman has a theatre company in Japan where he stages plays when film commitments permit. He asked Sherman to adapt the film as a play; they could test it in Tokyo. The first week in June 2008, the playwright devised a stage version for him to do with his Japanese company. ("I had a free week," Sherman quips.) Boasting a cast of 26, this play, featuring Rei Asami, opened at the Parco on March 1, 2009. Sherman loved it. He therefore reduced the cast size to permit the film to enjoy further stage reincarnations, including a possible London 2011 opening.

18. India (2000–2002)

In November 2000, while Sherman juggled projects, Meckler asked him to dramatize E.M. Forster's 1924 novel, *A Passage to India*, for her company Shared Experience. She explains, "Martin would be great on the Indian-ness and it would be interesting for a gay writer to tackle a book written when the author's gayness had to be hidden." Indeed Meckler felt drawn to this novel partly because "there is so much repression in the characters' lives. This lends itself to theatrical expression of the hidden."

Shared Experience had a first-rate reputation for moving fiction classics from page to stage, and Sherman had adored working with Meckler. How could he refuse? Ignoring the dictates of self-preservation and common sense, he agreed. They scheduled for late April 2001 a workshop with actors to stimulate his imagination, and then Sherman flew to Greece to begin writing. When he returned to London on June 6, he had drafted *Passage*.

Sherman intended not to foreground the novel's "gay subtext," but he felt it "permeates the book. The novel's last section is never included in any dramatization, yet is its core. It is spiritual and mysterious and deals with Hindu ritual, whereas the rest is Islamic."

The Marabar Caves interested him least. Sherman understands Forster wrote about a friendship developed and lost, not an assault in a cave. "People go on too much about the caves' 'mystery.' It's not a mystery. It's clear Aziz didn't assault Adela. Forster wisely didn't disabuse people of that fascination, but it wasn't about that."

Like the novel, the play progresses in short episodes, most lasting only a minute or two. Yet Sherman restructures the novel to help viewers understand it. He transposes to the beginning material from the concluding section, Part III, called "Temple," which takes place two years later. The Hindu Godbole, who appears in the earlier Chandrapore segments but plays no major role, functions as a central character in this Mau portion.

Sherman selects Godbole to narrate the opening of both acts as well as to interact with others. The Hindu tells us about the Mau legend concerning the origin of two shrines to head and to heart. This encourages us to observe the contrast of uptight Brits and more sensual and emotional Indians.

Godbole doesn't struggle to understand—a struggle that causes endless misunderstandings between the novel's Muslims and Christians. And he embraces a paradoxical ritual in which God's birth occurs almost simultaneously with discarding him. This rapid "passage" parallels Aziz's emotional shifts toward Fielding.

Sherman then dramatizes (like Pinter's *Betrayal*) a relationship's end, as Aziz rejects his dear friend Fielding. Thereafter, Sherman shows them meeting and moves chronologically, as they closely bond, then disengage in the trial's aftermath.

Those who believe *A Passage to India* concerns Adela and Mrs. Moore and the former's accusation of sexual assault in the Marabar Caves will find Sherman's approach unsettling, even irritating. Aukin believes, however, Sherman understands the book's "very essence. One of the criticisms of the novel is that it falls apart after the trial, but this is a misreading. Martin's adaptation makes this clear as the emotional journey continues through to the end."

By turning the play into a flashback framed by the Hindu professor, Sherman avoids such "misreading." We view the conflicts between Islamic and Christian characters from a slight remove. Godbole's perspective makes both Chandrapore groups "the other," and yet both worthy of affection, because "God si love," as his misprinted Hindu banner proclaims (6). It provides ironic contrast to the schism that propels India towards independence as well as sundering into separate countries. Forster created this irony; Sherman foregrounds it.

He doesn't employ all Forster's scenes. He omits, for instance, the section in which Fielding arrives at the Marabar Caves and tries to learn where Adela is, while Aziz, unaware anything has gone wrong, chats.

A particularly important scene dramatizes the beginning of the friendship we already know has ended. When Aziz enters, Fielding hasn't finished dressing. Speaking through the partition, Aziz expresses his admiration for the host he hasn't yet met: "The fact is I have long wanted to meet you. I have heard so much about your warm heart.... I used to wish you to fall ill so we could meet that way" (26). After Fielding damages his collar stud, Aziz offers his own, wrenching it off his collar, then lying that it's a spare so as to assist his new friend.

Forster shows us nothing of Adela's experience in her cave. Sherman, however, takes us in to share the darkness, the lit match, the echoing "BOOM" (54). Meckler stages her panic because her company shares characters' inner experience. The actors who form the cave's walls lightly touch her as she bumps against them. This doesn't suggest a rape. It does convey her inner hallucinatory panic and the possibility of a momentary sexual arousal that nothing in her priggish life has prepared her to handle.

At the end, Fielding hopes they can resume their friendship, prompting Aziz to declare "Clear out, you fellows, double quick, I say. We may hate one another, but we hate you most. If I don't make you go, my children will. If it's fifty or five hundred years we shall get rid of you, yes, we shall drive every blasted Englishman into the sea, and then ... (Half kisses him.) And then you and I shall be friends" (99). Fielding begs, but Aziz won't relent. The play has led to this outcome, which has far more impact than the trial. Forster would love it.

Complex tensions doom the relationship of Aziz and Fielding or, by extension, of East and West.

As Guy Mannes-Abbott explains in program notes for performances at the Brooklyn Academy of Music, Forster's own experiences suggested to him his locales and characters. This doesn't make the novel autobiographical, but does reflect his love for Sir Syed Ross Masood—a love not reciprocated. The novelist also drew upon his 1912–13 visit to the British Raj and his later employment by a small Hindu state's maharajah. Forster modeled Chandrapore on Bankipore and Mau on Dewas.

Forster accurately observes hostilities between rulers and ruled that led to the British departure. Eventually religious and cultural factionalism caused the subcontinent's division into today's India, Pakistan, and later Bangladesh. Forster presciently reflects those divisions. His *Passage* details more than just his experience of Islamic India. His Godbole brings Hindus into the volatile mix, and, by setting the latter part of the novel in Hindu Mau, an independent state, Forster uses his experience in that contrasting region to comment on more than Muslim-Christian conflicts.

By emphasizing *Passage*'s Hindu aspects, Sherman helps us appreciate Forster didn't write a novel about Adela or Adela and Mrs. Moore. He didn't, indeed, focus on the British. He wrote about two men, one British and one Indian, who meet, love each other across a cultural divide, then lose each other during the subcontinent's passage to nationhood, achieved 23 years later. The personal experience of men who form, enjoy, and destroy a friendship reflects the region's experience.

Sherman believes the protagonists don't recognize a physical attraction, but Forster hints at it. The playwright's program notes remark, "The scene where they meet ... is a classic courtship scene, albeit a rather adolescent one, and yet is entirely unconscious." Thus, Aziz, the Indian more in touch with his sensuality than any of the British characters, nevertheless experiences his own repression, similar to Fielding's and Adela's.

One can choose to notice the homoerotic subtext created by this closeted gay novelist or to see only the growth and death of a friendship. Adela's panic in the cave serves, not as the novel's subject, but as the catalyst for destroying the men's affection, whether or not based in erotic impulse.

Novel and play prove relevant today. Western imperialism causing resentment, interpersonally patronizing treatment of others that denies their humanity, cultural clashes based in ignorance and arrogance—these continue in the post–9/11 world just as they affected U.S. policy predating the terrorist attacks. Those bewildered souls who asked in autumn 2001, "Why do 'they' hate us?" should read Forster's novel or Sherman's play. Or, if a real history lesson would better serve, read about the slaughter Forster's compatriots carried out during the years he wrote his novel. The carnage the British wrought in India in 1919 especially turns the stomach.

Forster and Sherman indict with satire and small-scale pathos, not bullets. Yet the behavior they condemn springs from racism and xenophobia, mutual prejudices and distrusts that beget violence.

Sherman completed *Passage* before 9/11, yet events that day enhanced its relevance. The animosities it dramatizes have contemporary parallels. Spectators gasp when Dr. Aziz speaks of his Afghani ancestors, yet Forster wrote that line and Sherman put it into his adaptation before this took on 21st-century significance.

Sherman employs his usual genre of drama and comedy, the latter comprised of satire, irony, and Aziz's sly wit. He faithfully reflects how Forster turns the tables racially. Previous writers caricatured Indians, but this novelist presents Indians sympathetically and instead satirizes imperialists. Yet Forster and Sherman employ cultural misunderstandings and clashes to dramatic effect as well.

Sherman dramatizes his usual themes: survival and "the other." British "justice" threatens Aziz's survival, the climate and disease threaten the colonialists, and distrust and cultural conflicts imperil everyone. Mrs. Moore loses first her centering values and then her life. Aziz and Fielding's friendship perishes, as does the "truth."

Each group in *Passage* distrusts the other, whether Hindu, Muslim or Christian, master or servant, a different gender or class, dissimilar cultural quirks, or distinctions in indulging or repressing eroticism. Even attractiveness or plainness separates. Everybody serves as somebody else's outsider, and, despite impulses of respect and affection, fear of difference (especially racism) drives them. Ronny Heaslop even claims "the Jews" fomented recent unrest. Bigots blame L'Etranger.

This script reflects the male world of Forster's novel. Although Mrs. Moore and Adela engage our sympathies, they don't play central roles. Forster poses the question: Are two men of different races, one among the rulers, the other among the ruled, doomed to sacrifice friendship? When rulers suffer an inability to respect and feel compassion, a cross-cultural friendship perishes.

Both cultures confuse lies and truth, believing bigoted conjectures and ignoring facts. Forster and Sherman highlight mutual distrust, suspicion, fear, deception, and self-deception. Each culture assumes the worst about the other.

The play lasts two and three quarter hours. While watching a performance, we don't notice omissions. Sherman lifts a few sentences from one section and a few more from another, seamlessly stitching them into a scene we would swear Forster wrote. What Sherman doesn't verbalize, Shared Experience supplies. The ensemble use their bodies and voices to convey inner experiences and as substitutes for high-tech effects found in expensive productions.

Sherman employs a suitable presentational style. No slice-of-life drama on a box set, *Passage* permits Meckler's troupe to create exotic India through simple means, flipping from Asian to Western roles and switching from a garden party to a train, an elephant, several boulders, or a mob. They evocatively stage Adela's cave horror, which the novel omits.

Meckler selected the composer she had used for *Alive and Kicking*, Peter Salem, to devise the music performed by violin and tabla. Liz Ranken, that film's choreographer, provides "company movement" for the play. Niki Turner's minimalist set features beaten bronze and a cloth backdrop that shimmers like metal. She also employs versatile platforms and a few props. Actors wear white costumes and switch from rulers to ruled by swapping pith helmets for turbans. At right and left we observe competing shrines, to head and heart, providing a visual reminder the characters fail to balance reason and emotion or repression and sensuality.

A few critics, instead of asking, "Given Shared Experience's goal and methods, do they accomplish their tasks well?" simply condemn this theatrical style. These reviewers prove the exception; most applaud this stage version.

Passage received its world premiere at the Richmond Theatre outside London from September 19–21, 2002, followed by a one-month tour.

It played to enthusiastic audiences, but no London theatres became available, and the ensemble production, which boasted no star, seemed likely to die. However, Riverside Studios booked it to begin January 20, 2003.

Excellent notices had helped prompt the London engagement. Kingston admires every aspect but especially appreciates Sherman's use of Godbole as narrator framing the action. "We are drawn into the misadventures of the characters and are then drawn out of them by his detachment. It is a thrilling, dramatic feature within a thrilling, dramatic experience" (Features, 25). Gardner calls the production "magic" and Sherman's adaptation "clever," noting it "cracks open the novel and teases out its themes." She also approves how Sherman "provides both a comic edge and a philosophical and political framework."

The other tour critics published raves. Herman calls the "magic" as "rich and many-faceted as the Koh-i-Noor diamond." She judges Sherman's play "a new work both faithful to the old and urgently topical." Dungate effervesces, "Simply story-telling at its most magical" and "Intriguing and challenging in its complexity.... It is all quite, quite, lastingly beautiful."

Such enthusiasm while a production plays out of town risks backlash to "hype" when a show comes into London. A dozen positive reviews greeted it, however, while five proved mixed or slightly negative. Herbert approves, "Sherman's Forster adaptation sets a formidable standard. It achieves a great deal with very simple resources ... a remarkably detailed, believable picture of the many sides of colonial India" (4). Nightingale judges Sherman's script "able" and "as gripping as it is spare yet inventive." Brown begins, "Martin Sherman's adaptation ... is a triumph. It brings to thrilling, moving and engrossing theatrical life the racial, class and cultural tensions of India under British rule and—even more complex—the workings of the human heart." Clapp, too, loves *Passage*, terming it "spellbinding" (Review, 12).

Gross declares this the best stage adaptation of the novel and "an unusually rewarding evening" (Review, 9), and de Jongh begins by bashing Lean's 1984 film before praising Meckler's "beautifully imagined" production and Sherman's "cleverly distilled adaptation," which convey "Forster's essence."

Taylor, likewise, details Lean's flaws, which he contrasts to the play's merits, calling it "refreshingly scrupulous and lucid" as well as "bold." He praises Sherman's adaptation as "excellent" and values its "economy and incisiveness." He lauds an aspect some fault, the "early flash forward to the novel's end" which foreshadows the "central tragedy: the love between these men that will be destroyed." Taylor judges, "The production is very moving, but not at all sentimental."

Loveridge terms *Passage* "an enriching experience ... not to be missed" which "deserves to find a world-wide audience." She calls Sherman's version "a faithful adaptation" and "an intense and evocative portrayal." Logan describes it as "a languid, elegant telling of Forster's Raj drama which occasionally bursts into choreographed expressionist life" (143). He seems squeamish, however, about the sexuality, both Adela's and the men's. Woddis enthuses over how Sherman and Meckler render Forster's "metaphysical conundrums" and compares the text's "subtle and homoerotically poised reworking" to Eliot's *Four Quartets*. Nathan says production and "insightful" adaptation especially illuminate the pair's conflicts and "the real triumph of this production lies in leaving me with the sense of having visited a time before I was born and a country I've never seen."

Morley rhapsodizes about Sherman's script as the only dramatization of Forster's novel ever to remain true to it, by providing "no ready-made solutions" and by seeing events "through Indian rather than colonial eyes" (48). Sherman understood, argues Morley, "Forster was writing about the national identity and political and religious awareness of India."

Five critics publish mixed or more negative reviews. Sierz evaluates from a revolutionary perspective. Thus he observes Aziz and Fielding's relationship "strained by the ingrained attitudes of domination and subordination" and demands to know "how can we take action and change society?" At the most political moments, however, he feels "like cheering" and finds the show "highly stimulating" (21).

Marlowe calls it "a partial success," a "robust and inventive theatrical approach," but also lacking subtlety. She terms Sherman's adaptation "serviceable" but complains he presents "most of the British characters as crude stereotypes." Marlowe doesn't recall this comes from Forster's satire, not from Sherman's pen. She judges it "cannot fail to compel." Fisher finds dramatizing the book "dangerous" because this cannot vie with the film. He believes Forster wrote a novel about Adela and, hence, finds Sherman's play odd. Still, he judges "it provides much food for thought."

Other reviews veer towards negative. Spencer complains, "Its donnish mysticism, bossy political correctness and homo-erotic undercurrents all seem rather absurd" (23). He finds in the final few scenes "full-blooded dramatic life" but otherwise judges this "a plodding adaptation of a seriously overrated novel."

Where Spencer regards the novel with contempt, Peter suffers from a misconception concerning Forster's attitudes and themes. He has noticed no satire in the novel. Instead, he believes, "EM Forster's novel is about being English. India is less a place than a moral parade ground where you can take pride and pleasure in the English virtues of strength, leadership and responsibility" (Culture, 20). Having gotten Forster's position backwards, he can only praise "Meckler's visual flair" while deciding "it is the wrong way to take you inside the mystery that Forster was haunted by."

Meckler remounted *Passage* with another cast in 2004. Before visiting the U.S., this ensemble toured.

Bhagat greets this *Passage* rapturously, "Shared Experience bring the sights and sounds of India brilliantly to life." He singles out as the "most striking element of this play ... the portrayal of EM Forster's insight into the racism and cultural ignorance of the British colonists." He finds Sherman's adaptation "particularly accomplished" in its focusing through Hindu eyes, and he concludes, "Not just a good story, but a wonderful experience." Orme acclaims, "Martin Sherman can hardly do any wrong," the playwright "has wisely resisted the temptation to make the stage version too complex." "It's a stylish, admirable performance."

Passage received a less enthusiastic reception when it appeared November 2–6, 2004, in Brooklyn. Considering how beleaguered many New Yorkers felt while fearing terrorist attacks and taking precautions unlikely to protect them, perhaps their dismay when asked to sympathize with Muslim characters while disliking western Christian characters shouldn't surprise us.

CurtainUp reprinted Loveridge's London review. "Seen & Heard" doesn't pretend to have read the novel, but likes this, the "kind of play rarely produced by an American company and BAM gets kudos for continually bringing this kind of work to our shores." Dace commends, "Sherman's delicious sense of irony suits Forster perfectly, and Sherman and Meckler both bring to a satiric novel about the serious subject of bigotry exactly the right combinations of whimsy, ridicule and dramatic tension" (34–36).

Wolf approves, "Sherman's adaptation ... grasps key elements of the story and wraps them in theatrical magic.... He has striven for visual methods of conveying atmosphere and feeling, as well as finding a textual path." Wolf buttresses his praise with examples other New York critics use to condemn the work: framing it with Godbole, physical techniques he feels impart "beauty," and "hints" of homoeroticism.

Noh's mixed remarks call it "enthralling" and "magically directed" but term the script "merely serviceable" and condemn undue emphasis on "homoerotic tension" and Godbole as narrator of "the whole thing"—Noh's error, since the Hindu narrates little. Incensed by this imaginary total narrative, he calls it "most intrusive, tiresome and superfluous" (38).

"Unlike most bare-bones stage versions of great literary classics, Martin Sherman's adaptation of E.M. Forster's 1924 *A Passage to India* provides auds enough substance to chew on," writes Stasio (11). She continues, "There is also much to relish in Nancy Meckler's stylized visual treatment.... But in virtually ignoring Forster's deeper ruminations on the sociopolitics of colonialism, this production has the nutritional value of eye candy." She likewise objects to the "homoerotic impulses arbitrarily imposed" on Fielding, details her dislike of the physical theatre Shared Experience creates (despite her earlier praise), and misses Forster's "deep thought."

Feingold first recommends the show as a "Voice Choice"—based on its "high acclaim in England"—and then, after seeing it, pans it as "slow-moving and schematic, with mostly tinny acting and heavily signaled messages" (73). He doles out one dollop of praise by adding, "Some of Sherman's scenes, particularly those between Adela and Ronny, had the crisp clarity of his best writing," yet he believes the novel probably cannot be adapted for theatre. Rather than ask "Does Meckler's company excel at this?" Shaw condemns the genre: "Beware theater that describes itself as 'physical'" (23). She hates *Passage*. Manish doesn't care for it and calls Shared Experience a "Brooklyn theater company," but all other words he posts he has lifted from Isherwood's review.

That pan calls it "a cartoon" (E5). He supports his view by arguing Forster's novel makes a poor choice for dramatizing. Isherwood objects the rape doesn't work, Sherman shouldn't have restructured the book or used Godbole to supply some narration, and the homoeroticism "is odd and pointless." He finds the text "a simple reduction of the novel, not a reimagining of it"—despite his complaints about Sherman reimagining it. Isherwood errs by naming Sowmya Gopalan as composer, rather than Peter Salem.

DaVinci Nichols' negative review contains more perplexing errors. She refers to Dr. Aziz as "Anglo-Indian," but this term applies to the British in India, or to the offspring of an English and an Indian parent, which doesn't include the Indian Aziz, descended from Afghani ancestors. Nichols complains Fielding "stands around doing little or nothing in the drama." In fact, he plays the same large role in the play as in the novel, speaking, making decisions, acting in the same proportion. She continues, "He may be a bigger loss than the novel's clash of Hindu and Mau religions, which is thinly represented by two, nearly silent secondary characters." "Mau" designates the Hindu "native state" where Godbole begins both acts and play and novel end. A location isn't a religion, so the religious contrast she attempts here vanishes when she pits Hindu religion against Hindu state. She faults the uniformly British cast for using "fake British accents."

In April 2008, Vitalist Theatre and Premiere Theatre and Performance mounted *Passage*. Weiss terms this version "a true 'jewel in the crown'" (29). She likewise dubs it "a seductive voyage of discovery" and classifies it "highly recommended." Morgan disagrees. Although he calls the production "gorgeous and creatively staged," he finds the script "strangely unmoving" and everything other than caves and trial extraneous. He prefers Lean's film.

When *Passage* reached New York, *The Boy from Oz* had long since opened.

19. Oz (2001–2003)

On March 5, 1998, *The Boy from Oz* opened in Sydney and ran, there and touring, two years. It featured Todd McKenney and others singing Peter Allen hits strung together in a slim libretto by Nick Enright. More a revue than a book musical, it glossed over Allen's sexual orientation, instead dwelling on his Aussie roots.

Australian producer Ben Gannon teamed with London producer Robert Fox to put *The Boy from Oz* on Broadway. Or rather, they backed a new show of the same title. They sought developed characters and a more substantial and American plot.

They hired a new director, American Philip Wm. McKinley. He worked with two consecutive librettists to devise a book stressing Allen's U.S. career. Finally Fox suggested Sherman and flew McKinley to London, where he loved Sherman's intelligence and "divine sense of humor." The Broadway version would star Hugh Jackman, who had turned down the role in 1998 and had since become a superstar. His schedule required their workshop and backers performance occur in April 2002, plus McKinley and Sherman had to work around their own commitments in late 2001.

The playwright studied MacLean's biography and did additional research. He chose to represent Allen in performance, recounting his life story. Because the show would consist primarily of musical numbers, he had to make each contribute to characterization and advance plot. He selected songs to do that, some different from those used in Australia, or used in different places, or sung by different characters, sometimes in different arrangements. "Don't Wish Too Hard," disco for Liza and Peter in Australia, became Judy's ballad. Working with McKinley, Sherman constructed a plot, placing songs in events of Peter's life, choosing dramatic moments.

After McKinley returned home, they continued fine-tuning this outline. Then Sherman crafted his book. In a New York rehearsal studio, McKinley prepared the workshop and Sherman continued revising. McKinley recalls, "While directing a scene I would say to Martin, 'We need a section to take us to this moment.' Martin would leave and return with the exact needed instant, not five pages. Often it would only take him twenty minutes. Brilliant! I loved his brevity and his exactness with character."

McKinley knew "he was the right choice. He had that wicked wit that was also Peter's. And he's a collaborator, even loves rewriting. We never had cross words. That's rare in theatre collaboration."

Illustrating how Sherman's wit contributed, McKinley reveals a secret: "It's what permitted him to write all those wonderful Peter 'ad-libs' people think are made up on the spot by the performer. They're not. Martin wrote them. They worked as well in Japan as in America."

None of the creative team had participated in the Australian musical. In addition to McKinley and Sherman, Joey McKneely signed on as choreographer. For the workshop, Jackman played Allen, Mitchel David Federan played the Boy, Patti Allison appeared as Allen's mother, Ruthie Henshall took Liza, and Isabel Keating channeled Judy Garland.

During the workshop, producers requested a change. Sherman had revealed the father's suicide in its chronological place. The producers asked him to save the suicide for the end. That position corresponds to its spot in Enright's script. Any other resemblance between the books by Enright and Sherman derives from their use of the same sources, primarily the biography. McKinley explains, "We were careful to avoid any discussion of what had come before."

Broadway casting differed for two major roles. Beth Fowler took over as Marion, and Stephanie J. Block as Liza.

The Boy from Oz joins Sherman's other gay love stories *Passing By*, *Bent*, *Some Sunny Day*, *Alive and Kicking*, and *A Passage to India*. He provides a musical comedy laced with drama, but dominated by playful narrator Peter, who, as part of a concert, talks of his life's highlights. This conceit links episodes.

Sherman bookends the bio with "All the Lives of Me" and "Once Before I Go." He provides a flippant coda, the over-the-top production number "I Go to Rio." This gives Peter a Carmen Miranda moment (as in *Some Sunny Day*). Standing ovations punctuate the evening, but this number guarantees audiences go wild at the end.

Sherman dramatizes in this musical biography his usual two themes. They don't get much more "other" than Allen—the gay, resident alien, son of a suicide, product of a dysfunctional family who nevertheless remained an exponent of joie de vivre. His flamboyance and increasing openness about his sexuality especially set him off from other entertainers of the time.

AIDS snuffed out 48-year-old Allen's life in 1992, shortly before scientists provided effective drugs to combat the disease. Three other deaths also keep us focused on the survival theme. Judy dies of an overdose, Greg succumbs to AIDS, and Peter's father shoots himself. Sherman uses Allen songs effectively to enhance the pathos: "Quiet Please, There's a Lady on Stage" for Garland; "Love Don't Need a Reason" when Greg falls ill because "what we don't have is time"; "I Honestly Love You" as Greg's ghost consoles Peter about the entertainer's illness; "Don't Cry Out Loud" after the father's suicide; and "Once Before I Go" prior to Peter's demise.

The Boy from Oz examines survival from the other side. Allen's cheerful spirit helps him persevere and exude infectious joy for others. He likewise employs a survival kit of humor to keep himself and others laughing. Allen's refusal to put into words a declaration, "Yes, I'm gay," serves as a mechanism, in that gay-bashing era, to protect him.

Forced to cram his plot, character development, and dialogue between—and often in—production numbers, Sherman uses songs, strategically placed, to propel the action. He economically places spoken lines where music and lyrics won't do the trick.

Sherman invents his dialogue. He doesn't lift it from interviews or film clips—that is, from the characters' real lives—and he doesn't borrow from Enright's book.

Despite the dialogue's economy, it contains humor. When his mother protests 16-year-old Petey running off to a place "filled with beach bums, alcohol, drugs and sex," he responds, "I'm trusting that you're telling me the truth, Mum." When Peter tells Judy he had a difficult childhood, she retorts, "You're saying that with a straight face to Judy Garland?" When Peter is dying, Greg's ghost quips regarding the fiasco *Leg's Diamond* that even in heaven they heard about the *Times* review.

Sherman creates a Garland who fits so well her wisecracking image that we accept her authenticity immediately. Peter taps into her sense of humor and she into his. They have fun, which makes her death more poignant. Sherman characterizes Greg quickly by giving him the line, "You better realize if I move into this apartment, it's a lifetime commitment." He conveys Marion's acceptance by the reply she gives to the news he's fallen for a man, "That's lovely, too."

Narcissist Peter talks about himself. He focuses on his needs, even if it means letting his wife leave, choosing a lover who can help advance his career, and firing his agent to get what he wants. Though not Max, he tends—as Greg notes—towards self-absorption. Yet he protects Liza from Judy and from life's obstacles and disappointments and builds a close bond with her. This Peter Allen has more than one dimension.

Sherman traces Allen's sexual orientation. Petey has the passion for musicals and zest for imitating divas we expect. At 18, he tells us, he had girlfriends, but "my testosterone did tend to be more experimental." After Peter sleeps with an important television producer and tells people about it, he must take foreign bookings and get out of Sydney. When Judy's husband, Mark Herron, approaches him, we learn they have just had sex.

After she dies, as soon as the tribute song ends, Peter says,

> The night of her funeral the police raided the Stonewall, a gay bar in the Village, and the guys who were there, who were still mourning Judy, turned their grief into rage and fought back. They were led by a group of drag queens charging forward in battle—what a wonderful sight it must have been! And in a way, at that moment, the world as it was, changed. I didn't realize it at the time, but for me things would never be the same.

While dressing after sex, Greg tells him, "Ambiguity's clever, but you don't look comfortable on a fence. That's why gay audiences consider you an Uncle Tom. And straights think you're a screaming queen. Keep it up and you've got no future." But Peter asks Greg to move in, and, for the rest of the show, Allen leaves no doubt about his orientation.

The Boy from Oz uses factually accurate material to celebrate the success of a boy from nowheresville. It doesn't attempt psychoanalysis or put the singer/songwriter on trial. However, the *New York Times* assigned a feature article to a man who wouldn't settle for less.

Several facts made Gross unsuited to this assignment. He had never published about theatre. Most seasoned theatre writers wouldn't contend a musical must portray every facet of its protagonist's life. This young man (born in 1970) also hadn't experienced pre–and post–Stonewall. The son of a farm-animal veterinarian, he grew up in rural Illinois in a conservative family, a background unsuited to understanding swinging late-'60s, early-'70s Manhattan. Steeped in political conservatism leading to service as a Republican speechwriter, he also attended the Presbyterian Princeton Theological Seminary.

He convinced a *Times* editor his publication in 2000 of a derogatory article about Judy Garland and gay men gave him expertise concerning a Broadway musical about Peter Allen. It gave him, instead, experience trashing men like Allen. By attacking both man and musical, he departs from the usual format for such pieces which gives the article's subject a chance to talk about his or her show. Instead, he saw and rejected *Oz* right after it began previews. He didn't interview artists connected with it; he interviewed people he hoped would make it look bad.

His headline—"The Boy from Oz You Won't Meet on Broadway"—suggests a focused indictment the article oddly fails to support. His allegation—"Its portrait of him is, to say the least, highly selective"—although unsupported, convinced many readers Sherman's libretto must lie about Allen.

Gross supplies surprisingly few details as evidence. He says Allen "grew up in Tenterfield." That error establishes Gross hasn't read the MacLean biography, which explains that, although born there, Allen grew up in the larger, less remote town of Armidale. Because Allen's fans enjoyed thinking he came from Outback, he didn't correct the misconception, but MacLean does. Gross suggests Sherman leaves out important information but failed to read the source of the information.

When Gross finally reaches an accusation of an actual omission, he says the libretto should show Allen and Herron continuing an affair while married to Liza and Judy. He quotes Gerald Clarke's Garland biography as saying this "most likely" happened. He doesn't say why Clarke thinks so, and he doesn't acknowledge the difference between speculation and fact.

After wondering whether Liza suspected Allen's sexual orientation before she married him—guesswork not buttressed by that biography he hasn't read—

he quotes Liza's half-sister, Lorna Luft. She asserts her mother acted as matchmaker. He doesn't explain Luft's age at that time, 12, or the fact she didn't observe this. The couple met in London and had gotten engaged before Luft met Allen in New York. The biography explains that (100).

Gross quotes Luft because he wants to prove Sherman has the facts wrong when his Garland objects to the marriage. The biography delineates three phases to her reaction: approval, disapproval, and back to approval. Thus Gross, who accuses Sherman of selectivity, gives as an example Sherman's inclusion of all those phases.

Then Gross devotes five paragraphs to Allen's sophisticated nightlife and complains *Oz* "plays down this aspect of Allen's life to some extent." That qualification deflates the message, as it must, because the libretto includes "Continental American," which portrays Allen's gay sex and drug use. The opening lyric about getting high sets the tone, and Liza catches him with a man. This doesn't "play down" Allen's hedonism.

Gross barely refers to Allen and Connell's "open" relationship. He merely mentions one of "Peter's other boyfriends" attending Radio City. If Gross knew the biography, he would have read instead about Greg bringing a date to see Allen perform there (230). Perhaps Gross could try writing a drama containing both incidents—if, indeed, he hasn't confused one with the other. They don't, however, fit into the musical's concert format.

Gross switches gears and devotes two paragraphs to Allen's love for Connell. The libretto includes that, so what point does he intend? Then he protests omitting Allen's appearance on *The Tonight Show* shortly after Connell died. Maybe Sherman has already established Allen's "show must go on" attitude?

Gross suggests a final omission by quoting Allen's sister, who heard "despair" in his voice the day he died. Are *Times* readers supposed to find this surprising or even germane to a musical celebrating Allen's life and career? Sherman chooses more useful, earlier instances of grief to dramatize: Judy's death, Peter's lover's death and his father's suicide.

Gross concludes by quoting the sister about Allen as "happy," as well as "hilariously funny and very upbeat." He implies some untruth on her part. Perhaps he didn't read the biography because he didn't want to deal with all the others who assess Allen that way.

Gannon and Fox replied that they'd been true to Allen's spirit and times "while portraying domestic violence, alcoholism, drug use, promiscuity, suicide and two of the leading characters dying as a result of contracting the AIDS virus. Despite all of the above, Peter Allen brought entertainment and joy" to others, and they strive "to honor that spirit as honestly as we can" (sec. 2, 4). *The Boy from Oz* still hadn't opened then, didn't open, indeed, until October 16. The producers might have pointed out that, until opening night, revisions on the script continued.

Gross naïvely confuses art and documentary. Would anybody have required footnotes for *The Sound of Music* or *Annie Get Your Gun*? *Fiorello!* won the 1960 Pulitzer Prize for drama, not biography. Sherman can verify every fact in *Oz*, but that doesn't constitute a valid test for musical comedy.

Sherman met Allen a couple of times, lived across the street from Reno Sweeney, and saw Allen perform. More importantly, he spoke to many people who knew the entertainer and was struck by how everybody loved him; nobody had a negative word to say about him.

Perhaps what really rankles Gross stems from lack of historical perspective. Born after Stonewall, maybe he doesn't get why gay men once hid. They didn't live in the same world he inhabits. If they hadn't straddled that fence, would Gross have felt so free to reject a closet? He fails to understand the gradual process by which men like Allen, ever freer and more open, and men like Sherman, never closeted, made the world safer for him.

Another historical perspective he lacks concerns sexual freedom and recreational drug use in the mythic '60s and '70s. A child on a farm during the era of the gay baths and Studio 54, he seems only marginally aware many people, both straight and gay, not just showbiz types, at that time rejected monogamy and instead embraced swinging and partied through those years in Manhattan. "Normal" meant a life so alien to Gross he would fancy he had landed on another planet if he could travel back in time. He failed to understand his subject.

Sherman doesn't flinch from telling truths about Allen, and Gross makes no case that he does. Too bad many readers only scan headlines.

Believing the *Times* torpedoed Sherman's book, critics entered the Imperial knowing the newspaper of record told them to distrust it. Sherman therefore received some pans.

Street wisdom regarding *Oz* contends critics love Jackman but trash the book. 'Tain't necessarily so. A couple of favorable reviews don't mention the book, but many others praise it. Sherman's detractors don't outnumber his admirers. Yet the fact some critics penned vitriolic notices spawned mythology.

Those who focus on performers include Ansen, Lyons, and Reed. The latter adores Jackman. His paean concludes, "Here is a star with the power to render the critics impotent" (28).

Barnes observes, "Sherman handles the incidental figures neatly, provides some snappy dialogue, and doesn't shy from Allen's flamboyant homosexuality." Gardner responds to Allen's "unshakable zest for life" and "affectionate tenacity" in fulfilling his dreams, and to the scenes between Allen and both Liza and Greg, calling these "imbued with tenderness and humor." She likes the "flashes of levity and wit." Scheck argues *Oz* "doesn't quite match its subject's legendary flair, but, like its subject, it's hard to really dislike." He finds Allen interacting with Garland and Minnelli "the most entertaining." "The scenes depicting the often bitchy, showbiz-tinged banter among the three characters play like a surreal sitcom" he calls "inspired."

Sommers feels *Oz* achieves its goals. He calls it "airy puff pastry with a delicious Hugh Jackman center" and continues, "Martin Sherman's flossy script establishes Allen as the jaunty emcee of his own life, setting up the scenes and commenting on the action" (29). Sommers notes, "Cleverly using a batch of 24 appealing songs ... the musical sketches his main bio-events." After describing the flashy finale, he asks, "Well, why the heck not? The musical presents Allen as a goodtime Mr. Show Biz who wouldn't want audiences to go home all bummed out over his demise. So a tutti-frutti finale proves true to the show's frisky attitude toward life, love and whatever comes after." He judges, "Peter Allen would love it."

Osborne similarly praises *Oz* for accomplishing its objectives. He writes, "Some critics knocked the show, clearly missing the point—it was obviously intended as a bouncing, flashy Broadway entity (like Allen himself), not a deep-rooted, docu-inspection." He urges it "should be the first stop for anyone that's Broadway-bound between now and 10/2004."

Wolf writes, "Martin Sherman's book ... strives to give authenticity to the characters and their lives and at times the strain shows and slows the action, but there is plenty of fun when the dialogue is snappy and the gag lines earn laughs." He praises a sequence he finds "outstanding" and "amusing" and inquires regarding the finale, "Who can argue with that?" *Oz* packs "abundant glitz but also is moving."

Dace notes, "Producers ... chose a wizard for their *Oz* and got more than their money's worth, a book so unobtrusive it fits into pauses between vocalist refrains and into segues to the next song.... Because Sherman peppers the script with delicious wit, he can also wring tears from us."

Roca raves, "Sherman has written a superb book.... The playful tenderness of Liza and Peter's scenes in Act 1 rings true, and the tragedy of a young life cut down too soon in Act 2 as Peter and his lover Greg Connell face AIDS rises to tragic dimensions. Portraying real-life characters is tricky, but Sherman's book rings true. *The Boy from Oz* is a serious musical that happens to be fabulously gay."

Hatza likewise appreciates the libretto as drama "really about the gay rights movement from the 1950s to the 1990s. Moreover, Allen serves as a metaphor for that journey. His initial love of Hollywood ... spurs a personal voyage along his own yellow-brick road to fame and fortune with Judy Garland as his guide." He regards Allen's marriage to Minnelli as a "sham"—something Sherman disagrees with—but the playwright would surely concur that Allen belongs with Connell. Hatza feels the musical argues "gay people can have a real relationship grounded in love and mutual respect."

Heilpern posits, "Camp and its sister in exaggerated artifice, kitsch, are the moving spirits behind *The Boy from Oz*. The likable show pulls off the same, near impossible balancing act" Allen did. "Jackman and Co. have deftly sent up the over-the-top glitz of an escapist showbiz world, yet found a touching innocence in the wreckage." Heilpern argues, "A few reviewers have missed the point by taking a sour political stance toward the show. It's just a *show*." He calls the script "smart" and argues "the surprise of the good-natured production is that it can be hard-edged when it wants to be," and he cites the protagonist's narcissism.

Kissel begins, "When you die, the next best thing to going to heaven may be having a musical based on your life in which you are played by Hugh Jackman" (45). He understands *Oz* "uses Allen's songs to tell his story, but laments the time constraints truncating Sherman's book, which he nevertheless finds "full of sharp humor."

In a season wrap-up, Holden writes, "*The Boy from Oz* does a better job than most at fitting Peter Allen's often vague, moony sentiments to specific situations." Holden follows that remark with two additional pleasant paragraphs about this musical his paper trashed.

Coveney writes, "The show is ... written by Martin Sherman as an old-fashioned trio-musical—small town Aussie boy lives out a dream—with a difference. The difference is Jackman. This is the sort of knockout display likely to get camp a seriously good name" (55). Daniel approves, "Rest assured that Sherman ... trots out Judy Garland and Liza Minnelli characters in *Oz*—not to mention Aussie X-man Hugh Jackman, who plays Allen. After untangling from Minnelli, Allen spent 11 years with model Gregory Connell until AIDS took center stage. May he finally sleep serenely—and successfully—to the lullaby of Broadway."

Silas Kain, not closeted, doesn't excoriate Allen for his ambiguous status, and he approvingly quotes lyrics from "Bi-Coastal," which left "many Americans mortified." Clearly, Kain admires Allen's comparative openness instead of rebuking him for failing to come out years before a popular U.S. entertainer dared do so. Kain notices "Everything Old Is New Again" as a "necessary bridge to the last phase of Peter's life." He also appreciates the use *Oz* makes of "I Honestly Love You" to dramatize Greg's devotion to Peter.

Most negative reviews also praise Jackman and even other performers, but bash the book. This frothy musical prompts furious yet contradictory invective. For instance, some pans object to it covering too much, while others revile Sherman for leaving out something.

Brantley derides "an indisputably bogus show" (E1, E30). He dubs Allen a "cipher" and chides Sherman because *Oz* "seems never to have met a showbiz cliché it didn't like." Brantley objects to songs "being jimmied into the plot." He attacks what Heilpern embraces, the "gay camp" and "showbiz kitsch."

Brantley's review prompted protest from Davis, who terms it "cruel" and accuses him of wanting to close the show. She protests, "The show is *supposed* to be twinkly razzle-dazzle and a rollicking good time. Hell, that is what the late Peter Allen was all about. Yes, he had his dark side, and that is alluded to in the play, but Allen ... wanted to spread joy and fun. And that is precisely what *BFO*'s creative team set out to give Broadway audiences ... theatergoers *do* get it."

Perhaps Davis also has in mind Kuchwara's AP notice, which sneers at "less-than-lively material pushed unimaginatively around the stage.... Maybe that's because book writer Martin Sherman has come up with a turgid, by-the-numbers 'resume' plot." He castigates too much material (i.e., Allen's life) "sandwiched between Allen songs" and scolds Sherman for sins such as Allen announcing his own death. He fails to mention audience enthusiasm throughout and wild cheering at the end. Instead he reports, inaccurately, *Oz* "is a show filled with aimless energy rather than inspiration, leaving theatergoers exhausted rather than entertained."

Isherwood's U.S. review calls it "this pitifully flimsy musical." He decries the script as "an outline for a book, not the thing itself" and later elaborates, "A series of bare-bones scenes advance the story from turning point to turning point with dreary obviousness." He concedes Sherman's book "has its share of verbal wit" but echoes Gross's fulminations that it "doesn't come close to baring the soul of its subject."

Another taking his agenda from Gross, Frascella alleges, "This musical frustratingly dodges all the deeper, messier aspects of the driven artist's life." He feels, "The play turns its queer eye in a more open, honest direction" when Sherman drops Liza and dramatizes Greg and Peter. Allen himself did that; Sherman chronicles what Allen did. The Gross-refrain returns when Frascella complains *Oz* "clearly maintains that it's better to entertain than reveal." This critic doesn't notice Allen as narrator must remain in character and say only what he would or did say, not what somebody wishes he had.

Mandelbaum suffers similar *Times*-induced false assumptions. He demands a serious play, not a musical celebrating Allen's life. He hates the creative team's objective. He refers to "the risible dialogue," labels the show "mostly preposterous," and, of course, offers Gross's refrain, "Any dark side the real Allen possessed is conveniently left offstage."

More echoes emanate from Finkle, who mentions "The Lives of Me" but claims, "Some of those lives don't jibe with what is known about Allen." He continues, "Much of the information is dubious and/or misleading, perhaps even outright wrong." He oversimplifies Garland's attitude towards her daughter's engagement exactly as Gross does. He blasts the libretto for presenting Liza "as a paragon of stability." Again he oversimplifies by choosing the word "paragon" and because Liza warns Peter about instability. Someone can exhibit stability *and* instability, and a troubled person can provide support for a dying ex-husband. Throughout the biography readers discern a couple mutually supportive, not only during the marriage but afterward. One of Liza's sources of stability came from him.

Finkle offers two other instances of falsifying the record: Sherman omits

Allen's sister, and he doesn't show us Allen collaborating on songs. Because Allen left home young, bringing his little sister on to bid goodbye wouldn't have revealed anything. Dragging in collaborators would have provoked outrage at time wasted and boredom induced. The program provides collaborative credits.

Finkle summarizes all four accusations as "discrepancies" distorting the truth. These he feels prove "illumination of Allen's complexities was not a topmost concern." Yet the accusations don't involve secrets. Abandoning consistency, he derides including "Continental American" to depict "debauchery." Would he prefer leaving out drugs and promiscuity? He asserts the team that wrote the theme song from "Arthur" received a single Oscar "statuette." Had he checked MacLean he would have learned each received one (236–237). Allen gave his to his agent.

Both barrels blazing, Simon hates even Jackman and, as Allen's younger self, Federan, whom he terms "unappealing." He pronounces the show "vulgar" and "stifling, staggering, and finally stultifying." He compares Enright's and Sherman's use of Allen's songs, as though he finds the new book (which he terms a revision) unnecessary. Then he fulminates songs "are preexistent and shoehorned in, not germane and apropos."

Marks dubs *Oz* "Hugh Jackman's Chest Hair! The Musical" (Style, C01). He complains because "strategic shirt selection figures as a plot point." Yet it brought Allen success and contributes to dramatizing his relationship with Greg. The critic derides "show business cliché," castigates "Don't Cry Out Loud" after Petey's father's suicide, and mocks the time devoted to gay icon Judy Garland (who gave Allen his break, toured with him, and became his mother-in-law). Marks demands to know, "Would outside ambition, or a desperate desire to fit in, have coaxed a gay entertainer into marriage?" Allen's performance style doesn't exemplify trying to fit in. Marks ignores that Allen adored Liza and had sex with her. The biography suggests Peter and Liza later had an affair (233–234). Marks might want to reconsider the notion everyone fits neatly into categories of 100 percent straight or 100 percent gay. He flaunts his cleverness, ending, "Fine by me if he wants to stop another show. Just please, someone stop this one."

Cote also attacks Sherman for not slamming Allen's marriage. He rejects *Oz* as "a gaudy patchwork of coming-of-age-drama, a-star-is-born camp, AIDS play and Las Vegas floorshow. Barely held together by a spotty book and too many power-pop climaxes, it leaves you breathless but remarkably unmoved."

Winer argues Allen doesn't "deserve such a celebration." She concedes Jackman possesses "talent to distract from the labored wax museum mediocrity" of this musical, which "steps into every cliché the form embraces." Feldberg mocks "a wearying barrage of gay jokes" and derides the Allen-Minnelli courtship as "possibly the least persuasive ever presented" (17). McCarter hates Allen's songs, confessing, "I happen to respond to them the way others do to shellfish or bee stings" (18). Als prefers the lighting to script, Jackman and direction. Lemon finds it a lemon and wishes producers had opted for a revue. Le Sourd labels the book "morose" (1E), while Teachout calls it a "comic strip" (W15). Feingold reveals he already regarded *Oz* as "mediocre" before he saw it, though he finds "crisp pungency" in the libretto (81).

Other negatives come from radio and television critics. Bergen complains the "thin" book "just skims over the major events" in Allen's life. Collins praises Jackman but argues "everything else about this sorry production should have been burned on the Barbie." Torre labels *Oz* "pleasant if uninspired." Hamburg gushes over Jackman and says the script "doesn't matter." She complains Sherman doesn't mention Allen had just "had a fling with" Garland's husband before he met her. In fact, Sherman includes that. Later she ridicules the book as "sappy. I mean those lines were so ridiculous."

Of the negatives, only Richardson doesn't blame the book. He gets facts wrong, especially with the mega blooper that Allen dated Garland before marrying her daughter. He castigates producers for not dazzling spectators with "spectacular effects and scenery."

Although he doesn't review *Oz*, columnist Riedel attacked it, beginning before it opened and continuing to its closing. As its run ended, he assured readers, "Jackman had to make do with garbage" (New York Pulse, 047).

McKinley knows its book helped make *Oz* a crowd-pleaser. He feels, "Martin should be recognized for his contribution to its success and the success of Hugh Jackman's performance. As George Abbott once told me, without the script there can be no performance."

Jackman likewise says, "If I'm speaking what must be 50 percent of the book, how could you literally trash the book and give me praise? I've been in dogs before, and I never felt that here. And that's why I was shocked by the venom against the show" (sec. 2, 3).

Oz succeeded. It made a ton of money. It cost $9 million to mount, and by ten days before opening it had a $10 million advance sale. It made a $250,000 profit (above running costs) on its performances prior to its opening.

That fall many Broadway shows failed, and Sondheim's musical *Bounce* folded out of town after receiving poor notices in D.C. and Chicago. Yet during this difficult autumn for Broadway, Sherman's musical was one of the top ten grossing shows the week it opened, bringing in $273,125 despite press and comp seats. It opened on a Thursday and sold out that weekend.

Thereafter *Oz* kept breaking Imperial house-records: for the week ending November 9, $869,515; for the week ending November 30, $888,023; the next week $894,330; the next week $903,804. By the week ending January 4, 2004, its new house record hit $920,846. While thriving during the following months, it set another kind of record, raising more money for Broadway Cares/Equity Fights AIDS than any previous Broadway show: $1,172,056.

When ticket sales might have tapered off during the summer, they rose and kept rising, setting more house records: $982,845.37 for the week ending June 20; the next week $989,605; the week ending July 18, $1,021,931. On the week ending August 29, it grossed $1,062,910.84 and the next week it topped that at $1,085,923.19. When it played its final performance on September 12, 2004 (after 32 previews and 365 regular performances), *Oz* had proven phenomenally popular.

It also scored high on nominations and awards. Jackman won the Drama Desk Award, the Outer Critics Circle Award, a Drama League Award, a Theatre World Award, and the Astaire Award. Mitchel David Federan as young Peter won a Theatre World Award, and Isabel Keating took home two awards, Drama Desk Best Featured Actress and Theatre World. Outer Critics Circle nominated Joey McKneely for Outstanding Choreography, and the cast album snagged a Grammy nomination. *Oz* also made the *Advocate*'s Ten Best List and received five Tony nominations: for Best Musical (against *Caroline, or Change*, *Wicked*, and *Avenue Q*), for Best Actor, Isabel Keating for Best Featured Actress, Beth Fowler for Best Featured Actress, and Sherman for Best Book of a Musical. The moderately maligned libretto beat out several other musicals for a spot on the Tony ballot.

Sherman shared this nomination with Nick Enright. The contracts with Sherman and Enright gave the latter a playbill credit, preceded by "original book." This confused some critics into thinking Enright participated in what they saw. Contracts demand respect, yet why put into Tony nomination a man who wrote another book? That, too, stems from a contractual provision.

When the show's publicists, Boneau/Bryan-Brown, sent out press releases regarding the nominations, one bore the statement "*The Boy from Oz* is the first Australian musical to come to Broadway." Yes, the show dramatizes the career of Peter Allen, an Australian who also contributed to the songs' music and/or lyrics. But Americans otherwise comprise the creative team.

When Jackman accepted his Tony, he referred to his vehicle as an Australian musical and then, amazingly, he thanked, not Sherman, who wrote the show, but Enright, who didn't.

Asked if Jackman understood that he wrote the script, Sherman says, "Yes, completely." Asked if the two got along okay, Sherman replies, "Yes. Very well." Sherman won't comment further. Did Jackman thank the wrong writer from Australian chauvinism? Did he curry favor with Australians who revere Enright's memory?

Producers had wanted Jackman to perform Sherman's version in London, but he refused and agreed instead to perform Enright's in his country. Marketing there convinced Australians Enright's show had garnered a Tony nomination and helped Jackman win a performance Tony. Gannon and Fox revived Enright's show in huge arenas around Australia, beginning August 3, 2006. Kenny Ortega, not McKinley, directed. Producers advertised *Oz* replete with Tony claims.

But those false claims had unexpected consequences. Some of those who saw the revival of the Enright book knew the U.S. libretto. They complained the Australian management had cut what they saw in 2003–2004. Sherman's libretto includes Garland's fourth husband, Mark Herron, as an Allen trick, gives Liza and Greg much more substantial roles, and traces Allen's sexual orientation throughout.

These spectators recognized what they saw in 2006 as much sketchier than the Broadway book, and they launched protests because producers had "censored" the kiss. Of course, Enright had downplayed Allen's gay orientation and therefore never penned a kiss. Only Sherman wrote a scene in which one occurs. To explain its absence, Murray Bartlett (Greg in this arena production) says, "We just wanted to keep it very simple and very pure." Even Dish didn't notice what had happened, but instead dutifully reported the "kiss has been taken out" (46). The bait-and-switch succeeded.

In the huge arenas Jackman played, Enright's skeletal book made sense. Nearly all singing and dancing, little talking, goes over better in such venues. Ticket buyers came to see their Australian star sing their Australian songs, in a libretto written by their Australian author.

But Jackman should never have thanked the wrong writer. One can only imagine that Sherman felt foolish sitting at the Tony ceremony wondering if he had crossed into some parallel universe in which he didn't write *The Boy from Oz*.

In September 2004, when Jackman left *Oz*, it closed. Know-it-alls nodded sagely, saying nobody else could fill the role. McKinley, however, says the team had compiled a list of performers "who had the talent. Two facts helped us agree to close: First, it would take at least $500,000-$600,000 to advertise the replacement and rehearse. The show had recouped and was returning a profit. Why put it in debt again? Second, several critics weren't happy the show had succeeded despite their declarations. The replacement star would be subjected to these same critics. Why give them the opportunity? Why not go out on top?"

On June 10, 2005, a production featuring a Japanese cast performing a Japanese translation of Sherman's book opened at the Aoyama in Tokyo. McKinley directed, McKneely choreographed, and boy band-star Masayuki Sakamoto played Allen. The show received glowing reviews. It did such big business a revival occurred with longer scheduled runs, beginning September 2006. It played both Tokyo and Osaka, as did the next revival, opening on October 5, 2008. Those who said *Oz* couldn't have succeeded without Jackman must eat their words.

20. Laura (2003–2005)

In spring 2003, Norma Heyman commissioned Sherman to write another show-biz script. He would depict Laura Henderson and her historic Windmill Theatre. Heyman had first worked with Sherman on *The Summer House*. She explains, "After Judi Dench and Bob Hoskins and I agreed to embark on this film, I rang Stephen Frears and asked if he would consider directing it. He asked who would write it, and I asked what he thought. He said, 'What would you think of your friend Martin?'"

Frears got to know Sherman at her home and teaching at Equinoxe. He loved Sherman's humor and felt Sherman "would have a feeling for that world. I also thought he'd be good at writing for the girls."

Sherman responded he could only take it on if he could wait until after *The Boy from Oz* opened on Broadway in October. When he said he couldn't begin for six months, the producers told him they would have to choose another writer. But Frears said, "No you're not. You're going to wait for Martin." Sherman thought about the film and did some research, but only settled into serious work in late October. He completed his script two months later.

He experienced unusual pressure on this project because all elements had fallen into place without his having written a word. That never happens. The film had producers, a top director, two top stars, and funding from BBC and Pathé. Everyone waited only for the screenplay. In addition to developing a plot and populating it, he had to research variety acts at the Windmill.

Yes, Sherman chose the songs (or rather, often, sets of lyrics, because music hadn't survived) and placed them in the screenplay, with one exception. George Fenton, who composed the new music—such as "The Babies of the Blitz"—suggested "The Girl in the Little Green Hat."

Judi Dench reports, "When I learned Martin was writing the script, I knew the dialogue would be exceptionally accessible. I could not resist working with him and also with Stephen." Sherman didn't disappoint her.

Heyman calls his screenplay "wonderful, a great tribute to music hall," and refers to the musical numbers' "innocence. Martin made them so beguiling." She terms Laura "an enigma. Very little was known about her. She had no surviving children, no grandchildren. She vanished from theatrical history.

Martin's love of women and his imagination helped him to fabricate a character who feels so true and a film which reeks of the period."

Heyman ponders Frears's commitment. He wanted to do it, but "he won't tell a writer what to do. So it's not until he gets the first draft that he decides whether he wants to do it. I sent him the script, and I didn't hear from him. After three days, I rang him and asked, 'You like it, don't you?' He said, 'Yes' and that he felt trapped." Frears adds, "The script was good. I couldn't just say no. It had such wit and vivacity and it created such an entertaining character."

Heyman loves the screenplay because "it's rigorous. There isn't a spare word or line. It has nuances. It's delicate, delicious, naughty, and incredibly relevant. It has the mixed moods of *Clothes in the Wardrobe*. It's multi-textured. You take so many things away from it."

As soon as Sherman submitted it and Frears approved it, they went into pre-production. The team had begun with Dench and Hoskins in place, so Sherman had written their roles for them. Indeed, his star feels in tailoring the lines for her "he succeeded 100 percent. He has incredible skill with dialogue. He makes it accessible, concise, and very witty."

The remaining casting went smoothly. This includes the larger parts—such as Christopher Guest playing Lord Cromer, Kelly Reilly as Maureen, and Thelma Barlow making her film debut (after 50 years in show business) as Lady Conway—and the tiny parts, such as Doraly Rosen, spot-on as Maggie, Richard Syms as chauffeur Ambrose, and Thomas Allen as Eric Woodburn. Choosing soloists took longer. Finally they selected Will Young, who surprised his pop fans with his period style, and they found Camille O'Sullivan, adept at Jane's cabaret styling. Sherman describes his cast as "a dream."

The producers also hired a stellar off-screen creative team: Fenton for music; Oscar-winner Jenny Shircore for make-up and hair; two time Oscar-winner Sandy Powell for costumes which won her an Academy Award nomination; Hugo Luczyc-Wyhowski for production design; Eleanor Fazan and Debbie Astell as choreographers.

Powell's wardrobe evokes period, characters, and extras. She clothed denizens of both the fantasy world of Windmill performances and the real world backstage and outside. She complemented Dench's blue eyes with touches of blue and aqua in her dresses, jackets, and jewelry. She also put Dench in the same outfit and the same necklace and earrings more than once, a true-to-life touch.

Heyman again found Sherman "a joy to work with. I'd do it every day of my life if I could." Frears concurs: "He is very, very bright. When I worked out there was a problem, he would invent something imaginative and unexpected and with life and vitality. It would delight me because it wasn't prosaic but had flourish."

Dench remembers, "I have an abiding impression of Martin always being on set. I would glance up, and he would be there, smiling. He was cheering to have there, with a glorious sense of humor and always available to help." Additional pluses involved her getting to dance in a panda costume and snap lines like "I'd rather drink ink."

Frears recalls Sherman's tact, discretion and lack of ego: "He was always generous to others. He would have a strong opinion, but was delicate in the way he handled everybody. He was conciliatory, not looking for a fight. Yet he was courageous; he wouldn't just do what anybody wanted."

Sherman likewise enjoyed collaborating with Frears. "We worked together closely and made changes up to and through post-production. The changes were, in film terms, minimal, but nonetheless had huge impact. I was always on the set, and Stephen included me in all stages of post-production."

Those who assume Sherman wrote a biopic get it wrong. Only "inspired by true events," the film dramatizes a fabricated character based on the little known about Laura, a scenario based on information about the Windmill, which "never closed," and Sherman's imagination.

The screenwriter examined everything available about both woman and theatre, including, for her, the autobiographies by Van Damm and his daughter, and, for the theatre, the archival information concerning songs used, acts which appeared there, surviving scripts, film shorts of musical numbers, and details regarding the theatre's evolution. He used what he found helpful; he invented

Sherman at an Equinoxe screenwriting workshop, April 26–May 3, 2004, Marrakesh. (Photograph: Susan B. Landau.)

whatever strengthened his plot, characters, and comedic or dramatic impact. He omitted events extraneous to the Windmill, such as Mrs. Henderson founding what became the English National Ballet or Van Damm briefly leaving to produce elsewhere.

He took from the public record these facts: Henderson's son died in World War I. She bought a theatre. She hired Van Damm. The Windmill eventually presented nude tableaux—not her idea, and possibly not Van Damm's either, although he claims credit for it (86). The Lord Chamberlain approved this, but Sherman invented how she persuades him. The theatre remained open during the Blitz.

The autobiographies don't focus on Laura. Neither book provides a plot. Van Damm describes the extensive and serious injuries—26 separate wounds— a Windmill girl suffered when a bomb hit the café across the street (191), and his daughter mentions this bomb killed everyone in the café and also injured two others from the theatre in a nearby pub (96–97). Sherman bases Maureen's death on this. Van Damm also mentions an incident when a Windmill girl had just left a café and everyone remaining inside died (163).

Sherman altered a few facts, changing the year her husband died and she purchased the theatre from 1931 to 1937 and the age of her son at his death from 27 to 21. He diminished the number of years covered to reduce the sprawl of "and then, and then" and to avoid requiring actors to age. Changing her son's age made his death more poignant and her story about why she decided to do nude revues more plausible.

The nude tableaux begin before any signs of war. This could undermine her story about young men going off to the front without ever seeing a naked woman, but nobody watching seems to notice. The real Mrs. Henderson didn't come up with this idea, which seems designed to increase ticket sales. Yet Sherman intends her to speak truthfully about her motive, and she even tells Van Damm she had wanted to suggest nudity at the outset, but "I too lack courage."

Neither autobiography mentions the family's Jewishness, yet Van Damm's granddaughters say the family observed the Jewish holidays. Given the period's anti-Semitism, Sherman seized Van Damm's real circumspection on the subject as a useful plot element for developing Laura's character. It also provides the basis for a big laugh. After Maureen insists Van Damm also strip, Laura enters, smiles, and observes "Why, Mr. Van Damm, you *are* Jewish!"

She had eccentricities for a woman her age, in her era, and Sherman incorporates these. She went boating, took airplane joy rides, and went to the Windmill wearing Chinese garb and auditioned dressed as a dancing bear.

Sheila vouches for the "endless ding-dong battles" Mrs. Henderson fought with Van Damm and notes when she brought her friends backstage the mirrors gave them a nude back view of the showgirls (20, 24; also VD, 164).

She supplies a quotation from Laura: "In this enterprise I shall be carrying on the work of my husband who, during his life, spent a great deal of time and money in helping stage people" (46). Sherman incorporates this in the sherry party scene. He also includes an incident of a girl making a defiant gesture towards a bomber during the Blitz (63; Van Damm 190). He uses a bit of Sheila's discussion of business losses during 1934 (82–83) as well as Laura wanting a new hat (96).

Sherman invented numerous details. He made up her developing a crush on Van Damm, roughly 30 years her junior, as well as her jealousy of his wife. He reduced the age difference between the two by lowering hers and increasing his. The real Laura died shortly before her 82nd birthday in 1944. Given the character's statement to her friend Margot in 1937 "I'm nearly 70," we can assume the cinematic Laura dies at 76. In the final scene, during the Blitz, that would make Sherman's Mrs. Henderson 72 or 73 at most. (The Blitz began on September 7, 1940, and ended on May 11, 1941.) Sherman invents everyone except VD, Laura, and Lord Cromer, and he embroiders their personalities. Van Damm provided important insight: "She had a delicious brand of unrestrained impertinence" (76).

Sherman invents Laura's lateness and rudeness when she meets Van Damm. He invents Van Damm knowing anything about live theatre; he previously ran cinemas. He invents Van Damm suggesting nonstop vaudeville, devising the name Revudeville, and conducting the auditions and booking the acts. The reality would have required additional roles and reduced Hoskins' part. Van Damm ran the business and left creativity to others.

Sherman also invents Laura's boredom with good works. The real woman participated in and provided money to philanthropic activities. He invents Lord Cromer closing the theatre, Laura mounting a soapbox, and his relenting. He invents Mrs. Henderson vowing she will never enter the theatre again. He invents her talking about her son's death; according to Van Damm, she kept this her "tragic secret" (75).

As part of the fictional attraction between Van Damm and Laura, he invents their dance on the roof as well as her going to the roof during air raids. And Sherman invents everything concerning his fictional Maureen, from her falling into the river, to her giving the Luftwaffe two fingers, to Mrs. Henderson interfering with her life, to her pregnancy and rushing to her death.

Sherman underscores with "All the Things You Are" Maureen with Paul intercut with Laura facing mirrors framing herself with a feathered fan. He needed music widely recognizable and romantic. He selected Jamie Hammerstein's favorite of his father's songs. Oscar wrote it while wooing Jamie's mother. Sherman's friendship with the family made obtaining the rights affordable.

Mrs. Henderson Presents contrasts the fantasy theatre world and real life, where the Depression and three cemetery scenes intrude. The Blitz and other reminders of war provide more reality checks. These include such anti-war elements as Maureen's dead body (such a contrast to her beauty), Laura on her soapbox saying victims of war die in vain, and the son's grave amidst thousands of gravestones.

Following Maureen's death, the camera pans the dressing room. One woman runs her hand along her left eyebrow, either purposely or accidentally echoing Horst's gesture of love to Max. The camera pauses at the fifth place, occupied now only by Maureen's photograph. Laura rows down the river, then stops, grief-stricken.

Despite such serious moments, Sherman mostly writes like Sturges or Hawks. Although critics compare his sparring partners to Tracy and Hepburn, he feels "it's more Cary Grant and Hepburn. It's very Sturges. Mrs. Henderson isn't dissimilar to the Mary Astor character in *Palm Beach Story*."

Sturges employed the mixed moods and social implications typical of Sherman. Like *Sullivan's Travels*, this film depicts social issues and wrenches hearts in mid-hilarity. It addresses hypocrisy, anti–Semitism, racism (India), classism, sexism, and war. It indicts the ruling class's values, their insulation from hard knocks, bigotry, snobbery, and barring of ladies from meaningful endeavors. Reacting to that double standard, Mrs. Henderson's contemporary Virginia Woolf wanted a room of her own. Laura buys a theatre.

Sherman mocks conventions Laura flouts. He satirizes Lord Cromer, especially when he reveals he hates artistic imagination (this from a censor wielding power to destroy works of art) and during luncheon, when his prudery hilariously contrasts Laura's frankness. Sherman also provides so many witty lines fans argue over their favorites. Yet in the privacy of her boat, Laura grieves both her husband and Maureen, and her eyes tear as she watches Eric Woodburn sing the "Marseillaise" after France falls.

Sherman employs an episodic structure, sometimes spinning out scenes and sometimes reducing them to montages ("Goody Goody" and "The Babies of the Blitz"). The action falls into four segments: (1) Mr. Henderson's funeral and its aftermath; (2) Laura purchasing the theatre, hiring a manager and, with him, planning and launching their nonstop musical revue; (3) the decision to add a few nudes, negotiating the license, and success with that format; (4) the Blitz and the Windmill's survival. Within each section, suspense builds as to how Laura and then her theatrical family will fare.

The strong through-line, easily missed by laughing viewers, begins with Laura leading a pampered life that gives her no clue what ordinary women face. She continues grieving her son's death and privately mourns her husband, but won't allow strangers in a passing boat to observe it and jokes about widowhood. She dreads a purposeless future. When she attempts "good works," she attends a meeting to establish a refuge for unwed future mothers, but ridicules this effort by calling the expected offspring "future bastards." She insults her intended manager about his Jewishness. Yet when Nazis round up Dutch Jews she appreciates he still has family in Holland and sympathizes, speaking of helplessness in the face of what one cannot change.

She has made little progress, however, regarding the relative plights of young men and young women. Still sympathizing with her dead son, she shoos her prize performer into Paul's arms. When the bounder impregnates Maureen, then says he will return to his girlfriend, Laura's victim tells her "You live in your own world, Mrs. Henderson." After Maureen dies during the air raid, Van Damm says something similar—"You don't know anything about the real world, do you?" We can see on her face she feels the truth of his words. Finally, Laura explains her motive for the nude tableaux, finding her son's French postcard. She then apologizes.

During her four years owning the Windmill, she has dropped her blinders, grown, developed into a person less impetuous, willful, and selfish. Would we ever have expected the woman who treats Van Damm so rudely to have called her own actions "foolish" or to have said, "I do, in my very soul, regret" about anything? Yet Sherman has taken us on this journey to where she does.

Seeing hungry variety artists auditioning, learning from Hitler the murderous aspect of anti–Semitism, knowing a real unwed mother and seeing her death up-close help her appreciate the world doesn't revolve around her. As she experiences empathy, she starts turning into a human being. The screenwriter embeds all those moments in such hilarity we don't notice, but this subtext unifies the four years it covers.

Sherman characterizes her as more than a privileged but tactless matron. A narcissist who does what she pleases, she also possesses Sherman's wit, plus an attractive free spirit. When she buys a theatre, turns a joy ride into a flight to France, or disrobes a few performers, we delight in her daring. Decades ahead of her time, she refuses to accept marginalization, relegated to embroidery and buying necklaces and earrings. Laura exhibits independence and resourcefulness and achieves successes that resonate with 21st-century viewers. She takes her place among Sherman's strong female protagonists.

Once more, Sherman dramatizes outsiders. Mrs. Henderson flouts period expectations for her class and gender. Add good girls who pose nude, gay Bertie, and Jewish Van Damm, then plop them into show biz—itself a world apart—and we have characters and a milieu alien yet charming.

The film provides a potent lesson in respecting those different by virtue of class, income, religion, or sexual orientation. Mrs. Henderson's anti–Semitism—designed to create discomfort—gives way to respect, sympathy, even love for a man outside her world.

Sherman again dramatizes survival—of grief, death, war. After needlepoint and good works fail, Mrs. Henderson adopts the survival mechanism of buying a business. She inadvertently creates an extended family common to the gay community and the performing arts. Those for whom she provides work need her, but Laura also needs them. They nurture and comfort each other. Van Damm tells Maureen he will keep her on the payroll; Laura would have supported mother and child.

Mr. Henderson died, Alec died, Maureen dies, many of those who make up the Windmill's audiences will die, war's victims. Yet the Third Reich's efforts to obliterate the city will fail, as the Windmill becomes a symbol of determination to survive the Blitz as well as a refuge from it.

Sherman employs his usual irony. This selfish lady who finds helping unwed mothers boring, by pursuing her own agenda, makes a woman face unwed pregnancy. Ironically, despite her wealth, the real world has encroached on Laura. Ironically, she gleefully anticipates auditions, then finds them barbaric. Ironically, the obnoxious anti–Semite develops a crush on her Jewish manager.

Filming occurred between mid–September and early December 2004 in Shepperton Studios, Surrey; in France; in Buckinghamshire (Cliveden House and Coombe Hill); and on Chester Terrace, Regent's Park and elsewhere in London.

In late spring 2005 Frears and Sherman shot a new scene between Dench and Reilly, in which the women sip gin from coffee cups and discuss that Maureen alone among the girls doesn't go out with the soldiers. In the next scene, Mrs. Henderson sets about fixing her up with Paul. Thus, the addition establishes the romantic producer violates Maureen's desire to avoid a broken heart. As she puts it, she prefers remaining "a naked spinster." She adds, "Who would have dreamed that standing onstage without any clothes on would be the safest place to be?" This scene also contains Maureen's joking appraisal of Van Damm. She replies to Laura's noting the Luftwaffe no longer bomb during the tableaux, he has "sent Hitler our programme. Professional courtesy between Fuehrers."

As the film screened at festivals (see Appendix G), the buzz grew.

Publicists included interviews with former Windmill girls in the press kit. Several women they spoke to couldn't have met Mrs. Henderson since they joined the Windmill after she died, yet they speak about her as though they knew her. Another woman who claims to have worked there only in 1930 appears unaware that Laura Henderson bought the theatre in 1931 and didn't begin nonstop revues until 1932. Given the inaccuracies, the press agents might have thought to screen the comments. Their failure to do so led to a misconception among some critics. In her "memory" of events from 71 years earlier, Jean Kent claims Van Damm fired her in order to replace her with his girlfriend.

We can't know whether this accusation represents an unsubstantiated but possibly accurate account, sour grapes, or fabrication. Those critics who accuse Sherman of leaving out the girlfriend take the allegation as gospel. The other former Windmill girls all vouch for the theatre's propriety. Doris Barry, a Windmill Girl from 1932 to 1940, says Van Damm "provided strict chaperons." His granddaughter Jane Kerner says he treated the girls "as if they were his own children." Stanistreet quotes Linda Carroll saying she saw Van Damm as "a father figure" and quotes Charmian Macintosh recalling "Van Damm ran the place like a nunnery" (49–51). More importantly, these critics confuse fiction with documentary; they believe "inspired by true events" means true.

The film opened all over the U.K. on November 25, 2005. *Mrs. Henderson Presents* showed at eight cinemas in central London, more than the new *Harry Potter and the Goblet of Fire*.

Given the hype, Sherman and Frears might well have feared backlash. Four critics indeed pan the film. Ten reviews qualify as mixed, with two tipping slightly in the direction of favorable. That leaves 27 positives, many of these raves.

Shoard calls Laura "witty" but the plot "thin" (18). She terms Dench's character "skeletal" and scolds her use of the f-word and "a slightly superior type of porn." Quinn complains, "Martin Sherman's script doesn't offer them much in the way of firecracker dialogue" (Film, 6). Bradshaw slams the acting and labels the film "an insidiously ghastly piece of Blitz-kitsch nostalgia, reeking with chirpiness" (sec. 10, 7). He damns scenes "chock-a-block with terrible moments" and "porridgy" dialogue. He pleads, "Come friendly bombs and fall on our native film industry now." French objects to "a series of comic dialogues of a somewhat anachronistic kind," Van Damm and other men stripping "in an unlikely, highly embarrassing scene," and to "falseness and sentimentality" once the war starts (Review, 10).

Fitzherbert's mixed review says of the soapbox speech "the picture generates a sense of purpose" and calls it a "touching climax" (60). Yet he finds the movie "something of a let-down, not least because it is based on a fun idea and features a larger-than-life character at its centre." He calls Laura "essentially a Right-wing, snobbish, bigoted old bossy boots who expected everyone to do her bidding." He doesn't perceive she changes.

L.F. likes Henderson's "gleeful sense of adventure" and praises Dench for delivering "every one-liner with a tart but impish twinkle that's consistently winning." He deplores a tendency "to be in a perpetual panic to create drama" and dislikes the musical numbers. Porter feels "Dench knows exactly what to do with the mixture of barbed and scatty lines" but also chides the attempt at "poignancy" because it fails "to lay foundations" (Culture, 11). Ide appreciates "a towering performance" in which Dench fires "devastating broadsides at her long-suffering manager" and harries "him like a terrier." She objects to underdeveloping Young and Reilly's roles and to a "hurried" ending.

Malcolm faults it for cheating "a bit with the facts" (Review, 35). He says, "Insubstantial fare, perhaps, but nostalgic all the same for those who remember the Windmill's heyday—and entertaining for those who don't." He likes "witty dialogue" but can't handle shifting moods. He concludes it "gives more than a little pleasure to those tiring of vast enterprises laden with special effects." Barber judges "the first half is a hoot" and "Martin Sherman's screenplay is a jewel box of epigrams and put-downs" but deplores the evening "drifting to the conclusion that, during the Blitz, a girly show can 'fortify London in a way that sandbags cannot.' It's as embarrassing as the sight of a starkers Bob Hoskins" (ABC, 8).

Edwards finds it "so-so," complains of "too many subplots" but loves "Dench and Reilly." Andrews accepts it as "charming piffle" and "a nice enough show" (16). He wonders why "Jewish persecution" figures. Mottram terms it a "flawed-but-fun period piece" and judges "Frears just about keeps it on track, balancing out the poignant moments with a raspy wit." O'Hara awards three stars for performances, an "intriguing subject," and the "well written" relationship between Laura and Van Damm, but dismisses "a welter of subplots."

The 27 positive U.K. reviews began when it screened at the Toronto Film Festival. Winter extols, "Rich in period detail and choice witticisms ... a sweet and salty testament to creative widowhood and wartime endurance." She likes its "beguiling innocence, both bright-eyed and can-do." Robey, who terms it a "Pick of the Week," explains, "Stephen Frears, directing Martin Sherman's witty screenplay, mounts this as a very watchable showcase for his cast" (19). He adds "the redoubtable Dench ... makes it hard to resist."

Sandhu analyzes "a winning musical drama" which mocks "the prudishness and blinkered attitudes of the Lord Chamberlain" (27). He commends "agreeable and often charming fare that never descends into nostalgia." Tookey applauds "a charming comedy with a warmly nostalgic feel for the period and show business, and a refreshingly matter-of-fact attitude towards sex" (58). He calls Henderson's speech to the soldiers "a memorable moment in cinema" and concludes, "I enjoyed it a lot."

Bond calls it "the deliciously charming new comedy" that "manages to be funny, sweet and unexpectedly moving" and "a beautifully made and wonderfully evocative delight" (66–67). Hunter terms it "an absolute gem. Polished to perfection, frightfully funny and also rather moving, it is a jaunty stroll down memory lane with some unexpected lessons for our less innocent age" (44). He says of Laura, "Frank and fearless, she speaks her mind with all the wit of a British Auntie Mame," and he delights in "a sparkling slice of entertainment" replete with "brilliant one-liners and bitchy asides" but also "parallels with events in London this past year."

Sun enthuses a "Wonderful story of true Brit grit" ("Mrs. Henderson Presents"). *Cosmopolitan* praises "one-liners" and exclaims, "Heartwarming fun, take your mum" ("Mrs. Henderson Presents," 79). *Company* acclaims a "witty wartime winner" ("Mrs. Henderson Presents," 221). D.C. celebrates the mixed moods as "both moving and terrific fun" and praises the "naughty, epigram-laden script" as well as "compassion at the heart."

Brown observes, "Fantasy and reality are finely balanced" and "It's hard not to link the images of ordinary people being indiscriminately bombed with contemporary events" (71). He notices, "Without resorting to dowdiness, all is filmed in underwhelming tones that desentimentalise the story and its songs.

It works all of a piece with Martin Sherman's sharply written screenplay." Turner terms it "crowd-pleasing" and "very enjoyable to watch." He relishes its "genuinely fascinating slice of history" and commends "an enjoyable drama with a witty script, some imaginative musical numbers and superb performances from its cast." Utichi judges it "overflowing with charm" and "one of the best British films of the year." He enjoys the mix of "acerbic wit" and "touching drama" and loves the "chemistry" between Van Damm and Laura. Hennigan explains the film qualifies as "good clean fun" and adds, "It's impossible not to warm to this movie." Graham recommends it (47), as does cricket batsman Ed Smith, who terms it "funny and moving" (102).

Critics publishing outside London filed almost uniformly laudatory notices. *Irish Times* demurs slightly on the serious section, but otherwise finds it thoroughly entertaining, especially Sherman's "elegantly barbed wit" ("That Saucy Dame Judi").

Hunter published two other reviews. One reads "Sherman has done a splendid job," compares this to "backstage classics like *To Be or Not To Be* (1942) and *The Last Metro* (1980)," and pronounces it "one of the best British films of the year and an evening of pure entertainment" ("That's Entertainment"). Hunter's *Scotsman*'s review matches his others' enthusiasm.

Leicester Mercury, calling it "a soaraway hit," raves about "scintillating, sparkling entertainment, and a rare treat to see a British movie exuding such easy charm and finesse" boasting "bundles of humour." Pratt concludes, "Director Stephen Frears, more usually associated with more dramatic fare, shows he has a sense of humour after all" (10). Manning explains, "The will-they, won't-they element of Laura and Vivian's relationship forms the Central backbone of the story and is nicely handled by writer Martin Sherman" (Features, 3). He judges "it's virtually impossible to dislike this movie. Go see."

Davies calls it "marvelous sophisticated comedy," compares the leads to Tracy and Hepburn, and praises it as "sharply written, with keen attention to character and social subtext.... Oscar nominations are likely, a BAFTA for Dench seems a foregone conclusion." Dougan terms it a "glorious experience," declares "This may be Dench's best screen performance to date," and describes the plot as "full of sentiment" but never "sentimental" (4). Young applauds "thoroughly entertaining," with a "script sharp and witty and the performances spot on." He judges it "British film-making at its best." Key commends it as "gentle, often humorous" and "a charming slice of theatrical life from a time of innocence." Riley praises Dench's "tour-de-force theatrics" and relishes "the fruity dialogue" (*Liverpool Echo*). In a longer version, Riley declares Sherman's "delicious screenplay arguably his finest work since *Bent*" (*Western Daily Press*).

The Weinsteins spent $10 million for U.S. and German rights. Unfortunately, they ran the wrong kind of ad, emphasizing naked women. By running a misleading ad, the Weinstein Company ensured its natural audience of older viewers—especially women—would stay away. Fortunately, good reviews alerted some who would enjoy it to turn up anyway, but others never realized they would have loved it. Free plugs the Weinsteins should have gotten mostly didn't materialize. Harvey told Eaton the *Today* show, *Good Morning America*, and *The View* all turned down Dench because "she didn't fit their demographics."

The film opened in NYC and L.A. on December 9, 2005, two weeks earlier than planned. It received limited release in several other cities on Christmas day, then began opening elsewhere after the New Year. Most U.S. critics loved it. (See Appendix G.)

The 2005 British Independent Film Awards honored it with eight nominations, including one for Sherman for Best Screenplay, plus Hoskins as Best Actor, Dench as Best Actress, the movie as Best British Independent Film, Frears as Best Director, Reilly as Best Supporting Actress/Actor, Powell for Best Technical Achievement, and Barlow for Most Promising Newcomer.

Also in the U.K., it won a 2006 Empire Award (Kelly Reilly as Best Newcomer in this as well as *Pride & Prejudice*) and also won a 2006 London Critics Circle Film Award (Reilly, as British Newcomer of the year). The latter organization nominated Dench for British Actress of the Year, Frears as British Director of the Year, and the movie as British Film of the Year.

Most important in Britain, its four prestigious 2006 BAFTA nominations include one—the Anthony Asquith Award for Film Music—for Fenton, one for Powell for Best Costume Design, one for Dench for Best Performance by an Actress in a Leading Role, and one for Sherman for Best Original Screenplay.

In Italy, the picture received a 2006 David nomination as Best European Film from the David di Donatello Awards, Italy's major cinema prizes. In Thailand, a Golden Kinnaree Best Film nomination went to Stephen Frears.

In the U.S., the film received three 2006 Golden Globe nominations (Best Motion Picture, Musical or Comedy, plus nods to Hoskins and Dench), two 2006 Broadcast Film Critics Association nominations (one for Dench as Best Actress; the other for Best Comedy Movie), one 2005 Satellite Awards nomination (for Dench), and one 2006 Screen Actors Guild nomination (for Dench). Its two Academy Awards Nominations went to Sandy Powell for Best Achievement in Costume Design and Dench for Best Performance by an Actress in a Leading Role. It won the National Board of Review's 2005 award for Best Acting by an Ensemble, Frears won the Hollywood Film Festival's 2005 Hollywood World Award, and Dench came in as runner-up to Vera Farmiga in *Down to the Bone* for the Los Angeles Film Critics Association Best Actress award.

After the film started screening in the U.S. Heyman began receiving calls asking about turning it into a Broadway musical. "We've had phenomenal interest," she acknowledged. "The phone is off the hook with people who want to partner with me."

During the 2006 Christmas season, BBC1 screened *Mrs. Henderson Presents* as a holiday special. Among the top ten films on British network television for 2006, it came in at fourth place. *Pirates of the Caribbean: The Curse of the Black Pearl* topped the list, followed by *Calendar Girls*, and *Bruce Almighty* at number three (ukfilmcouncil.org.uk/information/statistics/yearbook/?y=2006& c=12). Eliminating foreign competition puts *Calendar Girls* in first place with eight million viewers and Sherman's film in second place with seven million. On this list, two Harry Potter films won the numbers six and seven spots with 5.1 million and 4.9 million viewers respectively. BBC2 aired Sherman's film the following year, again winning high ratings.

Wouldn't Laura Henderson delight in knowing she and the Windmill became a holiday treat?

21. More Controversy (2005–2011)

Early in 2005, Gordon Davidson left L.A.'s Mark Taper Forum. Because he hated Sherman's work, L.A.'s major theatre hadn't presented it. New Artistic Director Michael Ritchie chose Mathias to mount *Cherry Orchard*. For his mostly American cast, he wanted an American dramatist writing American English, one who had an affinity for Chekhov's mixed moods, so he hired Sherman.

Often translators use archaic language to provide period flavor; Sherman creates an idiomatic version. He attended rehearsals from December 27 for a February 12, 2006 opening. Annette Bening and Alfred Molina starred, and Lothaire Bluteau played Gaev. Prior to glowing reviews, the entire run had sold out. Sherman hadn't adapted the play, but only supplied a contemporary, actable translation. Yet critics often praise his text.

Mufson writes, "The many plot lines are kept lively by Martin Sherman's new and riveting translation." Weinstein commends "the current production, in a brisk new translation by Martin Sherman, delivers more humor and contemporary style than can be recalled." Welsh terms this version "lively and mostly idiomatic." Griffin finds it "in keeping with the rest of the sleek production" (128). Ochlan writes, "This new translation by Martin Sherman breathes just enough updating into the play to further showcase its relevance." Henerson applauds "Mathias' *Cherry Orchard* genuinely deserves full houses ... and the *Orchard* gang know exactly what they're about.... 'Such bad taste,' sniffs a dismissive Ranyevskaya." McNulty likes the text, but Hodgins's pan opts for museum-piece treatment and thus rejects Sherman's colloquialisms.

If the stars' schedules had permitted, they might have moved to Broadway, but by April they couldn't, so only L.A. saw this hit *Orchard*, which closed March 19.

Early in 2005, construction had begun on Sherman's home 90 minutes outside Athens. In Melitsina, Sherman wrote a new play, a commission from Aukin called *Aristo*, which he completed on November 20, 2006. By this time, however, the third major London production of *Bent* had begun previews on September 22 at the Trafalgar Studio 1, opening on October 5.

When producer Sonia Friedman approached Sherman, he agreed provided 29-year-old wunderkind Daniel Kramer could direct. Sherman wanted a young

(Left to right) Dena Hammerstein, Ian McKellen, and Sherman, January 7, 2007 in a boat on the Thames, headed to Greenwich for Alan Cumming's wedding to Grant Shaffer. (Photograph: David Gwinnutt.)

director to reinvent *Bent* for a young audience. In Kramer he got youth but also cutting-edge theatrical sensibility.

Kramer had a fresh vision. *Bent* might have run longer had he treated the Nazis more traditionally, but nobody who saw his production will forget his approach.

His enthusiasm for *Bent* began in high school, where this "formative text helped me come out of the closet and dream of another space and time where I could find my own happiness." He praises how *Bent* "captures sudden inhales of joy and pain—beyond any other."

They asked the Pet Shop Boys' Chris Lowe to score "Streets of Berlin" and assembled a cast headed by Alan Cumming, who liked "how Martin managed to be opinionated yet charming and fun. He's so full of life, so clever and able to communicate such huge ideas in his work in such a spare and affecting way. I love listening to him. He's a gag machine producing so many aces."

The cast, straight and gay, and their author went together to Paris Disneyland, organized by Cumming, who explains, "We were close enough to embrace it and not be cynical. Ten of us ran around like little kids. You can only do this with people you're really close to because then you're not afraid to let go."

Cumming assesses the script as the most affecting he's done: "It takes the audience on an almost unbearable journey, gets to their very core in a rare

(Left to right) Simon Callow, Ian McKellen, and Sherman, January 7, 2007 in a boat on the Thames, returning from Greenwich from Alan Cumming's wedding to Grant Shaffer. (Photograph: David Gwinnutt.)

visceral way. Playing the character who leads the audience on that journey is one of those once-in-a-lifetime experiences." He regards *Bent* as a powerful weapon against shame, which "is so damaging and so rife. Max finally overcomes his. *Bent* is one of the greatest plays because it affects people to their core. I defy anyone to see it and not be changed forever."

Kramer encouraged his actors to unearth the humor because it's "always been a way of surviving, and it's profoundly Jewish." Yet he explains he and his four actors playing Nazis quickly found the SS "were a group of thug boys. We've seen the imagery from Abu Ghraib and U.K. military hazing rituals that killed three soldiers. These are ignorant young men trained to hate and kill. Every soldier I interviewed described hysteria, chaos, punishing the enemy. Rage and sick power descend over the eyes, and men spit, kick, beat, stab, mock, laugh, scream. They're like the terrifying gang who operate across the street—lost, angry, cruel, looking for the next piece of glass to smash. My Nazis enjoyed the sadistic power."

This revival received numerous favorable reviews, plus more praising *Bent* but expressing reservations concerning the production. Indeed, only four critics pan it.

Morley announces Trafalgar Studios "has its first blockbuster hit" (41). He acclaims the play as "brilliant" and "raw in its tragedy and almost unwatchable in its brutality." He writes of Cumming as "breathtaking" and the production's "intense power." Shenton concurs, terming this "an immensely moving, dignified and historically important play," and adds concerning the mounting, "In Daniel Kramer's intimate, intense new production, Alan Cumming and superb newcomer Chris New ... bring a brave, bold brilliance to the play" (62). Shenton also reviews *Bent* elsewhere and disagrees with another critic. He judges it "as important as ever" and asserts the production "played out with an operatic intensity and intimacy, has a shattering power" (38).

Brown pronounces this "soul-wrenching," "first-rate," and "theatre at its thought-provoking best." It left him "close to tears at several junctures." Yet he notes the scene "where Wolf is killed in Max's flat shows them whooping like kids playing 'cowboys and Indians,' and one waves to the audience when exiting in a gesture that has more in keeping with farce, or a silent comedy. I'm not sure what the intention was here, unless ... to show the Nazis playing deadly and horrific 'games'—which in a sense is true."

Marlowe agrees. She praises Cumming for playing Max "with riveting complexity" (Times2, 17) and awards the evening four stars. She judges "Kramer's effective revival employs a motif of theatricality; at its best, it is shattering." She adds "the production has huge impact at its most restrained." Yet she objects Kramer's "approach has a significant drawback: he extends the theatrical metaphor" to the Nazis.

Coveney writes, "The play is presented with a defiant flourish, smoke and flame bursting through fissures with a Wagnerian soundtrack suggesting the apocalypse." He adds, "Just as we have entered a place of no return, the second act friendship of Max and Horst lugging their stones in the bleak compound restores our faith in humanity." The lovemaking scene "leaps at you with undiminished fervor and power."

Clapp raves "enthralling" (Review, 22). She observes, "It was not only the subject that made *Bent* explosive. It was its queasy, courageous mixture of terrible events and flippant sentences." She praises Cumming and New and says, "Kramer tautens every moment that could be soggy. That Dachau sex exchange—all grey, quietly lit, with the two men totally still—is spellbinding."

Nathan observes, "It has prompted a row ... as to whether the play portrays Jewish suffering in the camps as being less brutal than that experienced by homosexuals. But the play does not attempt to reflect Jewish suffering under the Nazis, but that of homosexuals in the mid-1930s, before the Nazis had perfected their 'Final Solution' for Jews" (45). He calls the evening "hugely powerful, as is Sherman's lesson, that love can be a defiant rejection of persecution."

Nathan's remark about Jewish suffering having considerably post-dated the period *Bent* dramatizes has as its target Letts's review. It ostensibly praises the evening, awarding it four stars. He extols the production's "flair" (53). Yet he proclaims it fails to touch his "heterosexual heart" because of his "suspicion that the suppression of homosexuality, even when it was this brutal, was not quite as bad as the agony suffered by Jewish people" because "Max and Horst are lone adults with the option of choice. Jewish parents had to see their children sent to their death." Choice? Has Letts heard nothing about genetic coding of sexual orientation? Does he think the pair freely chose on some whim to violate a law that could doom them? Would he say the same of straight but childless couples? Do breeders have a better right to live than non-breeders? The Nazis thought so, but should critics side with them? And what of their parents, grieving the loss of their sons? What about Jewish homosexuals? Somehow, Letts has let his homophobia slip out under the guise of defending Jewish sensibilities Nathan doesn't feel.

Shenton posted a challenge to Letts, where he argues "his review proves that the play is as necessary as it ever was, since it's the ignorant and ugly prejudice of that review, not the play, that now shocks me to the core."

Shuttleworth faults Kramer for choosing "to make his Nazis real monsters, whooping, bellowing, reveling in their inhumanity. It makes for a lot of terror ... but at the expense of more potent moral horror" (11). Billington likewise objects, saying Kramer's "revival has an aura of flamboyant excitability at odds with a movingly restrained play" (40).

Another of these mixed reviews, taking for granted *Bent*'s classic status but faulting the mounting, comes from De Jongh, who rebukes Kramer for an "under-powered production" and for donning "the velvet glove of restraint when the play turns nastiest" (17). He joins his colleagues in scolding the "ridiculously camp Gestapo officers." He explains *Bent* "left me scarcely less horrified, disturbed and revolted by its violence and cruelty" than in 1979. De Jongh likewise appreciates the relevance to broader atrocities: "In today's terrorist age, with state-sanctioned torture in Guantanamo and religious fundamentalists eager to blood gay men, Sherman's play seems more about human-beings' inherent savagery and capacity for hatred than homosexuality."

Burke objects to Sherman having "decided to suggest that the torture suffered by homosexuals at the hands of Nazis was worse than that of every other imprisoned outcast." She makes factual errors, which include her designating Wolf, not his executioners, SS. She says the Nazis arrest Rudy and Max "on the dangerous city streets" instead of in the forest. She also believes Max dies because he finds the loss of Horst "too much to bear and life without love is not worth living," a misconstruing of his final action. Despite her failure to understand it, Burke praises *Bent* as "grueling" and pronounces it a "hit."

Tayler notes "the play stands up well, in part because its message about being true to yourself is pretty timeless, and in part because of Sherman's skillfully carpentered script and grasp of theatrical spectacle" (Seven, 36). Eccles muddles history, saying Sherman sets his play in "Weimar Republic late 1930s" (21–22). She admires "the grim historical reality of *Bent*'s no-holds-barred truths" and compliments several of the actors. Yet she believes Kramer intends his Nazis as gay men, not heterosexual bullies.

Bevan also faults the staging. After praising the script, especially Act 2, where "the genius of Sherman's writing really takes hold," he writes, "Director Daniel Kramer has created a slick and visually striking production, but transforming the Nazis into a surreal troupe with almost balletic posturing was indulgent and inappropriate." Bevan cites an officer who writhes "like a demented robot." He stresses "this is my only bugbear in a play that is nevertheless brilliantly produced and acted," especially by Cumming and New, who "carry the colossal emotional weight of this gut wrenching morality tale."

Halliburton notes, "It's impossible not to be moved by the terrifying emotional and physical spiral Max descends" but complains about some "scrappy" dialogue (141). She concludes, "Switching between inscrutability and tortured pain, Cumming delivers a magnetic—if sometimes over-restrained—performance. Despite its undoubted flaws, this is an unforgettable evening." She picks it as a Critics' Choice.

Bassett terms *Bent* a "tragedy" but declares it "has not fully stood the test of time. Sometimes it's rushed, sometimes repetitive, sometimes too calculatedly tear-jerking" (11). She finds Trainor's Rudy "camp" and "tiresome" and complains, "When the persecution gets serious, the leering Gestapo keep looking like crude caricatures." Then she switches to praising Cumming, New, and the text in the latter half, only to complain about Max killing himself just after "standing up to be counted."

Taylor hasn't seen the play before and finds this mounting "at once highly accomplished and, given the subject matter, a little too confident in its deployment of 'theatrical effect'" (20). He understands the text, yet he lacks the historical knowledge to avoid complaining about the "pecking order among the ranks of the reviled and persecuted."

Wolf on theatre.com regards *Bent* as "flawed," objecting to "lurid passages and variable tone" and questioning its "all-male text that doesn't probe any of its individuals very intently. And yet, to see a full-house rise spontaneously to its feet—especially for a non-musical in London—is to witness a narrative whose gut-level affect is undimmed by time." He praises the staging. Wolf writes more vituperatively for bloomberg.com, where he regards Cumming as miscast and damns the text because it hasn't "stood the test of time." He refers to "Kramer's smartly designed and conceived staging."

Only four critics pan it. Brown feels Sherman uses the Holocaust "to wave a banner saying Glad To Be Gay" (Review, 75). She inaccurately describes Rudy and Max at play's start as "closet 'fluffs'" and dismisses Act 2, saying, "Max realizes his sexuality is an essential part of his humanity, and the play becomes crudely sentimental."

Sierz in *Tribune* challenges "a programme which compares the plight of the Guantanamo Bay detainees with those of Hitler's death camps. Am I the only one to find this distasteful" (23). He believes Max and Horst meet at Dachau instead of during transport. He says Max "swaps the yellow triangle for the pink star"—whoops—and he denounces the conclusion thus: "You're left with a heroic image of gay identity as a suicidal act of self-immolation," which he denounces as "retro, banal and deeply repellent." He concludes, "Keep your hankies, but pass the sick bag."

The final two reviews drew charges of homophobia.

One of these doesn't appear on the newspaper's website, which suggests editorial disapproval. Spencer attacks the curtain call because the stars kissed and objects to Sherman giving "a lachrymose tribute to Tom Bell, who appeared in the original production and died this week"—misleading since he died the night before (21). Spencer continues, "The mood of showbiz sentimentality was overwhelming and struck me as entirely disgusting." He challenges the play's existence because "sober documentary is the only appropriate response" to the subject and "Nazi death camps should never become the stuff of standing ovations." He finds *Bent* "titillating" and verging "on the pornographic" and supports his position by approvingly quoting Peter Hall's verdict, "*Bent* is a Manhattan fag's fantasy." After more bashing *Bent*, Spencer concludes, "The whole piece feels false and exploitative, as the dramatist bums a lucrative lift on the Holocaust."

Hart begins, "Seedy, trivial, superficial and ludicrous, *Bent* insults gay men and Holocaust victims alike" (Culture, 21). He blames victims, insisting, "The individualistic anarchy of these solipsistic bores often leads to a tyrannical backlash." Would Hart condemn to death every straight promiscuous person? Oddly, Hart assumes Sherman approves of Max at the start: "We're supposed to see Gay Berlin as wonderfully hedonistic and liberated, a happy place of sexual permissiveness and excess before the beastly Nazis shut it down." He feels *Bent* begins "trivial" and progresses to "repellent." He denounces portraying the guards as "screaming queens," after first condemning poor acting, set, dialogue, and direction. Then he reaches what especially revolts him, the sex scene. He concludes with a paragraph designed to damn the play's offensive "vile untruthfulness." Each item he labels a lie comes from accounts of the Holocaust written by survivors.

Callow, the director's partner, responded to three reviews. He takes Spencer to task for using the word "fag" and asks if he would use "kike" or "nigger" without discomfort. He explains to Hart the production presents Nazis as "sociopathic children, an interpretation with which anyone who has seen the footage of Abu Ghraib will find it hard to quarrel." He tells both critics Sherman presents documented truths, not distortions. He takes issue with Letts about Jewish children. He explains *Bent* makes the same point as *Rock 'n' Roll*: "The only real defiance of totalitarianism is by refusing the terms of the tyrant." Finally, he reminds these critics, "It is our history too."

Playwrights don't usually respond to reviews, and Sherman doesn't, but when interviewers ask about homophobic biases of critics, he replies. Sherman tells Roberts the reviews by Spencer and Hart "were outside of the bargain."

Concerning Spencer's insistence only documentary can provide an appropriate response to the Holocaust, Roberts challenges this stricture because it denies artists' right "to interpret horror, to create art in response to life's vilest tragedies. Sober documentary has its place, but is no substitute for Gorecki's Symphony Number 3, the achingly beautiful film *Vita e Bella*, or Primo Levi's *The Periodic Table*. And sober documentary could certainly never tell the tale of the courage of love, the triumph of hope over brutality that the two lead characters of *Bent*'s Dachau convey." Responding to Hart's remarks about the Nazis, Roberts quotes his designating them "screaming queens," then notes Kramer's knowledge of French physical theatre and use of "Bouffons" to indict Nazis.

Cumming speculates, "I think critics don't like the feeling they're not in control. They often have become inured to experiencing theatre on an emotional level, in the way the rest of the audience does. There also is a lot of homophobia in our society, albeit insidious, and something so bold as *Bent* allows this homophobia a release. Homophobia and sometimes internalized homophobia are rife amongst white, male, English, middle-aged, middle class theatre critics."

Sherman says Kramer's Nazis

> are the kind of taunting yobs on the street who participate in racist or homophobic attacks. I call them the Clockwork Orange Nazis. When you see the photos of Abu Ghraib, it's impossible to believe the guards behave with controlled decorum. They're behaving like hysterical monsters. A military expert who served in the British army in Northern Ireland plays one of the Nazis. He swears this is the way soldiers behave in extreme situations. He and Daniel are touching on something much truer than the clichéd, sinister Nazi we usually get. People fantasize their neighbors or children would corrupt with more gentility. Some critics have called them camp, immediately branding extreme behavior as gay. Instead, when the Nazi at the beginning of act 2 leads Horst onstage with his truncheon in Horst's mouth, that's a direct reference to the photos from Iraq—and chilling. Iraq and Guantanamo have given us a new understanding of how young men behave in war.

Sherman hoped Kramer's direction would attract young audiences, and it succeeded. This presented a problem. Young people purchased discounted tickets. Producer Friedman needed to sell more full-price tickets to pay *Bent*'s running expenses. It competed for those more costly tickets with a glut of West-End musicals, as did a concurrent mounting of *Summer and Smoke*. Both had to close early, despite Underground poster space donated to *Bent*.

Bent played to enthusiastic houses and generated the weeping and standing ovations accorded earlier productions, but it closed on December 9, 2006, instead of January 13, 2007. (Lyall mistakenly reports it closed in mid–November.)

Several London newspapers bemoaned two excellent productions of fine plays reducing their runs. At the 52nd annual *Evening Standard* awards, Brown reports that newspaper's De Jongh noted as the event's theme the fear "straight plays are in danger of being squeezed out of the West End."

Bent attracted three award nominations: New for the Milton Shulman Award for Outstanding Newcomer by the *Evening Standard* Awards; Cumming for Best Actor in the Whatsonstage.com Theatergoers Choice Awards; and New in the same awards for London Newcomer of the Year. Gould's season wrap-up praises "superb recreations of classic plays such as Martin Sherman's harrowing and poignant *Bent* at the Trafalgar Studios and Eugene O'Neill's *A Moon for the Misbegotten* at the Old Vic." Gould likewise selected for his short list of "great performances" Cumming as Max.

Sherman regretted the revival didn't run longer, but felt 12 weeks "very respectable on the West End." He rejoiced because many young people who hadn't seen it before saw this version, and he judged Cumming excellent, thrilling, as well as "very moving and painfully honest," and Chris New "astonishing, revelatory. We discovered a major talent who has the potential of being the most exciting actor of his generation."

Sherman intended Horst as 25. "Instead of being played as a wise older man, a rock of sanity and nobility, he's a kid who has his head screwed on about important things, brave but not noble, who can also be hysterical, pouting, manipulative, a pain. This makes the Max-Horst relationship more layered."

In early December 2006, Sherman took meetings in L.A. arranged by his motion-picture agent, Brian Siberall. While there, he agreed to write two films. For director Frears and producer Laura Ziskin he would update Ernst Lubitsch's *Trouble in Paradise*, and for HBO and Sigourney Weaver he would write about Gypsy Rose Lee. He would base that on Eric Lee Preminger's memoir *Gypsy and Me*.

Sherman went to Israel to give, on May 10, 2007, a lecture at Tel Aviv University that included excerpts from *Bent*, *Messiah*, and *Rose* performed by Cameri Theatre actors. The trip brought back memories—of the impact *Bent* had on Israeli law regarding homosexuality, the controversy *Messiah* caused in Haifa, and the outrage some New Yorkers felt at *Rose*'s condemnation of an Israeli murder of a nine-year-old girl.

In June, Sherman went to Evian to tutor screenwriters for Equinoxe again. He had been doing this for over a decade and would again in late November. He also serves on the board of the British Independent Film Awards. Also in June, Sherman revised *Aristo* for a July 6 reading with Robert Lindsay playing Aristotle Onassis.

That summer Sherman became involved in creating a ballet and a film, both starring Carlos Acosta in a new version of *The Red Shoes* against the background of the Cuban revolution. Elated, Sherman created a scenario involving a pair of ballet slippers cursed by voodoo and a man gripped by passions for ballet and revolution. The ensuing recession prevented funding these projects.

Before year's end, the Chichester Festival had agreed to premiere *Aristo* in September 2008, with Lindsay. Over the next six months, Aukin, Meckler, and Sherman assembled the cast. They chose Chichester's smaller theatre, the Minerva, preferring its intimacy.

For this his third work set entirely or partly in Greece, Sherman selectively takes his facts from Peter Evans's bestseller *Nemesis*, a shocker about Aristotle Onassis paying the PLO to assassinate Robert Kennedy. He also draws upon Evans's previous biography *Ari*. What Sherman derives from Evans he rearranges. He begins in medias res, as any Greek tragedian would, then supplies back-story.

A lesser writer would have used more *Nemesis* and achieved less. Sherman omits, for example, almost everything about Jackie's sister Lee, although Evans recounts damning details that might have sidetracked another playwright. In short, Sherman doesn't dramatize *Nemesis*.

An original, sometimes funny Greek tragedy, *Aristo* indicts those who maneuver themselves into positions of mega power and wealth, where they operate without a moral center, ruthlessly disregarding others.

From hundreds with whom Evans populates his book, the playwright chooses title character and protagonist Onassis, son and foil Alexandro, Jackie Kennedy, Maria Callas, and five chorus members—the shipping magnate's employees. At Chichester, three puppets enacted the sole onstage murder to hilarious effect. Aristo's daughter Christina doesn't appear, nor does Bobby Kennedy.

By cutting RFK and substituting narrative, Sherman makes it more Greek, creates the possibility Aristo lies about their encounter at JFK's wake, and permits Jackie to contrast Bobby's ethical center to Aristo's amorality. In her narrative, RFK emerges a finer man and statesman than he does in the deleted scene between him and Jackie. Cutting this character also saves a star's salary.

Sherman constructs *Aristo* in two acts, the first in a choral prologue and 15 scenes and the second in 18, all unnumbered. Act 1 dramatizes the tycoon's dangerous choices, driven by hubris. In Act 2, he reaps the consequences. The episodic structure reflects Greek practice.

Like Greek tragedians, Sherman employs frequent foreshadowing, foreboding, and fear of fate, destiny and angry gods who will strike down father and son. If we know 20th-century Greek and American history, this creates suspense of form, making us dread what we expect to occur and anticipate the way Sherman will treat these events. If we don't recall historical details, then it also engenders plot suspense.

Following a prologue by Costa, Ari's second in command, Onassis and guest Jackie Kennedy in 1963 (before JFK's assassination) deftly spar on his yacht. He admits he frequently lies. She compares him to Captain Hook, "dangerous and in danger at the same time—I mean that ticking clock" (6). His badinage often concerns sex or sometimes his fate, when he brags, "I never have to turn around to know what's behind me. Or ahead of me, for that matter" (10). Jackie presciently responds, "Tick-tock ... tick-tock...." Aristo wants her to desire him. Sherman has established suspense.

Scene 2 launches Costa into a comic gem recounting the sexual interconnections among politicians, stars, and powerful men of mega-wealth like Ari. It supplies the key to Aristo's obsessions: "I would call Niarchos Onassis' nemesis, but that word is better applied to Bobby Kennedy" (14).

In 3, Callas strides on to demand her due and insist, "The rest are pygmies!" (17). She grills the housekeeper. Did her lover sleep alone? Dimitra lies, but Costa confirms Ari and Jackie "consummated their flirtation on the Ionian Sea" (18). Maria and Aristo fight, then laugh and embrace. She disputes Costa's warning Aristo will jilt her "for the one woman in the world more famous than you" because Jackie "is married" (20), but gunshots begin scene 4.

Aristo describes the wake and Bobby's fury because he stayed at the White House for JFK's funeral. This scene leads to a suspense-generating declaration reminiscent of the Atreus-versus-Thyestes conflict underlying the *Oresteia*: "And I'll fuck him and eat him too and spit him out and little pieces of him will scatter over the earth and land on outdoor barbecues in Minnesota and Dubrovnik and Thessaloniki and be consumed as little specs of ash on second-rate, undercooked souvlaki! Get my goat! My 'goat' has just begun!" (25).

In 5, Aristo discusses with Theo his distress at learning everyone loves Alexandro. "There has never been a *nice* Onassis!" he fumes (26). "You have no idea how *dangerous* it is to be nice in my world. I am afraid for him." After this foreshadowing, Costa speaks of Alexandro's lover Fiona.

Aristo scolds Alexandro regarding his fidelity to her in 6, and suspense builds when father threatens to get rid of her if son doesn't. Scene 7 finds Alexandro worrying Aristo will have Fiona killed. Each chorus member prays to a different Greek deity in 8. They fear for the son, the father, and the new romance.

In 9, Aristo woos Jackie to wed him, which her affair with Bobby could derail. She notes, "You don't want to have me, you want to *steal* me" (34), and she contrasts Bobby's "distaste for social wrongs" with her Greek lover perpetrating wrongs. He continues to tempt her appetites for sex and security.

Scene 10 features gunshots "almost as famous" (37). Yanni relates Bobby's assassination. Aristo had sung an elegy at JFK's wake about killing "the golden eagle." This time Costa sings it.

In 11 Alexandro insists his father mustn't marry Jackie. He swears he won't attend the wedding and that he hates his father yet worries about him. This succinctly expresses the philos/aphilos (love/hate) relationship between them that permeates this play and underlies its tragedy. Subsequent to *Aristo*'s publication and its Chichester mounting, Sherman moved a section to this spot as the twelfth scene. Here Aristo and Jackie discuss "joint ownership of fig trees" (42).

In 13, Maria prays to Apollo about his giving her the glorious voice she destroyed and his punishing her with Aristo's marriage to Jackie. She implores Apollo to destroy Aristo, turning her prayer into a chilling curse. She emerges from her trance and wishes the couple "nothing but happiness" (41). Dimitra offers comfort, but Maria imperiously declines, snapping, "You're the chorus!" (42). This amusing response momentarily distracts us from the doom we fear awaits the lover who abandoned her.

Aristo joins the chorus on his wedding night in 14. He explains he and his bride enjoyed their "honeymoon night several hours before the marriage ceremony" (44). This upsets his companions because it tempts "fate." He notes, "My wife has cost me a lot," which we infer means the cost of his having RFK killed. The price, says Aristo: "I'm talking about my *soul*" (44). He explains that Hamshari owns it and admits he deceived Costa and Yanni about the amount paid the Palestinian and what he paid for.

In 15, Aristo confesses to Costa that Hamshari wanted to kill "a prominent American" and deduced Aristo might want to fund the murder of RFK. He agreed. "It wasn't just revenge," he explains. "It was expediency as well. Bobby would never have allowed me to marry her.... And I most certainly don't regret it, that little cocksucker had it coming. But it does take a rather prominent place in my thoughts, on this evening, the evening of my marriage. I did, after all, pay for the murder of the only man my wife ever really loved" (48). He wishes his conversation with Hamshari hadn't been overheard. When Costa asks who could have, Aristo replies, "The gods, my friend, the gods" (49). That suspenseful line ends Act 1.

Sherman has cut the production's first second-act scene with the puppets and substituted Alexandro telling the chorus his aunt Eugenia has died. "My family are all mad; they're killing each other," he laments (*Onassis*, 46).

Alexandro in scene 2 confronts Aristo, who has tapes that could destroy Niarchos's alibi for his wife's murder. The son has received evidence from his mother Aristo hired the PLO to kill RFK plus Fiona and Niarchos—"some kind of package deal" (56). Alexandro warns his father if Fiona dies, he will expose Aristo. And Aristo warns his son he mustn't know what his mother has told him "because it's dangerous" (57). Son threatens blackmail; father fears for son's life.

In 3, Alexandro tells the chorus he will move in with Fiona. In 4, Aristo publicly insults Jackie, but she maintains her composure. Spectators most enjoy the exchange in which he tells her "sleeping with you is like fucking an ironing board" and she replies, "What would you know ... about an ironing board?" (61). Her riposte amuses even Aristo. She feels dismayed because he openly sees Maria again.

Aristo reveals to Costa in 5 he seeks a divorce and Hamshari has died because he "knew too much" (63). Aristo learns in 6 that his private jet crashed. These two scenes lead us to suspect Fiona and Niarchos face less danger than do Aristo and Alexandro.

They again confront each other in 7. The young man grieves the pilots' deaths, while the father observes, "When you have enemies, there's no such thing as an accident" (65). Alexandro starts to insist this plane crash has nothing to do with RFK, but suddenly says, "I'm sorry," and Aristo in a rare moment of humility concedes, "I am too" (65). Aristo gives him a helicopter.

Foreboding 8 finds Aristo uneasy, saying he and the gods are waiting. Dimitra warns, "Nothing is certain except for this—the gods will fuck you up" (69). She sings of destiny.

In 9, Alexandro asks Jackie to tell his father he is "taking the Piaggio out one more time" before claiming ownership of the Puma, and she explains what draws her to his father—"The contradictions. The uncertainty. Treading on quicksand" (70). Like Rose, Jackie must avoid sinking.

In 10, Alexandro says he will make "one last flight" in the Piaggio, and Theo reiterates, "We all have a future already written /It is called destiny" (72). We anticipate what inevitably will occur.

In a scene which begins comically, Yanni reveals the Piaggio has suffered "engine failure" and "dropped ... from the sky," killing Alexandro (75). Aristo lunges at Yanni and tries to strangle him, then howls in anguish.

In 12, for the third time, we hear the "golden eagle" elegy (77). In 13, Aristo says the air force found the Piaggio had taken off with its cables reversed and wonders who hated him so much they "killed my Alexandro to get to me" (80). He regrets interfering with "natural order" and mourns his son (82).

Costa speculates, "I think he's dying" (83). Jackie frightens Costa by announcing she *knows*, but relieves him by revealing she has learned, not about RFK's murder, but about Aristo smuggling heroin. "He needed cash," Costa tells her, for "a divorce" (84). Jackie quotes Hook's crocodile as Aristo's avenging fate—"Tick-tock ... tick-tock" (85).

Yanni announces ex-wife Tina has died, another victim of Niarchos. We can infer this rival outdoes Aristo in evil. Jackie's husband hasn't killed his partners.

Considerably revised since its 2008 publication, the ending finds Aristo at his son's grave begging forgiveness and Maria striving to understand why she "gave up so much" and wondering, "How could we love such a man?" (*Onassis* 77). Aristo appears, vigorous, to dance at the diva's request. Early on Sherman dramatizes how Aristo seduces Jackie, so he closes with Maria reflecting about the erotic power he has wielded over her. The final image shows the virility that attracts both.

Like Sherman's other contemporaneous work, *Aristo* dramatizes an era in the life of a celebrity, in this case accompanied by two other superstars. Onassis resembles Max, but Max taken to ruthless extreme. Ari makes deals. He lacks ethics, scruples, conscience. He does as he pleases. As a youth, he behaved this way to survive, but subsequently he has done it from greed for money, power, sexual conquests. Max peddles small quantities of drugs; Ari ships it in tankers. Especially he lusts for revenge. He makes Max look like a Boy Scout.

Although Sherman sets a philosophic tone, generally Sophoclean, for his Greek tragedy, he ventures into black comedy, satire, and farce as well. He uses interrelationships in Onassis's life to amusing effect, and he provides both witty lines and humor from unwittingly witty remarks, as when the messenger begs Aristo not to kill the messenger or Costa provides his amusingly long-winded—like Polonius—revelations about amorality among the jet set. He keeps nine of ten murders offstage, but uses puppets to black-comic and satiric effect when Niarchos demonstrates to the policeman how he battered and bruised his wife while trying to "revive" her. (This vanishes from the revision.)

In using vengeance as the engine to bring down the house of Onassis, Sherman's script resembles Aeschylus's *Oresteia*. Two parallel furies, the title character and one of his victims, Maria, seek revenge. The play's ten murders suggest the bloodier Euripidean tragedies, or Seneca's, or some of the Jacobeans'. Theatre historians will enjoy tracing the play's lineage.

Never has Sherman written a play so presentational—all part of Greek tragedy's conventions.

In this his second portrayal of Callas, Sherman puts her more in control of her life and death or limbo. She's no passive victim. Jackie also proves a worthy sparring partner for Aristo. She never learns her husband has killed the only man she loved, but she does carry off a commercial transaction in her marriage and briefly enjoys her Captain Hook. And while treading quicksand, she doesn't sink. Among the onstage characters, only father and son, foils, perish because of Ari's hubris.

Aristo's dramatic action consists of duplicity and betrayal, driven by greed and passion for vengeance. Durrell's ghost haunts events, set in Greece, amidst intersecting intrigues, refracted through our shifting perceptions of reality. The protagonist, seemingly the most powerful man in the world, can do anything, have anything or anyone, but his house falls. This highly sexualized man's line will die out.

Sherman dramatizes his twin themes of outsiders and survival. He includes three kinds of women as "other." The chorus women, like their male counterparts, worry about surviving after their master's death. The conniving offstage wives of vying shipping tycoons, sisters, despite their own treachery, die. The onstage celebrity women, however, stay atop the quicksand. Jackie gets a short-lived romance and a fortune, and Maria takes back her man from the former first lady and takes revenge upon her faithless lover, who made her forfeit her voice. Ironically, they survive and thrive.

Exiled from Turkey to Argentina and then Greece, Aristo embodies the "other." His obscene wealth and narcissism likewise emphasize his differences from mere mortals.

What brings Aristo down? He destroys his family and his life. He doesn't know Maria curses him. He likewise knows nothing of the prayers each member of the chorus directs to an ancient deity. He does suspect, however, the gods' caprice or fate or his choices doom him. This all-powerful man, ironically, lacks the power to save himself and his line. We see what he only fleetingly glimpses: His hubris has brought about his suffering, and we experience catharsis of pity and fear. We also instinctively appreciate the resemblance between Onassis and the 21st-century's amorality, whether politicians or corporate heads or stars. Lindsay, for instance, cites Tiger Woods' confession "he was so rich and powerful that he felt he could get away with anything" (Franklin 4).

Sherman dedicates *Aristo* and *Onassis* to Mimi Denissi and family.

That winter Sherman wrote his first draft of *Trouble in Paradise*. In June 2008 he revised *Gypsy and Me* and heard Ziskin liked his May rewrites of *Trouble in Paradise*. So did Frears.

The screenplays have in common women who became celebrities because of sex. An historical figure chronicled by her son, Gypsy Rose Lee earned fame as a stripper. The fictitious perfume manufacturer in Samson Raphaelson's screenplay for Lubitsch's film, however, although sexy, ostensibly comports herself as a lady. Sherman changed that, taking inspiration from Paris Hilton. He recognized the original seems old-fashioned because a naïve woman allows her male secretary—a con artist—to take over her life. He averts a sexist situation by turning the heiress into a boozing, coke-snorting, seemingly mindless bimbo who nevertheless takes control of her fortune and bests the conman.

In adapting Preminger's *Gypsy and Me*, Sherman makes boy and mother initially four years younger. In the biography, Gypsy decides to stop stripping in chapter one. Sherman uses more of her life as comedienne/stripper and gets comic mileage from her actual patter. Sometimes he lifts dialogue from the book. Elsewhere he reads events took place and creates them. The screenplay concludes with an upbeat scene of Gypsy entertaining the troops, omitting her illness and death.

Rehearsals for *Aristo* began on August 4, 2008. Starring Lindsay, Elizabeth McGovern, and Diana Quick, it would begin performances on September 11 and open on September 25.

Lindsay embraced his character, and his hot scenes with McGovern's Jackie conveyed their lust without either removing garments. Katrina Lindsay's interior picture-frame proscenium evoked both yacht and taverna settings. Pool and sky reflected lighting designer Paul Pyant's sunlight and moonlight; timeless ocean lapping in Lorna Heavy's projections brought the Aegean on stage. Early preview audiences responded appreciatively. *Aristo* seemed destined for success.

Fickle Fate, however, threatened otherwise. On September 22, three days before the scheduled opening, disaster struck. Robin Soans, who played the second-largest male role, Costa, fell ill and left the cast. All performances had sold out before previews, and nobody had an understudy. Ticket holders expected to see *Aristo* Monday night, Tuesday night, Wednesday night, and Thursday afternoon, and critics expected to review it Thursday night.

Performances couldn't cease while another actor rehearsed Costa. Aukin, Meckler, and Sherman took the actor cast in the smallest male role, Theo, and moved him into Soans' part. They also deleted some of Theo's lines and gave the rest to Yanni. This diminished the group scenes' effectiveness and forced Julius D'Silva, the original Theo, into a role not ideal for him. Miscast, he heroically kept the play performing. Without his cooperation, *Aristo* would have closed. His courage paid off: No critic crucified him; a couple praised him.

The press office rescheduled critics to October 1. A new actor began performing Theo two days before the new opening. John Hodgkinson as Yanni, after playing some of Theo's role as well as his own for a week, unlearned extra lines.

Rescheduling the opening produced assignment alterations. Some periodicals could no longer review *Aristo*. The tally came to two negatives, six mixed, and five positives. Least damaged in reputation by Soans' ill-timed departure, Lindsay received glowing notices.

Nightingale praises the Euripidean trappings and "sharp, cutting dialogue" as well as Costa's "droll description of the interwoven sex lives of Onassis, Niarchos, the Kennedys and assorted Hollywood stars," and he lauds Lindsay (38). Peter suggests, "Imagine a Greek tragedy written by Tom Wolfe," champions a play that "crackles with wit, intelligence, even compassion," praises McGovern and Quick, and terms Lindsay's Onassis "a work of art ... vulgar but exciting—riveting and doomed."

Brown relishes Sherman's "bold new play" and "jolly good story" (sec. 2, 19). She feels "Meckler's production is overlong, but it's always absorbing." (Others who mention the length include Gardner and Spencer in negative notices and, in mixed, Taylor, Cooter, and Roberts. Sherman took this to heart and trimmed the text.) Marmion gives it four stars and refers to "Sherman's mischievous Sixties bio drama" (63). He calls Meckler's production "an elegant dream." In *Aristo*'s other favorable notice, Sell lauds it as "an evening of interesting and acute writing."

Gardner's negative review deplores, "You could almost fly to Greece in the time it takes for Martin Sherman to relate this story about Aristotle Onassis, and you would be guaranteed a better time when you arrived." Spencer rails against *Aristo* as a "bizarre and indigestible confection" and "shrill and pretentious"(31). He objects to its basis in conspiracy theory and demands dramatized evidence.

Six critics leaven rebuke with applause. Callan discerns an "oddity of a play ... curiously constructed." (53). "The piece is intermittently fascinating," Taylor writes. He finds "cleanly and clearly presented in Nancy Meckler's sleek, spare production," the play "lunges between the focused and the hokey." This mixed review assigns it three stars out of five. So does Thorncroft, who terms Aristo a "very modern anti-hero" and enjoys Lindsay (21). He deplores omitting "the feminine viewpoint" and complains the playwright chases "a multitude of hares." Thrice he laments Aristo "dominates." He wants another play, except he finds the "minimalist design nicely evokes an Aegean warmth."

In another three-star review, Cooter calls *Aristo* "years out of date" because Princess Diana "superseded" Jackie, who "means little to anyone under 40." Himself out of touch with autumn 2008, Cooter avers, "Onassis's ruthless business methods seem particularly out of sync right now." Ignoring extensive documentation in *Nemesis*, he accuses Sherman of speculating "wildly." He extols Lindsay as "mesmerizing." Mountford finds Sherman's "meaty new biodrama ... less digestible than it should be." She faults failure to explain how Onassis went from rags to riches (false), but likes set and video projections. She concludes, "*Aristo* isn't the best but it's an ambitious finale nonetheless." Roberts praises performers, designs, and the script's imagination and dialogue, yet felt bored.

Nobody reviewed it in the U.S. David Benedict, who had planned to, couldn't accommodate the schedule change.

When *Aristo* closed on October 11, no suitable West-End theatre came vacant, and Lindsay's father fell ill. Despite a global financial crisis, producers remained committed.

Sherman tightened it, pruning anything extraneous, repetitious, tangential. Most tellingly, he trimmed whatever he could after Alexandro's death. Like Lear ranting on the heath and later mourning Cordelia, Onassis, after the bad news, raves, grieves, dies. Yet he returns to vital life while Maria ponders why they all loved him.

Nevertheless, the Haymarket fell through when another show booked it, and others occupied appropriate West End theatres. Then the Haymarket became available, but not on a schedule which would permit recasting, rehearsing, and marketing.

In 2009, Sherman learned Universal wouldn't film *Trouble in Paradise* and HBO wouldn't make *Gypsy and Me*. Pathé saw his Greek tragedy as a hot property, so he adapted it for film and revised this, but it also languished. That year Garnett dedicated *Savage Adoration* to him.

Producers arranged to open *Aristo* (revised, recast—Jackie, Lydia Leonard; Maria, Anna Francolini—and re-titled *Onassis*) in the West End in autumn 2010. In February he began a screenplay based on Rose Tremain's *Music and Silence* for director Lone Scherfig, and talks began for a West-End *Roman Spring*.

Martin Sherman at home, 2010. (Photograph: David Gwinnutt.)

Onassis ran in Derby from September 9 through 25, selling out and eliciting only favorable reviews. Some critics raved ("witty, literate script," Wheeler; "a treat," Orme; "great writing," Jenner). Talk hummed of a Broadway transfer.

Given Sherman's topic and his risk-taking throughout his 50-year career, when it opened on October 12, 2010 at the Novello, it of course provoked his trademark controversy. Wildly divergent reviews say "brilliant ... an outstanding venture" (Bassett 60), "modern Greek tragedy ... a colourful cautionary tale" (Coveney, whatsonstage.com), and "brilliantly exposes Onassis's obvious hubris" (Moss) or reprove it as "ridiculous" (Billington 14), "dismally dull" (Shenton 66), and "static" (Hitchings 31). Its mixed moods infuriate some; its monster protagonist upsets others, who evidently forget Oedipus, Lear, and Macbeth also behave badly. Some critics spew venom, such as Spencer's "the brain begins to lurch and the stomach to turn" (31). Yet audiences loved it and gave it nightly standing ovations. Producers passed on an option to extend for a month. An early press-release error giving the extension date caused multiple press mistakes regarding an "early" closure, but it played its full scheduled run through January 8, 2011.

On October 30, Lavren died of cancer after hanging on until after her friend's opening.

The dramatist celebrated his 72nd birthday knowing *Onassis* had survived. But would anybody mount it again? A prominent Greek wants to produce it in Athens, where the play has done what the book didn't—caused a mini-scandal. The Onassis Foundation has denounced its protagonist's portrayal, but Aristo's relatives felt Sherman has captured Onassis exactly—apart from financing murder—especially his relationship with his son.

If prospective backers heed newspaper naysayers, perhaps the play has no future. If they listen to enthusiastic critics or audiences, however, others will mount it. It's a Sherman paradox: What makes the play great also makes it a hot potato. Sherman never plays it safe.

Appendices

A. *Bent* on Stage

At least 54 countries have presented *Bent*: Argentina, Australia, Austria, Belgium, Brazil, Bulgaria, Canada, Czech Republic, Chile, China, Colombia, Croatia, Denmark, England, Estonia, Finland, France, Germany, Greece, Hungary, Iceland, India, Irish Republic, Israel, Italy, Japan, Luxembourg, Mexico, Moldova, Netherlands, New Zealand, Northern Ireland, Norway, Panama, Peru, Philippines, Poland, Portugal, Puerto Rico, Romania, Russia, Scotland, St. Lucia, Singapore, Slovakia, Slovenia, South Africa, Spain, Sweden, Switzerland, Trinidad, United States, Venezuela, Wales.

Cities mount it repeatedly, and multiple municipalities in a country produce it. Every major German city has seen it, e.g., thrice in Essen, four times in Berlin. The Nationaltheatre in Manheim opened its production—the first outside the U.K. and U.S.—on April 19, 1980. The same day, the Coliseum Theatre in Oldham opened their first U.K. regional production, and the Palace Theatre in Southend on Sea, Essex, followed on April 23.

Coliseum's Artistic Director, Taylor, reports, "Many people told me I was moving too fast, Oldham wouldn't take it, I'd lose the audiences we had built up. On the first night I witnessed the first standing ovation I had ever seen at Oldham, the play was a sellout" (53). This audience response typifies reactions. No matter what critics say—and generally they prove supportive—spectators weep and cheer.

By August 1979, foreign producers contracted for productions in German-speaking Europe, Holland, the five Scandinavian countries, Australia, and France. By winter 1980, another Australian producer, one in Belgium, and two in Dublin had followed suit. The spring brought two more Australian producers under contract, and the summer added two mountings in New Zealand.

Belfast got a production in September 1980, as did Essen. Australia, Scandinavia, Greece (Athens), and Brussels (a French production) followed in the autumn. By then, in November 1980, the Out and About Theater in Minneapolis presented the U.S. regional premiere, and both the Theatre Royal, York, and R.A.D.A. opened productions.

Bent played Brazil in 1981 and thereafter. When Roberto Vignati presented it in São Paulo in a theatre seating 359 people, 420 spectators crammed in. This production recouped its investment in two months. When Vignati returned the show to São Paulo after touring, it played the 700-seat Teatro da Hebraica. It proved the most popular play ever before performed in Brazil, and the producer extended his contract to mid–April 1984. Another contract gave Brazil *Bent* for 18 months in 1986–1987. Eventually, in March 1999, the play's popularity prompted a São Paulo ballet (in translation *Bent: The Jailed Song*) inspired by Sherman's landmark drama.

In January 1981, *Bent* opened at the Civic in Chelmsford, at Wisdom Bridge in Chicago, and at Warehouse in Winnipeg. Other Canadian theatres quickly followed with openings in March in Vancouver, Toronto, and Edmonton. The Vancouver version broke box-office records and extended, which also occurred at Atlanta's Alliance Theatre that spring.

Bent opened in Berlin in February 1981, Detroit in March, Paris in September, at the Empty Space in Seattle in October, that month also in Hamburg, and in Stuttgart the next.

A 1981 sampling includes Barcelona, France, Belgium, and Luxembourg, and for 1982 Pittsburgh, Washington D.C., Lausanne, Nottingham, Ilford, Houston, Barcelona, and Boston. A projected California production, cast in 1982, never happened because of the producer's skullduggery, but Tom Cruise auditioned.

During 1983–84, *Bent* continued popular in, among others, Richmond, Cleveland, Columbus, Slovenia, Surrey, Kansas City, Denver, New Orleans, Aachen, Long Island, Orebro, Erie, Racine, Geneva, Albuquerque, and Tokyo. Producers contracted for productions in Rome, Sydney, Yugoslavia, Spain, and Mexico City.

Formerly fascist countries have loved *Bent*: Cities in Germany, Japan, and Italy frequently produce or revive it. Rome, for example, staged it in April 1985.

When the Caldwell Playhouse in Boca Raton presented it in February 1985, it proved a smash hit, and they had their best box-office returns in their ten-year history.

Bent finally got California productions in 1986, at California State University and at the Bowery Theater in San Diego, both in October. The Bowery version extended its run. Riddle writes, "You will not be the same person when you leave as when you entered" (16). The San Francisco Repertory soon followed, as did the Coast Playhouse in West Hollywood. Grant directed this version and, with about a week left of rehearsals, had to take over Max. Tate Donovan played Rudy and Peter Frechette essayed Horst. Lassell writes, "It's a brilliant play in a stunning production—the kind of event that fills you with the love of life at the same time it crushes you with the pain of living. It's remarkable, enduring, important, visionary" (B1, B5).

U.S. cities as different as Honolulu, Anchorage, and Omaha did *Bent*. As Max and Horst discover or retain their humanity while undergoing dehumanizing treatment, find meaning while engaged in a meaningless task, and behave courageously while Nazis terrorize them, the play's universal appeal works regardless of locale. Small cities in central Florida have presented the play four times in three decades. Most recently, in 2007, the Holocaust Memorial in that region asked Orlando's Empty Spaces to stage it in support of the museum's exhibit, "Nazi Persecution of Homosexuals." Before *Bent*, museums didn't schedule such exhibits because few people knew such persecution had occurred.

Atlanta got its second production in January 1988, Boston in June 1991, New York and San Francisco in September 1992, San Diego in October, and Pittsburgh and Richmond the following year. London had its first major revival in January

1990 (see Chapter 11), but that didn't stop that city's small Good Night Company from doing it the following year, and a U.K. provincial tour went out earlier, in 1988–89. *Bent* premiered in Lisbon in 1994.

When Buffalo's Ensemble Theatre staged *Bent* in March 1991, Chase greeted it as a season highlight and gave it 4 ½ stars. When the Gallery Players of Brooklyn did it in March 1996, Portantiere raved, *Bent* is "one of the finest plays of the past quarter-century" (38).

Often *Bent* revivals receive awards. For example, Thierry Lavat's Paris revival received four 2002 Moliere Award nominations, and it won the Moliere Meilleur Spectacle Repertoire Award. Although house lights came up quickly, spectators continued applauding through more than a dozen curtain calls.

Those cities that have produced this audience favorite more than once include Santa Fe, Lausanne, Minneapolis, Raleigh, Brussels, Berlin, Essen, Athens, Madrid, Barcelona, Tokyo, Paris, Sydney, Hamburg, Rio de Janeiro, Milwaukee, Stockholm, Washington D.C., Bucharest, Los Angeles, San Diego, Vancouver, Quebec, Toronto, and others. Moore hails a Denver revival, "*Bent* is a play about a pile of rocks, and it will hit you like a ton of bricks."

Although Tokyo has hosted several large professional productions, Ackerman also directed it there in 2003 with unknowns. Because a big revival would run simultaneously, he could only obtain the rights if his group gave away tickets. They played to over 100 percent capacity. He remembers,

> People were sitting in the aisles, on the radiators, anywhere they could put down a cushion. It's a bit of a theatre legend in Japan.
> It was extraordinary coming back to the play. It was so moving to do it with this young cast who knew virtually nothing about the Holocaust or gay life. They were unafraid of the subject and unashamedly gave themselves to the play. Their passion was so great every rehearsal was a joy. Seeing it with young men made it all the more tragic. They were just starting their lives but were imprisoned and murdered because of their sexuality. Martin turned to me during the performance and whispered, "You know this is better than the Broadway production." "What do you expect?" I replied. "I've had 20 years more experience."
> At the sayonara party for Martin the night before he returned to London, we were all a bit drunk, and we told everyone Martin wasn't really Martin at all. After all, none of them had met him before. We said Martin was his cousin Marvin Sherman and that he had really enjoyed this free trip to Japan. It became a big joke, and since then many theatre people in Japan affectionately refer to Martin as Marvin.

During the opening decade of the 21st century, producers have steadily presented *Bent*, including the Philippines (second time), Spain (twice), Germany, Italy, Scandinavia, Athens, Peru, Bath, Catford (Kent), Oxford, Cambridge (MA), Amarillo, Albuquerque, Columbia SC, Colorado Springs, the Catskills, Fort Collins, Eau Claire, Santa Ana, Long Beach, Orlando, Miami, Los Angeles (thrice), Paris (thrice), Bucharest, Tallinn, Dublin, Dallas, Tokyo (twice), Binghamton, Cincinnati, Las Vegas, San Francisco, Indianapolis, Chicago, Louisville, St. John's, St. Paul (twice), St. Louis (twice), Vancouver (twice), Rio de Janeiro (twice), Sydney, and London (both multiple fringe mountings and West End).

The play has continued to please crowds at amateur theatres. Samuel French, Inc., has licensed it to such companies 100 times between 2000 and 2009. Many of these productions have occurred in small communities or in locations (such as Idaho) not famous for progressive positions on controversial issues. Often schools lead the way in broadening minds.

In the U.K., Samuel French, Ltd., licensed 37 amateur productions between 1996 and 2009, plus numerous amateur productions in other parts of the world. The latter included, for example, 34 performances presented in Singapore in July and August 2003.

In October and November 2004, fully appreciating Sherman's understanding of "the other," disabled company Graeae toured *Bent* in the U.K. and Bulgaria.

Bent has become a staple of the acting school Bet Zvi outside Tel Aviv, which has mounted three productions and toured two to Russia. It has presented the only known performances of *Bent* in Russia.

New York got another revival in 1997. Schools there, such as the New School for Social Research and the dramatist's alma mater Actors Studio Drama School, have presented it. Seven productions occurred in NYC between 2001 and 2009. It has not, however, had a Broadway revival because Broadway economics discourage selections other than comedies, musicals, and imports of current West-End hits. Perhaps New York producers don't trust potential audiences to handle the material, despite *Bent*'s enduring power and appeal.

B. *Messiah* on Stage

Before *Messiah*'s December 1984 U.S. premiere, it had received productions in Germany, Austria, Belgium, Holland, Scandinavia, Australia, and Switzerland. The latter mounting, in French, featuring Yiddish songs and klezmer music, received raves.

For Manhattan Theatre Club's December 1984 production, Sherman asked for Ackerman, who had mounted it in Haifa, but he had a schedule conflict. The playwright therefore requested British director David Leveaux. Thus Sherman brought a British director to New York to helm an American production at the same time he selected an American director to bring his next play, *When She Danced*, to London.

The playwright insists this makes sense because "I'm between two cultures. My plays are very emotional, which is an American quality. That's rare in England. But I deal with larger issues than domestic ones. They have a sense of a larger world, and that's very English, very European." This has prompted some negative reviews by English critics who reject the emotional impact and some negative U.S. reviews prompted by his failure to write domestic drama.

Casting took an unusual five weeks. Diane Venora, who had played Hamlet for Joe Papp at the Public Theater not long before, took Rachel. Sensual Sarah went to Margaret Gibson, and handsome Mark Blum got Asher. Karen Ludwig, who had played leading roles, accepted the small character part of Tanta Rose.

After a difficult search, Mabou Mines's experimental actor David Warrilow won Reb Ellis. He brought inventiveness and comedic skill to his performance and received excellent reviews, but he also proved unpredictable. The other actors didn't know what he would say, or when he would say it, or whether he would say it.

As Rebecca, Viveca Lindfors didn't last; during rehearsals, the director fired her. Sherman calls her a "thrilling" actor, but her hearing loss frightened her, and that, in turn, caused Leveaux to regard her as difficult. Bloom had wanted to play Rebecca, but her audition had seemed too young. After Lindfors left, however, "David and Martin came to my house and practically begged."

Performances began on December 11, 1984, but, before the play opened on December 23, Sherman left for Japan to catch the final week of *Bent*'s second production there.

When he returned, he read some reviews baffled by its genre or its style or the sheer difference between it and the plays the critics usually judged. What were they to make of its quicksilver moods but huge philosophical issues? A silent God plays straight man in the comedy of Rachel's life, but, although she gets the punch lines, she must roll with the punches, and the men out of misguided fanaticism die. The fact that men wrote most of the reviews couldn't have improved these notices. Perhaps surprisingly, many do praise *Messiah*.

Leading the opposition, Barnes fulminates "scarcely a second coming, hardly worth a first visit. I lost sympathy with it about one minute and 23 seconds into the first act. I lost interest soon after" (36).

Watt's pan reveals he tuned out before Act 2 since he suggests the entire "boring religious mystery play" takes place in Yultishk (13). Hummler, substituting vague invective for specificity, bashes actors, director, and author, saying: "inert, lugubrious, unenlightening," "endless," "inept writing," "a lifeless bore.... This *Messiah* is a mess" (54).

Nobody else whacks it that hard, but many reflect frustration with a work so difficult to pin down, so varied in genre, style, and construction. Smith terms it "distracted and unwieldy" (37).

Rich admits, "Mr. Sherman remains a frustrating playwright. *Messiah* ... is a failure, but it can't be summarily dismissed. While there are plenty of writers today who trivialize historical nightmares for melodramatic ends, Mr. Sherman is not one of them" (36). Yet Rich rejects nearly every aspect of the play and its mounting.

Most other reviews qualify as mixed.

Christian Science Monitor admires the designs, but treats this supremely Jewish play as alien territory, terming it "bizarre" and "obscure" and assigning it to the wrong century ("Messiah" 28–29).

Rabbi Isaac, steeped in Judaism, doesn't cheer either, because he wants Sherman to write about Sabbatai—"a thundering epic about a mystical false messiah"— and cannot abide combining drama and comedy. He praises the "aria" in which Rebecca details "horrors of Jewish persecution," but believes it's a dead cat sewn into her husband's stomach. Isaac admires much about the script and performances but cannot conceal his disappointment that Sherman didn't write a different play (11).

Fink assumes Sherman's characteristically contrasting first and second acts reveal a failure "to find a unifying dramatic voice" and a "coherent theatrical realm," although he praises the playwright's "prose that rings with both lyric and dramatic poetry" (370–371).

Syna confuses the second act's location, naming Constantinople rather than

Gallipoli, but he cites details to demonstrate *Messiah*'s "electrifying" and funniest moments. He praises somewhat more than he finds fault, then concludes, "Sherman's play deserves a viewing" (5B).

Simon reveals more about himself than the play. He attacks *Bent*, then alludes to other writers (12 in 5 paragraphs) to show off his education and wit (as in "I.B. Singer sewing machine"). Ivo Pogorelich (a Croatian pianist whose talent Simon judges bogus) seems an obscure allusion, but no more difficult than the word "thaumaturgist" (the alternative form of the preferred "thaumaturge," meaning miracle worker) which he uses to describe Sabbatai. His more positive comments about the script include "not without interest," "generates a fair amount of wit, pathos, theatricality, and suspense," and "in a season that has tended to be aggressively mindless, an adroit production of a play that at least flirts with ideas is not to be casually dismissed" (54).

Novick warns that some spectators disagree with him, but he admires the "flawed, uncomfortable, preposterous (but the facts of the matter are preposterous!), fascinating work." His thoughtful analysis leads him to judge "for me this is the kind of brave, extravagantly faulty big play that is worth a dozen neat safe little ones" (72, 74). Kissel finds more to praise about both play and production (12).

Women tend, largely, to like it. Lamont concludes, "Despite its flaws, the play lingers in the mind" (34). Dace praises it as "fiery, bold and provocative" (38). Thrall appreciates it, but oddly seems to assume directors write the scripts. She terms *Messiah* "one of the season's liveliest productions" (14A).

Messiah received sporadic productions elsewhere. Yugoslavia, for instance, in the region now known as Slovenia, during the 1984-1985 season became the first Eastern European country to present it.

A Chicago-area mounting so irritated Christiansen he reviewed it vituperatively. He trashes *Bent*, then mocks combining comedy and drama. That Sherman trademark always has made some critics uneasy. He lards his notice with loaded language like "mumbo-jumbo" and "Rachel making goo-goo eyes at Asher" (sec. 5, 5). Saunders greets this production less stridently, yet calls *Messiah* philosophically "a mess" because it fails to reach a conclusion about faith (41).

A woman reviewed the next Chicagoland mounting; Weiss loves it. She begins, "From Moses the lawgiver to Tevye the milkman, it has been men who have most often spoken directly to God in Jewish history and fable. But in Martin Sherman's dramatic *Messiah*, which opened Monday night in an enchanting production at Skokie's National Jewish Theater, the voice that questions, confesses, consults and rages in conversations with God is that of Rachel (Lisa Dodson), a smart and feisty but terribly homely 28-year-old" (45).

More German productions and one in L.A. occurred. Although the playwright terms the latter "dreadful," he praises a two-performance reading at a London church organized by the National Theatre Studio in May 1995 which cast major performers in every role. Linda Marlowe played Rebecca and Lindsay Baxter took Sarah; the scene between them succeeded as never before because of their extraordinary skill.

In the mid–90s, some Sherman friends clamored for a London revival. Pope and Callow hoped to see it; Luscombe and Meckler hoped to direct it. Finally Meckler sent the script to Heyman, who had produced a Sherman television film as well as a film Meckler had directed. Just after she had dispatched the script to Heyman, however, Meckler accepted Sherman's film *Alive and Kicking*.

Instead of Meckler reviving *Messiah* in London, the Birmingham School of Speech and Drama, after mounting it in that city, gave it a performance at the West-End Criterion Theatre in July 1997. In January and February 1999, the L'Khaim Theatre mounted a small revival at the Hackney Empire Studio.

A German theatre presented *Messiah* in the late '90s, a Paris theatre revived it in spring 2004, and New Yorkers enjoyed it in March and April 2006, when Workshop Theater Company revived it. In the U.K., Chichester College presented *Messiah* in March 2007, and Cygnet staged it in Exeter in July 2008.

Messiah's Hebrew publication has prompted amateur productions in Israel (for instance, by the Beit Zvi school in 1987), and Rachel's monologues have yielded audition pieces. The BeerSheba Municipal Theatre revived *Messiah* during Christmas week 2008.

Several Americans have written theses about the play.

C. *When She Danced* on Stage

In New York in February 1990 at Playwrights Horizons, Luscombe directed, Elizabeth Ashley starred, and Jonathan Walker played Sergei. The pair conveyed appropriate sexual electricity.

But others gave better performances: Marcia-Jean Kurtz inhabited Belzer brilliantly, and Robert Sean Leonard as Greek Alexandros caught the play's nearly lunatic frenzy, but also its quiet intensity.

As for Ashley, what she lacked in timing she made up for in sensuality and charisma. Critics who praised her found her star quality right for Isadora. However, she couldn't master the lines. Because the play's economy and wit require actors to speak those exactly, she failed Isadora. When she wandered too far afield, the other actors evinced skill keeping scenes on track.

New York critics disagree about the play, but only one published a negative review. Apart from Kurtz's Belzer, Hummler fumes, "There's no reality or truth in sight." He assumes Sherman portrays Duncan and Esenin inaccurately because such extreme people couldn't have existed. He terms it "meretricious and annoying," a "bungle" and "grimly unfunny."

Simon's mixed review pummels the play and Ashley, but calls Leonard's Alexandros and Kurtz's Belzer "outstanding." He illustrates "crudeness of execution" by asking, "Can you believe that the spouses could not convey a single word to each other?"

Some other critics—Watt, Barnes, Winer, and Kirkpatrick—published mixed reviews that applaud Ashley.

Novick expresses reservations: "Mr. Sherman and his adroit director, Tim Luscombe, are well aware that the overripe romanticism of Isadora and her men folk has its comic, even farcical side" (19). He likes that, especially "quite a satisfying food fight. The pathetic parts of the play, however, are less successful."

Novick's colleague disagrees. More interested in dance, this dancer, and Sherman's conviction "words are inadequate to describe the ineffable effects of dance in performance," Resnikova enjoys it (19).

Feldberg judges it "a literate, intelligent work" that fails to interest us in characters other than Belzer. Nelsen faults the first act's pacing, which he finds "slow, despite a great deal of witty banter" (33). Yet he likes the play, says the Tower of Babel "works," and loves the second act's farce.

Rich understands and praises the play. He says of the dinner party, "As written by Mr. Sherman, the scene is an imaginative amalgam of Marx Brothers and Chekhov—a circus of food fights, unrequited lust and ineffectual attempted suicide" (C15). Rich writes a mixed review because he faults Luscombe, for not doing justice to the text, and most actors, particularly a miscast Ashley.

Popkin begins his favorable notice, "*When She Danced* makes farce out of personal tragedy, but then life does that too" (41). He judges the play "works extremely well." Kuchwara praises Sherman for his "special skill at evoking the joy Isadora's dances brought to people" as well as Luscombe for his handling of "the shift in action from tragedy to melodrama to farce" (14).

Oliver writes Duncan "never set foot on the stage of Playwrights Horizons, and that we accept her there at once is just one of Mr. Sherman's accomplishments in this remarkable play" (98). Regarding Belzer's monologue, she feels, "This small incident is just one instance of the playwright's subtle, telling indirection." Raidy fears Sherman has trouble "winding things up," but judges this "a fascinating work" and "staged with great élan" (28). Sommers raves, "Writing with grace and subtle humor, Martin Sherman quite lovingly depicts Isadora Duncan during her twilight years" (52A). He continues, "This often funny, ultimately very moving play benefits from the mercurial subtlety of the acting ensemble."

Feingold publishes a longer rave about Sherman's "mordant, shimmeringly complex play" (105–106). He praises its "fidelity to this extravagance, this delight in extreme behavior and extreme language for their own sake. The stylistic excess ... is elegantly and carefully tracked, each grandiose version of it slightly different from the others." After further applause, Feingold observes Sherman's use of foreign languages without translation "is a tour de force of playwriting in itself and helps ... to twist the bleak events into a bitter madcap farce, a *Room Service* of the International Set." Feingold rejoices concerning the text for several more paragraphs, culminating in terming it "Sherman's best play to date."

Sherman had suggested Liza Minelli play Isadora. Wendy Wasserstein reports Minelli attended the play "and afterwards told Martin, 'I would love to be at the party in your head.' Martin imagined himself serving drinks in his brain." A few years later he would create Minelli as a character in his musical *The Boy from Oz*, so she would attend that party.

When She Danced has received other U.S. productions—in Philadelphia, L.A., Chicago (thrice), Helena, and Harrisburg, for instance—at least two other U.K. mountings (in Strathclyde in May 1992 and at London's Central School of Speech and Drama in June 1998), and numerous other mountings 'round the world—in Australia, Brazil, Canada, Japan, Paris, Madrid, Scandinavia, in German-speaking and Italian-speaking Europe, in Holland and Flemish Belgium, and widely in Central and Eastern Europe.

As *Ked'tancovala*, it ran in 1996 in Bratislava, Slovakia. The Czech Republic mounted it in 1999, the National Theatre of Romania presented it in 2002–2003, and the Czech Republic revived it later in the decade. Polish television aired it, on July 1, 1998, starring the famous Teresa Budzisz-Krzyanowska. It even opened as a musical in Budapest, Hungary, on March 7, 2008, thanks to its fan lyricist-librettist-producer Atilla Galambos. This theatre kept it in the repertory the following season.

In 2005, Joe Mantello asked to mount it on Broadway with Patricia Clarkeson, but only if he could do it without using a proscenium theatre. When that fell through, Stanley Tucci, in 2008, began discussing staging it with Clarkeson.

The play remains one of Sherman's most produced works.

D. *A Madhouse in Goa* on Stage

The play received a second U.K. production in March 1990 at the Oldham Coliseum, where Linda Marlowe directed. Productions also occurred in Germany, Switzerland, Scandinavia, and Italian-speaking Europe.

Another U.K. mounting followed in 1991, when Millstream Touring presented *Madhouse* from May 2 through June 29, 1991. The tour returned to the Yvonne Arnaud in July.

Madhouse reached New York in fall 1997. Wasserstein had midwifed this production, which opened on November 17, by suggesting the play to Carol Rothman, Second Stage's Artistic Director. Rothman might have misunderstood the play's mixed genres and its tones that switch on a dime. Second Stage also got the date wrong for its London premiere, which the New York program lists as August 28, 1989, instead of April 28.

Although Sherman says little about this *Madhouse*, most critics and even some of the playwright's friends give it low marks. The problem lay with the director, Nicholas Martin.

He specializes in farce, satire, and parodying the classics, which he did in an infamous Broadway *Hedda Gabler* starring Kate Burton that undermined Ibsen rather than interpreting him. Evidently convinced Sherman wrote *A Table for a King* as Williams' parody, Martin encouraged Judith Ivey to play Mrs. Honey as an over-the-top lower-class Southern ditz.

Some spectators at Martin's *Hedda Gabler* recognized the director had made a fine play appear incompetent because they knew the script. New Yorkers had no such advantage with *Madhouse*.

Sherman confirms he didn't intend *Madhouse* as a send-up of Williams, whom he admires. A decade after the misguided Second Stage production, Sherman begins his endorsement of the New Directions collection of Williams' poetry: "I did not think it possible to love or respect Tennessee Williams more than I already did" (2007). Sherman reserves his sharpest satiric venom instead for Barnaby Grace, the Hollywood producer. He especially doesn't mock Mrs. Honey who, along with Ivey's other character, Heather, and male nurse Oliver, embodies Sherman's own humane wisdom and concerns for humanity. He created Mrs. Honey as an authentic Southern lady.

In Salonika in September 1997, Sherman pruned *Madhouse* towards the end plus inserted a reference to the Chernobyl nuclear explosions that occurred on April 26, 1986. He had completed *Madhouse* that year.

Director Martin made a damaging change. The script specifies Oliver fails to locate the source of the loud noises as the play ends, but Daniel, whose aphasia has muddled his speech but not his wits, recognizes the volcano as the sounds' source. After he says "The apricot is erupting," he must laugh, ruefully, wryly and with relish, because they will quickly die (80). The director cut the laugh.

Critics in 1989 had described Redgrave's Mrs. Honey with such adjectives as "ineffably dignified Southern lady" (Wardle), "dreamy, desolate" (C. Edwards), "an elderly but graciously imperious Southerner" (Watt), "a delicate Southern blossom" (Kissel), "fading Southern belle" (J. Edwardes), "autocratic American matron" (Tinker), "wistful" (Coveney), "a pathetically dignified Mississippi matron" (Henry). These descriptions convey the contrast of the character Sherman wrote and Redgrave played to the weirdo Ivey concocted, what Southerners would have labeled "poor white trash."

Where Redgrave brought dignity and wisdom to the role and left us devastated when David betrays her, Ivey caused us to dislike her and that, in turn, left us indifferent to her fate. Instead of locating Mrs. Honey's inner core and inhabiting her skin, Ivey had seen a strange woman and determined to imitate her externally—bizarre hair, frowsy dress, and all.

Gussow quotes Ivey: "'I just looked up and there was Mrs. Honey, with her black hair and silver streak,' she said. 'I stopped still in my tracks and memorized as much about her as I could'" (E1). She drew a picture of that woman for the costume designer. Ivey imposed the wrong external details on the role. She created a crude caricature, not a real person.

Her Mrs. Honey's lack of dignity went beyond her wig and costume. She brayed and fidgeted. Her matron flirted salaciously with Nikos. She kept sticking out her tongue and grinning after pulling the lady's bell out of her bra. She seemed three years old. Alas, under misguided direction, even Ivey's second-act performance misfired as her braying and wiggling continued during her Heather. She invented silly business, like making swimming motions when she mentioned fish on a menu. She turned the voice of sanity bonkers.

Confronted with a misdirected production, most critics fault the play. Eight write mixed reviews. One other pans everything. Three critics praise it.

Barnes saw *Madhouse* in London, where he reviled it. Now he dismisses it as lacking "the life that might be bestowed upon it by the conviction of some basic touch with reality" (67). He finds it improbable and employs a homophobic slur concerning the "limp-wristed male nurse" Oliver.

Canby terms it "earnest, foolish" and advises, "The collapse of civilization deserves better" (sec. 2, 26). Evans begins, "Watching Martin Sherman's *A Madhouse in Goa* is like sharing a bus ride with a ranting lunatic: You know it's crazy, but you can't look away. Fuzzy surrealism mingles, sometimes awkwardly, with nightmarish reality" (72). He describes Mrs. Honey as "loud" and "a Tennessee Williams parody."

Winer avers the dramatist "does not appear to be on the brink of renewing interest in the rest of his work" (B9) and adds, "This is too bad, because Sherman has a welcome sense of scale, of the bigger picture around personal dramas." She laments she "feels jerked around." Marks bashes *Madhouse* as "listless and sardonic" and "dated" satire that tries to deal "with virtually all the problems of the world" (E1, 6). He assumes Sherman spoofs Williams.

Russo concedes, "So many of the pieces are cannily crafted that, with all its imperfections, *A Madhouse in Goa* is still provocative and rich" (99). Simon likes the play but trashes Ivey, saying she "overacted ferociously" (76). O'Toole objects to the ending, where he feels, "It is suddenly as if the Hollywood producer had emerged from the plot and taken over the writing" (45). Yet he also judges, "This contains a fascinating reflection on politics, art and truth."

In the negative notice, Lyons calls Act I a "downmarket *Suddenly, Last Summer*" in which Ivey "screechily overdoes Mrs. Honey" (A12). He gets several facts wrong, such as "Daniel is now dying of an unspecified malady and has authorized his friends to sell his tale to a vulgar movie producer." He concludes, "Neither half of the play transcends its chosen brand of rhetoric."

In the positive review, Rosenberg accepts the false premise Sherman has written a Williams' satire. Yet he also compares it to *Bent*, finding them "equally hypnotic" (35). He feels both have "a cumulative effect that sits unyieldingly on a viewer's conscience."

Stone and Feingold promote *Madhouse*. Prior to its review dates, Stone judges, "It's wonderfully strange, comical, and scary" and calls Ivey "excellent" (16). Without having seen it, Feingold writes, "What the event has to do with potential is self-evident, since Sherman's also the author of *Bent* and the delicious, underrated *When She Danced*" (3).

Vanessa Redgrave graciously went backstage and complimented Ivey's performance, and some of Sherman's friends preferred the U.S. mounting, perhaps because their views of the world's dangers had caught up with the play's pessimism.

Following this U.S. premiere, Samuel French, Inc., published it in January 1998. This has made possible other U.S. productions, such as those presented in Atlanta, Ft. Lauderdale and Pittsburgh in 2000.

From August 6 to 30, 1998, Sherman's friend Tim Miller presented *A Table for a King* as a one act starring film celebrity Susan Tyrrell at his Highways Performance Space in Santa Monica. Highways brought Sherman to L.A. for the production, and he found it "wonderful, because Tyrrell was a haunting Mrs. Honey and because director David Schweitzer was so in tune with the play."

In 2008, a Barcelona theatre presented *Madhouse*, and the University of Wisconsin Press published *A Table for a King* in an anthology of gay travel writing.

E. *Rose* on Stage

In a city boasting many Jewish critics, *Rose* received a somewhat smaller proportion of positive reviews on Broadway than in London, but some came from

Jewish reviewers. Novick feels Rose's story must be told. He approves her individuality, her "resilience, her shrewdness, her strong sense of moral responsibility," and her "wisecracking wit, her gift for irony" (11–12). He notes, "For her, the essence of Jewishness is not belief but skepticism" and reflects, "Some may question the prominence given ... to Jewish violence against Arabs.... Others will find this, as I did, the most piercing of all Mr. Sherman's ironies." He concludes *Rose* serves a noble function of theatre, one "deepening our understanding of history, politics and ideas by making them real to us in poignant terms of felt experience."

Lieberman rebukes anyone feeling "this important show" presents "nothing new." She argues, "American born Jews whose parents have shielded them from an ugly past" need to hear *Rose* and "so too should these horrific events be emblazoned on each generation's psyche.... 'Are these horrors destined to be repeated?' is the question of the piece and a timely one for all nationalities."

Epstein praises the "deliciously self-deprecating sense of humor that keeps Martin Sherman's painstakingly crafted one-woman play from becoming mired in pathos" (37). She urges, "When you go to the Lyceum, and you must, leave your own baggage at home. Olympia Dukakis' feisty, unforgettable Rose has enough for us all."

The Siegels relish the fact "emotions sweep across the stage and over the audience with the tidal wave of her testimony. Her life story is bracketed by ... a young girl's shocking murder; both tales define our time and challenge our humanity." They continue, "Sherman gives us a heroic tragedy of heartbreaking simplicity." They conclude, "Rose—and the play named after her—retain their integrity. In the end, the play asks us to retain ours, as well."

Sommers judges Sherman "creates a feisty character—tough, wry and tender all at once" and "makes her experiences so touching and memorable to hear. Somehow she magically becomes the grandmother of us all, regardless of creed or origin" (70). Ledford writes Sherman "has created another superb character study ... the most captivating hours you are likely to applaud on Broadway this year" (p.s.v.-7). Sheward focuses on the "rich performance" in this, one of three plays in this column that "have the power to awaken the sleeping minds of Broadway playgoers."

Zoglin, although averse to solos, praises "a magnificent performance" and "a moving evening" ([80]). Stevens lauds its "sad reminiscences, sprinkled with Jackie Mason type humor." Katavolos commends "delicate and majestic material" and "a tragicomedy, perfectly formulated." Loney gives it four stars. Raymond proclaims, "Rose blooms."

Burke relishes Sherman's "dazzling and gut-wrenching one-woman play *Rose*.... You've got to hand it to those Brits; they know talent and theatrical genius." He observes, "Sherman's play is sharp and focused, detailing in exquisitely chosen words the life story of one feisty Jewish woman." He advises, "Bring a handkerchief. You *will* be sobbing before the evening is over."

Fanger praises Dukakis and her character, who "has retained her dignity and sense of humor, despite" her odyssey (17). Cunningham predicts "at the very least a nomination for a Tony." He praises the work's drama and humor and calls it "never ever predictable.... Sherman has written this singular wonder, the wonder of singularity, so wisely and so well."

Fintan O'Toole reasons, "This quietly harrowing one-actor play offers what was missing from all the celebrations—a somber reflection on the 20th century" (54). He continues, "*Rose* tells the story of a century in which everything changed except the violence of the strong against the weak. This is one of those rare plays in which there is no gap between what it says and how it works." He praises Sherman for grasping "the power of understatement."

Contrast these critics to those who skewer a turkey. Lyons labels *Rose* "an insufferable lecture ... Martin Sherman's coy imagining of the past, not surprising from one who imagined himself a gay victim of the Nazis" (46). He resents Sherman turning Israel into "the latest version of Nazi Germany" and rejects the work as "a hip, '90s gay-leftist take on modern history." He twice drags in the dramatist's sexual orientation to evaluate a heterosexual play. His details include errors: He thinks a German soldier shot Esther; he believes Rose married Mort; he confuses chronology and identity.

Le Sourd also provides inaccuracies and drags in Sherman's sexual orientation. He accuses Sherman of deceiving viewers into believing Rose sits shivah for her daughter Esther with a "bait-and-switch which seems alarmingly dishonest," and he distorts Sherman's perspective: "The good guys, now, you see, are Palestinians" and "history's significant dead are now apparently Palestinian, not Jewish. Oh" (1E, 5E).

Webber accuses Sherman of lecturing; he mocks "Yes, Grandma. Now can we go out and play?" (E1, E5). He avers, "The production has a finger-wagging quality." He faults Sherman for "grave and intrusive sentimentality" and wisecracks "not all that clever." Winer wishes a Yiddish-theatre actor had starred (sec. 2N, B2–B3). She rejects the script as "generic ... connecting the historical and psychological dots of 20th-Century Judaism." Gamerman finds *Rose* boring. "I realized with a sinking heart that she was starting in the 1920s and working her way forward. Slowly" (A28). Musto similarly fulminates, "I paid half price for a ticket to *Rose* and sure enough got half a show, bolting gloriously to freedom at intermission. The nonhappening ... recalls her entire fucking life ... with equal parts strained humor and pretend pathos" (12). Simon also admits he "squirmed" and "left early" (73). Lindstrom dislikes one-person shows.

A fifth bored critic, Richardson, condescends "people interested in this type of ethnic performance" should see it off-Broadway. He packs errors into his one-minute radio review and refers to "the life of a Jewish girl" of 80. Kuchwara finds the evening "exhausting" and feels, "For all its narrative, the tale is strangely superficial, despite the emotionalism of its subject matter." Zinoman alerts readers to audience enthusiasm, but he hates the script, composed "in the flowery voice of an awkwardly written first novel" (160). He berates the dramatist, "Adding to the general false tone of the script are Sherman's annoyingly contrived one-liners." He adds, "It should be said that the audience heartily enjoyed these jokes and rewarded Dukakis with a standing ovation."

Several negative reviews misunderstand the play and its author's view of Israel. Leon accuses *Rose* of "a subtext stealth agenda" (15). She elaborates, "Rose bristles with dissonant notes, even questioning the Jews' claim to Israel by positing, 'Perhaps we don't belong anywhere.'" This line does *not* appear in *Rose*. Rose doesn't object to Israel's existence. She longs for the Promised Land. When she arrives there, she kisses the ground and resists soldiers who drag her away to deport her. She wishes she could live in Israel and visits her family there. Leon ignores all these sections of text in order to convict Sherman of views he and Rose don't hold. She attempts to disprove a "lie," the "predictions of the demise of Yiddish" by citing Yiddish banners at a Seder. She fails to notice she and Sherman agree in appreciating Yiddish culture.

N. Siegel levels similar allegations: "Dramatic license slips into thematic manipulation on the part of an agenda-driven writer" and calls Sherman "facile." She complains Rose sits shivah, not "for her grandson Doron ... but only for the dead child." She further rebukes, "Remarkably, Doron's name is only invoked as the girl's brutal murderer" instead of serving as a second reason for sitting shivah. Siegel errs. Doran hasn't died.

Rosenberg praises only the section that angers Siegel. Initially he calls it "a clunker of an evening" (D6). He terms it "tedious," says it "clobbers the audience with a shallow, joke-filled portrayal," but then continues, "Only toward the end, as his heroine weighs the moral imperatives of Israelis trying to balance freedom and security, does Sherman suggest depths the rest of the evening avoids."

Backalenick publishes two pans. She calls opening-night enthusiasm "tepid" (5, 7). She errs in twice saying the play ran for a year in London, and she locates the shtetl in Poland rather than Ukraine. Because "we've heard it all before," she tells readers to spend their money on some other Broadway show. In another review, she opines, "This long monologue does not display the best of playwright Sherman's talents" (31).

Feldberg's mixed review awards Sherman "an A for ambition" (YT-4). He faults Sherman's mixed moods, damns "extremely heavy" irony, and concludes, "*Rose* has its touching moments, and even a few deeply moving ones.... But almost everything the play has to say is familiar and predictable, and has been presented before to greater dramatic effect."

Isherwood praises Dukakis but finds "there's something pat and even rote about this cozy tour through the highs and lows of a woman's life" (2, 7). He would prefer Sherman cover less, to linger and probe. He complains *Rose* "does not make for a lively evening of theater" and dubs it "Danielle Steel's Diaspora," his response to mixed moods. Yet Isherwood also praises the play: "Rose's tough, unsentimental voice is convincingly rendered by Sherman's colloquial, often piquantly funny writing."

Feingold applauds Dukakis but faults Sherman for writing monologue, not play. He objects, "We sense the carpentry: each episode carefully wrought" (79). He concedes, "Some of these segments are gorgeously written." He complains about Rose's memory of a film she saw 60 years earlier and condemns "The first time I ate ice cream was in Atlantic City" because "by 1937, they had ice cream in Eastern Europe."

Schaap praises "potential" and acknowledges, "There are flashes of brilliance in Dukakis's performance, and in the writing, but too often you are aware that it is a performance." Rinn prefers first act to second, finding the latter "more sentimental and more predictable." She also faults Rose not changing (35).

Two other mixed reviews voice the opposite preference, for the second half over the first. Schifrin observes Rose "instinctively realizes the absurdity of her life, indeed of life in general, and tells some marvelous stories." He continues, "But

Rose can also be a bit tiring." He loves the U.S. half "where a Singer-like magic realism intersects with bourgeois Jewish pretensions." He feels as a whole "we get a passionate history lesson more than passionate theater," but he praises, too.

Pisarra terms the first half "sleep-inducing," yet says of the second, "Slowly, deliberately, her tale begins to incorporate the past tragedies that continue to haunt her. By the time Rose relates her attempt to get her first (Old World) husband's soul to inhabit her body.... Dukakis and Sherman suddenly attain a brilliant combination of hilarity and anguish typical of emotional extremes." He concludes, "The first half makes you wish you'd never come. But the second makes you glad you stayed."

Twelve years after she rehearsed *Rose*, Dukakis continues to tour it in the U.S. and occasionally abroad. U.S. theatres have staged productions, for instance, in Foxboro and Watertown (MA), Chimney Rock (NC), Portland (OR), St. Paul, Baltimore, Washington, Sarasota (twice), Buffalo, Hartford, Asheville (twice), San Francisco and L.A.

Abroad *Rose* has been produced in Israel, Argentina, Uruguay, Brazil, Panama, Greece, the Netherlands, Belgium, Austria, multiple locations in Germany, France, Spain, Sweden, Denmark, Finland, Greenland, Italy, both the Republic of Ireland and Northern Ireland, Canada, South Africa, Australia, Romania, Czech Republic, Hungary and other parts of Central and Eastern Europe. In some cities the play has returned for additional seasons. For instance, it became a staple in the repertory in Budapest for more than half a decade. In 2009, Vanessa Redgrave asked to revive the play in the West End, with Meckler directing and Fox producing.

Danish actor Pia Rosenbaum wrote Sherman on December 29, 2001, "I finished the *Rose* tour ... and ... it was a huge success. The reviews were overwhelming, and so were the audiences.... And once when there should have been a discussion afterwards, it was cancelled because the audience was weeping too much."

The Israeli production at the Camerei in Tel Aviv began in early 2000, even before the Broadway run. Their staging, starring Gita Munte, put Rose's shivah on sand, which suggested Israel, Atlantic City, Miami Beach, the Arizona desert where she encounters a ghost from her past, the shifting sands of time, even the quicksand over which Rose remarks those outsiders struggling to survive must skip. This production encountered a problem, but not with Sherman's requiem after an Israeli murder of a Palestinian; spectators accepted that, and *Rose* garnered wonderful reviews and did excellent box office. Yet the director initially cut Rose and her son's argument about Yiddish.

The director's suggestion that this pivotal sequence would bore his audiences confirmed the playwright's point: Yiddish culture wouldn't survive much past Hitler's murder of Yiddish speakers and Israel adopting Hebrew. Sherman says Kaddish for the culture.

F. Films on Screen

Only four U.S. critics panned *The Summer House*. Derryberry scoffs at "a depressingly snide comedy of mores" (28). The other three don't understand the flashbacks. Millar condemns it as "a snoozer" and "a bit slight" (9C). Paul Sherman dismisses it as "a slight English ensemble comedy." Stark labels it "muddle-headed" and "ghastly" (3C).

Because these critics don't understand the flashbacks, they can't follow the film. Like all Sherman's scripts, this one requires paying attention. What happened to Margaret in Egypt provides the key to understanding her actions later. These, in turn, motivate what everybody else does, especially Lili's final choice, which Stark mocks as "Moreau doing an impression of Salome's demented grandmother."

Some U.S. critics publish mixed reviews. The flashbacks puzzle some, but several feel uncomfortable with the sexual content. Alice Thomas Ellis and Sherman satirize bourgeois hypocrisy, and this doesn't sit well with bourgeois prudish critics. Thus Hicks lauds "wonderful performances" yet complains of "one long setup for a cheap, vulgar punchline" (W3). Likewise, Movshovitz misunderstands it as "essentially a one-joke film about the liberating power of guilt-free sex" (Weekend, 6). Where does Anderson find animal intercourse and cross-dressing? Perhaps this is standard libel on gospelcom.net to disparage films deemed immoral? She awards the movie a -2 for "acceptability" and a +2 for "entertainment," so she intends her notice as "mixed."

Armstrong loves "the chemistry" between Moreau and Plowright and "the well-written dialogue" but fails to comprehend the Egypt segments (D3). Yet he finds it superior to *Enchanted April*. Jones also faults the flashbacks, and Meyers ignores their nightmarish content, for he describes Margaret as "happy" in Egypt (C2).

Some critics seem uncomfortable with Sherman's trademark combination of humor and drama. Renshaw, who says he "laughed quite a lot" and praises "quotable one-liners" and "good lines by screenwriter Martin Sherman," objects the writer "burdens the humor with an unnecessarily dark and cumbersome story structure." He likewise complains of "distracting flashbacks" and "disturbing undercurrents—intimations of child abuse, an unexplained violent death—which seem grossly out of place and entirely unnecessary." Berardinelli, Campbell, and Lyman also lambaste the film's mixed moods, found in Sherman's source.

Smith complains of failing to understand "what happened" in Egypt and "why," and then continues, "The ending of the *Summer House* is spelled out all too clearly. It's shocking." Then Smith fails to understand Ellis's viewpoint, and thus Sherman's, and thus the film's: "As the obnoxious fiancé, Mr. Threlfall gets precious little slack from the screenplay. While all the other characters are given their due in humanity, his is but a cardboard buffoon from beginning to end. Not only is that not fair play, it damages any sense of emotional logic" (1C-2C). The writers of mixed reviews fail to enjoy the satire; Smith expresses discomfort with feminist satire.

Nearly all mixed reviews find the film funny. DN, however, lodges a singular and puzzling objection, that the script lacks "the specific, wrung-dry wit of Alice Thomas Ellis" (BB-6). Sherman uses all the Ellis jokes and adds others. The only U.S. critic who suggests he has any familiarity with Ellis, DN nevertheless misremembers her.

Matthews praises "lively characters, marvelous dialogue" but wonders whether "you find the joke at the end worth the time it takes to get there" (51). Brown calls it a "whimsical, immensely slight movie" (50). Sterritt faults Moreau as "frantically flamboyant" (14).

Other U.S. critics love *The Summer House*.

Schickel understands this comedy offers "a rather sober meditation on life's tendency to disappoint" (108). He knows Margaret's efforts "to be a dutiful daughter" are "costing her her sanity" and "gets" the mixture of humor and drama. He appreciates discovering "a movie in which everything is not foreshadowed, underlined, commented upon. In other words, *The Summer House* is disciplined in the way that British theatrical productions often are. As a result, the story's somewhat surprising conclusion actually surprises."

Adams calls it "a thoroughly delightful comedy of manners" (41). She praises: "Wickedly funny but never mean-spirited, Martin Sherman's screenplay is wise and life-affirming.... Sherman breathes life into his characters while managing to startle and surprise." Thomas prefers it to *Enchanted April*, calling it "less talky" and "lots livelier," as well as "wry and delightful" (Calendar, 10). James enthuses "tremendous fun to watch" (C19). McCarthy loves this "comic audience pleaser" and Sherman's "zippy dialogue and character humor, extended by the extravagantly talented cast" (32).

Variety lists Jami Bernard's review as favorable, despite the critic's uneasiness with the "ribald" repartee, etc. (53). It likewise categorizes Hirsch's rather bland notice as positive, because it employs words such as "droll," "delight," "effective," and "fascinating" (11). Kauffmann ignores the subversive feminism, but finds it "amusing" and likes Sherman's "nippy dialogue" (31). Carr declares, "It's fun sharing the cast's relish" and terms it an "impeccably crafted period piece" (24). Kempley praises "this droll British comedy" and judges its screenplay "wickedly witty and idiosyncratic" (C1). Paton loves this "wonderful film" (10).

Several television critics awarded it high marks, but didn't preserve their comments for posterity. McAlister, however, posted her radio review online, for instance, "It is filled from beginning to end with women's discourse, by which I don't just mean that women are doing the talking, but that they are articulating a female world view, in particular the world view of crones like Lily and Mrs. Monro who have lived long and learned a lot about life and who no longer bother to play by patriarchy's rules. They have earned the right to say and do what they really think—about life, men, and marriage. And they do so with such warmth, charm, and wit, it's delightful—and very funny. I was laughing out loud a lot."

The Brussats praise Sherman for his "fine job" adapting Ellis. They call Lili "the capstone role of Jeanne Moreau's illustrious career" and elucidate the "spiritual message" thus: "No woman should live down to the expectations of others. Dare to be yourself and let what happens happen. *The Summer House* is a total delight."

The dvdlaser.com critic judges, "The pleasure of the film is in its individual scenes ... both in Britain ... and in Egypt.... Throughout ... you also keep wondering how she is going to get out of this awful marriage, and sure enough there is a delightful climactic scene where all her problems are solved" ("The Summer House").

Steinmetz writes, "Sherman ... has produced the richest, most satisfying screenplay of the year" (Friday sec., L). Baumgarten dotes on the actors, but especially Moreau. Ebert gets some facts wrong, but likes the "odd and amusing comedy of manners" and the "final scene of poetic justice as perfect as it is unexpected." Rosenbaum approves, "Apart from offering a juicy star turn to Moreau, the movie has a lot of mordantly funny things to say about the conventionality of suburban English life."

Neman praises it as "a joy," "delightful and wryly observed," a "thoroughly engaging movie" boasting "the most delicious ending to any film in recent memory." Arar approves the "credible job balancing social satire and the darker, erotic drama behind Margaret's emotional paralysis," and she likes the "sparkling dialogue" (L.A. Life, 4). Turnquist calls it "a movie that's as light and likable as a June afternoon" (L9). Denerstein applauds "Witty and well-acted" and adds, "The dialogue and scathingly sharp characterizations all lead to a fine and surprising payoff" (8D).

Schwarzbaum terms this an "odd and oddly engaging story," describes it enthusiastically, and concludes, "Give me a movie where Plowright and Moreau knock back whiskey and giggle any day, and let young brides take notes on what it's like to gulp down life." Byerley posts, "It is a slight but charming little English comedy of character," praises the cast as "fabulous," and judges Moreau as "at her most effervescent." Moss lauds "a finely observed story about marriage, lust and sex that is as endearing as it is smart" (R-82, 83).

Film Journal gives the cover of its Oct.-Nov. issue to *The Summer House*. Two stills fill that cover, which also praises Moreau, Plowright, and Walters and describes the movie as a "delightful new comedy." This issue's "Film Journal Yearend Preview" terms it "this disarming comedy" (137). The same issue's "Jeanne Moreau Shakes Up Goldwyn's Summer House" calls Sherman "a keenly observant Yank" (12, 56).

Finally, Ringel proclaims, "This exquisite English comedy offers some of the best acting and wittiest writing of 1993" and notes, "The terrific cast tears into this neo–Restoration comedy material with joyously well-crafted abandon" (P/3). She concludes, "Watching these two great actresses getting happily sloshed together in a pub is as enthralling as anything at the movies all year."

Alive and Kicking Film Festivals

It premiered at the Locarno International Film Festival on August 8, 1996. Sherman says, "The festival audience received it wonderfully." Elley gives it a mixed notice, calling it "an upbeat dramatic comedy" and "often likable, sometimes involving, but ultimately uneven," with a "bumpy" script (121).

It screened on Long Island at the Hamptons Film Festival (October 17–20), where it won the Audience Award, and later it won the same award (the only one given) at the London Film Festival. On March 27, 1997, it closed the London Lesbian and Gay Film Festival, and in May it garnered approval from Gorringe in its Seattle International Film Festival showing. She pronounces it "much better" than Meckler's earlier *Sister, My Sister*, and goes on to call it "thoughtful without being maudlin, witty without being snide." She praises it for "making the prospect of extracting as much joy as possible from hopeless circumstances an exhilarating exercise."

New Zealand saw it in Wellington's Lesbian and Gay Film Festival Out Takes

97 on May 28 and Canterbury's Out Reels 97 on June 1, 1997. The Big Apple got its first glimpse on June 7 in the New York Lesbian and Gay Film Festival, and San Francisco's similar festival showed it on June 23. After its release in the U.K., the U.S., and Canada, it continued to play at festivals, including those in Ireland, Portugal, Spain, Germany and Czech Republic.

Callas Forever Premieres and Reviews

It opened in France and Belgium on September 18, 2002 (following a Paris premiere on September 16), Italy September 20, Israel September 28, Greece November 8, Spain November 15. In 2003 they added Russia on June 29, Japan on July 19, Denmark on August 14, Lithuania on October 24, Brazil on November 21. In 2004, Bulgaria followed on March 19, Mexico on June 25, the Czech Republic on August 26 (after the Karlovy Vary Film Festival the previous month), and Canada on September 27.

Producers usually don't release films in Lithuania before doing so in the U.S. and U.K., but Giovannella Zannnoni and Riccardo Tozzi perhaps had difficulty finding distributors there, plus feared poor reception, so they milked the box office elsewhere for two years before entering those markets. Zeffirelli had shown it for a Columbus Day benefit in New York in 2002, and, over two years, seven U.S. film festivals, mostly gay, screened it. But it didn't open in the U.S. until November 5, 2004, in limited release. It went into general release in the U.K. on November 29, 2004. The U.S. DVD appeared on June 21, 2005. Hungarian television aired it on July 15, 2005.

Some *Callas* reviews leave Sherman with undeserved egg on his face. Critics in Britain especially savage it.

Bradshaw trashes "a camp extravaganza of such exquisite awfulness, such unembarrassable silliness, that you watch it hypnotized" (Friday Review, 17). Russell writes, "Reducing Callas' final days to unintentional comedy, Franco Zeffirelli comes not to honour the diva but to bury her in a deluge of sniggering giggles." Bullock terms the film "a monumentally frustrating exercise in overblown camp." Bullock likes the Carmen, as does Megahey, who calls it "simply stunning" but lambastes the "poor script and dialogue." Peters concurs, concerning the "precious mess of a picture" and the Bizet's value. Smith complains, "Alas, the octogenarian Zeffirelli directs so sluggishly the title feels only too appropriate." M.H. lashes out at "dialogue ... drowned by the thuds of cliché hitting earth."

Kermode and G. Hall pen somewhat milder, yet unfavorable notices.

In the U.S., Davis condemns the script as "frequently clunky." Buell calls it a "flimsy 111-minute soaper" that makes him wonder whether he "wouldn't be better off washing the dog.... Here pooch!" Rabin complains it "promises high drama but instead settles for high camp."

Vice rejects it as "overripe cheese." L. Thomas terms it "cheese machine" and "goopy melodrama" and von Rhein "silly." Von Busack dubs it, "Maria, Full of Disgrace." P. Hall's pan concludes, "A better argument against multinational cooperation cannot be imagined."

It bores some critics who get important details wrong. Callahan thinks Larry, from Michael's apartment, makes his 2 A.M. call to Callas rather than to Keller.

Would he really ask the diva, "Where does she get the pills?" Thomson thinks the movie was shot in another language and dubbed in English dialogue he describes as "wooden"; he likewise finds the script "dull" (WE42). Ebert and Paris incorrectly identify Larry as Callas's former director.

Both hate the film, as does Ed Gonzalez, who finds the plot "cliché-ridden" and the *Carmen* "all artifice, no emotion." Blaylock dismisses it as "camp" (66). McDonagh calls it "poky, oddly uninvolving" and judges it will make viewers dislike Callas because she throws "herself a world-class pity party." Holden derides *Callas Forever* as "essentially a piece of highbrow karaoke" (E17).

Some reviews especially fulminate regarding the screenplay. Jankowicz judges Ardant works with "a bad script," while Noh excoriates it as "bottom-feeding, lowbrow tabloid fodder."

Where critics applaud Ardant and the opera sections, most still reprove the script, from mildly (Shen regarding "a faintly campy script") to more specifically (Fernandez's "Love interests spark and fade into the background, characters drop out in obvious oversight only to reappear to prop up the story"). You would think Fernandez had watched Zeffirelli skipping scenes.

In another mixed notice, Blank complains about the poorly developed affair between Larry and Michael and then objects to "the singer's misgivings about the dishonesty of lip-synching." He explains, "Virtually all European movies were totally dubbed until quite recently and ... with the rarest of exceptions, all singing for all musicals is prerecorded for logistical reasons anyway. Has been since the 1930s." Several other critics mention this problem. Why did Zeffirelli make the basis of his film an objection Callas would have no reason to raise and Larry could so easily have refuted?

In other mixed reviews, Young faults its "flat, expository dialogue" (32). Arnold judges "the action tends to become tiresome and predictable." Erickson, after noting the movie "falls back on ancient showbiz clichés," perceives, ironically, it "is a display of kitsch that concludes by lecturing the audience about the pitfalls of kitsch." They fault the screenplay.

So do such critics as Knight ("dramatically clunky," "ill-conceived," "static pacing"), Clifford (who complains of little character development for Sarah, Marco, and Michael), Musetto ("campy and clichéd"), Bernard ("campy and stagey"), Ebiri ("light on story and substance"), Rebello ("clumsily contrived script"), and Esther ("this butchering of singer Maria Callas").

Ruhe terms the film a "camp-filled fantasy" (H5). Burr regards the script as "overheated" and a "grave robbery." Atanasov targets the subplot involving Larry and Michael (the most frequently faulted section) and finds the whole scenario a "grotesque" attempt at a Callas tribute. Prescott deems the plot "fatally flawed." Harrison writes, "The story as a whole ... doesn't hold together, primarily because the imaginary characters and situations that surround her are so inadequately sketched."

Reed terms the script "intelligent but perfunctory" and especially expresses misgivings about the ending (26): "This sudden burst of suicidal integrity is noble, but not entirely convincing." Reed unerringly identifies undeveloped plot points the director's failure to film several key scenes caused.

Even the positive reviews don't enhance Sherman's reputation because those invariably praise Ardant and/or *Carmen* and the other operatic selections. White doesn't ridicule the script, but he never mentions Sherman (28). Schrader does the same, as do Widdifield and Cherryl. The anonymous favorable review from the United States Conference of Catholic Bishops likewise ignores Sherman's part. Curiously, this critic—clearly an opera buff—places *Callas Forever* in the middle of five morality rating categories and mentions Larry and Michael's affair without condemning it.

Kauffmann raves, "Zeffirelli's *Carmen* sequences here are thrilling" and "Ardant is marvelously genuine," but ignores the screenplay except for revealing his distaste for Larry and Michael's relationship (29). LaSalle, who adores the film, nevertheless perceptively notes the script's "weaknesses": "Everything else is rendered in shorthand, so the story often seems ungrounded" (E-3). Small wonder, because the director left holes, also duly noted by Di Nardo ("non–Callas scenes are a little sloppy and even irrelevant"). Two favorable reviews, by Wegg and K. Thomas, name Sherman.

G. *Mrs. Henderson Presents* on Screen

Mrs. Henderson Presents screened at numerous festivals, including those in Toronto, Brazil (the Rio de Janeiro International Film Festival), Chicago, France (the Dinard Festival of British Cinema), Austin, Milwaukee, Savannah, Rochester (the High Falls Film Festival), Marrakech, Inverness (its U.K. premiere), Leeds, Israel (British Film Festival), the European Union Film Festival (in both Canada and the Czech Republic), Thailand (Bangkok International Film Festival), Hungary (Alba Regia International Film Festival), and Mexico (Morelia Film Festival). In addition, it served as the surprise film, a crowd-pleaser, at the London Film Festival.

It attracted distribution in Switzerland, Australia, Italy, Belgium, France, the Netherlands, Israel, Greece, Iceland, Norway, Portugal, Singapore, Finland, Brazil, Panama, Spain, Argentina, Hong Kong, Sweden, Russia, Czech Republic, Mexico, Venezuela, Austria, Germany, Hungary, Japan, and Poland.

Too many U.S. publications reviewed *Mrs. Henderson Presents* to examine each. The numbers skew sharply towards positive notices: in this sampling, 7 negatives, 11 mixed, and 52 favorable.

Taylor writes, "All is joyful vulgarity until World War II churlishly bursts in, generating oodles of Dunkirk spirit and swelling Martin Sherman's awful script into such orgies of cliché, you want to bottle it" (88). Missing the anti-war attitude, Hewitt fulminates, "We have to sit through a bunch of sanctimonious war speeches so we can hear the clever quips." He dislikes the mixed moods and, strangely, decries the interaction between Henderson and Van Damm as "oddly sketchy— apparently, we are supposed to notice that she's falling for him, but neither the script nor the actors lets us in on that."

Kelly gets facts wrong, setting the entirety during World War II, referring to Mrs. Henderson's merchant husband as a "diplomat," calling the Windmill a "burlesque house"—an American, not British practice. He mocks the film as "toothless and forgettable—an episode of *The Golden Girls*" and "so slight it seems in danger of fading away right before our eyes."

Clark likewise lobs ageist and sexist missiles. He laments the movie seems "made for blue-haired ladies who want to be shocked just enough to go 'tee-hee' before they go to a brunch where tea is served with crustless white bread." He finds the story identical to *Tonight and Every Night*, which reveals he hasn't seen that one, since their plots and characters share only a music-hall setting. He bashes Sherman's screenplay as "lumberingly old-fashioned" and "flatfooted," with "lackluster direction," and he jokes, "You spend as much time looking at your watch as what's on screen."

Gleiberman finds it "dull" and gripes, "There is no drama, unless you count the wallflower romance of Hoskins and Dench, doing the Britcom shtick that's become her version of autopilot." Travers dismisses the film from his opening question, "Has a movie featuring full-frontal female nudity ever been this goody-goody?" He rebukes Frears, doesn't mention Sherman, but judges it "stays content to do the trite thing." Dargis refers to "a period British comedy laced with a dash of tragedy and straining with uplift" (E13). This critic would have preferred a different film—one about burlesque instead of vaudeville, one set in 1948, four years after Mrs. Henderson died.

The most succinct mixed review comes from Tucker, reporting from the Toronto Film Festival. His roundup says it "got more laughs and applause than any other movie I saw at Toronto. I was not among the laughing/clapping—it seemed like a long BBC sitcom to me."

Muller begins, "*Mrs. Henderson Presents* is a lively period piece elevated by a winning pair of leads." He continues, "Outside the Dench/Hoskins dynamic, the film is nothing special, but it rushes along when they're on-screen together." Muller prefers Sherman's funnier and more spirited scenes to his drama—a view common in the mixed notices. He admonishes it for providing "threadbare special effects showing the Blitz as well as a soap-opera subplot.... The screenwriter resorts to shorthand and the movie's credibility sags." Yet he explains, "The movie is worth seeing, if just for a couple of scenes," and he chooses the men removing their clothes and Laura mounting her soapbox.

Myers finds it "wickedly funny" until "along comes the brutish World War II, and this bit of froth, nicely whipped together by Judi Dench and Bob Hoskins, curdles." Thomas, likewise, dislikes the mood mixture. He praises "a raucous, bawdy and playful look at life in London's theater district before and during World War II.... Unfortunately, it's not consistently riveting when it veers away from its humorous elements."

Carr calls the title character "fun, outrageous, impulsive" and Dench's performance offered "with dryness, sparkle and boatloads of style. It's fun to watch her trample Christopher Guest's Lord Chancellor" (36). Reservations temper his enthusiasm. Means opines the "comedy drama" offers "such an odd mixture of old-fashioned sentiment and bare skin that it's either the dirtiest clean movie or the cleanest dirty movie ever made."

Rooney, covering the Toronto Film Festival, expresses chagrin at finding Frears making a "bland" film instead of his usual edgy work. He faults Sherman for lack of "tangible conflicts or satisfyingly developed characters," yet enjoys his "facility for barbed, Wildean dialogue" and Dench's match for that in her "deliciously dry manner." He notes the script lacks "narrative backbone," but enjoys the luncheon scene with the Lord Chamberlain and judges "the film's real strength is in its portrait—and Dench's feisty embodiment—of a reckless, independent spirit.... Her galvanic speech in the final act touches the right emotional chords."

Some reviews castigate the film's "patriotism," which makes them uncomfortable despite Hitler's best attempts to annihilate the British during the Blitz. Oddly, they seem not to notice its anti-war stance. Sarris, for instance, while conceding "chuckles" and amusement and praising Guest's Lord Chamberlain, blasts "a silly orgy of nostalgic patriotism and the titillating naughtiness of stationary nudity" (23). Rapold chides, "Ms. Dench's comic take on aristocratic whimsy is sharp and winningly nutty. Sadly, it is cut short by the film's precipitous nosedive into one of the sillier appeals to patriotism in some time" (15).

Subsequent to the Toronto Film Festival, Winter offers some of her former praise, then lambastes "a queasy fascination with the question of Vivian's Jewishness," "a bathetic motivation behind Laura's promotion of smut," and "Laura's deep insulation from the realities of working life as a form of beguiling innocence." One might argue these elements contribute to Sherman's characterization of her growth.

Tobias mischaracterizes the vaudeville at the Windmill as "an all-nude revue" rather than a musical revue with a few nude tableaux posed as museum works. He finds Dench "ideally cast" and judges the movie "gets by for a while on its genial naughtiness. But when the war intrudes and Dench reflects on the loss of her son in World War I, the frivolity abruptly ends, and the movie perishes along with it." Tobias forgets the film ends almost immediately afterwards.

Baumgarten finds it a bit dull before the war livens it up, although she judges this "too little, too late." She calls it "staid music-hall drama." She terms Dench "very good and likable" but finds problematic "the film's awkward mixture of drama, comedy, and music-hall numbers."

Fifty-two other critics, occasionally with reservations, pile on the praise. Cook calls it "marvelous," gives it four out of four stars, and pleads, "Please head out and see it." Christiancritic.com doesn't record the shock we might anticipate. Instead, M. Elliott commends "the relationship dynamic that deliciously drives the movie," explains the nudity "is tastefully and artfully done," and overall calls it "a charming and entertaining film."

The Brussats agree in praising this "clever comedy" and single out Laura's "whiz-bang speech" on the soapbox and the "excellent" scene when "van Damm tells the women posing nude that they should not be ashamed of their bodies, because they were given to them by God as a gift." Rainer concurs, applauding, "Screenwriter Martin Sherman is at his brittle best in these exchanges.... The film is supremely well crafted." He assigns it an "A" and concludes it concerns "the exhilaration of a life in the theater—a life lived at full pitch."

The United States Conference of Catholic Bishops Office for Film and Broadcasting concedes "it can't be denied that the Windmill did provide a morale-boosting service and was so respectable (as were the girls themselves) that it attracted families with children." The analyst finds the film "as decorous as anything on 'Masterpiece Theatre,'" doesn't disapprove the nudity, and even praises Frears and

Sherman for tugging "at the heartstrings" and presenting "a convincing recreation—musical numbers and all—of a small but significant chapter in London's brave resistance to Hitler's relentless bombardment."

Morales feels it wins "our jaded hearts with its effortless charm" and "avoids cheap sentiment." Morgenstern extols "a scintillating script ... one of the wittiest comedies to come our way in a very long time." He rejoices because "*Mrs. Henderson Presents* truly is a comedy, first and foremost, but it's also tender, serious, joyously musical and marvelously unpredictable. Every time you think you know where a scene is going, something comes along to surprise you. Bare breasts share the screen with naked feeling."

Toppman explains "there will always be room for the gentle pleasures this kind of British movie provides: steady chuckles, sudden tears that dry as quickly as they flow, acting whose predictability is one of its joys." He concludes, "It's a welcome exponent of a valued tradition." Gillespie, speaking of Dench, calls the film "a tailor-made showcase for her particular brand of tart good-heartedness" (E1). She feels Dench and Hoskins "put on a darn good show" and "couldn't be more nimble." She enjoys their "trading semi–Wildeian one-liners and skirting (kind of) the ever-present issue of a possible romance."

Longino finds three reasons to see it: The comedy; the costumes; Dench (H12). He calls the title character "fun, breezy, witty and slightly naughty." Gallo praises the "studied British theatricality and sharp wit," its "bitchy bons mots" and "elegant aphorism." He enjoys the "Tracy and Hepburn" style "barbed, beautifully timed exchanges" and the assault upon Lord Cromer. He concludes the film "hits all its marks, well worn though they be, and Dench fans will once more find themselves glorying in her reckless spirit."

Garner feels it "moves along at an enjoyable clip, and Dench grabs hold with every acidic line of dialogue and every sharp-eyed glance." Hartman describes it as "a delightful dramatic comedy" and "a charming piece that entertains without getting heavy, yet dares to make poignant statements when the moment is right." Hanke terms it "no dry study of history" and "a little treasure." He credits this "delightful confection" to "its stars, a wonderful screenplay by Martin Sherman ... and the assured direction of Frears." He finds the story "engaging" and praises "the way the film normalizes sex and sexuality in a refreshing manner." Williams perceptively discusses Mrs. Henderson's anti–Semitism and its place in her character development before concluding, "Filled with delightful dialogue from beginning to end, there's chemistry and tension aplenty in this bittersweet character study."

Newman finds it "full of life." He judges the title character worthy of Evelyn Waugh and says this "is one of the rare pictures that makes you feel as if the writer actually was inspired." He explains, "The wickedly funny Mrs. Henderson the movie presents is the creamy creation of writer Martin Sherman" and calls the luncheon with Lord Cromer "one of the funniest scenes of the year."

Thompson loves the Cromer scene and respects the Windmill's family. Westbrook enjoys it as "nakedly sweet for a film containing full-frontal nudity." He continues, "The shows are a hit, and the film should be, too." He judges the musical numbers "a delight" and the film a "warmhearted fable." He adds, "For those who love the family of the theater, this postcard from its past is worth framing in your heart."

Wirt recommends it as "terrific entertainment." He explains regarding Van Damm and Laura: "The feisty anger, jealousy and affection they express earn them a place among the great couples in 2005 movies." Gronvall acclaims, "Posh meets prole in this period drama elegantly directed by Stephen Frears." She notes Dench's "bons mots and trenchant ripostes come courtesy of writer Martin Sherman ... who reaches beyond nostalgia to riff on the relationship between commerce and art and on the transcendent power of beauty."

Phillips calls this "a dear film, sentimental and fond, full of beautifully acted British resolve." He quips, "The movie has more going on, however, than it has coming off." Sherman "juices up the roles of Henderson and Van Damm." He adds, "'Mrs. Henderson Presents' can be extremely moving." Ebert dwells upon his visit to the Windmill in 1961. He loved the vaudeville, and he describes the cinematic version as "a fond show-biz tale" populated by Dench and Hoskins, their characters "both high-spirited and stubborn." He concludes, "*Mrs. Henderson Presents* is not great cinema, and neither was the Windmill great theater, but they both put on a good show."

Arnold asks, "How can it miss?" and answers his own question, "Actually, it doesn't.... You have to have a very hard heart indeed not to find it irresistible: It's funny, touching and crammed to the rafters with clever dialogue, splashy production numbers and stiff-upper-lip charm." Macdonald calls the picture "a shamelessly entertaining bonbon, with a welcome mix of tartness and sugar." She praises the music hall as "frothy fun" and continues by noting the film, particularly "in its first half, has a charmingly playful tone to it, as if everyone involved were on holiday."

Lumenick calls it "one of the year's best" and "a classy crowd-pleaser." He feels Hoskins delivers his "best performance in decades." He praises Maureen's "tragic romance with a soldier" which "provides the movie's most poignant moments." He applauds Frears and Sherman for crafting a "stirring ode to British show business (there are several well-staged musical numbers) and Londoners' pluck during the Luftwaffe raids." Bernard writes, "For a spot of nearly naughty fun, you can't go wrong with *Mrs. Henderson Presents*, a sweet tidy movie that offers the unusual combination of Judi Dench and a bevy of bare, bouncing breasts. You don't see that every day." Bernard correctly labels it as "loosely inspired by a real vaudeville theater" and also finds it "clean as a whistle, despite the R rating." Denby dubs it "a valentine to British vaudeville in a gently risqué period."

Reed rejoices,

> When 2005 is over, the movie I will remember that gave me the most pure and unfiltered joy is *Mrs. Henderson Presents*. This upscale revelation—brilliantly written by the accomplished playwright Martin Sherman (*Bent*), meticulously directed by the great Stephen Frears, and stylishly acted by a marvelous cast headed by Judi Dench and Bob Hoskins— is a diamond-sparkling, Kleenex-grabbing, jaunt down memory lane [22].

Seymour says, "Always with Frears, it's the not-so-obvious graces that separate his genre films from everyone else's ... when the cameras cut away to an audience of servicemen, it really does feel as though you're staring at a vintage 1940s photograph of pale, weathered faces brought eerily to life."

Chagollan explains it concerns "characters who thumb their noses at convention and in the process, triumph over adversity." He feels Sherman "keeps things light with the suggestion of a stiff upper lip—a kind of posh English patois that's always agreeable to the ear."

Wolf raves, "A glorious, immensely entertaining semi-musical ... is among the best films of 2005 ... consistently delightful, often very funny and at times touching." He admires the "drama, warmth and a sense of time and place" he finds "packed into the film." He understands the function of Van Damm's Jewishness, and he elaborates, "Sherman's screenplay is rich in plot and characterization." He concludes the movie "affords tons of pleasure in so many ways."

Sragow explicates, "The whole movie is about priming the sap that makes life worth fighting for." He understands the dual function of Laura's remarks about Van Damm's Jewishness, that they ignite "the movie's funniest joke as well as its most understated and moving display of compassion." After praising Guest, he continues, "The profoundly wacky Dench is the vital core of the movie. She brings to life a headstrong, cultivated woman who at heart is both romantic and profane."

Rickey explains "a successful alliance between blueblood and blue-collar" created the Windmill Theatre. She calls it a "confection," describes the screenplay as "catnip for theater lovers," praises the Dench and Hoskins rhythms, but prefers the Dench and Guest interaction. She notes, "In its juxtaposition of voluptuous nudity with the horrors of war, in its evocation of idealized beauty draped like gods and goddesses of Grecian art, the film invokes classical ideas about how the life force asserts itself most aggressively in the face of death." D. Elliott says it "favors patriotism, family values and nude girls. Hip, hip, hooray!"

Burr observes Frears "gives us a sweet, old-fashioned study of time and place and one unsinkable woman" fueled by "a raging curiosity about the world after a lifetime of crushing good behavior." He judges the inaudible conversations at her son's grave "the film's most moving scenes." Hornaday calls it "a whimsical period piece" in which "humor and warmth abound." She believes, "The film's most oddly moving sequence is also its most amusing, when as a tribute to their French allies the dancers assume a righteous homage to Liberte, Egalite, and Decollete." Ogle terms it "hilarious and poignant."

Stein praises Dench's performance as "worthy of Oscar consideration" and commends its "old-fashioned feel, as if it had been made in the period of its setting. I mean this as a compliment." She finds it "well crafted," offering "an innocence and wry, gentle humor." She especially enjoys as "the loveliest dance" the one between Van Damm and Henderson as the picture ends. Turan begins, "Just as there will always be an England, there will always be a certain kind of English film: the highly polished entertainment, well-acted, genteelly amusing and impeccably turned out." He calls it "especially satisfying" and Sherman's script "smartly good-natured." Regarding Dench's performance, he asserts, "This tart-tongued role is one of her very best."

Rechtshaffen pronounces this "another keeper" from Frears. He judges it "an absolute delight ... with wittily acerbic dialogue, pitch-perfect performances and terrific production numbers." He elaborates concerning a "gorgeous script by Martin Sherman ... splendid entertainment which ... doesn't shrink away from the darker impulses generated by the onset of World War II. Sherman's words and Dench's delivery are a match made in movie heaven."

McDonagh begins, "Say what you will about feel-good films anchored by feisty old broads, the English have a knack with them and Stephen Frears' ... is delightful." He relishes the title character's frankness and concludes "this is the Dench and Hoskins show ... bickering, bantering and sniping at each other with genteel glee." Corliss advises readers the picture "is an utterly charming fiction based on fact." He labels it a "holiday treat." Ansen judges, "It's seriously fun" and argues, "Sherman is good at writing witty one-liners with a Wildean snap. When you dangle one of these in front of an actor with Dame Judi's formidable technique, the question is not whether she'll knock it out of the park, but how far."

Garcia says Dench's "twinkling eye and twitching upper lip divulge a mischievous and risqué femininity reminiscent of American screwball comedy." She praises "uniformly excellent performances," the "virtuoso direction," and the "witty screenplay ... refreshingly uncomplicated." She judges it "beautifully crafted." Doughton declares, "Hoskins is a hoot, and so is the film," praises "a poignant character study" and later explicates "the story of an older woman making up for lost time. Trading decades of muzzled vitality for a new lease on subversive spirit, Laura Henderson proves that it's never too late to live a little." Schneider believes "the British keep proving they're far ahead of us when it comes to infusing 'adult' material with tenderness and humor." Regarding Laura, he rhapsodizes, "You hang on her every stinging word."

Zacharek explains it concerns "artful draping and wartime valiance, in precisely that order. This is a shimmery beaded curtain of a movie, a slight, charming picture that's almost all façade. But what a façade!" She admires the "jazzy syncopation" of the Dench/Hoskins scenes and pronounces them "a pleasure to watch." And "you're left marveling at how Frears has kept the whole thing so crisp and so fun." Alter notes "moviegoers tend to expect a more 'authentic' (i.e., graphic) depiction of war. But it would be a mistake to write *Mrs. Henderson Presents* off as a frivolous diversion. A pervading sense of loss underlines all of the snappy repartee and double entendres. By the time the credits roll, the film has managed to show the toll of war without a single onscreen death."

Berardinelli applauds the mixed genres and continues, "*Mrs. Henderson Presents* is at times funny, at times poignant, and at times uplifting.... It offers a feel-good experience, but without the heavy dose of schmaltz that often accompanies such a production." Leeper likewise enjoys that it "deftly touches a wide range of emotions. Certainly it is by turns funny, sentimental, and powerful.... Martin Sherman's screenplay offers delightful dialog ... a real gem." Granger begins "For sheer, sophisticated delight, you can't do better than this deliciously wicked comedy." She raves, "Written with acerbic wit ... and cleverly directed ... it's a dual tour-de-force for Judi Dench and Bob Hoskins.... On the Granger Movie Gauge of 1 to 10, *Mrs. Henderson Presents* is a poignant yet utterly charming 10. It's a classy, laugh-out-loud crowd pleaser." And Malcolm recommends it, despite his paper's previous pan.

Selected Bibliography

Chapter 1

Molotsky, Irvin. "You Can Take the Boy Out of Camden." *New York Times*, 23 April 2000: NJ4.

Sherman, Martin. Editorial. *Record* 48 (Christmas 1955): 5.

———."Socrates Jones." *Record* 46 (Christmas 1953).

———. "Socrates Jones in 'Tickets, Please.'" *Record* 47 (Christmas 1954): 20–21.

Chapter 3

Cooke, Richard P. "Wilted Wycherly." *Wall St. Journal*, 13 December 1965: 16.

<Core-online.org/History/freedom-summer.htm>.

Gottfried, Martin. "The Country Wife." *Women's Wear Daily*, 10 December 1965: 25.

Hipps, Edward Sothern. "Restoration Play Redone." *Newark Evening News*, 10 December 1965: 62.

Sherman, Martin. "Things Went Badly in Westphalia." *The Best Short Plays: 1970*. Ed. Stanley Richards. Philadelphia: Chilton, 1970, [371]–408.

Chapter 4

Sherman, Martin. "Foreword." *Stonewall 25: The Making of the Lesbian and Gay Community in Britain*. Eds. Emma Healey and Angela Mason. London: Virago, 1994, 1–2.

———. "Passing By." *Gay Plays*, I. Ed. Michael Wilcox. London: Methuen, 1984, [99]–120.

Chapter 5

Baker, Rob. "Back at Home Base." *Daily News*, 20 June 1977: 43.

Barnes, Clive. "The Theater: 'Cracks.'" *New York Times*, 11 February 1976: 35.

Church, Michael. "Passing By." *Times*, 20 June 1975: 13.

Coveney, Michael. "Cracks." *Financial Times*, 19 October 1981: 11.

Da Silva, Beatrice. "Whodunit?" *Villager*, 12 February 1976: 9.

Eder, Richard. "'Cracks' Has Holes." *New York Times*, 22 June 1977: C22.

Feingold, Michael. "Critic Cracks 'Cracks' Critics." *Village Voice*, 23 February 1976: 106.

———. "Waving Her Psychic Scars." *Village Voice*, 29 November 1976: 97.

Gilbert, W. Stephen. "Gay Sweatshop." *Plays and Players*, August 1975: 36.

Glover, William. AP. 11 February 1976.

Gold, Sylviane. "'Cracks' Earns Its 2nd Chance." *New York Post*, 24 June 1977: 42.

Gottfried, Martin. "It Cracked Under Poor Direction." *New York Post*, 11 February 1976: 5.

Harris, William. "Off and On." *Soho Weekly News*, 23 June 1977: 48–49.

Kingston, Jeremy. "Calling Time on the Californian Freaks." *Times*, 4 May 1993: 34.

Lipton, Victor. "Off-Broadway: Passing By." *Show Business*, 14 March 1974: 21.

Madden, John. "Cracks." *Variety*, 18 February 1976: 120.

McFerran, Ann. "Lunchtime: Almost Free Theatre." *Time Out*, 27 June–3 July 1975: 15.

Nellhaus, Arlynn. "'Cracks' Hits Loony World." *Denver Post*, 21 November 1975: 26.

Oliver, Edith. "The Theatre: Off Broadway." *New Yorker*, 23 February 1976: 82.

Peter, John. "Theatrecheck." *Sunday Times*, 2 May 1993: sec. 9, 23.

Proctor, Roy. "'Couple' Much the Better Half in Evening of One-Acts." *Richmond Times-Dispatch*, 10 September 1994: B7.

Sharp, Christopher. "Cracks." *Women's Wear Daily*, 11 February 1976: 26.

Sherman, Martin. *Cracks*. London: Samuel French, 1986.

Shorter, Eric. "Not Knowing Whodunnit." *Daily Telegraph*, 23 October 1981: 17.

Syna, Sy. "'Cracks' a Hilarious Mystery Spoof." *Wisdoms Child*, 5 July 1977: 12.
Venning, Nicola. "The Way We Were." *What's On*, 5 May 1993: 55.
Wardle, Irving. "A Post-Communist Kafka." *Independent on Sunday*, 2 May 1993: 21.
Watt, Douglas. "'Cracks' a Whodunit Comedy That Misfires." *Daily News*, 11 February 1976: 78.
Watts, Richard. "The Season's Worst Disaster." *New York Post*, 16 February 1976: 13.
Wolf, Matt. "Cracks." *Variety*, 17 May 1993: 106.

ADDITIONAL REVIEWS OF CRACKS AT KING'S HEAD

Armistead, Claire. "Cracks, King's Head." *Guardian*, 5 May 1993: sec. 2, 6.
Coveney, Michael. "A Musical Moll Collecting Husbands." *Observer*, 2 May 1993: Arts 4, 55.
De Jongh, Nicholas. "Watching the Defectives." *Evening Standard*, 5 May 1993: 56.
Eley, Esther. "And the Sexy Seventies Revisited." *Mid Week*, 13–17 May 1993: xx.
James, Christopher. "Cracks." *Time Out*, 5–12 May 1993: 115.
Macaulay, Alastair. "Cracked Up in California." *Financial Times*, 1–2 May 1993: sec. 2, xx.
Morley, Sheridan. "Flanders Mare." *Spectator*, 8 May 1993: 38.
_____. "London Theater." *International Herald Tribune*, 5 May 1993: 9.
Tinker, Jack. "A Cracker of a Spoof on Wicked Times." *Daily Mail*, 26 May 1993: 40.

ADDITIONAL REVIEWS OF RIO GRANDE

Gregory, Don. "Rio Grande." *Show Business*, 25 November 1976: 17.
_____. "Rio-Not So-Grande." *Our Town*, 3 December 1976: 12.
Nelsen, Don. "The Warning Sign Goes Unheeded." *Daily News*, 18 November 1976: 108.
Stasio, Marilyn. "Rio Grande." *Cue*, 11–24 November 1976: 50.

Chapter 6

Barber, John. "What Makes a Play." *Daily Telegraph* 23 July 1979: 8.
Bettelheim, Bruno. *The Informed Heart: Autonomy in a Mass Age*. New York: Avon, 1971; orig. Free Press, 1960.
Chambers, Colin. *Peggy: The Life of Margaret Ramsay, Play Agent*. London: Nick Hern, 1997.
Heger, Heinz. *The Men with the Pink Triangle*. London: Gay Men's Press, 1980; New York: Alyson, 1980.
Kogon, Eugen. *The Theory and Practice of Hell: The German Concentration Camps and the System Behind Them*. Trans. Heinz Norden. New York: Farrar, 2006; orig. Farrar, 1950.
McKellen, Ian. "When Stage Horror Is Not Sensationalism." *Daily Telegraph*, 28 July 1979: 14.
Plant, Richard. "The Men with the Pink Triangles." *Christopher Street*, February 1977: 4–10.
"Plays and Players 1979 Awards." *Plays and Players*, January 1980: [12]–13.
Renault, Mary. *The Mask of Apollo*. New York: Pantheon, 1966.
Sherman, Martin. "Bent." *Martin Sherman: Plays 1*. London: Methuen, 2004, [51]–142.
_____. *Bent*. New York: Samuel French, 1979.
_____. *Bent*. Charlbury: Amber Lane, 1979.
Two Gay Sweatshop Plays. London: Gay Men's Press, 1981.

LONDON *BENT* REVIEWS

Negative

Bennett, Peter. "Upstage." *Gay News*, 17–30 May 1979: 33–34.
King, Francis. "Turn of the Shrew." *Sunday Telegraph*, 6 May 1979: 14.
Shulman, Milton. "Horror Story of the Gay Kind." *Evening Standard*, 4 May 1979: 15.
Simo. "Bent." *Variety*, 25 May 1979: 98.
Stewart, Ian. "Odd Men Out." *Country Life*, 24 May 1979: 1634.
Trewin, J.C. "New Plays." *Lady*, 24 May 1979: 931.
Young, B.A. "Bent." *Financial Times*, 4 May 1979: 21.

Mixed

Barnes, Clive. "London's 'Bent' an Actor's Play." *New York Post*, 25 September 1979: 40.
Brown, Geoff. "Bent." *Time Out*, 18–24 May 1979: 31.
Chaillet, Ned. "Bent." *Plays and Players*, June 1979: 23–24.
Coveney, Michael. "Bent." *Financial Times*, 12 July 1979: 23.
Cushman, Robert. "Time Passes." *Observer*, 6 May 1979: 14.
Elsom, John. "Camp Ordeal." *Listener*, 17 May 1979: 689–90.

Hepple, Peter. "Bent at the Royal Court." *Stage*, 11 May 1979: 13.
Hirschhorn, Clive. "Theatre." *Sunday Express*, 13 May 1979: 22.
Tinker, Jack. "When Gay Meant Grief." *Daily Mail*, 11 July 1979: 3.

Favorable

Barber, John. "Nazi Persecution of Homosexuals Shown." *Daily Telegraph*, 4 May 1979: 9.
Billington, Michael. "Bent." *Guardian*, 4 May 1979: 10.
———. "Exclusive Report from London." *New York Theatre Review*, June 1979: 24.
De Jongh, Nicholas. "Bent." *Guardian*, 12 July 1979: 11.
[Editors]. "Gay News Comments." *Gay News*, 17–30 May 1979: 16.
Gilbert, W. Stephen. "In the Web." *Gay News*, 12 July 1979: 33.
Grant, Steve. "Bent." *Time Out*, 27 July–2 August 1979: 30.
Leech, Michael. "Pink Triangle Life Under the Nazis." *Where to Go*, 17–23 May 1979: 50.
Morley, Sheridan. "Bent Double." *Punch*, 3 May 1979: 908.
Nightingale, Benedict. "In the Lime-Pit." *New Statesman*, 11 May 1979: 692.
Reed, Rex. "A Harrowing Hit from Britain." *Sunday News*, 11 November 1979: Leisure 3, 12.

Chapter 7 and Appendix A

"'Bent,' a 'Play That Has to Be Done.'" *New York Times*, 22 August 1979: C20.
Clum, John. *Acting Gay: Male Homosexuality in Modern Drama*. New York: Columbia University Press, 1992; rev. ed. 1994.
———. "Review: Queer Music." *Performing Arts Journal* 18.2 (May 1996): 118–126.
———. *Still Acting Gay*. New York: St. Martin's Press, 2000.
"Co-Producer Steinlauf Has 88G Piece of 'Bent.'" *Variety*, 12 December 1979: 83.
Grau, Gunter, ed. *Hidden Holocaust: Gay and Lesbian Persecution in Germany 1933–45*. Trans. Patrick Camiller. London: Cassell, 1995.
Hammermeister, Kai. "Inventing History: Toward a Gay Holocaust Literature." *German Quarterly*, 70.1 (Winter 1997): 18–26.
Harris, Michael. "Now Playing: Theatre." *Globe and Mail* [Toronto] <theglobeandmail.com> 7 November 2007.
Heger, Heinz. *The Men with the Pink Triangle*. London: Gay Men's Press, 1980; New York: Alyson, 1980.
Henry Hook Trivia Crostics (vol. 1). New York: Random House, 2001: 21.
"Love Against the Odds." *Bromley Times*, 12 December 2007.
Plant, Richard. "The Men with the Pink Triangles." *Christopher Street*, February 1977: 4–10.
———. *The Pink Triangle: The Nazi War Against Homosexuals*. New York: Holt, 1986.
Pollack, Joe. "'Bent' Defunded in St. Louis." *Back Stage*, 6 October 2000: 2.
Rector, Frank. *The Nazi Extermination of Homosexuals*. New York: Stein and Day, 1981.
"School Drama Over Bent." *Pink Paper*, 9 February 1991.
Seifert, Dorthe. "Between Silence and License: The Representation of the National Socialist Persecution of Homosexuality in Anglo-American Fiction and Film." *History and Memory: Studies in Representation of the Past* 15.2 (Fall/Winter 2003): 94–129.
Sherman, Martin. "Bent." [abridged] *Best Plays of 1979–80*. Ed. Otis L. Guernsey, Jr. New York: Dodd, Mead, 1980, 164–181.
———. *Bent*. New York: Samuel French, 1979.
Smith, Liz. "Liz Smith." *Daily News*, 9 November 1979: 8.
Sterling, Eric. "Bent Straight: The Destruction of Self in Martin Sherman's Bent." *Journal of European Studies* 32.4 (December 2002): 369–88.
Sumner, Ben. "A Spectacular Electrified Fence." *Technical Design Solutions for Theatre*: *The Technical Brief Collection*. Ed. Ben Sammler and Don Harvey (vol. 2). Woburn: Focal Press, 2002, 199–200.
Woods, Gregory. "The Pink Triangle." *A History of Gay Literature: The Male Tradition*. New Haven: Yale University Press, 1988, [247]–256.
"Why Are There So Many Off-Broadway Shows" *Show Business*, 18 September 1980: 1, 3.

Broadway *Bent* Reviews

Negative

"Bent." *Christian Science Monitor*, 21 December 1979: 19.
Currie, Glenne. "Homosexuals in Dachau Theme of New Broadway Play." 11 December 1979, UPI.
———. 25 June 1980, UPI.
Gerard, Jeremy. "Bent." *Our Town*, 20 January 1980: 18.

Goldfarb, Alvin. "Bent." *Theatre Journal* 32.3 (October 1980): 398–399.
Kauffmann, Stanley. "Friends and Lovers." *Saturday Review*, 2 February 1980: 30, 32.
[Morrison,] Hobe. "Bent." *Variety*, 5 December 1979: 88.
Munk, Erika. "Cross Left." *Village Voice*, 10 December 1979: 104.
Sharbutt, Jay. "Drama of Nazi Attack on Gays." *San Francisco Examiner*, 4 December 1979: 23.
Simon, John. "Campy Dachau, Plywood 'Mahagonny.'" *New York*, 17 December 1979: 110–111.
Stasio, Marilyn. "York's 'Bent' Out of Place." *New York Post*, 19 June 1980: 30.
Watt, Douglas. "'Bent' Is Shocking But Not Moving." *Daily News*, 3 December 1979: 29.

Mixed

Barnes, Clive. "'Bent' Reveals One More Nazi Horror." *New York Post*, 3 December 1979: 19.
Bowne, Alan. "Theater: Bent." *Gotham*, 12 December 1979: 7.
Brustein, Robert. "A Theater for Clever Journalists." *New Republic*, 5–12 January 1980: 23–24.
Eaker, Sherry. "Bent." *Back Stage*, 21 December 1979: 51.
Feingold, Michael. "Two Political Fables." *Village Voice*, 10 December 1979: 105.
Kroll, Jack. "Love Among the Ruins." *Newsweek*, 17 December 1979: 115.
Mackay, Patricia. "*Bent:* Flight and Confinement." *Theatre Crafts*, May–June 1980: 6.
Rich, Frank. "Stage: Michael York Heads New 'Bent' Cast." *New York Times*, 19 June 1980: C16.
Richardson, Jack. "Three from London." *Commentary*, March 1980: 71–75.
Wallach, Allan. "Theater: Prison Camp Drama." *Newsday* [Melville, NY], 3 December 1979: sec. 2, 32.
Watt, Douglas. "Fresh Cast Gives 'Bent' a New Slant." *Daily News*, 19 June 1980: 79.
Wilson, Edwin. "Holocaust and Homosexuality Suffuse New Play." *Wall Street Journal*, 5 December 1979: 22.

Favorable

Bell, Arthur. "Bell Tells." 26 November 1979: 39.
Cizmar, Paula L. "Finding Dignity at Dachau." *Books & Arts*, 8 February 1980: 23.
Clurman, Harold. "Theater." *Nation* 29 December 1979: 701–702.
Gill, Brendan. "The Theatre: Surviving." *New Yorker*, 17 December 1979: 100.
———. "The Theatre: Happy Liar." *New Yorker*, 30 June 1980: 55.
Johnson, Malcolm L. "'Bent': A Strong Play That Hartford Lost." *Hartford Courant*, 9 December 1979: F1, F9.
Kalem, T.E. "Walpurgisnacht." *Time*, 17 December 1979: 84.
Kerr, Walter. "For the 'Serious' Theatergoer." *New York Times*, 16 December 1979: sec. 2, 3, 34.
———. "Stage: 'Bent,' Starring Richard Gere." *New York Times*, 3 December 1979: C15.
Kissel, Howard. "Bent." *Women's Wear Daily*, 3 December 1979: 12.
Molyneaux, Gerard M. "Bent." *Library Journal*, 1 July 1980: 1536.
Ortleb, Charles. "Sharing the Holocaust." *Christopher Street*, January 1980: 10–11.
Patterson, John S. "Theatre Notes: Bent on Bent." *Villager*, 6 December 1979: 14.
Rabkin, Gerald. "Wearing the Pink Triangle." *Soho Weekly News*, 6 December 1979: 65–66.
Raidy, William A. "Love-hate Tragedy Is an Intense Triumph of the Soul." *Star-Ledger* [Newark], 3 December 1979: 24.
Reed, Rex. "*Bent* a Deep & Brilliant Blockbuster." *Daily News*, 5 December 1979: 56.
Smith, Liz. "Liz Smith." *Daily News*, 4 December 1979: 8.

Appendix A

Taylor, Kenneth Alan. "Getting Them Young." *Plays and Players*, October 1981: 53–4.
Riddle, January. "Live Performances." *Uptown* [San Diego], January 1987: 16.
Lassell, Michael. "Gripping, Brilliant 'Bent' Leaves Audience Stunned." *Los Angeles Herald Examiner*, 6 April 1987: B1, B5.
Chase, Anthony. "Smash Performance: 'Bent' Is a Triumph of the Season." *Buffalo News*, 8 March 1991: Gusto, 22.
Portantiere, Michael. "Beyond Broadway." *Theater Week*, 6 May 1996: 38.
Moore, John. "Hunger's 'Bent' Best of the Year." *Denver Post*, 22 April 2003: F04.

Chapter 8 and Appendix B

Messiah Reviews

Amory, Mark. "Theatre: Women Alone." *Spectator*, 18–25 December 1982: 48–49.

Asquith, Ros. "Messiah." *City Limits*, 11–17 February 1983: 50.
Barber, John. "In Search of the Messiah." *Daily Telegraph*, 13 December 1982: 11.
———. "Rachel the Indomitable." *Daily Telegraph*, 3 February 1983: 13.
Barkley, Richard. "Theatre." *Sunday Express*, 12 December 1982: 22.
Barnes, Clive. "Non-musical 'Messiah' Is Too Hard to Handel." *New York Post*, 26 December 1984: 36.
Billington, Michael. "Messiah." *Guardian*, 10 December 1982: 10.
Carne, Rosalind. "Messiah/Aldwych." *Financial Times*, 4 February 1983: 15.
Christiansen, Richard. "Playwright Falls Short in 'Messiah.'" *Chicago Tribune*, 6 November 1985: sec. 5, 5.
Cushman, Robert. "Hoping for a Miracle." *Observer*, 12 December 1982: 29.
Dace, Tish. "Messiah." *New York Native*, 14–27 January 1985: 38.
De Jongh, Nicholas. "Messiah." *Guardian*, 3 February 1984: 12.
Edwards, Christopher. "Lost Chance." *New Statesman*, 17–24 December 1982: 52.
Elsom, John. "Theatre." *Mail on Sunday*, 12 December 1982: 35.
Fenton, James. "London's Most Moving Play." *Sunday Times*, 12 December 1982: 40.
Fink, Joel. "Messiah." *Theatre Journal* 37 (October 1985): 370–71.
Gordon, Giles. "Women's Worlds." *Spectator*, 19 February 1983: 25.
Grant, Steve. "Messiah." *Time Out*, 17–30 December 1982: 105.
Handelzalts, Michael. "Stage Animal: When Theater Could Ruffle Feathers." <haaretz.com/hasen/objects/pages/1068574.html> 4 March 2009.
Herbert, Ian. "Prompt Corner." *London Theatre Record*, 1–28 January, 1983: 4.
Hirschhorn, Clive. "Theatre." *Sunday Express*, 6 February 1984: 23.
Howes, Keith. "Carrying the Can." *Gay News*, 3–16 May 1979: 15–16.
Hummler, Richard. "Messiah." *Variety*, 26 December 1984: 54.
Isaac, Dan. "Troubled Lives." *Westsider*, 17 January 1985: 11.
King, Francis. "Theatre: Messianic Failings." *Sunday Telegraph*, 12 December 1982: 12.
Kissel, Howard. "Messiah." *Women's Wear Daily*, 26 December 1984: 12.
Lamont, Rosette C. "Messiah." *Stages*, February 1985: 34.
Masters, Anthony. "Messiah." *Times*, 4 February 1984: 11.

"Messiah." *Christian Science Monitor*, 8 January 1985: 28–29.
Morley, Sheridan. "The Gift of Big Writing." *Times*, 11 February 1983: 10.
———. "Look Back in Anger." *Punch*, 9 February 1983: 44.
———. "'Messiah' Explores Nature of Faith." *International Herald Tribune*, 15 December 1982: 6.
Nightingale, Benedict. "Face to Face." *New Statesman*, 11 February 1983: 32–33.
Novick, Julius. "Prisoners of Hope." *Village Voice*, 1 January 1985: 72, 74.
Pascal, Julia. "Messiah." *City Limits*, 17–23 December 1982: 55.
Petty, Moira. "Calling up God for a Chinwag." *Daily Mail*, 3 February 1983: 25.
Rich, Frank. "Theater: Sherman's 'Messiah.'" *New York Times*, 24 December 1984: 36.
Roper, David. "At the Theatre." *Daily Express*, 3 February 1983: 13.
Saunders, Dick. "*Messiah*'s Salvation Is Some Good Acting." *Chicago Sun-Times*, 4 November 1985: 41.
Sherman, Martin. "Messiah." *Plays*. London: Methuen, 2004: [143]–200.
Shulman, Milton. "Saved by the Pen." *Evening Standard*, 10 December 1982: 30.
Simon, John. "False Messiah, Fake Diamonds." *New York*, 7 January 1985: 54.
Smith, Patricia Keeney. "Theatre of Extremity." *Canadian Forum* 65 (April 1985): 37–38, 40.
Stewart, Ian. "An Irresistible Magnet?" *Country Life*, 24 February 1984: 447.
Syna, Sy. "Provocative 'Messiah' Disturbing but Flawed." *New York City Tribune*, 1 January 1985: 5B.
Thrall, Judy. "Messiah." *Back Stage*, 4 January 1985: 14A.
Wardle, Irving. "Messiah." *Times*, 10 December 1982: 11.
Watt, Douglas. "'Tis Not the Season for This 'Messiah.'" *Daily News*, 24 December 1984: 13.
Weiss, Hedy. "A Feminist's 'Messiah': Woman at Center of Jewish Theater Production." *Chicago Sun-Times*, 22 June 1994: 45.
Young, B.A. "Messiah/Hampstead." *Financial Times*, 10 December 1982: 12.

Chapter 9

Duncan, Isadora. *Isadora Speaks*. Ed. Franklin Rosemont. San Francisco: City Lights, 1981.
———. *My Life*. New York: Liveright, 1927.

300 Selected Bibliography

Kinel, Lola. *This Is My Affair*. Boston: Little, Brown, 1937.
Sherman, Martin. *When She Danced*. Charlbury: Amber Lane, 1988.

GUILDFORD REVIEWS

B., P. "Play About Isadora Duncan a Little Too Sedate." *Herald*, 6 December 1985: 6.
"Isadora Play Is Full of Ironies." *Surrey Advertiser*, 29 November 1985: 23.
Tatlow, Peter. "Language of Dance." *Stage and Television Today*, 12 December 1985: 24.
Tims, Hilton. "Trauma Laced with Comedy." *Midweek Comet*, 4 December 1985: 9.

KING'S HEAD REVIEWS

Mixed

Edwards, Christopher. "On the Edge of Preciosity." *Spectator*, 24 September 1988: 44–45.
Gardner, Lyn. "When She Danced." *City Limits*, 29 September–6 October 1988: 77.
Hurren, Kenneth. "Back to the Bad Old Days." *Mail on Sunday*, 25 September 1988: 38.
King, Francis. "Raucous Fun as Burlesque Returns." *Sunday Telegraph*, 25 September 1988: 18.
Peter, John. "A Star Who Can't Give You Anything but Fun." *Sunday Times*, 25 September 1988: C11.
Wardle, Irving. "Terpsichore to Take on Trust" (alt. "Terpsichore to Be Taken on Trust.") *Times*, 21 September 1988: 20.

Favorable

Billington, Michael. "The Broken Butterfly." *Guardian*, 21 September 1988: 17.
Chamberlain, Lesley. "Free-Style Fervour." *TLS*, 30 September–6 October 1988: 1072.
Coveney, Michael. "When She Danced." *Financial Times* 20 September 1988: 25.
Edwardes, Jane. "When She Danced." *Time Out*, 28 September 1988: 51.
Hiley, Jim. "Grin and Bare It." *Listener*, 29 September 1988: 45.
Hirschhorn, Clive. "Rooney and Miller." *Sunday Express*, 25 September 1988: 19.
Kemp, Peter. "Dancing Through Bohemia." *Independent*, 21 September 1988: 12.
MacDonald, Caroline. "Duncanesque." *What's On*, 28 September–5 October 1988: 41.
Morley, Sheridan. "Broadway Babies." *Punch*, 7 October 1988: 66.
Nathan, David. "Rise and Fall of a Goddess of Dance." *Jewish Chronicle*, 30 September 1988: 12.
Shulman, Milton. "A Flame Burns Out." *Evening Standard*, 20 September 1988: 43.
Spencer, Charles. "The Passions of Isadora." *Daily Telegraph*, 22 September 1988: 10.
Tinker, Jack. "The Free Spirit Who Was Imprisoned by Passion." *Daily Mail*, 5 October 1988: 32.

APPENDIX C: PLAYWRIGHTS HORIZONS

Negative

Hummler, Richard. "When She Danced." *Variety*, 7 March 1990: 62.

Mixed

Barnes, Clive. "Sheerly Lovely Isadora." *New York Post*, 20 February 1990: 22.
Feldberg, Robert. "A Day in the Swirl of Isadora Duncan." *Record* [Bergen], 20 February 1990: B-6.
Kirkpatrick, Melanie. "Isadora Off- and On-Stage." *Wall St. Journal*, 28 February 1990: A14.
Nelsen, Don. "Isadora: Barefoot in the Dark." *Daily News*, 20 February 1990: 33.
Novick, Julius. "'When She Danced': Duncan Preened When She Didn't." *New York Observer*, 5 March 1990: 19.
Resnikova, Eva. "Miss Margarida's Way: Parsons Passes, Audience Flunks." *New York Observer*, 5 March 1990: 19.
Rich, Frank. "A Comic Portrait of Duncan in Her Gloomy Final Years." *New York Times*, 20 February 1990: C15.
Simon, John. "Not Made in Heaven." *New York*, 5 March 1990: 56–7.
Watt, Douglas. "Three Good Actors in Not-so-good Plays." *Daily News*, 2 March 1990: 39.
Winer, Linda. "Isadora Duncan After the Dance." *Newsday* [Melville, NY], 20 February 1990: sec. 2, 5, 13.

Favorable

Feingold, Michael. "Let the Artist Live." *Village Voice*, 6 March 1990: 105–106.
Kuchwara, Michael. "Ashley as Duncan in 'When She Danced.'" *New York City Tribune*, 21 February 1990: 14.
Oliver, Edith. "Portrait of the Artist on the Wane." *New Yorker*, 26 February 1990: 98.
Popkin, Henry. "When She Danced." *Theater Week*, 12–18 March 1990: 41.
Raidy, William A. "'When She Danced' Captures the Spirit of Eccentric, Legendary

Isadora Duncan." *Star-Ledger* [Newark], 20 February 1990: 28.
Sommers, Michael. "When She Danced." *Back Stage*, 16 March 1990: 52A.

Chapter 10

Clum, John M. *Staging Gay Lives*. Boulder: Westview Press, 1996.
Durell, Lawrence. *Balthazar*. New York: Penguin, 1991.
Kurth, Peter. *Isadora: A Sensational Life*. Boston: Back Bay, 2002.
"Londoner's Diary: Martin Seeks Asylum from Goans." *Evening Standard*, 2 June 1989: 6.
Redgrave, Vanessa. *Vanessa Redgrave: An Autobiography*. New York: Random House, 1994.
Sher, Antony. *Beside Myself: An Autobiography*. London: Hutchinson, 2001.
Sherman, Martin. *A Madhouse in Goa*. Charlbury: Amber Lane, 1989.

A MADHOUSE IN GOA REVIEWS

Arditi, Michael. "Laughing All the Way to the Camps." *Punch*, 12 May 1989: 46.
Barnes, Clive. "The Worst of the West." *New York Post*, 1 September 1989: 32.
Billington, Michael. "Tall Tales from World's End." *Guardian*, 1 May 1989: 21.
Coveney, Michael. "Blithe Spirit." *Financial Times*, 16 June 1989: 19.
———. "A Madhouse in Goa." *Financial Times*, 2 May 1989: 19.
Dace, Tish. "The Ultimate Apocalypse." *New York Native*, 31 July 1989: 38.
Edwardes, Jane. "A Madhouse in Goa." *Time Out*, 21 June 1989: 49.
Edwards, Christopher. "Shouted Down." *Spectator*, 13 May 1989: 43.
Henry, William A. III. "A Trio of Triumphs in London." *Time*, 3 July 1989: 59.
Hepple, Peter. "Hammersmith." *Stage and Television Today*, 11 May 1989: 11.
Herbert, Ian. "Prompt Corner." *London Theatre Record*, 23 April–6 May 1989: 527.
Hiley, Jim. "Playing for Time." *Listener*, 11 May 1989: 31.
Hirschhorn, Clive. "Bit Too Much on the Bone to Suit My Taste." *Sunday Express*, 18 June 1989: 19.
Hornby, Richard. "The London Theatre." *Hudson Review* 42.4 (Winter 1990): 629–36.
Hurren, Kenneth. "Vanessa Is Lost in Doom and Gloom." *Mail on Sunday*, 7 May 1989: 36.
Hutera, Donald. "A Madhouse in Goa." *Time Out*, 3–10 May 1989: 40.

Kissel, Howard. "From Madhouse to Majesty, London Stage Is Robust." *Daily News*, 6 September 1989: 35.
McAfee, Annalena. "Turning Tables." *Evening Standard*, 2 May 1989: 41.
Morley, Sheridan. "Martin Sherman's Coherent 'Madhouse.'" *International Herald Tribune*, 10 May 1989: 7.
Nathan, David. "Short on Credibility." *Jewish Chronicle*, 12 May 1989: 15.
Paton, Maureen. "Portrait of Obsession." *Daily Express*, 19 June 1989: 32.
Pitman, Jack. "A Madhouse in Goa." *Variety*, 28 June 1989: 65.
Ratcliffe, Michael. "Boney in Zoomerset." *Observer*, 7 May 1989: 41.
Renton, Alex. "Accidental Tourists." *Independent*, 1 May 1989: 13.
Rich, Frank. "Some West End Efforts to Repel the New American Invasion." *New York Times*, 27 June 1989: C15, C20.
Roberts, Peter. "A Madhouse in Goa." *Plays International*, June 1989: 26.
Robinson, Tim. "A Madhouse in Goa," *City Limits*, 11–18 May 1989: 71.
Shorter, Eric. "Critics Choice: Theatre." *Daily Telegraph*, 13 May 1989: xx.
Smith, Rupert. "A Madhouse in Goa." *20/20*, August 1989: 132.
Spencer, Charles. "Ragbag of Fashion." *Telegraph*, 1 May 1989: 17.
Tinker, Jack. "Now Redgrave Dares All." *Daily Mail*, 10 May 1989: 30.
Tyler, Rupert, and Patrick Gale. "Saying It with Panache." *Gay Times*, June 1989: 76.
Wardle, Irving. "Finally It's Too Much." *Times*, 1 May 1989: 14.
Watt, Douglas. "Hoffman Falls a Bit Shy as Shylock." *Daily News*, 28 July 1989: 45.
Wearing, Catherine. "Living Dangerously." *What's On*, 10–17 May 1989: 36.

WHEN SHE DANCED AT THE GLOBE REVIEWS

Bayley, Clare. "Veiled Insults." *What's On*, 14–21 August 1991: 34.
Billington, Michael. "Divine Accident of True Genius." *Guardian*, 7 August 1991: 29.
Coveney, Michael. "Vanessa Takes Possession of the Soul of Isadora." *Observer*, 11 August 1981: 49.
Edwardes, Jane. "When She Danced." *Time Out*, 14–21 August 1991: 102.
Edwards, Christopher. "Bohemian Rhapsody." *Spectator*, 10 August 1991: 40–41.

Gore-Langton, Robert. "In Paris with the Original Champagne Socialist." *Daily Telegraph*, 8 August 1991: 15.
Gross, John. "A Resistible Legend." *Sunday Telegraph*, 11 August 1991: XII.
Hirschhorn, Clive. "Vanessa Dances to a Wild Tune." *Sunday Express*, 11 August 1991: 60.
Hurren, Kenneth. "Vanessa Trips up Leading Such a Dance." *Mail on Sunday*, 11 August 1991: 33.
Koenig, Rhoda. "Isadora Bunkum." *Punch*, 14 August 1991: 42.
Linford, Matthew. "When She Danced." *Pink Paper*, 31 August 1991: 11.
Lipman, Amanda. "When She Danced." *Good Times*, 16–22 August 1991: 15.
Macaulay, Alastair. "When She Danced." *Financial Times*, 8 August 1991: 9.
McVay, Gordon. "When She Danced." *Plays and Players*, October 1991: 33.
Morley, Sheridan. "History as Pantomime." *International Herald Tribune*, 14 August 1991: 7.
Nathan, David. "Breaking Language Barriers." *Jewish Chronicle*, 9 August 1991: 20.
Newman, Barbara. "Another Opening, Another Show." *Dancing Times*, September 1991: 1115–1116.
Nightingale, Benedict. "Kindred Spirits in the Mirror." *Times*, 7 August 1991: 16.
O'Connor, Patrick. "Shadow Dancing." *TLS*, 23 August 1991: 17.
Paton, Maureen. "Dreary Vanessa Ends Up with Ego on Her Face." *Daily Express*, 7 August 1991: 29.
Peter, John. "In the Steps of Star Quality." *Sunday Times*, 11 August 1991: sec. 5, 9.
Pitman, Jack. "When She Danced." *Variety*, 26 August 1991: 92.
Raymond, Gerard. "When She Danced." *Theater Week*, 2 December 1991: 30.
Shulman, Milton. "After the Dance." *Evening Standard*, 7 August 1991: 36.
Shuttleworth, Ian. "When She Danced." *City Limits*, 15–22 August 1991: 57.
Taylor, Paul. "Fallen Comet." *Independent*, 8 August 1991: 15.
Tinker, Jack. "Vanessa Triumphs on the Rack of Ruin." *Daily Mail*, 7 August 1991: 3.
Wardle, Irving. "Born to Be a Great Pantomime Director." *Independent on Sunday*, 11 August 1991: 15.

Chapter 11

Cotton, Ian. "John's Hall of Fame." *Observer Magazine*, 11 December 1988: 46–49, 51.

Sherman, Martin, and Antony Sher. "Honour That Removes Gay Fears." *Guardian*, 9 January 1991: 18.
Summers, Claude. *Gay and Lesbian Literary Heritage*. New York: Routledge, 2002; orig. Holt, 1995.

Bent Reviews

Billington, Michael. "Carrying the Torch." *Guardian*, 22 January 1990: 38.
Cook, William. "Bent." *Midweek: Free Thinking*, 1 February 1990: 33.
Coveney, Michael. "Loving Men to Death." *Observer*, 28 January 1990: 60.
"Critics Choice." *Time Out*, 24–31 January: 37.
Edwards, Christopher. "Striking Camp." *Spectator*, 17 January 1990: 45–46.
Gross, John. "The Yellow Star and the Pink Triangle." *Sunday Telegraph*, 28 January 1990: 49.
Herbert, Ian. "Prompt Corner." *London Theatre Record*, 2–28 January 1990: 59.
Hewison, Robert. "Gestures of Gay Pride Drained of Defiance." *Sunday Times*, 28 January 1990: E7.
Hiley, Jim. "Sherman's March." *Listener*, 1 February 1990: 43.
Hirschhorn, Clive. "Property Deal That Sells Out on Friendship." *Sunday Express*, 28 January 1990: 38.
Hoyle, Martin. "Bent." *Financial Times*, 22 January 1990: 13.
Hurren, Kenneth. "Pall of Berlin and Brutality." *Mail on Sunday*, 21 January 1990: 32.
Kemp, Peter. "Making Commitments." *Independent*, 22 January 1990: 11.
Koenig, Rhoda. "Camp Cliché." *Punch*, 2 February 1990: 42.
Mars-Jones, Adam. "Intimate Encounters with Death." *TLS*, 26 January 1990: 91.
Miller, Carl. "Wages of Sin." *City Limits*, 25 January–1 February 1990: 76.
Morley, Sheridan. "'Bent' Is Back, Chillingly Relevant." *International Herald Tribune*, 24 January 1990: 7.
Nathan, David. "In the Hell Hole of Dachau." *Jewish Chronicle*, 26 January 1990: 18.
Nightingale, Benedict. "A Glimpse of Hell." *Times*, 20 January 1990: Review, 41.
Osborne, Charles. "Acts of Violence." *Daily Telegraph*, 22 January 1990: 13.
Paton, Maureen. "A Cautionary Tale of Casual Cruelties." *Daily Express*, 22 January 1990: 37.
Rees, Caroline. "Timely Revival." *Tribune*, 26 January 1990: 9.
Shulman, Milton. "Moral shocker." *Evening Standard*, 22 January 1990: 33.

Smith, Rupert. "On 'Bent.'" *Time Out*, 24–31 January 1990: 37.
Tinker, Jack. "A Metaphor for All the Cruelties of Man." *Daily Mail*, 20 January 1990: 3.
Van Werson, Gerard. "Leading by Example." *Stage and Television Today*, 1 February 1990: 14.
Williams, Hugo. "Gay Journey into the Jaws of Hell." *Sunday Correspondent*, 28 January 1990: 38.

Chapter 12

Ellis, Alice Thomas. *The Summer House*. New York: Penguin, 1994.

U.K. REVIEWS (ALL FAVORABLE)

Amery, Colin. "Television: Let Enthusiasts Do Their Own Thing." *Financial Times*, 20 January 1993: 17.
Anwar, Farrah. "Clothes in the Wardrobe." *Sight and Sound*, March 1993: 55.
Catchpole, Charlie. "Charlie's Choice: Bonk Saves Bride." *News of the World*, 24 January 1993: 34.
Day-Lewis, Sean. "Pick of the Day." *Sunday Telegraph*, 17 January 1993: xxvi.
P., E. "Screen Two." *Time Out*, 13–20 January 1993: 253.
Paterson, Peter. "Skeletons in the Wardrobe." *Daily Mail*, 18 January 1993: 34.
Paton, Maureen. "Moreau Mixes an Erotic Cocktail in Croydon." *Daily Express*, 18 January 1993: 31.
Payne, Sally. "Critics' Choice: Screen Two." *Sunday Times*, 17 January 1993: sec. 8, 27.
Peachment, Chris. "Old Swingers Stroll Down Memory Lane." *Daily Telegraph*, 18 January 1993: 13.
"10.00 Screen Two," *Observer*, 17 January 1993: 54.
"10.00 Screen Two." *Times*, 16 January 1993: 17.
Venning, Harry. "Television Review." *Stage and Television Today*, 28 January 1993: 23.
Wilson, A. N. "When Hope Springs Interminable." *Sunday Telegraph*, 24 January 1993: xii.

U.S. REVIEWS

Negative

Derryberry, Jil. "The Summer House." *Interview*, January 1994: 28.
Millar, Jeff. "'The Summer House' Is a British TV Snoozer." *Houston Chronicle*, 25 December 1993: 9C.
Sherman, Paul. "Star Cast Is Never at Home in Dull 'House.'" *Boston Herald*, 25 December 1993: 023.
Stark, Susan. "Jeanne Moreau Puts a Chill on 'Summer House.'" *Detroit News and Free Press*, 24 December 1993: 3C.

Mixed

Anderson, Alice. "The Summer House." <gospelcom.net>.
Armstrong, David. "Two Great Actors Under One Roof." *San Francisco Examiner*, 24 December 1993: D3.
Berardinelli, James. "The Summer House." <reelviews.net/movies/s/summer_house.html>.
Brown, Georgia. "Love and Marriage." *Village Voice*, 4 January 1994: 50.
Campbell, Bob. "'Summer House' Is an Overloaded 'Holy Mess.'" *Star-Ledger* [Newark], 21 December 1993.
Hicks, Chris. "Each of 3 Foreign-Made Films Has Something to Recommend It: 'The Summer House.'" *Deseret Morning News* [Salt Lake City], 21 January 1994: W3.
Jones, Bill. "Moreau's Delectable Acting Makes 'Summer' Appetizing." *Phoenix Gazette*, 24 December 1993: Marquee, 14.
Lyman, David. "'Summer House' Sweet, but Vacant." *Cincinnati Post*, 24 December 1993: 3B.
Matthews, Jack. "Jeanne Moreau's 'House.'" *Newsday* [Melville, NY], 21 December 1993: 51.
Meyers, Joe. "French Star Moreau Saves 'Summer House' from Ruin." *Connecticut Post* [Bridgeport], 24 December 1993: C2.
Movshovitz, Howie. "Vibrant Moreau Spices Up 'The Summer House.'" *Denver Post*, 24 December 1993: Weekend, 6.
N., D. "The Summer House." *Film Journal* January/February 1994: BB-6.
Renshaw, Scott. "Summer House, The (1993) (TV)." <IMDb rec.arts.movies.reviews news group>
Smith, Russell. "Veteran Actresses Tame Flighty Plot." *Dallas Morning News*, 24 December 1993: 1C-2C.
Sterritt, David. "Freeze Frames." *Christian Science Monitor*, 11 March 1994: 14.

Favorable

Adams, Thelma. "Can This Bride Be Saved?" *New York Post*, 21 December 1993: 41.
Arar, Yardena. "Grande Dames Strike Gold with 'The Summer House.'" *Los Angeles Daily News*, 21 December 1993: L.A. Life, 4.

Baumgarten, Marjorie. "The Summer House." *Austin Chronicle*, 7 January 1994: 38–39.
Bernard, Jami. "'Summer' & the Laughing Is Easy." *Daily News*, 21 December 1993: 53.
Brussat, Frederic, and Mary Ann. "The Summer House." <spiritualityandpractice.com/films/films.php?id=4952>.
Byerley, Jim. "Film Reviews." HBO. <Hbo.com> <IMDb>.
Carr, Jay. "Moreau Brings Heat to 'Summer House.'" *Boston Globe*, 24 December 1993: 24.
[Cover], *Film Journal* October-November 1993.
Denerstein, Robert. "Moreau's Performance Heats Up Witty 'Summer House.'" *Rocky Mountain News* [Denver] 24 December 1993: 8D.
Ebert, Roger. "The Summer House." *Chicago Sun-Times* <rogerebert.suntimes.com> 24 December 1993.
"Film Journal Year-end Preview." *Film Journal*, October-November 1993: 26, 28, 30, 137.
Hirsch, Neil. "Were Men Put on Earth to Torment Women?" *New York Law Journal*, 23 December 1993: 11.
James, Caryn. "A Quiet English Setting, 1959: Enter, the Exotic Jeanne Moreau." *New York Times*, 21 December 1993: C19.
"Jeanne Moreau Shakes Up Goldwyn's Summer House." *Film Journal*, October/November 1993: 12, 56.
Kauffmann, Stanley. "Changings." *New Republic*, 10 & 17 January 1994: 30–31.
Kempley, Rita. "The Summer House." *Washington Post*, 24 December 1993: C1.
McAlister, Linda Lopez. "The Summer House." WMNF-FM, Tampa, 6 February 1994. <mith2.umd.edu/WomensStudies/FilmReviews/S/summer-house-mcalister>.
McCarthy, Todd. "The Summer House." *Variety*, 8 November 1993: 32.
Moss, Marilyn. "The Summer House." *Boxoffice*, December 1993: R-82, 83.
Neman, Daniel. "A Joyful 'Summer House.'" *Richmond Times-Dispatch*, 22 January 1994: B7.
Paton, Dean. "Four Actresses Shine in the Summer House." *Seattle Post-Intelligencer*, 24 December 1993: What's Happening, 10.
Ringel, Eleanor. "A Summer Breeze: British Comedy Puts the Accent on Wit." *Atlanta Journal-Constitution*, 24 December 1993: P/3.
Rosenbaum, Jonathan. "The Summer House." <onfilm.chicagoreader.com/movies/capsules/11708_SUMMER_HOUSE.html>.
Schickel, Richard. "Bourgeois, But No Bore." *Time*, 31 January 1994: 108.
Schwarzbaum, Lisa. "Great Dames." (alt. "The Summer House.") *EW Magazine* <ew.com> 11 February 1994.
Steinmetz, Johanna. "Screenplay Matches Wits with Moreau in 'Summer.'" *Chicago Tribune*, 24 December 1993: Friday, L.
"The Summer House." <dvdlaser.com/search/detail.cfm?id=23394>.
Thomas, Kevin. "'House': Wry, Delightful English Comedy." *Los Angeles Times*, 21 December 1993: Calendar, 10.
Turnquist, Kristi. "Moreau Holds Up 'House.'" *Oregonian* [Portland], 25 December 1993: L9.

Chapter 13

Denby, David. "Not Kids' Stuff." *New Yorker*, 28 May 2007: 86.
Everett, Rupert. *Red Carpets and Other Banana Skins: The Autobiography*. New York: Warner, 2006.
Geller, Uri. *My Story*. London: Robson, 1975.
Grossman, David. *See Under: Love*. Trans. Betsy Rosenberg. New York: Farrar, 1989; London: Cape, 1990.
Reynolds, Nigel. "Did Uri Geller Bend the Theatre Critics' Minds?" *Daily Telegraph*, 27 June 1996.
Sherman, Martin. *Some Sunny Day*. Charlbury: Amber Lane, 1966.

SOME SUNNY DAY REVIEWS

Negative

Herbert, Ian. "Prompt Corner." *Theatre Record*, 8–21 April 1996: 449–450.
Hirschhorn, Clive. "Some Sunny Day." *Theatre Week* 17–23 June 1996: 42.
———. "Wartime Fantasy About Gay Aliens Is a Risk Too Far." *Sunday Express* 24 April 1996: 59.
Morley, Sheridan. "Barbican Director and Star Tame Shakespeare's Difficult Shrew." *International Herald Tribune* 17 April 1996: 11.
———. "A Tawdry Singalong." *Spectator* 20 April 1996: 50.
Nathan, David. "Play on Weirdos." *Jewish Chronicle* 19 April 1996: 38.
Peter, John. "Clouding the Issue." *Sunday Times* 21 April 1996: 10*14.

Mixed

Cash, Jonathan. "Theatre." *Gay Times* May 1996: 94.

Christopher, James. "Some Sunny Day." *Time Out*, 17 April 1996: 121.

De Jongh, Nicholas. "Unearthly Visitor Has an Earthy Appetite." *Evening Standard*, 12 April 1996: 7.

Hanks, Robert. "Enter Stage Left, Talking Far Too Much." *Independent on Sunday*, 14 April 1996: Critics, 15.

Hughes, David. "Sun and Games." *Mail on Sunday*, 21 April 1996: Review, 34.

M[urray], D[avid]. "Theatre: Some Sunny Day." *Financial Times*, 17 April 1996: 25.

Nightingale, Benedict. "Only the Alien Is Out of Place." *Times*, 13 April 1996: 17.

Poole, Steven. "Don't Call Me Darling in Daylight." *TLS*, 3 May 1996: 19.

Sierz, Aleks. "Wilting in the Heat of War." *Tribune*, 26 April 1996: 9.

Smurthwaite, Nick. "Review: Some Sunny Day." *Midweek*, 22–25 April 1996: 24.

Trevelyan, William. "Play of the Week." *Camden New Journal*, 18 April 1996: 17.

Favorable

Barnsley, Jon. "Twist in the Bending." *News of the World*, 14 April 1996: 16.

Benedict, David. "Theatre: Some Sunny Day." *Independent*, 15 April 1996: sec. 2, 26.

Billington, Michael. "Making a Drama out of a Crisis." *Guardian*, 12 April 1996: 2.

Gross, John. "The Eve of El Alamein—and the Blob from Outer Space." *Sunday Telegraph*, 14 April 1996: 9.

Harley, Kevin. "First Nights: Some Sunny Day." *Pink Paper*, 19 April 1996: 17.

Kellaway, Kate. "Overboard in Cairo." *Observer*, 14 April 1996: 11.

Paton, Maureen. "Stirring Satire with a Casablanca Feel." *Daily Express*, 12 April 1996: 7.

Rieden, Juliet. "Theatre." *Ms London*, 29 April 1996: [6].

Selavie, Sasha. "Theatre: Some Sunny Day." *Thud* [London], 19 April 1996.

Spencer, Charles. "A Wartime Drama Full of Fun and Intrigue." *Daily Telegraph*, 12 April 1996: 14.

Thaxter, John. "Splendidly Starry Lift to an Astonishing Night." *Stage*, 18 April 1996: 12.

Tinker, Jack. "Treasures for All at This Bizarre in Cairo." *Daily Mail*, 12 April 1996; alt. "Pick of the Theatre." *Daily Mail*, 19 April 1996: 52.

Wilson, Kevin. "Theatre." *QX*, 24 April 1996: 28.

Woddis, Carole. "Some Sunny Day." *What's on in London*, 17 April 1996: 52–53.

Wolf, Matt. "Some Sunny Day." *Variety*, 22–28 April 1996: 100–101.

Chapter 14 and Appendix F

Feinstein, Howard. "Artificial Aids." *Guardian*, 6 June 1997: 12.

Holden, Stephen. "It's Not All Popcorn and Car Chases." *New York Times*, 6 June 1997: C18.

Sherman, Martin. "Right of Reply." *Independent*, 12 December 1995: sec. 2, 7.

Taylor, Jeffrey. "Out of Step." *Independent*, 29 November 1995: sec. 2, 8.

FESTIVAL REVIEWS

Favorable

Gorringe, Carrie. "Common Themes, a Promising First Start, and a Side Order of Chopsocky." *Nitrate Online*, 30 May 1997.

Mixed

Elley, Derek. "Indian Summer." *Variety*, 9 September 1996: 121.

U.K. REVIEWS

Favorable

Bradshaw, Nick. "Alive and Kicking." *Time Out*, 4–11 June 1997: 79.

Brown, Geoff. "No Real Need to Watch This Space." *Times*, 5 June 1997: 37.

Cameron-Wilson, James. *Film Review 1997–8*. London: Virgin, 1997, 16.

Childs, Carole. "Alive and Kicking." *Movie Plus Magazine* July 1997: 15.

Clinch, Minty. "Alive and Kicking." *Hello!* 7 June 1997: 86.

"Do Not Miss Films." *Times*, 7 June 1997: 21.

Gilbey, Ryan. "New Films." *Independent*, 7–13 June 1997: Eye, 8.

Hamilton, Jake. "Alive and Kicking." *Empire*, July 1997: 46.

Malcolm, Derek. "Cruising for a Bruceing." *Guardian*, 6 June 1997: Review, 9.

———. "Indian Summer." *Moving Pictures International* January 1997, Reviews, 11.

Robinson, Nigel. "Alive and Kicking." *Film Review*, July 1997: 23; repr. *Film Review Special Yearbook 1997/98*, January 1998: 16.

Thompson, Ben. "Crash: Did We Wait So Long for This." *Independent on Sunday*, 8 June 1997: Review, 11.

Tyler, John. "Alive and Kicking." *Attitude*, June 1997: [25].

Wilson, Kevin. "Reviews: Film." *QX*, 28 May 1997: [8].

Mixed

Allan, Vicky. *Sight and Sound*, July 1997: 35.
Leith, William. "Any Excuse to Dress Up as an Insect and Behave Badly." *Observer*, 8 June 1997: Review, 12.
Richards, Luke. "Cinema." *Pink Paper*, 6 June 1997: 18.
Stimpson, Mansel. "Alive and Kicking." *Gay Times*, June 1997: 93.

Negative

"Dancing Queens." *Boyz*, 7 June 1997: 26.
Landesman, Cosmo. "Rest of the Week's Films." *Sunday Times*, 8 June 1997: sec. 11, 5.
Walter, Alexander. "Lightweight Dance of Death." *Evening Standard*, 5 June 1997: 26.
Richards, Luke. "Express." *Pink Paper*, 4 April 1997: [cover].
_____. "Film Festival Ends in a Celluloid Whimper." *Pink Paper*, 4 April 1997: 2.

U.S. REVIEWS

Mixed

Byrne, Bridget. "Alive and Kicking." *Boxoffice Online*.
Donadoni, Serena. "Alive and Kicking." metrotimes.com [Detroit], 1 October 1997.
Elliott, David. "With Pathos: Gotta Dance, Gotta Die." *San Diego Union-Tribune*, 28 August 1997: Night & Day, 8.
Lim, Dennis. "Summer Camp." *Village Voice*, 29 July 1997: 78.
Schwarzbaum, Lisa. "Alive and Kicking." <ew.com> 8 August 1997.
Stamets, Bill. "Stumbling Character Trips Up Alive and Kicking." *Chicago Sun-Times*, 19 September 1997: NC 37.
Williamson, Bruce. "Movies." *Playboy*, August 1997: 22.

Favorable

Bernard, Jami. "A Dancer Stumbles Upon Love." *Daily News*, 25 July 1997: 68.
Bleiler, David. *TLA Video and DVD Guide 2005: The Discerning Film Lover's Guide*. New York: TLA, 2005. 13.
Bookey, Seth. "Indian Summer." <geocities.com/Athens/2679/kino.html> 27 July 1997.
Brophy, Stephen. "Beauty and the Burly Therapist." *Bay Windows*, 31 July1997: 20, 30.
Brussat, Frederic, and Mary Ann. "Film Review." *Spirituality and Practice*, July 1997.

Drobnic, Angie. "Alive and Kicking." *Weekly Alibi* [Albuquerque], <weeklywire.com/filmvault/alibi/a/aliveandkicking1.html> 20 October 1997.
Farber, Stephen. "Screen Heat." *Movieline*, August 1997: 38.
Feeney, F.K. "Alive and Kicking." *Mr. Showbiz*, <mrshowbiz.go.com/reviews/moviereviews/movies/AliveandKicking_1997.html>.
Graham, Renée. "Refreshing Love Story at Heart of 'Alive.'" *Boston Globe*, 1 August 1997: D4.
Hartl, John. "*Alive and Kicking* Clicks with Sharp Dialogue." *Seattle Times*, 22 August 1997: G7.
Holden, Stephen. "Full of Life and Love as Time Runs Out." *New York Times*, 25 July 1997: C14.
Huisman, Mark J. "Poz Picks." *Poz*, July 1997: 59.
Hunter, David. "Alive and Kicking." *Hollywood Reporter*, 25–27 July 1997: 5, 33.
Hunter, Stephen. "*Alive and Kicking* with True Heroics." *Washington Post*, 12 September 1997: Weekend, 42–3.
Jessica Film Junkie. "Dancers and AIDS." <matchflick.com/movie-review/16860-3617> 11 March 2007.
Kauffmann, Stanley. "Intimacies." *New Republic*, 4 August1997: 26–7.
Keough, Peter. "Alive and Kicking." *Boston Phoenix* <bostonphoenix.com/archives/1997/documents/00524520.htm> 31 July 1997.
Lyons, Jeffrey. WNBC-TV. July 1997.
Maltin, Leonard. <us.IMDb.com/Maltin?0116631>, from *Movie and Video Guide*. New York: Signet, 1998.
Martin, Mick, and Marsha Porter. *DVD and Video Guide 2005*. New York: Ballantine, 2004, 21–22.
McBride, Joseph. "Alive & Kicking." *Sidewalk San Francisco*, August 1997. <sanfrancisco.sidewalk.com/detail/2796>; also <hbo.com/Filmreviews/reviews/bent.shtml>.
Millar, Jeff. "Alive and Kicking Is a Powerful Film." *Houston Chronicle* <chron.com> 9 September 1997.
Ramos, Steve. "Alive and Kicking." *Citybeat* <citybeat.com/archives/1997/issue349/filmindex.html> 1997.
Reed, Rex. "Family Matters: Death and Pimps." *New York Observer*, 4 August 1997: 29.
Ringel, Eleanor. "The Dances of Life, Love and Death." *Atlanta Journal and the Atlanta Constitution*, 7 November 1997: 18.
Roca, Octavio. "Romance and Dance in 'Kicking': AIDS Drama Elicits Heartfelt Laugh-

ter, Tears." *San Francisco Chronicle*, 22 August 1997: D3.
Satuloff, Bob. "Alive and Kicking." *Advocate*, 8 July 1997: 67.
Shulgasser, Barbara. "The Dance of Life—and AIDS." *San Francisco Examiner*, 22 August 1997: C5.
Sigesmund, B.J. "Alive and Kicking." <Newsweek.MSNBC.com> 11 August 1997.
Skir, Leo. "Alive and Kicking." <gaytoday.badpuppy.com> 22 September 1997.
Smith, Russell. "Alive and Kicking." *Austin Chronicle* <austinchronicle.com> 26 September 1997.
Summer, Jane. "Alive and Kicking Delivers a Gay Love Story with Heart." *Dallas Morning News*, 26 September 1997: 5C.
Thomas, Kevin. "Dancing for Lives on the Border of Death." *Newsday*, 25 July 1997: B9.
_____. "Despite AIDS' Toll, Love Stays Alive." *Los Angeles Times*, 25 July 1997: F12.
Worth, Larry. "Pair of Aces Is Draw for Gay Tale." *New York Post*, 25 July 1997: 51.

Chapter 15

BENT CANNES REVIEWS

Corliss, Mary. "Ghosts." *Film Comment*, July/August 1997: 2, 4.
Hunter, Allan. "Bent." *Screen International*, 30 May 1997: 15.
Levy, Emanuel. "Bent." *Variety*, 26 May 1997: 66.

U.S. REVIEWS

Negative

Adnum, Mark. "Concentration Camp." <outrate.net/?p=475#more-475>.
Bennett, Dan. "Bent." *San Diego Reader*, 26 November 1997: 101.
Bookey, Seth. "Bent." <Geocities.com> November 1997; <IMDb rec.arts.movies.reviews> 1997.
Donsky, Seth Michael. "Bent." *New York Press*, 3 December 1997: 58.
Ebert, Roger. "*Bent* Out of Shape for Its Nazi Setting." *Long Beach Press Telegram*, 16 November 1997: D2.
_____. "*Bent* Takes Viewer on Manipulative Ride." *Chicago Sun-Times* <rogerebert.suntimes.com> 26 November 1997.
_____. "Something's Lost in Translation." *Record* [Bergen], 26 November 1997: 403.

_____. [summary]. *Daily Breeze* [Torrance, CA] <dailybreeze.com> 26 November 1997.
_____. [summary]. *Outlook* [Santa Monica], 26 November 1997.
Elliott, David. "Bent." *San Diego Union Tribune*, 27 November 1997: 12.
Fine, Marshall. "*Bent* Fails to Keep Up with the Times." *Gannett Newspapers*, 26 November 1997: F8.
Gerhard, Susan. "First Runs." *San Francisco Bay Guardian*, 26 November 1997: 85.
Karten, Harvey S. "Bent." <www.IMDb.rec.arts.movies.reviews> November 1997.
Kehr, Dave. "From 'Nutcracker' to Nazi Camps and Cops." *Daily News* [NY], 26 November 1997: 48.
Noh, David. "The Men with the Pink Triangles." *New York Blade*, 28 November 1997: 27.
Null, Christopher. "Bent." <filmcritic.com> 2001.
Patterson, Alex. "Bent." <eye.net> 18 December 1997.
Rabin, Nathan. "Bent." <avclub.com> 10 April 2002.
Rozen, Leah. "Bent." *People* 8 December 1997: 22.
Saravia, Jerry. "Bent." <reviews.imdb.com/Reviews/228/22890> 1997.
Shulgasser, Barbara. "Bent: Almost Unwatchable." *San Francisco Examiner*, 26 November 1997: C3.
Taylor, Ella. "Bent." *L.A. Weekly* <laweekly.com> 28 November–4 December 1997.
Weitzman, Elizabeth. "Bent." *Interview*, December 1997: 82.
White, Armond. "Bent." *New York Press*, 3 December 1997: 58.

Negative/Mixed

Holden, Stephen. "Transported from Gay Berlin to Labor at Dachau." *New York Times*, 26 November 1997: B3.
Scheck, Frank. "*Bent*: Camp Prisoners Become Friends." *Oakland Tribune*, 26 November 1997: Cue 1–2.
_____. "Rocky Night Getting 'Bent.'" *Hollywood Reporter*, 25 November 1997: 18.
Strauss, Bob. "How Play Gets 'Bent' into Film." *Daily News* [L.A.], 26 November 1997: 12.
_____. "Screen Adaptation Blurs 'Bent' Message." *Cincinnati Enquirer*, 23 January 1998: Weekend, 22.

Mixed

Adams, Sam. "Does This '70s Drama of Gay Identity Hold Up in the '90s?" *City Paper*

[Philadelphia], <citypaper.net> 4–11 December 1997.
Adams, Thelma. "'Bent' Offers a New Take on the Holocaust." *New York Post*, 26 November 1997: 47.
Alspector, Lisa. "Bent." *Chicago Reader*, 7 November 1997: sec. 2, 12.
"Bent." <screenit.com> 24 November 1997.
Berardinelli, James. "Bent." <reelviews.net/movies/b/bent.html> November 1997.
Byerley, Jim. "Bent." <HBO.com> and <Max.com> November 1997.
Clifford, Laura. "Bent." <reelingreviews.com/reel168.htm> 1997.
Clifford, Robin. "Bent." <reelingreviews.com/reel168.htm> 1997.
Dermody, Dennis. "Lost and Found: Bent." *Paper*, December 1997: 125.
Fine, Marshall. "*Bent* Adapts the Play, but Not Well." <usatoday.com/life/enter/movies/lfilm08.1.htm> 17 December 1999.
Fox, Ken. "Bent." <movies.tvguide.com/bent/review/132472> 8 December 1998.
Garner, Jack. "Despite the Fine Acting, This Tale of Nazi Horrors Was Better Told Onstage." <RochesterGoesOut.com> 20 March 1998.
Hearty, Kitty Bowe. "Bent." <Cinemania Online.seattle.sidewalk.com/detail/36553> 3 December 1998.
Henrickson, Lisa. "Bent." *GQ*, December 1997: 91.
Howe, Desson. "Bent." *Washington Post*, 28 November 1997: Weekend, N62.
Johnson-Ott, Ed. "A Little Dated." *Nuvo Newsweekly* [Indianapolis], 5–12 February 1998: 8.
Kauffmann, Stanley. "Scheming Then and Now." *New Republic* <tnr.com> 1 December 1997.
Litton, David. "Bent." <movieeye.com> 27 July 2002.
Maltin, Leonard. "Bent." <IMDb.com> 1998.
Martin, Mick, and Marsha Porter. "Bent." *DVD and Video Guide 2005*. New York: Ballantine, 2004. 88.
Millar, Jeff. "Time Not Kind to *Bent* Drama." *Houston Chronicle* <chron.com> 22 December 1997.
Morgan, Curtis. "Modern Attitudes Toward Gays Dilute Bleak Film's Power." *Miami Herald*, 26 November 1997: D2.
Potter, Alicia. "Bent." *Boston Phoenix* <bostonphoenix.com> 26 November 1997.
Rickey, Carrie. "Bent Lets Down in the Third Act." *Knight-Ridder Newspapers*, 20 February 1998.
Savlov, Marc. "Bent." *Austin Chronicle*, 20 February 1998: 60–61.

Schwarzbaum, Lisa. "The Company of Men." *Entertainment Weekly*, 28 November; "Bent." 5 December 1997.
Susman, Gary. "Bent." *Rough Cut*, November 1997.
Tatara, Paul. "Poignancy of *Bent* Plays Better on Stage." <CNN.com> 4 December 1997.
Tatum, Charles. "Bent." <efilmcritic.com> 3 June 2004.
Williamson, Kim. "Bent." <Boxofficeonline.com> November 1997.

Favorable

Baltake, Joe. "*Bent* Cries Out Against Bigotry." *Sacramento Bee* <movieclub.com/reviews/archives/98bent/bent.html> 27 February 1998.
"Bent." *E! Online* <eonline.com/Reviews/Movies/Leaves/0,20,510,00.html> November 1997.
Bernstein, Abbie. "Bent." *Drama-Logue* 27 November–3 December 1997: 9.
Bleiler, David. *TLA Video and DVD Guide 2005*. New York: TLA, 2005. 56.
Brussat, Frederic, and Mary Ann. "Bent." <spiritualityandpractice.com> November 1997.
Burliuk, Greg. "Acting in *Bent* Is Oscar Worthy." *Kingston Whig-Standard* <southam.com> 16 January 1998.
———. "The E Files: 'Bent.'" *Southam New Media*, 16 January 1998. <southam.com/vancouversun/cgi/efiles.pl?section=movies&subsection=reviews&file=Bent&article=review2>
[Calomese, Heather]. "Appointments." *New York Blade*, 28 November 1997: 32.
Canaan, Lee. "Bent." *Entertainment News Syndicate*, November 1997.
Charles, Goldie. "Bent." *Jewish Week* [New York] <thejewishweek.com> 21 November 1997.
Chase, Andrea. "Bent." *Movie Magazine International* <reviews.shoestring.org> 26 November 1997.
Chuck. "Bent." <chuckthemovieguy.com/reviews/bent.htm> 1999.
Craig, Jeff. "Bent." *Sixty Second Preview* (radio), 2 December 1997.
De Wolfe, Cheryl. "Bent." *Apollo Guide*, 1998 <apolloguide.com/mov_print.asp?CID=1198> and *Apollo Leisure Guide*, June 1999 <apolloguide.com/mov_revtemp.asp?Title=Bent>.
Dickson, Mary. "Defiantly Bent." *City Weekly* [Salt Lake City], 11 May 1998 <weeklywire.com/ww/05-11-98/slc_cinema.html>.

Graham, Renée. "*Bent*: A Trip to the Dark Side of Cabaret." *Boston Globe*, 26 November 1997: E4.
Guthmann, Edward. "Love in a Time of Genocide." *San Francisco Chronicle*, 26 November 1997: E8.
Hammond, Alice. "Bent." *New York Rock* <newyorkrock.com> November 1997.
Hartl, John. "Contemporary Edge Raises the Impact of *Bent*." *Seattle Times*, 26 November 1997: E3.
Hershenson, Karen. "*Bent* Tale of Gay Affirmation, Surpassing Nazis' Persecution." *Contra Costa Times*, 26 November 1997: F04.
Hitchens, Christopher. "Mick at Night." *Vanity Fair*, 448, December 1997: 140.
Hofler, Robert. *Buzz*, December 1997.
Jessica Film Junkie. "Bent." <matchflick.com> 11 March 2007.
Johnston, Andrew. "Bent." *Time Out New York*, 27 November 1997: 77.
Judell, Brandon. "Bent." *PopcornQ* <rottentomatoes.com> 19 August 2003.
———. "Clivewire." *Detour*, December 1997/ January 1998: [138].
Keogh, Tom. "A Tragic Paradox." <film.com> November 1997.
Kirkland, Bruce. "Nightmarish Brutal *Bent* Will Make You Squirm." *Toronto Sun*, 19 December 1997: 119.
Maynard, Kevin. "Bent." *Mr. Showbiz* <IMDb.com> November 1997.
Maynez, Michael A. "Bent." *Merry-Go-Round* <casenet.com/michael/bent.htm> 1997.
Meek, Tom. "Bent." *Film Threat Weekly* <filmthreat.com> 1 December 1997.
Monk, Katherine. "'Bent' Shows Us Our Human Core." *E Files: Vancouver Sun*, 19 December 1997.
"Movie Review: Bent." <hppub.com/mrbent.htm> 1997.
Natale, Richard. *Buzz Weekly*, 21–27 November 1997.
Nechak, Paula. "'Bent' Views Holocaust from Gay Perspective." *Post-Intelligencer* [Seattle], 26 November 1997: D4.
Obejas, Achy. "A More Open 'Bent' Film Loses Play's Claustrophobia But None of Its Power." *Chicago Tribune*, 27 November 1997: Tempo, 9.
———. "A Reel Treat." *Chicago Tribune*, 7 November 1997: C.
Period, Grace. "Our Queer Year: Get Bent." <gay.net> 19 December 1997.
Pickett, Jim. *GAB* [St. Cloud, MN], 5 November 1997.
Pinsker, Beth. "Bent." *EW Magazine* <ew.com> 4 June 1999.

Polunsky, Bob. "Bent." *Midland Daily News* [Michigan] <ourmidland.com> November 1997.
Potter, Chris. "Bent." *Michigan Live* <mlive.com> 1998.
Provenzano, Tom. "Screen Scene." *Drama-Logue*, 27 November–3 December 1997: 3.
Reed, Rex. "A Spirit Bent Is Not Broken." *New York Observer*, 1 December 1997: 45.
Satuloff, Bob. "Bent." *Film Journal International* <filmjournal.com> November 1997.
Sokolowski, Brenda. "Bent." *Anchorage Press*, 9–15 April 1998: 21.
Steinberg, David. "To Be Fully Alive or Not to Be, That Is the Question." *Spectator* <sexuality.org> 3 April 1998.
Stuart, Jan. "The Darkest Age." *Advocate*, 9 December 1997: 77–78.
Taubin, Amy. "Altered States" *Village Voice*, 2 December 1997: 84.
Thomas, Kevin. "Bleak 'Bent' Makes Smooth Move to Screen." *Los Angeles Times*, 26 November 1997: F8.
———. "Finding the Will to Live and Love at Dachau." *Newsday* [Melville, NY], 26 November 1997: B10.
Thompson, Luke Y. "Bent." *New Times* <rottentomatoes.com/m/1087747-bent/> 3 February 2003.
Travers, Peter. "Digging Deeper." *Rolling Stone*, 11 December 1997: 85.
Valez, Andrew. "Bent." *H/X Magazine* [NYC], 28 November 1997.
Verniere, James. "'Bent' Is Stagey but Powerful." *Boston Herald*, 26 November 1997: 048.
Vitello, Barbara. "Love's Power Endures in the Brilliant *Bent*." *Daily Herald*, 26 November 1997: O48.
Warren, Steve. "Weimar Than You Bargained For." *Weekly News* [Miami], 26 November 1997: 27.
Whitty, Stephen. "'Bent' Sets Pride Against Prejudice." *Newhouse Newspapers*, 26 November 1997.
Williams, Albert. "The Hidden Holocaust." *Chicago Reader*, 7 November 1997: 48.
Williamson, Bruce. "Movies." *Playboy*, January 1998: 19.

U.K. REVIEWS

Negative

Billson, Anne. "Fairytale Hits the Right Buttons." *Sunday Telegraph*, 8 March 1998: Review, 12.
Brown, Geoff. "Calculated Charm Does Not Add Up." *Times*, 5 March 1998: 37.

Hemblade, Christopher. "Bent." *Empire*, April 1998: 44.

Walker, Alexander. "Gay Pride Takes a Fall." *Evening Standard*, 5 March 1998: 26.

Mixed

Andrews, Nigel. "Simple with No Need for Extra Spice." *Financial Times*, 5 March 1998: 22.

"Bent out of Shape." *Mirror*, 5 March 1998: Screen, 5.

Fisher, Nick. "Jagger Dragger." *Sun*, 7 March 1998: 30.

French, Philip. "Who's Clever Boy?" *Observer*, 8 March 1998: Review, 12.

Gilbey, Ryan. "Bent." *Independent*, 7–13 March 1998: 19.

———. "The Nazis' Camp Was Never Like This." *Independent*, 6 March 1998: Eye, 6.

Johnston, Trevor. "Bent." *Time Out*, 4–11 March 1998: 73.

Simpson, Mansel. "Bent." *Gay Times*, March 1998: 94.

Sweet, Matthew. "No Wonder It Knocked Them for Six." *Independent on Sunday*, 8 March 1998: sec. 2, 6.

Van Kruyssen, Helen. "Bent: Film Review." *Total Film* <totalfilm.com/cinema_reviews/bent> April 1998.

Williams, Richard. "Never Cry Woolf." *Guardian*, 6 March 1998: sec. 2, 7.

Favorable

Cameron-Wilson, James. *Film Review Special* #26, Yearbook 1998/99: 44.

Kimberly, Nick. "Bent." *Sight and Sound*, March 1998: 39–40.

Porter, Edward. "Bent." *Sunday Times*, 8 March 1998: sec. 2, 11.

Appendix D: Madhouse in Goa *New York Reviews*

Gussow, Mel. "It Takes All Sorts to Make the World of Judith Ivey." *New York Times*, 1 December 1997: E1.

Negative

Lyons, Donald. "Theater: Eccentricity and Deception." *Wall St. Journal*, 26 November 1997: A12.

Mixed

Barnes, Clive. "Maddening *Madhouse*." *New York Post*, 18 November 1997: 67.

Canby, Vincent. "A Madhouse in Goa." *New York Times*, 30 November 1997: sec. 2, 26.

Evans, Greg. "A Madhouse in Goa." *Variety*, 24 November 1997: 72.

Marks, Peter. "Morally Sightless, a Writer Loses His Words as Well." *New York Times*, 19 November 1997: E1, 6.

O'Toole, Fintan. "It's Too Far to 'Goa.'" *Daily News*, 18 November 1997: 45.

Russo, Francine. "Raining Big Themes." *Village Voice*, 2 December 1997: 99.

Simon, John. "Miracle on 33rd St." *New York Magazine*, 15–30 December 1997: 76.

Winer, Linda. "A Madhouse Indeed." *Newsday* [Melville, NY], 18 November 1997: B9.

Favorable

Feingold, Michael. "Choices." *Village Voice*, 4 November 1997: 3.

Rosenberg, David A. "A Madhouse in Goa." *Back Stage*, 12 December 1997: 35.

Stone, Laurie. "Choices." *Village Voice*, 28 October 1997: 16.

Chapter 16

Carter, Jimmy. *Palestine Peace Not Apartheid*. New York: Simon, 2006.

"Legit Grosses." *Variety*, 22–28 May 2000: 61.

Wesker, Arnold. *The Birth of Shylock and the Death of Zero Mostel*. London: Quartet, 1997; New York: Fromm, 1999.

Wolf, Matt. "London Petal Power." *Variety* <findarticles.com> 13 September 1999.

ROSE REVIEWS, LONDON

Mixed to Negative

Barnes, Clive. "A Swell 'Unwell.'" *New York Post*, 29 August 1999: 32.

Billington, Michael. "Through the Past Darkly." *Guardian*, 26 June 1999: 21.

Clapp, Susannah. "All the Town's a Stage." *Observer*, 27 June 1999: Arts, 8.

De Jongh, Nicholas. "Scene Stealer Is Show Maker." *Evening Standard*, 25 June 1999: 10.

Gore-Langton, Robert. "One Woman Who's a Tragic History Lesson." *Daily Express*, 25 June 1999: 35.

Macaulay, Alastair. "Ingratiating Junk." *Financial Times*, 28 June 1999: 20.

Morley, Sheridan. "Sherman Maps a Jewish Century." <*International Herald Tribune* iht.com> 7 July 1999.

Spence, Martin. "Review: Rose." *Midweek*, 12 July 1999: [20].

Wardle, Irving. "Passions of Middle Age." *Sunday Telegraph*, 27 June 1999: Review, 8.
Wolf, Matt. "Rose." *Variety* <variety.com/review/VE1117914414> 19 July 1999.
———. "Taking the Temperature of London's Theatrical Summer" *Star-Telegram* [Fort Worth], <star-telegram.com> 27 July 1999.

Favorable

Brown, Georgina. "Battling in Vain with Olympian Emotions." *Mail on Sunday*, 4 July 1999: Review, 73.
Butler, Robert. "The Theme of This Play Is Acting." *Independent on Sunday*, 27 June 1999: 6.
Coveney, Michael. "At Last Night's First Night." *Daily Mail*, 25 June 1999: 23.
Dace, Tish. "Rose." *Plays International*, September 1999: 22.
Eaker, Sherry. "Center Stage." *Back Stage*, 12 November 1999: 7.
Edwardes, Jane. "Rose." *Time Out*, 30 June–7 July 1999: 144.
Foss, Roger. "Rose." *What's On*, 30 June 1999: 62.
Hepple, Peter. "Rose." *Stage*, 1 July 1999: 12.
Herbert, Ian. "Prompt Corner." *Theatre Record*, 20 July 1999: 797.
Jennett, Mark. "Rose." <culturevulture.net> June 1999.
Kingston, Jeremy. "Tour of Gentle Force." *Times*, 28 June 1999: 19.
Nightingale, Benedict. "A London Season as Unsettling as the Weather." *New York Times*, 29 August 1999: Arts, 6.
Spencer, Charles. "This Miniature Epic Emerges as a Triumph of Olympian Proportions." *Telegraph*, 28 June 1999: 19.
Taylor, Paul. "The Story of a Survivor." *Independent*, 28 June 1999: 10.
Wright, Michael. "Rose." *Sunday Times*, 4 July 1999: sec. 11, 22.

Appendix E: Rose Broadway Reviews

Favorable

Burke, Thomas. "Broadway Reviews: Rose." *Talkin' Broadway*, 13 April 2000.
Cunningham, Dennis. WCBS Channel 2 <cbs 2ny.com/now/story/0,1597,184012-207,00.shtml> April 2000.
Epstein, Arlene. "Vintage Mamet, Remarkable 'Rose.'" *Nassau Herald* [Lawrence, NY], 4 May 2000: 37.
Fanger, Iris. "Broadway Dramas Explore Truth, Survival." *Christian Science Monitor*, 14 April 2000: 17.
Katavolos, Terenia. "Spotlight on Broadway. *Putnam County News and Recorder* [Cold Spring, NY], <pcnr.com/news/2000/0503> 3 May 2000.
Ledford, Larry. "Olympia Dukakis Triumphs as Rose." *Bergen News*, 10 May 2000: p.s.v-7.
Lieberman, Jeanne. WFAS AM radio, 16 April 2000.
Loney, Glen. "Loney's Show Notes." <nytheatre-wire.com/lt00051t.htm> 2000.
Novick, Julius. "Another Mother Courage." *Jewish Daily Forward* [NY], 21 April 2000: 11–12.
O'Toole, Fintan. "Beauty of 'Rose': Its Thorny Truths." *Daily News* [NY], 13 April 2000: 54.
Raymond, Gerard. "Sherman's Rose Blooms." *Advocate*, 23 May 2000: 101–102.
Sheward, David. "Back Stage Notes." <Backstage.com> [NY], 20 April 2000.
Siegel, Barbara, and Scott Siegel. "Rose." <TheaterMania.com> 19 April 2000.
Sommers, Michael. "'Rose' in Full Bloom." *Star-Ledger* [Newark], 13 April 2000: 70.
Stevens, Gary. "Mighty Mixture." (Syndicated in 62 newspapers) April 2000.
Zoglin, Richard. "Theater." *Time* 24 April 2000: [80].

Negative

Backalenick, Irene. "Rose." *Back Stage* 21 April 2000: 31.
———. "'Rose' Not the Best Pick." *National Jewish Post and Opinion* [Indianapolis], 26 April 2000: 5, 7.
Gamerman, Amy. "Theater: A Tom Stoppard Revival." *Wall Street Journal*, 19 April 2000: A28.
Kuchwara, Michael. "Survivor." Associated Press, 12 April 2000.
Leon, Masha. "Masha Leon." *Jewish Daily Forward* [NY], 28 April 2000: 15.
Le Sourd, Jacques. "Dukakis Shines in Convoluted 'Rose.'" *Journal News* [White Plains, NY], 13 April 2000: 1E, 5E.
Lindstrom, Pia. Channel 5, [12 April] 2000.
Lyons, Donald. "'Rose' Lost in Time." *New York Post*, 13 April 2000: 46.
Musto, Michael. "La Dolce Musto." *Village Voice*, 25 April 2000: 12.
Richardson, David. WOR (radio), 18 April 2000.
Rosenberg, David A. "Drama Is the Name of the Broadway Game." *Sunday Hour* [Norwalk, CT], 7 May 2000: D6.

Siegel, Naomi. "Political Agenda Takes Over in 'Rose.'" *New Jersey Jewish News* [Whippany], 20 April 2000.
Simon, John. "The Music Woman." *New York*, 15 May 2000: 73.
Webber, Bruce. "In 'Rose,' a Survivor Living on the Other Hand." *New York Times*, 13 April 2000: E1, E5.
Winer, Linda. "A Jewish Rose of Many Other Names." *Newsday* [Melville, NY], 13 April 2000: sec. 2N, B2–B3.
Zinoman, Jason. "Rose." *Time Out New York*, 20–27 April 2000: 160.

Mixed

Feldberg, Robert. "So Many Hats, and So Much Ground to Cover." *Record* [Bergen] 13 April 2000: YT-4.
Feingold, Michael. "Agenda Bending." *Village Voice*, 25 April 2000: 79.
Isherwood, Charles. "Rose." *Variety* 13 April 2000: 2, 7.
Pisarra, Drew. "Rose." <newyork.citysearch.com/E/E/NYCNY/0014/71/02> 2000.
Rinn, Miriam. "'Rose' Is a Rose Is a Rose— and Not Much Else." *Jewish Standard* [Teaneck, NJ], 24 April 2000: 35.
Schaap, Dick. "World News Now." ABC TV [12 April] 2000.
Schifrin, Daniel. "Reinventing Rose." *Jewish Week* [NY], 21 April 2000: 41.

Chapter 17

Sherman, Martin. *Absolutely! (perhaps)* London: Methuen, 2003.

Callas Forever

U.K. REVIEWS

Bradshaw, Peter. "Callas Forever." *Guardian*, 19 November 2004: Friday Review, 17.
Bullock, Saxon. "Callas Forever." <channel4.com>.
H., M. "Callas Forever." *Time Out* <timeout.com> 17–24 November 2004.
Hall, George. "Callas Forever." *Sight and Sound*, January 2005: 45–46.
Kermode, Mark. "Bergmanesque Superheroes? Come Off It." *Observer*, 21 November 2004: Review, 9.
Megahey, Noel. "Callas Forever." *DVD Times* <dvdtimes.co.uk> 6 May 2003.
Peters, Patrick. "Callas Forever." *Empire* <empireonline.com>.

Russell, Jamie. "Callas Forever." <bbc.co.uk> 14 November 2004.
Smith, Neil. "Callas Forever." *Total Film* <totalfilm.com> January 2005.

U.S. REVIEWS

Negative

Blaylock, David. "Callas Forever." *Village Voice*, 3 November 2004: 66.
Buell, Richard. "Callas Forever." *Boston Phoenix* <bostonphoenix.com> 26 November–2 December 2004.
Callahan, Dan. "Callas Forever." <ToxicUniverse.com> 28 October 2004.
Davis, Steve. "Callas Forever." *Austin Chronicle* <austinchronicle.com> 25 March 2005.
Ebert, Roger. "Callas Forever: What Becomes a Legend Most?" *Chicago Sun-Times* <rogerebert.suntimes.com> 26 November 2004.
Gonzalez, Ed. "Callas Forever." *Slant Magazine* <slantmagazine.com> 20 October 2004.
Hall, Phil. "Callas Forever." *Film Threat* <filmthreat.com> 14 November 2004.
Holden, Stephen. "Ode to an Opera Star, in a Movie She Never Made." *New York Times*, 5 November 2004: E17.
Jankowicz, Mia. "Callas Forever." <PopMatters.com> 17 December 2004.
McDonagh, Maitland. "Callas Forever." <TV Guide.com> 2005.
Noh, David. "Callas Forever." Film Journal International <filmjournal.com> 2005.
Paris, Barry. "'Callas Forever' Is Out of Sync." *Pittsburgh Post-Gazette* <post-gazette.com> 18 March 2005.
Rabin, Nathan. "Callas Forever." *Onion* <avclub.com> 23 November 2004.
Thomas, Lindsey. "Movies: Callas Forever." *City Pages* [Minneapolis/St. Paul] <citypages.com> 2004.
Thomson, Desson. "'Callas': For Fans Only." *Washington Post*, 26 November 2004: WE 42.
Vice, Jeff. "Callas Forever." *Deseret Morning News* [Salt Lake City] <deseretnews.com> 4 February 2005.
Von Busack, Richard. "Swan Song: Franco Zeffirelli's 'Callas Forever': Maria, Full of Disgrace." *Metro* [San Jose] <metroactive.com> 24–30 November 2004.
Von Rhein, John. "'Callas' Silly Enough to Raise the Dead." *Chicago Tribune*, 26 November 2004: Movies, 2.

Mixed

Arnold, William. "One for the Opera Buffs." *Seattle Post-Intelligencer* <seattlepi.nwsource.com> 26 November 2004.
Atanasov, Svet. "Callas Forever." <dvdtalk.com> 24 June 2005.
Bernard, Jami. "Callas Forever." *Daily News*, 5 November 2004: 56.
Blank, Ed. "Cast Cannot Overcome Flaws Inherent in 'Callas Forever.'" *Pittsburgh Tribune-Review* <pittsburghlive.com> 18 March 2005.
Burr, Ty. "Zeffirelli Courts Camp in 'Callas.'" *Boston Globe* <boston.com> 26 November 2004.
Clifford, Robin. "Callas Forever." <reelingreviews.com> 2004.
Ebiri, Bilge. "Callas Forever." *New York Sun*, 5 November 2004: 16.
Erickson, Glenn. "Callas Forever." Turner Classic Movies <tcm.com> 2005.
Esther, John. "That Lip-Synching Feeling." *Gay and Lesbian Review* 12.1 (2005): 50.
Fernandez, Enrique. "Melodrama Doesn't Befit This Opera Tale." *Miami Herald* <miamiherald.com> 2004.
Harrison, Eric. "Callas Forever." *Houston Chronicle* <chron.com> 25 February 2005.
Knight, Tim. "Callas Forever." <Reel.com>.
Lobo. "Callas Forever: She Put the 'D' in Diva." <Judithwolfe.com/lobosmoviereviews>.
Musetto, V.A. "Callas Forever." *New York Post*, 5 November 2004: 46.
Prescott, Judith. "Callas Forever." *Hollywood Reporter* <hollywoodreporter.com> 21 October 2002.
Rebello, Stephen. "Callas Forever." *Advocate*, 9 November 2004: 56.
Reed, Rex. "Callas, Ray Hit High Notes." *New York Observer*, 8 November 2004: 26.
Ruhe, Pierre. "What-If Tale of Diva Callas Hits Too Many False Notes." *Atlanta Journal-Constitution*, 11 February 2005: H5.
Shen, Ted. "Callas Forever." *Chicago Reader* <chicagoreader.com> 2004.
Young, Deborah. "Callas Forever." *Variety*, 23 September 2002: 24, 32.

Favorable

Cherryl. "Callas Forever." <themoviechicks.com> 2005.
Kauffmann, Stanley. "Rites of Stardom." *New Republic*, 29 November 2004: 28–29.
LaSalle, Mick. "'Callas Forever' Cloaks the Soprano in Fantasy and Pain." *San Francisco Chronicle*, 24 November 2004: E3.
Schrader, Kristin. "Callas Forever." <filmmonthly.com> 19 November 2004.
Thomas, Kevin. "Franco Zeffirelli Gets to Honor His Old Friend in This Aria to a Diva." *Los Angeles Times* <caldendarlive.com> 5 November 2004.
United States Conference of Catholic Bishops. "Callas Forever." <usccb.org/movies> 2004.
Wegg, S. James. "High Tech No Match for High Art." <jamesweggreview.org> 17 May 2004.
White, Armond. "Callas Forever." *New York Press*, 10 November 2004: 28.
Widdifield, Joan K. "Movie Review: Callas Forever." *Movie Magazine International* <shoestring.org> 4 November 2004.

ABSOLUTELY! (PERHAPS) REVIEWS

Negative

Evans, Lloyd. "Creaky Bauble." *Spectator*, 31 May 2003: 42, 44.

Favorable

Brown, Georgina. "Hot Gossip and a Very Cool King." *Mail on Sunday*, 25 May 2003: 69.
De Jongh, Nicholas. "Mirrors of Madness." *Evening Standard*, 21 May 2003: 42.
Foss, Roger. "'Absolutely! (perhaps)' and 'Extremities.'" *What's On in London*, 28 May 2003: 47.
Gross, John. "Reality, or What You Will." *Sunday Telegraph*, 25 May 2003: Review, 7.
Macaulay, Alastair. "Absolutely! (perhaps)." *Financial Times*, 22 May 2003: 17.
Nightingale, Benedict. "Absolutely! (perhaps)." *Times*, 21 May 2003: 21.
Peter, John. "Rest of the Week's Theatre." *Sunday Times*, 25 May 2003: Culture, 18.
Spencer, Charles. "A Touch of Class from Zeffirelli." *Daily Telegraph*, 21 May 2003: 20.

Mixed

Bassett, Kate. "Who Can You Trust? Absolutely No One." *Independent on Sunday*, 25 May 2003: 12.
Billington, Michael. "Zeffirelli Dazzles and Puzzles." *Guardian*, 21 May 2003: 24.
Clapp, Susannah. "Confusion Without a Conclusion." *Observer* <guardian.co.uk/theobserver/2003/may> 25 May 2003.
Coveney, Michael. "At Last Night's First Night." *Daily Mail*, 21 May 2003: 9.
Gore-Langton, Robert. "The Weekend Starts Here." *Daily Express*, 30 May 2003: 45.

Koenig, Rhoda. "Jokes Overshadow Poignancy of Relationships." *Independent*, 21 May 2003: 10.
Maxwell, Dominic. "Absolutely (perhaps)." *Time Out*, 28 May 2003: 144.
Nathan, John. "Absolutely! (perhaps)." *Jewish Chronicle*, 30 May 2003: 51.
Shenton, Mark. "British Women Rule the Stage." *Sunday Express*, 25 May 2003: 64.

THE ROMAN SPRING OF MRS. STONE REVIEWS

Negative

Garvin, Glenn. "Muddled Script Withers Showtime's 'Roman Spring of Mrs. Stone.'" *Miami Herald*, 3 May 2003: 3E.
Lazere, Arthur. "The Roman Spring of Mrs. Stone." <culturevulture.net> 2003.

Favorable

Fries, Laura. "The Roman Spring of Mrs. Stone." *Variety* <variety.com/review/VE1117920644> 1 May 2003.
Gardella, Kay. "Mirren's 'Spring' Fling Worthy of Emmy." *Daily News* [NY], 3 May 2003: 63.
Gilbert, Matthew. "Mirren Gives 'Mrs. Stone' a Sensual, Sad Touch." *Boston Globe*, 1 May 2003: D1.
Mason, M.S. or Connors, L.L. "What's on TV." *Christian Science Monitor*, 2 May 2003: 18.
Richmond, Ray. "TV Review: The Roman Spring of Mrs. Stone." *Hollywood Reporter* <hollywoodreporter.com> 30 April 2003.
Rosenberg, Howard. "'Mrs. Stone' Shares the Pain." *Los Angeles Times* <latimes.com> 3 May 2003.
Smith, Nancy De Wolf. "Another Spring for Mrs. Stone." *Wall Street Journal*, 2 May 2003: W11C.
Stewart, Susan. "Hits and Misses." *TV Guide*, 3 May 2003: 49.
Storm, Jonathan. "Depth of Perception on Old Folks." *Philadelphia Inquirer* <philly.com/> 3 May 2003.

Mixed

Gates, Anita. "Tennessee Williams's Rome in Gritty Sepia." *New York Times*, 2 May 2003: E27.
Meyer, Carla. "Autumn Passion Burns in Showtime's 'Spring.'" *San Francisco Chronicle*, 3 May 2003: D1, D6.

Chapter 18

Sherman, Martin. *E. M. Forster's A Passage to India*. London: Methuen, 2002.

PASSAGE REVIEWS
FIRST U.K. PRODUCTION

Tour

Dungate, Rod. "A Passage to India." <Reviews Gate.com> 23 October 2002.
Gardner, Lyn. "A Passage to India." *Guardian* <guardian.co.uk/stage/2002/oct/15/theatre> 15 October 2002.
Herman, Judi. "Passage to India." *What's on Stage* <whatsonstage.com> 14 October 2002.
Kingston, Jeremy. "A Passage to India." *Times*, 12 October 2002: Features, 25.

London, Favorable

Brown, Georgina. "The Samurai Bard with a Cutting Edge." *Mail on Sunday*, 26 January 2003: 77.
Clapp, Susannah. "Hytner Turns Down the Heat." *Observer*, 26 January 2003: Review, 12.
De Jongh, Nicholas. "Passage to India." *Evening Standard* <thisislondon.co.uk/theatre/review-30> 24 January 2003.
Gross, John. "Spiritual Crisis Stays Earthbound." *Sunday Telegraph*, 26 January 2003: Review, 9.
Herbert, Ian. "Prompt Corner." *Theatre Record* 18 February 2003: 4.
Logan, Brian. "A Passage to India." *Time Out*, 29 January 2003: 143.
Loveridge, Lizzi. "A CurtainUp London Review: A Passage to India." <curtainup.com/passagetoindia.html> 24 January 2003.
Morley, Sheridan. "Through Indian Eyes." *New Statesman*, 17 February 2003: 48.
Nathan, John. "Pass the Duchess." *Jewish Chronicle* <website.thejc.com> 31 January 2003.
Nightingale, Benedict. "Story of Racism Still Resonates." Alt. "A Passage to India." *Times* <timesonline.com> 24 January 2003 late editions; 25 January 2003.
Taylor, Paul. "A Passage to India: More Metaphors for Being Human." *Independent* <independent.co.uk/arts-entertainment> 29 January 2003.
Woddis, Carole. "A Passage to India." *Herald* <heraldscotland.com> 31 January 2003.

Mixed or Negative

Fisher, Philip. "A Passage to India." *British Theatre Guide* <britishtheatreguide.info/reviews/passageindia-rev.htm> *2003*.

Marlowe, Sam. "A Passage to India." *What's on in London*, 29 January 2003: 52.
Peter, John. "A Passage to India." *Sunday Times*, 2 February 2003: Culture, 20.
Sierz, Aleks. "Fair Crack of the Cultural Whip." *Tribune*, 7 February 2003: 21.
Spencer, Charles. "It Ain't Half Dull, Mum." *Daily Telegraph*, 25 January 2003: 23.

SECOND PRODUCTION, U.K.

Bhagat, Adrian. "A Passage to India." Left Lion <leftlion.co.uk/articles.cfm/id/342> 10 October 2004.
Orme, Steve. "A Passage to India." *British Theatre Guide* <britishtheatreguide.info/reviews/passagetoindia-rev.htm> 2004.

BROOKLYN REVIEWS

Favorable

Dace, Tish. "Tish Dace in New York." *Plays International*, December 2004: 34–36.
Feingold, Michael. "Voice Choices." *Village Voice* <villagevoice.com> 24 October 2004.
Loveridge, Lizzi. "Passage to India Makes a Brief Visit to Bam." <curtainup.com/passagetoindia.html/> November 2004.
"Seen and Heard." livedesignonline.com/news/seen_heard_nov5/, 5 November 2004.
Wolf, William. "A Passage to India." *Wolf Entertainment Guide* <wolfentertainnmentguide.com> November 2004.

Mixed

Noh, David. "Laughs, Please, However They Come." *Gay City News* [NY], 11 November 2004: 38.
Stasio, Marilyn. "A Passage to India." *Variety*, 5 November 2004: 11.

Negative

DaVinci Nichols, Nina. "A Passage to India." <culturevulture.net/Theater/Passage.htm> 6 November 2004.
Feingold, Michael "Sightlines." *Village Voice*, 10 November 2004: 73.
Isherwood, Charles. "A Minimal Meeting of Forster's Twain." *New York Times*, 4 November 2004: E5.
Manish. "A Passage to Brooklyn." <sepiamutiny.com/sepia/archives/000639.html> 4 November 2004.
Shaw, Helen. "Delhi Platter." *New York Sun*, 4 November 2004: 23.

CHICAGO REVIEWS

Morgan, Scott, C. "Inventive Staging Saves Meandering 'Passage.'" <dailyherald.com> 18 April 2008.
Weiss, Hedy. "'Passage' Connects Love and Politics Brilliantly." *Chicago Sun-Times*, 10 April 2008: 29.

Chapter 19

Bartlett, Murray, quoted in Sams, Christine. "Boy from Oz Gives Gay Kiss a Miss." <theage.com.au> 6 August 2006.
Dish. "Censorship Down Under." *Washington Blade*, 11 August 2006: 46.
Gannon, Ben and Robert Fox. "'The Boy from Oz': True to Allen's Spirit." *New York Times*, 12 October 2003: sec. 2, 4.
Gross, Michael Joseph. "The Boy from Oz You Won't Meet on Broadway." *New York Times*, 5 October 2003: sec. 2, 5.
Jackman, Hugh. Quoted in Green, Jesse. "Theater: Debriefing: Eight Days a Week." *New York Times*, 5 September 2004: sec. 2, 3.
MacLean, Stephen. *Peter Allen: The Boy from Oz.* Sydney: Random Australia, 1996.
Riedel, Michael. "Hugh Go, Boy!" *New York Post*, 10 September 2004: New York Pulse, 047.

REVIEWS

Favorable

Ansen, David. "Jackman's 'Oz' Fest." *Newsweek* <newsweek.com/id/61910> 27 October 2003.
Barnes, Clive. "'Oz' All About Hugh." *New York Post*, 17 October 2003: New York Pulse, 051.
Coveney, Michael. "From Mutant to Marvelous." *Daily Mail*, 7 November 2003: 55.
Dace, Tish. "Tish Dace in New York." *Plays International* December-January 2003–4: 36–38.
Daniel, Dennis. "For Pete's Sake." *Poz*, October 2003.
Davis, Natalie. "Culture: Broadway Baby." *BC: Blogcritics Magazine* <blogcritics.org> 21 October 2003.
Gardner, Elysa. "Jackman Makes 'Boy from Oz' Sing." *USA Today* [McLean, VA], 17 October 2003: E09.
Hatza, George. "A Voice of Dissent on 'The Boy from Oz.'" *Reading Eagle* <readingeagle.com> 2003.

Heilpern, John. "Jackman Triumphs Arm in Arm with Camp and Kitsch." *New York Observer*, 22 October 2003: 21.
Holden, Stephen. "Yellow Brick Road Leads Show Tunes Down a New Path." *New York Times* <theater2.nytimes.com> 28 May 2004.
Kain, Silas. "Experiencing Peter Allen Again—The Boy from Oz." <blogcritics.org/archives/2005/09/18/023520.php> 18 September 2005.
Kissel, Howard. "We Honestly Love Hugh." *Daily News*, 17 October 2003: 45.
Lyons, Jeffrey. Channel 4 WNBC, 17 October 2003.
Osborne, Robert. "Rambling Reporter." *Hollywood Reporter* <hollywoodreporter.com> 21 October 2003.
Reed, Rex. "Shattered Glass Is Quietly Shocking: Loving Hugh Jackman." *New York Observer*, 3 November 2003: 28.
Roca, Octavia. "Gay Plays Head Straight to Broadway and Beyond." *Miami Herald* <miami.com/mld/miamiherald/entertainment/8034519.htm> 26 February 2004.
Scheck, Frank. "The Boy from Oz." *Hollywood Reporter* <hollywoodreporter.com> 17 October 2003.
Sommers, Michael. "Sassy Musical Bonbon." *Star-Ledger* [Newark], 17 October 2003: 29.
Wolf, William. "The Boy from Oz." <wolfentertainmentguide.com> 17 October 2003.

Negative

Als, Hilton. "Down Underdog." *New Yorker*, 27 October 2003: 108–109.
Bergen, Annie. Bloomberg Radio WBBR-AM 1130, 20 October 2003.
Brantley, Ben. "Flash of '70's Sequins." *New York Times*, 17 October 2003: E1, E30.
Collins, Pat. UPN-9TV, 16 October 2003.
Cote, David. "The Boy from Oz." *Time Out*, 23–30 October 2003: 176.
Feingold, Michael. "Personal Bestings." *Village Voice*, 22–28 October 2003: 81.
Feldberg, Robert. "Where's Glinda When You Need Her?" *Record*, 17 October 2003: 17.
Finkle, David. "The Boy from Oz." <TheaterMania.com> 17 October 2003.
Frascella, Lawrence. "Glitter and Be Gay." *Entertainment Weekly*, 24 October 2003: 114.
Hamburg, Joan. WOR Radio, 17 October 2003.
Isherwood, Charles. "The Boy from Oz." *Variety* <variety.com> 16 October 2003.
_____. "The Cheesy Way Out." *Times* <entertainment.timesonline.co.uk> 17 October 2003.
Kuchwara, Michael. "Theater: The Boy from Oz." Associated Press, 16 October 2003.
Lemon, Brendan. "The Boy from Oz." *Financial Times*, 17 October 2003: 12.
Le Sourd, Jacques. "'Oz' Is a Big Loser (with a Z)." *Journal News* [White Plains, NY], 17 October 2003: 1E–2E.
Mandelbaum, Ken. "The Insider: Not the Boy Next Door." <broadway.com> 16 October 2003.
Marks, Peter. "'Oz': A Mess Instead of a Myth." *Washington Post*, 17 October 2003: Style, C01.
McCarter, Jeremy. "Legs Diamond's Revenge." *New York Sun*, 17–19 October: 18.
Richardson, David. WOR Radio, 17 October 2003.
Simon, John. "All Petered Out." *New York*, 20 October 2003: 83.
Teachout, Terry. "A Friend-in-Law of Dorothy." *Wall Street Journal*, 17 October 2003: W15.
Torre, Roma. "New York One." Channel 1, 16 October 2003.
Winer, Linda. "Irresistible Hugh to the Rescue." *Newsday* [Melville, NY], 17 October 2003: B2, B12.

Chapter 20 and Appendix G

Eaton, Phoebe. "Revenge of the Weinsteins." *New York Magazine* <nymag.com/news/features/15591> 6 February 2006.
Stanistreet, Michelle. "How the Windmill Girls Kept the Blitz at Bay." *Express on Sunday*, 20 November 2005: 49–51.
Van Damm, Sheila. *We Never Closed: The Windmill Story*. London: Robert Hale, 1967.
Van Damm, Vivian. *Tonight and Every Night*. London: Stanley Paul, 1952.

U.K. REVIEWS

Negative

B[radshaw], P[eter]. "Come Friendly Bombs." *Guardian*, 25 November 2005: sec. 10, 7.
French, Philip. "Her Naked Ambition." *Observer*, 27 November 2005: Review, 10.
Quinn, Anthony. "A Very British Scandal." *Independent*, 25 November 2005: Film, 6.
Shoard, Catherine. "Cinema." *Sunday Telegraph*, 27 November 2005: 18.

Mixed

Andrews, Nigel. "How to Defeat the Devil with Post-Feminism." *Financial Times*, 24 November 2005: 16.
Barber, Nicholas. "Mrs. Henderson Presents,"

Independent on Sunday, 27 November 2005: ABC, 8.

Edwards, David. "Movies: Mrs. Henderson Presents." *Mirror* <mirror.co.uk/tv-entertainment/film/200> 26 November 2005.

F., L. "Mrs. Henderson Presents." *Radio Times* <radiotimes.com> November 2005.

Fitzherbert, Henry. "Jodie's Vanishing Girl." *Sunday Express*, 27 November 2005: 60.

Ide, Wendy. "Mrs. Henderson Presents." *Times* <timesonline.com> 24 November 2005.

Malcolm, Derek. "Presenting Glitz, Glamour and Girls with No Clothes." *Evening Standard*, 24 November 2005: Review, 35.

Mottram, James. "Mottram on Movies." *What's On in London* <whatsoninlondon.co.uk/cinema.htm> 23 November 2005.

O'Hara, Helen. "Mrs. Henderson Presents." *Empire* <empireonline.co.uk> 25 November 2005.

Porter, Edward. "There Ain't Nothing Like a Dame." *Sunday Times* 27 November 2005: Culture, 11.

Favorable

Bond, Matthew. "Flesh of Genius." *Mail on Sunday*, 27 November 2005: 66–67.

Brown, Stephen. "Mrs. Henderson Presents." *Sight and Sound*, December 2005: 71.

C., D. "Mrs. Henderson Presents." *Time Out* <timeout.com> 23 November 2005.

Davies, Mike. "Variety Is the Spice of Life." *Birmingham Post* NewsBank Newspapers–U.K., 24 November 2005.

Dougan, Andy. "Dame Judi's Good Nudes." *Evening Times* [Glasgow], 24 November 2005: 4.

Dwyer, Michael. "That Saucy Dame Judi." *Irish Times* <irishtimes.com/newspaper/theticket/2005> 25 November 2005.

Graham, Polly. "Mrs. Henderson Presents." *News of the World*, 20 November 2005: 47.

Hennigan, Adrian. "Mrs. Henderson Presents." <bbc.co.uk/films/2005> 22 November 2005.

Hunter, Allan. "So Nice to Be Naughty with Judi and Her Girls." *Daily Express*, 25 November 2005: 44.

———. "That's Entertainment in the Raw." *Scotland on Sunday* [Edinburgh] <news.scotsman.com> 20 November 2005.

———."That's Entertainment in the Raw." *Scotsman* [Edinburgh] NewsBank Newspapers–U.K., 20 November 2005.

Key, Philip. "The Big Picture: The Show Goes on as the Clothes Come off." *Daily Post* [Liverpool], NewsBank Newspapers–U.K., 25 November 2005.

Manning, Jo. "Paunch and Judi." *South Wales Echo* [Cardiff], 26 November 2005: Features, 3.

"Mrs. Henderson Presents." *Company*, December 2005: 221.

"Mrs. Henderson Presents." *Cosmopolitan*, December 2005: 79.

"Mrs. Henderson Presents." *Leicester Mercury*, NewsBank Newspapers–U.K., 24 November 2005.

"Mrs. Henderson Presents." *Sun*, NewsBank Newspapers–U.K., 26 November 2005.

Pratt, Steve. "When a Plot Totally Takes Flight." *Northern Echo* [Darlington], NewsBank Newspapers–U.K., 24 November 2005: 10.

Riley, Joe. "Mrs. Henderson Presents." *Liverpool Echo*, NewsBank Newspapers–U.K., 25 November 2005.

———. "Mrs. Henderson Presents." *Western Daily Press* [Bristol], NewsBank Newspapers–U.K., 25 November 2005.

Robey, Tim. "Pick of the Week." *Daily Telegraph*, 19 November 2005: 19.

Sandhu, Sukhdev. "Bosom Buddies." *Daily Telegraph*, 25 November 2005: 27.

Smith, Ed. "Frears Inspired by Hammond More Than Hollywood." *Times*, 26 November 2005: 102.

Tookey, Chris. "Mr. Frears Presents His Naked Nostalgia." *Daily Mail*, 25 November 2005: 58.

Turner, Matthew. "Mrs. Henderson Presents." *View* <viewlondon.co.uk> 14 November 2005.

Utichi, Joe. "Mrs. Henderson Presents." *Film Focus* <filmfocus.co.uk> 25 November 2005.

Winter, Jessica. "Mrs. Henderson Presents." *Guardian*, NewsBank Newspapers–U.K., 13 September 2005.

Young, Graham. "Naughty but Nice." *Evening Mail* [Birmingham], NewsBank Newspapers–U.K., 25 November 2005.

U.S. REVIEWS

Negative

Clark, Mike. "'Mrs. Henderson' Should Be Covered Up." *USA Today* <usatoday.com> 8 December 2005.

Dargis, Manohla. "Come On In, Dearie, for Gaudy Skits and Artsy Nudes." *New York Times*, 9 December 2005: E13.

Gleiberman, Owen. "Mrs. Henderson Presents." <ew.com/ew/article/0,,1138549,00.html> 7 December 2005.

Hewitt, Chris. "It's the Graceful Segue That's Barely There." *St. Paul Pioneer Press* <ae.miami.com> 13 January 2005.

Kelly, Christopher. "Mrs. Henderson Presents." *Fort Worth Star-Telegram* <ae.miami.com> 13 January 2006.

Taylor, Ella. "Film: Current Releases." *L.A. Weekly*, 23–29 December 2005: 88.

Travers, Peter. "Mrs. Henderson Presents." *Rolling Stone* <rollingstone.com/reviews/movie> 6 January 2006.

Mixed

Baumgarten, Marjorie. "Mrs. Henderson Presents." *Austin Chronicle* <austinchronicle.com> 3 February 2006.

Carr, Jay. "Dench Is Just Not Enough." *A.M. New York*, 9 December 2005: 36.

Means, Sean P. "Mrs. Henderson Presents." *Salt Lake Tribune* <film-finder.com> 9 December 2005.

Muller, Bill. "Mrs. Henderson Presents." *Arizona Republic* [Phoenix] <azcentral.com> 3 February 2006.

Myers, Randy. "'Henderson' Presents a Misstep." *Contra Costa Times* [Walnut Creek, CA], <contracostatimes.com> 23 December 2005.

Rapold, Nicolas. "Taking It Off for England." *New York Sun*, 9 December 2005: 15.

Rooney, David. "Mrs. Henderson Presents." *Variety* <variety.com/review/VE1117928134.html> 9 September 2005.

Sarris, Andrew. "Dame Judi's F-Bombs." *New York Observer*, 26 December 2005: 23.

Thomas, George. "'Henderson' Beholden to Dench and Hoskins." *Beacon Journal* [Akron], <ae.miami.com> 2 February 2006.

Tobias, Scott. "Mrs. Henderson Presents." *Onion* <avclub.com/content/node/43281> 7 December 2005.

Tucker, Ken. "The Tip Sheet from Toronto." *New York* <nymag.com> 26 September 2005.

Winter, Jessica. "Mrs. Henderson Presents." *City Pages* [Minneapolis/St. Paul] <citypages.com>.

Favorable

Alter, Ethan. "Mrs. Henderson Presents." *Premiere* <premiere.com> 9 December 2005.

Ansen, David. "Judi, Judi, Judi! The Divine Ms. D Delivers." *Newsweek* <msnbc.msn.com/id/10414367/site/newsweek> 19 December 2005.

Arnold, William. "'Mrs. Henderson' Is Simply Irresistible." *Seattle Post-Intelligencer* <seattlepi.nwsource.com> 13 January 2006.

Berardinelli, James. "Mrs. Henderson Presents." <reelviews.net/movies/m/mrs_henderson.html/> 2005.

Bernard, Jami. "'Mrs. Henderson' Presents a Charming Bawdy of Work." *Daily News* [NY], <nydailynews.com> 9 December 2005.

Brussat, Frederic, and Mary Ann. "Mrs. Henderson Presents." *Spirituality and Practice* <spiritualityandpractice.com/films/films.ph p?id=10124>.

Burr, Ty. "Dench Makes an Enjoyable 'Mrs. Henderson.'" *Boston Globe* <bostonglobe.com> 13 January 2006.

Chagollan, Steve. "Mrs. Henderson Presents." *Variety* <variety.com> 15 November 2005. <christiancritic.com/mov2005/mrshpres.asp>.

Cook, Linda. "Mrs. Henderson Presents." *Quad City Times* [Davenport], <qctimes.com> 1 February 2006.

Corliss, Richard. "We Offer a Bird's Eye View of the Big, the Bad, and the Barest Movies of the Holiday." *Time* <time.com> 11 December 2005.

D[enby], D[avid]. "Mrs. Henderson Presents." *New Yorker*, 26 December 2005: 36.

Doughton, K.J. "Mrs. Henderson Presents." *Film Threat* <filmthreat.com> 19 December 2005.

Ebert, Roger. "Mrs. Henderson Presents." *Chicago Sun-Times* <rogerebert.suntimes.com> 13 January 2006.

Elliott, David. "'Mrs. Henderson' Is Delightfully Starkers." *Union-Tribune* [San Diego], <signonsandiego.com> 3 February 2006.

Elliott, Michael. "A Movie Parable: Mrs. Henderson Presents." Christiancritic.com/.

Gallo, Bill. "The Nude Bomb: Mrs. Henderson Shakes Up War-Torn Britain with an Assault of the Flesh." *Dallas Observer* dallasobserver.com 12 January 2006.

Garcia, Maria. "Mrs. Henderson Presents." *Film Journal* filmjournal.com 18 July 2007.

Garner, Jack. "Regal Yet Ribald, Judi Dench Once Again Shows Why She's Screen Royalty." *Rochester Democrat and Chronicle*, 3 February 2006.

Gillespie, Eleanor Ringel. "3 Daring Dames (well sort of): For Dench, the Show Goes on in Wartime." *Atlanta Journal-Constitution*, 13 January 2006: E1.

Granger, Susan. "Mrs. Henderson Presents." <Modamag.com> 21 December 2005.

Gronvall, Andrea. "Mrs. Henderson Presents." *Chicago Reader*, <onfilm.chicagoreader.com/movies/capsules/28709_MISSUS_HENDERSON_PRESENTS> 2005.

Hanke, Ken. "Mrs. Henderson Presents." *Mountain Xpress* [Asheville, NC], <mountainx.com> 1 February 2006.

Hartman, Forrest. "'Mrs. Henderson Presents' a Burlesque Show, and It's a Hit." *Reno*

Gazette and Journal <news.rgj.com> 3 February 2006.

Hornaday, Ann. "Mrs. Henderson Presents." *Washington Post* <washingtonpost.com/ac2/wp-dyn/cityguide/profile?id=1106229>.

Leeper, Mark R. "Mrs. Henderson Presents." <rec.arts.movies.reviews> 21 December 2005.

Longino, Bob. "Mrs. Henderson Presents." *Atlanta Journal-Constitution*, 21 April 2006: H12.

Lumenick, Lou. "Dame Judi and Nudies Boost Blitz Morale." *New York Post* <nypost.com> 9 December 2005.

Macdonald, Moira. "War and Tease: A Plucky Matron Brings Joy to WWII London." *Seattle Times* <seattletimes.nwsource.com> 13 January 2006.

Malcolm, Paul. "The Complete Mr. Arkadin, A.K.A. Confidential Report." *L.A. Weekly*, 19 April 2006.

McDonagh, Maitland. "Mrs. Henderson Presents." <tvguide.com/movies/mrs-hendersonpresents/review/197905>.

Morales, Jorge. "Mrs. Henderson Presents." *Village Voice* <villagevoice.com> 6 December 2005.

Morgenstern, Joe. "'Brokeback Mountain' Brings an Open, Epic Sweep to Cowboys' Hidden Love." *Wall St. Journal* <online.wsj.com> 9 December 2005.

Newman, Bruce. "Risque Business." *Mercury News* [San Jose] <mercurynews.com> 23 December 2005.

Ogle, Connie. "Presenting a Fun, Moving Tale." *Miami-Herald* <ae.miami.com> 3 February 2006.

Phillips, Michael. "Mrs. Henderson Presents." *Chicago Tribune* <metromix.chicagotribune.com/movies/mmx-060113-movies-review-henderson.0.3801451.story?coll=mmx-movies_top_heds>.

Rainer, Peter. "Dame Judi at Her Comedic Best." *Christian Science Monitor* <csmonitor.com> 9 December 2005.

Rechtshaffen, Michael. "Mrs. Henderson Presents." *Hollywood Reporter* <hollywoodreporter.com> 13 September 2005.

Reed, Rex. "London Calling! Mrs. Henderson Has Me Crowing." *New York Observer*, 28 November 2005: 22.

Rickey, Carrie. "Baring It All (Chastely) Was Good for Morale." *Philadelphia Inquirer* <philly.com> 13 January 2006.

Schneider, Steve. "Mrs. Henderson Presents." *Orlando Weekly* <orlandoweekly.com> 2 February 2006.

Seymour, Gene. "Two Old Pros Barely Get By." *Newsday* [Melville, NY] <newsday.com> 9 December 2005.

Sragow, Michael. "'Presents' Strips Away Pretense of Art: It Simply Entertains." *Sun* [Baltimore] <baltimoresun.com> 3 February 2006.

Stein, Ruthe. "Dench Bares Her Talent as Eccentric Mrs. Henderson." *San Francisco Chronicle* <sfgate.com> 24 December 2005.

Thompson, Gary. "BBC Meets Burlesque in 'Mrs. Henderson.'" *Philadelphia Daily News* <philly.com> 13 January 2006.

Toppman, Lawrence. "Dench Nails 'Mrs. Henderson.'" *Charlotte Observer* <ae.charlotte.com> 2 February 2006.

Turan, Kenneth. "Mrs. Henderson Presents." *Los Angeles Times* <calendarlive.com> 9 December 2005.

United States Conference of Catholic Bishops. "Mrs. Henderson Presents." <usccb.org/movies/m/mrshendersonpresents.shtml> 2005.

Westbrook, Bruce. "Fun and Sentimental, Even with All the Nudity." *Houston Chronicle* <chron.com/disp/story.mpl/ent/movies/reviews/3577775.html> 2006.

Williams, Kam. "Mrs. Henderson Presents." *Dallas Black* <dallasblack.com> 6 February 2006.

Wirt, John. "Mrs. Henderson Presents." *Advocate* [Baton Rouge] <2theadvocate.com/entertainment/movies/reviews/2252827.html> 2006.

Wolf, William. "Mrs. Henderson Presents." <wolfentertainmentguide.com/pub/filmsearch.asp?record=3377> 2005.

Zacharek, Stephanie. "Mrs. Henderson Presents." <Salon.com> 9 December 2005.

Chapter 21

THE CHERRY ORCHARD REVIEWS

Griffin, Bradley W. "The Cherry Orchard." *Theatre Journal* 59.1 (March 2007): 126–129.

Henerson, Evan. "The 'Cherry Orchard' More Than Ripe for the Picking." *Daily News* [LA] <dailynews.com> 15/2/2006.

Hodgins, Paul. "Theater: Rich Pickings Show 'Orchard' Weakness." *Orange County Register* [Santa Ana] <ocregister.com> 14 February 2006.

McNulty, Charles. "The Essence of Chekhov." *Los Angeles Times* <calendarlive.com> 14 February 2006.

Mufson, Ariana. "The Cherry Orchard." <curtainup.com> February 2006.

Ochlan, P.J. "Arts Report." 105.1 KMZT <kmozart.com/lifeleisure/artsreport.asp> 17 February 2006.
Weinstein, Karen. "The Cherry Orchard." <culturevulture.net> 15 February 2006.
Welsh, Anne Marie. "'Cherry Orchard' Is Too Peachy." *Union Tribune* <signonsandiego.com> 14 February 2006.

BENT

Brown, Mark. "Plea for Serious Drama as Stoppard Rocks West End." *Guardian* <arts.guardian.co.uk> 28 November 2006.
Callow, Simon. "That's Not Bent, That's Twisted." *Times* <timesonline.co.uk> 16 October 2006.
Crick, Jamie. "Martin Sherman: Bent." <rainbownetwork.com> 6 November 2006.
Gould, Robert. "Out with the Old, In with the New." <broadwayworld.com> December 2006.
Lyall, Sarah. "Musicals Drown Out Plays in West End of London." *New York Times* <nytimes.com> 9 December 2006.
Roberts, Erica. "I Wanted *Bent* Re-Imagined for a Different Generation." *Pink Paper* <pinkpaper.com> 19 October 2006.

REVIEWS

Favorable Reviews

Brown, Peter. "Bent." <Whats-on-in-london.com> 5 October 2006.
Clapp, Susannah. "A Queer Courage in the Face of Death." *Observer*, 8 October 2006: Review, 22.
Coveney, Michael. "Bent." <WhatsonStage.com> 6 October 2006.
Letts, Quentin. "Bent on Living: A Love Even the Nazis Couldn't Crush." *Daily Mail*, 6 October 2006: 53.
Marlowe, Sam. "Bent." *Times*, 9 October 2006: Times 2, 17.
Morley, Sheridan. "Raw, Brutal and Totally Brilliant." *Daily Express*, 6 October 2006: 41.
Nathan, John. "Don't Come to This Cabaret." *Jewish Chronicle*, 13 October 2006: 45.
Shenton, Mark. "Bent." *What's on in London*, 12–19 October 2006: 38.
———. "Bent as Necessary as Ever." <thestage.co.uk/newsblog/2006/10/bent_as_necessary_as_ever.php> 6 October 2006.
———. "A Little Britain of What You Fancy." *Sunday Express*, 8 October 2006: 62.

Mixed

Bassett, Kate. "The Wrong Kind of Camp." *Independent on Sunday*, 8 October 2006: ABC, 11.
Bevan, Richard. "Bent." <rainbownetwork.com> 9 October 2006.
Billington, Michael. "Moving Play Needs No Flames or Wagner." *Guardian*, 6 October 2006: 40.
Burke, Karen. "Bending the Rules for Emotion-Filled Tour de Force." <london24.com> 20 November 2006.
De Jongh, Nicholas. "Harrowing *Bent* Casts New Light on Man's Savagery." *Evening Standard*, 6 October 2006: 17.
Eccles, Christine. "At Bent." *Plays International* December–January 2006–7: 21–22.
Halliburton, Rachel. "Bent." *Time Out*, 11–18 October 2006: 141.
Shuttleworth, Ian. "The Critics: Bent." *Financial Times*, 9 October 2006: 11.
Tayler, Christopher. "Bent." *Sunday Telegraph*, 8 October 2006: Seven, 36.
Taylor, Paul. "Still Packing a Terrible Punch." *Independent*, 9 October 2006: Extra, 20.
Wolf, Matt. "Bent." <Theatre.com> 10 October 2006.
———. "Nazis Conquer London Theater with 'Cabaret,' 'Bent.'" <bloomberg.com> 13 October 2006.

Negative

Brown, Georgina. "Bent Has to Be Played Straight." *Mail on Sunday*, 8 October 2006: Review, 75.
Hart, Christopher. "Why Did They Have to Camp It Up?" *Sunday Times*, 8 October 2006: Culture, 21.
Sierz, Aleks. "Bent Out of Shape: Over the Top and Overblown." *Tribune*, 13 October 2006: 23.
Spencer, Charles. "Suffering Made Sentimental." *Daily Telegraph*, 7 October 2006: 21.

ARISTO

Evans, Peter. "Night of Aristo." <newyorksocialdiary.com/node/60189>
Sherman, Martin. *Aristo*. London: Methuen, 2008.

REVIEWS

Favorable

Brown, Georgina. "Searching for Ari's Skeletons." *Mail on Sunday*, 5 October 2008: sec. 2, 19.
Marmion, Patrick. "Onassis, the Original Babe Magnate." *Daily Mail*, 3 October 2008: 63.
Nightingale, Benedict. "Killer Performance of

a Man Who Could Do Anything." *Times*, 3 October 2008: 38.
Peter, John. "Aristo." *Sunday Times* <entertainment.timesonline.co.uk> 12 October 2008.
Sell, Michael. "Aristo." *Stage* <thestage.co.uk/reviews/review.php/21969/> 6 October 2008.

Negative
Gardner, Lyn. "Theatre: Aristo." *Guardian* <guardian.co.uk> 3 October 2008.
Spencer, Charles. "Tiresome Lesson in Ancient Greek." *Daily Telegraph* 3 October 2008: 31.

Mixed
Callan, Paul. "Dark Side of Oily Onassis." *Daily Express*, 3 October 2008: 53.
Cooter, Maxwell. "Aristo." <WhatsOnStage.com> 6 October 2008.
Mountford, Fiona. "Last Years of Onassis." *Evening Standard* <thisislondon.co.uk/theatre/review-2356> 2 October 2008.
Roberts, Peter. "In Chichester." *Plays International*, December-January 2008–9: 30–31.
Taylor, Paul. "Aristo." *Independent* <license.icopyright.net> 13 October 2008.
Thorncroft, Antony. "Aristo." *Financial Times* 5 October 2008: 21.

ONASSIS

Edge, Simon. "Did Aristotle Onassis Kill Bobby Kennedy?" <Express.co.uk> 15 September 2010.
Franklin, Ashley. "A Home Run: Meeting Robert Lindsay." *Derbyshire Life*, September 2010: 2–5.
Jury, Louise. "O No! Family Protest Over Play That Accuses Him of Murder Plot to Marry Jackie." *Evening Standard* <thisislondon.co.uk/theatre/article-23890663> 22 October 2010.
Leon, Ruth. "A Letter from London." <Playbill.com> 18 October 2010.
"Lindsay's Hit as Onassis Destined for a Sell-Out." Amber Sound 107.2 FM <ambersoundfm.com> 16 September 2010.
Nathan, John. "Interview: Martin Sherman." <thejc.com> 14 October 2010.
Sherman, Martin. *Onassis*. London: Methuen, 2010.

DERBY REVIEWS
[ALL FAVORABLE]

Hirst, Amy. "Crowds Flock to See Robert's Play." <ilkestonadvertiser.co.uk/lifestyle/crowds_flock_to_see_robert_s_play_1_16183 59> 24 September 2010.

Jenner, Steve. Ashbourne Radio. Aired 15 September 2010.
Orme, Steve. "Onassis." <britishtheatreguide.info/reviews/onassis-rev.htm> 15 September 2010.
Powlson, Nigel. "Onassis at Derby Theatre." *Derby Evening Telegraph* <thisisderbyshire.co.uk> 14 September 2010.
Rogers, Jan. BBC Radio Derby, 15 September 2010.
Wheeler, Mike. "Onassis." <theatreworldinternetmagazine.com> 15 September 2010.

LONDON REVIEWS

Favorable
Bassett, Kate. "The Greeks Have a Word for It—Brilliant." *Independent on Sunday*, 17 October 2010: 60.
Callan, Paul. "First Night Review." *Daily Express*, 13 October 2010: 31.
Coveney, Michael. "Onassis." <whatsonstage.com/reviews/theatre/london/E8821223284748/Onassis.html> 13 October 2010.
———. "A Ship-Shape Turn from Lindsay." *Independent*, 14 October 2010: Viewspaper 17.
Moss, Ben. "Robert Lindsay as Aristotle Onassis." <westendextra.com/reviews/theatre/2010/oct/theatre-review-robert-lindsay-aristotle-onassis> 21 October 2010.
Tanitch, Robert. "Onassis." <morningstaronline.co.uk/news/content/view/full/97096> 1 November 2010.
Topalova, Maria S. "Onassis at West End or If Wikileaks Existed 40 Years Ago." <grreporter.info/en/onassiswest_end_or_if_wikileaks_existed_40_years_ago/3884> 2 January 2010.
Woddis, Carole. "Onassis." <reviewsgate.com/index.php?name=News&file=article&sid=53 14> 13 October 2010.

Mixed
Billen, Andrew. "Onassis." <newstatesman.com/theatre/2010/10/onassis-sherman-play-tragedy> 28 October 2010.
Broadbent, Giles. "Review: Onassis, Novello Theatre." <wharf.co.uk> 23 October 2010.
Buteux, Ariane. "Onassis." <westend.broadwayworld.com> 12 October 2010.
Hemming, Sarah. "Onassis." <FT.com> 14 October 2010.
McGinn, Caroline. "Onassis." *Time Out*, 21–27 October 2010: 129.
Portman, Jamie. "No Punches Pulled in Onassis Play." <ottawacitizen.com> 22 October 2010.

Purves, Libby. "Oh, for a Bit More Wit and Less of a History Lecture." *Times*, 13 October 2010: 18.
Thaxter, John. "Onassis." <thestage.co.uk> 13 October 2010.

Negative

Benedict, David. "Onassis." <variety.com> 13 October 2010.
Billington, Michael. "No Drama, Just Exorbitant the Greek." *Guardian*, 13 October 2010: 14.
Brown, Georgina. "Short-Changed by the Super-Rich." *Mail on Sunday*, 24 October 2010: Review 22–23.
Evans, Lloyd. "Thank God for the Critics." <spectator.co.uk/arts-and-culture/featured/6391608/theatre-greek-myth-.thtml> 22 October 2010.
Hitchings, Henry. "Even Lindsay Can't Keep Onassis Ship Afloat." *Evening Standard*, 13 October 2010: 31.
Jays, David. "Playing the Fame Game." *Sunday Times*, 17 October 2010: Culture 18–19.
Letts, Quentin. "Onassis." *Daily Mail*, 13 October 2010: 34.
Shenton, Mark. "It's a Shaw Thing." *Sunday Express*, 17 October 2010: 66.
Spencer, Charles. "A Laughable Greek Tragedy." *Daily Telegraph*, 13 October 2010: 31.
Thompson, Warwick. "Onassis Plots to Kill Kennedy, Hamlet Goes Grungy." <Bloomberg.com> 14 October 2010.
Tripney, Natasha. "Onassis." <theatermania.com/london/reviews/10-2010/onassis_31253.html> 15 October 2010.
Walker, Tim. "Return of Loadsamoney." *Sunday Telegraph*, 17 October 2010: Seven 22.
Wolf, Matt. "Onassis, Novello Theatre." <theartsdesk.com> 13 October 2010.
Zozo. "Theatre Review: Onassis." <londonlist.com/2010/10/theatre_review_onassis_the_novello.php> 13 October 2010.

Index

Absolutely! (perhaps) 203, 206, 210
Ackerman, Robert Allan ix, 36, 40, 50–51, 67–69, 73, 75, 81, 91, 96, 101–102, 104, 109, 115, 120–121, 125, 206–209, 211, 269–270
Acosta, Carlos 255
Actors Studio 18, 21, 25, 26, 28, 270
Adams, Sam 182
Adams, Thelma 181, 283
Adelphi (theatre) 127, 134
Adnum, Mark 180
agents *see* Dolan, Mary; Erhardt, Tom; Fifi-Oscard; Fishbein, Frieda; Lane, George; Ramsay, Peggy; Siberall, Brian
Albery, Ian 66
Alexandria Quartet 19, 23, 106, 150, 152
Alive 41
Alive and Kicking 31, 88, 95, 105, 146, 156, 158, 159–172, 176, 178, 216, 222, 273, 284–285
"All the Things You Are" 238
Allam, Roger 207–208
Allan, Vicky 167–168
Allen, Jonelle 29
Allen, Peter 27, 221–233
Allen, Thomas 235
Almagor, Gila 102
Als, Hilton 231
Alspector, Lisa 182
Alter, Ethan 293
Altman, John 211
Amery, Colin 144
Amory, Mark 89
Anderson, Alice 282
Andre, Jill 39
Andrews, Nigel 185, 243
Ansen, David 226, 293
An-ski, Shloyme 158–159, 187
anti-war 238, 287, 289
Anwar, Farrah 144
Apollo (theatre) 105
Arar, Yardena 284
Arbatt, Alexander 102
Arditi, Michael 118
Ari 256–257, 260
Aristo 247, 255, 256–261, 262–263, 265

Armstrong, David 282
Arnold, William 286, 291
Arvanitis, Yorgos 174
As Time Goes By 45
Asami, Rei 125, 211
Ashley, Elizabeth 273, 274
Asquith, Ros 91
Astell, Debbie 235
Atanasov, Svet 286
Atlantic City 4, 5, 159, 188, 192, 280, 281
Attitudes 11
Aukin, David ix, 49, 88, 89, 127, 146, 160, 161, 162, 174, 213, 247, 256, 262
awards 53, 66, 70, 79, 94, 122, 128, 135, 145, 146, 171, 179, 184, 194, 203, 206, 211, 232, 235, 245, 255, 269, 284

B., P. 102
Back, Daryl 103
Backalenick, Irene 280
Baker, Rob 44
Baldwin, James 10, 19
Baltake, Joe 183
Balthazar 106
Bancroft, Anne 206–207, 208, 211
Bando, Tomasabaru 125
Barber, John 64, 65–66, 89, 91
Barber, Nicholas 242
Bark-Jones, David 152
Barkley, Richard 90
Barlow, Thelma 235, 245
Barnes, Clive 40, 64, 75, 116–117, 194, 226, 271, 273, 276
Barnsley, Jon 154
Bassett, Kate 206, 252, 265
Bassett, Linda 162
Baumgarten, Marjorie 283, 289
Bayley, Clare 123
BBC 51, 83, 126, 137, 143, 144, 160, 187, 188, 234, 246, 288
Beatty, Warren 207
Beckett, Samuel 52, 56, 86, 136, 181, 188
Beersheba Municipal Theatre 94, 273
Before the Act 127, 174
Beit Zvi 273
Bell, Arthur 76–77

Bell, Tom 53, 61, 64, 253
Benedict, David 72, 154, 263
Bening, Annette 247
Bennett, Dan 180
Bennett, Peter 62
Bent (film) 156, 158, 159, 172, 173–186, 244
Bent (play) 2, 32, 36, 36, 37, 42, 44, 45–82, 83, 86, 88, 89, 91, 92, 95, 102, 118, 119, 126–136, 153, 161, 164, 165, 173, 174, 181, 211, 222, 247–255, 267–270, 271, 272, 277, 291
Berardinelli, James 182, 282, 293
Bergen, Annie 231
Berlin 2, 56, 65, 66, 68, 174, 176, 177, 248, 253, 267, 269
Berman, Ed 36, 37
Bernard, Jami 170–171, 283, 286, 291
Bernstein, Abbie 185
Bertish, Suzanne 102, 174–175
Bettelheim, Bruno 46–48, 55, 56
Bevan, Richard 252
Bhagat, Adrian 218
Billington, Michael 64, 89, 103, 117, 124, 131–132, 153, 195, 206, 251, 265
Billson, Anne 185
Bishop, Andre 125, 197
Blackout 49–50
Blair, Clay, Jr. 41
Blank, Ed 286
Blaylock, David 286
Bleiler, David 171, 183
Block, Stephanie J. 222
Bloody Sunday 19–20
Bloom, Verna ix, 8, 9, 25, 26, 28, 30, 35, 43, 93, 271
Blum, Mark 270
Bluteau, Lothaire 174, 179, 180, 247
Bond, Matthew 243
Bookey, Seth 171, 180
Boston University 7–10, 146
Bouffons 254
Bowne, Alan 75
Boy from Oz 27, 30, 207, 210, 220, 221–233, 234, 274
Bradshaw, Nick 167
Bradshaw, Peter 242, 285
Brantley, Ben 228
Brophy, Stephen 169
Brown, Geoff 63, 167, 185
Brown, Georgia 282–283
Brown, Georgina 196, 205, 217, 252, 262
Brown, Peter 250
Brown, Stephen 243
Brussat, Frederic 171, 185, 283, 289
Brussat, Mary Ann 171, 185, 283, 289
Brustein, Robert 75, 76
Bubble 81
Budzisz-Krzyanowska, Teresa 275
Buell, Richard 285
Bullock, Saxon 285

Burge, Stuart 53, 54
Burke, Karen 251
Burke, Thomas 278
Burliuk, Greg 184
Burr, Ty 286, 292
Burton, Kate 275
Butler, Robert 196
Byerley, Jim 181, 284
Byrne, Bridget 168

C., D. 243
Cairo 91, 106, 147, 150, 151
Cali, Joseph 35
Callahan, Dan 285
Callan, Paul 263
Callas, Maria 199, 200–201, 202–203, 206, 256, 257, 260, 285–287
Callas Forever 199, 200–203, 206, 285–287
Callow, Simon ix, 36, 37–38, 49, 79, 86, 122, 127, 135, 151, 249, 253, 272
Cameri (theatre) 197, 200, 255
Cameron-Wilson, James 167, 186
Campbell, Bob 282
Campbell, Cheryl 152
Canaan, Lee 184
Canby, Vincent 276
Carmen Miranda 148, 222
Carne, Rosalind 91
Carpenter, Larry 44
Carr, Allan 33, 35, 40–41, 137, 196
Carr, Jay 283, 288
Carter, Jimmy 197
Casablanca 150
Cash, Jonathan 153
Cashman, Michael 127, 130, 135
Catchpole, Charlie 144
Chagollan, Steve 291
Chaillet, Ned 63
Chamberlain, Lesley 103
Chambers, Colin 54
Chaney, James Earl 18
Change 29, 30
Changing Scene (theatre) 39
Channel 4 160, 162, 174
Channing, Stockard 35
Chapman, Gerald 36
characterization 19, 27, 34, 42, 43, 55, 56, 57, 62, 65, 71, 74, 76, 84, 85, 86, 96, 97, 99, 100, 107–108, 110–113, 116, 147, 150, 151, 154, 159, 165, 175, 192, 207–208, 212, 213, 216, 221, 223, 229, 235, 237–238, 240, 260, 275–276, 278, 284, 289, 290, 292, 293
Charles, Goldie 184
Charleson, Ian 127
Chase, Andrea 185
Chase, Anthony 269
Chekhov, Anton 86, 100, 114, 120, 247, 274
Chernobyl 198, 276
Cherry Orchard 247

Index

Cherryl 287
Chetwyn, Robert ix, 52, 53, 54, 61, 62, 66, 75
Chichester (theatre) 256, 257, 273
Childs, Carole 167
choice 43, 56, 57, 58, 71, 99, 107, 108, 111, 112, 113, 175, 178, 189, 256, 261, 282
Chopin, Frédéric 98
Christiansen, Richard 272
Christie, Agatha 34, 44
Christopher, James 153
Chuck 185
Church, Michael 36
Cizmar, Paula L. 78
Clapp, Susannah 195, 206, 217, 250
Clark, Max Stafford 49
Clark, Mike 288
Clarkeson, Patricia 275
Clause 28 70, 126, 128, 132, 133, 134, 135
Clea 41, 106
Clifford, Laura 182
Clifford, Robin 182, 286
Clinch, Minty 167
Clothes in the Wardrobe 91, 137–145, 235
Clum, John 73, 119
Clurman, Harold 25, 28, 77
Cocks, Jay 30, 93
Codron, Michael 90, 133
Collins, Pat 231
Collins, Pauline 101, 102
Collins, Steven 36
comedy 2, 5, 17, 19, 21, 30, 31, 34–35, 36, 37, 39–40, 44, 49–50, 52, 55, 56, 58–60, 63, 65, 68, 74, 79, 80, 86, 90, 91, 97, 98, 100, 102, 107, 113, 114, 117, 121, 123, 124, 132, 134, 144, 151, 152, 153, 154, 170, 203, 205, 206, 215, 222, 226, 243, 244, 245, 250, 260, 271, 272, 278, 281, 282, 283, 284, 285, 288, 289, 290, 293; *see also* farce; satire
coming out 31, 53, 55, 57, 63, 80, 126, 128
Connors, L.L. 210
Cook, Linda 289
Cook, William 131
Cooke, Richard P. 21
Cooter, Maxwell 262, 263
CORE 11, 17, 18
Corliss, Mary 178
Corliss, Richard 293
Costa-Gavras 173
Cote, David 230
Cottesloe (theatre) 194, 197
Country Wife 20–21, 22
Coveney, Michael 44, 63, 103, 118, 124, 131, 196, 206, 228, 250, 265, 276
Coward, Noel 17, 63, 107, 136
Cracks 24, 27, 30, 33–35, 38–40, 41, 43–44, 68, 88, 114, 151
Craig, Jeff 185
Crane, Ichabod 14, 28

Criterion (theatre) 62, 63, 66, 273
Cronin, Pat 16, 18, 19
Cryer, David 29
Cumming, Alan ix, 248–250, 252, 254, 255
Cunningham, Dennis 73, 278
Currie, Glenne 73, 75
Curry, Tim 52
Curtis, Simon 187, 188
Cushman, Robert 63, 89

Dace, Tish 119, 196, 218, 227, 272
Dachau 2, 32, 46–48, 55, 56, 57, 59, 60, 64, 65, 70, 72, 76, 80, 94, 127, 129, 130, 174, 176, 177, 178, 180, 181, 182, 184, 250, 253, 254
Daily, Irene 43
Dance 14, 40, 41, 57, 95–104, 120, 121–125, 142, 147, 148, 161–171, 201, 236, 238, 259, 274, 292
Daniel, Dennis 228
Dargis, Manohla 288
Da Silva, Beatrice 40
Davidson, Gordon 247
Davies, Mike 244
Davies, Oliver Ford 204, 205, 206
Da Vinci Nichols, Nina 219
Davis, Natalie 228–229
Davis, Steve 285
Day-Lewis, Sean 144
Dead Zero 188, 196
De Angelis, Rosemary 39
decision 47, 58, 94, 99, 113, 189, 219, 239
Declements, Barthe 81
De Jongh, Nicholas 64, 91, 153, 194, 205, 217, 251, 255
De la Tour, Frances 121, 122
De Laurentis, Dino 200
Delta Lady 29, 30–31
Del Valle, Peter 36
Dempster, Curt 30, 35
De Munn, Jeffrey 50, 67
Denby, David 156, 291
Dench, Judi ix, 101, 127, 234, 235, 241, 242–244, 245, 288–293
Denerstein, Robert 284
Denissi, Mimi 261
Dennehy, Brian 207
depression 23, 25, 58, 113
Derby 265
Dermody, Dennis 181
Derryberry, Jil 281
Desti, Mary 97, 98, 100, 123
De Wolfe, Cheryl 184
Dexter, John 53, 101, 187–188
Dickinson, Michael 36
Dickson, Mary 184
Dignam, Arthur 105
Dolan, Mary ix, 26, 28, 34, 39
Donadoni, Serena 169
Don't Call Me Mama Anymore 33

Dougan, Andy 244
Doughton, K.J. 293
dramatic action 55, 56, 57, 99, 189, 260; see also choice; decision
Drobnic, Angie 171
D'Silva, Julius 262
Dudley, Bill 152, 155
Dukakis, Olympia ix, 8, 145, 193–196, 197, 198, 278, 279, 281
Dukes, David 67, 68, 75, 79
Duncan, Isadora 95–103, 120–125, 273–275
Dungate, Rod 216
Durrell, Lawrence 18, 19, 23, 41, 105, 106, 107, 137, 150, 152, 203, 206
dybbuk 30, 34, 35, 39, 146, 156, 158, 159, 164, 187

Eaker, Sherry ix, 75–76, 195–196
Ebert, Roger 179–180, 283–284, 286, 291
Ebiri, Bilge 286
Eccles, Christine 251–252
Eddison, Robert 128
Eder, Richard 44
Edwardes, Jane ix, 103, 118, 123, 196, 276
Edwards, Christopher 89, 91, 103, 117, 123, 129, 276
Edwards, David 243
Egypt 91, 106, 138–140, 142, 143, 144, 147, 151, 202, 282, 283
Eight to Hate 8, 9
Eikenberry, Jill 36, 39
Elley, Derek ix, 284
Elliott, Cass 33
Elliott, David 169, 180, 292
Elliott, Michael 289
Ellis, Alice Thomas 137–144, 282–283
Elsom, John 63, 89
Elyot, Kevin 102, 103
Emperor's New Clothes 11, 14
Enchanted April 282, 283
Engel, Lehman 29
Enright, Nick 221, 222, 223, 230, 232–233
Ensemble Studio Theatre 30, 35, 49–50, 51
Epstein, Arlene ix, 278
Equinoxe 146, 234, 236, 255
Erhardt, Tom ix
Erickson, Glenn 286
Erikson, Claris 30
Esenin, Sergei 27, 96–100, 102–103, 120, 121–122, 124, 125, 273
Esther, John 286
Eugene O'Neill Theatre Center/National Playwrights Conference 30, 38–39, 49, 50–51, 67, 69
Evans, Greg 276
Evans, Lloyd 205
Evans, Peter 256
Everett, Rupert 151, 153, 154–156
Evers, Medgar 16
Exodus 1947 189, 191

Eyre, Richard 127
Eyre, Ronald 88–89

F., L. 242
Fanger, Iris 278
Farber, Stephen 171
farce 14, 34, 39, 40, 58, 86, 90, 97, 99, 101, 114, 125, 151, 204, 210, 250, 260, 274, 275
Fassbinder, Rainer Werner 173
Fat Tuesday 16–19, 21, 27, 42, 85, 106, 148
Fazan, Eleanor 235
Federan, Mitchel David 222, 230, 232
Feeney, F.K. 171
Feingold, Michael 40, 43, 75, 76, 219, 231, 274, 277, 280
Feldberg, Robert 230, 274, 280
Fenton, George 234, 235, 245
Fenton, James 89
Fernandez, Enrique 286
Fiennes, Ralph 127, 128
Fierstein, Harvey 33, 109
Fifi-Oscard 52
Fine, Marshall 180
Fingerhut, Arden 67
Fink, Joel 271
Finkle, David 229–230
Fishbein, Frieda 16
Fisher, Nick 185
Fisher, Philip 218
Fitzherbert, Henry 242
Fleming, Sue 107
Flemyng, Jason 161, 168, 169
Florentines 199, 200
Fly in the Ointment 138
Folan, Francesca 105
Forster, E.M. 212–219
Foss, Roger 196, 205
Fowler, Beth 222, 232
Fox, Eytan 81
Fox, Ken 182
Fox, Patrick 29
Fox, Robert ix, 104, 119, 120, 125, 146, 154–156, 157, 197, 221, 225, 232
Francolini, Anna 263
Frascella, Lawrence 229
Frears, Stephen ix, 145, 234, 235, 236, 241, 242, 243, 244, 245, 255, 261, 288, 289–290, 291, 292, 293
French, Philip 185, 242
Friedman, Sonia 247, 254
Fries, Laura 210

Gaetani, Raimonda 207
Galambos, Atilla 275
Gale, George 131
Gale, Patrick 119
Gallo, Bill 290
Gamerman, Amy 279
Gannon, Ben 221, 225, 232
Garcia, Maria 293

Index

Gardella, Kay 210
Gardner, Elysa 226
Gardner, Lyn 103, 216, 262
Garland, Judy 29, 222, 223, 224, 225, 226, 227, 228, 229, 230, 231, 233
Garner, Jack 181, 290
Garnett, Gale Zoe ix, 39–40, 41, 43, 51, 53, 83, 84, 110, 125, 263
Garrick (theatre) 128
Garvin, Glenn 210
Gates, Anita 210
Gay Sweatshop (theatre company) 36–38, 44, 45, 49
Geller, Uri 152, 153, 156–157
genre 18, 86, 100, 103, 114, 116, 168, 169, 170, 203, 206, 215, 219, 271, 275, 291, 293
Gerard, Jeremy 74
Gere, Richard 67, 68, 79, 173, 180
Gerhard, Susan 180
Gershwin, Ira 14
Giambalvo, Louis 39
Gibbs, Matyelok 89
Gibson, Margaret 270
Gilbert, Matthew 210
Gilbert, W. Stephen 36, 51–52, 65, 83
Gilbey, Ryan 166, 185
Gill, Brendan 77
Gillespie, Eleanor Ringel 290
Giordano, Tony 38, 39–40
Gish, Sheila 102–103, 123
Glass, Philip 174, 177, 178, 184
Gleiberman, Owen 288
Glover, William 40
Gold, Sylviane 44
Goldfarb, Alvin 75
Goldwyn, Samuel 26, 144, 158, 159, 178, 179, 284
Gonzalez, Ed 286
Goodman, Andrew 18
Gordon, Giles 91
Gore-Langton, Robert 123, 195, 206
Gorringe, Carrie 284
Gottfried, Martin 21, 40
Graham, Polly 244
Graham, Renée 169, 183
Granata, Dona 211
Granger, Susan 293
Grant, David Marshall ix, 50, 51, 54, 67–68, 69, 79, 81, 268
Grant, Richard E. 127
Grant, Steve 65, 66, 89
Grau, Gunter 72
Graves, Rupert ix, 105, 107, 115, 175
Greece 23–24, 25, 40, 88, 96, 97, 105, 108, 110, 148, 151, 156, 163, 164, 168, 202, 212, 256, 260, 262, 267, 281, 285, 287
Greig, Noel 45
Grey, Joel 33
Grifasi, Joe 39
Griffin, Bradley W. 247

Griffiths, Drew 36, 38, 45, 49
Gronvall, Andrea 291
Gross, John 123, 129, 154, 205, 217
Gross, Michael 67
Gross, Michael Joseph 224–226, 229
Grossman, David 157–158
Guest, Christopher 235, 288–289, 292
Guthmann, Edward 183–184
Gypsy and Me 255, 261, 263

H., M. 285
Haifa 91, 92, 101, 255, 270
Haifa Municipal Theatre 73, 91, 95, 102
Hall, George 285
Hall, John 126
Hall, Peter 23, 130, 253
Hall, Phil 285
Halliburton, Rachel 252
Hamburg, Joan 231
Hamilton, Jake 167
Hamilton, Robert 30
Hammermeister, Kai 73
Hammerstein, Geraldine (Dena) 38, 51, 175, 248
Hammerstein, James (Jamie) ix, 4, 38, 39, 40, 42, 50, 51, 55, 175, 196, 238
Hammond, Alice 184
Hampstead (theatre) 36, 49, 88, 89, 90, 91, 104, 119, 146, 154, 155, 161
Hampton, Christopher 158, 199, 200
Handelzalts, Michael 93
Hanke, Ken 290
Hanks, Robert 153
Hardin, Joseph 36
Harding, Alex 83
Harley, Kevin 154
Harris, Fox 28
Harris, Michael 79
Harris, William 44
Harrison, Eric 286
Hart, Christopher 253–254
Hartford Stage Company 67
Hartl, John 170, 183
Hartman, Forrest 290
Hatza, George ix, 227
Hawks, Howard 166, 239
HB 26, 28
HBO 187, 255, 263
Hearty, Kitty Bowe 182
Heavy, Lorna 261
Heger, Heinz 46, 79–80
Heilpern, John 227–228
Hemblade, Christopher 185
Henderson, Laura 234, 236–244, 246, 287–293
Henerson, Evan 247
Hennigan, Adrian 244
Henrickson, Lisa 182
Henry, William A. III 119, 276
hepatitis 31–32, 37, 38, 54

Hepple, Peter 63, 117, 196
Herbert, Ian ix, 90, 116, 131, 150, 152, 196, 216
Herman, Judi 216
Hershenson, Karen 185
Hewison, Robert 129, 135
Hewitt, Chris 287
Heyman, Norma ix, 137, 143, 144, 145, 234–235, 245, 272–273
Hicks, Chris 282
Higgins, Anthony 162
Hiley, Jim 103, 116, 129–130
Himmler, Heinrich 45, 60, 70–72
Hipps, Edward Sothern 21
Hirsch, Neil 283
Hirschfeld, Magnus 60
Hirschhorn, Clive 63, 91, 103, 118, 123, 129, 152
Hitchens, Christopher 185
Hitchings, Henry 265
Hitler, Adolf 45, 46, 60, 65, 70–72, 134, 180, 184, 190, 240, 241, 252, 281, 289, 290
HIV 31
Hodgins, Paul 247
Hodgkinson, John 262
Hofler, Robert 184
Holden, Stephen 166, 169, 180, 181, 228, 286
Holocaust 45, 46, 50, 62, 63, 71, 72, 73, 74, 75, 84, 157, 159, 182, 184, 185, 191, 196, 252, 253, 254, 268, 269
Holt, Thelma 156
Holzer, Adela 39–40, 68
Hornaday, Ann 292
Hornby, Richard 118
Hoskins, Bob 234, 235, 243, 245, 288, 290, 291, 292, 293
Howe, Desson 181
Howes, Keith 83
Hoyle, Martin 130
Hughes, David 153
Huisman, Mark J. 169
Hummler, Richard 271, 273
Hunter, Allan 178, 243, 244
Hunter, David 171
Hunter, Stephen 170
Huntington's Chorea 3, 26
Hurren, Kenneth 103, 118, 123, 129
Hussein, Waris 143
Hutera, Donald 118
Hytner, Nick 156, 158, 159

Ide, Wendy 242
Indian Summer 160, 163, 165, 166, 169; see also *Alive and Kicking*.
Inter-Action 37
interval (intermission) 2, 56, 60, 86, 88, 106, 112, 130, 134, 194
irony 34, 57, 71, 80, 86, 89, 90, 99, 101, 108, 109, 112, 115, 132, 140, 151, 157, 177, 190, 194, 202, 204, 213, 215, 218, 241, 260, 261, 278, 280, 286
Isaac, Dan 271
Isherwood, Charles 219, 229, 280
Israel 24, 26, 27, 73, 81, 91, 92, 93, 101, 102, 104, 107, 121, 137, 157, 189, 190, 192, 195, 197, 200, 255, 267, 273, 279–280, 281, 285, 287
Ivey, Judith ix, 275, 276, 277

Jackman, Hugh 221, 222, 226, 227, 228, 230, 231, 232, 233
James, Caryn 283
Jankowicz, Mia 286
Jarman, Derek 135–136
Jenner, Steve 265
Jennett, Mark 196
Jennings, Alex 127
Jerusalem 4, 24, 26, 27, 28, 42, 85, 92, 104, 106, 187
Jessica Film Junkie 171, 185
Johnson, Malcolm L. 78
Johnson-Ott, Ed 182
Johnston, Andrew 184
Johnston, Trevor 185
Jones, Bill 282
Judell, Brandon 185
Jules and Jim 17, 20, 31, 143
Justine 106

Kahn, Madeline 36
Kain, Silas 228
Kalem, T.E. 78
Karlin, Miriam 109
Karten, Harvey S. 180
Katavolos, Terenia 278
Kauffmann, Stanley 74, 171, 182, 283, 287
Keating, Isabel 222, 232
Keeps Rainin' All the Time 108
Kehr, Dave 180
Keitel, Harvey 30
Kellaway, Kate 153
Kelly, Christopher 287
Kemp, Peter 103, 129
Kempley, Rita 283
Kennedy, John F. 28, 256, 257
Kennedy, Robert F. 28, 256, 257, 258, 262
Keogh, Tom 185
Keough, Peter 169
Kermode, Mark 285
Kerr, Walter 77
Kestelman, Sara 152
Key, Philip 244
Kimberly, Nick 186
Kinel, Lola 96
King, Francis 62, 89, 103
King, Martin Luther 16, 28
King Konstantinos II 108
King's Head (theatre) 44, 102, 103, 104, 120, 123, 124

Kingston, Jeremy 44, 196, 216
Kirkland, Bruce 184
Kirkpatrick, Melanie 273
Kiser, Terry 26
Kissel, Howard 78, 117, 228, 272, 276
Klaff, Jack 89
Klein, Stewart 73
Klyne, Tracy 128
Knesset 73, 92
Knight, Tim 286
Koenig, Rhoda 123, 129, 206
Kogon, Eugen 46, 47, 72
Kramer, Daniel ix, 247–248, 249, 250, 251, 252, 254
Kresley, Ed 11, 29
Kroll, Jack 75, 76
Kuchwara, Michael 229, 274, 279
Kulukundis, Eddie 49, 53, 61, 62, 90, 101
Kurtz, Marcia-Jean 273

Lamar, Eddy 152
Lamb, Larry 105
Lamont, Rosette C. 272
Landesman, Cosmo 168
Lane, George 199
LaSalle, Mick 287
Lassell, Michael 268
Lavren, Christine ix, 13–14, 16, 17–19, 20, 21, 22–24, 33, 34, 69, 91, 97, 101, 265
Lazere, Arthur 210
Ledford, Larry 278
Lee, Gypsy Rose 255, 261, 263
Leech, Michael 65
Leeper, Mark R. 293
Leigh, Vivien 207
Leith, William 168
Lemon, Brendan 231
Lenya, Lotte 12, 207
Leon, Masha 279–280
Leonard, Lydia 263
Leonard, Robert Sean 273
Le Sourd, Jacques 231, 279
Letts, Quentin 250–251, 253
Leveaux, David 270, 271
Leveaux, Marie 17
Levy, Emanuel 178
Lewis, Stephen Brimson 174, 175, 181
Lieberman, Jeanne 278
Liepa, Andris 125
Lim, Dennis 168
Limato, Ed 67
Lincoln Center 20–21, 125, 197
Lindsay, Katrina 261
Lindsay, Robert 255, 256, 261, 262, 263
Lindstrom, Pia 279
Linford, Matthew 124
Lipman, Amanda 124
Lipman, Maureen ix, 87–90, 91, 127
Litton, David 182
Livingston, Jorie 26, 35, 41, 42

Livingston, Leila ix, 26, 35, 41, 57
Lloyd, Christopher 39
Logan, Brian 217
Loney, Glen 278
Longino, Bob 290
Loquasto, Santo 67
Lorente, Isabelle 174
Loveridge, Lizzi 217, 218
Lowe, Chris 248
Lubitsch, Ernst 255, 261
Luczyc-Wyhowski, Hugo 235
Ludwig, Karen 270
Lumenick, Lou 291
Luscombe, Tim ix, 44, 80, 102, 103, 135, 272, 273, 274
Lyman, David 282
Lynn, Vera 146
Lyons, Donald 277, 279
Lyons, Jeffrey 73, 171, 182, 226
Lyric Theatre, Hammersmith 104, 105
Lyttleton (theatre) 128

Macaulay, Alastair 123, 194, 205
MacDonald, Caroline 103
Macdonald, Moira 291
Mackay, Patricia 75
MacKenzie, Julia 44
Madden, John 40
Madhouse in Goa 4, 13, 23, 25, 27, 30, 35, 41, 104–119, 120, 125, 127, 137, 159, 151, 178, 179, 275–277
Magdalany, Philip 43, 107
Malcolm, Derek 293
Malcolm, Paul
Malcolm X 28
Maltin, Leonard 171, 182
Mandelbaum, Ken 229
Manhattan Theatre Club 93, 94, 270–272
Manish 219
Manning, Jo 244
Mantello, Joe 275
Maori 147
Marabar Caves 212, 213
Mark Taper Forum 247
Marks, Peter 230, 277
Marlowe, Linda 272, 275
Marlowe, Sam 217–218, 250
Marmion, Patrick 262
Mars-Jones, Adam 130
Marshall, Frank 41
Martin, Mick 171, 182
Martin, Nicholas 275, 276
Martinez, Olivier 207
Mason, M.S. 210
Masters, Anthony 91
Masters, Ben 39, 50, 51
Mathias, Sean ix, 52, 127, 128, 130, 131, 173–179, 180, 181, 247
Matthews, Jack 282
Mauer, Judy ix, 39, 40, 44, 61, 69

Maxwell, Dominic 206
Maynard, Kevin 184
Maynez, Michael A. 185
McAfee, Annalena 118–119
McAlister, Linda Lopez 283
McBride, Joseph 170
McCarter, Jeremy 230
McCarthy, Todd 283
McClure, Michael 50
McDonagh, Maitland 286, 293
McFerran, Ann 36
McGovern, Elizabeth 261, 262
McKellen, Ian ix, 2, 49, 51, 52, 53, 54, 60, 61, 62, 64, 65–66, 68, 70, 80–81, 126–128, 129, 130, 131, 132, 134, 135, 136, 174, 248
McKinley, Philip Wm. ix, 221–222, 231, 232, 233
McKneely, Joey 222, 232, 233
McNulty, Charles 247
McVay, Gordon 124
Meadow, Lynne 94
Means, Sean P. 288
Meckler, Nancy ix, 88, 89, 160, 161–162, 163, 166, 168, 170, 171, 193, 194, 195, 212, 213, 216, 217, 218, 219, 256, 262, 263, 272, 273, 281, 284
Meek, Tom 185
Megahey, Noel 285
melodrama 19, 58, 62, 64, 73, 74, 75, 76, 77, 86, 89, 114, 116, 129, 131, 169, 170, 184, 203, 210, 271, 274, 285
Menshikov, Oleg 121–122, 125
Mercer, David 113
Messiah 4, 27, 30, 42, 83–94, 95, 101, 160, 187, 191, 255, 270–273
Meyer, Carla 210–211
Meyers, Joe 282
Miami 17–18, 31, 188, 192, 269, 281
Michell, Roger ix, 151, 155
Michener, James 104
Miles, Christopher 66
Miles, Sylvia 28, 29, 30–31, 34
Milhaud, Darius 12
Millar, Jeff 170, 181, 282
Miller, Carl 130
Miller, Tim ix, 81, 277
Mills College 12, 13–14, 16
Minerva (theatre) 256
Minskoff, Lee A. 67
Mirren, Helen ix, 206, 209, 210, 211
Mitchell, Eileen ix, 9, 11
mixed moods 19, 86, 91, 99, 100, 101, 114, 168, 235, 239, 243, 247, 265, 271, 280, 282, 287, 289
Molina, Alfred 247
Molyneaux, Gerard M. 77
Monk, Katherine 184
Moore, John 269
Morales, Jorge 290

Moreau, Jeanne 143, 144, 160, 282, 283, 284
Morgan, Curtis 182
Morgan, Scott C. 220
Morgenstern, Joe 290
Morley, Sheridan 65, 66, 90, 91, 103, 118, 123, 132, 152, 195, 217, 249
Morrison, Hobe 74
Moscow 96, 100, 105, 120, 159
Moscow Jewish Theatre 105, 159
Moss, Ben 265
Moss, Leland 42
Moss, Marilyn 284
Moss, Robert ix, 35, 43
Mostel, Zero 187
Mottram, James 243
Mountford, Fiona 263
Mountolive 106
Movement 83, 137, 160
Movshovitz, Howie 282
Mowbray, Malcolm 143
Mrs. Henderson Presents (film) 238, 242, 243, 287, 288, 290, 291, 293
Mrs. Henderson Presents (musical) 245–246
Mufson, Ariana 247
Muller, Bill 288
Munk, Erika 74
Munte, Gita 281
M[urray], D[avid] 153
Musetto, V.A. 286
Music and Silence 263
Musto, Michael 279
Myers, Randy 288

N., D. 282
narcissism 26, 27, 34, 57, 76, 98, 99, 110, 149, 150, 151, 202, 223, 228, 240, 261
narrative 35, 52, 65, 78, 99, 106, 118, 138, 139, 157, 169, 189, 190, 195, 208, 212, 216, 219, 222, 229, 252, 256, 279, 289
Natale, Richard 184
Nathan, David 103, 118, 123, 131, 152
Nathan, John 206, 217, 250, 251
National Theatre 22, 24, 70, 104, 127, 128, 130, 131, 132, 135, 136, 143, 173, 193, 197, 202, 272
Nazi 45, 46, 47, 48, 52, 55, 56, 57, 58, 60, 62, 64, 65, 70, 71, 72, 73, 74–75, 79, 82, 106, 127, 129, 130, 131, 133, 134, 148, 151, 159, 174, 175, 177, 178, 180, 181, 182, 186, 189, 190, 191, 195, 239, 248, 249, 250, 251, 252, 253, 254, 268, 279
Nechak, Paula 183
Nellhaus, Arlynn 39
Nelsen, Don 274
Neman, Daniel 284
Nemesis 256, 257, 263
New, Chris 250, 252, 255
New York, New York 36
Newell, Mike 157, 158
Newman, Barbara 123

Newman, Bruce 290
Newmark, Judith 70
Next Year in Jerusalem 4, 24, 26–28, 42, 85, 187
Night Before Paris 28, 30, 49
Night of the Long Knives 45, 60, 63, 70, 180
Nightingale, Benedict 64, 66, 91, 123, 131, 152–153, 196, 205, 217, 262
Nighy, Bill 162
Noh, David 180, 219, 286
Novick, Julius 272, 273–274, 278
Null, Christopher 180

Obejas, Achy 183
Obscure Revue 8
Ochlan, P.J. 247
O'Connor, Kevin 26
O'Connor, Patrick 124
Ogle, Connie 292
O'Hara, Helen 243
Oliver, Edith 40, 274
Olivier, Laurence 22, 24, 53, 79, 109, 122, 135, 194, 206
Olympics 31, 54, 59
Onassis 88, 105, 114, 258, 259, 261, 263, 265
Onassis, Aristotle 27, 165, 201, 255, 256–263, 265
Onassis Foundation 265
Oresteia 257, 260
Orme, Steve 218, 265
Ormerod, Ben 128
Ortega, Kenny 233
Ortleb, Charles 79
Orton, Joe 86
Osborne, Charles 130
Osborne, Robert 227
O'Sullivan, Camille 235
Oswald, Lee Harvey 28
O'Toole, Fintan 277, 279
Our Town 136, 150
Oval House (theatre) 83
Owen, Clive 174, 180, 183
Owen, John 70

P., E. 44
Papp, Joe 51, 270
Paragraph 175 60, 71, 72
Paris 23, 25, 31–32, 41–42, 45, 83, 96, 106, 114, 124, 160, 173, 188, 197, 200, 201, 202, 248, 268, 269, 273, 274, 285
Paris, Barry 286
Parish, Diane 162, 169
Pascal, Julia 90
Passage to India 88, 206, 212–220, 222
Passing By 28, 29, 30, 31–33, 35, 36–38, 45, 222
Paterson, Peter 144
Paton, Dean 283

Paton, Maureen 116, 122, 132, 144, 153
Patrick, Robert 36
Patterson, Alex 180
Patterson, John S. 77
Payne, Sally 144
Peachment, Chris 144
Perlow 30
Peter, John 44, 103, 123–124, 152, 205, 218, 262
Peters, Bernadette 29
Peters, Patrick 285
Peterson, Alan 163
Petty, Moira 90
Phillips, Michael 291
Piccadilly (theatre) 127
Pickett, Jim 183
Pierrepont Hotel 4, 159
Pinsker, Beth 185
Pinter, Harold 30, 66, 127, 136, 213
Pirandello, Luigi 118, 200, 203, 204, 205, 206
Pisarra, Drew 281
Pitman, Jack 117, 125
Plant, Richard 45, 70–71, 72, 79–80
Playwrights Horizons 35, 36, 42–43, 44, 69, 88, 107, 125, 273
Pleasence, Angela 101–102, 103
plot construction 32, 39, 41, 55–57, 64, 65, 76, 78, 84, 91, 112, 118, 119, 130, 142, 147, 150, 157, 161, 165, 189–190, 204, 212, 219, 221, 239–240, 256, 263, 271
Plowright, Joan ix, 101, 127, 141, 143, 200, 201, 203, 205, 206, 282, 284
Point Blank 83
Pollack, Joe ix, 70
Polunsky, Bob 183
Poole, Steven 153
Pope, Alan ix, 37, 38, 45, 49, 52, 61, 66, 69, 83, 107, 164, 272
Pope, Martin 160, 161, 162
Popkin, Henry 274
Portantiere, Michael 269
Porter, Edward 185, 242
Porter, Marsha 171, 182
Potter, Alicia 181
Potter, Chris 183
Powell, Sandy 235, 245
Pratt, Steve 244
Pratt, W.W. 11
Preminger, Eric Lee 255, 261
Prescott, Judith 286
Pressman, Kenneth 43
Proctor, Roy 37
Provenzano, Tom 185
Public Theater 51, 270
Pyant, Paul 261

Quam, Mylo 19, 26
Quarshie, Hugh 127
Quick, Diana 261

quicksand 1, 189, 192, 259, 281
Quinn, Anthony 242

Rabin, Nathan 180, 285
Rabkin, Gerald 78
Radclyffe, Sarah 173
Radner, Gilda 36
Raidy, William A. 79, 274
Rainer, Peter 289
Ramos, Steve 171
Ramsay, Peggy 26, 30, 36, 42, 49, 51, 52, 104, 146, 164
Ranken, Liz 162, 216
Rapold, Nicolas 289
Ratcliffe, Michael 117
Raymond, Gerard 124, 278
Rebello, Stephen 286
Rechtshaffen, Michael 292
Rector, Frank 72
Red Carpets and Other Banana Skins 156
Red Shoes 255
Redgrave, Corin ix, 125, 151, 152, 153, 155, 156
Redgrave, Vanessa ix, 103, 104–105, 109, 115, 116, 117, 118, 119, 120, 121, 122, 123, 124, 125, 126, 127, 276, 277, 281
Reed, Rex 65, 78, 171, 184, 226, 286, 291
Rees, Caroline 132
Reilly, Kelly 235, 241, 242, 243, 245
Renault, Mary 54
Renshaw, Scott 282
Renton, Alex 119
Resnikova, Eva 274
Rhys, Paul 128
Rich, Frank 75, 76, 119, 271, 274
Richards, Lloyd 38, 50
Richards, Luke 168
Richardson, David 231, 279
Richardson, Jack 75, 76
Richardson, Tony 122
Richmond, Ray 210
Rickey, Carrie 182, 292
Rickhards, Dominic 128
Riddle, January 268
Rieden, Juliet 154
Riley, Joe 244
Rimkus, Stevan 128
Ringel, Eleanor 170, 284
Rinn, Miriam 280
Rio Grande 34, 35, 41–43, 85, 95, 106, 147, 164
Riverside Studios 216
Roberts, Peter ix, 117, 254, 262, 263
Robey, Tim 243
Robinson, Amy 187
Robinson, Nigel 167
Robinson, Tim 118
Roca, Octavia 227
Roca, Octavio 170
Roehm, Ernst 70, 180

Roman Spring of Mrs. Stone 198, 200, 206, 210, 211, 263
Rome 23, 37, 199–200, 207, 208, 210, 268
Rooney, David 288
Roper, David 90
Rose 27, 30, 71, 88, 111, 145, 158, 159, 188–194, 195–197, 198, 200, 255, 259, 277–281
Rose Theatre 105
Rosen, Doraly 235
Rosenbaum, Jonathan 284
Rosenbaum, Pia 281
Rosenberg, Alan 50
Rosenberg, David A. 277, 280
Rosenberg, Howard 210
Rosian, Adela 40
Roswell 158
Rothman, Carol 275
Rothman, Tom 144
Royal Court 2, 49, 53–54, 60, 61, 62, 63, 66, 104
Rozen, Leah 180
Ruby Wax Stressed 198
Rudman, Michael 30, 36, 49
Ruhe, Pierre 286
Russell, Jamie 203
Russo, Francine 277
Russom, Jacqueline ix, 12, 14

Sakamoto, Masayuki 233
Salem, Peter 162, 216, 219
Sandhu, Sukhdev 243
Sarandon, Chris 36, 50
Sarandon, Susan 36
Saravia, Jerry 180
Sarris, Andrew 289
satire 6, 8, 9, 28–29, 35, 36, 39, 40, 44, 86, 100, 103, 108, 114, 144, 151, 154, 188, 204, 215, 218, 239, 260, 275, 277, 282, 284
Satuloff, Bob 169, 185
Saunders, Dick 272
Savlov, Marc 181
Sayer, Philip 52
Schaap, Dick 280
Scharf-Wilner, Josef 83
Scheck, Frank 181, 226
Scherfig, Lone 263
Schickel, Richard 283
Schifrin, Daniel 280
Schindler's List 173
Schlesinger, John 41
Schlissel, Jack 51, 53, 67
Schneider, Steve 293
Schrader, Kristin 287
Schuman, Howard ix, 51–52, 61
Schwarzbaum, Lisa 169, 182, 284
Schwerner, Michael 18
Scorsese, Martin 30
Scott, Ann 157
Scott, Dennis 50
Sears, Ian 105

Second Stage 37, 179, 275
See Under: Love 146, 157, 158, 164, 187, 196
Seifert, Dorthe 73
Selavie, Sasha 154
Sell, Michael 262
Semel, Nava ix, 73, 93
Seventeen and in Between 81
Sevi, Sabbatai 83, 84–85, 86, 88, 89, 92, 271, 272
Seymour, Gene 291
Shaffer, Peter 66
Shapiro, Elizabeth 159, 188
Sharbutt, Jay 74
Shared Experience 212, 215, 216, 218, 219
Sharkey, Jimmy 53
Sharp, Christopher 40
Shaw, George Bernard 113, 136, 151
Shaw, Helen 219
Sheen, Michael 121
Sheiness, Marsha 43
Shen, Ted 286
Shenton, Mark 206, 250, 251, 265
Shepperd, Drey 29
Sher, Antony ix, 33, 37, 38, 80–81, 109, 127, 135–136, 161, 162–163, 168, 169, 171
Sherman, Joseph T. 3, 4–5, 7–8, 10, 11, 19, 24, 26–27, 36, 69, 84, 158, 159, 187, 196–197
Sherman, Julia Shapiro 3, 4–5, 8, 9, 10, 19, 26–27, 192
Sherman, Laura Daisy 3, 17, 31, 69
Sherman, Paul 282
Sheward, David ix, 278
Shircore, Jenny 235
shivah 188, 189, 190, 191, 192, 198, 279, 280, 281
Shoard, Catherine 242
Shorter, Eric 44, 119
Showtime 200, 206, 207
Shulgasser, Barbara 170, 180
Shulman, Milton 62, 90, 103, 123, 128, 129, 255
Shuttleworth, Ian 123, 251
Shylock 187–188
Siberall, Brian 255
Siegel, Barbara 278
Siegel, Naomi 280
Siegel, Scott 278
Sierz, Aleks 153, 217, 252
Sigesmund, B.J. 171
Silverman, Stanley ix, 8, 9, 10, 11–15, 16, 20–21, 25–26, 68–69
Simo ix, 62
Simon, John 74–75, 230, 272, 273, 277, 279
Simon, Neil 38, 52, 62, 66
Simpson, Mansel 185
Skeleton in the Cupboard 138
Skir, Leo 169
Smith, Ed 244
Smith, Liz 67, 74

Smith, Maggie 22, 132
Smith, Nancy De Wolf 210
Smith, Neil 285
Smith, Patricia Keeney 271
Smith, Rupert 118, 129
Smith, Russell 170, 282
Smurthwaite, Nick 153
Soans, Robin 262
Soaps 36
Sokolowski, Brenda 183
Solinger, Michael 173
Solitary Thing 12–15, 16, 17
Some Sunny Day 17, 27, 42, 106,, 119, 144, 146–158, 164, 195, 222
Sommers, Michael 227, 274, 278
Spence, Martin 195
Spencer, Charles 103, 117, 153, 196, 205, 218, 253, 254, 262, 265
Sragow, Michael 292
Stamets, Bill 168
Stark, Susan 282
Stasio, Marilyn 74–75, 219
Stein, Ruthe 292
Steinberg, David 183
Steinlauf, Steven 67
Steinmetz, Johanna 283
Sten, Anna 26, 28
Stephens, Robert 22
Sterling, Eric 73
Sterritt, David 283
Stevens, Gary 278
Stewart, Ian 62, 91
Stewart, Job 30
Stewart, Susan 210
Stigwood, Robert 41
Stimpson, Mansel 168
Stone, Laurie 277
Stone, Oliver 30
Stonewall 29–30, 45, 127, 223, 224, 226
Stoppard, Tom 66, 105, 136
Storm, Jonathan 210
"Stormy Weather" 108
Strasberg, Lee 25, 28
Strauss, Bob 181
Streep, Meryl 39
Street Scenes 30
Streisand, Barbra 83
Stuart, Jan 183
Sturges, Preston 97, 100, 166, 201, 239
style (representational, presentational) 22, 42, 52, 56, 68, 86, 98, 112, 146, 157, 167, 171, 174, 175, 177, 181, 184, 216, 230, 235, 247, 260, 271, 276, 281, 288, 290
Summer, Jane 170
Summer House 106, 137–145, 157, 160, 234, 281, 284
Supervivientes de los Andes 40–41
Survive 41
Susman, Gary 181
Suspense 19, 35, 41, 57, 65, 77, 86, 113, 117,

142, 150, 165, 176, 239, 256, 257, 34, 258, 272
Sweet, Matthew 185
Swift, Clive 89
Symonds, Robert 20–21
Syms, Richard 235
Syna, Sy 44, 271

Table for a King 107, 108, 111, 112, 117, 275, 277
Tatara, Paul 182
Tatlow, Peter 102
Tatum, Charles 181
Taubin, Amy 184
Tayler, Christopher 251
Taylor, Ella 180, 287
Taylor, Jeffrey, 166
Taylor, Kenneth Alan 267
Taylor, Paul 124, 196, 217, 252, 262, 263
Teachout, Terry 231
Teale, Owen 103
Tel Aviv 44, 81, 197, 200, 255, 270, 281
Ten-Minute Hamlet 105
Ten Nights in a Barroom 11–12
Thatcher, Maggie 61, 70
Thaxter, John 154
Theatre Communications Group 39
Theatre De Lys 39–40
theme 19, 33, 41, 55, 60, 62, 63, 64, 76, 78, 81, 84, 86, 89, 90, 95, 103, 106, 107, 109, 130, 144, 151, 165, 169, 170, 176, 178, 185, 191, 203, 204, 215, 216, 218, 222, 255, 260
Things Went Badly in Westphalia 28–29, 30, 31
Third Time Lucky 83
Thomas, George 288
Thomas, Kevin 170, 184, 283, 287
Thomas, Lindsey 285
Thompson, Ben 167
Thompson, Gary 167
Thompson, Luke Y. 185
Thomson, Desson 286
Thorncroft, Antony 263
Thrall, Judy 272
Threlfall, David 143, 282
Tiernan, Kip 10
Tims, Hilton 102
Tinker, Jack 63, 103, 118, 124, 131, 153
title 12, 13, 18, 28, 34, 48, 79, 90, 92, 95, 105, 107, 138, 140, 146, 155, 160, 165, 166, 169, 176, 188, 199, 204, 205, 206, 207, 221, 256, 260, 263, 285, 288, 290, 293
Tobias, Scott 289
Tobin, Jerry 36
Tokyo 106, 211, 233, 268, 269
Tookey, Chris 243
Topper, Jenny ix, 119, 146–147, 155–156
Toppman, Lawrence 290
Torre, Roma 231
TOSOS 36

Tracking Jack 187, 196
Trafalgar Studio 1 247, 249, 255
tragedy 8, 34–35, 52, 57–58, 63, 74, 78, 79, 86, 88, 91, 114, 123, 131, 132, 140, 184, 196, 205, 206, 210, 217, 227, 249, 252, 256, 257, 260, 261, 263, 265, 274, 278, 288
Train to Happiness 105
Travers, Peter 184, 288
Traverse Theatre 30, 49
Tremain, Rose 263
Trevelyan, William 153
Trewin, J.C. 62
Trouble in Paradise 255, 261, 263
Tucci, Stanley 275
Tucker, Ken 288
Tumarin, Boris 26
Turan, Kenneth 292
Turner, Matthew 244
Turner, Niki 216
Turnquist, Kristi 284
Tutin, Dorothy 101, 161, 168, 169
Tyler, John 167
Tyler, Rupert 119

Uchovsky, Gal 81
Ukraine 84, 188, 280
United States Conference of Catholic Bishops 287, 289
Unseen Angels 92, 95
Utichi, Joe 244

Vale, Michael 128
Valez, Andrew 185
Van Damm, Sheila 236–238
Van Damm, Vivian 236–238, 240, 241–242, 243, 244, 289, 291, 292
Van Kruyssen, Helen 185
Van Werson, Gerard 130
Venning, Harry 144
Venning, Nicola 44
Venora, Diane 270
Verniere, James 183
Vice, Jeff 285
Vitello, Barbara 183
Voight, Jon 173
Volkoff, Vladimir 83
Von Busack, Richard 285
Von Rhein, John 285
Voodoo 17, 148, 150, 255
Voss, Philip 162
voter registration 17, 18

Walker, Alexander 185
Walker, Jonathan 273
Wallach, Allan 75
Walter, Alexander 168
Wardle, Irving ix, 44, 90, 103, 117, 123, 195, 276
Warner, David 23
Warren, Steve ix, 183

Warrilow, David 270–271
Warsaw 71, 133, 188, 189, 190, 191, 192
Wasserstein, Wendy ix, 158, 198, 274, 275
Waterford 38–40, 51
Waters, Aiden 162
Watt, Douglas 40, 73–74, 75, 117, 271, 273, 276
Watts, Richard 40
We Love Adventure 11
Wearing, Catherine 118
Weaver, Sigourney 255
Webber, Bruce 279
Wegg, S. James 287
Weiner, Michael 9, 16, 19, 20–21, 22–24, 25, 33, 69
Weinstein, Karen 247
Weiss, George 157
Weiss, Hedy 220, 272
Weitzman, Elizabeth 180
"We'll Meet Again" 146, 148
Welsh, Anne Marie 247
Wesker, Arnold ix, 30, 187–188
Westbrook, Bruce 290
Wheeler, Mike 265
When She Danced 27, 92, 95–103, 104, 120–125, 137, 151, 164, 191, 270, 273–275, 277
Whitcover, Walt 26, 28
White, Armond 180, 287
Whitman, Peter 37, 44, 45, 49, 52, 61
Whitty, Stephen 184
Widdifield, Joan K. 287
Wiener Library 45
Williams, Albert 83
Williams, Hugo 130
Williams, Kam 290
Williams, Richard 185
Williams, Tennessee 4, 19, 107, 136, 143, 200, 206, 207–210, 211, 275, 276, 277, 290
Williamson, Bruce 169, 182
Williamson, Kim 181
Wilson, A.N. 144
Wilson, Doric ix, 33, 36
Wilson, Edwin 75
Wilson, Kevin 154, 167
Wilson, Lanford 33
Windmill Theatre 234, 235, 237, 239, 240, 241, 242, 246, 287, 289, 290, 291, 292

Winer, Linda 230, 273, 277, 279
Winter, Jessica 243, 289
Wirt, John 291
wisdom 38, 49, 86, 101, 111, 112, 119, 130, 146, 163, 183, 191, 194, 196, 198, 255, 276, 283
wit 9, 12, 14, 37, 38, 39, 58, 65, 84, 99, 101, 107, 114, 119, 125, 134, 137, 151, 168, 169, 187, 203, 206, 215, 222, 226, 227, 229, 235, 240, 243, 244, 262, 272, 273, 278, 282, 283, 290, 293
Woddis, Carole 153, 217
Wojewodski, Robert 67
Wolf, Matt 44, 154, 180, 195, 197, 252
Wolf, William 218–219, 227, 292
Woods, Gregory 73
Woods, James 35
Woodstock 28, 34
World War II 62, 170, 181, 182, 287, 288, 292
Worth, Larry 168–169
Wright, Michael 196
Wurlitzer Foundation 34
Wycherley, William 20–21, 58
Wyndham's (theatre) 66

Yiddish 4, 90, 97, 158, 159, 188, 189, 190, 192, 195, 196, 270, 279, 280, 281
York, Michael 79
Young, B.A. 62, 89
Young, Deborah 286
Young, Graham 244
Young, Will 235, 242
Yultishka 3, 84, 158, 159, 188, 191, 192, 271
Yvonne Arnaud (theatre) 101, 275

Zacharek, Stephanie 293
Zaks, Jerry 35
Zang, Ed 39
Zavani, Franco 40, 93, 96, 109, 120
Zeffirelli, Franco 199, 200, 201, 202–203, 205–206, 285, 286, 287
Zinnemann, Fred 83, 137
Zinoman, Jason 279
Ziskin, Laura 255, 261
Zoglin, Richard 278

www.ingramcontent.com/pod-product-compliance
Lightning Source LLC
Chambersburg PA
CBHW051207300426
44116CB00006B/459